HENRY RAND HATFIELD:
HUMANIST, SCHOLAR, AND ACCOUNTING EDUCATOR

Studies in the Development of Accounting Thought

Gary John Previts and Robert J. Bricker,
Series Editors

Volume 1: *Henry Rand Hartfield: Humanist, Scholar, and Accounting Educators,* by Stephen A. Zeff

HENRY RAND HATFIELD: HUMANIST, SCHOLAR, AND ACCOUNTING EDUCATOR

by Stephen A. Zeff

Jesse H. Jones Graduate School of Management
Rice University

Emerald

United Kingdom – North America – Japan
India – Malaysia – China

Emerald Group Publishing Limited
Howard House, Wagon Lane, Bingley BD16 1WA, UK

British Library Cataloguing in Publication Data
A catalogue record for this book is available from the British Library

ISBN: 978-0-7623-0622-0
ISSN: 1479-3504 (Series)

INVESTOR IN PEOPLE

Contents

To Beth,
with thanks

List of Illustrations

Preview

Some years ago, Professor Zeff came to Berkeley as a visiting faculty member. Shortly after his arrival, we introduced him to the Hatfield Collection in the business school on the University of California campus. Along with showing him this collection, we dropped a hint or two about the need for a biography of Henry Rand Hatfield. He was impressed with the richness of the material available to a biographer. This "biographical study" is the result.

Even though I knew Hatfield personally (for example, he guided me in my master's thesis on "consolidations"), I had been unaware of his earlier life. His educational background reflected his broad intellectual interests, including the formal study of several foreign languages, such as Latin and German. His preparation lacked any formal study of accounting, but this was offset in part by some practical business experience before he became an academic. As a result, Professor Zeff starts his examination of Hatfield's career with a detailed account of the man's background, especially who his father was, what he did in his life, and the influence it had on the young Henry Rand Hatfield. This study gives us much more than Hatfield's academic career. Zeff expands his account to give us a detailed recounting of the life of a member of a scarce breed: a person of high intelligence, broad education, and high moral values that he took for granted, who was conscious of his place in society and his obligations to that society, and "liberal" in the best sense of that term. The reason for Hatfield's leadership becomes much clearer in the light of this background material.

Hatfield was more than a leading professor who wrote in a fine literary style. Mainly, his influence was felt in his personal relationships. He liked people, and he would meet with them in person. When it was not possible to meet, he would carry on a voluminous correspondence. He was in great demand as an after-dinner speaker, and he kept in close touch with his teaching assistants, graduate students, and colleagues all over the world. His political conservatism had a strong underpinning in nineteenth-century liberalism, which stood him in good stead during the Great Depression of the 1930s.

All of this and more is discussed in this biographical study. For this, we are all indebted to Professor Zeff.

Maurice Moonitz

Preface

During the first half of the twentieth century in the United States, Henry Rand Hatfield was known as the "dean of accounting teachers." He played a major role in shaping the early accounting literature. To study Hatfield's career is to come to understand the early evolution of accounting as an academic and professional field, for he was a significant contributor to both.

Hatfield was born in 1866, studied classics at Northwestern University, and obtained a Ph.D. in political economy and political science from the University of Chicago in 1897. Since he had worked in a bond house for several years during the 1880s, he was tapped to coordinate Chicago's new program in commerce from 1898 to 1904, when he left for the University of California at Berkeley. At Chicago, he had begun to offer coursework in accounting, before Berkeley hired him to direct its nascent program of accounting instruction. He became the first full-time academic at an American university with a professorial rank in accounting, and he served as dean of both the Chicago and Berkeley colleges of commerce as well as dean of the faculties at Berkeley.

In 1909, Hatfield published *Modern Accounting: Its Principles and Some of Its Problems*, the first major U.S. textbook to explore in depth the principles and practices of financial accounting. As much a treatise as a textbook, it drew extensively on the views of authorities in the United States and Europe, and it did much to shape the field. He published a revised edition in 1927. The book was widely cited and has since been reissued by reprint houses.

In 1919, Hatfield was president of the American Association of University Instructors in Accounting (later the American Accounting Association), which he had helped found in 1916. In the same year, he became the only accounting academic ever to serve as vice president of the American Economic Association.

He had a deep interest in both bookkeeping history and the relation between accounting and the law, and as an author he was an implacable critic of slipshod terminology, illogical thinking, and unprincipled reasoning. His critical faculty was on display in the many book reviews he published. He spoke out against behavior by practicing accountants that did not comport with the public interest. In many ways, he was the conscience of the accounting profession. He also possessed a pungent sense of humor, which was reflected in many of his writings, including his best-known article, "An Historical Defense of Bookkeeping," published in 1924.

Hatfield became even better known as the coauthor, together with Thomas H. Sanders and Underhill Moore, of *A Statement of Accounting Principles*, which was commissioned by the Haskins & Sells Foundation and published in 1938 by the American Institute of Accountants.

He could read several languages, traveled widely, published poetry, and was celebrated for his scholarship, wit, and erudition. Among U.S. accounting academics, Hatfield was a Renaissance figure. He received honorary doctorates from both Northwestern and Berkeley.

After a long and active career that extended even beyond his retirement from the Berkeley faculty in 1937, he died in 1945 at age 79. In 1951, he was inducted into the Accounting Hall of Fame.

A chronology of Hatfield's career is given in an appendix to this Preface.

BACKGROUND AND ACKNOWLEDGMENTS

I became interested in doing a biographical study of Henry Rand Hatfield in 1963, when Maurice Moonitz, a Berkeley accounting professor and a former student of Hatfield's, encouraged me to spend some time examining Hatfield's many files of correspondence, manuscripts, notes, and clippings that were stored in the Berkeley business school. I decided to take a leave from my university during the fall semester of 1964, which, along with spending the summers of 1964 and 1965 in Berkeley, allowed me to pore through the Hatfield papers in detail. The Haskins & Sells Foundation gave me a small grant to support my work, and I was also assisted by Berkeley's Institute of Business and Economic Research. Their support allowed me to conduct scores of interviews and correspond with many of Hatfield's former students, colleagues, and professional acquaintances both in the United States and overseas. In addition, I had numerous chats with his children and other close relatives. The Berkeley business school graciously permitted me to take with me many of his files when I returned to my home institution (then Tulane University).

Since I was also doing research in 1964-1965 on the 50th anniversary history of the American Accounting Association (AAA), I benefited from interviews with such early AAA leaders as William A. Paton, A. C. Littleton, Eric L. Kohler, Fayette H. Elwell, Russell A. Stevenson and Howard C. Greer—all of whom knew Hatfield.

In the summer of 1966, thanks to an invitation from Sidney Davidson, I served as a visiting associate professor at the University of Chicago, where I studied archival materials at both the University of Chicago and Northwestern University and conducted a number of interviews.

My plan was to compose a biographical study of Hatfield that would include a number of his previously unpublished manuscripts as well as reproductions of some of his more important published writings. Since I am not qualified to judge his interest and writings in bookkeeping history, I asked Basil Yamey, a professor at the London School of Economics and a distinguished accounting historian, to write an analysis for the book. This he kindly consented to do, and I sent him the pertinent notes and correspondence from Hatfield's files. Yamey's contribution is included in Chapter 5.

But the incessant demands of teaching and a series of administrative assignments, together with a stream of research projects that had firm deadlines, prevented me from making any further progress until the latter 1980s. By then, Yamey's contribution was in hand, and I firmly resolved to begin the drafting. I completed the first chapter and a bit of the second, but then the Hatfield project was again shelved owing to a research commitment in The Netherlands.

In 1996, I dedicated the summer and a sabbatical leave during the fall semester to an acceleration of work on the book, which included further data-gathering visits to Chicago and Berkeley. By then, the Hatfield project had become an obsession, and I was determined to bring it to completion. One explanation of the prolonged period of drafting is that the book has been so much fun to research and write!

Beginning in 1996, I became the beneficiary of precious collaboration with Elizabeth Tebeaux, a professor of English at Texas A&M University who was on a three-year, part-time visit to Rice University. In conversations, she had become intrigued by the Hatfield project, and she asked to see the draft chapters. Thereupon, she began to make immensely valuable suggestions about the organization and writing of the book. In addition, she volunteered to do research on American Methodism and, especially, the writings of Hatfield's father, an activist minister of the faith. She thus contributed a major section at the beginning of Chapter 1 on Hatfield's Methodist upbringings. She also did most of the research and drafting of Chapter 6, on the personal Hatfield, and she is responsible for the comments on Hatfield's use of rhetoric. Beth has been an indispensable adviser on all that is in this book.

In the late 1980s and mid-1990s, I exposed my chapters to critical comment from accounting colleagues. Their remarks and suggestions have helped me in a great many ways. The commentators were Rob Bricker, Phil Brown, Kees Camfferman, Ray Chambers, Bill Cooper, Sid Davidson, Tom Dyckman, David Forrester, Lou Goldberg, Chuck Horngren, Yuji Ijiri, Paul Kircher, Maurice Moonitz, Bob Parker, Lee Parker, Gary Previts, David Solomons, George Staubus, Steve Walker, and Geoff Whittington. The Hatfield family—especially Emily Benner, Sally Chappell, John S. Hatfield, Henry Glover and Betty Werther (all grandchildren), and Jon Glover (great-grandson)—have commented on drafts and have generally been wonderful counselors. When I began the project in 1964, Henry Rand Hatfield's son and daughter and their spouses—John G. and Margaret Hatfield, and Charles A. and Elizabeth Glover—were very helpful and supportive.

Academic colleagues from related fields have also made important contributions. Through correspondence, Alfred H. Bornemann, J. Laurence Laughlin's biographer, and A. W. Coats, a historian of economic thought at the University of Nottingham, offered many useful insights. Herman Freudenberger, also a historian of economic thought and a friend and former colleague from Tulane University, provided valuable perspectives and advice. James E. Kirby, professor of church history at Southern Methodist University's Perkins School of Theology, and Rev. Caroll Fancher, minister *emeritus* of the First United Methodist Church, Bryan, Texas, provided important background understanding of the evolution and principles of Methodist theology during the nineteenth and early twentieth centuries.

During my visits to Berkeley in 1964-1965, Hector R. Anton, chairman of the accounting area, provided me with office space and the opportunity to finance my research by teaching a section of the intermediate accounting course in each of my three terms of residence. Ann White, the secretary in the Berkeley business school, expertly typed my correspondence and memoranda. Allan Bortel, then an undergraduate at Berkeley, performed yeoman service in tracking down Hatfield's publications as well as references to him and his works. Beth Nguyen, Brett Shobe, and Brent Voorhees, three undergraduates at Rice University, provided valuable assistance in the latter stages of the project. My secretary, Delia Jennings, was very helpful throughout the 1990s.

The following archivists, librarians, and registrars went the extra mile to respond to my many queries:

- Patrick M. Quinn, archivist, Northwestern University;
- James R.K. Kantor and William M. Roberts, successive university archivists, University of California, Berkeley;
- Krista L. Ovist, archives assistant, Department of Special Collections, Joseph Regenstein Library, University of Chicago;
- Kathy Robinson Hillman, librarian, Moody Memorial Library, Baylor University;

- Bill Page, documents librarian, Evans Library, Texas A&M University;
- Ann Daily, business librarian, Texas A&M University;
- Joseph Capobianco, registrar, Columbia University;
- Jill Parchuck, business librarian, Watson Library of Business & Economics, Columbia University;
- Chris Anderson, assistant commerce librarian, University of Illinois at Urbana-Champaign;
- Diane Grundy, librarian, Henry Buhl Library, Grove City College;
- Katherine Edwards Art, archivist, First United Methodist Church of Evanston; and
- William K. Beatty, librarian/archivist, Frances E. Willard Memorial Library, Evanston.

Throughout the research and writing, Maurice Moonitz has been my unfailing guide and source of encouragement. He has graciously written a Preview for the book.

It is my hope that this biographical study will throw light not only on the contributions of Henry Rand Hatfield but also on the developments in academic and professional accounting that paralleled his career.

Stephen A. Zeff
Rice University

Henry Rand Hatfield

HENRY RAND HATFIELD: OUTLINE OF HIS PROFESSIONAL CAREER

Summary of Academic Posts

1894-1898: Washington University
1898-1904: University of Chicago
1904-1945: University of California

1866 Born in Chicago on November 27, the last of five surviving children of Rev. Dr. and Mrs. Robert M. Hatfield.

1883 Entered Northwestern University, enrolling in the classical course.

1886 Dropped out of Northwestern to take employment in the bond house managed by his brother-in-law, in Chicago. Also worked in New York City for the bond house, remaining with the firm until 1890.

1891 Reentered Northwestern University.

1892 Received A.B. degree from Northwestern. Entered doctoral program in the newly reopened University of Chicago.

1894 Became instructor in political economy at Washington University, St. Louis, while continuing his studies part-time at the University of Chicago. Remained on faculty of Washington University until 1898, though was on leave in 1896-1897 as a fellow at the University of Chicago.

1897 Received Ph.D. degree *magna cum laude* in political economy and political science from the University of Chicago, July 1. His thesis title was "Municipal Bonding in the United States."

1898 Married Ethel Adelia Glover (Ph.D., University of Chicago, 1898), June 15. Became instructor in political economy and political science, University of Chicago. Principal teaching duties were in the new curriculum resulting from the establishment in 1898 of the College of Commerce and Politics. Became a member of the American Economic Association.

1900 On leave for two quarters during 1900-1901, which included a three-month visit to several business schools on the European Continent.

1901 Academic title was changed to instructor in commerce.

1902 Promoted to assistant professor of political economy, and was made first dean of the College of Commerce and Administration.

1903 At the annual meeting of the American Economic Association (AEA), in New Orleans on December 30, presented a brief paper—as discussant of another paper—in which he remarked on proper accounting practice. Reproduced in *Papers and Proceedings of the Sixteenth Annual Meet-*

ing, Third Series, Volume V, Number 1 (February 1904), pp. 272-77. It was the first discussion at an annual meeting of the AEA on accounting theory.

1904 Appointed associate professor of accounting (on the Flood Foundation) in the department of economics, University of California, to take charge of the accounting courses in the College of Commerce. Thus became the first full-time academic with a professorial title in accounting.

1908 Beginning with the March issue, became one of a dozen associate editors of *The Journal of Accountancy*. The *Journal* discarded this category after the issue of December 1914.

1909 D. Appleton and Company published *Modern Accounting: Its Principles and Some of Its Problems*, which was a pioneering textbook in a virtually barren accounting literature.

Published "Zwei Pfadfinder" (Two Pioneers) in the *Zeitschrift für Buchhaltung*, an Austrian journal.

Promoted to professor of accounting (on the Flood Foundation) and was appointed secretary of the College of Commerce, functioning as dean throughout his term (1909-1916).

1910 On May 26, was elected the first honorary member of the California State Society of Certified Public Accountants.

1911 Prepared a paper titled "Some Variations in Accounting Practice in England, France, Germany and the United States," which was presented at the annual meeting of the American Association of Public Accountants, in San Francisco on September 20. The paper was published posthumously in 1966. It was the first paper presented in the United States on the divergent accounting practices in different countries.

1913 Instrumental in organizing national Beta Gamma Sigma, the honor society for business students. Served as national vice president, 1913-1922. Was elected honorary member of the Alpha of Wisconsin chapter, 1913.

1916 Appointed acting dean of the faculties for the period from January to June. Was also appointed dean of the College of Commerce, retaining that title until 1920.

Served on the executive committee of the newly founded American Association of Collegiate Schools of Business, until 1920.

Active participant at the organization meeting, in Columbus, Ohio, on December 28, of the American Association of University Instructors in Accounting (AAUIA). Was elected vice-president for 1917 and 1918.

Became a member of the Berkeley Club, a university discussion group. Presented 11 papers between 1920 and 1942.

1917 Appointed dean of the faculties for 1917-1918.

In charge of conducting four six-week training schools, in Berkeley, for the Ordnance Field Service of the War Department, October to May 1918.

1918 In July, went on leave to become director of the Division of Planning and Statistics for the War Industries Board, in Washington, D.C. Assignment terminated in December.

1919 From May to July, served as an expert with the Advisory Tax Board in Washington. Returned to Berkeley in August.

Served as president of the AAUIA and as vice-president of the AEA. Was the only accounting educator ever to serve as an officer of the AEA.

1920 Resigned as dean of the College of Commerce on November 30 to become dean of the faculties, remaining in that position until June 30, 1923.

1922 Directed preparation of the university's budget for 1922-1923.

Elected Senator of Phi Beta Kappa, and served until 1928.

1923 Received an honorary LL.D. degree from Northwestern University.

Presented a paper, "An Historical Defense of Bookkeeping," at the eighth annual meeting of the AAUIA, in Columbus, Ohio, on December 29. The presentation was a huge success. The published paper has been widely reprinted and is Hatfield's best-known work.

1927 D. Appleton and Company published *Accounting: Its Principles and Problems*, a revision of *Modern Accounting*.

Served as acting dean of the College of Commerce, 1927-1928.

Presented a paper, "What is the Matter with Accounting?" at the annual meeting of the American Institute of Accountants, in Del Monte, California, on September 21.

1928 Beta Alpha Psi, the national accounting fraternity, presented Hatfield with its Award of Merit for "the most outstanding contribution to the literature of accountancy for the year ended May 1, 1928" for his book *Accounting*.

1929 Presented a paper and represented United States at the International Congress on Commercial Education, in Amsterdam, September 2-5. Was discussant at the Third International Congress on Accounting, in New York, September 11-14.

1930 Became a consultant to Professor Henry W. Ballantine (of the School of Jurisprudence) on the drafting of provisions relating to capital, surplus, and dividends in California's General Corporation Laws of 1931 and 1933.

1933 A discussant and United States representative at the Fourth International Congress on Accounting, in London, July 17-21.

1935 At the invitation of the Haskins & Sells Foundation, began collaboration with Thomas H. Sanders and William O. Douglas to write "an independent and impartial study" of "the body of accounting principles."

Presented a paper, "What They Say About Depreciation," at the annual meeting of the AAUIA, in New York City, on December 27.

1937 Retired from the active faculty of the University of California.

Presented a paper, "A Critique of the Tentative Statement of Accounting Principles Underlying Corporate Reports," at the annual meeting of American Accounting Association, in Atlantic City, New Jersey, on December 29. (The paper was never published.)

1938 The American Institute of Accountants published *A Statement of Accounting Principles*, written with Sanders and Underhill Moore (who had replaced Douglas).

1939 Presented a paper, "A Survey of Developments in Accounting," at the annual meeting of the American Institute of Accountants, in San Francisco on September 21. Also prepared an exhibit of rare bookkeeping books for the annual meeting.

1940 Ginn and Company published *Accounting Principles and Practices*, written with Sanders and Norman L. Burton.

Received an honorary LL.D. degree from the University of California.

1942 Delivered the annual Dickinson Lecture in Accounting, "Surplus and Dividends," at the Harvard Business School on April 21 and 23. (Published as a book under same title in 1943.)

1945 Died on December 25.

1951 Inducted into the Accounting Hall of Fame at Ohio State University.

Chapter 1

Beginnings, 1866 to 1904

This chapter provides a brief history of the Hatfield family, beginning with an emphasis on the life and Methodist value system of Rev. Robert M. Hatfield, whose principles were reflected in the life and work of Henry Rand, his youngest son. The narrative then focuses on Henry's early life, his undergraduate experience at Northwestern University, and his five-year employment with a bond house. Next, it takes up his five years both as a doctoral student in political economy and political science at the University of Chicago and as an instructor at Washington University. The chapter then considers his seven years as an instructor and assistant professor at Chicago and as the first dean of the College of Commerce and Administration, and it assesses the influence of key Chicago faculty members on his development as a teacher, thinker, and scholar. It was in his last three years at Chicago that accounting came to be his primary field of teaching and research. By 1904, he had become discouraged with the slow progress in the development of the college and left to take charge of the accounting work in the equally young College of Commerce at the University of California.

A study of Henry Rand Hatfield and his contributions to accounting must begin with his Puritan Methodist upbringing. The religious tradition of the six previous generations of intensely Protestant Hatfields who lived and died near White Plains, New York, is an inextricable part of our understanding of who he was, his commitment to higher education, his approach to accounting as an emerging field, and the disciplinary and ethical principles of accounting that he helped define. In short, we cannot separate Henry Hatfield from the New England Protestant mind, which, as American history shows, shaped the lives and contributions of many others in the centuries up to and during the time in which he lived. In Hatfield's case, New England Puritanism, combined with a classical education, produced a man who was an articulate and disciplined scholar, one whose deep commitment to his concept of accounting exemplified traditional Protestant ethics. Thus, the shaping of Hatfield's self-image as an accounting educator and scholar reveals the imprints of the Colonial and nineteenth-century American intellectual landscape.

THE HATFIELD FAMILY

Henry Hatfield, as an individual, echoes many of the values articulated by his father, Rev. Robert Miller Hatfield (1819-1891), a classic embodiment of eighteenth- and nineteenth-century American Methodism. As James Taft Hatfield, Henry's elder brother and a Germanist at Northwestern University, noted at the beginning of his unpublished biographical essay on their father,[1] trying to tell the life story of one who represents the authentic Puritan-Methodist tradition is difficult. The controlling value system of the world has now changed, even more than it had by 1938, when James Hatfield, by then 76 and converted to Unitarianism, described his father's life and values. And with that change has been lost an awareness of the power that the Protestant tradition wielded in the lives, beliefs, and values of those who wore and championed its mantle. Yet, as a survey of the facts of the Hatfield family will suggest, the Puritan-Methodist tradition constituted a powerful force in defining Henry Hatfield's life.

The Hatfield family, according to genealogist Abraham Hatfield, is thought to be descended from Thomas Hatfield, an Englishman who followed the Puritan exodus to Leyden, Holland, in the early seventeenth century.[2] Available evidence suggests that a son, Thomas, made the Atlantic crossing as a colonist sometime in the middle of the century and settled in New Amsterdam, which was then part of New Netherland (which would become the state of New York). Later, Hatfield moved to Mamaroneck, on Long Island Sound at the southeastern edge of Westchester county, and eventually his descendants migrated five miles north to White Plains, a settlement that was established in 1683 and which eventually became the seat of Westchester county.

The importance of Protestantism in the Hatfield lineage recurs frequently in the genealogy. Thus, beginning the story of Henry Rand Hatfield by alluding to the family's inextricable connection with Dutch Reformed Protestantism and later American Methodism offers an appropriate framework through which we can view these intellectual and religious traditions that shaped the family. As Abraham Hatfield noted, the name of Peter Hatfield, the son of Thomas the younger, appeared on the 1719 list of petitioners who sought permission to form a Presbyterian Church in White Plains, which would remain the locus of the Hatfield family for nearly 200 years.

As James Taft Hatfield wrote, Methodism became established in White Plains in 1787, only six years before his great-grandfather, Robert Miller Hatfield, and his wife joined the church.[3] The family's commitment to Protestantism ran deep: James's and Henry's grandmother was the daughter of a Methodist minister, and their father, also named Robert Miller Hatfield, was converted at age 17 in the Old Methodist Meeting House in White Plains. From James's portrait of their father, we see a minister who, though having little education, nevertheless felt God's irresistible call to preach. During the years of his ministry, he regularly strengthened his spiritual leadership through self-education opportunities offered by the

Methodist Conferences, which until 1954 were the main source of courses and examinations furnished to ministers for their continued development.[4] As James said of his father, "His most striking trait was his thirst for knowledge" (p. 4).

ROBERT MILLER HATFIELD—GOD'S FAITHFUL SERVANT

James Hatfield described his and Henry's father as one who, from an early age, displayed a strong sense of justice and an equally strong dedication to articulating his views of what he considered to be just. This sense of justice was Biblically based. From his early school days, he rejected slavery and alcohol. Before quitting public school, he had already shown extraordinary oratorical ability. In a school composition, he wrote: "Unfortunate, unhappy the man who first imported slaves into America. He fastened a stain upon her fair escutcheon which will be washed out only with the blood of her unborn sons" (p. 3). Although the pontifical diction later was used less effusively in his sermons and articles, his flair for Latinate diction and picturesque word choice, destined to be emulated by Henry Rand, was evident in his early sermons.

After leaving school, his mental acquisitiveness continued unabated. As the son of a devout Methodist who "was far more anxious to live justly with God and man than to increase his possessions" (p. 5), he regularly attended church class meetings, prayer meetings, and revivals and "was soundly and happily converted" (p. 9) just short of his 17th birthday. At age 22, he entered the ministry and through self-study prepared himself for the Conference examinations. From the inaugural year of his ministry, he was deeply committed to preaching the Word of God. As a youth in a household directed by Puritan values, he had known a life of hard farm work, morning prayer before breakfast, and few social pleasures, but increasing spiritual commitment. This background undoubtedly fostered his effective pastoral efforts, from his first pastorate onward. That he was successful was confirmed in a lengthy obituary.[5]

In the first year of Rev. Hatfield's ministry at a little church in Pawtucket, Rhode Island, membership increased from 109 to 162, a testimony to his fervid devotion and to the rapid growth of Methodism during this period. As James wrote, "He preached every Sunday morning and afternoon, held prayer- and class-meetings, assisted elsewhere at camp-meetings and revivals, and, in general, spent himself unstintedly [sic] in his chosen calling" (p. 9). According to James, his father recorded in his diary that "The Word of God was 'a burning fire in [my] bones'" (p. 12).

Robert and Elizabeth Ann Taft (1824-1903), his third cousin and a distant relation to the Tafts of Ohio,[6] were married in 1843. She was as devout as Robert, but "she was troubled by the thought that her own devoted piety did not measure up to the fiery zeal of her husband" (p. 17).

Throughout the years of Rev. Hatfield's ministry, the family moved regularly: itinerancy was a founding principle of Methodism—to encourage the spread of the Gospel—and the Hatfields relocated approximately every three years. Robert Hatfield's fame as a powerful orator continued to grow. Each move resulted in his leading a larger church, and he was soon regarded as one of the notable personages among Methodist ministers.

ROBERT MILLER HATFIELD—CHRISTIAN ABOLITIONIST

The late 1850s were a time of great tension in the country. As James Hatfield wrote:

> The country was in a feverish state: *Uncle Tom's Cabin* had been read by everybody, the Dred Scott decision had been announced, John Brown's raid and execution had stirred up universal excitement, secession was in the air, awaiting only the election of Abraham Lincoln to flare into the great national conflagration (p. 22).

In May of 1860, a Methodist General Conference was held in Buffalo, New York. This took place less than two years after the celebrated Lincoln-Douglas debates, and the burning issue at the Conference centered on whether Church members could hold slaves. Although the southern states had withdrawn from the Church in 1844, delegates from the border states attended. Perhaps Robert Hatfield's greatest claim to lasting stature—or, in some eyes, derision—among the great Methodist ministers was his famous speech on slavery delivered at the Conference. In a speech to the assembled delegates near the close of its lengthy debate, Hatfield argued eloquently and courageously against slave-holding, calling it an "abomination" (p. 25). James Hatfield characterized his father's speech thus: "The masterly style, the forceful diction, the profound seriousness of Hatfield's speech placed it at the very top of all the discourses made at the time. It evoked applause and hearty Methodist 'Amens'" (p. 23). The Conference approved an amendment prohibiting slave-holding by a vote of 139 to 74 (p. 25). Similar speeches by Hatfield followed in the wake of this success, which marked him as a leader among the abolitionist preachers.

The Civil War began in 1861, and in April 1865, the month in which General Robert E. Lee surrendered at Appomattox to end the war, Hatfield went west to assume an important pastorate at Chicago's Wabash Avenue Church. In view of his earlier impression of Chicago on a trip west in 1857, it is a wonder that the Hatfields moved there at all. According to James, his father had regarded Chicago with contempt:

> Chicago waxes worse and worse. It is without exception the meanest and dirtiest hole of a city that I have ever seen. The streets are like a bed of mortar, and are flanked on either side by pools of green and fetid water.... *It is a miserable hole* (p. 21).

However, the Chicago that greeted the Hatfields in 1865 was much improved over the conditions that had appalled Robert Hatfield in 1857. In a series of bold actions, the city had paved its principal thoroughfares, was well along the way toward solving the twin problems of its unsatisfactory drainage and inadequate plumbing, and was nearing completion of a sanitary water system. The demands of the Civil War had established Chicago as the assembly point for desperately needed grain shipments, thus adding to its standing as the country's rail transportation center. In 1864, the Union Stockyards were built, and by the mid-1860s, the city's factories were humming.[7]

After settling in Chicago, one of Rev. Hatfield's first acts was to deliver a eulogy on President Abraham Lincoln, who was assassinated five days after Lee's surrender, on April 14.

Notwithstanding his series of addresses on the moral evils of slavery, Robert Hatfield cannot be described as radical. An astute observer of human nature, he saw the reconstruction of the South in realistic terms. Prejudice, he stated in a series of front page articles in *The Independent*, a weekly that was probably the most influential church paper in the country and a trumpet of Radical Republicanism, continued to be deeply rooted in all people of the South: even former slaves segregated themselves according to the intensity of skin color and would worship only with those of their own ethnic subgroup; former slaveholders lacked economic skills to transform the war-ravaged land; former slaves had no new system of values to enhance their new freedom and to build new lives; and employers engaged in fraudulent actions to withhold pay from former slaves. As he wrote on March 4, 1869:

> An old and radical Abolitionist as I am, candor compels me to say that many of those who were once slaves are disposed to do almost anything else rather than eat their bread in the sweat of their faces. For this they are to be pitied rather than blamed. During all the years of their bondage, labor and slavery were in their vocabulary almost synonymous terms; and freedom meant nothing less than exemption from work and a perpetual holiday. It is not to be expected that the freedman should at once escape from the influences of these errors. Life on the plantation was hard and cheerless, and nothing is more natural than that the emancipated slaves should flock to the cities in quest of lighter work and more excitement....
>
> It is a slander of colored people to say, as their former masters are in the habit of doing, "They are all dishonest, the best of them will steal": but there are localities in which it is almost impossible to raise and secure crops, owing to their thieving propensities.[8]

Hatfield further argued in this series of articles that education launched by Christian churches was the only solution to what he termed "colorphobia." Solutions to the ravages of slavery and the Civil War would not be quick or easy, he stated—a stance not popular with many political theorists of the day. In another article, he wrote:

> Unless Christians extend a helping hand to the black man, and aid him in securing the qualifications essential to his new position, most of the blessings promised him in his emancipation will be lost.

> It was right and expedient to place the ballot in the hand of the freedman; but the value of the elective franchise as a means of improving his character and condition has been greatly exaggerated by visionary politicians and philanthropists. If the colored people of the South are doomed to an inferior position by their ignorance of their vices, they and their votes will be controlled by the more cultivated and competent whites; and no plans of reconstruction, no legislation at Washington can permanently prevent this. In the long run, capacity is sure to secure position and power. The thing to be done at once, and on a scale hardly yet dreamed of by the churches of the North, is to send a supply of competent teachers and preachers of the Gospel to all parts of the South.
>
> We are met at this point by the question, Whether, in prosecuting our evangelistic efforts in the South, it is possible to bring the whites and blacks together in the same congregations? After what I saw during my recent journey, I am compelled to doubt whether the thing is expedient, or even possible, to any considerable extent. The colored people themselves are, in many cases, violently opposed to it. There is a colorphobia of the South that is not by any means confined to the Anglo-Saxons. In one city that I visited I found the colored people divided, not with rigid exactness, but pretty accurately, into three distinct classes; and these distinctions they carried into their places of worship. The octoroons and Quadroons had a church almost entirely to themselves, and in which few whites or pure Africans are ever seen. I found a second church, crowded with a congregation a few shades darker; and was told of a third, where the worshipers were almost all full-blooded blacks. These people, in choosing their church relations, follow prejudices and affinities over which we have little control. And these prejudices are as inveterate as they are unreasonable.[9]

Although Robert Miller Hatfield exemplified fundamental Methodism in his sermons and articles during the 1860s, his interest in the role of Methodism and Christianity as ideologies for rectifying social problems places him among the leaders of those who advocated the principles later codified in the Social Gospel. The Methodist Social Gospel, which was formalized in 1916, advocated not only the importance of personal religious experience but also the impact that Christians should have on society. According to the Social Gospel, society will change if individuals are spiritually transformed. Rev. Hatfield's contributions to *The Independent* during the 1860s initially focused on slavery but then moved on to display his views on emerging social and religious issues such as women's rights, the evils of wealth, secularism, and business ethics. It was during this period that Henry Rand Hatfield was born.

When Robert Hatfield died in 1891, Henry was 25. The range of his father's religious, political, and social interests during the period from 1860 to 1885, which were the final active years of Rev. Hatfield's ministry, suggests that Henry Hatfield grew up in the period when the Methodist Social Gospel was first taking shape. Undoubtedly immersed in his father's views on Christianity and politics, Henry would have been affected by the emerging Methodist position that concern for salvation of the individual was not sufficient. As Norwood noted in *The Story of American Methodism*:

> Recurrent financial crises which threw many good people to disaster, the labor battles of the 1880s and 1890s, the overawing power of organized corporate business, the stresses of impe-

> rialistic adventures, the new and sometimes strident voices of women—these forces required something more than a lifesaving boat.[10]

Liquor, gambling, "improper diversions," ungodly literature, and desecration of the Sabbath remained critical, fundamental issues, but some ministers—and Rev. Hatfield was likely one of this group—were beginning to see the importance of the need for Christians to understand economic life in the new industrial age. The first advocates of the Social Gospel learned these lessons from the results of labor disputes, frequent financial panics, and depression and recession. These showed the deleterious effects of laissez-faire policies on the working class, which had historically been the group to which Methodism appealed.[11]

James wrote, "For some ten years, during and following the Civil War, Hatfield's leading articles were a feature of [*The Independent*], then at the height of its influence.... These articles made their author a national figure, and until the end of his life he was a prized contributor to many religious journals"[12] (pp. 28, 29). All of Rev. Hatfield's articles appeared on the front page of *The Independent*. In many issues, his articles appeared alongside those written by such well-known figures as the Quaker poet John Greenleaf Whittier, the preacher and reformer Henry Ward Beecher (founding editor of *The Independent*), the abolitionist William Lloyd Garrison, the author Harriet Beecher Stowe, and the editor and publisher (and founder, in 1841, of the *New-York Tribune*) Horace Greeley. These fellow writers were all leading voices in the national dialogue on social problems during and after Reconstruction, and all expoused the need for a sustained, Biblically based value system.

ROBERT MILLER HATFIELD—THE FINAL YEARS

During his pastorate at Wabash Avenue Methodist Church in Chicago, beginning in 1865, Rev. Hatfield preached some of his greatest sermons on political corruption, Romanism, the saloon, and the theater—issues that share a common theme: the importance of mental, moral, and spiritual self-discipline and adherence to Biblical guidelines. As James remarked, "The three years at Wabash Avenue marked a high point in influence and success" (p. 31). The church, located in the best residential area, was visited by many important guests, including the evangelist Dwight L. Moody, Henry Ward Beecher, and the abolitionist pamphleteer and black leader Frederick Douglass. It was during this pastorate that Henry Rand was born, on November 29, 1866.

After six years in Chicago, the Hatfield family sought an escape from the city's rigorous climate. They left not a moment too soon. In October 1871, six months after their departure, "a fire swept across the heart of the city, destroying its whole commercial district, gutting most of its fine neighborhoods, and leaving a third of its people homeless."[13]

The Hatfield family spent three years in Cincinnati, followed by three in Philadelphia. Then, in 1877, Rev. Hatfield accepted the pastorate at the First Methodist Church of Evanston. This was to be his last major assignment, and his family finally gave up its nomadic behavior. This fledgling suburb of Chicago, a devout Methodist enclave which in 1900 would become the home of the Woman's Christian Temperance Union,[14] was the seat of Northwestern University, where Hatfield would serve as a trustee and fund raiser from 1878 onward, his sons James and Henry would take their first degrees, and James would be, for 44 years, a professor of German and head of department.

The town of Evanston, located 12 miles north of Chicago's commercial center, fronted on Lake Michigan. Chicago was rebuilding itself energetically in the aftermath of the Great Fire of 1871, this time with iron and steel instead of wood. By the end of the 1870s, most of the earlier momentum had been recaptured, and Chicago was poised to begin a new cycle of expansion and development.[15] James, who was 15 when the family moved there, described the Evanston of 1877 as follows:

> Evanston was a favored village of a few thousand inhabitants, with many of the features of a New England town. None of the streets were paved, sidewalks were of wood, mail was received twice a day in a one-storied shanty on the main street. The town had been laid out in the midst of primeval forests by the Methodist-founders of the University in 1854, and attracted people interested in education, as well as numbers of retired preachers, teachers, and missionaries. The imposing black church, seating some 1,200 persons, cared for the spiritual needs of most of the population; it was the Methodist cathedral of the region (p. 39).

Even then, the Evanston church was known for its great pulpiteers. During his tenure, Hatfield brought the church back from Unitarianism to mainstream Methodism. As had been characteristic of the churches he had led, attendance soared. James remembered:

> the great prayer-meeting filled the lower room every Wednesday night, and was a social institution of unique significance: all sorts and conditions united there for prayer, song and testimony; professors, capitalists, impecunious theological students, shop-keepers, tradesmen—all had a chance to ventilate their religious experiences, and used it without restraint. The quality of their offerings was always vivid, not infrequently racy (p. 40).

After three years of service at the First Methodist Church, Robert Hatfield gave his farewell sermon in October 1880. His pastorate is commemorated by a portrait, painted in 1868 by Theodore Pine, which is displayed in a passageway of the church, located at the corner of Church Street and Hinman Avenue in central Evanston.

During the first half of the 1880s, Hatfield was pastor of two Chicago churches,[16] and from 1878 to 1891, he was an active trustee and one of the most influential members of the executive committee of Northwestern University. He helped raise funds for the Science Hall and for the first men's dormitory, which, following his death, was named for him.[17]

Hatfield preached regularly and worked diligently in the great revival campaigns of evangelists such as Dwight L. Moody (p. 36). Among his sermon themes were: "The state of the unrepentant after death; prayer; Christian deportment under losses, the antidote to care; reaching the desired haven; to young men; home-piety; suicides, their causes and cure" (p. 40). In 1883, he had occasion to give one of his thumping orations at a hearing into charges that a fellow minister had advanced heretical doctrines. James reported that it was a "forceful speech, stating, 'with sledge-hammer blows,' the fundamental beliefs of the Methodist Church in regard to the Scriptures, the atonement, and probation after death" (p. 41).

Rev. Hatfield died on April 1, 1891, at the age of 72.

THE SPIRITUAL LEGACY

Robert Miller Hatfield's strength lay in his unswerving commitment to his fundamental Methodist convictions; his practical vision concerning the role of the Church in leading social change; his belief that the Protestant Church should articulate the value system of the United States; and his remarkable ability to unite people, wherever he served, through his oratory and unflinching adherence to fundamental Christian values. His vision of a theology that combined individual accountability with social leadership made him exceptional among Methodist ministers. His refusal to deemphasize fundamental Methodist Protestantism in any area of life and his determination to describe with unflinching directness the dark side of the Reconstruction controversy, in which both blacks and whites were bound by deeply rooted prejudice, likely cost him the stature that, as a practical visionary, he richly deserved. He was never reticent and had little patience with those who acted with political expediency and refused to take a stand. He is credited with having said, "Call me a savage, a disturber, or anything else, but do not dishonor me by calling me 'a safe man'."[18]

Free of ulterior motives, he was willing to argue for his beliefs with little thought of the consequences to his career. As one of the eulogizers said at Hatfield's funeral sermon, "he was a straightforward, upright, manly disciple of Christ. He was absolutely incapable of that diplomatic speech which conceals one's true belief."[19] He believed that the sermon was a powerful instrument for change; that change must be sanctioned by the Gospel, which was the sole arbiter of truth; and that ethics were inviolable and should pervade every aspect of human experience. For example, a sermon he gave on temperance to the Evanston Citizens' League in 1886 illustrates the directness of his style:

> Now, in spite of the charter of our university, in defiance of the state law, in disregard of the village ordinances we are disgraced and cursed by grog shops here in Evanston, and some of lowest and meanest and dirtiest kind....

> Now, I submit to every candid man and woman that there is something wrong in this, grievously wrong, outrageously wrong. A rum seller has no more right or business in Evanston than a horse thief or counterfeiter, and any man who comes here and violates the law, and outrages public sentiment, by endeavoring to sell intoxicating drinks would have no just ground of complaint if some of our indignant citizens should dump him and his whole concern into Lake Michigan the first day he enters upon his business. It is an insufferable insult to every decent man in this community, and if the law has no relief for us, if there were no legal way of meeting this, I should stand up here or elsewhere and say the people would be justified in falling back on their natural reserved rights and treating these scoundrels as they deserve. I am righteously indignant. Every drop of blood in my veins tingles when I think of the insult and injury put upon us by these worthless vagabonds, who are not worth as much as the cost of the powder it would take to blow them up.[20]

It was into the home of this venerable Methodist minister, who lived what he preached, that Henry Rand Hatfield was born. We can infer from the letters, articles, and speeches made by Henry Hatfield during his career, as well as his views on accounting principles, accounting practice, and accounting education, that his father's values were powerful forces in molding his own values. Both men exemplified lifelong commitments to the highest moral standards for their respective vocations. Both believed in living and working according to these ethical standards. Both were visionaries who nevertheless recognized the reality of human frailties and the limits that those frailties place on the high ethical calling that both believed should be the goal of all individuals. Both advocated a practical idealism that recognized the value of education for a democratic society—one of the fundamental tenets of Methodism.

Like his father, Henry Hatfield possessed remarkable skills in the written and spoken word. And (as I discuss further in Chapter 6) his father's Methodism, which was evident in his own life, can be felt reverberating through the style as well as the values that are reflected in many of his speeches and essays.

THE PURITAN METHODIST FOUNDATION OF ECONOMIC PRINCIPLES

In tracking the influence of his family's Protestant and Methodist lineage on Henry Hatfield, we cannot ignore the fundamental Puritan economic value system that pervaded the Puritan-Methodist tradition. The fundamental principles of Methodism were more than theological and moral: they also included specific views on economics and financial accountability. An oath of poverty was never the goal, yet a virtuous use of wealth was mandated. For example, *The Methodist Armor* of 1912, one of the principal theological guidebooks of Methodism during the emergence of the Social Gospel, stated: "It is surely a Christian duty in every man who has power over natural law so to organize his affairs as to enlarge and make more bountiful the property foundation on which his household stands, for property is the absolute condition of civilization."[21]

We have only to consider capitalism's sanction of the rightness of wealth in the natural order of human endeavor, to see that Methodism and capitalism existed in a symbiotic relationship. The central doctrine of Protestantism was justification by faith, not works. Nevertheless, works were important; but they had to be done in the spirit of doing good within society. Justification by faith led to freedom for the individual believer, who no longer depended on the intervention of priests to be made right with God. Because grace became manifested in good works, good works and productivity became signs that an individual had received grace. As Thomas Taylor, the renowned English Puritan divine, stated in 1653, "We teach that only Doers shall be saved, and by their doing though not for their doing."[22] Honest economic practices, performed by the sanctified individual, manifested God's blessings. Hard work and industry that led to productive economic activity for the common good was the highest human endeavor. From the Protestant and capitalist perspective, negligence in business was believed to harm the public welfare.[23]

From a purely Scriptural standpoint, visible fruits were sanctioned by the Parable of the Talents and the Olivet Discourse. Christ stated that believers were to seek first the Kingdom of God and his righteousness, and all other things would follow. Thus, material blessings were seen as a sign that the successful believer had indeed received Grace and divine blessing.

Education was critical to the salvation process. The individual believer, responsible for working out his own salvation through faith and then manifesting this faith in good works, needed knowledge, available initially through study of the Scriptures and, later, in classical works that echoed the main values of Scripture. Without continued study and increasing knowledge of God's word, the inner Light of Grace could be darkened and the nourishment of the whole person diminished. Study of Scripture and Godly works yielded knowledge of God's will for the individual believer.

Thus, Methodism launched Sunday schools as early as the 1790s, and colleges and universities in the decades before the Civil War, including Wesleyan University, Emory College (today Emory University), Indiana Asbury University[24] (today DePauw University), Union Institute (today Duke University), Ohio Wesleyan University, Iowa Wesleyan College, and Northwestern University (where the three sons of Robert Miller Hatfield received their undergraduate education). After the war, the Methodists founded Drew University, Syracuse University, and Central University of the Methodist Episcopal Church, South (today Vanderbilt University), among others. "In 1880," Norwood wrote, "the M. E. Church alone had forty-four colleges and universities, as well as eleven theological seminaries and institutes and one hundred thirty secondary schools of various sorts. It had a board of education responsible for all the many aspects of the work."[25]

Thus, because individuals grow by work and education, Methodism advocated commercial law as being necessary to organize the active forces of society for the good of its citizens. Wealth could be a byproduct of properly directed, disciplined work habits: "You sharpen men by industry ... and you gain freedom from bondage to matter by property, which gives men the opportunity of reflection and of refinement. Property as our master is a tyrant, and mean enough; but as your servant, it is God's noble gift."[26] According to Methodist theology, the Gospel inspires industry, which in turn sharpens the intellect; but, at the same time, it strictly forbids prodigality:

> He has made the earth, and stored it with all its wealth; he has created the natural forces and laws which are used in the creation of wealth, and he has put all these at my service. My labor is his because I am his handiwork; because I am dependent upon him for my existence; because, therefore, my supreme allegiance is due to him; and all that by means of my labor I get out of the earth is his. All the wealth which is dug out of the earth ... or which is directly produced ... by the wafting winds of commerce, is gathered from stores which he has accumulated and made valuable by means of powers with which he has endowed us. To take these stores and employ these powers for our own uses and purposes is just as truly an act of dishonest defalcation as for the clerk to take money from his employer's till for his own pocket.[27]

This perspective remained a sustaining principle in American Methodist theology. Repeatedly, the Methodist faith and message, as stated in the many versions of the Methodist *Discipline*, argued for an approach to living that advocated balanced economic progress with accountability for wealth: "Do not forget that man has temporal as well as spiritual needs," recites the 1886 edition of the *Methodist Church Member's Manual.*[28] In the Methodist *Discipline*, published in 1864, members were admonished "to avoid evil, do no harm, avoid borrowing without intent or capability to repay, spending money on costly apparel, unholy diversion, and self-indulgence."[29] Yet, Methodism, in all its theological guidebooks, emerges as an active faith that calls for full development of the individual within the confines of the Gospel and the Church:

> You have not entered the church simply to escape the world.... God has not set his condemnation upon any of our natural faculties and endowments; and it is no virtue to crush or strangle them. Religion gives them all, scope and right direction.[30]

Like Christ, the Christian should condemn all false principle, revile when reviled, seek the highest good of all people, and oppose everything that hinders the realization of society's highest good. The Christian is to "seek the public good" as "the most good is finally accomplished by doing always the good which may be done in the present."[31] Methodism was not an ascetic religion but one that sought to raise the standards of the world by application of Christian principles to all walks of life:

> Take the world as it is. Do not lay out for yourself an eccentric path. Do not suppose that to be a Christian you must cease to be a good farmer, or merchant, or physician. The world needs all honest employment. Do not lead others, in their aspirations for holiness, to despise these things. The holiness that cannot be presserved [sic] in the common employments of life is not strong enough to save the world. It is in the sanctifying of all our human relations that Chris-

tianity must save mankind. The more, therefore, you can bring your own example within the common life—the life of the great multitude, the more inspiration will there be in it for all.[32]

In Methodism as well as in Puritanism, education was defined as essential to salvation and prosperity:

[The Gospel] inspires industry, sharpens the intellect, forbids prodigality, all of which tend to the accumulation of property. Educated mind *finds* the hidden gold, silver, coal, oil, and utilizes the resources of nature, which lie neglected by a savage people.... The richest nations on earth are Christian nations.[33]

Thus, Christianity has the power to reform economics for the betterment of humanity. This ongoing mandate for education as critical for spiritual, moral, and economic salvation clearly manifested itself in the life of Robert Miller Hatfield and was carried into the life of Henry Rand Hatfield, whose views on economics, education, and accounting, as will be shown, echoed these fundamental Puritan-Methodist principles.

While the thesis of Max Weber's landmark study *The Protestant Ethic and the Spirit of Capitalism*[34] is not the focus of this study, readers will note that many of the features of nineteenth-century Methodism which defined both Robert Miller Hatfield's and Henry Rand Hatfield's views of the world, mirrored many of the critical features of Puritanism defined by Weber. First, economics had high moral significance. For both Hatfields, their individual callings in life, their chosen careers, became an affirmation of their worth as individuals. They pursued their work with earnestness and not just for monetary gain. For Henry Hatfield, business and the conduct of business should reflect the highest of moral and rational values. This principle became the focus of many of his essays (see Chapter 7). Stated another way, both father and son sought and found social and moral significance in their life callings, which were guided by clearly defined moral principles. These principles did not merely supply a set of pragmatic rules to use in the pursuit of a utilitarian end. Both men believed that accumulating wealth was concomitant with an obligation to make careful use of possessions. Methodist theology, as shown through its guidebooks, advocated the attainment of wealth while assiduously arguing for moral stewardship in the gain and use of that wealth. Both Hatfields followed this tenet. Robert Miller Hatfield argued for this perspective in the pulpit, while Henry Hatfield argued for it in his essays on the proper conduct of accounting. Each, in his own way, argued for high moral principles, diligence in pursuit of one's life's work, and careful use of wealth. Their value systems reflect the Protestantism that, according to Weber, influenced Capitalism. Since the Hatfields' combined lives spanned more than 12 momentous decades (1819-1945) and covered the period when American capitalist enterprise emerged in full force, we can see their lives against that economic landscape. In both, we can see what James Taft Hatfield called the Puritan-Methodist tradition shadowing all they did, although in different ways. In Henry Hatfield, we see these goals

Rev. Robert Miller Hatfield and his family in about 1879. From left, standing: Henry, Anna (wife of Samuel A. Kean), Emily, and James; sitting: father Robert, Marcus, and mother Elizabeth. Rev. Hatfield was pastor of the First Methodist Church of Evanston, and Henry was about 12 years old.

manifested in his high moral vision of accounting; in Robert Miller Hatfield, we see them in his commitment to the efficacy of the social gospel. In short, what Weber identified and what both Robert Miller and Henry Rand Hatfield exemplified was a capitalistic social ethic inspired by Puritan religious values. It was a social ethic that defined the conduct of their lives and work. Methodist theology, clearly an offshoot of the New England mind (as described by Perry Miller[35] in his landmark work), became the catalyst for their values and actions.

EARLY LIFE AND EDUCATION OF HENRY RAND HATFIELD

Little is known of Henry's early life. He was the youngest of nine children born to Robert and Elizabeth Hatfield. Four of these children died before their fifth birthday.[36] The other four children who grew to adulthood were Marcus Patten (1849-1909), who became a practicing and academic pediatrician; Anna Rebecca

(1851-1931); Emily Marcia (1860-1928), who was a church missionary in China; and James Taft (1862-1945), a classicist and professor of German at Northwestern University, who served as president of the Modern Language Association in 1934.

All three brothers—Marcus, James, and Henry—were humorous, perhaps Marcus the most of all. James's humor tended to have a sting.[37] In this respect, Henry followed.

Ill health, which plagued the family, was a factor in Henry's early life. He suffered from bad eyesight from an early age. In his teens, he spent one or two summers as a cowboy on a Dakota ranch, apparently to build up his health. He spent another period out west, erecting barbed wire along railroad tracks. He enjoyed travel and once accompanied his sister Emily on a trip to Hawaii, when she was en route to China as a missionary.[38]

Based on information about the family in James's biography of his father and on fleeting comments in Henry's extant speeches (see Chapter 7), we can assume that the Robert Miller Hatfield household was guided by strict Methodist principles: religion was "the very life and soul of the family, ever-present, pervading, regulating, and sanctifying all events."[39] From Rev. Hatfield's sermons, we can infer that Scripture reading held a dominant position in the family regimen, as did weekly class meetings (devoted to mandatory discussion of each individual's spiritual deficiencies), regular attendance at all church services—most likely characterized by two-hour sermons—Sunday School, and camp meetings. Education, in addition to extensive reading, was stressed. Writing, as a means of preserving the family heritage, was also a Hatfield tradition, and Rev. Hatfield was a regular contributor to a variety of Methodist publications until shortly before his death. Based on Rev. Hatfield's antipathy toward the theater, we can assume that the reading matter available to Henry and his siblings was tightly controlled. That the Methodist emphasis on education was integral to the Hatfield household can be seen in the careers chosen by Marcus, James, and Henry. Rev. Hatfield's sermons clearly showed his interest in the classics and the Christian humanist tradition.

Thus, it is hardly surprising that Henry enrolled in the three-year classical course at the Northwestern University Preparatory School. Considering the emphasis that Methodism placed on the classics—the result of John Wesley's influence on the character of Methodism—as well as Rev. Hatfield's love of learning, Henry's choice was not unusual.

In 1883, at the age of 16, Henry completed the classical course. Of the 27 units that constituted the Preparatory School's classical course, nine were in Latin, six in Greek, five in mathematics, and seven in history, English grammar, natural philosophy, and physiology. Henry continued this line of studies by enrolling in the classical course at Northwestern University.

In choosing the classical course instead of science, Henry may have been influenced not only by the example of his father but also by the interests and aptitudes

Henry Rand Hatfield as a young man. Photograph probably dates from the late 1880s, when he was in his early 20s and was employed in S.A. Kean & Co.

of his brother James, four years his senior. James loved foreign travel and eagerly sought to acquire foreign languages. James had completed Northwestern's classical course and received his bachelor's degree in 1883. Three years later, he was awarded a master's degree in Latin and then proceeded to Johns Hopkins University, where he obtained a Ph.D. in the same subject. In 1890, the year in which his doctorate was conferred, James accepted a chair in German language and literature at his alma mater, Northwestern University, which brought the number of full professors in the university to 16.[40]

James was known for his wit as well as erudition. To underscore the universality of his declaration that no one, regardless of national origin, should tramp on his lawn, he installed signs with "please" rendered in a Babel of seven languages to warn people against treading on his lawn. On another occasion, when he and a colleague watched the university president, Henry Wade Rogers, splash along a campus sidewalk after a heavy rain, Hatfield remarked, "See Henry wade!"

After two years at Northwestern, young Henry Hatfield left to join the well-reputed private banking firm of S. A. Kean & Co. in Chicago, which was also a bond house. Samuel Axtell Kean, his sister Anna's husband, was known as the "praying banker" becuase each Thursday he held a half-hour prayer meeting before opening for business.[41] From September 1885 until December 1890, Henry was employed successively as a bookkeeper, clerk, manager of the bond department, and, in his last year, manager of the New York branch office. It was during this period that he became acquainted with the matters of finance and accounting that would engage his interest during most of his academic career.

Why would Henry have left in the middle of his university studies to begin working in a business in which he had no previous experience? The Hatfield family genealogy attributes Henry's decision to "trouble with his eyes."[42] Yet one wonders whether the small print in financial documents would have been any easier on his eyes than Greek and Latin texts. Another reason might have been financial. His father was retired from the ministry; his brother James was studying for his master's degree; and his oldest brother Marcus was in the early stage of his career as a professor of medicine and had three young children. Moreover, perhaps Henry was tiring of studying the classics, and he may have viewed joining his brother-in-law's firm as an intriguing diversion or a means of finding his profession.

By 1890, S.A. Kean & Co. was "the largest private banking house in Chicago, and one of the oldest."[43] As a private bank, it did not come under state or federal supervision. On December 17, 1890, the bank was unable to meet its depositors' claims, and the firm closed its doors. Allegations appeared in the Chicago press that S.A. Kean had irresponsibly managed his firm's affairs. The unsatisfied creditors brought an action against Kean and his firm in county court, and the trial was extensively covered in the press.[44] By the end of the trial, which lasted two weeks, terms such as "fraud" and "swindle" were being used to describe Kean's practice of appropriating depositors' funds to finance speculations in the bond market. He had doctored his financial statements so that unsuspicious readers would not realize that his firm's assets were insubstantial in relation to its debts. As manager of the New York branch, Henry Hatfield was mentioned in the press, as creditors anxiously awaited his arrival in Chicago to hear his view of the state of the firm's finances. Hatfield was a witness in the trial. In the end, a syndicate of S.A. Kean's "friends," probably members of the Methodist community, arranged to pay creditors 35 cents on the dollar. While criminal proceedings were instituted and Kean was required to answer to a grand jury, it seems that no criminal trial was held.[45]

With this sobering exposure to the world of finance behind him, Henry resumed his studies at Northwestern in January 1891.[46] His brother's example, as well as a possible declining interest in the classics, may have prompted Henry's decision, made in his senior year, to major in German.

Henry's course of study at Northwestern included 23 quarter/hours[47] of Latin, 27 hours of Greek, 31 hours of German, 20 hours of mathematics, 21 hours of philosophy (including metaphysics and logic), and lesser concentrations in rhetoric, composition, orations and elocution, literature, and science. As already noted, he chose German as his major field. Nine hours of political economy and six hours of law, all taken in his senior year, were the only social sciences. These latter-day selections doubtless were the consequence of his sojourn in banking and were a clue to the fields he would choose for his doctoral studies.

Henry's instructor in the nine-hour sequence in political economy was Robert D. Sheppard, Professor of History and Political Economy, whose two earned degrees were in theology and who had previously been a Methodist minister.[48] Sheppard was a Northwestern trustee who served as the university's business manager from 1893 to 1903.[49] The six hours of law were taught by university president Henry Wade Rogers, who had previously been dean of the University of Michigan law school.

Following his brother's lead, Henry became a member of both the Beta Theta Pi social fraternity and the Adelphic literary society. He participated in several oratorical contests and served as treasurer of his graduating class. He was a writer as well, contributing to *The Northwestern* (the weekly student magazine) and *The Syllabus* (the school yearbook). In an article titled "The Bank Clerk" in the September 25, 1891, issue of *The Northwestern*, Henry drew on his experience with S.A. Kean & Co. to extol the qualities that a person develops as a bookkeeper in the course of training to become a bank teller:

> The book-keeper learns persistence and the power of all-absorbing attention, and finds in his formidable ledgers the same satisfaction and the same training gained from college mathematics, while the pursuit at night of an elusive shortage has the interest of a game of chess. This persistency is not gained so well in college. We puzzle for awhile over an obscure construction, but if the point is unimportant we let it pass if the solution is not soon found. In a bank there is no relative importance in mistakes. The difference must be found and the amount is absolutely unessential.

His concluding words were autobiographical and echoed the mental and spiritual discipline that was ingrained in his Methodist upbringing:

Undated photograph of Henry Hatfield, probably in his upper 20s, when he was a graduate student at the University of Chicago.

> I have shown that the discipline received in a banking office is such as to train and develop the faculties most needed in future life. And this is becoming known by many, so that it is no uncommon thing for young men to take a course of a few years in a city bank who have no purpose or desire to make that their life's work.[50]

It was not generally known that Henry was the author of an unsigned satirical thrust at President Henry Wade Rogers in the 1892 *Syllabus*. The first president of Northwestern who was not a minister of the Methodist Church, Rogers was a forceful personality and a controversial figure on the campus. In 1892, he dared to move the university's Commencement (i.e., graduation) ceremony from Evanston's First Methodist Church to the Chicago Auditorium, an action that would not have been appreciated by possessive Evanstonians. Henry's prize-winning essay, which was written in Renaissance prose, poked fun at the President's girth ("Henreweighed" was the sobriquet for Rogers), his windy inaugural address in 1891, and his promotion of varsity football.[51] Many years later, Hatfield said that he did not want it known that he was the author of the work because "it nearly did me in."[52]

Throughout his four years of study at the university, Hatfield's grades were consistently in the 90's (on a 100-point scale), and often in the high 90's, and in 1892 he was admitted to membership in Phi Beta Kappa. On June 13, 1892, Henry participated in an Oratorical Contest for the Kirk Prize, speaking on "The Sabbath." Three days later, at the Commencement ceremony held in the Chicago Auditorium, he was among 19 recipients of the A.B. (*Artium Baccalaureus*, or Bachelor of Arts) degree from Northwestern University.

During his senior year at Northwestern, Henry received two offers of employment from banking firms. Once again, however, he may have been inspired by his brother James's example. James had just received his Ph.D. from Johns Hopkins and was about to accept a faculty appointment at Northwestern. He was the second of the Hatfields (after Marcus) to embark on an academic career, and Henry's love of learning may have pointed him in the same direction. Perhaps prompted by his banking experience, he chose political economy and political science as the fields in which he would study, and he decided to enter the new University of Chicago.[53]

CHICAGO IN THE 1890S—A DYNAMIC COMMERCIAL LANDSCAPE AND A NEW UNIVERSITY

In 1892, when Henry Hatfield entered the doctoral program of the University of Chicago, the city had matured as a capital of industry and culture.

In the period of recovery after the Great Fire of 1871, Chicago was bursting with creative energy and civic pride. Industry and commerce quickened their pace. Architects such as Louis Sullivan, Daniel H. Burnham, John Wellborn Root, and William Le Baron Jenney conducted bold experiments in the art of office building design. The city known as the nation's rail hub developed the world's most extensive street railway system, with cable cars replacing horsedrawn cars in the early 1880s, followed by gradual electrification beginning in the 1890s. In 1889, the Auditorium, the biggest architectural project in the history of the city, was completed and quickly established Sullivan's credentials as a world-class designer.[54] The Newberry Library opened three years later, and in 1897 the Chicago Public

Library moved into a capacious Greek Renaissance building on Michigan Avenue. In 1893, the Art Institute began to flourish in its new building on the lake front. In 1891, Theodore Thomas left the New York Philharmonic to found the Chicago Orchestra (renamed the Chicago Symphony Orchestra in 1913).

In 1889-1990, Chicago competed successfully to bring to the city the World's Columbian Exposition, which honored the four-hundredth anniversary of Columbus' discovery of the New World. The Exposition's "White City" of buildings and attractions (including the first Ferris Wheel) occupied Jackson Park and the Midway Plaisance, on the doorstep of the projected University of Chicago, thus taking advantage of the extensive park system recently created for the city. Chicago's leaders paid little attention to Rudyard Kipling's unflattering remark about the city ("Having seen it, I urgently desire never to see it again. It is inhabited by savages")[55] in the confident knowledge that it was on the threshold of becoming a great metropolis. The fair was held from May to October 1893.[56]

In the midst of this exciting period of civic progress, leaders of Chicago's Baptist community enlisted the financial backing of John D. Rockefeller, "the world's richest Baptist,"[57] to found the second University of Chicago. The first University of Chicago had been opened in 1858, when the city's population of 84,000 was struggling to recover from the Panic of 1857. The mid-century decade of the 1850s was notable for the establishment of several institutions of higher education, with the University of Chicago being the third university founded in the Chicago area during the decade. Northwestern University, a Methodist enterprise, had been launched in 1851, and Lake Forest University, founded by the Presbyterians in the town of Lake Forest, 30 miles to the north of Chicago, had opened in 1857.

The first University of Chicago managed to survive the Great Fire of 1871 and the Panic of 1873, but it eventually succumbed to unwise financial policies. The university was being operated on borrowed money. In 1886, when the indebtedness was called, the university foundered and closed its doors. It was an embarrassment to all, and especially to the Baptists of Chicago. As Storr wrote, the university had "jeopardized its trust—and consequently any hope of becoming great—by anticipating greatness."[58]

In 1890, Chicago's population reached a million, partly from the annexation of outlying areas but mainly from the waves of immigration from Europe. "By 1890," wrote Mayer and Wade, "nearly seventy-eight percent of Chicago's population was foreign-born or children of the foreign-born."[59] In September of that year, the new University of Chicago was incorporated. John D. Rockefeller had given the University $600,000 (with more to follow), and William Rainey Harper (1856-1906), a Biblical scholar and a man possessed by a vision of a great university, accepted the presidency. Wesley Clair Mitchell (1874-1948), who received A.B. and Ph.D. degrees in political economy from Chicago in the 1890s and who later became one of the foremost students of business cycles, recalled the early days at Chicago as follows:

> The University of Chicago opened in October, 1892, and I was one of the aborigines, as we called the first entrants. It had perhaps the most distinguished faculty then to be found in any American university—such men as Michelson in Physics, Nef in Chemistry, T.C. Chamberlain in geology, G.H.Moore in mathematics, Paul Shorey in Greek, William Vaughn Moody in English, and John Dewey [who arrived in 1893] in philosophy. These men were drawn from all over the country and Europe.[60]

Harper's new university was not greeted with enthusiasm on all sides. A.W. Coats, a British economic historian, reported that "radical journalists and politicians had no hesitation in bestowing upon the new institution the opprobrious title of 'the Standard Oil University'."[61] Harper's practice of buying distinguished professors from other universities was viewed with a jaundiced eye by those who feared a capitalist intrusion in the ivory tower. Harper brought J. Laurence Laughlin (1850-1933) from Cornell to head the department of political economy.[62] Laughlin, in turn, populated the department with men of diverse personalities and ideologies. As Friedman wrote:

> Laughlin's emphasis on quality rather than ideology was combined with an emphasis on research by his faculty, as well as by graduate students in their training. A corollary was his belief in personal teaching as opposed to formal lecturing.... Though himself a hard-money man of rigidly conservative views, he demonstrated an extraordinary degree of tolerance for divergent views in staffing and guiding the Department.[63]

Laughlin's initial appointments included Adolph C. Miller (1866-1953) as an associate professor, the controversial institutional economist Thorstein B. Veblen (1857-1929) as a fellow, and William Caldwell (a philosopher whom Laughlin and Miller hoped to interest in economics) as a tutor. Laughlin's biographer wrote:

> When the University opened in October 1892, the Department of Political Economy was the best equipped in the country. Nineteen courses were offered; *The Journal of Political Economy* was to be published; and Laughlin was in a position to foster an interest in practical questions.[64]

Yet, as Coats suggested, "Had Harper deliberately set out to confirm the suspicions of those who regarded the University of Chicago as a tool of the business interests, he could hardly have made a better choice" than Laughlin, whom Coats describes as "one of the most conservative economists in the country."[65]

HATFIELD'S DOCTORAL STUDIES AT CHICAGO AND INSTRUCTORSHIP AT WASHINGTON UNIVERSITY

Courses Taken at Chicago, 1892-1893

In 1892, when Henry Hatfield, bachelor's degree in hand, was deciding where to take his doctoral studies in political economy and political science, the new Uni-

The three Hatfield brothers in 1896. From left: James, Henry, and Marcus. Henry was 29 years old and an instructor at Washington University, on leave from the University of Chicago's doctoral program.

versity of Chicago seemed the obvious choice. Northwestern had only Robert D. Sheppard, a close friend of the Hatfield family, who had never published any research. At Chicago, Hatfield would have colleagues and the inspiration of an academic enterprise whose driving force, President Harper, had assembled a distinguished faculty with the active financial backing of Chicago's civic leaders and no less a captain of industry than John D. Rockefeller. Wisely, Hatfield chose Chicago.

In his first year of graduate study, Hatfield took the following courses[66] and seemed, at first, to be taking a minor field in English:

Autumn Quarter 1892	
Principles of Political Economy	Miller
Railway Transportation	Laughlin
Shakespeare's "Tempest" Interpreted (first half-term)	R. G. Moulton
Literary Masterpieces and Their Interpretation (second half-term)	Moulton
Winter Quarter 1893	
Advanced Political Economy	Miller
Taxation	Miller
Studies in Poetry of Cowper, Coleridge, Burns, etc. (first half-term)	W.D. McClintock
[Title of English course unknown] (second half-term)	McClintock
Spring Quarter 1893	
Socialism	Veblen
Tariff History of the United States	Miller
Unsettled Problems of Economic Theory	Laughlin

No courses were offered at the university during the summer of 1893. In fact, students were not allowed to attend four quarters consecutively without their physician's permission.[67]

In 1893-1894, Hatfield took courses only during the autumn quarter, choosing the following selections:

[Public] Finance	Miller
Money and Practical Economics	Laughlin
Comparative Politics	Harry Pratt Judson

Comparative Politics was Hatfield's first course in the department of political science. Harry Pratt Judson, who was to become the university's president in 1907 following Harper's death at age 50, had been a history professor at the University of Minnesota prior to becoming head professor of political science and a member of the University of Chicago's original faculty.

At Washington University, 1894-1896

In January 1894, Hatfield took a leave from the Chicago doctoral program and joined the faculty of Washington University, St. Louis, as an instructor in political economy, with the intention of acquiring experience as a teacher. For the next two-and-a-half years, he taught at Washington University, with the important exception of the summer of 1894, when he enrolled in the following three courses at Chicago:[68]

Civil Government in the United States	Judson
History of Political Economy	Miller
Scope and Method of Political Economy	Caldwell

It was in Judson's civil government course that Hatfield met his future wife, Ethel Adelia Glover, of Washington, D.C., who had received an A.B. from Wellesley College in 1890. After teaching high school for several years in Washington, she matriculated on July 2, 1894, at the University of Chicago as a doctoral student in political science and history. During her first summer at Chicago, she and Henry Hatfield sat next to each other in Judson's course, and they became acquainted at a fudge party given by Judson during the term. Henry fell in love, although it seems that the feeling was slow to become mutual. Henry pursued Ethel "with more or less assiduity" (as he later wrote in a "notarized affirmation" of his love), and during his years in St. Louis, he wrote her a steady stream of affectionate letters.

At Washington University, Hatfield gave courses during the second half of the 1893-1894 academic year and during the succeeding two years. In the spring of 1894, he offered a course in political economy and another in psychology. In each of the following two years, he was responsible for five courses:

- Principles of Political Economy,
- Advanced Political Economy,
- Descriptive Political Economy,
- Financial History of the United States, and
- Tariff History of the United States.

Showing Laughlin's influence, Hatfield used Mill's *Principles of Political Economy* in the first course. He used Marshall's *Principles* in the Advanced course.[69]

Back at Chicago, 1896-1897

Hatfield arranged a leave from Washington University in 1896-1897 to return to the University of Chicago. He worked on his dissertation, took 11 courses, and continued to court Miss Ethel Glover (not necessarily in that order of importance). His courses were as follows:

Summer Quarter 1896	
International Law —War	Judson
American Constitutional Law[70]	Judson
Autumn Quarter 1896	
History of Political Economy	Veblen
Seminar	Laughlin
Diplomatic History of the United States	Judson
Winter Quarter 1897	
Federal Administration	Edmund J. James
Seminar	Laughlin
Scope and Method of Political Economy	Veblen
Spring Quarter 1897	
Diplomatic History of Europe, 19th Century	Judson
Seminar	Laughlin
American Agriculture	Veblen

Whether Judson's two courses on diplomatic history and James's course on federal administration were prescribed for Hatfield's doctoral program is not known, but their attractiveness may have been enhanced somewhat by the fact that Ethel Glover was enrolled in all three.

Influence of Laughlin and Veblen on Hatfield

Hatfield's intellectual development at the University of Chicago can largely be attributed to his colleagues and mentors there. While documented evidence of this influence is lacking, we can nonetheless infer something of the roles of both Laughlin and Veblen.

In political economy, Hatfield took six courses from Miller, four from Veblen, and three plus a year-long seminar from Laughlin. In the seminar, Laughlin met individually with the graduate students to discuss the development of their theses. Of Laughlin, Wesley Clair Mitchell wrote:

> He was not an original thinker of great power. He did not enrich economics as did, for example, the elder Clark, Irving Fisher, Veblen, and John R. Commons—to name only fellow-countrymen. He did not even keep abreast of current developments in economic theory. Mill and Cairnes were the models to which he clung.[71]

Yet Mitchell regarded Laughlin as a superb teacher. He evinced a great interest in his students, and he was determined to make them think independently: "Veblen and [philosopher John] Dewey might open fascinating new vistas to the mind; Laughlin forced one to face intellectual conflicts in his own mind and find out where he stood in the world of ideas."[72] Laughlin believed in the seminar as a means of guiding and stimulating graduate students in the writing of their theses. In an *Atlantic Monthly* article, Laughlin described his approach, which Hatfield came to embrace in his own teaching and writing:

> The purpose of study is not the absorption of a given author, but the understanding of a subject through many sources and many authors. Instructed to report upon a given topic, the student is obliged to learn methods of work and study of far greater importance than any acquired information; he learns how to use books, and he learns to weigh and discriminate between statements. Instead of accepting a carefully prepared exposition by the lecturer, with its logic and its resulting conclusions fully worked out, he is taught how to prepare the data, to exercise himself in the application of principles, and to draw his own conclusions. Instead of having the ground covered for him in a masterly way by the instructor, he is obliged to cover it himself, to learn by his own mistakes, and to gather experience from the fate of his own performances under the most rigorous criticism. The purpose of such a system is the acquisition of independent power and methods of work, rather than any specific beliefs. Indeed, the instructor may never know what the final beliefs of his students are.[73]

In Mitchell's view, Adolph Miller, a neoclassicist, was more up to date in economics than Laughlin. "All in all," wrote Mitchell, "[Miller] had the finest gift of exposition of any academician I have ever listened to at length."[74] Miller's intellectual impact on Hatfield is difficult to judge, but he seems to have been the inverse of Laughlin in terms of teaching method. Laughlin's example may have stimulated in Hatfield the urge to drive students to understand their own minds and research their own conclusions. In his approach to teaching (as well as in his textbooks and articles), Hatfield continually questioned authority and authorities, and he challenged students to defend their beliefs. Again, Hatfield's propensity to question beliefs and the principles on which they rest emulated his father's sermons and articles.

Veblen's well-known idiosyncratic manner may have redoubled Laughlin's influence on Hatfield's approach to teaching. Mitchell assessed Veblen the teacher as follows:

> To a well-brought-up scion of American culture, taking one of Veblen's courses meant undergoing vivisection without an anesthetic. Those who could stand the treatment, and not all could, came out with a much more critical attitude toward economic theory, and toward themselves—a critical attitude that included Veblen's own methods of arriving at conclusions—not at all a comfortable state of mind, but one that has marked advantages if one wishes to do scientific work.[75]

Veblen's biographer quoted another of Veblen's students as follows:

> It was [Veblen's] feeling always that a man should follow his bent as the surest guarantee of his accomplishing whatever he might, by any chance, have in him the possibility of doing and becoming. He was never more in earnest about anything than about helping a man to discover his true bent by first drawing him out and then bringing to bear upon the view or interest expressed a unique combination of quizzical scepticism and sympathetic interpretation. He had a very genuine and strong interest in any bold and fresh hypothesis backed by conviction and by evidence honestly sought, whatever the field of inquiry or whoever the inquirer might be.[76]

Reflecting this influence, Hatfield, in his articles and teaching, professed skepticism toward conventions unless they could be shown to emerge from a defensible theory. Hatfield's continual questioning of conventional practice and conventional explanations was consistent with Veblen's showing that economists' conclusions could be understood only in the light of their questionable premises and conceptions. Hatfield's many book reviews were a blend of sympathetic interpretation and penetrating critique.[77]

One student recalled that Veblen "had the wonderful faculty of discussing without prejudice and with such fairness an extremely controversial subject [such as socialism] that the students received not the slightest inkling of his own belief or conviction,"[78] a trait that many of Hatfield's students have also attributed to him.

Maurice Moonitz, in his remarks on Hatfield's unpublished papers (see Chapter 7), detects Veblen's influence in Hatfield's "involved" writing style and "his tendency to use long, unusual words in place of those more colloquial at the time."[79] Thus, it would seem that Laughlin's and Veblen's influence on Hatfield can be seen more in the latter's approach to writing and teaching than in the substantive views he espoused. As Hatfield made his career in accounting and not in economics, it is more difficult to discern their influence on his substantive views and values. In later years, Hatfield's few references to Veblen were almost reverential. In a paper presented in 1937, "Moriturus Vos Saluto," which was mostly a series of reflections on his Berkeley experiences, Hatfield mentioned only Veblen from his Chicago days.[80] Veblen, he said, had a "commendable" attitude toward students' facility with foreign languages, by which he meant that students had a responsibility to learn them. Hatfield confided, "I happened to be on rather intimate terms with Veblen, even though he was my instructor."

Another impact on Hatfield is probably traceable to Laughlin. Hatfield may have been impressed with the importance that Laughlin attached to assembling a department with diverse personalities and ideologies. In his many years in the economics department at the University of California, Hatfield, himself a conservative like Laughlin, succeeded in forming close relationships with faculty colleagues, including those in other departments, across the entire spectrum of political beliefs.

Completion of the Degree

On July 1, 1897, Hatfield completed his dissertation and received the degree of Doctor of Philosophy *magna cum laude*. The honors were based on his final oral examination. His examining committee consisted of Laughlin, Judson, and Albion W. Small (head professor of sociology). His final examination took place on June 17, 1897.[81] His thesis, "Municipal Bonding in the United States," was reported to be a tome of 1,923 pages.[82] It was never published, and no copies have survived.[83] The abstract of the thesis was as follows:

> A consideration of the elements which make municipal bonds attractive to investors, and of the various features of bonding as they affect the issuing municipality. The general economic principles which should determine the purpose, the amount, and the form of municipal debt are considered, as well as the effect of the various statutory restrictions. A sketch is given of the operation of an early syndicate organized to control the western bond market. The material of this thesis is derived mainly from the private records of several bond dealers of the time.[84]

Hatfield probably chose this topic as a result of his experience in the banking house of S.A. Kean & Co. between 1885 and 1890.

Final Year at Washington University, 1897-1898

In the autumn of 1897, Hatfield returned to Washington University and offered a course in psychology, an introductory treatment similar to the course he gave there in the spring of 1894. His textbook was Harald Höffding's *Outlines of Psychology*, with collateral readings taken from William James's *Psychology*. During 1897-1898, he also offered the following range of courses,[85] which illustrates the broad scope of work for which Hatfield was responsible:

- Elementary Economics,
- Financial History of the United States,
- Advanced Economics,
- Money and Banking,
- Descriptive Economics,
- Tariff History of the United States,
- Economic History since 1763, and
- Social Economics.

Hatfield viewed Washington University as a testing ground for a possible academic career. There, he confirmed his interest in teaching and enjoyed the opportunity to sample a range of courses and to direct their development. He was the only instructor in the department of economics. But his about-to-be fiancée was in Chicago, completing work on her own doctorate. In his frequent correspondence with Ethel, he compared the merits of going to Northwestern or to Chicago, as a stepping stone to a position in the new American University, in Washington, D.C. American University represented the fulfillment of the dream of Bishop John Fletcher Hurst, who had purchased the land and begun the massive fund-raising drive in 1891.[86] The university was to be limited to graduate studies. By 1897, it had not yet opened, but the completion of its first building in December 1897, to house the College of History, excited Hatfield's interest. Like Northwestern, American University had been conceived and nurtured by Methodists. In the end, Hatfield rejected Northwestern, writing to Ethel as follows:

> I would always feel in Evanston that my personal pull with Dr. Sheppard and Mr. Crandon [secretary of the university], and my relationship to my father had gotten me the place and that is not quite gratifying.... And if [American University] ever amounts to anything, I am sure Chicago will be a much better recommendation than Evanston [for a position at American].... And the opportunities in Chicago are all that one needs ask for. The mere fact of having to hold one's own against other men in the same department, is a help and a stimulus, which I would not have were I the sole economist at Evanston.[87]

But would Chicago be interested in him? Hatfield knew that Laughlin had been endeavoring since 1894 to found a school of commerce, evidently with Harper's sympathy. In a letter to Ethel dated December 3, 1897, he reported that he had told "Larry" Laughlin that "when [the proposed College of Commerce opens] and he wanted to get someone who united a fine economic training with a practical business experience," he was available. At the same time, Hatfield wrote to President Harper as follows:

> In accordance with your request that I sometime submit in writing the substance of my last conversation with you, I hand you the following: In so large an institution as the University there must be a number of positions in which a person with a thorough business training could be of service to the institution. Should there at any time be a vacancy in such a position, I beg that you will consider me as a possible applicant.
>
> As to my qualifications, I would state that I have had a training of more than five years in the best business school, a banking house. In the fourth year of this schooling I acted as manager of the bond department in the main office in Chicago; in the fifth year I was manager of the New York branch office, so that my experience covers much more than mere matters of detail.[88]

Hatfield proceeded to identify an investment house, a bank, and a manufacturing corporation that had offered him employment in 1891 and 1895. He then stated, "These were all refused as I did not wish to desert entirely the scholar's life." Harper forwarded Hatfield's letter to Laughlin with the handwritten note: "Mr. Laughlin—Why might Hatfield not be a man for our College of Commerce & Politics? WRH." Laughlin replied, also by hand, "Very good suggestion. But probably not for statistics. JLL."

Harper's reply to Hatfield has not survived, but it prompted the following letter from Hatfield, written a month later:

> My idea was that there might be some position in connection with the administration of the finances in which I could be of service to the University. I presume that the bulk of such work is done by the Comptroller. It would seem to me that, in so large an institution, there would be more than one man could attend to, and that my experience in managing a banking office

Henry Hatfield, probably around 1900-1902, when he was an instructor at the University of Chicago. In 1902, he became an assistant professor and the first dean of the university's College of Commerce and Administration.

> would be of service in attending to some branch of the University's finances. In addition to a knowledge of general business methods, my past training has made me familiar with the proper methods of keeping accounts, and has given me experience in attending to investments.
>
> I do not, however wish to "desert the academic ranks," as is evidenced by my refusal of several desirable business offers. I *must* teach. But I should not be averse to finding a place where I could combine some teaching with some work in practical finance.[89]

Hatfield's persistence paid off. On February 24, 1898, he wired Ethel, who was in Washington, "Uncle Larry writes that we get Chicago. Job date not given. H.R.H."[90] He resigned from Washington University at the end of the 1897-1998 academic year and was hired as instructor of political economy and political science in the University of Chicago. That Hatfield was succeeded at Washington University by Robert F. Hoxie, also a doctoral student in political economy at the University of Chicago, suggests that Laughlin may have had an arrangement by which his students could obtain teaching experience at the St. Louis institution.[91]

In May 1898, Hatfield published his first article as an academic. The four-page article, titled "Paper Money for War Expenses," appeared in *Student Life*, the monthly publication edited by the students of Washington University. Hatfield's argument, which would have been applauded by Laughlin, was that the government should not finance the Spanish-American War by printing money. In fact, the article was a paper that Hatfield had written in one of Laughlin's classes.[92]

On June 15, 1898, Henry and Ethel were married at her parents' home in Washington, D.C. Henry was 31 and Ethel was six weeks shy of her 31st birthday. Afterward, they rented an apartment across the Midway from the Gothic campus of the University of Chicago. Ethel received her Ph.D., also *magna cum laude*, on July 1, 1898, her thesis being a study of the U.S. Interior Department. Her major field was political science, with history as a minor. Even though she was far from being the first woman to receive a Ph.D. from an American university (the first was awarded in 1877),[93] such an occurrence was hardly commonplace during the last quarter of the nineteenth century.[94] There is no evidence that she engaged in teaching or research following the receipt of her doctorate.

HATFIELD ON THE CHICAGO FACULTY, 1898-1904: THE COLLEGE OF COMMERCE—AND UNIVERSITY POLITICS

The autumn term of 1898 began with Henry Rand Hatfield as the first faculty member whose appointment was ostensibly concerned with the fledgling College of Commerce and Politics.

At Chicago, the distinction between a college and a school had not yet clearly been established. While graduate students were registered in their respective departments, undergraduates were enrolled in one of three colleges: Arts, Literature, or Science. Each college was composed of a junior college for freshmen and sophomores, and a senior college for juniors and seniors. All of the junior colleges came under the aegis of the dean of the Junior Colleges, and all of the senior colleges fell under the jurisdiction of the dean of the Senior Colleges. Each of the three junior colleges and senior colleges had its own dean, but they seem to have been minor figures. Faculty appointments were in the departments, which were responsible for mounting all of the courses. The powers in the university, apart from the President and the Senate, were the head professors of the departments, not the deans of the colleges. A professional school (e.g., the School of Education) would have a status parallel to that of a department. It would have a faculty of its own, ordinarily under the headship of a dean.

The history of the efforts to gain recognition for a college of commerce illustrates the confused relationship between the colleges and schools. In February 1894, Laughlin placed before the Senate a plan for a "School of Commerce and Industry." It was approved in principle as a "College of Commerce and Industrial Science," later revised as "School of Commercial and Political Science," then titled the "College of Commercial and Political Science," and finally, in 1898, changed to the "College of Commerce and Politics." A quadripartite grouping of the departments of political economy, political science, history, and sociology administered the college. Laughlin, as head of political economy, was first among equals, as the college was regarded as his "baby."[95]

The only precedent for the college was the Wharton School of Finance and Economy (as it was then known), which had opened in 1881 at the University of Pennsylvania. Prior to 1904, the Wharton School did not have a director or dean and was merely a grouping of courses within the general college. The faculty members who taught the Wharton courses held their appointments in discipline departments.[96] Significantly, the Wharton faculty member who "was the leading force in the new school" from 1883 to 1895,[97] Edmund Janes James (1855-1925), had joined the Chicago political science faculty in 1896. James, who had taken his Ph.D. in Germany, cofounded the American Economic Association in 1885 and established the American Academy of Political and Social Science in 1889. At the behest of the American Bankers' Association (ABA), James had gone to Europe to study institutions for educating businessmen. His report, *Education of Business Men in Europe*, published by the ABA in 1893, attracted widespread interest. He was, without question, one of leading figures in the early movement to introduce business education in American universities. (James left Chicago in 1902 to become president of Northwestern University, and in 1904 he became president of the University of Illinois.)

While Hatfield had been hired for his usefulness to the College of Commerce and Politics, his faculty appointment was in the departments of political economy and political science. Most of Hatfield's other colleagues in the two departments were not strangers to him: in political economy, Laughlin, Miller (who left in 1902 for the University of California), Veblen, and William Hill (who had joined the faculty in 1893); and in political science, James, Judson, and Ernst Freund (a recent arrival from Columbia).

During the three academic years 1898-1901, Hatfield taught eight different courses: Civil Government in the United States seven times, Descriptive Economics twice, Social Economics twice, and one offering each of Processes of Leading Industries, American Constitutional Law, Principles of Political Economy, Commercial Geography, and Technique of Trade and Commerce.[98] All of the courses except Processes of Leading Industries were standard-bearers in the curricula of the political economy and political science departments; Processes was new, apparently having been designed for the college. Particularly intriguing was a new course that Hatfield was scheduled to give in 1898-1899 but which was cancelled. Titled "Railway Accounts, Exchanges, etc.," it carried the following description in the 1897-1898 *Register*:[99]

> 32. Railway Accounts, Exchanges, etc.—Lectures, Reading, and Reports
>
> Mj. Autumn Quarter, '98; 8:30
> Dr. Hatfield
>
> A study is made of the financial methods of leading railways as shown by an analysis and examination of their accounts. In the interests of both investor and manager the training in methods of railway accounts and auditing will be valuable, but this can be done to advantage only after taking the courses treating of the general problems of railway management (Courses 30 and 31).
>
> Together with this work, grouping allied topics, the student will be trained in a study of the construction of bond tables, the causes regulating the prices of bonds and securities, the various forms of state, municipal and railway securities at home and abroad, the calculation of foreign and domestic exchange, and an introduction to annuities.[100]

This would have been the first course offered by Hatfield with a significant accounting content. It would appear that the major portion of the course grew out of Hatfield's dissertation research, yet it is interesting that the course was designed to emphasize the importance to both the investor and the manager of an understanding of the methods of accounts and auditing. Laughlin's decision to have Hatfield offer the course may have been made out of lack of any other viable candidate, because the subject of accounting was not mentioned in their correspondence of 1897-1898.[101] Hatfield's experience with the accounts of S.A. Kean & Co. likely qualified him for the task, for he had never taken a course in the subject. Hatfield had vaunted his practical knowledge of accounts in his correspondence with President Harper, which Laughlin had seen. Years later, Hatfield told an interviewer how he happened into accounting:

> Asked how he came to specialize in accounting, Professor Hatfield disclaims anything so picturesque as an "inner urge," and says it was an accident. The authorities decided that business courses should have a place in the University curriculum, and he was called upon because of his previous business experience.[102]

The apparent successor to the Railway Accounts course (it carried the same course number: 32) was titled Technique of Trade and Commerce. It was offered for the first time, by Hatfield, in the spring quarter of 1901. The course description was as follows:

> 32. Technique of Trade and Commerce.—Weights and measures; customs regulations; exchange and price quotations; commercial documents; foreign and domestic exchange; accounts; investment securities; insurance, etc.
>
> Mj. Spring Quarter
> Dr. Hatfield
>
> An attempt to familiarize the student with the actual forms and methods used in modern exchange. Especial attention will be given to the interpretation of railway and other corporation accounts, and to the use and construction of exchange and conversion tables, cambists, bond values, annuity tables, etc.[103]

By contrast with Railway Accounts, which was never offered, Technique of Trade and Commerce seemed to contain less of an accounting emphasis. Yet it was the only course in the curriculum of the College of Commerce and Administration, prior to 1901-1902, that had any accounting content at all. No course syllabi survive from this early period, so it is not possible, apart from the course description, to judge the amount of time that was devoted to particular topics.

On July 1, 1899, the Beta of Illinois Chapter of Phi Beta Kappa was installed at the University of Chicago, and Hatfield became its secretary. His brother James Taft came down from Northwestern to officiate at the installation.

The Hatfields' first son, John Glover, was born on January 24, 1900, in Washington, where Ethel was staying with her parents, the John J. Glovers. During the winter quarter of 1899-1900, Henry Hatfield did not offer any courses at Chicago. After spending January with his wife in Washington, he paid a call on acquaintances at the Wharton School and spent most of February and March studying the manufacturing and refining operations of industrial companies in the Northeast and interviewing their executives, evidently to develop materials for his courses.[104]

The year 1900-1901 was pivotal in Hatfield's development. Apparently influenced by James, who had made a tour of European universities in the early 1890s, Hatfield conducted a three-month European tour of his own (and at his own expense) during the winter quarter, departing in early October and returning to United States in mid-January 1901.[105] He spent time in Belgium, France, and Germany.[106] Upon his return to the university at the end of March, he was interviewed by the press. A reporter for *The Chicago Sunday Tribune* wrote:

> As a result of the trip [Hatfield] will introduce several innovations and in a short time a prospectus of the new department known as the "College of Commerce and Administration" will be issued. The work in this department has never been completely organized, but with the return of Professor Hatfield steps will be taken to bring it up to the standard of the European schools.

In the news report, Hatfield outlined the proposal for the college:

> The idea of the system at Chicago is to provide a plan of education which will fit students for a business as well as a professional career. In doing this we do not wish to establish an ordinary business college, but a school that will aid in developing the student. Direct and immediate attention will be paid to the modern languages. This is necessary, as in time the United States will be at the head of the world's commerce. This work includes a drill in English. A course will be given in modern history, especially in that which relates to America. Elementary courses in physics, chemistry, and mathematics will be provided, together with advanced courses in the same subjects if there is any call for them. Special attention will be paid to political economy. Law, both commercial and common, will be taught.
>
> My work will include following new courses: History of commerce, commercial geography, technique of commerce, business organization.[107]

Nowhere in the article, or in another report that appeared in a different newspaper, was accounting mentioned.[108] Yet, in a letter written in 1937, Hatfield recalled that he had developed a course in accounting "as a result" of his trip to Europe:

> The beginnings were feeble. I think you can ignore the courses in 1898-1901. I returned to the University in April, 1901 from a six-months' leave, during which I went to Europe to see what the Colleges of Commerce in France and Germany were doing. As a result I offered 47. Accounting on my return and continued to give the course until I left Chicago for California in January, 1904.... We used no text book. The class was small. I followed largely the earlier writings of Professor J. F. Schär.[109]

In the academic year 1901-1902, Hatfield's faculty title became instructor in commerce, with an appointment only in the department of political economy. He was the sole member of the departments of political economy and political science with "Commerce" in his faculty title. Hatfield was still the faculty member most concerned with the operation of the College of Commerce and Administration, although Laughlin continued to be a force behind the scenes.

In 1901-1902, Hatfield's entire teaching load, except for a summer offering of Principles of Political Economy, were commerce courses: Commercial Geography, Accounting, Modern Industries, Banking (the latter three all being new courses), and Technique of Trade and Commerce. Turner wrote that Hatfield "versatilely grappled with a number of different courses in his years at the University, so that innovations in the commercial studies were often directly due to him."[110]

The description of Accounting, which was the course that Hatfield developed upon his return from Europe, was as follows:

> 47. Accounting.—A study of the underlying principles. Some practice work under the guidance of an expert auditor of accounts will be given, but only with a view to illustrating the principles discussed in the lectures. Emphasis will be placed on the interpretation of balance sheets and the problems implied therein.
>
> Mj. Winter Quarter; 9:30
> Dr. Hatfield and Mr. Arnett.[111]

Trevor Arnett (1870-1955), who was born in England, was the University of Chicago's chief accountant in 1899-1900 and its auditor from 1901 to 1922. He had been an accountant and chief clerk in the auditor's office of the Chicago & Great Western Railway from 1893 to 1896 and was a student in two of Hatfield's classes in 1898-1899 (even though he had received his A.B. from Chicago in 1898). Five students enrolled in the course, of whom one dropped it. Hatfield offered the course only one more time, in the winter quarter of 1902-1903, when it carried a description that emphasized it as useful for businessmen rather than as technical preparation for bookkeepers:

> 47. Accounting.—A study of underlying principles from the point of view of the business man rather than that of the professional bookkeeper. Examination will be made of the published accounts of railroad and other corporations, and emphasis will be placed on the interpretation of balance sheets and the problems implied therein. Practice work under the guidance of an expert auditor will be given, not with the purpose of training the students to be bookkeepers, but to illustrate the principles discussed in the class-room.
>
> Mj. Winter Quarter; 11:00
> Assistant Professor Hatfield
> and Mr. Arnett.[112]

Laughlin had never been satisfied with the ambiguous organizational niche which the College of Commerce and Politics occupied. A jurisdictional dispute had arisen among the four governing departments in 1900, prompting Laughlin to appeal to President Harper for a stronger form of organization. All that resulted was a change in the name (once again) to the College of Commerce and Administration, implying that it would, in the future, be more closely linked to the department of political economy than to the other three departments. Turner has remarked that the college "scarcely existed, in its first years of life, except as a paper rearrangement of courses which already formed a part of the offerings of the regular departments of the University."[113]

In 1902, an organizational change was implemented that led directly to Hatfield's promotion to the rank of assistant professor of political economy and to his appointment as dean of the College of Commerce and Administration. In 1901, at Laughlin's urging, the Senate had set up a committee to advise whether the College of Commerce and Administration should be reorganized as a professional school with its own faculty and dean. The committee, whose members were Laughlin, Judson, Small, E.H. Moore (mathematics), and James, reported in March 1902 that it favored the reorganization. The Senate received the committee's report but refused to transform the college into a school. Instead, the college was redefined as a "technical college," a term that was without precedent in the university and which endowed the college with few of the attributes of a professional school apart from its separate existence. There was no provision for appointing a dean, but Laughlin and President Harper were already in correspondence on the subject. On March 4, 1902, Laughlin wrote to Harper:

> The University of Ill. is offering Mr. Hatfield higher salary and higher rank than he has here to enter their new College of Commerce just established.
>
> I advise an exhibition of appreciation of his work done here; also, the plan I suggested before: an advance of $200 next year, and a letter promising him the promotion to Asst. Professor the year following. I think that will hold him.

On March 8, 1902, Laughlin wrote again to Harper:

> As to the Deanship of the College of Com. and Adm., it looks as if it should go to [Hatfield] on competitive merits; he has done all the work hitherto of a practical & efficient kind, he is familiar with all the organization, and he has decided executive ability. I should favor it.

Harper replied to Laughlin on March 13:

> I think if we give the deanship to Hatfield it would be well to give him the assistant professorship this year. The deanship would carry with it a salary of $300. This would make a total of $2,000.[114]

In the end, Hatfield remained at Chicago and was advanced in rank and appointed the first dean of the College of Commerce and Administration.[115]

The establishment of colleges of commerce in American universities was not free of controversy, and one of the staunchest opponents of such programs was Thorstein Veblen, who had been promoted to the rank of assistant professor in the department of political economy in 1900.

Veblen's presence among those with whom Hatfield needed to reach a consensus probably doomed the Chicago experiment from the beginning. Veblen, philosopher turned social critic, was beginning to attract attention from his monumental book, *The Theory of the Leisure Class*, published in 1899.[116] As Hatfield already knew from his days as a graduate student at Chicago, Veblen was at best an iconoclast and at worse the *enfant terrible* of higher education. Veblen's anti-collegiality with both faculty and undergraduates was legendary, as was his philandering, which would cost him positions at both Chicago and Stanford.[117] Like his father, Hatfield was known for his moral and political conservatism, and it is likely that Veblen's acrid rejection of Christian values and even minimal academic deportment created a tension between the two men.

Veblen's own philosophies, as expressed in *The Theory of the Leisure Class* and, later, in *The Higher Learning in America*,[118] were diametrically opposed to any education that was vocational or utilitarian. As Diggins observed, Veblen felt that "Schools of commerce were too imbued with the 'business animus,' and law schools too steeped in the study of the strategic use of knowledge to explore its theoretical foundations."[119] In *The Higher Learning*, Veblen wrote, "A college of commerce is designed to serve an emulative purpose only—individual gain regardless of, or at the cost of, the community at large—and it is, therefore, peculiarly incompatible with the collective cultural purpose of the university. It belongs in the corporation of learning no more than a department of athletics."[120]

Thus, Hatfield's attempt to strengthen the College of Commerce represented the essence of what Veblen detested: another manifestation of capitalist culture and the university's increasingly stark devotion to pecuniary goals.

Ironically, however, in some respects Hatfield's Puritan Methodist conservatism coincided with Veblen's vision: both men were destined to become the consciences of capitalist business enterprises, moralists with elitist sensibilities and egalitarian sympathies. Both wanted to save higher education from the effects of purely pragmatic education. Both rejected praxis not based on sound theory and principles. Both valued the study and mastery of languages, and Hatfield admired Veblen's intellect.[121] Both "opposed the careerist tendencies of college life that would turn the university into a well-heeled agency for the production of well-adjusted young corporation men."[122] Both believed in the possibility of high ethical standards in the conduct of business. Yet, at the same time, Hatfield—arguing from the Methodist tradition which shaped his values—sought to achieve this ascetic level of business and industry by an ideology that was foreign to Veblen, who passionately believed that profit-seeking, organized religion, capitalism, and nationalism were detrimental to society. The individual's idle curiosity, Veblen argued, if allowed full expression, would emancipate individuals and permit their true productive powers to operate. From Hatfield's perspective, nothing could have been more antithetical to his thinking and that of the Puritan Methodist milieu of the nineteenth and early twentieth centuries, which valued self-discipline, highly nationalist education, patriotism, and Christian-based standards of government as the basis for capitalism.

Veblen continued unrelentingly throughout his troubled career to reject the accumulation of wealth and the business preoccupation with profit. In contrast, Hatfield, a byproduct of New England Puritanism, saw ethical accumulation of wealth as an acceptable, God-ordained result of hard work and disciplined living. While Hatfield, as we shall see, viewed the need for principled accounting practices as concomitant with the goal of effective and ethical business operation, Veblen would have seen accounting as simply another pecuniary tool for focusing on the enhancement of profit and for distorting and obscuring the noneconomic motives of profit. Hatfield's statement, published in 1927, that "accounting attempts to exhibit ... the amount the proprietor is worth, and how his wealth increases or decreases from time to time ... [and is concerned] with the abstract quantity of wealth, and how, and why that net wealth changes in amount"[123] would have been viewed by Veblen with pure antipathy as the essence of what he sought to eliminate in his larger argument for the rejection of capitalism.

Paradoxically, perhaps Veblen, even more than Hatfield, saw the ethical dangers in developing a class of well-educated professionals who, in their commitment to administering other people's money, would surely develop a new, less noble code of corporate ethics and a new role for themselves that was less accountable to society and more accountable to the amoral goals of the corporate machine.

Incongruous as it may have seemed, Veblen's name appeared on the initial roster, published in 1902-1903, of faculty members who were associated with the College of Commerce and Administration.[124] One could hardly envy the lot of a commerce dean who would have Veblen as a faculty colleague.

During the following two academic years, 1902-1904, Hatfield's teaching load did not involve the development of any new courses. He offered Commercial Geography and Banking three times each, Principles of Political Economy twice, Accounting and Modern Industries once each, and Modern Business Methods (which was a revised version of Technique of Trade and Commerce) once. Administrative matters consumed considerable time. One of Hatfield's duties was to coordinate a series of lectures given in the university by "representatives of great business institutions."[125] He edited a volume titled *Lectures in Commerce*, which contained a selection of the lecturers' papers.[126]

In his report to the President submitted in 1904, Dean Hatfield drew attention to changes in the curriculum and to a number of "pressing needs," which included the following:

> A group of specialized courses designed to train accountants. The course now given in accounting is entirely different in scope and purpose, being adapted to give the understanding of accounts which might be demanded by the business man whose interest is that of manager or proprietor, and not the technical training needed for the professional accountant.[127]

Hatfield had been placed in a difficult position as dean of a college that existed more on paper than as a self-directing unit. Support from the university administration was minimal, and the availability of faculty members to teach particular courses depended on the generosity of discipline departments such as political economy and political science. The appointments of any of the faculty who might teach commerce courses were in their respective departments. Even Hatfield's appointment as dean was in political economy. In his report to the President submitted in 1904, Hatfield referred diplomatically to persistent tensions between the college and the all-powerful departments: "there are still needed courses which the present force of instructors cannot give without abandoning other equally important work."[128]

Whether the university was genuinely prepared to support the college is open to question. In his decennial report in 1902, President Harper alluded to sources of resistance to furthering commercial studies in the university:

> Notwithstanding the early date at which the movement [to establish the College of Commerce and Administration] was started, the development of the work as distinguished from that of other undergraduate work has been slow. This has been due to the purpose of the University—the desire of the authorities being not to lay too great emphasis upon work of this character, in contrast with the longer-established college work, in the early years of the history of the University.[129]

This passage calls to mind the numerous efforts since 1894 to establish a professional school of commerce, all of which were rebuffed until finally, in 1898, a college without a dean or faculty, and subject to the collective governance of four discipline departments, was reluctantly approved. Four years later, the Senate again refused to install Commerce as a professional school, instead denominating it as a "technical college" even though its courses were intended to prepare businessmen and not technical specialists. A dean was appointed, but the teaching faculty was still to be borrowed from the departments. Although President Harper, in his 1902 report, affirmed a desire to appoint new instructors so that the commerce offerings might be placed on a sounder footing, Hatfield found it necessary to complain two years later that the college continued to exist at the mercy of the departments. College enrollment had increased from 109 in 1901-1902 to 152 in 1902-1903 and 181 in 1903-1904—a two-thirds increase in two years—yet the dean of the college did not possess the authority to call upon additional faculty to offer a full program of courses.

In March 1902, coincident with Hatfield's appointment to the deanship, one of the college's supporters departed. Edmund Janes James left to become president of Northwestern University. Hatfield used James's new position to argue that, "if the University of Chicago is to maintain its dignity in the line of commercial education, it is necessary to extend our line of operations very materially," as otherwise Northwestern, under its new leadership, was likely to advance to the fore in serving the needs of Chicago industry and commerce.[130] But nothing came of this effort by Hatfield to strengthen the college's financial and academic standing.

The lack of commitment from important quarters must have been an unremitting source of frustration to Hatfield. Others knew of his predicament, including Adolph C. Miller, who had gone to the University of California in 1902 as head of the department of economics, and Wesley C. Mitchell, who had left Chicago for Berkeley at the end of 1902 to take up a position as assistant professor of commerce. In March 1904, Miller wrote to Hatfield, urging that he consider an appointment to the Berkeley faculty. In a pointed reference to Chicago's half-hearted support of its College of Commerce and Administration, Miller wrote, "There is the finest opportunity in the country here for a real College of Commerce and we want you to have a big share in engineering its development."[131] The College of Commerce at Berkeley had been established in 1898, and the Flood Foundation, established in the same year, enabled the university to attract promising scholars to the college. Hatfield affirmed his willingness to accept an offer. On April 6, University of California President Benjamin Ide Wheeler wired Hatfield the offer of an associate professorship, and Hatfield wired his acceptance the following day. On April 13, Wheeler wrote to Hatfield, "your appointment as Associate Professor of Accounting in the University of California was duly approved at yesterday's meeting of the Regents."

On April 8, Miller wrote again, assuring Hatfield that the two universities' colleges of commerce were not to be compared:

> You are coming to a place of great opportunities for your line of work. The College of Commerce is a serious affair—not a mere name—we have unequalled resources, a good staff, a fine lot of students, and the unqualified support of the President. Yours will be a big responsibility in the College, and you want to bring your full boiler-capacity with you.[132]

Miller and his Berkeley colleagues wanted Hatfield to take charge of the work in accounting, although they were not insistent. Miller wrote, "It seemed desirable to emphasize the subject of *accounting* in the title of your professorship, but if you like something else better, that can be arranged in the future."[133] Hatfield's title was settled: associate professor of accounting. His was the first full-time professorial appointment in accounting at a U.S. college or university. Although six accounting and auditing professorships had been established at New York University in 1900, these were given to five practitioners and a banker who taught on a part-time basis,[134] and the appointments of accounting instructors at other universities were either at the level of lecturer (in the case of Durand W. Springer, at the University of Michigan)[135] or were professorial positions in economics, commerce, or related fields.[136]

Personal factors also played a role in Hatfield's decision to leave Chicago. A second son, Robert Miller, was born on August 16, 1902, and a third child was expected in the autumn of 1904. Ethel was not happy in Chicago, mainly because of its harsh climate and the limitations imposed by city life on a young family. For Henry, his family ties to Evanston had been loosened somewhat by the death of his mother on May 28th of the previous year. As for their plan to move eventually to Washington, D.C., American University was showing no signs of making its debut (it did not begin giving classes until 1914).

On the professional side, the University of California offered a College of Commerce with an endowment of $175,000 (per Miller's letter of April 8), the full support of the faculty and the president, and even funds with which to purchase books for the library. Moreover, Hatfield would be joining two friends from his early days at Chicago, Miller and Mitchell (who had received his Ph.D. in 1899). And his salary would be increased to $2,500, coupled with an advancement in rank.

Hatfield may have been eager to escape the tense debates at Chicago. Veblen would not have been an easy colleague in a program of studies in commerce. Laughlin was not on good terms with Small, and President Harper was inclined to snub Laughlin in favor of Small.[137] Laughlin's practice of staffing the department of political economy with doctoral students and faculty members who held conflicting ideologies could well have placed severe strains on the civility of collegial discourse. Barber refers to "the turbulence that surrounded the Department of Political Economy in its first decade an a half."[138] Hatfield, as dean of the College of Commerce and Administration, was in the unenviable position of a supplicant for faculty to teach the courses in his curriculum. An assistant professor, he had the daunting task of negotiating with head professors. It could not have been easy to maintain stable relations with all of the principals. In this sense, the climate that Laughlin had created may have been a factor in driving Hatfield away.[139] On the other hand, Hatfield's career as a pioneer accounting academic owed much to Laughlin's influence (and to Adolph Miller's as well). As Bornemann wrote, "It is probable that, as a result of exposure and receptivity to 'practical questions' [as fostered by Laughlin], the early graduate students leaving Chicago for college teaching posts elsewhere were factors of some importance in the development of business offerings in the United States."[140] Bornemann cites Hatfield as a prime example of Chicago's influence.

Hatfield gave his final courses at Chicago during the winter quarter of 1903-1904. Although his resignation took effect on October 1, accrued vacation credit enabled an earlier departure. In the late spring or early summer of 1904, he and his family moved west.

FURTHER INFLUENCES ON HATFIELD: THE ROLES OF JAMES AND SCHÄR

During his six years (1898-1904) as an instructor, assistant professor, and dean at the University of Chicago, Hatfield seems likely to have been influenced by his colleague, Edmund J. James;[141] also, as he himself affirmed, he was much influenced by the writings of Johann Friedrich Schär (1846-1924).

James was, without question, the preeminent advocate of higher commercial education in the United States from the 1880s to the first decade of the twentieth century.[142] He had played a leading role at the first American business school, the Wharton School of Finance and Economy, and had written a monograph on the progress made in commercial education in Europe. That he held passionately to his views and possessed a strong personality can be discerned from the bold advocacy in his published writings.

Yet James's position in the university was anomalous. Laughlin had opposed his initial appointment in 1895, which explains why James spent his first year, 1895-1896, as a professor in the Extension Division. The following year, James accepted a professorship in the department of political science, even though his appointment could also have been in political economy. As Barber wrote, "Harper steered clear of Laughlin when arranging James's assignment."[143] James's biographer wrote, "his Chicago years appear in subdued tones, and their major points of interest center in his ever-increasing concern with the problems and potentials of higher education."[144] Laughlin managed to distance James from the College of Commerce and Administration. In 1901, however, President Harper wanted to bring James into closer involvement with the college,[145] which is perhaps why James was named by the Senate in 1901 to the committee studying the possible reorganization of the college as a professional school; he was the only member who was not a head professor.

While documentary evidence is lacking, it seems likely that James counseled Hatfield, his young colleague in the department of political science, on matters relating to the development of the commerce curriculum.[146] This conclusion rests on four observations. First, in 1898, Hatfield joined the American Economic Association, which James had helped found, even though Laughlin, Hatfield's department head, refused to have anything to do with the association until 1904, when he finally he applied for membership.[147] Second, James and Hatfield shared an interest in the educational preparation of the businessman, even though Hatfield was also concerned with the development of technical specialists, such as accountants and insurance professionals. Third, James's views on the teaching of accounting seem to have influenced Hatfield. While Hatfield's background in accounting was limited to his experience as a onetime keeper of the accounts of S.A. Kean & Co., James had supervised the work of several teachers of bookkeeping and accounting at the Wharton School. James did not believe in offering courses that dwelled on bookkeeping technique. Nor did Hatfield, as will be shown below. In 1888, James gave the following description of the Wharton course in accounting (of which he approved):

> A course in the Theory of Accounting, to which are devoted four hours a week throughout the junior year. Practical work is insisted upon only so far as it is necessary to understand the theoretical aspects of the subject and the general principles which underlie all special systems.[148]

The descriptions of the two accounting courses with which Hatfield was associated at the University of Chicago strike a similar chord. Fourth, James was not reluctant, even when addressing academic audiences, to vaunt the merits of instruction in practical subjects. In particular, he held accounting in high regard. In a speech in 1900 to the American Economic Association, James said:

> I should accept any practical subject which can be made a serious intellectual pursuit, if by so doing, I could advance practical knowledge and increase intellectual training. Thus, for instance, the whole system of accounting, or as it is some times called with a sneering connotation "bookkeeping," I should make an element in all such [commercial] curricula. The theory of accounting is as strictly a scientific subject as the theory of political economy itself, and steady application to this subject offers a stimulating and valuable mental discipline. It is, moreover, an efficient means of presenting the facts of industrial organization in a concrete and direct way. The study of bookkeeping brings to light, in one form or another, the deeper underlying problems in connection with the organization of business. The study of municipal accounts offers, for example, a direct road to understanding the difficulties and the mechanism of public corporations.[149]

Few educators of the period could be found who would give such a ringing endorsement to the intrinsic value of accounting study, and James might well have impressed on Hatfield the importance of accounting instruction in higher commercial education.

One final link between James and Hatfield is worth noting. James probably played a role in Hatfield's decision to study commercial education in Europe.[150] During his three-month European tour in the winter of 1900-1901, Hatfield, who was proficient in the German language, seems to have spent the most time in Leipzig, where the first German business school, or *Handelshochschule*, had been founded in April 1898.[151] While there, he read *Versuch einer wissenschaftlichen Behandlung der Buchhaltung* (An Attempt at a Scientific Analysis of the Treatment of Bookkeeping) (Basel, 1890) by J.F. Schär, who, though lacking any university education, was said to be "the most significant accounting theorist of the pre-World War I German era."[152] Schär, a Swiss, had studied to become a primary school teacher and was employed in commerce and as a teacher in a secondary commercial school in Basel before moving to professorial posts at the Universität Zürich in 1903 and the Handelshochschule Berlin in 1906.[153]

The Handelshochschule Leipzig, which was affiliated with the Universität Leipzig, attracted students who were destined to become among the most eminent German business economists, specializing in accounting, of the early twentieth century. Eugen Schmalenbach, Ernst Pape, Heinrich Nicklisch, Hermann Grossmann, and Balduin Penndorf graduated from the Handelshochschule in the spring of 1900, several months before Hatfield's arrival. Hatfield could hardly have chosen a more propitious time to learn firsthand about the pioneering developments in German commercial education.

In his biographical sketch in the University of Chicago's *Register* for 1902-1903 (p. 28), Hatfield inserted the following notation: "Student, University of Leipzig, 1900." In his reading of Schär's tract on single- and double-entry bookkeeping, Hatfield discovered a theory of double-entry bookkeeping that was far superior to what he called the "naïve personalistic theory" used in most American textbooks. Schär's approach appealed to him because it considered bookkeeping entries "in reference to the effect which they will have in the final showing" rather than merely as a mechanistic process by which debit and credit are depicted "as showing personal relationships with non-existent and purely hypothetical personalities."[154] In the preface to his textbook *Modern Accounting*,[155] Hatfield disclosed his "indebtedness to J.F. Schaer whose clear writings have done much to put bookkeeping on a more rational basis."[156]

During his European tour—in conversations, at lectures, and through reading—Hatfield more than likely began to acquire an interest in the early history of bookkeeping It is known that by 1904, he had acquired a knowledge of Pacioli's "De computis et scripturis."[157] Hatfield's classical education, including a knowledge of several languages, would have facilitated his study of the medieval roots of double-entry bookkeeping and its subsequent diffusion through Europe.

During his European tour, Hatfield also became aware of a European literature that compensated for the absence of authoritative writings in the United States, such as Herman Veit Simon's *Die Bilanzen der Aktiengesellschaften und der Kommanditgesellschaften auf Aktien* (The Balance Sheets of Publicly Held Corporations and Limited Partnerships) (Berlin, 1899), which he cited several times in *Modern Accounting* and in his 1911 address, "Some Variations in Accounting Practice."[158] (Hatfield was apparently unaware of Charles Ezra Sprague's series of articles in 1889 on the "The Algebra of Accounts.")[159] In *Modern Accounting* and the 1911 address, he made liberal references to the German and French, as well as British, literature on accounting.[160] Hatfield was well in the forefront of his American contemporaries in acknowledging the importance of the European literature on accounting.

Despite all that he had learned on his enriching tour of European commercial centers, Hatfield was reluctant—as he always was—to profess certainty about his knowledge of accounting. He would cite others, draw attention to incongruities and inconsistencies, and synthesize the literature. However, he could not bring himself to champion definitive answers, an approach or attitude of mind that may have been a product of his classical education. His knowledge of classical rhetoric can be found in essays in which he states his position and then proceeds to posit arguments in support of his position—a technique he undoubtedly absorbed from his father's sermons and essays. It is almost as if, as a literary scholar, he was content with interpreting and criticizing texts composed by others.

In other instances, however, he would take an entirely different tack: with an even hand, he would posit conclusions as questions, only to use these interrogatives to destroy the conclusions. This approach has the earmarks of Platonic dialectic, in which the rhetor does not preach the truth but asks hearers (or readers) to discover the truth for themselves or to examine from a different perspective the premises of the arguments that they had hitherto accepted as true. This truth, which the rhetor often reveals by questioning (which is the basis of Socratic method), does not expound truth but provides a scaffolding by which truth can be discovered. Thus, standard exposition proceeds along discursive and logically reasoned lines, while dialectic is antidiscursive. Standard exposition is comforting, as it builds on accepted notions, but dialectic is disturbing because it challenges hearers' accepted beliefs and urges them to continue to seek answers.

As will become evident in chapters 3 and 4, in many speeches Hatfield often told his audiences what they did not want to hear, to force them to see themselves clearly—to persuade them, ultimately, to accept the view that he, the rhetor, presented. This technique, from Plato's *Gorgias*, prods the individual mind toward the rigorous examination of the notions to which it has ascended, often without careful examination, to refine and, eventually, refute them. The end of the dialectic, as Hatfield would have learned from classical rhetoric, is not the orderly disposition of ideas—which is the goal of expository essays—but the transformation of the hearer's mind into an instrument capable of seeing things for what they are: imperfect reflections on a larger truth, often shifting and uncertain, which must be carefully sought. In Platonic dialectic, the reader's attention should move from the text—what is said on the page—to what is happening in the mind of the reader. The best dialectic is successful when it points away from itself as text and toward a larger truth, which is the object of inquiry.[161] For example, in February 1903 at a gathering of business academics held in Ann Arbor, Michigan, Hatfield was heard to say:

> What is the difference between "bookkeeping" and "higher accountancy"? It is true that while bookkeeping was formerly held in poor repute no one was familiar with the subject and it was denied that it had a place in the college curriculum. I am told that there are college professors not a thousand miles from this town [Ann Arbor, Michigan] who would not admit bookkeeping into their curriculum unless over their dead bodies.
>
> What is the difference and what is its place? I do not know. I am teaching "accounting" myself, and I can say freely that I don't know what it is and I don't know where to place it.[162]

As was also typical of his writings, Hatfield preferred to propound questions rather than assert a confident knowledge of answers.

A PARTING TOUCH: DOUBLE-ENTRY BOOKKEEPING AS MATHEMATICS

In 1903, at the outset of his last year at Chicago, Hatfield succeeded in persuading the university's mathematics department to offer a noncredit course on the Principles and Practice of Bookkeeping.[163] The course was cited in a note appended to the description of the Accounting course for which it was a prerequisite, and also in the curriculum listing of the College of Commerce and Administration.[164] References to the bookkeeping course no longer appeared in the university's *Annual Register* after 1908. Who actually was to teach the course is not known. Indeed, it is not known for certain that the course was ever taught.[165] Hatfield later wrote that "the unquestioned academic standing of the Mathematics Department would remove some of the odium or reproach attached to a course in bookkeeping."[166] The ardor of the mathematics department was less than Hatfield's, for the course was nowhere mentioned in the section of the university's *Annual Register* in which the department's courses were presented. By this time, Hatfield was surely aware that a distinguished fifteenth-century mathematician, Luca Pacioli, had written the first printed work on double-entry bookkeeping as part of a treatise on arithmetic, algebra, and geometry, and he may well have known that another distinguished mathematician, Arthur Cayley of Cambridge, had published a slender book on the same subject less than 10 years earlier.[167] Hatfield's success in establishing such a course in Chicago's mathematics department was a suitable display of bravura by the man who would later argue the historical defense of bookkeeping.

NOTES

1. James Taft Hatfield, "Robert Miller Hatfield" (unpublished manuscript, 1938), 46 pages, on deposit in the Northwestern University Archives.

2. Abraham Hatfield, *The Hatfields of Westchester, A Genealogy of the Descendants of Thomas Hatfield of New Amsterdam and Mamaroneck, Whose Sons Settled in White Plains, Westchester County, New York* (New York Genealogical and Biographical Society, 1935), p. 7.

3. James Taft Hatfield, *op. cit.*, p. 1. Most page references to this work are inserted parenthetically in the text.

4. Beginning in 1922, a high school diploma was required for ordination. By 1934, a college degree was required, although a seminary degree was not required for ordination until 1954. Interview with James Kirby, Professor of Church History, Southern Methodist University, September 4, 1997.

5. The obituary was published in the *Northwestern Christian Advocate*, April 8, 1891.

6. Interview with Elizabeth Hobart (daughter of Henry Hatfield's sister Emily), February 2, 1964. She "was one of the Ohio Tafts," according to an article titled "Westchester's Hatfield Family Has Fought in All U.S. Wars," *The Herald Statesman*, Yonkers, NY, August 21, 1951.

7. Harold M. Mayer and Richard C. Wade, *Chicago: Growth of a Metropolis* (Chicago, IL: University of Chicago Press, 1969), pp. 94-102; and *Illinois: A Descriptive and Historical Guide* (Chicago: A.C. McClurg & Co., 1939), p. 198.

8. Robert Miller Hatfield, "The Present Condition of the South," *The Independent*, March 4, 1869, p. 1.

9. Robert Miller Hatfield, "The Colored People of the South," *The Independent*, March 18, 1869, p. 1.

10. Frederick A. Norwood, *The Story of American Methodism* (Nashville, TN: Abingdon Press, 1974), p. 342.

11. *Ibid.*, pp. 342-344.

12. *The Independent*, which was founded in 1848 as a Congregationalist newspaper that printed secular as well as denominational news and comment, "became famous as a radical antislavery paper." Frank Luther Mott, *American Journalism: A History of Newspapers in the United States through 250 Years, 1690 to 1940* (New York: The Macmillan Company, 1941), p. 378.

13. Mayer and Wade, *op. cit.*, p. 106.

14. In 1855, at the request of the Methodist founders of the university, the Illinois legislature amended the university's charter to prohibit the sale under license or otherwise of "spirituous, vinous or fermented liquors" within four miles of the university. William A. Dyche, "The Four-Mile Limit," in Robert D. Sheppard and Harvey B. Hurd, eds., *History of Northwestern University and Evanston* (Chicago, IL: Munsell Publishing Company, 1906), p. 317. The establishment of this four-mile limit "made Evanston a choice haven for temperance advocates for the next hundred years." Harold F. Williamson and Payson S. Wild, *Northwestern University: A History, 1850-1975* (Evanston, IL: Northwestern University, 1976), pp. 5, 6. Also see Michael H. Ebner, "The Result of Honest Hard Work: Creating a Suburban Ethos for Evanston," *Chicago History*, Vol. XIII, No. 2, Summer 1984, pp. 48-65.

15. Mayer and Wade, *op. cit.*, pp. 117-124.

16. The first of his two pastoral assignments in Chicago was at the Langley Avenue Church. James Taft Hatfield wrote, "On Sundays and Wednesdays he made the trip to the city [from his home in Evanston], and found shelter and hospitality at the home of Mr. William H. Rand, near the church." *Op. cit.*, p. 41. Robert Hatfield may have been befriended by Rand shortly after arriving in Chicago in 1865, and Henry Rand Hatfield, who was born in November 1866, may have been named after him.

17. *Ibid.*, p. 44; also see James Taft Hatfield, *op. cit.*, p. 40.

18. *Northwestern Christian Advocate*, April 8, 1891.

19. *Ibid.*

20. Robert Miller Hatfield, Address, Union Meeting, in Evanston, of Four Churches, under the Auspices of the Citizens' League Temperance Association, February 14, 1886 (Evanston "Index" Print, p. 3). The transcript reports that the quoted passage provoked laughter.

21. *The Methodist Armor* (Nashville, TN: Publishing House, Methodist Church South, 1912), p. 78.

22. Quoted in Christopher Hill, *Change and Continuity in Seventeenth-Century England* (Cambridge, MA: Harvard University Press, 1975), p. 89.

23. *Ibid.*, pp. 81-102.

24. In 1866, the year of Henry's birth, Indiana Asbury University awarded his father an honorary Doctor of Divinity degree.

25. Norwood, *op. cit.*, p. 304.

26. *Ibid.*, p. 79.

27. *The Methodist Armor, op. cit.*, pp. 164-165.

28. *The Methodist Church Member's Manual* (St. Louis, MO: South-Western Methodist Publishers, 1886), p. 58.

29. "The General Rules," *The Doctrine and Discipline of the Methodist Episcopal Church* (New York: Carlton and Porter, 1864), Chap. 18.3.

30. "Relation to the World" in *The Methodist Church Member's Manual, op. cit.*, p. 54.

31. *Ibid.*, p. 58.

32. *The Methodist Church Member's Manual* , *op. cit.*, p. 59.

33. *The Methodist Armor, op. cit.*, p. 165.

34. Max Weber, *The Protestant Ethic and the Spirit of Capitalism*, translated by Talcott Parsons (London: G. Allen & Unwin, 1930). Weber's work was first published in German in 1904-1905.

35. Perry Miller, *The New England Mind* (New York: Macmillan Company, 1939).

36. In addition to the nine identified children in the Hatfield genealogy, it is stated that: "Four other children died young, of whom there is no record." Abraham Hatfield, *op. cit.*, p. 152.

37. Interview with Elizabeth Hobart, February 2, 1964.

38. Interview with John G. and Margaret Hatfield (Henry Rand Hatfield's son and daughter-in-law), August 23, 1964. Also, letter to the author from Elizabeth Hatfield Glover (Henry Rand Hatfield's daughter), dated November 1965.

39. *The Methodist Armor, op. cit.*, p. 286.

40. Williamson and Wild, *op. cit.*, p. 55.

41. "'Praying Banker' Kean Dead," *The Chicago Record-Herald*, July 12, 1913 (an identical article appeared in *The Chicago Daily Tribune* on the same date), as modified by "Tribute to Samuel A. Kean, Former Banker, Who is Dead," *The Chicago Sunday Tribune*, July 13, 1913, Part VIII, p. 18.

42. Abraham Hatfield, *op. cit.*, p. 177.

43. F. Cyril James, *The Growth of Chicago Banks* (New York: Harper & Brothers, 1938), pp. 557-558. Kean conducted daily religious services as inspiration for the staff. *Ibid.*, p. 516.

44. The following titles of articles appearing in *The Chicago Daily Tribune* convey a sense of the changing tide of opinion on Kean: "Will Not Open Today," December 18, 1890, pp. 1-2; "Banker Kean Arrested," December 19, 1890, pp. 1-2; "Banker and Creditors," December 20, 1890, pp. 1-2; "The Kean Failure" (editorial), December 20, 1890, p. 4; "Assets Take a Tumble," December 23, 1890, p. 2; "S.A. Kean's Business Methods" (editorial), December 24, 1890, p. 4; "Another Drop in Assets," December 27, 1890, p. 11; "Where Did the Money Go?" (editorial), December 31, 1890, p. 4; and "Kean Should Be Prosecuted" (editorial), January 2, 1891, p. 4. Beginning with front-page articles titled "Facts of a Failure!" and "Banker Kean Arrested" on December 18, 1890, the *Chicago Journal* and *The Chicago Daily News*, respectively, also covered the Kean insolvency and trial extensively. *The New-York Times*, for its part, gave the matter almost daily attention. An extensive collection of press clippings on the Kean failure may be found in Scrapbook 48 in the Frances E. Willard Memorial Library, Woman's Christian Temperance Union, Evanston, IL.

Redlich correctly speculated that the firm broke down "probably for lack of capital." Fritz Redlich, *The Molding of American Banking: Men and Ideas* (New York: Johnson Reprint Corporation, 1968), part II, p. 391.

Although in the year 1891 "there occurred throughout the United States more bank failures than in any previous year since the creation of the national banking system," Chicago was said to have been comparatively immune from casualties. The Kean failure, occurring just before the turn of the year, was a troubling exception. See James, *The Growth of Chicago Banks*, *op. cit.*, p. 557.

45. See "Will Friends Aid Him?" *The Chicago Daily Tribune*, December 30, 1890, p. 8; "He Knows No Shame," *The Chicago Times*, January 1, 1891, p. 3; "Kean Fraud Settled," *The Chicago Times*, January 3, 1891, p. 1; and "Mr. Kean Prepares to Settle," *The Chicago Daily Tribune*, January 3, 1891, p. 3.

46. The Kean episode did not rob Henry Hatfield of all interest in banking. In March 1902, during his senior year at Northwestern, the State Bank of Evanston was incorporated, and Henry's name appeared among the list of stockholders. See William G. Hoag, "Evanston Banks," in Sheppard and Hurd, *op. cit.*, p. 290. Sheppard, a close friend of the Hatfield family, was one of the incorporators of the new bank.

47. Quarter/hours refer to the number of hours per week of instruction in a quarter. Then, as now, Northwestern was on the quarter system, and the average course load per quarter seems to have been about 15 hours. Three quarters of study were offered each year, as summer terms were not held until 1914. Henry graduated with a total of 181 quarter/hours over a period of four years, an average of just above 45 hours per year.

48. Biographical data on Sheppard may be found in *ibid.*, pp. 477-478.

49. Williamson and Wild, *op. cit.*, p. 120.

50. The quotations are from *The Northwestern*, Vol. XI, No. 21, September 25, 1891, p. 267.

51. "Chronicles," *The Syllabus*, Vol. VIII, 1892, pp. 167-172.

52. Notice in *Rho's Rhomer*, of Beta Theta Pi, March 1940.

53. It is not known whether Henry's initial plan was to study political economy alone or both fields. That he might have initially planned on political economy alone is suggested by the fact, as will be seen below, that he did not take any courses in political science until his fourth quarter at the University of Chicago.

54. Donald L. Miller, *City of the Century: The Epic of Chicago and the Making of America* (New York: Simon & Schuster, 1996), p. 358.

55. Arrell Morgan Gibson, ed., *American Notes—Rudyard Kipling's West* (Norman, OK: University of Oklahoma Press, 1981), p. 139.

56. See, for example, Stanley Applebaum, *The Chicago World's Fair of 1893: A Photographic Record* (New York: Dover Publications, 1980).

57. Miller, *op. cit.*, p. 395.

58. Richard J. Storr, *Harper's University: The Beginnings* (Chicago, IL: University of Chicago Press, 1966), p. 4.

59. Mayer and Wade, *op. cit.*, p. 152.

60. Notes written by Wesley Clair Mitchell in 1945, excerpted in Lucy Sprague Mitchell, *Two Lives: The Story of Wesley Clair Mitchell and Myself* (New York: Simon and Schuster, 1953), p. 85. Mitchell's spellings were a bit awry: the names were T.C. Chamberlin and E.H. Moore.

61. A.W. Coats, "The Origins of the 'Chicago School(s)'?," *The Journal of Political Economy*, Vol. LXXI, No. 5, October 1963, p. 488.

62. For an account of Harper's aggressive program for launching the university and, in particular, bringing economists on board, as well as his frequently strained relations with Laughlin, see William J. Barber, "Political Economy in an Atmosphere of Academic Entrepreneurship: The University of Chicago," in William J. Barber, ed., *Breaking the Academic Mould: Economists and American Higher Learning in the Nineteenth Century* (Middletown, CT: Wesleyan University Press, 1988), Chap. 10. Barber wrote that "Harper was frequently reminded that Laughlin was perhaps the least pliable of his head professors" (p. 259).

63. Milton Friedman, "James Laurence Laughlin (1850-1933)," in John Eatwell, Murray Milgate, and Peter Newman, eds., *The New Palgrave: A Dictionary of Economics* (London: Macmillan Press Ltd., 1987), Vol. 3, pp. 139, 140.

64. Alfred Bornemann, *J. Laurence Laughlin: Chapters in the Career of an Economist* (Washington, DC: American Council On Public Affairs, 1940), p. 3.

65. Coats, *op. cit.*, p. 489.

66. The titles of the courses that Hatfield took as a student and taught as a member of the faculty are those reported in the *Examiner's Grade Reports* in the Department of Special Collections, Joseph Regenstein Library, University of Chicago. For courses having a given number, the title indicated in the grade reports was frequently at variance with the title in the university's *Annual Register*. Some of these variances may have resulted from carelessness in the completion of the grade reports, while others may have reflected last-minute modifications in course content.

67. Letter to the author from Mrs. Maxine L. Sullivan, Registrar of the University of Chicago, dated January 5, 1965.

68. Veblen's biographer refers to "the startling innovation of summer school." The 1894 summer quarter may have been the first summer term at an American university. Joseph Dorfman, *Thorstein Veblen and His America* (New York: Augustus Kelley, 1961; originally published in 1934), p. 101.

69. *A Catalogue of the Officers and Students of Washington University, with the Courses of Study for the Academic Year 1893-94*, pp. 13, 23, 36; *A Catalogue...for the Academic Year 1894-95*, pp. 13, 22.

70. David P. Barrows, later to become president of the University of California, also was enrolled in this course. In remarks made at the retirement dinner for Hatfield, he said, "We studied cases of the Supreme Court. [Hatfield] would get up and talk about them. I sat, modest and silent, always. He did not hesitate to attack the Supreme Court with impunity, and delighted in dissenting opinions." (Remarks from the transcript of proceedings, "Dinner Honoring Henry Rand Hatfield and Carl Copping Plehn," April 30, 1937.) Even at that early stage, Hatfield took the side of the critic, another indication that he had absorbed the Methodist social doctrines so thoroughly inculcated by his father.

71. Wesley C. Mitchell, "J. Laurence Laughlin," *The Journal of Political Economy*, Vol. XLIX, No. 6, December 1941, p. 879.

72. *Ibid.*, p. 880.

73. J. Laurence Laughlin, "Teaching of Economics," *The Atlantic Monthly*, Vol. LXXVII, May 1895, p. 685. Also see Laughlin, "The Economic Seminar," *The Journal of Political Economy*, Vol. 20, No. 2, February 1912, pp. 169-175; and Bornemann, *op. cit.*, Chap. III.

74. Notes written by Wesley Clair Mitchell, excerpted in Lucy Sprague Mitchell, *op. cit.*, p. 86.

75. *Ibid.*

76. Dorfman, *op. cit.*, p. 119.

77. During the period from 1899 to 1905, when Veblen was managing editor of *The Journal of Political Economy*, he published 15 book reviews written by Hatfield, chiefly of works relating to commerce.

78. *Ibid.*, p. 120. Also see Wesley C. Mitchell, "Thorstein Veblen: 1857-1929," *The Economic Journal*, Vol. XXXIX, No. 156, December 1929, pp. 646-650.

79. Moonitz (born 1910), currently professor *emeritus* of accounting at Berkeley, knew Hatfield personally from 1934 to 1945, when Hatfield died. He took Hatfield's Seminar on Accounting Theory, but Hatfield was not a member of his dissertation committee.

80. The paper is reproduced in Chapter 7.

81. *University Record*, Vol. II, No. 11, June 11, 1897, p. 103.

82. *Xerox University Microfilms Comprehensive Dissertation Index 1861-1972* (Ann Arbor, MI: Xerox University Microfilms, 1973), Vol. 34, p. 939.

83. As indicated in the abstract, most of the data in Hatfield's thesis were obtained from confidential sources, and it seems plausible that it was deliberately withheld from circulation because of the sensitivity of the information thus obtained. In a paper titled "The Inner Workings of a Pool," delivered in 1931 to the Berkeley Club, Hatfield refers to the confidentiality and sensitivity of the informa-

tion reported therein, even three decades later. It seems likely that the paper was drawn from Hatfield's doctoral thesis.

84. In the same place where this abstract is reported, the title of Hatfield's thesis is given differently: "Municipal Bonding: A Study of the Western Bond Market for the Years 1886-1895." *The President's Report, 1892-1902* (Chicago, IL: University of Chicago Press, 1904), p. 15. One infers that Hatfield himself contributed this bibliographical information, and the difference in the two thesis titles is a mystery.

85. *A Catalogue of the Officers and Students of Washington University, with the Courses of Study for the Academic Year 1897-98*, pp. 31-32.

86. Ethel's father, John J. Glover (1835-1914), who was employed in the Department of Justice, was not related to the banker Charles C. Glover, who was treasurer, trustee, and one of Bishop Hurst's first backers in the development of the plan for the university. (Information about John J. Glover's employment was supplied by the National Archives at College Park, Maryland, of the National Archives and Records Administration, in a letter dated November 8, 1996. In 1900, Glover, who was a lawyer, became Chief of the Division of Accounts in the Department of Justice. During the Civil War, he had served in the Ohio Volunteer Infantry.

Information about the Glover family may be found in Elizabeth (Hatfield) Glover and Dorothy (Boake) Young, *A Glover Family History: Descendants of Amos and Ann Katherine (Smith) Holmes Glover* (Privately printed, 1984).

87. Letter to Ethel Glover from Hatfield, dated January 7, 1898 (shown to the author by John G. Hatfield, in 1964, in Berkeley). By then, Sheppard had taken over the position of business manager at Northwestern.

88. Letter to Harper from Hatfield, dated December 7, 1897 (Harper Papers, Department of Special Collections, Joseph Regenstein Library, University of Chicago).

89. Letter to Harper from Hatfield, dated January 5, 1898 (Harper Papers).

90. The telegram is preserved in Hatfield Scrapbook No. 1.

91. An alternative explanation is that Otto Heller, a noted Germanist at Washington University, had come to know James Taft Hatfield, Henry Hatfield's older brother who was a German professor at Northwestern, and that Heller had recommended the younger Hatfield for the instructorship at Washington University. The history of Washington University is silent on the instruction given in economics and psychology during the 1890s. See Ralph E. Morrow, *Washington University in St. Louis* (St. Louis, MO: Missouri Historical Society Press, 1996).

92. Letter to Ethel Glover from Hatfield, undated but evidently written in the spring of 1898 (collection of John S. Hatfield, Burlingame, CA).

93. The degree was given by Boston University. Emilie J. Hutchinson, *Women and the Ph.D.* (Greensboro, NC: The North Carolina College for Women, 1930), p. 20.

94. Ethel Glover Hatfield was one of five women who received a Ph.D. degree at the University of Chicago Convocation on July 1, 1898. Before that date, 10 women had received Ph.D.s from the university. Information supplied by the Department of Special Collections, Joseph Regenstein Library, University of Chicago. From 1877 to 1924, the University of Chicago, with 144, was second only to Columbia University, with 171, in the number of Ph.D.s granted to women. The University of California was twelfth, with 22. See Hutchinson, *op. cit.*, p. 22.

95. Most of the discussion of the organizational issues within the university, including the history of the proposals leading up to creation of the College of Commerce and Politics, has been drawn from Chapter One, "J. Laurence Laughlin and the Early Years," of the unpublished manuscript "A History of the School of Business of the University of Chicago," by R. H. Turner (n.d.), on file at the Graduate School of Business and in the Department of Special Collections of the Joseph Regenstein Library, both at the University of Chicago. Storr, *op. cit.*, pp. 135-141, also has a useful discussion, but it is less detailed than Turner's.

96. Edward Potts Cheyney, *History of the University of Pennsylvania, 1740-1940* (Philadelphia: University of Pennsylvania Press, 1940), pp. 288-295.

97. *Ibid.*, p. 289. See also Steven A. Sass, *The Pragmatic Vision: A History of the Wharton School 1881-1981* (Philadelphia: University of Pennsylvania Press, 1982), p. 85.

98. This enumeration of courses is based on the *Examiner's Grade Reports* for the three academic years, rather than on the listings in the *Annual Register*. The information was supplied by the Department of Special Collections, Joseph Regenstein Library, University of Chicago.

99. The courses listed in a given year's *Register* were those to be given in the following year. The designation "Mj," for Major, signifies that a course was to meet for the full 12-week quarter.

100. *Annual Register of the University of Chicago, 1897-98*, p. 187.

101. Yet Trevor Arnett, who would assist Hatfield in offering the first accounting course in the winter quarter of 1901, recalled, "I do not think that Laughlin was much interested in accounting or in courses in commerce and business." (Letter to Alfred H. Bornemann, dated February 16, 1939, copied to the author by Bornemann.) A senior member of the department of political economy who might have nudged Hatfield into accounting was Adolph C. Miller, professor of finance, who, as mentioned above, left for the University of California in 1902. It was Miller who, in early 1904, recruited Hatfield to Berkeley to take charge of the work in accounting.

102. "Builders of the West—XCV," *Journal of Electricity and Western Industry*, Vol. 46, No. 4, February 15, 1921, p. 210.

103. *Annual Register of the University of Chicago, 1899-1900*, p. 169. Hatfield offered the course twice more, in the spring quarters of 1901 and 1902.

104. Letter to the author from John S. Hatfield, dated November 29, 1996, based on a reading of Henry Hatfield's letters to his wife during that period.

105. He sailed on the S.S. "Columbia" from New York City to Cherbourg, departing on October 4, and returned to New York City on January 17, 1901 on the S.S. "Minnehaha" from London. (Information in Hatfield Scrapbook No. 1.) While most of his time was spent studying programs of commercial education, he did tour some manufacturing establishments, including Fried. Krupp in Essen.

106. See his unsigned report on a conference he attended at the University of Göttingen, in *The Nation*, February 21, 1901, pp. 158-159.

107. "Returns to Teach Trade," *The Chicago Sunday Tribune*, March 31, 1901, p. 13. Hatfield's assessment of the state of commercial education in Europe is of interest: "The school at Leipsic [*sic*] is the most important one in Germany. While not actually a part of the university there, it may be regarded as an affiliated school. In Belgium the school of the greatest importance is located at Antwerp. This is regarded as almost the most important in existence. Austria is influenced by the schools at Prague and Vienna. England is backward in this respect, but the people are becoming aroused, and an advance will soon take place in that country, as well as in France and Italy."

108. *Ibid.* The other article to appear, headed "Means to Teach Commerce," is likely to have been in *The Chicago Daily News*. Clippings of both articles appear in Hatfield's Scrapbook No. 1.

109. Quoted in Jeremiah Lockwood, "Early University Education in Accountancy," *The Accounting Review*, XIII, No. 2, June 1938, p. 138. The remainder of his six-month leave was spent on the East Coast.

110. Turner, *op. cit.*, p. 45.

111. *Annual Register of the University of Chicago, 1900-01*, p. 187.

112. *Annual Register of the University of Chicago, 1901-02*, p. 201.

113. Turner, *op. cit.*, p. 13.

114. The letters from which these excerpts are taken form part of the Harper Papers, Department of Special Collections, Joseph Regenstein Library, University of Chicago. Storr wrote that, in the early years of the university, "Some professors received as little as half, or even less, of the $7,000 which head professors [such as Laughlin] received; and not all of them received that. Instructors were paid about one-sixth or one-fifth as much." Storr, *op. cit.*, p. 82. Hence, the salary offered to Hatfield compared favorably to Chicago's standard.

115. The appointment was announced in the *University Record*, April 1902, p. 389.

116. Thorstein Veblen, *The Theory of the Leisure Class: An Economic Study of the Evolution of Institutions* (New York: The Macmillan Company, 1899).

117. John P. Diggins, *The Bard of Savagery: Thorstein Veblen and Modern Social Theory* (New York: The Seabury Press, 1978), pp. 169-189.

118. Thorstein Veblen, *The Higher Learning in America: A Memorandum on the Conduct of Universities by Business Men* (New York: Hill and Wang, 1957, originally published in 1918), p. 154, footnote omitted.

119. Diggins, *op. cit.*, p. 174.

120. Veblen, *The Higher Learning*, *op. cit.*, p. 154. In his preface to the book, which is dated March 1916, Veblen wrote, "It is something more than a dozen years since the following observations on American academic life were first assembled in written form." Hence, the views he expressed in the book began forming at the time Hatfield was at Chicago.

121. In "Moriturus Vos Saluto," an unpublished paper given in 1937, Hatfield commended Veblen's idiosyncractic method, used when Hatfield was a graduate student at Chicago, to encourage a graduate student to master French before the graduate language exams. Hatfield also recalled that, as a graduate student at Chicago, he was "on rather intimate terms with Veblen, even though he was my instructor."

122. Diggins, *op. cit.*, p. 154, in reference to Veblen.

123. Henry Rand Hatfield, *Accounting: Its Principles and Problems* (New York: D. Appleton and Company, 1927), p. 1.

124. *Annual Register of the University of Chicago, 1902-1903*, p. 111. The faculty of the college "consists of all instructors offering courses in the curriculum of the College, and five members of the University at large appointed by the Board of Trustees." The published list of the college faculty consisted of 35 names, including that of the president.

125. *University Record*, April 1902, p. 389.

126. Henry Rand Hatfield, *Lectures in Commerce* (Chicago, IL: University of Chicago Press, 1904). The book was republished the following year under the title *American Commerce and Finance*.

127. "The College of Commerce and Administration," *The President's Report 1902-04*, pp. 137, 138.

128. *Ibid.*, p. 138.

129. *The President's Report, 1892-1902*, *op. cit.*, pp. lxxxix-xc.

130. Letter to Harper dated October 25, 1902, as quoted in Turner, *op. cit.*, p. 61.

131. Letter to Hatfield from Miller, dated March 16, 1904 (Hatfield Papers, University of California, Berkeley). In his letter, Miller began by alluding to another possible attraction, "Assuming that your good judgment will not permit you to become a candidate for the vacancy in Economics at Texas."

132. Letter to Hatfield from Miller, dated April 8, 1904 (Hatfield Papers, University of California, Berkeley).

133. *Ibid.*

134. Lockwood, *op. cit.*, p. 142.

135. *Ibid.*, p. 140.

136. The first full-time professorial appointments in accounting at the University of Pennsylvania, Dartmouth College, the University of Illinois, and Harvard University were later than 1904. In 1908, John Christie Duncan became the first assistant professor of accounting at Illinois. At Harvard, William Morse Cole, a full-time instructor in the department of political economy, in 1900-1901 began teaching an accounting course that was "open to undergraduates in their senior year ... as a vocational aid for students who were expecting to go into business." See Melvin T. Copeland, *And Mark an Era: The Story of the Harvard Business School* (Boston: Little, Brown and Company, 1958), p. 22. Upon the opening of Harvard's Graduate School of Business Administration in 1908, Cole joined its faculty as assistant professor of accounting. See Jeffrey L. Cruikshank, *A Delicate Experiment: The Harvard Business School 1908-1945* (Boston: Harvard Business School Press, 1987), pp. 26, 41.

In 1907, Joseph French Johnson, dean of New York University's School of Commerce, Accounts and Finance, in an article surveying the catalogues of a number of major American universities for the amount of accounting coursework offered, made the following remark, as if to suggest a "first": "In the University of California there is a professor of accounting." "Professional Accountancy and Education," *The Journal of Accountancy*, Vol. 5, No. 2, December 1907, p. 121.

137. Letter to Ethel Glover from Hatfield, dated January 7, 1898. Also see Turner, *op. cit.*, fn. 47.

138. Barber, *op. cit.*, p. 265.

139. Cookingham wrote, "The Chicagoans [i.e., Miller, Mitchell and Hatfield] migrated to the West with the expectation that they would have wider scope for scholarly pursuits there than would be the case in a department dominated by J. Laurence Laughlin." Mary E. Cookingham "Political Economy in the Far West: The University of California and Stanford University," in William J. Barber, ed., *Breaking the Academic Mould: Economists and American Higher Learning in the Nineteenth Century* (Middletown, CT: Wesleyan University Press, 1988), pp. 277-278.

140. Alfred Bornemann, "The Development of Economics and Administration in the School of Business," *The Journal of Business*, Vol. XXX, No. 2, April 1957, p. 132.

141. James's father, like Hatfield's, was a Methodist preacher. James, like Hatfield, was a graduate of Northwestern University.

142. See his "Schools of Finance and Economy," an address before the Convention of the American Bankers' Association, Saratoga, N.Y., September 3, 1890 in *Education of Business Men.—I and II* (New York: American Bankers' Association, 1892), pp. 9-26; *Education of Business Men in Europe* (New York: American Bankers' Association, 1893); and "Relation of the College and University to Higher Commercial Education," *Papers and Proceedings* of the Thirteenth Annual Meeting of the American Economic Association, December 27-29, 1900, Third Series, Vol. II, No. 1, pp. 114-165. James's biographer wrote that "James can probably be described as the 'father' of higher business education in the United States." Letter to the author from Richard A. Swanson, dated January 31, 1965.

143. Barber, *op. cit.*, p. 255. At Wharton, James's title had been professor of public finance and administration.

144. Richard Allen Swanson, "Edmund J. James, 1855-1925: A 'Conservative Progressive' in American Higher Education," doctoral dissertation in history (University of Illinois, 1966), p. 125.

145. Turner, *op. cit.*, fn. 54.

146. Yet Swanson wrote, "I have found nothing indicating any particular relationship between [James] and Hatfield." Letter to the author from Richard A. Swanson, dated January 31, 1965.

147. See A.W. Coats, "The First Two Decades of the American Economic Association," *The American Economic Review*, Vol. L, No. 4, September 1960, p. 572; and a letter to the author from Dana M. Coleman, Office of the Secretary of the American Economic Association, Nashville, TN, dated August 24, 1989. Coats wrote, "I should imagine that you are quite right in thinking that James had a considerable influence over the development of the College of Commerce at Chicago." Letter to the author from Coats, dated November 24, 1964. Coats has also written on the early years of Chicago's department of political economy; see fn. 59 *supra*.

148. James, quoted in Lockwood, *op. cit.*, p. 136.

149. James, "Relation of the College and University to Higher Commercial Education," *op. cit.*, pp. 158-159.

150. Hatfield's interest in European higher education may also have been encouraged by his brother-in-law Franklin Paine Mall (1862-1917), a distinguished anatomist. Mall, who married Ethel Glover's sister Mabel in 1895, had done postgraduate work in Heidelberg and Leipzig before joining the Chicago faculty in 1892 and then proceeding to The Johns Hopkins University upon the opening of its medical school the following year.

151. For a discussion of German higher commercial education, see August Wilhelm Fehling, "Collegiate Education for Business in Germany," in L.C. Marshall, ed., *The Collegiate School of Business: Its Status at the Close of the First Quarter of the Twentieth Century* (Chicago, IL: University of Chicago Press, 1928), pp. 305-361. Also see James, *Education of Business Men in Europe*, *loc cit.*;

Fritz Redlich, "Academic Education for Business: Its Development and the Contribution of Ignaz Jastrow (1856-1937)," *The Business History Review*, Vol. XXXI, No. 1, Spring 1957, pp. 35-91; David A.R. Forrester, *Eugen Schmalenbach and German Business Economics* (New York: Garland Publishing, 1993), pp. 73-80; and Robert R. Locke, *The End of the Practical Man: Entrepreneurship and Higher Education in Germany, France, and Great Britain, 1880-1940* (Greenwich, CT: JAI Press, 1984), Chap. V. The author is indebted to R.H. Parker for drawing his attention to Locke.

152. *Ibid.*, p. 115.

153. *Ibid.*, p. 216. See also the chapter on Schär in Edmund Sundhoff, *Dreihundert Jahre Handelswissenschaft* (Köln, Germany: Wirtschaftsverlag Bachem, 1991), pp. 162-195. The author is grateful to W.H.A.M. Hendriksen for bringing this work to his attention.

154. These quotations are taken from a letter to Stephen W. Gilman from Hatfield, dated September 8, 1912. While Hatfield does not mention Schär by name, the letter includes a description of the difference between the personalistic theory and the approach recommended by both Schär and Charles Ezra Sprague.

155. Henry Rand Hatfield, *Modern Accounting: Its Principles and Some of Its Problems* (New York: D. Appleton and Company, 1909).

156. *Ibid.*, p. vii.

157. A report in the *Berkeley Daily Gazette* of September 23, 1904, p. 2, of an address given by Hatfield at the weekly meeting of the College of Commerce refers to Pacioli's work without naming its author. The report paraphrased Hatfield as saying, "The first treatise on bookkeeping appeared in Italy at the same time the first work on algebra was published."

158. Henry Rand Hatfield, "Some Variations in Accounting Practice in England, France, Germany and the United States," published posthumously in the *Journal of Accounting Research*, Vol. 4, No. 2, Autumn 1966, pp. 169-182.

159. *The Office*: May 1889, pp. 91-92; July 1889, pp. 122-123; August 1889, pp. 144-145; and September 1889, pp. 166-167. This series of articles had been published earlier, in July-August 1880, in *The Book-Keeper*.

160. As indicated in Chapter 2, Hatfield returned to Europe for several months during the fall of 1907.

161. See Stanley E. Fish, *Self-Consuming Artifacts* (Berkeley, CA: University of California Press, 1972), pp. 1-7.

162. Discussion, in *Convention of Educators and Business Men for Discussion of Higher Commercial Education*, held under the auspices of the Michigan Political Science Association, February 5-7, 1903, Ann Arbor, Michigan (also cited as *Publications of the Michigan Political Science Association*, Volume V), pp. 183-184. Hatfield wrote that "now some of our friends in the East" prefer "accountancy" (p. 183).

163. In some listings, its title was given as "Theory and Practice of Double Entry Bookkeeping."

164. The *Annual Register, 1903-04*, was the first in which reference to the course appeared (pp. 112-113, 218, 411).

165. The university's Registrar could find no information in her files concerning the course. "This is perhaps because the course was non-credit ... [and] there were no grade reports" (letter to the author from Mrs. Maxine L. Sullivan, Registrar, dated November 11, 1965).

166. Paraphrased from a letter written by Hatfield, in Lockwood, *op. cit.*, p. 133. In a 1952 article, Devine wrote that the failure of economists to recognize the "economic implications" of the accounting field "is evidenced by the struggle of Professor Hatfield to get a course in accounting recognized at the University of Chicago. The fledgling course emerged as a course in mathematics!" Carl Thomas Devine, "Integration of Accounting and Economics in the Elementary Accounting Course," *The Accounting Review*, Vol. XXVII, No. 3, July 1952, p. 330. There is nothing, however, to suggest that Hatfield had a "struggle" in gaining acceptance for an accounting course. Moreover, the course offered through the department of mathematics was labeled "bookkeeping." It was Devine, in conversation, who alerted the author to the existence of this course.

167. A. Cayley, *The Principles of Book-keeping by Double Entry* (Cambridge, UK: The University Press, 1894). In his "Historical Defense," delivered in 1923, Hatfield said, after quoting Scott and Goethe, "Cayley, scientist beyond question, even more significantly declared, 'Bookkeeping is one of the two perfect sciences'." Henry Rand Hatfield, "An Historical Defense of Bookkeeping," *The Journal of Accountancy*, Vol. XXXVII, No. 4, April 1924, p. 253.

Chapter 2

At Berkeley and in Washington, 1904 to 1919/1920

During this period, Hatfield took charge of the work in accounting at the University of California, gradually built the curriculum, headed the College of Commerce, and eventually became acting dean of the faculties. He formed an alliance with John F. Forbes, a leading San Francisco practitioner, to elevate the quality of the accounting profession. A major event was the publication in 1909 of his pioneering textbook, *Modern Accounting*. He played a role in the founding and early governance of Beta Gamma Sigma, the AACSB, and the AAUIA, and during the World War he served in the War Industries Board and with the Advisory Tax Board. He was tempted by offers to move east, but in the end his affection for the University of California, its surroundings, and culture won out.

> *In this, I think, lies the real difficulty of practically all American bookkeeping. There is no attempt to show the pupil what he is trying to do, and why he does it. There may be alleged principles, or rules, or theories, but these all have no connection with what is the real purpose or the real result of the bookkeeping process.*
>
> —*Some Heretical Views on the Method of Teaching Bookkeeping* (1913)

ARRIVAL IN BERKELEY

In 1904, when the Henry Rand Hatfields moved from Chicago to Berkeley, a journey of 2,100 miles, the family viewed life on the western fringe of the continent with some uncertainty. Years later, Hatfield recalled the transition:

> When I was preparing to move, I looked at the census and saw that the population of Berkeley was 13,214, a pleasant suburban community, it seemed to me, after the noise and the bustle of Chicago, infested with elevated trains, factory chimneys and stockyard odors.... When I came to Berkeley, the unpaved streets were thick with dust. The dust was full of fleas. The fleas were endowed with malignant mordacity which made life something of a burden to the non-immunized tenderfoot. I found at that time that many of the residents obtained water by means of windmills erected in their back yards, and heated it by means of sun heaters erected on the

> southern slopes of their roofs.... There was at that time no proper restaurant in Berkeley.... There was no real hotel in Berkeley; one had to put up temporarily in a hotel in Oakland.... And one did his shopping in Oakland or in San Francisco, because of the then inadequacy of Berkeley shops.[1]

Berkeley was a 40-minute ride by train and ferry across the bay from San Francisco. (The San Francisco–Oakland Bay Bridge did not open until 1936.)

In the U.S. Census for 1900, California was the 21st most populous of the 45 states, smaller even than Alabama, North Carolina, or Tennessee. California, still an agricultural and trading state with but considerable urbanization, had not yet burgeoned into an industrial state. It was hardly a haven for large corporations. The state constitution made shareholders liable for a proportionate share of the debts of their corporation. Limited liability did not come to California until 1930. In 1900, San Francisco, with a population of 342,782, ranked as the ninth largest U.S. city and was the most important city west of St. Louis. It was the financial and cultural center of the West. Los Angeles, still a junior metropolis, ranked 36th with 102,479 inhabitants.

THE UNIVERSITY AND THE COLLEGE OF COMMERCE, C. 1904

In 1904, the University of California was prospering under its eighth president, Benjamin Ide Wheeler, a philologist who had come to Berkeley from Cornell in 1899. The year prior to Wheeler's arrival, the university had established its College of Commerce. The drive to create the college had been led by Arthur Rodgers (1848-1902), an 1872 graduate of the university, a well-known San Francisco lawyer, and a member of the university's Board of Regents. Establishment of the college also had the support of the powerful Merchants' Association of San Francisco.[2] At the university's Commencement in May 1898, Edmund Janes James spoke on "The Functions of the Modern University and its Relation to Modern Life" and devoted much of his address to the merits of university education in commerce.[3] Whether by design or inadvertence, James's address served to prepare the university for its new college.[4]

Carl C. Plehn (1867-1945), who had come to the university in 1893, was appointed associate professor of finance and the first dean of the college, occupying the cramped quarters of Room 17 in the basement of North Hall. Plehn, one of the fathers of California's system of public finance and taxation, became in 1923 the first Westerner to be elected president of the American Economic Association. The organization structure of the University of California shared one similarity with the University of Chicago, namely, that the faculty power base resided in the departments, not in the colleges. A student's course of study was taken in the college of his or her choice, such as Letters, Social Sciences, Chemistry, or Commerce. Professors whose courses formed part of the academic program offered by one or more colleges would be members of those colleges' faculties, but their tenurable appointment was in a department. The dean of a college, unlike the chairman of a department, was not concerned with hiring and promoting faculty members. The faculty of each college "chooses a dean to advise with and guide the students in the college, to take charge of certain matters of discipline, and to care for the special interests of the college."[5]

In his inaugural report to the university, delivered in 1898, Dean Plehn made a valiant attempt to defend the curriculum of the new College of Commerce as culturally broad and scientifically rigorous.[6] He differentiated the breadth of the Berkeley undertaking from its counterpart at the University of Chicago, where, he said, only four departments—political economy, political science, history, and sociology and anthropology—serviced the commerce curriculum. Lest skeptical members of the university faculty have failed to appreciate the lofty academic plateau at which the new college's curriculum was to be offered, Plehn gave an assurance that the mundane subject of accounting would be denied a place:

> The things to be taught [in the College of Commerce] are more important than book-keeping and accounting.
>
> The mere arts of the counting-room do not belong to the list of studies. The student will be encouraged to acquire a knowledge of them elsewhere, possibly before entering college. Thus the College of Commerce will supplement, not compete with, the work of the older business and commercial schools. It is not by their skill as book-keepers that the merchant princes have won their title to fortune and to fame. They have been men who could see beyond the pages of their ledgers, and who understood something of the nature of the great forces which govern the commerce of the world.[7]

The subject of economics was slow to develop at Berkeley, and the emergence of accounting as a proper university subject necessarily was tied to the standing of economics. At the time of Dean Plehn's *apologia* in 1898, his academic appointment was in the department of history and political science. It was not until 1902, when Adolph C. Miller arrived from Chicago, that a department of economics was created, and Miller became its chairman. In January 1903, Miller brought Wesley Clair Mitchell, also from Chicago, to the department.[8] Miller was aware of Hatfield's experimentation with accounting instruction at Chicago, and he, like Hatfield, may have been persuaded of its importance by James. The origin of accounting coursework at Berkeley may be traced to Miller's appointment. In his initial year as chairman of economics, accounting instruction was offered for the first time, and in 1904 it was Miller who successfully recruited Hatfield to the department as associate professor of accounting.

Hatfield's ill-fated experience in 1885-1890 with the banking firm of with S.A. Kean & Co. continued to follow him. In the univerity's announcement of his appointment, as reported in *The Daily Californian* (the student-run newspaper), he was described as "a University of Chicago professor and practical banker, to be assistant professor of accounting at $2500 a year."[9]

Even before Miller's arrival, Plehn had evidently reconsidered his position that accounting would not be offered in the college, since accounting was mentioned as one of the areas in which courses must be taken in 1900-1901 and 1901-1902.[10] Yet no course with accounting content was actually offered until 1902-1903. Ironically, the instructor was none other than Dean Plehn. In that year, Plehn, whose reputation would eventually come to rest on his work in public finance and taxation, offered a three-hour course, Economics 14, "Corporation Finance and Accounting." No course description was reported in the university's *Register*, but the following description was given in 1903-1904 for Economics 14, also offered by Plehn:

> 14. Accounting and Corporation Finance [2 hours]
>
> The principles of accounting and credit as illustrated by the methods of large corporations and of the government; a study of negotiable securities, and a critical examination of bank statements, railroad accounts, and available corporation (and "trust") accounts.[11]

Plehn's reflections on his experience as the first instructor to offer work in accounting at Berkeley were not recorded, but it is likely that he was relieved to have Hatfield take charge of coursework in the area in 1904.

HATFIELD'S INITIAL YEARS AT BERKELEY, 1904-1909

In 1904-1905, 125 students were enrolled in the College of Commerce. The Berkeley campus of the university had 2,469 undergraduate students and 104 faculty of professorial rank, including four in the department of economics.[12] Hatfield's appointment was the first to be made under the Flood Foundation's grant. In 1898, Miss Cora Jane Flood, the daughter of James Clair Flood, one of the bonanza kings who made an enormous fortune in Nevada's Comstock Lode, gave the university a grant valued at more than $460,000 to support "some branch of commercial education."[13] The term of Hatfield's appointment began on July 1, 1904, by which time Miller had also been placed under the Flood Foundation's grant. The appointments of Plehn and Wesley C. Mitchell were added to the Foundation early in 1905.

In 1905-1906, the College of Commerce moved into newly completed California Hall, which Miller characterized as "the spacious and dignified home."[14] Although Hatfield's appointment was in accounting and President Wheeler was soon to report that "The important work in accounting has been put upon an effective basis by the appointment of a special instructor in this branch, Associate Professor Henry Rand Hatfield, who came to us two years ago after a successful career in the University of Chicago,"[15] his teaching load continued to run the gamut of commerce courses. During his first five years on the Berkeley faculty, Hatfield offered a broad array of nonaccounting courses:[16]

- Introduction to Commercial Geography (1904-1905),
- Geography of International Trade (1904-1905),
- Practical Banking (1904-1908),
- [Invited] Lectures on Commerce (1905-1907),
- Municipal Finance (1905-1907 and 1908-1909),
- Corporation Finance (1905-1909),
- Commercial Reviews and Trade Journals (1905-1906),
- Economics of Industry (1906-1907), and
- Theory and History of Banking (1908-1909).

Hatfield developed most of these courses.

Building the Accounting Curriculum and Ties with the Profession

In stages, Hatfield began to evolve the coursework in accounting. He offered Economics 14 in the fall semester of 1904—the course that Plehn had given twice in conjunction with work in finance—but he confined it to accounting, retaining his Chicago orientation toward the preparation of nonspecialists:

> 14. Principles of Accounting
>
> The interpretation of accounts with regard to the need of the business manager rather than those of the accountant. The formation and meaning of the balance sheet. The profit and loss statement. The various accounts appearing in the balance sheet and errors frequently found therein.[17]

In the fall of 1905, the course was retitled Introduction to Accounting and became a staple in the curriculum. No adequate American textbooks were available. Initially, Hatfield chose to use a book written by a Scot: George Lisle, *Accounting in Theory and Practice* (Edinburgh: William Green & Sons, 1900). Hatfield praised the book as "perhaps the best single volume treating the entire subject which has appeared in English."[18]

In 1904 and again in 1905, Hatfield gave talks to Bay Area bookkeepers' associations on the subject of "What Are Profits?" A report on a 1904 meeting said, "He treated the subject from the standpoint of an accountant and gave many legal decisions to illustrate his points."[19]

During this period, Hatfield met John F. Forbes (1876-1965), a San Francisco practitioner who was to become a leading member of the accounting profession in California and in the nation.[20] Hatfield had no such contacts in Chicago, where his associations outside the university were mostly with the owners and managers of industrial, commercial and banking concerns. In San Francisco, Hatfield became aware of the work of accountants in public practice and their needs for academic preparation. He joined with Forbes in "an unofficial committee of two" to set about raising the standards of the accounting profession in California, including the development of accounting courses at the University of California.[21]

Soon after Forbes opened his office, Hatfield came to see him. They agreed on the importance of attracting people of quality into the profession, and they saw the university as central to their effort. Their first aim was to "straighten out" the State Board of Accountancy, whose secretary had been accused of trying to sell CPA certificates.[22] Forbes became a member of the State Board in 1909 and used his influence with the Governor to have good men appointed to serve with him.[23] For his part, Hatfield took an interest in placing good men with the accounting firms.[24]

While Hatfield hesitated to assert his authority on proper accounting practice, he had no difficulty in defining the standard of proper professional conduct. In remarks made to a meeting of San Francisco CPAs sometime in 1905-1906, he challenged his listeners to rise to that standard:

> The ... need of the profession is the establishing of the highest possible standard for its members. I plead not merely for technical dexterity in the investigation of accounts and the detection of frauds; not merely for knowledge derived from prolonged study of the principles of accounting and the legal and economic factors inherent thereto; not merely for a high standard of personal probity which will make men willing to intrust to the accountant their intimate business secrets, nor the high code of professional ethics which should reflect this character. The profession should claim all these, but much more.
>
> I am thinking rather of the public role which you must occupy and the high standard which you should set in that respect. Let me mention a single illustration. The most important problem before the public is the regulation of corporations. There are many sides to this problem but most of them center about the finances, the questions of investment and of profits. In a word, they are questions of accounting. But there is no other country where such vicious principles of corporation accounting are countenanced as in the United States. In proof of this, look at the text book on corporation accounting recommended by the N.Y.C.P.A. This explicitly states that there is no objection (I quote the words literally) to listing the assets acquired by stock purchase at twice their actual value. In the English and German texts there is no hint that any one ever thought of such an improper course, except perhaps where the author is referring to confessedly fraudulent manipulations. Is the C.P.A. prepared to take a stand for accuracy in corporation accounts? May not C.P.A. stand for Conscience, Probity, Accuracy?[25]

Coincident with Hatfield's increasing involvement with the profession, specialist accounting courses began to appear in the curriculum of the College of Commerce. In 1905-1906, a one-semester course titled Advanced Accounting ("A consideration of the more complicated problems of accounting")[26] made its debut, and it was joined in 1906-1907 by Accounting Practice. In 1908-1909, a course in auditing was added.[27] With one exception, these accounting courses were given by Hatfield. The lone exception occurred in the fall of 1907, when Hatfield was on leave, and Lincoln Hutchinson, an instructor in commercial geography, taught Introduction to Accounting. Similarly, Hatfield had taken over Hutchinson's courses in geography when the latter was on leave in 1904-1905.

Early Forays in the Accounting Literature

Hatfield's final year at Chicago and his initial five years at Berkeley constituted his first productive period as a pioneer contributor to the accounting literature. In December 1903, he discussed a paper by Edward S. Meade[28] at the annual meeting of the American Economic Association. Meade, who had been a graduate student in political economy at the University of Chicago from 1896 to 1898 (he received his Ph.D. in 1899 from the University of Pennsylvania), delivered a paper on "The Management of the Surplus Reserve." Hatfield was one of three discussants, and he criticized Meade for associating a company's "surplus reserve" (in today's parlance, "retained earnings") with specific assets:

> Why should the surplus have a special corresponding item among the assets? It almost seems at times as though the author were misled by the use of his pet phrase "surplus reserve," and thought because there is a surplus, there must needs be a specific reserve, such as is meant when we speak of the bank reserve. Is a fund of ready cash, or of easily negotiated securities, desirable in the assets of a corporation? Is it not equally desirable whether the corporation have a surplus or not?[29]

Hatfield, always quick to skewer injudicious terminology, identified the choice of the term "reserve" as the culprit in Meade's analysis.

Further, when Meade argued that an expenditure for the betterment of plant should be charged against earnings if it were not expected to produce a return in the immediate future, but that it should be capitalized if it were likely to be immediately productive, Hatfield bridled at a policy that would systematically understate earnings:

> Expedience, public policy perhaps, frequently justify the hiding of earnings because the temptation is generally toward exaggeration rather than toward depreciation of profits, but the ideal goal of accounting is exact accuracy, and a hidden surplus is in its very term a confession of an inexact balance sheet.[30]

This was Hatfield's initial published utterance on accounting theory, and it was the first time that a technical accounting issue was discussed at an annual meeting of the American Economic Association, which was then the only yearly occasion when academics interested in accounting would congregate.

Also in 1903-1904, while he was still at the University of Chicago, Hatfield signed a contract with D. Appleton and Company to write a textbook on accounting. For a number of reasons, including Hatfield's adjustment to a new university in an unfamiliar part of the country, progress on the book was slow. Further, even then, Hatfield's approach to authorship was to draw heavily on the views of authorities in the field. But in the middle of the first decade of the new century, an American literature on accounting (as opposed to bookkeeping) hardly existed, and the situation in Britain, where a literature was just beginning to emerge, and on the Continent was not much better.

Personal factors also intervened. While the Hatfield family was buoyed by the birth of a daughter, Elizabeth, on September 21, 1904, Henry Hatfield suffered a heart attack in 1905 and his wife, a miscarriage in 1906.[31]

The disastrous San Francisco earthquake of April 18, 1906 caused only minor damage in Berkeley. Yet, owing to the massive destruction of property in San Francisco, the university suffered financial losses that were "calamitous."[32] Following the tragedy, "refugees poured into Berkeley and the town experienced a boom."[33] Hatfield served in the relief effort. In a letter to family and friends in Baltimore, Ethel Hatfield wrote:

> Prof. Hatfield has been down town all day every day, working in the main office of the relief committee; getting subscriptions, authorizing expenditures; hunting up cash, which is terribly scarce, as all banks are closed; getting credit wherever possible, and organizing a system of accounts for the committee. He seems to be standing it well, but I hope the work will let up a little soon.[34]

During the first half of the academic year 1907-1908, Hatfield spent six months in New York and Europe on a leave of absence,[35] evidently doing research for his forthcoming book. Upon his return, he began composing his book in earnest. It was said that he wrote most, if not all, of the book in the Sierras during vacation periods, standing at an improvised table. He hunt-and-pecked away on his trusty Hammond typewriter.[36]

In 1908, Hatfield was one of a dozen academics appointed as associate editors of *The Journal of Accountancy*, a monthly publication begun in November 1905 under the auspices of the American Association of Public Accountants. In the first issue of the journal in which his name appeared, Hatfield reviewed two books. He excelled in book reviewing because he relished the role as an objective critic of the evolving literature. From the 1890s to the 1940s, he wrote more than 50 book reviews, mostly in economics and accounting journals.

Apart from Hatfield, all of *The Journal of Accountancy*'s panel of associate editors were from Eastern and Midwestern universities.[37] One supposes that Hatfield's candidacy was advanced by Edward S. Meade, an associate editor who had served as coeditor of the *Journal* in 1905-1906. Meade and Hatfield were students in the doctoral program in political economy at Chicago in 1896-1897, and Hatfield had discussed Meade's paper at the AEA annual meeting in December 1903. Hatfield probably would have met Joseph French Johnson, the *Journal*'s editor, when he paid a call on the Wharton School, where Johnson was a professor, in February 1900. In 1901, Johnson became dean of the New York University's School of Commerce, Accounts and Finance. Hatfield's service as an associate editor terminated with the issue of December 1914, when the then-editor, A.P. Richardson, dispensed with the panel.

HATFIELD'S ACTIVITIES IN BERKELEY AND WASHINGTON, 1909-1920

Modern Accounting Makes Its Debut

Hatfield's *Modern Accounting: Its Principles and Some of Its Problems* was published by Appleton in 1909 (see the Appendix to this chapter for a discussion of the contents). Some 38,000 copies of the book were sold before 1927, when the revision was published.[38] *Modern Accounting* was the first American or British book on accounting (as distinguished from bookkeeping) to be published in a Japanese translation.[39]

Modern Accounting was the first of a genre. Charles E. Sprague's *The Philosophy of Accounts* (published by the author) and William Morse Cole's *Accounts, Their Construction and Interpretation* (Boston: Houghton Mifflin), both published the year before, had succeeded in improving upon, especially in America, what Hatfield later described as a bookkeeping literature consisting of "a dreary succession of banal directions, showing little originality, little systematic thinking."[40] Hatfield later wrote that "Cole's Accounts was the first significant and praiseworthy American treatise on accounting," since Sprague's book—which Hatfield much admired—was really "a series of essays [originally published in 10 monthly installments during 1907 in *The Journal of Accountancy*] rather than a systematic treatise."[41]

While Cole's *Accounts, Their Construction and Interpretation* carried the subtitle *For Business Men and Students of Affairs*, Hatfield attempted in *Modern Accounting* "to present the principles of accounting" in a "work [that] is mainly a discussion of the problems of practical accounting" (pp. v, vii). Cole had just become assistant professor of accounting in the Harvard Business School, and his book was published in the year in which the school began operations. Harvard Business School aimed to prepare managers, not accountants.[42] Hatfield, on the other hand, had been recruited by John F. Forbes to prepare able students for the accounting profession, and he wrote *Modern Accounting* as if to elevate the level of discussion in accounting classrooms and among accounting professionals. Cole's textbook, with its emphasis on the interpretation of accounts, unveiled what the author later called the "Where-got-gone statement," the progenitor of the modern-day cash flow statement.[43] Only about one-third of Cole's book treated the principles and problems of preparing the financial statements of a general-purpose enterprise. Hatfield, by contrast, devoted 13 of his 19 chapters to the balance sheet, the valuation of assets, intangible assets, depreciation, capital stock, liabilities, profits, surplus and reserves, sinking funds, and trading, manufacturing and income accounts. His was the first U.S. textbook to give such extensive coverage to the principles and practice of accounting (as distinguished from bookkeeping), and he continually reminded his readers of the importance of principled practice and accurate terminology.

Hatfield's first two chapters, on The Theory of Double Entry Bookkeeping, are of particular interest. Sprague and Hatfield are known for having presented the proprietary theory of accounts in its most complete form.[44] In *Modern Accounting*, Hatfield adopted the bookkeeping equation: Goods = Proprietorship, with Assets being Positive Goods, and Liabilities being Negative Goods. Hendriksen suggested that the proprietorship theory places greater emphasis on explaining changes in the balance sheet, while the entity theory is more oriented to explanations in terms of the income statement.[45] Hatfield subsequently adopted the equation: Assets = Liabilities + Proprietorship. He was not much impressed by the difference between his division of the right-hand side of the balance sheet into liabilities and proprietorship, and William A. Paton's later preference for a single category of "equities," although subsequent writers have made much of the distinction.[46] In 1925, when reviewing Paton's *Accounting* (The Macmillan Company, 1924), he wrote:

> To some it would seem that there is little significant difference between saying that the right-hand side of the balance-sheet contains two distinct categories, liabilities and proprietorship, and saying that it contains only equities, but these are divided into "two quite distinct elements."[47]

To Paton, however, the "managerial point of view" (which others called the "entity theory") required that interest be classified as a distribution of income, not as an expense in arriving at income. He placed primary emphasis on the return to all long-term capital suppliers, arguing that "there is no fundamental antithesis between payments to the stockholder (dividends) and return to the bondholder (interest)."[48] For this reason, Paton grouped liabilities and proprietorship under a common heading, which he denominated as "equities."

In *Modern Accounting*, as came to be typical of his writings, Hatfield did not press his views on the reader but instead distilled the views of the most respected authorities, judiciously interspersing his own as appropriate. He was more a perceptive annotator of the literature, especially with a keen eye for the ironic, than an unbridled advocate (as was Paton, for example) of what he believed to be correct.

Hatfield cast a wide net. The bibliographical notes at the end of his chapters contained no fewer than 149 entries to the works of American, British, German, French, and Swiss writers, occasionally with a pithy remark on the significance of the work. (By contrast, Sprague cited four works, and Cole, none.) Hatfield was in earnest: at the end of his two chapters on Capital Stock, he wrote, "For a more serious discussion of the principles involved see" and proceeded to cite extracts from one treatise written in French and two in German (pp. 182-183). He also referred in the book to 68 court opinions (mainly American and British) as well as to corporation statutes, Interstate Commerce Commission regulations, and the actual financial and accounting practices of companies and banks. Although a textbook, *Modern Accounting* possessed the character of a handbook.

Assessments of *Modern Accounting*

The reviews were generally favorable. In *The Journal of Accountancy* (September 1910, p. 387) Seymour Walton[49] adjudged it to be a "very excellent book" and said that he recommended it strongly to his students in Advanced Accounting at Northwestern University as "the best book they could obtain for collateral reading." In the *Journal of Political Economy* (November 1909, pp. 647-650), William Morse Cole described it as "an extremely valuable and interesting treatise," but he complained that "the author has given so much opinion of other people and so little of his own—especially when the opinions of others are so often contradictory of one another. He has raised many problems; and most of them are still problems when he leaves them." The book, he said, is "helpful to the lawyer preparing a brief, but is hardly convincing to the layman who needs sound principles.... The accountants should expect to lead, not follow the courts.... Mr. Hatfield's own point of view is uncompromisingly favorable to making the accounts show the exact truth, but he is not eager to argue for his own beliefs as to just what is the truth."[50] Cole aptly pointed out that "Mr. Hatfield's own opinion is usually implied in his comments on the other opinions expressed, and his opinion seems sane, but except for the close reader it is likely to be more or less swamped in the mass of confirmatory and contradictory opinion." Neither Cole nor Hatfield was a CPA, but they held very different conceptions on the role of the textbook author as authority.

An unsigned review in *The Nation* (June 10, 1909, pp. 584-585) said that "Professor Hatfield has produced the best treatise on accounting that has yet appeared in the United States, and it is difficult to find its superior in the English language.... It strikes a happy mean between the extremes of the theoretical and the practical, and presents what might be called a comparative study of accounting practice rather than any dogmatic scheme of the author's own." On this last point, Hatfield would have agreed.

Frederick A. Cleveland, a specialist in municipal accounts and finance (and, as a graduate student in political science at the University of Chicago from 1897 to 1899, an acquaintance of Hatfield's), wrote that *Modern Accounting* was "scholarly" and gave evidence of "wholesomeness and conservatism of principle" (*The Economic Bulletin*, Vol. II, 1909, p. 236).

In an unsigned review in *The New York Times* (May 8, 1909, p. 289), the reviewer observed:

> One thing that is made very clear in Mr. Hatfield's book is that accounting of the highest order is much more complicated than it used to be. The schemes which were good enough in the days

> of comparatively small concerns would be ridiculously inadequate now that capitalizations run into the hundreds of millions and ownership in the case of pretty near all of our great corporations is well separated from management.
>
> Mr. Hatfield writes intelligently about the changes in accounting that have come about through recent economic developments and gives an excellent exposition of the methods in use at the present day.

Joseph E. Sterrett, a partner in Price, Waterhouse & Co. and president of the American Association of Public Accountants (forerunner of the American Institute of Accountants), wrote that the value of the book was "not only as a text-book for students of accounting but as a hand-book for business men and for practicing accountants it must rank among the first books of its class" (*Political Science Quarterly*, June 1911, p. 346).

In retrospect, practicing accountants had high praise for *Modern Accounting*. Looking back in 1948, a nationally respected practitioner and author, Maurice E. Peloubet (1892-1976), wrote:

> Among the educational pioneers no one was more influential or stood higher than Henry Rand Hatfield.... [*Modern Accounting*] was one of the most important early books on the subject in this country. Many of us, who can go back thirty years or more, will remember very well having learned chapters of [*Modern Accounting*] practically by heart. It is still sound in principle and many of the basic theories which were first discussed in it are as valid today as they were then.[51]

Judson E. Krueger, a partner in John F. Forbes & Co. who took Elementary Accounting from Hatfield in 1913, has remarked that, prior to 1909, when *Modern Accounting* was published, no book in general circulation was more than a text on bookkeeping.[52]

Francis P. Farquhar, the senior partner in a medium-sized San Francisco accounting firm who was president of the California State Society of Certified Public Accountants in 1942-1943, recounts the following experience that took place in 1912, not long after he graduated from Harvard College:

> When I went to work for [Clinton H. Scovell & Co., a Boston accounting firm] the office secretary brought out a book from under the counter and said, "Have you studied this book?" I said, "No I haven't seen that." "Well, Mr. Scovell doesn't want anybody to work for him unless he's read this book. We have a stock of them here at the wholesale rate and you'd better buy one and if you haven't read it in two weeks, he's likely to fire you." And that book was *Modern Accounting* by Henry Rand Hatfield....
>
> Hatfield was one of the first professors to recognize modern trends in accounting. He grasped modern accounting and taught it and had a great influence on the development of accounting philosophy and accounting procedure. His book was a great contrast to the early books on accounting written largely by men who had come up through the English procedure of apprenticeship and had quite a different point of view from American accounting. I don't think Scovell ever met Hatfield, but he admired his book.[53]

An unsigned review in the *Evening Transcript*, published in Boston, testified to the impact of *Modern Accounting*. The review, published on July 2, 1927 and ostensibly about Hatfield's 1927 successor textbook, *Accounting: Its Principles and Problems*, is much more revealing about *Modern Accounting*:

> About the year 1909 a modest little book under the title of "Modern Accounting" first made its appearance. Rather prosaic was this volume, both in its dress and subject matter. Apparently, it was just another book on the constructive and analytical aspects of advanced bookkeeping, unfamiliarly known, as yet, as "Accounting." To the average person it would never occur that a book of this nature could possibly create something of a furore. But that was exactly what happened.
>
> Looking back in retrospect, one is intrigued to discover and isolate the elements which gained such instant approval for a treatise by a hitherto unknown author. Was it the realization that here was a writer that had gone beyond the simple limits of our own experience to those of the English, French and German for precept and example? Or, was it the ample evidence of a deep and scholarly knowledge of the historical, traditional, legal and present-day aspects of the subject? Perhaps it was a fusion of these ideas. Suffice, the book became—and remained—a classic authority on the subject of accounting.

It seems likely that the review was written by one of the city's accounting practitioners.

Academic accountants also esteemed the book. In 1972, William A. Paton testified to the impact that *Modern Accounting* had on his decision to choose accounting over economics:

> Some sixty years ago I happened to enroll in an accounting principles course at the University of Michigan. The instructor in charge was David Friday, a professor of economics who knew nothing about accounting. But Friday was an excellent teacher and understood the importance of keeping ahead of the class when embarked on strange waters. For some weeks our progress was slow. [Cole's *Accounting and Auditing*] was a confused presentation baffling to instructor as well as students.... Then one day our teacher came in beaming with two books of modest dimensions which he held up for us all to see and recommended strongly. One was *The Philosophy of Accounts* (1907) by Charles Ezra Sprague and the other was *Modern Accounting* (1909) by Henry Rand Hatfield.... In my case the availability of Sprague and Hatfield in connection with this course was crucial. It was these writings that aroused my interest in accounting, and without this spur I am quite certain that I would never have shifted from teaching economic theory to a career primarily in the accounting field.[54]

A.C. Littleton has written, "The appearance of Sprague's *Philosophy of Accounts* (1907), Hatfield's *Modern Accounting* (1909), and [J. Lee] Nicholson's *Factory Organization and Costs* (1909), may be said to mark the real beginning of American contributions."[55] Some years later, Roy B. Kester, who authored a series of major accounting textbooks from 1916 to 1946, wrote (in a testimonial to Hatfield upon the latter's retirement):

> Let me pay tribute in the humble mood of a student to a teacher, to the impetus given me in 1909 by your Modern Accounting shortly after its publication when I was struggling to secure

> preparation for work in this field. As there so well developed, the philosophy of the subject made a lasting appeal to me and to it I attribute the awakening of a really compelling interest to which may be traced the beginnings of any contribution which I may have made in that field.[56]

Finally, a close observer of the accounting profession assessed the book. John L. Carey, the longtime (1930-1969) chief administrative officer of the American Institute of (Certified Public) Accountants, although not a CPA himself, wrote that Sprague's *The Philosophy of Accounts*, Cole's *Accounts, Their Construction and Interpretation*, and Hatfield's *Modern Accounting* "were outstanding books on accounting ... which served as a basis for instruction at the universities, and to a considerable extent as authority for practitioners for many years to come."[57] He added, "In the first 30 years of its existence [i.e., from the 1880s onward], however, the American accounting profession had little native technical literature with which to work."[58]

Hatfield's First Article on Bookkeeping History

Also in 1909, Hatfield published an article in German in the Austrian journal *Zeitschrift für Buchhaltung*, titled "Zwei Pfadfinder" ("Two Pioneers").[59] The idea for the article was probably stimulated during one of Hatfield's trips to Europe. He argued that two American writers, Thomas Jones and B.F. Foster (who published between 1836 and 1852), had preceded two continental authors, G.D. Augspurg in Bremen and Georg Kurzbauer in Vienna (who had published almost simultaneously in the early 1850s), in clearly enunciating the significance of the proprietorship accounts, including profits and losses, as a necessary complement of the asset and liability accounts in the compilation of the ledger. This division of accounts, Hatfield wrote elsewhere, "constitutes the very essence of double-entry bookkeeping."[60] The article represented Hatfield's first foray into the history of bookkeeping.

On the Teaching of Bookkeeping

During the summer of 1909, Hatfield offered several accounting courses as part of the department of education's program to raise the level of teaching in the state's public schools.[61] The program may also have been a reflection of Hatfield's low regard for the instruction being given in bookkeeping by the high schools. In an unpublished paper, "Business Efficiency as a University Ideal," he wrote: "In my own work, those who come to me with two years of [high school] bookkeeping do no better than those who come with virgin minds." The courses in the summer program were Elementary Accounting, Advanced Accounting, and Conferences for Teachers ("A course dealing with the literature of accounting and discussing the methods of teaching the subject"[62]). Hatfield also taught the latter

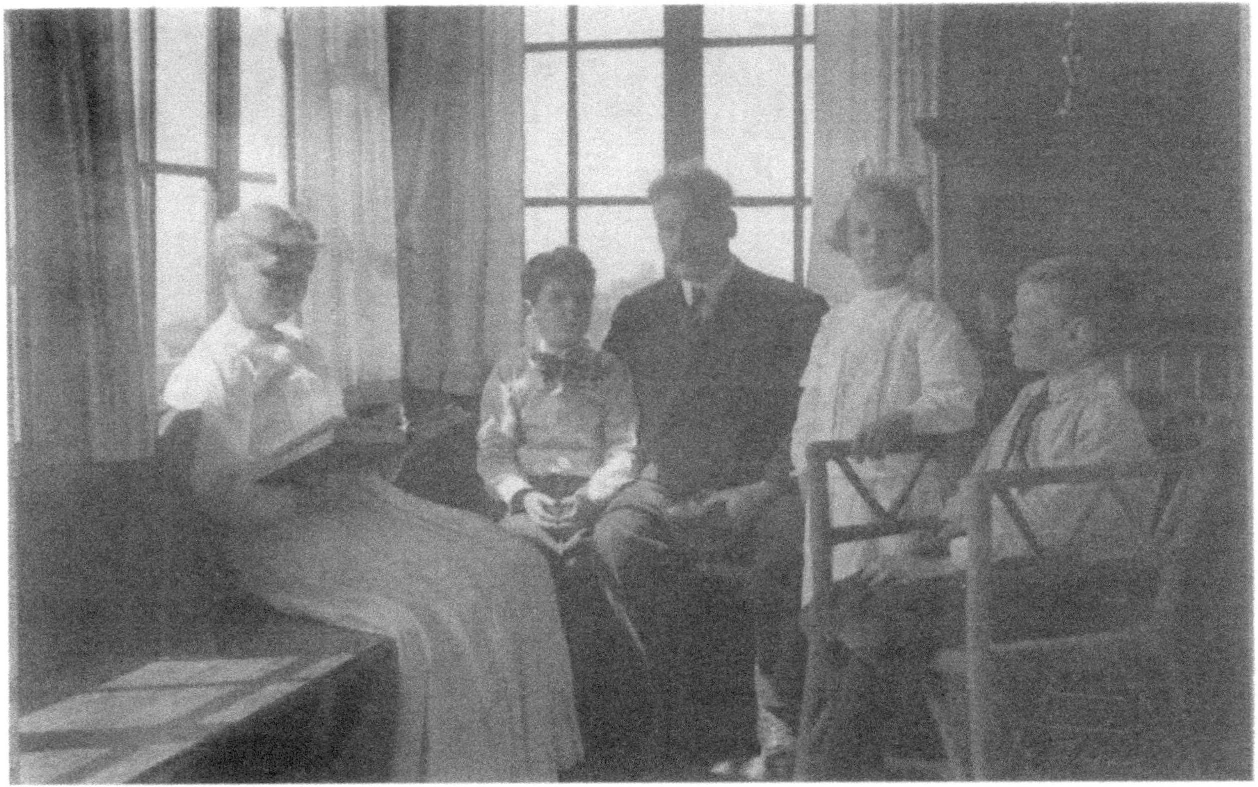

The Henry Hatfield family c. 1914. From left: Ethel, Robert, Henry, Elizabeth, and John.

The Henry Hatfield family at play, c. 1914. From left: Ethel, Elizabeth, Robert, John, and Henry.

course in the summer of 1915 (jointly with Stephen W. Gilman—see below) and during the 1916-1917 and 1917-1918 academic years, under the title of Teachers' Course. In 1913, Hatfield presented the paper "Some Heretical Views on the Method of Teaching Bookkeeping" to a meeting of high school teachers of bookkeeping. He emphasized that "the pupil [should be] taught to regard business transactions with reference to the way in which they really affect the proprietor, and not in accordance with some mere formula of comings and goings." In this paper, Hatfield was much influenced by Jones's work, discussed in his "Zwei Pfadfinder." "According to the underlying theory," he wrote in the 1913 paper, "double-entry bookkeeping is double, not because there are two columns in an account, nor because every debit has a credit, nor because there are two entries for each transaction, but because it attempts to make two parallel sets of records, leading to a double portrayal of essential facts."

A House of His Own

Also during the summer (and perhaps as early as the spring) of 1909, the Hatfields moved from rented lodgings into their newly constructed home on Le Conte Avenue, just north of the university campus. The Hatfield house was designed by Julia Morgan, who was "Berkeley's first woman architect and one of the State's most noted architects."[63] Hatfield's daughter, Elizabeth Hatfield Glover, wrote that while the house was going up, "Father used to go over to the place and 'save the country'—trying to keep the loose land from washing away in some of the spring floods. A nearby canyon overflowed until a culvert was made under the street."[64] Over the years, Hatfield planted numerous redwoods from Muir Woods and Mt. Tamalpais. He had a keen interest in the flora of the West.[65]

Continued Academic and Professional Activity

In 1909, Hatfield was promoted to professor of accounting, continuing on the Flood Foundation. After five years at $2,500, his salary was raised to $3,000. By then, the department of economics had increased in size to nine faculty with professorial rank (from four in 1904-1905).

Hatfield continued to teach a wide range of commerce courses, while gradually adding new accounting courses. He introduced a course in Cost Accounting in 1909-1910. The following year, Cost Accounting was split into a regular section and an honors section. From 1912-1913 to 1914-1915, he taught, in succession, Banking, The Investment Market, and Corporation Finance, as well as Municipal Finance and Commercial Reviews and Trade Journals (jointly taught with an associate professor of English). Following 1915, Hatfield's nonaccounting teaching was largely confined to Corporation Finance and Investments. In 1913-1914, Accounting Systems, taught by Hatfield, made its debut. By 1915-1916, the college's enrollment had almost doubled, from 177 in 1907-1908 to 340, keeping pace with the doubling of the university enrollment from 2,610 to 5,286 during the same period.

Hatfield always made it clear that the university's accounting courses did not attempt to prepare students for a professional examination. In a letter written in 1918, he said:

> The giving of the C.P.A. is not in the hands of the University but is given by the State Board of Accountancy. The University does not specifically prepare for the passing of such examination, but attempts rather to provide the training which it considers essential for the work of the public accountant not limiting itself to cramming for an examination.[66]

Scott H. Dunham, a prominent San Francisco CPA who served as Hatfield's teaching assistant in 1928-29, said that Hatfield emphasized principles and gave rein to the student's reasoning process in his courses. In Hatfield's view, accounting was not a technical body of knowledge to be memorized. Once the student entered practice, Hatfield maintained, he could learn the details of accounting while being paid. He believed that a student should have a thorough knowledge of accounting principles that reflected more than one point of view.[67]

Such was the regard in which Hatfield was held by the profession that he was made an honorary member of the California State Society of Certified Public Accountants in 1910,[68] one year after the society was founded as the result of a merger of three previous bodies.[69] John F. Forbes, the Society's secretary-treasurer and always a force in the affairs of the profession, arranged for the distinction to be conferred,[70] not only as a measure of his respect for Hatfield but also so that Hatfield could attend meetings of professional accountants in San Francisco and thus join with Forbes in raising the standard of practice.[71] On only one other occasion, in 1970, has the society conferred an honorary membership.[72]

Sabbatical in Europe

During the second half of 1911, Hatfield took the first of several sabbatical leaves overseas. In the summer, he taught two courses at Columbia University, one on corporation finance and the other on accounting.[73] He also spent some time doing research in the Library of Congress in Washington. Once in Europe, he spent most of his time in Munich, attending lectures by Willi Prion and others at the Handelshochschule (i.e., commercial college) and at the university. He visited colleagues at the Handelshochschulen in Leipzig and Berlin, where he met Professor Schär. He also spent some time in Edinburgh, where had lunch with Richard Brown,[74] and in London, where he visited the library of the Institute of Chartered Accountants in England and Wales.[75]

Address on International Accounting Practices at the AAPA's Annual Meeting

One of the consequences of his overseas tour was that an address he had prepared to deliver at the annual meeting of the American Association of Public Accountants, held on September 19-21 in San Francisco, had to be read by another. It seems likely that John F. Forbes, the California Society's secretary-treasurer, had recommended Hatfield as a speaker. Hatfield's address, titled "Some Variations in Accounting Practice in England, France, Germany and the United States," became perhaps the earliest comparative study covering countries with distinctly different accounting traditions. Much of the research for the paper seems also to have found expression in *Modern Accounting*. Hatfield never had the paper published, apparently believing that his research was not yet complete,[76] but in 1966, more than 20 years after Hatfield's death, I edited the paper and had it published in the *Journal of Accounting Research*. The paper, Hatfield's first article-length manuscript on accounting, was, with "An Historical Defense of Bookkeeping" (1923), the only major papers that he wrote between the publication of *Modern Accounting* in 1909 and the appearance of its successor, *Accounting*, 18 years later. Hatfield's views on the American accounting scene were perceptive. After reviewing the approaches to regulating accounting in England and on the Continent, he wrote:

> And as to America? Here is to be found accounting almost unregulated either by statutes or by courts. No authority recognized, almost every abuse apparently sanctioned by the practice of prominent if not always reputable concerns. Yet throughout all there is an exhibition of American adaptability and inventiveness. So successful have American accountants been in devising forms suited to the desired ends that on the continent any bookkeeping device recognized as having peculiar merit and originality is, irrespective of its actual origin, apt to be called "American" bookkeeping. Particularly advanced has been the development, in the United States, of cost accounting, and this may properly be spoken of as the greater characteristic contribution which the present generation has made to the science of accounting. As on the continent one looks to jurists, and in England to chartered accountants, in this country it is perhaps to engineers that one looks for the greatest stimulus and inspiration in accounting progress; for in large part the development of cost accounting is due to the initiative of engineers, although the public accountant has greatly contributed to its development.[77]

Continued Development of the Accounting Curriculum

At long last, in 1912, colleagues were appointed to help Hatfield teach the work in accounting. On the recommendation of Stephen W. Gilman at the University of Wisconsin,[78] Lewis Lilly arrived as an assistant in accounting, probably at a pittance of a salary. (Hatfield's salary continued at $3,000 in 1912-1913, plus a $300 allotment for summer teaching.) Lilly was made an instructor two years later. He and Hatfield jointly taught the Introduction to Accounting course, whose enrollment was expanding with the steady growth of the college. Lilly introduced a course in Fiduciary Accounting and also assisted Hatfield in Advanced Accounting. He resigned in 1916 to take over the accounting work at the University of Washington, and following the war he became a partner in a San Francisco firm which later merged with Haskins & Sells.[79]

Also in 1912, Hatfield succeeded in inducing John F. Forbes to offer courses in the college. Forbes joined the faculty in the spring semester of 1913 as lecturer in accounting and gave accounting courses on a part-time basis in all but four years until 1940.[80] He said that he never accepted any compensation.[81] Forbes was not, however, well regarded as a teacher.[82] In 1913-1914, Forbes took over the work in Cost Accounting and Auditing, and he introduced courses in Public Utility Accounts and Municipal Accounts in 1914-1915 and 1916-1917, respectively.[83] From 1915-1916 onward, he took the ferry from San Francisco to Berkeley on Wednesdays in time to teach Auditing (in the fall) or Cost Accounting (in the spring) that evening, stay overnight in a Berkeley hotel, and offer either Public Utility Accounts or Municipal Accounts (later renamed Governmental Accounts) at 8:00 the next morning, prior to catching the ferry back to the City.[84]

In 1913-1914, Hatfield introduced a course in Accounting Systems, which carried the description, "Principles of accounting as applied to different forms of enterprise."[85] Beginning in 1915-1916, his Advanced Accounting was retitled as Advanced Accounting Problems and became a full-year course (four credits versus its previous three), described as "Investigation and reports on suggested topics."[86] In the fall of 1917, Hatfield invited a group of honors students to join the course informally. His plan was "to read rapidly several of the leading texts. I thought we would start out with Cole, Esquerre, Dickinson, Dicksee."[87] He wrote the enrolled students, "Later in the term we may undertake original investigations."[88] From an early stage, a critical literature review was Hatfield's approach to his seminar. The title of his capstone seminar always referred to "Accounting Problems," not "Accounting Theory."

From 1915-1916 onward, the one-semester Introduction to Accounting course became a two-semester sequence titled Principles of Accounting, 14A and 14B, with the following description:

> While this course is a prerequisite for advanced work in accounting, it is also designed to meet the needs of those who do not expect to become professional accountants, and to furnish such an understanding of accounts as will be of service to the business man, the lawyer and the public official.[89]

In 1915-1916, the university's College of Mining began offering a course in Mine Cost-Accounting, followed in 1916-1917 with a course in Petroleum Cost Accounting.[90] In 1918, Hatfield tried unsuccessfully to persuade the College of Mining to allow the department of economics to offer the work in mine accounting.[91] As Moonitz wrote:

> This development is of significance because it highlights a problem in any large university, namely, the jurisdictional limits of basic disciplines. In the case of accounting, the College of Mining set up its own courses; later on, at Berkeley, Industrial Engineering began a similar move, but Business Administration apparently was able to keep control of accounting by setting up a course designed primarily to meet the needs of upper-division students in Engineering. There was also some accounting content in courses offered in the College of Agriculture in the field of Farm Management. The principal reason why schools and colleges other than commerce or business wanted to undertake the burden of teaching accounting was their unwillingness to require their students to take a year of lower-division introductory accounting before getting to the subject-matter of interest to them.[92]

In 1916, Charles C. Staehling (1883-1975), a graduate of the University of Chicago and a member of that university's select chapter of Phi Beta Kappa, came to the college as instructor in accounting, and replaced Lilly as Hatfield's associate in the offerings of Introduction to Accounting. Two years later, upon completing the Master of Science degree (he never enrolled for the doctorate) and passing the CPA examination, he was promoted to assistant professor of accounting. In 1917-1918, he began to offer the course in Partnership Accounts that was originally intended for Lilly. In 1918-1919, he began offering a course in Income Tax Accounting, which was becoming his major interest.[93] After taking a leave of absence from 1919 to 1922 to acquire experience in public accounting, Staehling returned as associate professor of accounting, although continuing as a part-time consultant to Haskins & Sells. He remained on the Berkeley faculty until his retirement in 1951, eventually becoming, in his final year, professor of accounting. Staehling never published any research or even a textbook on his own.[94] (Hatfield's exacting standard and penetrating criticism would have intimidated many junior colleagues.) Staehling's thinking and teaching were much affected by John B. Canning's *The Economics of Accountancy* (New York: Ronald Press, 1929), an influence that he transmitted to Maurice Moonitz, a student in Staehling's classes and later his teaching assistant.[95]

Participation in the University's Literary Clubs

Hatfield, educated in the classics, economics, and political science, had worked in the bond market, was addicted to detective novels, and regularly traveled overseas during leaves and occasionally in summers. A former student who knew Hatfield well wrote the following in 1964: "He read Latin as readily as English and wrote in their own tongue to his academic friends in Greece. He was fluent in German and French and had a working knowledge of Italian and Spanish."[96] Hatfield's interests were catholic. In those halcyon days of Renaissance scholars, universities would have one or more men's literary clubs at whose meetings members from diverse disciplines or practical backgrounds would partake of a wide-ranging discussion of the topic chosen for the evening. The best-known such club at the University of California was the Berkeley Club, founded in 1873.[97]

Members were expected to attend all meetings and to be responsible, in an agreed order, for opening the discussion of a subject. Hatfield was elected to membership in October 1916 and, except for war leave in 1917-1919, continued as a member in good standing until his death in 1945. Few other members of the department of economics were members, but Plehn was among them.

When serving as "opener" for the evening's discussion of a topic, Hatfield followed the practice of writing out a paper and reading it. As far as is known, in scheduled presentations at meetings of all kinds, even when delivering brief remarks or serving as toastmaster (for which he was in great demand), he read from a prepared script. Ten typescripts of papers (or derivations thereof) prepared for presentation to the Berkeley Club survive. Most have been resurrected and edited, and several are reproduced in Chapter 7. The papers that Hatfield presented to the Berkeley Club give vivid testimony to the range of his interests (copies of all but the 1929 paper have been found):

- "Experiences with the War Industries Board," 1920
- "The Corporation and the Public," 1921
- "De Computis et Scripturis," October 1923
- "Cui Lumen Ademptum," September 24, 1925[98]
- "Parliament and the Trade Unions," October 27, 1927
- "The International Congress at Amsterdam," December 19, 1929
- "The Inner Workings of a Pool," October 8, 1931
- "Germany of the Present Day," September 7, 1933
- "George Washington and Doctor Craik," August 30, 1934
- "Moriturus Vos Saluto," April 29, 1937
- "Of 'Loose and Lavender Language'," November 19, 1942

"De Computis et Scripturis" was an early version of his famous paper, "An Historical Defense of Bookkeeping." Hatfield wanted to establish the pedigree of accounting among his university colleagues, and this objective may be a reason why he gave papers on such a wide range of scholarly topics, with only one on the subject of accounting.[99]

Hatfield also belonged to the Kosmos Club, which was formed in 1901.[100] He joined the club sometime prior to 1910 and resigned in September 1920.[101] His papers presented to the Kosmos Club were as follows (only the 1912 paper has survived):

- "The Pragmatist's Conception of Reality," March 1, 1909
- "Business Efficiency as a University Ideal," November 4, 1912
- "War and Statistics," February 2, 1920.

Hatfield's "Business Efficiency as a University Ideal" was an amusing paper in which he took as his point of departure the uproar caused by a Carnegie Founda-

Henry Hatfield in the study of his Berkeley home. Photograph was taken in about 1914. Hatfield was professor of accounting in the University of California and secretary (in effect, dean) of the College of Commerce.

tion report that argued for greater effectiveness—indeed, efficiency—in the performance of university tasks. Hatfield provided several thinly veiled examples of incompetent and amateurish administration at the three universities with which he had been associated. "In the college world," he wrote, "the naturally inefficient administrator almost glories in his inefficiency, wears it as a badge of his high caste, and coddles and develops it far beyond its natural limits."

Hatfield prepared a paper on "Corporations and the Public" for a meeting of the Kosmos Club on February 4, 1918, but did not present it, perhaps because of the press of administrative commitments in the university. In 1921, he presented a paper with an almost identical title to the Berkeley Club. In it, he explored the public's distrust of corporations:

> One cannot take up a paper, serious or comic, without seeing some headline, cartoon, squib, editorial or article in some way portraying the evil of corporations. Why is it that civilization takes so little pride in its great invention; why is it, if corporations are so inherently vicious, that society continues to have them, for they are absolutely the creation of law, and would have no existence without legal sanction? Surely the public, Frankenstein-like, seems to have used its creative genius to produce a monster which, once in existence, seems only to plague its magician creator.

A short piece attached to the main paper discussed the importance of publicity of accounts as a remedy for financial misdeeds. He read an earlier version of this paper, perhaps in a somewhat different form, as one of a series of lectures in 1910 on "Phases of Corporation Finance" to the Oakland chapter of the American Institute of Banking. (Both papers are reproduced in Chapter 7.)

Administrative Assignments at Berkeley

Plehn's term as dean of the College of Commerce ended in 1909.[102] Hatfield then was named to the new position of secretary of the college. From 1909 to 1916, the dean's position was, at a formal level, encompassed within the newly created office of dean of the faculties, although Hatfield, as secretary of the college, carried out most of the dean's functions. Hatfield remained as secretary until 1916, when the deanship of the college was restored, a position that Hatfield occupied until 1920.

In addition, Hatfield served as acting dean of the faculties for the first six months of 1916 and became dean of the faculties for the academic year 1917-1918 (with a salary supplement of $500) when the incumbent, David Prescott Barrows (who would succeed Wheeler as president at the end of 1919), was on overseas leave.[103] The dean of the faculties was the second-ranking executive in the university.

Hatfield apparently built a reputation as a fair-minded and conscientious administrator, for such assignments continued to come his way in the 1920s.[104] As acting dean of faculties, one of his duties was to speak at the inauguration of the president of the University of Washington on March 21, 1916. His elegant address, scribbled on the back of hotel stationery, is reproduced in Chapter 7. Hatfield began by referring to "an event which took place in Berkeley last November," at which "it seems that there came down from the north a horde, valiant as Vikings, stalwart as the Goths, irresistible as Thor himself. Despite sacrificial fires burned on our Grecian altar, and stranger vigils kept beside our hallside, the fairest flower of California classical culture went down before that horde, and the place thereof knew it no more." Hatfield's allegory referred to the Big Game played between the University of California and the University of Washington.[105] The previous November, in the first Big Game between the universities, Washington's football team had trounced the lads from Berkeley, 72-0.[106]

Hatfield found that his double duty during 1917-1918 as dean of the college and dean of the faculties, even though fewer students were in attendance following the U.S. entry into the war, was more of a load than he had anticipated. One factor was his heavy involvement, from October 1917 to May 1918, in running several training schools for the Ordnance Field Service of the War Department (described below). In a letter to Professor C.B. Bradley dated October 17, 1917, Hatfield wrote:

> At the beginning of the year, somewhat against my wishes, I undertook to take over, in addition to my own duties, those which had formerly been performed by Professor Barrows [i.e., as dean of the faculties]. The only excuse for my doing so was the thought that with the lessened number of students [owing to the war] the administrative work would be considerably less than it had been formerly. I find, however, that while there are fewer students, the complications due to war conditions have really made more administrative work rather than less. In addition to this, I have just this week had put upon me by request of the War Department, the supervision of a special course of training for persons desiring to enter the Ordnance Department, which still further adds to my overcrowded schedule.

It was for this reason that, at his request, he was relieved from his duties as dean of the College of Commerce on April 1, 1918, while continuing as dean of the faculties.[107] Only a few weeks later, Hatfield wrote President Wheeler that the load of managing the university's instructional system during the trying wartime period, coupled with a project that he had just completed for the U.S. Shipping Board, had taken a toll on his health, and he resigned also as dean of the faculties.[108]

Hatfield's series of university administrative assignments from 1909 to 1918 does much to explain the paucity of his publications from 1910 to 1919. As will be seen, he was in Washington on war-related assignments in 1918-19. His output during these 10 years consisted of one article, "Some Neglected Phases of Accounting," given as an address to a convention of the American Electric Railway Accountants' Association in October 1915 in San Francisco, and reviews of 13 books, the last of which appeared in 1916.

In an administrative assignment outside the university, Hatfield served as president of the Berkeley Commission of Charities from 1914 to 1918.

Hatfield's Book Reviews

From his arrival in Berkeley until 1916, Hatfield wrote 17 book reviews, mostly in *The Journal of Accountancy* and the *Journal of Political Economy*. Apparently because of the demands of university administrative assignments as well as his war-related service in Washington, he published no further reviews until 1925.

Hatfield's three most significant reviews during this period were of books by Charles E. Sprague, Robert H. Montgomery, and Arthur Lowes Dickinson—three pillars of the profession. Hatfield praised Sprague's *The Philosophy of Accounts* as "the masterly little treatise, with which no other American work can properly even be compared, with which even the wide literature of Germany can furnish but few rivals" (*The Journal of Accountancy*, November 1908, p. 67). In *Modern Accounting*, Hatfield characterized Sprague's book as "the most important theoretical work which has appeared in English."[109]

To Hatfield, Sprague's book was a breath of fresh air in a literature that treated "each account as though it represented an actual relationship of debtor and creditor, carrying out the principle by a forced and unnatural personification." That was, until then, the "conventional explanation of the theory accounting," a shallow conception that led in its most extreme form to a rule to be memorized: "Debit all that comes in and credit all that goes out." To Hatfield, the acknowledged scholar among accounting academics, such reasoning was undignified and a debasement of the subject. He admired Sprague for having rescued accounting from this morass of mangled metaphors. Hatfield wrote an introductory note for the 1922 republication of Sprague's book, where he discussed the work at greater length. (This note is reproduced in Chapter 7.)

Montgomery was a founding partner of Lybrand, Ross & Bros. & Montgomery and president of the American Association of Public Accountants, and Hatfield hailed Montgomery's new auditing textbook in the opening sentence of his review (*Journal of Political Economy*, October 1913): "The primacy among treatises on auditing, which until the present has been held by Dicksee's work, now passes to Montgomery's *Auditing Theory and Practice*." The book, he said, was "scholarly, comprehensive, masterly." He added: "Throughout the book the author takes an advanced position on the question of professional ethics .... he always stands clearly for professional honor and personal integrity." This was the ultimate accolade from the son of a fire-breathing Methodist minister.

Notwithstanding this fulsome praise, Hatfield took issue with Montgomery's placement of the reserve for depreciation among the liabilities. In *Modern Accounting*, Hatfield's preference was to show the allowance for depreciation (he did not think the term "reserve" was apt, even though it was then widely used) as a deduction from the related asset—that is, as a Valuation Account, a term that he coined.[110] Eventually, in his fourth edition, published in 1927, Montgomery accepted "allowance" in place of reserve and recommended that the allowance for depreciation be deducted from the asset to which it relates.[111] Hatfield joyously welcomed Montgomery's *volte-face*.

Hatfield reviewed Dickinson's *Accounting Practice and Procedure* at length (*The Journal of Accountancy*, December 1914). Dickinson, a partner in Price, Waterhouse & Co. and a leader of the profession in both the United States and England, had criticized the inclusion of interest and rent in the cost of manufacture. He regarded rent and interest as divisions of profit, not elements of cost, which was to be divided among the three classes of capitalist: the owner of the rented facilities, the lender, and the owner of the company. In an earlier article, Dickinson had said, moreover, that "the manner in which capital is provided cannot affect cost of manufacture."[112] His arguments were rehearsed in this book.[113] In his review, Hatfield registered a dissent:

> The author's well-known views in regard to the exclusion of interest and rent from cost accounts may have certain merits in actual cost keeping. But the economic analysis by which he attempts to support his views is unsatisfactory. It is not the contractual feature which determines whether a distributive share is a part of profits; and wages, as well as interest, may be considered a commutation of a share in the product. It is also difficult to reconcile the author's statement that interest cannot enter into cost with his approval of charging to the construction account the interest actually paid out during construction. Perhaps he would frankly admit the inconsistency, but justify it on grounds of practical expediency.

In *Modern Accounting*, Hatfield seemed to support the charging of actually incurred interest to the construction account. In *Accounting* (1927), he sidestepped the issue, merely observing that the discussion on this point "has been almost interminable."[114]

By adopting this position on interest and rent, Dickinson qualified as a supporter of the "entity theory," since he defined profit as the return to all suppliers of capital, not just to the residual owners.

Beta Gamma Sigma, the AACSB, and the AAUIA: Hatfield as a Founder and Early Officer

The decade from 1911 to 1920 was an exciting period, during which one organization after another was formed to serve the needs of business schools and the community of accounting academics. Hatfield became a founder and early officer of Beta Gamma Sigma, the American Association (now Assembly) of Collegiate Schools of Business, and the American Association of University Instructors in Accounting (now known as the American Accounting Association).

In 1913, Beta Gamma Sigma, the national honorary society for business students, was established.[115] It was formed by the merger of scholarship societies at three universities: Beta Gamma Sigma at the University of Wisconsin,[116] Delta

Kappa Chi at the University of Illinois, and the Economics Club at the University of California. At the inaugural biennial convention of Beta Gamma Sigma in February 1913, Hatfield, who had attended the 1911 meeting where plans were laid for the merger of the three societies, was elected a vice-president of the new body. He served on the executive committee between 1915 and 1917, then remained as Grand Vice President until 1922, but it is not known whether he was present at any of the biennial conventions during those years.

With the rapid growth in the number of business schools in U.S. universities—40 schools, colleges, and other such programs had been opened by the end of 1915[117]—a conference was held on June 16 and 17, 1916, in Chicago to form an organization that could establish standards and promote improvements in the schools' offerings. Representatives of 17 business schools participated in the conference, at which the American Association of Collegiate Schools of Business (AACSB) was founded. The conference had been called by Edwin F. Gay, dean of Harvard University's Graduate School of Business Administration, Leon C. Marshall, dean of the University of Chicago's College of Commerce and Administration, and Alfred E. Swanson, acting dean of Northwestern University's School of Commerce. Lewis Lilly was the delegate from Berkeley. Gay was elected chairman of the conference and also was chosen to chair the provisional executive committee, once the delegates had approved the formation of the AACSB. Although not present, Hatfield was named to the executive committee, and he continued to serve on the committee for two further terms, from 1918 to 1920.[118] He made the long journey east to attend a preliminary meeting of the executive committee on December 4-5, 1916, in Cambridge, Massachusetts (which coincided with a meeting of Beta Gamma Sigma's executive committee); and in November 1919, he was present at the AACSB's first annual meeting, also held in Cambridge.

Hatfield became a major figure in a new association of university accounting academics. On December 28, 1916, at the time of the annual convention of the American Economic Association in Columbus, Ohio, he was one of perhaps two dozen academics who founded the American Association of University Instructors in Accounting (AAUIA).[119] Hatfield, the dean of the College of Commerce at Berkeley and previously the dean at Chicago, whose pioneering textbook, *Modern Accounting*, had come out seven years earlier, was, at age 50, the elder statesman among those in attendance. His dignified bearing and air of eloquence hardly belied that standing. Hatfield was made chairman of the committee on the constitution, and his committee's recommended draft was approved unanimously.[120] John R. Wildman of New York University, who had called the meeting, was elected president, and Hatfield was elected one of the three vice-presidents. Fayette H. Elwell of the University of Wisconsin, who had been instrumental in founding Beta Gamma Sigma (and was serving as its first Grand President), was chosen secretary-treasurer. He admired Hatfield and enthusiastically advanced his candidacy for the association's highest office. Elwell succeeded to the presidency in 1918, and Hatfield continued for a second year as vice-president. In the following year, Hatfield not only served as president of the AAUIA but also was a vice-president of the American Economic Association (AEA). He was the only accounting academic ever to become an officer of the AEA.

The AAUIA's early annual meetings were lightly attended, partly because of members' increasing involvement in activities relating to the war effort. At the third annual meeting, held on December 27, 1918 in Richmond, Virginia, when Hatfield was installed as president, the few members in attendance, a mere dozen, met for dinner in a private dining room in Mrs. Murphy's Cafe. Hatfield's exhibition of playful humor lifted the spirits of those attending and made the dinner a memorable event in the association's young history, one that may have done much to keep the flame of the association alight. Twenty years later, William A. Paton wrote to Hatfield:

> That one might be possessed of the erudition evident in *Modern Accounting* and still be a good fellow and a wit hadn't occurred to me, and seeing and hearing you kid the waitress at the historic dinner session in Richmond in 1918 was something of a revelation. You had a little competition from John Madden, but easily carried off the palm.[121]

The principal issue that arose during Hatfield's presidency was whether the association should have its own journal. Wildman and Elwell, the two past presidents, as well as Vice-President John T. Madden of New York University, and the secretary-treasurer, H. T. Scovill, of the University of Illinois, all favored a "Quarterly Journal of Accounting Instruction." But Hatfield opposed the initiative and sent the following telegram:

> MY VOTE IS AGAINST PUBLISHING INDEPENDENT JOURNAL. I THINK IT WOULD BE BETTER IN ALL RESPECTS TO COOPERATE IN PUBLISHING JOURNAL OF ACCOUNTANCY, MAKING ONE GOOD JOURNAL INSTEAD OF TWO WEAK JOURNALS.[122]

Hatfield believed that accounting academics should work closely with members of the profession, and he feared that an association journal would drive a wedge between the two. His opposition put an end to the campaign. It was not until 1926 that the association finally launched a journal, *The Accounting Review*.

It was the practice of the association's presidents to address the membership upon retiring from office, and Hatfield did so on December 30, 1919, even though his address was not announced in the official program or reported in the *Papers and Proceedings* of the fourth annual meeting. But the script of the address, scribbled in Hatfield's hand, as if it had been composed shortly before delivery, has been found among his papers. In his prepared remarks, Hatfield raised questions about whether "we, in the universities, are to emphasize the general principles or the more highly elaborated details of specialized technique" and whether the same accounting course "is suited to the needs of most of our students who are to be business and not professional men." He was perhaps the first to make a case for a professional school of accounting:

> In one respect accounting is in a peculiar, perhaps in an unfortunate position. It may be illustrated by comparing it with law. Courses in commercial law are given in Schools of Commerce, mining law in Schools of Mines, Roman law in Letters and Science, yet none of these courses train the lawyer. That is reserved for a professional School of Law. Similarly, Stevens Institute has some excellent lectures on accounting, our College of Agriculture gives a course in farm accounts, and any College of Commerce gives accounting. But in most universities there is no professional School of Accounting separate from the School of Business. Accounting, like law, is a profession, not a business. Schools of Business teach some law without becoming law schools. But for some reason professional teaching in accounting is relegated to Schools of Business, although it belongs there as little as professional law belongs in Commerce, Engineering or Agriculture.

Alluding to the controversy over an association journal, he intoned, "The closest possible cooperation is to be sought" with other organizations. In the event that the point was lost on any of his listeners, he added:

> The interests of accounting are greater even than the interests of teachers of accounting. There should be some significant publication in which all interested would cooperate—public accountants, teachers, economists. Such a publication would be expensive. It needs the widest backing. Splitting the field produces several weak organs. It is worth an effort to make one good national publication.

His final comment resonates even today: "Our best hope to be successful teachers is to stimulate scholarly research. Fundamental problems are awaiting solutions."

Hatfield's belief that "the interests of accounting are greater even than the interests of teachers of accounting" carried over into the effort to standardize and improve terminology. In 1917, he was made chairman of the AAUIA's Committee on Nomenclature. From the mid-1910s until 1922, however, he was preoccupied with university administrative assignments, as well as spending a year of war-related service in Washington, so it is perhaps not surprising that his committee never rendered a report. In 1922, Hatfield recommended that J. Hugh Jackson, then employed in the training office of Price, Waterhouse & Co., succeed him as chairman, since Jackson, a former professor at Harvard, then served on the Special Committee on Terminology of the American Institute of Accountants. The reason given by Hatfield was to promote cooperation between the two bodies,[123] and Jackson thereupon became chairman.

Hatfield Heeds the Call to Government Service

In 1917, after the United States entered the war in Europe, Hatfield became one of many academics to embark on assignments relating to the war effort. From October 1917 to May 1918, he directed four six-week training schools in Berkeley for the Ordnance Field Service of the War Department. In November, Hatfield confessed a restlessness:

> Since the University opened, a very considerable number have either been drafted or have volunteered their services, so that almost every day we find some student or member of the faculty leaving us for government service. My regret is that I seem destined to stay here, while others are getting off into work which seems more immediately appropriate to the national need.[124]

In January 1918, Edwin F. Gay, who was on leave from the deanship of the Harvard Business School to serve as director of the Division of Planning and Statistics at the U.S. Shipping Board in Washington, offered Hatfield a position at the board. Gay had come to know Hatfield through the work of the AACSB's provisional executive committee. Hatfield was willing to go but felt that his departmental colleague, Stuart Daggett (1881-1954), a specialist in transportation, was better suited. In the end, President Wheeler intervened to persuade Hatfield to remain in his important post as dean of the faculties. Then, in February, the Shipping Board's Emergency Fleet Corporation, based in San Francisco, asked Hatfield to make a survey of the available labor supply in the steel yards on the coast. Assisted by Ira B. Cross (1880-1977), associate professor of economics on the Flood Foundation (who had arrived from Stanford University in 1914) and three others from the department, Hatfield completed the report in a scant two weeks.[125]

A few months later, Gay issued a second call for Hatfield to join him in Washington, and this time it was accepted. The university granted him a six-month sabbatical leave of absence, at two-thirds salary, from July 1, 1918. (The leave was later extended to June 30, 1919.) Although Hatfield was officially dean of the College of Commerce during 1918-1919, Stuart Daggett (who had filled in for him during the spring of 1918) served as acting dean throughout the year.

Hatfield's assignment in Washington was to conduct an economic study of the effects of price-setting by the government, so as to contribute to improved policies. One of his colleagues on the project was to be Wesley C. Mitchell,[126] his friend from Chicago as well as a former economics department colleague (1903-1912) at Berkeley. As Lucy Sprague Mitchell characterized those days, "Washington was a confusing place,"[127] and, shortly after Hatfield arrived in Washington, he was instead made director of the new Division of Planning and Statistics of the War Industries Board, the massive agency headed by Bernard M. Baruch.[128] Hatfield wrote, "I have about one hundred and sixty in the Division and the work of organizing the Division and getting the staff has been one which has taxed all my powers."[129] In "Experiences with the War Industries Board," a paper read to the Berkeley Club in 1920 (reproduced in Chapter 7), he recounted his initial adjustment and gave his impressions of Gay:[130]

> I left Berkeley, having been called to the Shipping Board, to work under W.C. Mitchell in scientific work for which my studies in accounting seemed to fit me. When I reached Washington,

> I was set to work with the War Industries Board, nominally over, instead of under, Mitchell, and in purely administrative rather than academic work, being called Director of the Division of Planning and Statistics. The work was not in itself alluring, for there were many difficulties connected with the reorganization and expansion of a disrupted organization. But it was not easy to refuse a war task, especially when presented by E.F. Gay.
>
> Gay had, previously, organized the statistical work of the Shipping Board, with such eminent success that he was asked to supervise also the statistical work of the War Trade Board, the War Industries Board, and later the Central Bureau of Planning and Statistics. Tower of Chicago, Swanson, Dean of Commerce of Northwestern, and myself were respectively made directors of the statistical work of the three boards, each acting under the direction of Gay. In this way, the fullest co-operation was secured in the work of the three boards, to the great benefit of the service. It was one of my chiefest pleasures to be brought into such close contact with Gay of whom (since he has just become editor of the *New York Post* and hence is not even a Presidential possibility) I can now speak without suspicion of being his campaign manager. Mr. Gay's whole attitude was that action should be based on the fullest knowledge obtainable and not on the business man's "hunch." His instructions were, "Get all the facts that can possibly be gathered within the time limit, and then use a hunch for the rest." A born administrator, indefatigable in work, inspiring to his associates, fearless, outspoken yet diplomatic, he became real force in Washington.

What he did not say was that the Washington summer was insufferably hot (114° in the shade on one day in August!) and there was no air conditioning. Much of the investigative work had to be done in hotel rooms.[131]

Hatfield marveled at how people from different walks of life could quickly adapt themselves to new challenges in totally different fields, and he drew from it a lesson that supported his view, even as an accounting academic, that a general education, as he had enjoyed, was superior to technical specialization:

> One of the significant facts, and it may possibly be also a lesson, derived from wartime experience in Washington was that so many important positions were filled by persons of broad general education, but with no special technical training for their particular jobs. A college dean was Assistant Secretary of War, a Wall Street operator controlled industry, a miner regulated food, a Texas judge curtailed manufactures, a college president administered fuels, the editor of a provincial paper ruled over exports, and a manufacturer of pneumatic tools was autocrat over our imports. If the war was at all well managed, the experience may well be an argument against highly specialized and in favor of general cultural education.[132]

Following the Armistice on November 11, 1918, the work at the board wound down. On January 4, 1919, Hatfield wrote:

> I have ended my work with the Division of Planning and Statistics of the War Industries Board, and am planning to spend most of my time for the next six months in some academic writing, although I shall have a somewhat nominal advisory connection with closing up some of the war activities.[133]

The visit to Washington was made easier by the fact that Ethel Hatfield's mother, then 75, lived there. Although Hatfield's sabbatical leave was extended a further six months, he was reappointed dean of the College of Commerce as from January 1, 1919.

A further assignment came Hatfield's way. From May 7 to July 15, 1919, he served as temporary Special Expert in the Office of the Commissioner of Internal Revenue, in the Treasury Department, attached to the Advisory Tax Board. Hatfield wrote to his brother, James Taft Hatfield, in an undated letter apparently written in August 1919, that "My two months' work with the Advisory Tax Board was the most interesting thing I ever did, and I would have liked to stay longer." The board's task was "to develop rules for the calculation of taxable income which were reasonably consistent with sound principles of accounting."[134]

Hatfield Feels Pressures to Move East

In November 1917, Professor T.S. Adams wrote Hatfield

> to ascertain whether you would consider a call from Yale University. We shall need next year a new head for the business course or college recently established in the Sheffield Scientific School. The course has a modest but reasonably ample endowment provided by Mr. Vanderbilt, one of our alumni. The graduates of the institution, many of whom are prominent and influential men, are greatly interested in its success; and the course should have, with proper guidance, a very promising future.[135]

In a letter of reply, Hatfield expressed a modicum of interest and sought answers to a number of questions. But nothing seems to have come of the inquiry. The salary offered by Yale was $4,500, only $500 more than his professorial salary at Berkeley.

When wartime service in Washington removed Hatfield from his semi-isolation on the West Coast, he was courted for positions at Harvard University and Price, Waterhouse & Co. While in Washington, he wrote to President Wheeler that he had been offered a full professorship at the Harvard Business School, doubtless extended at Gay's suggestion.[136] While Hatfield said that he had received several tentative offers "generally at a considerable increase of salary" since coming to Berkeley, he had rejected them without even conferring with Wheeler. "But," he wrote,

> the present invitation is more troublesome. The work is to be entirely with graduate students, with less hours, more salary, more freedom from routine work [recall his "Business Efficiency and the University Ideal"], and opportunity and encouragement in carrying on research work. Furthermore, in my line of work, there is a certain advantage in being in the East, where the profession of accounting has a somewhat higher standing, and where contact with leaders of the profession is easier than in California. Altogether the offer was one which is not easily rejected. On the other hand, I do not wish to leave California. I have more affection for Berkeley and the University than I have ever had for any other place. Is it a case of weighing professorial advantages against the joy of living?
>
> Your resignation introduces another element of uncertainty. Will the work in Commerce be adequately supported in the future? Is there any assurance as to my future salary and as to conditions of work?[137]

Wheeler replied immediately with an impassioned plea:

> I cannot bear to contemplate any such thing as your leaving the University of California. I know how attractive it must be to go to Harvard and how suited to you the position which is offered to you is, and still you will be after all a specialist and you will not do the work which I know you do here with such evident interest. Delightful as it is to exercise the duties of a specialist, there is something about the work you always did here in keeping track of your individual students that appeals to me as worth while above everything. We have never meant to keep you from your special studies and work. But we have valued it highly that with your work you have been willing to blend a certain amount of care and oversight for individual lives. Pray do not think of leaving us. The place is here suited to you and waiting for you. Your salary next year will be forty-five hundred dollars and the five hundred dollars given for the Deanship will raise the total amount to five thousand dollars. I am sure you have no reason to have any solicitude regarding the support that would be given to the subject of Commerce by my successor. Who he will be I am sure I do not know, and I do not think anyone knows. Great care will be taken, however, in this election, and almost all the names which have been mentioned are of the better sort. I can hardly think of the University of California without you. You have come to be part and parcel of it. How can you think of leaving your home on the hillside?[138]

The discussions with Harvard and the entreaties from Berkeley lasted throughout the year and into January 1920, when, at long last, Wallace B. Donham, dean of the Harvard Business School, came to realize that Hatfield was not disposed to accept an offer.[139] That David Prescott Barrows, whom Hatfield had come to know as the onetime dean of the faculties, had been chosen to succeed Wheeler as president, together with Harvard's unwillingness to give him a salary crediting his 16 years of service at Berkeley, which would have exceeded the salary of even the most senior faculty at the Harvard Business School (which had begun in 1908), seemed to be among the factors weighing against the move.[140]

Then, in May 1920, George O. May, the senior partner of Price, Waterhouse & Co. (PW) and one of the leading figures in the accounting profession, invited Hatfield to consider taking over management of the firm's new school "for the practical education of the juniors on our staff."[141] Hatfield expressed interest and asked "whether it would be possible to make an arrangement whereby I should give all my time for nine months or a year to this organizing of such a school, thereafter having only a general supervision without giving up regular University work."[142] In his reply, May made it clear that he and his partners had in mind a permanent position,[143] and thereafter the discussions seem to have ended. It seems likely that one of May's partners, Joseph E. Sterrett (1870-1934), with whom Hatfield had worked at the Advisory Tax Board, had recommended Hatfield for the position. Sterrett had been president of the American Association of Public Accountants in 1908-1910 and was one of the elders of the profession. In 1911, he wrote a laudatory review of Hatfield's *Modern Accounting*, and May conveyed Sterrett's "kindest regards" in his second letter to Hatfield. Sterrett had written to Hatfield on July 12, 1919, just after Hatfield had left for Berkeley following his assignment at the Advisory Tax Board, "I cannot begin to tell you how sorry I am that you are no longer with us."[144]

As far as is known, these were the only occasions when Hatfield gave serious consideration to leaving the University of California.[145] His wife had a strong influence in these decisions, as she was averse to cold weather.[146] In the end, his affection for the university and Berkeley, for the nearby hills and Mt. Tamalpais, where he loved to hike, and for camping in the Sierra Nevada, overcame all enticements.

APPENDIX: SUMMARY OF HATFIELD'S *MODERN ACCOUNTING* (1909)

The purpose of this Appendix is to summarize the distinctive features of Hatfield's book.

A signal event of 1909 was the publication of Hatfield's pioneering textbook, *Modern Accounting: Its Principles and Some of Its Problems* (New York: D. Appleton and Company).[147] It was unlike any American accounting textbook then or since. Appleton's advertisement for the book placed it in the category of "Intermediary and Advanced Texts."

Merely laying out the chapters would have been a challenge, since it was only the second American textbook of its kind. The first such book, Cole's *Accounts, Their Construction and Interpretation* (Boston: Houghton Mifflin, 1908) did not come to Hatfield's notice until after he had completed his manuscript.

In the Preface, Hatfield catalogued the problems facing an author of a textbook at this early stage in the evolution of accounting practice and the literature. He complained of "a most embarrassing confusion in terminology, so that one can never be sure of just what is meant by a given account" (p. vi). "More serious still," he added, "is the uncertainty as to the correct principle to follow in many cases, as for instance in the valuation of fixed assets and the method of estimating depreciation" (p. vi). When in doubt about the correctness of usage, "there is no ultimate arbiter to whom appeal can confidently be made." He concluded, therefore, that "the comparative study of accounting practice will, perhaps, be a greater service to accounting science than a more dogmatic treatise."

What was remarkable (and, indeed, unique) for an American textbook is that he referred not only to American sources (rulings of the Interstate Commerce Commission, corporate financial statements, and leading accounting textbooks, of which there were few) but also to the writings of English accountants and to "the decisions of English and American courts, the commercial codes of Germany, France, Austria and the commentaries of the leading jurists of these countries." Precedents in Belgium and Switzerland, as well as in a number of the Latin American republics, were also mentioned in the book. He justified this wide sweep of authority with the following indictment of American writings and practice:

> Such attention to foreign authorities is all the more necessary since in this country far too little attention has been given to matters of principle. American accounting is famed for short cuts and practical efficiency. At the same time the accounts of American corporations, until very recent years, have been replete with questionable practices, oftentimes vicious in principle and misleading in their results.

Hatfield's *Modern Accounting* was not only a textbook but also a veritable annotation of the literature.[148]

Hatfield's assessment of a number of the American and British works listed in the bibliographical notes at the end of most of his chapters is worth recording:

- Garcke and Fells, *Factory Accounts*: "A pioneer work on the subject and still standard" (p. 315)
- Dicksee, *Goodwill and Its Treatment in Accounts*: "The most complete treatment of the subject" (p. 120)
- Dawson, *Accountant's Compendium*: "A valuable reference work in dictionary form" (p. 33)
- Dicksee, *Bookkeeping for Accountant Students* and *Advanced Accounting*: "The above two works form a comprehensive treatise. The latter contains an admirable collection of bookkeeping problems" (p. 34)
- Dicksee, *Depreciation, Reserves, and Reserve Funds*: "An important work" (p. 143)
- Lisle, *Accounting in Theory and Practice*: "This is perhaps the best single volume treating the entire subject which has appeared in English" (p. 33)
- Lisle, ed., *Encyclopædia of Accounting*: "A most valuable work of highest scientific standard" (p. 33)
- Pixley, "How to Read a Balance Sheet": "A valuable article by the former president of the Institute of Chartered Accountants" (p. 69)
- Sprague, *The Philosophy of Accounts*: "The most important theoretical work which has appeared in English" (p. 33)

Hatfield's light touch, so well represented in his later writings, becomes evident on pages 206-207, where he employed a character from a nursery rhyme to illustrate the nonpermanence of an enterprise organized to exploit wasting assets: "Like Nan Netticote, of the childish conundrum, the more brilliant its career, the sooner it ends; the more efficient its management the more quickly will its resources be exhausted."[149]

Hatfield's first two chapters deal with double-entry bookkeeping, and he acknowledges the influence of J.F. Schär, whose treatise he had studied during his visit to Leipzig in 1900. Hatfield emphasized the proprietorship interest by characterizing the double-entry equation as:

Goods = Proprietorship,

where Goods was "used in the technical economic sense of anything, material or otherwise, to which value attaches" (p. 1). He later made clear that Assets are Positive Goods and Liabilities are Negative Goods. Hatfield has been classified with Charles Ezra Sprague as one of the early proprietary theorists.[150]

As noted above, Hatfield's chapters concluded with bibliographical notes, and succinct comments were often appended to the more important works. True to the comparative focus that Hatfield announced in the Preface, 11 of the 16 works referenced at the end of Chapter II were of foreign origin.

In Chapter III, "The Balance Sheet," Hatfield referred to "Valuation Accounts." He wrote that this term adopts "the German nomenclature (Bewertungskontenten) as there is no well established English term. They may be defined as accounts introduced for the technical purpose of indicating that a sum is to be subtracted from some other account" (p. 50). In the second edition of the *Accountants' Handbook* (New York: The Ronald Press Company, 1933, p. 1778), Paton wrote that in *Modern Accounting*, "Hatfield designated contra or offsetting accounts in the balance sheet as 'valuation accounts' and this label has been employed by many writers since."

When discussing the valuation of assets, Hatfield seemed to support the inclusion of actually incurred interest among the costs of construction. He found the practice to be "not illogical, and the custom of so doing is gaining increasing legal sanction" (p. 76). He referred without criticism to the British Companies Act of 1907, "which virtually makes, not merely interest on bonds, but even dividends on capital paid in lieu of interest during construction, a part of the construction costs" (p. 77), a practice that was also acceptable in Germany. Hatfield tilted against the apparently widespread view that conservatism, even at the expense of truth, "is really a merit rather than a fault" (p. 84). He maintained that accuracy was the goal of accounting, adding: "to state that an absolute understatement is praiseworthy neglects the fact that fraud may surely be perpetrated in that manner."

After discussing the treatment of land, buildings and machinery in Chapter V, "The Valuation of Particular Assets," Hatfield argued that the preference for historical cost is less a *desideratum* than a device for avoiding manipulation of the accounts:

> In the foregoing pages there has been only one objective criterion of value, cost price, and that is confessedly faulty for it refers to an earlier and not to the present day valuation. But for investments that are quoted in a stock exchange there is a definite objective determination of to-day's value. The objection to making an independent valuation of one's lands or houses is that there may be an unconscious overvaluation, or that an intentional, and perhaps fraudulent, overvaluation cannot be easily detected. But where there is a definitely ascertainable market price, known to the public and fixed by outside interests, the objections just urged do not apply and it would seem that it might be safe and justifiable to ignore altogether the cost price, and alter the book value with every fluctuation in the market price (p. 90).

But Hatfield did not say whether he would credit an increase in market price to profit.

He defended the compound interest method of amortizing premiums and discounts on bond investments. "But accounting practice," he wrote, "has not fully accepted this principle. In many cases the annual writing off of premium paid is justified, but there is hesitation at writing up the bond bought at a discount. This is largely an evidence of the conservative tendency which looks askance at anything which tends to swell the value of assets, but encourages undervaluation" (p. 97). When recognizing the probable loss on bills receivable, he seemed to prefer "Allowance" over "Reserve" in the title of the valuation account (p. 100), thus being much in advance of his time. Later in the book, he used "Reserve" for Bad Debts (his quotation marks) to distinguish between a loss that "is practically certain to take place," thus being a reduction in assets, and a provision based on "a minimum certainty and a maximum of prudence," which is instead a reservation of profits (p. 239).

Hatfield's views on inventory valuation are of interest. On page 81, he wrote that "the general principle must be adopted that the basis of inventory values is the present value of the asset to the holders as a 'going concern'." He was concerned, however, about "preventing a self-deceiving exaggeration of values" (also p. 81). Later, on pages 101-102, after acknowledging that general practice "prescribes that merchandise on hand shall be inventoried at cost rather than at selling price" and that "Prudence further demands that merchandise which evidently cannot be sold except at a loss, be marked down even below the cost price," Hatfield stated his preference as follows:

> If one could count not only on good faith but as well on unbiased judgment in making inventories, the taking of the present market value, instead of the cost price would not be objectionable, but rather to be commended. Indeed, the first principle of valuation laid down above, that of the "going concern" in strict logic demands that merchandise for sale be valued at the present selling price, with a reduction to cover selling expenses.

In Chapter VI on "Immaterial Assets," Hatfield contributed a thoughtful 11-page discussion of goodwill. With a keen eye for vivid expression, he observed that "accountants have recognized that the purchase of Goodwill of an established firm may be a most valuable transaction, for it may save, as Guthrie has neatly put it, 'the period of perilous probation'" (p. 108). Further: "accounting practice prudently, though perhaps illogically, forbids the firm which created the Goodwill to place in the Balance Sheet any value on the *clientèle* which it has built up and which it could at any moment sell for a large sum" (p. 108). Using homely examples, Hatfield argued that an inveterate optimism by managers makes it necessary that assets be limited to a value that may be verified by appraisal:

> This conservative restriction is doubtless necessary to prevent a harmful exaggeration. Human nature is so incurably optimistic, especially when it comes to estimating one's own possessions. The boy's jackknife, the citizen's fatherland, the man's children, are in normal cases a little better than similar possessions of anyone else. The same phenomenon appears in the valuation of one's business assets, where the natural instinct to overvalue one's possessions is augmented by the fact that such overvaluation may be the means of overreaching some one else in a business deal. In proportion as it is difficult to verify values it is therefore customary to limit the value at which they are appraised. Cash being of definite value may be listed though it cost nothing; quoted securities or commodities may, according to some authorities, be listed at the market value even though that exceed the cost; but Goodwill, because of its vague nature and the difficulty of verifying its appraisal is to be excluded unless it has been purchased (pp. 108-109; footnote omitted).

Though acknowledging the disagreement among authorities over whether goodwill should be written off on a regular basis, Hatfield concluded: "Strict logic requires, at least where the price paid for Goodwill is definitely based on a number of years' purchase of excess earnings, that the valuation should be written off in the same number of years" (pp. 116-117). Hatfield would amortize goodwill "in proportion to the number of years figured in its valuation," but "where it is clear that the valuation of the Goodwill was erroneous, that it is not worth its book value, the best method of adjustment is that advocated by Dicksee, to offset the decline in its value by a reduction of capital, not by a charge against profits" (p. 117).

It is in the first paragraph of his chapter on "Depreciation" that Hatfield uttered his famous dictum:

> Depreciation is the law of nature.... All machinery is on an irresistible march to the junk heap, and its progress, while it may be delayed, cannot be prevented by repairs (p. 121).

Hatfield thus believed that depreciation and repairs were intertwined, and he confidently concluded, "The complete and scientifically correct method of figuring depreciation compels that there should be at the same time a recognition of the necessity of repairs and a simultaneous apportioning of both repairs and depreciation between the years irrespective of the time when the expense is actually incurred.... [T]here should be an equal apportionment of the sum of these two between the several years" (p. 135).

Hatfield complained that current practice with respect to depreciation was sadly negligent. He wrote: "Any recognition of depreciation at all being relatively uncommon in the accounts of American corporations, it is not to be wondered at that the few companies which show depreciation in prosperous years, when profits are large, grow faint hearted when business is poor" (p. 136). He also commented on the practice by some corporations to over-charge depreciation, thus creating a "Secret Reserve." He despaired at the different reactions to under- and over-depreciation: "To charge too little is considered dishonorable, to charge more than enough is considered a sign of conservatism and is not only done by the most reputable corporations, but where this occurs the action is very frequently praised by financial writers" (p. 137).

Hatfield became angered when discussing the accounting treatment of "stock watering," that is, valuing non-cash assets received in exchange for capital stock at the par value of the stock, when the worth of the assets is significantly less than that amount. He regarded stock watering as "in itself a fraud upon investors and a crime against the public" (p. 171). He was therefore nonplused that no less an authority than A. Lowes Dickinson, the senior partner of Price, Waterhouse & Co. and a leader of the accounting profession, wrote in support of valuing such assets by reference to the par value of the stock. Hatfield's appeal to the profession to raise its standard veritably leaped from the page:

> But despite the high authority opposed to the views set forth in this treatise, the claim is still made that to reject the standard of attempted accuracy is a confession of impotence, which, while it exhibits a commendable modesty on the part of professional accountants, seems, to the layman, to do scant justice to the ability of that profession (p. 171).

Hatfield's preferred treatment for discount on bonds payable, namely, to be shown as an asset (p. 188), strikes one as a concession to conservatism (i.e., not reducing the recorded amount of liabilities), whose distorting influence upon accounting practice is the object of criticism at numerous places in the book. At the end of his chapter on liabilities, Hatfield argued that "An agreement definitely made to pay pensions" should give rise to inclusion in the current period's expenses of "the amount necessary to provide for future pensions.... Evidently in such a case to omit such a liability from the Balance Sheet is incorrect" (p. 194). This view was well ahead of its time.

On page 196, Hatfield asserted that "the Balance Sheet interests more particularly the creditor, the Profit and Loss account the proprietor or stockholder" (p. 196). But he admitted that this distinction is relative, since both statements are needed by both creditors and owners.

In Chapters XI and XII on "Profits," he was totally preoccupied with the availability of profits for dividends, and he cited American and English court opinions extensively. Hence, the importance of realization is palpable. One can discern Hatfield's fascination with the verbal gymnastics engaged in by judges when justifying their sometimes inexplicable decisions in cases involving accounting terminology and concepts. Apparently the law intrigued Hatfield. He became an adviser to Professor Henry Winthrop Ballantine in the drafting of the first modern California corporation law, and he wrote several articles and gave a public lecture on the legal concepts of surplus, capital and dividends.

While seeming at first a supporter of charging major property losses (such as through destruction by fire without insurance) directly against capital, Hatfield instead is seen to support a charge against income. Those who would charge the loss to capital and thus allow dividends out of income to be unabated were said to counsel that "it might be an act of cruelty to dependent stockholders to stop dividends entirely until an exceptional loss is reimbursed" (p. 217) He concluded, however: "The hardship of going entirely without dividends for a series of years may perhaps be considered only a fair return for the exceptional privileges granted to stockholders" (p. 218).

As part of a disquisition on the proper treatment of reserves, Hatfield criticized the secret reserve, which he detected in the accounts of several banks and railroads:

> Again appears a case of justifying a practice abhorrent to accounting principles, yet not without certain practical merits. In the anxiety to escape the prevalent temptation to exaggerate the value of the assets, which in many cases has led to such disgraceful results, conservative financiers applaud an equally erroneous, but perhaps less dangerous tendency to understatement. But the creation of a Secret Reserve is not without its dangers. It may be used as a means of refusing to pay dividends really earned, which so far as it applies to holders of income bonds or non-cumulative preferred stock, may work an irreparable loss. Even where there are no such divisions of interests it may lead ignorant stockholders, thinking the Balance Sheet correct, to dispose of their stock at less than its real value (p. 254).

For a going concern, Hatfield did not question the propriety of the Reserve for Insurance, used instead of actually purchasing fire insurance, by which an "accurate estimate" of future losses is charged to a number of years in anticipation of the occurrence of any such loss. His rationale was that "so long as the company maintains its business and refrains from insuring, the Reserve is closely allied to a Depreciation account or a provision for bad debts. If the plant is sufficiently large and scattered the law of probabilities makes certain that a loss will some time occur" (p. 260).

Hatfield became frustrated when searching for wisdom in court opinions, as he set out to do in many of his chapters. He pined for "the day when the growing dignity of the profession of accounting shall cause its principles to permeate the ranks of bench and bar" (p. 231). He said that court opinions furnish many ... interesting illustrations of the difficulty which the legal mind finds in solving problems requiring accounting knowledge" (p. 33, fn. 1).

Modern Accounting did not include any homework problems, but in 1914, Samuel F. Racine published a *Guide to the Study of Accounting* (Seattle, WA: Western Institute of Accountancy, Commerce & Finance), which contained a series of questions intended to accompany five textbooks, including Hatfield's.

NOTES

1. Reminiscences contained in Hatfield's address, "Moriturus Vos Saluto," delivered in 1937 before the Berkeley Club, pp. 3-4 (of the original script). For another impression of Berkeley just after the turn of the century, see Lucy Sprague Mitchell, *Two Lives: The Story of Wesley Clair Mitchell and Myself* (New York: Simon and Schuster, 1953), Chap. 9.

2. F.W. Dohrmann, the president of the Merchants' Association, said that Rodgers "is the one who conceived, advocated and fathered the College of Commerce of the University of California." See F.W. Dohrmann, "The First College of Commerce in the World," and Arthur Rodgers, "Response" [to an address by Benjamin Ide Wheeler], in *Merchants' Association Review*, Vol. 4, No. 40, December 1899, pp. 4-5. Also see William Warren Ferrier, *Origin and Development of the University of California* (Berkeley: The Sather Gate Book Shop, 1930), p. 446; and E.T. Grether, "The Strategic Role of Arthur Rodgers," *CalBusiness*, Winter 1984, pp. 5-7, and "The College of Commerce, 1898: The Pioneering Predecessor of the Schools of Business Administration," *CalBusiness*, Fall 1984, pp. 5-7. (Ewald T. Grether (1899-1994) joined the economics department in 1924 as an instructor. He served as dean of the College of Commerce from 1941 to 1943, when it was reorganized as the Schools of Business Administration. He continued as dean until 1961.)

Only the Wharton School, begun in 1881 at the University of Pennsylvania, preceded the establishment in 1898 of Colleges of Commerce at both the Universities of Chicago and California.

3. James's address was published in the *University Chronicle*, Vol. 1, No. 3, June 1898, pp. 201-225.

4. Since the university's Board of Regents had known of James's writings on commercial education in Europe and the United States, and had exchanged correspondence with him on the subject, the invitation extended to him to address the Commencement in 1898 was probably the result of careful design. *Annual Report of the Secretary to the Board of Regents of the University of California for the Year Ending June 30, 1898* (Berkeley: The University Press, 1898), p. 35. Yet his biographer reports that James may have been considered a candidate to succeed Martin Kellogg as president of the university. Hence, the occasion of his address may have been to enable James "to see and be seen." Richard Allen Swanson, "Edmund J. James, 1855-1925: A 'Conservative Progressive' in American Higher Education," doctoral dissertation in history (University of Illinois, 1966), p. 130.

5. Carl C. Plehn, "Report of the Dean of the College of Commerce," *Biennial Report of the President of the University on behalf of the Board of Regents to His Excellency the Governor of the State 1896-1898* (Berkeley, The University Press, 1898), p. 55.

It was not until 1942 that a department of business administration was established. E.T. Grether, "1941-1961: Twenty Years That Transformed the School," *CalBusiness*, Spring 1988, p. 10.

6. A possible reason for Plehn's defense may have been that the College of Commerce was admitted to the university as one of the "Colleges of General Culture," not as a technical college. (In 1913-1914, the College of Commerce was reclassified as one of the "Colleges of Applied Sciences." E.T. Grether, "The College of Commerce, 1898: The Pioneering Predecessor of the Schools of Business Administration," *CalBusiness*, Fall 1984, p. 6.)

7. Plehn, *op. cit.*, pp. 51, 60.

8. For a historical review of the economics department until about 1920, see Mary E. Cookingham, "Political Economy in the Far West: The University of California and Stanford University," in William J. Barber, ed., *Breaking the Academic Mould: Economists and American Higher Learning in the Nineteenth Century* (Middletown, CT: Wesleyan University Press, 1988), pp. 273-280.

9. "Grant Higher Rank and Salaries to Faculty," *The Daily Californian*, Vol. XXIII, No. 79, May 18, 1904, p. 1.

10. The mention of the accounting elective in the college's curriculum in 1900 and 1901 does not indicate a department of origin. Upon Miller's arrival, the economics department stepped forward to offer the work in accounting.

11. *Register of the University of California 1903-1904*, p. 154. Observe that accounting came at the end of the course title in 1902-1903 but was advanced to the front of the title in the following year.

12. Verne A. Stadtman and the Centennial Publications Staff, compiler and editor, *The Centennial Record of the University of California* (University of California, 1967), pp. 216, 271.

13. Letter of transmittal from Cora Jane Flood, dated September 13, 1898, in "Report of the President of the University, *Biennial Report ... 1896-1898, op. cit.*, p. 11; also see "Flood Foundation Professorships in the School of Business Administration," in *Endowed Chairs of Learning* (Berkeley:

University of California, 1947), pp. 14-17, and E.T. Grether, "The Initial and Continuing Role of Cora Jane Flood," *CalBusiness*, Spring 1984, pp. 5-7.

14. Cited in the "Report of the President of the University," *Biennial Report of the President of the University on behalf of the Regents to His Excellency the Governor of the State 1904-1906* (Berkeley, CA: The University Press, 1906), p. 23.

15. *Ibid.*

16. *Registers of the University of California 1904-1905* to *1908-1909.*

17. *Register of the University of California 1904-1905*, p. 157.

18. *Modern Accounting: Its Principles and Some of Its Problems* (New York: D. Appleton and Company, 1909), p. 33.

19. "Professor Hatfield Talks to Bookkeepers' Club," *The Daily Californian*, Vol. XXIV, No. 71, December 1, 1904, p. 1; also see Hatfield Scrapbook No. 1.

20. Forbes was the most prominent California certified public accountant of the period, and he continued to be a professional leader throughout his career. He served as secretary-treasurer, 1909-1927, and president, 1934-1935, of the California State Society of Certified Public Accountants; he was a member of the State Board of Accountancy from 1909 to 1951; and he was vice-president, 1925-1926; president, 1932-1934; and a member of council for more than 40 years, of the American Institute of Accountants (renamed in 1957 as the American Institute of Certified Public Accountants). See Tindall Cashion, *The First Seventy Five Years* (The California Society of Certified Public Accountants, 1984), pp. 4-5. Forbes was devoted to the profession.

In 1912, Forbes consolidated his practice with that of Haskins & Sells and became the managing partner of the San Francisco office. *Haskins & Sells: Our First Seventy Five Years* (Haskins & Sells, 1970), p. 38. Thus began a long history of close contacts between Haskins & Sells and the university's accounting faculty.

21. John F. Forbes, "Observations of a CPA Examiner," *The Accounting Review*, Vol. XIX, No. 2, April 1944, p. 135.

22. *Ibid.*

23. Interview with John F. Forbes, September 5, 1963.

24. Interview with John F. Forbes, December 21, 1964.

25. These remarks have never before been published, and are reproduced in full in Chapter 7. "N.Y.C.P.A." apparently refers to the New York State Society of Certified Public Accountants.

26. *Announcement of Courses 1905-1906*, p. 36.

27. The auditing course, listed as Economics 14D, carried the following description: "Practice in the detection and tracing of fraudulent alterations in a set of actual books of a defunct concern." *Register of the University of California 1907-08-09*, p. 244. It was a bizarre piece of accounting pathology.

28. Meade later dropped the final e in the spelling of his surname.

29. Henry Rand Hatfield, Discussion, "The Management of the Surplus Reserve," by Edward S. Meade, in *Papers and Proceedings* of the Sixteenth Annual Meeting, New Orleans, La., December 29-31, 1903 (New York: American Economic Association/Macmillan, May 1904), Third Series, Vol. V, No. 2, Part II, pp. 274-275.

30. *Ibid.*, p. 276.

31. Letter to the author from Elizabeth Hatfield Glover (Henry Hatfield's daughter), dated December 1, 1965.

32. Verne A. Stadtman, *The University of California, 1868-1968* (New York: McGraw-Hill Book Company, 1970), p. 188.

33. George A. Pettitt, *Berkeley: The Town and Gown of It* (Berkeley, CA: Howell-North Books, 1973), p. 162.

34. The letter was reproduced in a Washington newspaper (clipping in Hatfield Scrapbook No. 2).

35. "Several Changes Made in Faculty," *The Daily Californian*, Vol. XXXI, No. 3, January 15, 1908, p. 3.

36. Interview with Charles C. Staehling, September 3, 1963.

37. Of the 12 associate editors, only Hatfield and Charles E. Sprague are viewed today as major accounting authors of the period.

38. This estimate is based on an inspection of royalty statements in Hatfield's files.

39. The translation (which ran to 350 pages but was described as abridged) was carried out by Takenosuke Ebihara and was published by Hakubunkan in 1912. In a letter to Yuji Ijiri dated September 8, 1965, Hiroshi Yoshida reports confirmation that the Japanese edition of *Modern Accounting* was the first such book to be translated. The author is grateful to Professor Ijiri for researching this question. Curiously, a second translation into Japanese was published in 1971. The translator was Kenkitsu Matsuo and the publisher was Tusho-do.The author is grateful to Professor Toshio Iino for information about this second translation. There is no sign that Matsuo was aware of the translation carried out almost 60 years earlier. The second translation was of the 1918 printing of Hatfield's 1909 book, but because the publisher presented the year of printing on the title page as if it were the year of publication, more than a few commentators have mistaken a later printing for a revised edition.

Nishikawa reports that H.B. Bryant and H.D. Stratton's *Common School Book-keeping, Embracing Single and Double Entry*, was published in a Japanese translation in 1873-1874. See K. Nishikawa, "The Early History of Double-Entry Bookkeeping in Japan," in A.C. Littleton and B.S. Yamey, eds., *Studies in the History of Accounting* (Homewood, IL: Richard D. Irwin, Inc., 1956), p. 384.

40. Introductory Notes to Charles E. Sprague, *The Philosophy of Accounts* (New York: The Ronald Press Company, fifth edition, 1922), p. xvii.

41. Letter to Cole from Hatfield, dated July 6, 1936. For Hatfield's review of Sprague's book, see *The Journal of Accountancy*, Vol. 7, No. 1, November 1908, pp. 67-69.

42. See Jeffrey L. Cruikshank, *A Delicate Experiment: The Harvard Business School 1908-1945* (Boston: Harvard Business School Press, 1987), pp. 55, 74.

43. William Morse Cole, *Accounts, Their Construction and Interpretation for Business Men and Students of Affairs* (Boston: Houghton Mifflin Company, 1908), pp. 97-102. The title "Where-got-gone statement" appears in the index of the revised and enlarged edition of Cole's book, published in 1915, on p. 445. In his discussion of the history of the funds statement, Anton incorrectly gives 1915 as the year in which Cole first presented his statement. See Hector R. Anton, *Accounting for the Flow of Funds* (New York: Houghton Mifflin Company, 1962), pp. 46-47.

44. Eldon S. Hendriksen, *Accounting Theory* (Homewood, IL: Richard D. Irwin, 1965), p. 24.

45. *Ibid.*, pp. 22-27.

46. See Stephen Gilman, *Accounting Concepts of Profit* (New York: The Ronald Press Company, 1939), Chap. 5; William J. Vatter, *The Fund Theory of Accounting and Its Implications for Financial Reports* (Chicago: The University of Chicago Press, 1947), Chap. I; Hendriksen, *op. cit.*, pp. 22-27; Stephen A. Zeff, *A Critical Examination of the Orientation Postulate in Accounting, With Particular Attention to Its Historical Development* (New York: Arno Press, 1978; originally written in 1961), Chap. IV; Louis Goldberg, *An Inquiry Into the Nature of Accounting* (American Accounting Association, 1965); Gary John Previts and Barbara Dubis Merino, *A History of Accounting in America* (New York: John Wiley & Sons, 1979), pp. 165-170 and 176-180; and Jenice P. Stewart, "The Significance of an 'Orientation Postulate'," *Abacus*, Vol. 25, No. 2, September 1989, pp. 97-115.

47. Henry Rand Hatfield, *The Journal of Accountancy*, Vol. 40, No. 5, November 1925, p. 389. In *Accounting*, the 1927 revision of *Modern Accounting*, Hatfield adopted Assets – Liabilities = Proprietorship as his bookkeeping equation, but pointed out that A = L + P reflects the arrangement of items in the balance sheet. *Accounting: Its Principles and Problems* (New York: D. Appleton and Company, 1927), p. 2.

48. William Andrew Paton, *Accounting Theory—With Special Reference to the Corporate Enterprise* (New York: The Ronald Press Company, 1922), p. 267.

49. Moonitz describes Walton as "a practicing accountant and the proprietor and driving force behind the Walton School of Commerce (primarily a correspondence school)." Walton edited the "Students' Department" in *The Journal of Accountancy* from 1914 to 1920, when he died. Maurice Moonitz, "Three Contributions to the Development of Accounting Principles Prior to 1930," *Journal of Accounting Research*, Vol. 8, No. 1, Spring 1970, pp. 147-148.

50. Roger J. Traynor, a student of Hatfield's who eventually became a highly respected Chief Justice of the Supreme Court of California, has written, "I still think that [Hatfield's] *Modern Accounting* is one of the greatest books I ever studied. I found it a masterpiece not only of craftsmanship but of literature. It was a real privilege to have his course and I owe him a great debt for the intellectual discipline it entailed." Letter to the author from Traynor (while Chief Justice), dated November 16, 1964. While Traynor's praise does not refer specifically to the usefulness of Hatfield's book in the preparation of a brief, it does suggest that the "intellectual discipline" of Hatfield's style of argument may be compatible with the mode of analysis favored in the law.

51. Maurice E. Peloubet, "The Imprint of Personalities on the Accounting Profession," in *Fifty Years of Service: 1898-1948* (Newark, NJ: New Jersey Society of Certified Public Accountants, n.d.), p. 19. Peloubet was president of the New Jersey Society of Certified Public Accountants in 1928-1929.

52. Interview with Krueger, October 19, 1964.

53. "On Accountancy, Mountaineering, and the National Parks," an interview with Francis P. Farquhar conducted by Willa Klug Baum (Berkeley, 1960), as part of the General Library/Berkeley Regional Cultural History Project, University of California, pp. 62-63 of typescript. The anecdote was confirmed in the author's interview with Farquhar, December 11, 1964.

54. W.A. Paton, Foreword to the Reissue, in Charles E. Sprague, *The Philosophy of Accounts* (Lawrence, KS: Scholars Book Co., 1972), p. iii.

55. A.C. Littleton, "The Development of Accounting Literature," *Publications of the American Association of University Instructors in Accounting*, Vol. IX, No. 2, December 1925, p. 12.

56. Letter to Hatfield, dated March 21, 1937.

57. John L. Carey, *The Rise of the Accounting Profession: From Technician to Professional 1896-1936* (New York: American Institute of Certified Public Accountants, 1969), p. 102.

58. *Ibid.* Carey was of the view that much of the literature relied upon by U.S. accounting educators and practitioners during this period was of English origin. See *ibid.*, pp. 101-102.

59. *Zeitschrift für Buchhaltung*, Vol. XVIII, No. 4 (205), April 1909, pp. 80-86. The article was translated into English by Richard H. Homburger and was accompanied by an article titled "The Relevance of 'Zwei Pfadfinder'," by Homburger and Gary John Previts, in *The Accounting Historians Journal*, Vol. 4, No. 1, Spring 1977, pp. 1-13. The author has found the original English version of "Zwei Pfadfinder" in Hatfield's files. Hatfield's version and Homburger's translation are very close.

60. *Modern Accounting*, p. 9.

61. *Register of the University of California 1909*, Part VI, Summer Session, p. 38.

62. *Register—Part VI, Summer Session; Announcement for 1909*, p. 38.

63. Pettitt, *op. cit.*, p. 159. Among Julia Morgan's many credits was the Hearst Castle, in San Simeon, California.

64. Letter to the author, dated November 1965.

65. Interview with Merion Daggett (son of Stuart) and his wife, November 23, 1964. Stuart Daggett (1881-1954), who was a specialist in transportation economics, joined the University faculty in 1909, became a close colleague of Hatfield's, and was dean of the College of Commerce from 1920 to 1927.

66. Letter to G.T. Paxton, dated April 23, 1918.

67. Interview with Dunham, of John F. Forbes & Company, September 5, 1963.

68. In the citation, Hatfield was praised for "his magnificent services rendered Accounts and Accountancy." See Cashion, *op. cit.*, p. 3.

69. Forbes claims credit for bringing about the merger. Interview with John F. Forbes, September 5, 1963.

70. Interview with John F. Forbes, December 21, 1964.

71. Hatfield regularly attended such meetings. Interview with John F. Forbes, December 21, 1964. Moonitz has written, "Although [Hatfield] was not a CPA and had never practiced as an accountant, he attended the monthly meetings of the San Francisco chapter of the California State Society of CPAs. It was his practice to take one of his graduate students with him to each meeting as his guest.... The message that Hatfield conveyed to us [Moonitz was Hatfield's guest on one occasion, probably in 1934] by this and other means was clear: keep in touch with the profession and take part in its activities." Maurice Moonitz, "Some Career Influences," *Issues in Accounting Education*, 1984, p. 3.

72. Cashion, *op. cit.*, p. 20.

73. *Catalogue and General Announcement 1911-1912*, Columbia University in the City of New York, pp. 94 and 399.

74. Brown was secretary of the Society of Accountants in Edinburgh and author of *A History of Accounting and Accountants* (Edinburgh: T.C. and E.C. Jack, 1905).

75. These particulars have been drawn from a diary kept by Hatfield. He was accompanied by his wife and three children and, for part of the trip, Ethel's parents.

76. Just prior to reading the paper in Hatfield's absence, George R. Webster said, "The Professor was in the hope that when he was in New York recently he would be able to get material for filling up some gaps regarding the laws and practice in those countries there. He finds that he has not been able to get the material and he asks us kindly not to print the paper because he would like it printed when he gets back from Europe, where he expects to spend more of his time in investigating the subject of the paper," *The American Association of Public Accountants, Twenty-fourth Anniversary Year-Book* (1911), p. 72.

77. "Some Variations in Accounting Practice in England, France, Germany and the United States," *Journal of Accounting Research*, Vol. 4, No. 2, Autumn 1966, p. 181. This article is reprinted in Chapter 7.

78. Gilman (1857-1930) and Hatfield were great friends. Gilman said that Hatfield was his best friend. From Hatfield's file of correspondence, it is evident that the two men were acquainted as early as 1907. From 1879 to 1896, Gilman worked in Chicago as an accountant and in the coal business, and perhaps they became acquainted during that period. In 1896, Gilman moved to Madison, where he studied law and became a practicing lawyer, and then, from 1908 to 1928, he was a professor at the University of Wisconsin's School of Commerce. During the summers of 1912 and 1915, Gilman taught at Berkeley, and in the spring of 1913, when Hatfield stopped in Madison, Gilman arranged for him to be inducted as an honorary member of the Alpha of Wisconsin chapter of Beta Gamma Sigma. Fayette H. Elwell (1885-1980), whose entire career was at Wisconsin, remarked on both men's gregarious manner and grand sense of humor, saying, "I never enjoyed anything more than when Henry Rand Hatfield would get together with Steve." Interview with Fayette H. Elwell, October 26, 1964. Also see Fayette H. Elwell, *The First 50 Years of Beta Gamma Sigma* (Homewood, IL: Richard D. Irwin, 1963), pp. 17-18, 89. Gilman, father of the better-known Stephen Gilman, author of *Accounting Concepts of Profit* (New York: Ronald Press, 1939), was the only academic colleague at another university whom Hatfield addressed in correspondence by first name ("My dear Steve"). His usual salutations for academic acquaintances of long standing were, for example, "My dear Littleton," "My dear Paton," or "My dear Professor Cole."

79. Maurice Moonitz, *History of Accounting at Berkeley* (Professional Accounting Program, Schools of Business Administration, University of California, Berkeley, December 1986), p. 13.

80. From 1926 to 1930, Forbes was in the executive office of Haskins & Sells in New York. *Haskins & Sells: Our First Seventy-Five Years, ibid.* From 1929 to 1933, Forbes's courses are shown as being jointly taught with Judson E. Krueger (a manager, then partner, in Haskins & Sells). Krueger recalls that he took the class almost half the time, since Forbes was busy or out of town. Interview with Krueger, October 19, 1964. From 1933 to 1939, C. James Hasson replaced Krueger in the course listings and probably had the same degree of involvement as Krueger. Hasson was a partner in John F. Forbes & Company (which Forbes formed after leaving Haskins & Sells in 1932). Both Krueger and

Hasson carried the title of lecturer in accounting. Krueger and Hasson were university graduates (in 1916 and 1927, respectively) and were Hatfield's former students. See also Moonitz, *History, op. cit.*, p. 24.

81. Interview with John F. Forbes, December 21, 1964.

82. Interview with Arthur A. Wender (a teaching assistant in 1925-1926), January 26, 1965.

83. *Ibid.*, pp. 13-14; *Register of the University of California 1912-1913*, Part II, p. 85, *1913-1914*, Part II, p. 91, and *1915-1916*, Part II, p. 93.

84. Moonitz, *History, op. cit.*, pp. 13-14.

85. *Register of the University of California 1912-1913 with Announcements for 1913-1914*, Part II, p. 85.

86. *Register of the University of California 1914-1915*, Part II, Announcement of Courses for 1915-16, p. 92.

87. Letter to Ralph H. Barr, dated September 6, 1917.

88. Letter to R.P. Rodolph, dated September 6, 1917.

89. *Ibid.*, p. 89.

90. *Announcement of Courses of Instruction, for the Academic Year 1915-1916*, p. 183; *Announcement of Courses of Instruction for the Academic Year 1916-1917*, p. 125.

91. Moonitz, *History, op. cit.*, pp. 18-19.

92. *Ibid.*, p. 19.

93. As discussed below in connection with Hatfield's 1919 work for the Advisory Tax Board, the accounting issues relating to the federal income tax were beginning to attract interest in 1918-1919, as a result of the increasing importance of the tax as a revenue-raising fiscal instrument during wartime. Staehling's may have been the first such course offered by any university. See C.E. Allen, "The Growth of Accounting Instruction Since 1900," *The Accounting Review*, Vol. II, No. 2, June 1927, p. 162.

94. Forbes said that Staehling "wrote an awful lot, but he never finished anything." Interview with John F. Forbes, December 21, 1964. Paton said that Staehling's problem was "that he was in awe of Hatfield." Interview with William A. Paton, October 27, 1964.

95. For a biographical sketch of Staehling, see Moonitz, *History, op. cit.*, pp. 14-15. See also Moonitz, "Some Career Influences," *op. cit*, pp. 2-3. For evidence of Canning's influence on Staehling and Moonitz, see their *Accounting: An Analysis of Its Problems* (Brooklyn, NY: The Foundation Press, 1950/1952), Chaps. 2, 5-7. The book, which followed the syllabus for Staehling's intermediate-level course, was dedicated "To the memory of Henry Rand Hatfield. Pioneer in accounting thought, constructive critic, steadfast friend and colleague." In *Accounting*, Hatfield endeavored to prod Staehling into getting out a book on partnership accounts, by including a footnote that announced the latter's "forthcoming book" on the subject (*op. cit.*, p. 408), but the volume never appeared. Staehling recalled the footnote as a "kick in the pants." Interview with Charles C. Staehling, January 24, 1965. However, in 1950, Staehling did write Chapters 19-21 on the subject of partnerships in the aforementioned *Accounting*, coauthored with his junior colleague, Maurice Moonitz. It was Moonitz who succeeded in having the book published.

96. Memorandum to Dow Votaw from Frank A. Waring, dated July 2, 1964, p. 2.

97. The bylaws and cumulative membership list of the club have been reproduced in a paper completed in 1957 by Roland W. Pinger (Bancroft Library Collection, University of California, Berkeley).

98. Hatfield presented a paper titled "The Scholar's View of War" at the installation of the Phi Beta Kappa Chapter at Occidental College, Los Angeles, on May 12, 1926. It was an abridged version of "Cui Lumen Ademptum." The latter paper has not survived.

99. Interview with Robert Gordon Sproul, January 15, 1965. Sproul, a member of the Berkeley Club from the mid-1930s onward, and was president of the university from 1930 to 1958.

100. The Kosmos Club was so spelled to follow the Greek and, also, to distinguish it from the well-known Cosmos Club in Washington, D.C. Originally, its emphasis was on science and the scientific method. Interview with Harry Torrey, December 2, 1964.

101. Interview with Jacob N. Bowman, January 19, 1965, and "J.N. Bowman, The Kosmos Club, University of California, 1901 to May 6, 1957," in a box titled "Kosmos Club, Records, 1901—" (Bancroft Library Collection, University of California, Berkeley).

102. As mentioned above, the university's principal administrative units were the departments, not the colleges. The dean of a college was concerned chiefly with sounding out faculty members on curriculum changes and then forwarding recommendations to the dean of the faculties and the president (or, after 1920, the Academic Senate's Committee on Courses, which had final authority), and with preparing the roll of candidates for graduation. Hence, a college's function related only to the curriculum and the granting of degrees. Personnel decisions were made by the departments. Interview with E.T. Grether, January 13, 1965.

103. The dean of the faculties was to be concerned with "the personal well-being and conduct of the student body as a whole and the provisions for their instruction." University Record, *University of California Chronicle*, Vol. XI, No. 3, July 1909, p. 270.

104. Joel H. Hildebrand (1881-1983), a distinguished professor of chemistry at Berkeley (after whom Hildebrand Hall was named), recalled that "Hatfield was a valuable man on the faculty because of his good sense and sense of humor. He had the quality of seeing both sides of a question, and with his humor he would see paradoxes. Thus, he would make a good dean." Interview with Hildebrand, December 4, 1964. Hildebrand himself served as dean of men from 1923 to 1926.

105. From 1915 to 1918, the annual football encounter known as the Big Game, which all would associate with California and Stanford, had to be contested with other universities. In 1906, the two universities agreed to drop American-rules football, as it had become too dangerous, and to replace it with rugby-rules football. The Big Game was thus contested in rugby football for nine years. Then, in 1915, when they could not agree on whether to continue freshman intercollegiate contests, the two universities terminated their varsity relations, and California had to look elsewhere on the West Coast for a Big Game opponent. To find one, California had to resume playing American football, since the other major universities on the coast still played that version of the game. Stanford stayed with rugby and delayed its resumption of American football until 1919. During those four years, Stanford played its Big Game with the University of Santa Clara, and California played the University of Washington. See S. Dan Brodie, *66 Years on the California Gridiron 1882-1948: The History of Football at the University of California* (Oakland, CA: The Olympic Publishing Company, 1949), Chaps. VI and VII; and Brick Morse, *California Football History* (Berkeley, n.p., 1924), pp. 127ff.

106. "California was deflated by Washington by a score unparalleled in the history of the Blue and Gold—72-0." This report appeared in "North Wins First Game by Big Score," *The Daily Californian*, Vol. XLVI, No. 62, November 8, 1915, p. 1.

107. Memorandum to Hatfield from R.G. Sproul, Acting Secretary of the Regents, dated April 10, 1918.

108. Letter to Hatfield from Benjamin Ide Wheeler, dated April 21, 1918. (Deposited in the Bancroft Library: CU-5, Box 1918: 257.)

109. Hatfield, *Modern Accounting*, *op. cit.*, p. 33.

110. *Ibid.*, pp. 50-54, 236-239.

111. Robert H. Montgomery, *Auditing Theory and Practice* (New York: The Ronald Press Company, 4th edition, 1927), pp. 313-317.

112. Arthur Lowes Dickinson, "The Economic Aspect of Cost Accounts and Its Application to the Accounting of Industrial Companies," in *Papers and Discussions of the Twenty-third Annual Meeting*, St. Louis, Missouri, December 1910, of the American Economic Association (Fourth Series, No. 2: Vol. I, No. 2, April 1911), p. 120. In his 1922 treatise, William A. Paton made an almost identical statement. See *Accounting Theory*, *op. cit.*, p. 268.

113. Arthur Lowes Dickinson, *Accounting Practice and Procedure* (New York: The Ronald Press Company, 1914), pp. 200-211.

114. Hatfield, *Accounting: Its Principles and Problems* (New York: D. Appleton and Company, 1927), p. 373.

115. The discussion of the early years of Beta Gamma Sigma is based on Elwell, *loc. cit.*

116. The Greek letters of the fraternity were taken from the names of the three "top" professors of commerce: D. Earle Burchell, Stephen W. Gilman, and William A. Scott.

117. L.C. Marshall, "The American Collegiate School of Business," in L.C. Marshall, ed., *The Collegiate School of Business: Its Status at the Close of the First Quarter of the Twentieth Century* (Chicago, IL: The University of Chicago Press, 1928), pp. 4-9, fn. 1.

118. Particulars about the early years of the AACSB have been drawn from *The American Association of Collegiate Schools of Business: 1916-1966* (Homewood, IL: Richard D. Irwin, 1966), Chap. VI and App. A.

119. The discussion of the early years of the AAUIA is based on Stephen A. Zeff, *The American Accounting Association: Its First 50 Years* (American Accounting Association, 1966, reprinted in 1991).

120. Minutes of the First Meeting of the American Association of University Instructors in Accounting, held December 28, 1916 at Hotel Deshler, Columbus, Ohio, pp. 6-7.

121. Quotation in Zeff, *op. cit.*, pp. 11-12. In a letter to the author dated April 9, 1974, Paton wrote that he first met Hatfield at the Richmond meeting. Paton was then an assistant professor at the University of Michigan.

122. *Ibid.*, p. 16.

123. Letter to J. Hugh Jackson from Henry Rand Hatfield, dated July 18, 1922.

124. Letter to Professor W.E. Hotchkiss (of the University of Minnesota), dated November 19, 1917.

125. *President's Report 1917-18*, p. 100.

126. "U.C. Prof. Joins Shipping Board," *San Francisco Journal of Commerce*, July 1, 1918 (in Hatfield Scrapbooks).

127. Mitchell, *op. cit.*, p. 296.

128. For a comprehensive study of the work of the War Industries Board, see Grosvenor B. Clarkson, *Industrial America in the World War: The Strategy Behind the Line, 1917-1918* (Boston: Houghton Mifflin Company, 1923). Also see Bernard M. Baruch, *American Industry in the War: A Report of the War Industries Board (March 1921)* (New York: Prentice-Hall, 1941). In his unpublished paper "War and Statistics," Hatfield wrote of the War Industries Board as follows: "It tried to get facts concerning the supply and consumption of war needed commodities, of productive capacity used and unused, of prices, for use in fixing prices, of stores of goods on hand, of possible sources of saving by substitution, of methods of eliminating waste. Its task was enormous. Such statistics had never before been gathered."

129. Letter to President Wheeler, dated September 25, 1918.

130. Also see Herbert Heaton, *A Scholar in Action: Edwin F. Gay* (Cambridge, MA: Harvard University Press, 1952), esp. Chap. III, "Wartime in Washington 1917-1919." Heaton quoted from Hatfield's "Experiences with the War Industries Board."

131. Interview with Merion Daggett (son of Stuart) and his wife, November 23, 1964. Stuart Daggett was also in Washington, as an expert in Hatfield's division.

132. "The State University and the Body Politic: The Southern Branch of the University of California," address delivered as dean of the faculties at the Charter Day Assembly, March 23, 1922, at the Southern Branch of the University of California (later renamed the University of California at Los Angeles). This address is included among Hatfield's unpublished papers in Chapter 7.

133. Letter to Mr. James Sutton, Recorder, University of California.

134. C.W. DeMond, *Price, Waterhouse & Co. In America: A History of a Public Accounting Firm* (New York: Privately printed, 1951), pp. 133-134.

135. Letter dated November 7, 1917. Adams, a noted tax authority, was then on leave from Yale and serving as an economic adviser to the Treasury Department in Washington.

136. Gay's role was confirmed in an interview with Charles A. and Elizabeth Glover (Hatfield's son-in-law and daughter), January 24, 1964. In fact, Gay wrote to Hatfield on April 15, 1919 in regard to his "right to pension if he transfers to Harvard." Letter in the Hatfield files.

137. Letter dated March 24, 1919. Wheeler, already in failing health, had advised the university Regents in February of his intention to resign. See Ferrier, *op. cit.*, pp. 511-515. For his part, Hatfield recommended Gay as a candidate to succeed Wheeler as president.

138. Letter dated April 1, 1919.

139. It was reported in the press that Harvard had offered Hatfield a salary of $7,000. The University of California had a maximum salary for professors of $5,000. By comparison, the salary ranges for full professors at selected other universities were: University of Washington, $3,200-$3,600; Stanford, $4,500-$7,500; and Yale University, $5,000-$8,800. ("Rivals' Bids May Cripple U.C. Faculty," *Oakland Tribune*, January 29, 1920, pp. 1, 4.) By stark contrast, when William Rainey Harper was recruiting faculty for the new University of Chicago in 1891-1892, "[t]he scale ultimately set for head professors was a salary of $7,000 per year (at a time when the senior professors at Harvard or Yale were seldom paid more than $4,000)." William J. Barber, "Political Economy in an Atmosphere of Academic Entrepreneurship: The University of Chicago," in Barber, ed., *op. cit.*, p. 245.

140. Letter to Hatfield from Donham, dated January 29, 1920.

141. Letter to Hatfield from May, dated May 19, 1920.

142. Letter to May from Hatfield, dated May 24, 1920.

143. Letter to Hatfield from May, dated June 8, 1920.

144. Sterrett was vice-chairman of the Board. C.W. DeMond, *op. cit.*, p. 133. In 1921, J. Hugh Jackson resigned as assistant professor of accounting at the Harvard Business School to become PW's director of professional training, the position for which Hatfield had been recruited. *Ibid.*, pp. 171-172. In 1923, Jackson returned to Harvard as professor of accounting, becoming the first graduate of the Harvard Business School to become a full professor there.

145. Another effort was made by Harvard in 1921 to persuade Hatfield to come east, but it is not known how seriously he took the entreaty. It was said that J. Hugh Jackson made the approach. Interview with Charles A. and Elizabeth Glover, January 24, 1964. It is also known that George O. May made a second proposition to Hatfield. Nothing is known of this initiative other than that it occurred sometime before 1934, when Hatfield wrote to May reminding him of the occasions on which "you in times past twice honored me by considering me for a possible appointment." See the section "Hatfield Seeks Position with the New SEC" in Chapter 4.

146. Interview with Charles A. and Elizabeth Glover, January 24, 1964.

147. *Modern Accounting* was reprinted nine times from 1911 to 1923. Harry C. Bentley and Ruth S. Leonard, *Bibliography of Works on Accounting by American Authors* (Boston, MA: Harry C. Bentley, 1935), Vol. II, p. 28.

The year of each reprinting was displayed at the foot of the title page as if it were the year of original publication. This prominence given to the year of reprinting has misled several commentators into citing a reprinting year as the year of publication, even though the year of copyright continued to be given as 1909 on the back of the title page. As far as can be ascertained, the book was not revised during the several reprintings. In his preface to *Accounting: Its Principles and Problems* (New York: D. Appleton and Company, 1927), Hatfield states that "the publication" of *Modern Accounting* occurred 18 years before.

148. In 1908, William Morse Cole published *Accounts, Their Construction and Interpretation* which, together with Charles Ezra Sprague's *The Philosophy of Accounts* (Privately published, 1908) and Hatfield's *Modern Accounting*, were the three most important book-length works on accounting theory and practice during the first decade of the century in the United States. Yet Hatfield nowhere cites Cole, as discussed above. Cole was assistant professor of accounting in Harvard University's Graduate School of Business Administration, which was established in 1908. In *Modern Accounting*,

Hatfield wrote that Sprague's book was "The most important theoretical work which has appeared in English" (p. 33). Sprague was president of Union Dime Savings Bank, in New York City, a CPA, and a part-time professor of theory of accounts at New York University's School of Commerce, Accounts and Finance, which opened in 1900. He had been an active contributor to the accounting literature since the early 1880s.

149. In the revision of this book, published in 1927, Hatfield corrected the name of the nursery rhyme character to Nancy Etticoat.

150. See Gary John Previts and Barbara Dubis Merino, *A History of Accounting in America* (New York: John Wiley & Sons, 1979), pp. 168-171.

Chapter 3

"Historical Defense" and Accounting, 1919/1920 to 1930

During the 1920s, Hatfield's interests in the relationship between law and accounting and in the early history of bookkeeping became more pronounced. He continued to occupy deanships in the University of California, and in 1929 the American Institute of Accountants again invited him to address its annual meeting. The decade was dominated, however, by the presentation and publication of his famous address, "An Historical Defense of Bookkeeping," and the publication of *Accounting: Its Principles and Problems*, which was the revision of *Modern Accounting*.

> *No matter if he is a houn'*
> *They gotta quit kicking my dog aroun'.*
>
> *Let us boldly raise the question whether accounting, the late claimant for recognition as a profession, is not entitled to some respect, or must it consort with crystal-gazing, sociology, chiropractic, pedagogy and palm-reading.*
>
> *Progress is being made. What better evidence is there than that even lawyers and courts are coming to appreciate that there are such things as accounting principles?*
>
> —*An Historical Defense of Bookkeeping*, 1924

ADMINISTRATION, TEACHING, AND LECTURING, 1919-1920

When Henry Hatfield returned to the University of California in July 1919 from his year's leave of absence in Washington, he resumed his duties as dean of the College of Commerce. In the fall, he wrote to his brother James, "The University is perfectly overrun. At present there are 8500 students here, about 50 percent more than ever before. It has caused the utmost confusion, trying to get class rooms, and assistants, and text books, etc. The worst is that, at the best, it means absurdly over-large classes and correspondingly poor work."[1] The enrollment in the College of Commerce had soared 45 percent, from 360 in 1917-1918 to 521 in

1919-1920, reflecting wartime and postwar conditions.[2] Hatfield offered a two-semester sequence in Commercial Reviews and Trade Journals, which was the last course he would offer outside of accounting and finance, as well as Corporation Finance, Investments, Accounting Systems, and Advanced Accounting Problems. Forbes and Staehling continued to teach courses in the evening, commuting by ferry from the city.

During January and February 1920, Hatfield gave a series of eight semi-weekly talks on "Corporation Organization and Accounts" to the Investment Bankers Club of San Francisco, intended "to develop the judgment of [the bond houses'] salesmen, and thus to put the business on a higher plane."[3]

In 1920-1921, Hatfield offered two new courses: Analysis of Corporation Accounts and Reports, and Seminar in Accounting Problems (the first accounting course to be given at the graduate level). He continued to offer the seminar almost every year, even after his official retirement in 1937. In 1919-1920 and 1920-1921, Hatfield's salary was $5,000 and $6,500, respectively, still less than the $7,000 that Harvard had offered him in January 1920 (see Chapter 2).

When Staehling returned to the full-time faculty in 1922, he took over Hatfield's Analysis course under a slightly different title, Analysis of Business Statements, resumed offering Partnership Accounting, and began teaching Accounting Systems.

Late in 1920, President David P. Barrows suddenly tapped Hatfield to become, once again, dean of the faculties, a post that had been vacant for some months. An annual stipend of $3,000 came with the position. Hatfield thereupon resigned as dean of the College of Commerce on November 30, the day before he was to begin his new appointment. He was succeeded as dean by Stuart Daggett. Hatfield's colleagues in the college "adopted a beautiful full-page resolution of congratulations to him and the University 'which is to enjoy the benefits of his services.'"[4] An extract from the resolution follows:

> The association of Dean Hatfield with the College of Commerce has been an unusual one. As Dean of that College he directed its affairs for years with the utmost skill and efficiency. It has grown from an experiment into one of the most important branches of the University. He has set before its students the ideal that commerce is a profession not only consistent with a broad cultural foundation, but incapable of being properly exercised without it. He has shown them that the highest qualities of mind and character are worthily employed in the solution of business problems and that trained businessmen owe to their community a civic responsibility which untrained men only imperfectly realize. Following the Ciceronian dictum bonus orator non est nisi bonus vir, he has maintained the principle that a good business man must first of all be a good citizen and a good man. If commerce students have really grasped this it is in large measure due to the teaching of Dean Hatfield.
>
> His colleagues unanimously testify to his constant tact, his courtesy, his unfailing sympathy. In the breadth of view, the keen sense of duty, the kindly humor which he always displayed, he exhibited those qualities of leadership which have now been called to a larger field.[5]

Henry Hatfield in the early 1920s, when he was dean of the faculties of the University of California. It was in December 1923 that he delivered his famous address, "An Historical Defense of Bookkeeping," to the annual meeting of the American Association of University Instructors in Accounting.

The resolution was signed by three members of the Commerce faculty: Max Radin (whose base was in the School of Jurisprudence), Ira B. Cross (economics) and Charles H. Raymond (English).

An edgy relationship existed between Hatfield and Cross, who were colleagues in both the college and the department. While their relations appeared cordial on the surface,[6] there was friction beneath. Hatfield was a political conservative of dignified bearing, but he had a refined sense of humor and a biting wit that could put others on the defensive in conversation. Cross, who had come up the hard way, was outgoing and rough-hewn. His outspoken, left-wing political views sometimes made him a *bête noire* of Bay Area businessmen. Cross regarded Hatfield not as a progressive department chairman but as one who preferred the status quo. They differed both in manner and ideology.[7] Once, perhaps in 1924-1925, the only year in which Hatfield was chairman of the department of economics, Cross stormed out of a departmental meeting after losing patience with Hatfield, who was presiding, and scribbled a message on the blackboard of a neighboring classroom: "Hatfield, see Hebrews 13:8." After the meeting ended, several faculty spied the message written in Cross's unmistakable handwriting. There was a rush to find a Bible. When one was found, they located the passage that expressed Cross's exasperation with Hatfield: "Jesus Christ the same yesterday, and to-day, and forever."[8]

HATFIELD AS DEAN OF THE FACULTIES

Hatfield became dean of the faculties on December 1, 1920. It was a difficult period in the history of the university. The Academic Senate had just successfully battled the University Regents in the "Revolution of 1919" and thus obtained broad authority over curricular matters and the right to be consulted on changes affecting professorial positions and on the appointments of deans and directors. Hatfield was one of those who organized the movement in October 1919.[9]

The awkwardness of the president's constricted prerogatives brought him into continuing friction with both the Regents and the Academic Senate. In addition, Barrows was not an effective administrator. Joel H. Hildebrand recalls that "he was not a consistent person;" he would change his mind frequently and forget his promises. Hatfield, he said, often mediated between the faculty and Barrows.[10] Hatfield would become irritated with Barrows, who would delay decisions, especially on the budget, until the last minute.[11]

In response to complaints and reports in the press that faculty salaries were below those of comparable universities, Barrows decided to raise salary levels across the board in 1920-1921,[12] which obliged him to project an operating deficit for the year, the first in the university's history.[13] The financial statements for the year revealed an operating deficit of some $283,000, which converted the previous balance-sheet surplus of just under $28,000 into an accumulated deficit of $255,000 on June 30, 1921.

It fell to Hatfield to plan the restoration of the accumulated surplus. This effort came at a time of unprecedented demand for university instruction. In the academic year 1921-1922, the university's enrollment continued to burgeon, as borne out by the following report in *School and Society*:

> The University of California maintains its lead in having the largest enrollment in the United States, and probably in the world, of full-time regular students, 11,505. The grand total enrollment is 17,909; counting the 22,145 citizens who are taking extension courses the University of California is giving instruction to a total of 40,054 persons.[14]

Columbia University ranked a distant second in full-time enrollment, with just under 9,800. Moreover, the University of California's summer enrollment of 7,864, second only to Columbia's 11,809, was well ahead of the University of Wisconsin's 4,547, in third position. The University of California did not charge tuition to Californians, yet the university had to staff the courses. From 1920-1921 to 1922-1923, the total number of faculty members in the university increased from 688 to 792, or 15 percent. In terms of number of faculty, the university's size had doubled in 10 years.[15]

Hatfield's financial planning was made more difficult by the narrow defeat of a proposed amendment to the California state constitution that would have provided a desperately needed additional source of university funding. But Barrows succeeded in getting the state legislature to raise the base of its annual appropriation to the university, and he persuaded the Regents to approve an incidental fee of $25 to be levied on students each semester.[16] The nation's run-up of inflation in 1917-1920 had taken its toll. Among Hatfield's responsibilities was fund-raising, and he was often on the ferry to San Francisco to talk to bankers and businessmen.

A thorny political problem complicated Hatfield's tenure. While President Barrows saw himself as responsible only to the Regents for the budget, the Academic Senate acted under the Regents' new Standing Orders to create a Committee on Budget and Inter-Departmental Relations that began submitting recommendations for the budget. The committee's chairman criticized Barrows for making changes in the 1921-1922 budget without consulting the Committee.[17] But Hatfield, who had allied himself with the Faculty Revolution of 1919, was apparently regarded as a trusted intermediary. Having to steer a cautious path between Barrows and the committee, it is small wonder that Hatfield listed his preparation of the University Budget for 1922-1923 as an achievement worthy of equal ranking with his publications. Devising a budget acceptable to both parties, as well as to the Regents, must have required negotiations of great delicacy. In the end, the university recorded an overall surplus of $119,300 in 1922-1923, and that, together with the $305,500 surplus posted the previous year, returned the university to a comfortable accumulated surplus of just under $170,000 on June 30, 1923.[18]

During the early 1920s, Los Angeles civic leaders pressed President Barrows to expand the recently established Southern Branch of the university there, entreaties that Barrows received coolly.[19] In 1919, the university had opened a Southern Branch in Los Angeles, replacing the Los Angeles State Normal School. One of Hatfield's duties as dean of the faculties was to represent the university on important occasions, and he gave a memorable address at the Charter Day Assembly held on March 23, 1922 on the campus of the Southern Branch. As in his 1916 address at the installation of the president of the University of Washington, he was every bit the classical scholar. He began, wisely, by stroking his audience:

> Los Angeles, smiled upon by Nature, enriched, not by the barren gold mines, but by the ever-replenishing gold of its groves, and by its inexhaustible and revivifying golden sunlight, has been even more richly endowed by its peculiar citizenry, a gathering together from all the states, of those who had somewhat of the initiative without the crudeness of the pioneers of '49—a people mature, successful, combining experience and adventure—a people of ideals and of hopes.

He then turned to a consideration of the "reciprocal rights and obligations" between the university and the state and examined "the conditions necessary to the welfare of the new importation," including freedom of inquiry and liberation from "the bondage of deadening, initiative-destroying routine." Perhaps thinking of the business interests in Los Angeles that were pushing for expansion of the Southern Branch, Hatfield argued with eloquence that the university should be concerned primarily with general, not specialized or practical, education (a belief that had been strengthened during his service with the War Industries Board):

> It must ever be borne in mind that the function of the University is not inculcation of practical facts, nor in mere training in dexterity of hand, or eye or mind, but in giving insight into fundamental matters, in stimulating the spirit of independent research, in training in right methods of thinking, in opening the mind of the youth to higher things—and these things are, of all things, the most practical.... Whether you are members of the faculty, or citizen supporters of the University, resist, I beg you, any tendency to overemphasize the obviously practical. I am myself a professor of accounting, and have for long been intimately concerned with commercial education, but even from my philistine view point, if a choice has to be made, mathematics is more important than accounting, literature is more important than stenography, philosophy than business practice, economic theory than foreign trade.[20]

Somewhat more than a year later, it became evident that Hatfield's term as dean of the faculties was nearing its end. To cope with the many problems of an expanding university, President Barrows "felt the need for greater initiative and authority than he had been allowed, by the Regents on the one hand and the faculty on the other."[21] In May 1922, a frustrated Barrows tendered his resignation as president, to take effect on June 30, 1923.[22] Hatfield, caught in the middle, resigned as dean of the faculties as of the same date.

DEPARTMENTAL ADMINISTRATION, TEACHING, AND WRITING, 1921-1923

During the 1921 summer session, William A. Paton visited from Michigan and taught Elements of Accounting and Advanced Accounting. Paton related an anecdote from that summer's visit:

> One morning Professor Hatfield walked into my advanced class, unannounced, about ten minutes before time to close, and sat down among the students. Unfortunately at that moment I was dealing with the rather dull technical problem of allocating the total paid in by investors in preferred shares, with a "bonus" of common shares in the package, to the two types of stock, for accounting and reporting purposes. Probably I was proposing to divide the total paid in proportion to the market values of respective blocks of shares at the approximate date of investment. Hatfield's sudden entrance, coupled with the tinge of awe with which I regarded him, resulted in a severe attack of self-consciousness and confusion. I kept on talking to the end of the hour but if I stayed on the beam at all it was purely accidental.[23]

John B. Canning, of Stanford's economics department, offered courses in economics and insurance at Berkeley during the 1920 and 1921 intersessions (i.e., the six-week term between the spring semester and summer session), and it seems likely that his contacts with Hatfield and Forbes prompted him to begin developing an accounting curriculum in his department as a means of preparing able students to enter the accounting profession in California. Moonitz explains why, from 1915 onward, Hatfield sought to bring academics from other universities to the summer session:

> Geographically speaking, Berkeley was isolated from virtually all of the leading academic and commercial centers of the country. Jet planes were not in commercial use until well after World War II. Travel was available, of course, but primarily by rail for trips to cities such as Chicago and New York. As late as the 1930s and 1940s, it took 40 hours from Oakland to Chicago by the fastest train available; and 48 hours by the standard overland trains. Twenty-four additional hours were needed to get to New York. In practical terms, this meant that a whole week away from Berkeley was needed to spend two days in a Midwest or Eastern city. The summer sessions were an attractive means of bringing people to Berkeley, and Hatfield made good use of those attractions (including taking visiting faculty to such places as Yosemite National Park).[24]

In the spring of 1921, at Hatfield's suggestion, the Paciolo Club was organized in the College of Commerce "to acquaint upper-division students, majoring in accounting, with each other and as far as possible to secure speakers of note from the professional accounting world."[25] In 1919, the national accounting fraternity Beta Alpha Psi had been founded at the University of Illinois, and in 1925 the Paciolo Club became the Lambda Chapter of Beta Alpha Psi.[26]

Hatfield confided to an interviewer in 1921 that he wanted to write a book "analyzing the nature of profits from the legal, economic and accounting standpoints."[27] It seems likely that a recent stimulus for this idea was his work at the

Advisory Tax Board in 1919, although he had evinced a strong interest in court opinions and legal treatises much earlier, in both his *Modern Accounting* and his address "Some Variations in Accounting Practice in England, France, Germany and the United States," delivered to the annual meeting in 1911 of the American Association of Public Accountants.

An unexpected and intriguing proposal came Hatfield's way in June 1921. He received a telegram from Herbert C. Hoover, Secretary of Commerce in the Administration of President Warren G. Harding. Hoover wrote, "Would you be open to enter service of Department of Commerce for the Summer in organization of effective service of production and other economic data and in general as economic adviser to department?" Hatfield's name had surely surfaced as a result of the work he did in Washington in 1918-1919. While he telegraphed back for further particulars, in the end he decided that his obligations as dean of the faculties prevented him from leaving for the summer.[28]

On September 12, 1922, Hatfield was elected a senator of Phi Beta Kappa at the society's Fourteenth National Council in Cleveland, Ohio. He was the only senator from west of Madison, Wisconsin, and he served until 1928.[29] On May 12, 1926, he gave an address, "The Scholar's View of War," when he officiated at the installation of the Delta of California chapter of Phi Beta Kappa at Occidental College, in Los Angeles. It was an abridged version of "Cui Lumen Ademptum," which he had presented in 1925 to the Berkeley Club.

Also in 1922, Ronald Press reissued Sprague's *The Philosophy of Accounts*, to which Hatfield contributed an introduction. In his review of the book in the November 1908 issue of *The Journal of Accountancy*, Hatfield had said (p. 67) that "the author has so combined scholarly erudition, philosophic thought and practical experience as to disarm any reviewer." The book, he said, was a "masterly little treatise." In *Modern Accounting* (p. 33), Hatfield wrote that Sprague's book was no less than "the most important theoretical work which has appeared in English." With the hindsight of 14 years since the original publication of Sprague's book, Hatfield observed in 1922:

> It is the contrast between "The Philosophy of Accounts" and what went before that gives significance to the work.... Sprague shows that the bookkeeper is not interested in a mere game of matching debits and credits, but that he is concerned in preserving an accurate record of assets, of liabilities, and of the changing proprietorship. He presents to the student an explanation of technique which relates itself to an obviously desirable end: knowledge of the status and progress of the business, grouping all around the balance sheet, "the groundwork of all accountancy, the origin and the terminus of every account."[30]

Most previous American works on the subject had been narrowly mechanical, with simple-minded rules to reinforce one's memory of the procedure. Hatfield noted Sprague's influence on subsequent writers and concluded, "The sanity and clarity introduced into accounting literature by Sprague is inestimable in its value, imperishable in its influence."[31]

Hatfield's note, prepared for the republication of Sprague's treatise, marked the end of a dry spell. His last previous publication had been a book review in March 1916. The succession of university administrative assignments both before and after the year spent in Washington had effectively kept him from doing any scholarly work.

EVENTS IN 1923: AN HONORARY DOCTORATE FROM NORTHWESTERN, AND THE BERKELEY FIRE

Not only was 1923 the year in which Hatfield resigned as dean of the faculties, it was also a year marked by: (1) receipt of an honorary doctorate from his alma mater, (2) a narrow escape from the ravages of the Berkeley Fire, and, as will be seen, (3) the delivery of his celebrated address, "An Historical Defense of Bookkeeping." Also, the year could be toasted for the removal of the College of Commerce to South Hall from cramped quarters in the basement of Wheeler Hall. Hatfield wrote, "At last we have a home, and although we are like a hermit crab moving into someone else's shell, we at last have a place to call our own."[32] The college's original home had been in North Hall, and then it had been moved to the new California Hall in 1905.

On June 18, Hatfield received an honorary Doctor of Laws (LL.D.) degree from Northwestern University, which was presented at a ceremony in Evanston by Ralph E. Heilman, dean of the School of Commerce. The citation read as follows:

> An alumnus of Northwestern University; Professor of Economics and Accounting, Dean of the College of Commerce, Dean of the Graduate School of the University of California; a scholar widely known for his writings in Accounting and Economics; an inspiring teacher; an able and efficient university executive; a public servant who has frequently been called to render expert service both to his state and national government.[33]

On September 17, a holocaust of fire swept mercilessly across Berkeley:

> Around noon on that hot and windy fall day, smoke began to billow over the top of the Berkeley hills, and in a relatively few minutes burning leaves, grass and shingles whipped down the hills setting new fires wherever they landed. Water mains and hydrants wouldn't yield enough water to stop the advance of the fire, and buildings were dynamited to bring the fire closer to the ground. Before the last sparks were finally extinguished 584 family residences, apartment houses, fraternities, sororities, and a firehouse were destroyed and one hundred more structures were damaged.[34]

Paton told how Hatfield reacted to the suddenness of the advancing blaze:

> The firemen were trying to burn a few houses ahead of the fire as a fire lane and decided that Hatfield's place must go. Henry got out on his roof with a loaded shotgun and warned them off. And just then the wind shifted and his house escaped.[35]

Hatfield, his sons John and Robert, and students from the university worked tirelessly to save the house from the encroaching fire. Hatfield's accounting books, manuscripts and other valuable belongings were carted off to safety. He later wrote the following report to his brother James:

> Our house, the one back to back with us (Mrs. Bolton's) and the two west of us were not burned, but everything else on the block went, as did every thing on many blocks north and west of us. There was a terrific wind, every thing dry and hot, and the water supply in the regular water pipes gave out long before the fire got to us.... We had some extraneous excitement, as when some frantic messenger came insisting that every one get off the roof as they were going to dynamite the house. But instead of getting off the roof, more students went up.[36]

HATFIELD'S "AN HISTORICAL DEFENSE OF BOOKKEEPING": ITS ORIGINS AND ITS RECEPTION

In October, a month after the Berkeley Fire, Hatfield gave a paper, "De Computis et Scripturis," to the Berkeley Club. Its object was to rescue accounting from the obloquy dispensed by colleagues in the established disciplines. But Hatfield believed that the paper deserved a wider audience. The previous year, William A. Paton, president of the American Association of University Instructors in Accounting (AAUIA), had pressed Hatfield to give a paper at the group's annual meeting in Chicago. Hatfield said he would try, but in the end he could not free the time even to attend. But in 1923, he fulfilled his intent by adapting the paper given to the Berkeley Club. After removing the many references to university personalities and making other substantial revisions, he presented the paper, retitled "An Historical Defense of Bookkeeping," to the eighth annual meeting of the AAUIA, held on December 28-29 at the New Southern Hotel in Columbus, Ohio. It is not known what reaction the original paper provoked at the Berkeley Club, but the revised version he presented at the meeting of accounting instructors caused a sensation. It became one of the most celebrated papers in the U.S. accounting literature, and it is the work for which Hatfield is best known.

In both presentations, Hatfield's mission was to persuade his audience of the respectability of accounting.[37] In "Historical Defense," he stated: "Three elements, if not conclusively proving, at least presumptively establish, respectability. These are, first, parentage and lineage; second, the company one keeps; and third, the services which one renders the community." At the AAUIA, he styled the argument for an audience of accounting academics, who had been enduring in their own universities demeaning remarks about the worthiness of accounting as a field of academic study. An extract from the initial paragraphs from his Berkeley Club paper suggests how he attuned his argument to a body of unbelievers from other disciplines:

> Mine is an attitude of apology. Not a mere apology for neglect to prepare a paper (which would be misleading), nor for incompetence in handling the subject, which would be useless, but a deeper abashment, fundamental and far-reaching, an *apologia pro vita mea*. Am *I* a member of the Berkeley Club? Is Saul also among the prophets. Many of you are philosophers, and to you I pay the homage of ignorance—*omne ignotum pro mirifico*, perhaps. To you whose eyes disclose the fires kindled at Attic altars I pay the reverence due from one who started out in that path, but whose feet have sadly strayed. Others of you are scientists, who can rede the riddle of the universe, and from such I do not even resent the condescension which he who deals in ponderabilities shows toward the rest of mankind. Theologians, men of letters and men of affairs, lawyers, engineers, publicists, physicians, knowers of the 6500 sounds in the Siamese syllabaries—before you I stand, a mere accountant....
>
> I who dabble in sordid figures of dollars and cents, instead of toying with infinities and searching for the elusive soul of things, doomed to consider how to record rather than how to perform deeds, puzzling over the costs rather than managing the affairs or receiving the profits of public utilities. It is true that my subject is often self-styled the Science of Accounts or the Art of Accounting, one book there is even called the Philosophy of Accounts....
>
> But it is not good for man's soul always to suffer under the inferiority complex. An explosion must occasionally take place, and to-night I propose to explode.... "It don't matter if he is only a hound. You've got to quit kicking my dog around." Yes, I am in the way of being an accountant. I deal not in philosophy, or theology, or mining, or politics or business, or law, yet I am not ashamed.
>
> The contempt which you feel for accounting is not limited to the intelligentsia, but is widespread, and is evidenced by the well-nigh universal ignorance of the subject, by condescension towards its devotees, and by its exclusion from polite literature.[38]

Even before he rallied his accounting colleagues to his side in Columbus, he had to "explode" before his peers at the Berkeley Club. Hatfield's "Historical Defense" thus fulfilled his own need to respond to the condescensions he himself was suffering.

The following hilarious passage from "Historical Defense," which also appears in the Berkeley Club version, follows his demonstration that bookkeeping could claim "an origin sufficiently academic to give respectability to this our 'houn' dog'":

> Perhaps I should adopt the language appropriate to the kennel and speak of bookkeeping as having been sired four hundred years ago by a monk, and today damned by thousands of university students.[39]

Three other memorable passages from "Historical Defense" are as follows (page references are to the version published in *The Journal of Accountancy*, April 1924):

> Let those who vaunt the superior merits of other disciplines remember that this presentation made by Paciolo was not crude and incorrect but contains the essentials of bookkeeping as we know it today, despite the fact that it was written at a time when chemistry partook of the vagaries of alchemy, biology was a weird collection of errors, and medicine had more in common with the medicine man than it has even today. It may be well to see how this discipline—I do not venture to call it science—compares in its antiquity with the more arrogant natural sciences (p. 246).

> But today business is a continuum. Machinery serves for many years, the factory building stands for a generation, the railroad is built to last forever. The industrial process is made up of a never-ending stream of raw materials, goods in process and finished commodities. Expenses are incurred in common and not like the expenses of a caravan solely in connection with one parcel of goods. But man is strangely agricultural in his tradition, even though society has become industrial. Time was when the recurring cycle of the year was of immense significance to him, for seed-time and harvest each came in connection with the course of the earth around the sun. And man still thinks that he must reckon results in terms of the accidental period involved in such a circuit. We demand to know how much a concern makes in a year. We must know, because the reciprocal rights of preferred and common stockholders may be altogether changed, depending on whether profit is to be attributed to the month of December or to the following January. We must know in order to satisfy the demands of the income-tax collector. And so accountants are asked to perform the hopeless task of taking this economic continuum, of chopping it up into arbitrary and meaningless lengths called a year and apportioning to each such year a proper part of the cost of a building which will last fifty years, of a machine which will be used for twenty years, of a blast furnace which will last ten, and of a stock of coal bought in December which will all be consumed before spring again appears (p. 252).
>
> I have tried to remove the stigma attached to accounting by showing that in its origin it is respectable, nay even academic; that despite its present disrepute it has from time to time attracted the attention of men of unquestioned intellectual attainment; that it justifies itself in that it has arisen to meet a social need. Its functions are to locate responsibility, to prevent fraud, to guide industry, to determine equities, to solve the all-essential conundrum of business: "What are my profits?"; to facilitate the government in its fiscal operations, to guide the business manager in the attempt to secure efficiency. Are not these efforts worthy of any man's attention? And so I close this paper with quotations from men whom all must respect: Scott, the romanticist, declared the profession of accounting "respectable"; Goethe, the universal genius, speaks of bookkeeping as "one of the fairest inventions of the human mind"; and Cayley, scientist beyond question, even more significantly declared "Bookkeeping is one of the two perfect sciences." With these I rest the defense of my houn' dog (p. 253).

"Historical Defense" was a consummate example of scholarly research and decorous prose, intended both to inform and to amuse, as well as to inspire, and it is not difficult to appreciate why the essay has been reprinted numerous times both in the United States and Great Britain. The distinguished British accounting theorist W.T. Baxter would write in 1949 that "Professor Hatfield is probably better known in this country than any other American writer on accounting. His works are characterised not only by a rare simplicity and penetration, but also by frequent glimpses of humour.... His *Accounting* and *Historical Defense of Book-Keeping* are perhaps his most familiar works."[40]

The reaction to Hatfield's presentation at the AAUIA's annual meeting has been described as follows:

> Hatfield's address, a rare mixture of wit and wisdom, was enthusiastically received; it evoked two ovations—including one later during the business session. The speech meant more to the Association than a landmark in eloquence. It lifted spirits and excited interest in the work of the Association. As [Howard C. Greer, who subsequently served as president of the Association] later confided, "I resolved then and there that an organization that could produce men like that and talks like that, was worthy of my attention and participation." George W. Eckelberry

> was to follow Hatfield with a discussion of the admissibility of the books of account as legal evidence. Amused by his unenviable role as the second speaker of the already electric morning, Eckelberry ad-libbed, "I don't know what function I can perform on this program after a speech like that unless I could appear as the zero that follows the one that makes it ten times as much as it was!"[41]

Paul C. Taylor, of the University of Illinois, recalled that the members of Hatfield's audience "laughed their heads off."[42] A.C. Littleton wrote that "his personality added 50% to a wonderful and masterful paper."[43] W.A. Paton wrote, "It was a great treat, one of the very best AAA sessions in our history."[44]

"Historical Defense" may have served to attract some young people into the accounting profession. A columnist in *The Saturday Evening Post* magazine made use of Hatfield's address to advise his readers that accounting is not a lowly occupation after all but has come "into a prominence and significance that cannot be denied."[45]

HATFIELD'S SPORADIC PARTICIPATION IN THE AAUIA

It is a curiosity that, following the 1923 annual meeting, Hatfield attended only three subsequent annual meetings of the association, in 1927, 1935 and 1937. At the historic 1935 annual meeting, when the members debated the proposal to change the organization's name to the American Accounting Association and broaden its mission, he was toastmaster at the banquet.[46] At all three annual meetings, he read papers. The 1927 paper, "Some Recreations of an Accountant," was in substance his article "An Accountant's Adventures in Wonderland," which was published in the December 1940 issue of *The Journal of Accountancy*."[47] The 1935 paper "What They Say About Depreciation" was published in the March 1936 issue of *The Accounting Review*. The 1937 paper was a biting criticism of the "Tentative Statement" issued by the association's executive committee the year before. This paper was never published, but it is included among Hatfield's unpublished papers in Chapter 7. All three papers are discussed in Chapter 4.

In 1932, Hatfield accepted AAUIA President Greer's invitation to serve as one of 19 eminent academics and practitioners on the newly created Council on Accounting Research, which was intended to suggest and guide research on accounting problems. He and John B. Canning, from Stanford, were the only Council members who were not from the East or Middle West. The Council met only once, at the time of the 1932 annual meeting, and it never fulfilled its ambitious aims.[48] It was one of a series of initiatives that foreshadowed the reorganization of the AAUIA as the American Accounting Association three years later.

Eric L. Kohler, the editor of *The Accounting Review* throughout the 1930s and the association's president in 1936, observed that Hatfield was "fairly withdrawn" from the association.[49] Hatfield had found himself at odds with the leaders of the association in the 1920s and 1930s, and that may have cooled his interest in the organization. As early as 1921, an effort was made to change the organization's name to the American Accounting Association (AAA) and thus to expand its membership base. Hatfield opposed the change, arguing that it would "cripple its usefulness." In December 1923, he wrote, "There are special problems relating to the teaching of accounting in the University which need to be carefully considered. I do not believe that participation by 'all who are interested in accounting' would lead to better results."[50]

At the 1935 annual meeting, the AAUIA membership again debated whether to change the organization's name and thus broaden its membership. On this occasion, however, the leaders of reform sought to authorize the association to provide the recently formed Securities and Exchange Commission with authoritative advice on sound accounting principles. One of the proposed bylaws of the newly named AAA was to be:

> To develop accounting principles and standards, and to seek their endorsement or adoption by business enterprises, public and private accountants, and governmental bodies.[51]

Hatfield (along with Thomas H. Sanders of Harvard) was among those who spoke against the proposal: "They believed that the Association should be oriented to the problems of the teacher—including research on theory that is necessary to doing a better job in class—and should not attempt to perform a function of the practitioners' organization."[52] Nonetheless, the proposal was overwhelmingly approved in a mail ballot.

In 1919, when Hatfield was AAUIA president, his opposition to a journal for the association was decisive. Seven years later, however, Paton and others succeeded in launching an association journal, *The Accounting Review*.

Hatfield, who was 20 or more years older than Kohler, Paton, Littleton, Greer, and the other reformers in the AAUIA during the 1920s and 1930s, was respected as "the dean of accounting teachers" but was probably perceived as a reactionary figure and one who "was more on the side of the Institute."[53] The reformers fervently believed that the association should become an activist organization, especially as regards research and the development of principles. Hatfield demurred. Most of the leaders of the movement for change were at institutions in the Midwest, and Hatfield's location on the West Coast would not have facilitated his participation in meetings even if he had shared their zeal.

HATFIELD'S INTEREST IN THE EARLY HISTORY OF BOOKKEEPING

As "Zwei Pfadfinder," published in 1909, was the first work testifying to Hatfield's interest in the history of bookkeeping, "Historical Defense" was a reaffirmation and deepening of this interest that continued into the 1920s. In a lengthy review of Pietro Crivelli's *An Original Translation of the Treatise on Double-entry Book-keeping, by Frater Lucas Pacioli*, in 1925,[54] he said: "There are some, few in number indeed and perhaps of perverted taste, who manifest an interest in the useless subject of the early history of bookkeeping.... I count myself one of the number." In the review, Hatfield stated his preference for Crivelli's more literal translation than that of J.B. Geijsbeek (*Ancient Double-Entry Bookkeeping*, 1914), and in some detail he assessed the two translations against the original, written in medieval Italian. Hatfield's review suggests that he had also read the translations of Paciolo (a spelling that Hatfield preferred to Pacioli) into modern Italian and German.

He kindled this antiquarian interest during a five-month trip in the late spring and summer of 1925 to Britain, where he spent much of his time in the British Museum and in the London library of the Institute of Chartered Accountants in England and Wales.[55] This research led to the writing of several short pieces in the mid-1920s. He published three letters in *The Accountant*, a weekly journal edited in London, in July and August 1925 and in August 1926. In the first letter, he congratulated the English Institute for adding to its library a valuable sixteenth-century book by Peele that was "the oldest English work on bookkeeping known to be in existence." In the letter, he displayed an extensive knowledge of writings stemming from Peele's work.[56] The following month, he contributed a lengthy letter on further aspects of Crivelli's translation of Paciolo, providing further evidence of his extensive reading of the early literature on bookkeeping.[57] One supposes that this letter originally formed part of his book review but was edited out by the American journal. In a brief letter in August 1926, he pointed out that the first use of the term "Balance Sheet" could be traced as far back as 1777.[58] Finally, in a note published in the *Quarterly Journal of Economics* in which he made use of his German and French language skills, Hatfield reviewed the uses of the term "capital" in bookkeeping tracts of the sixteenth century.[59] He also discussed early bookkeeping history in an address in December 1926 to the San Francisco chapter of the California State Society of Certified Public Accountants "on the development of the theory of accounts during the past 400 years with particular reference to the progress of the theory of accounts since 1908."[60]

From January to July 1927, Hatfield was on sabbatical leave in Europe "doing further research in the early history of bookkeeping and accounting."[61] Charles A. Gulick, Jr., a departmental colleague, has said, "My remembrance is that he once wanted to write a history of bookkeeping."[62] Hatfield himself professed such an interest, but it was never consummated. He continued to write short pieces on the early history of bookkeeping in the 1930s and 1940s but, as Basil Yamey suggests in a paper written for this volume (which appears in Chapter 5), bookkeeping history was apparently no more than "a side interest, although a beguiling side interest," to Hatfield.

In 1930, Hatfield reviewed David Murray's *Chapters in the History of Bookkeeping, Accountancy & Commercial Arithmetic* (*The Journal of Accountancy*,

July 1930, pp. 63-64) and pronounced: "The book is both scholarly and entertaining, indispensable to those particularly concerned in the history of accounting, of value to all accountants who are interested in anything beyond the technique of their profession." Coming from Hatfield, a critic *extraordinaire*, this was high praise indeed.

TEACHING, ADMINISTRATION, AND CONTINUING INTEREST IN LAW, 1923-1930

From 1923 to 1930, Hatfield continued to offer both Economics 14A and 14B, Principles of Accounting, the Seminar in Accounting Problems, and the two-credit courses in Corporation Finance and Investments. It was not until 1929-1930 that his teaching load consisted exclusively of courses in accounting.

In the *Announcement of Courses* for 1923-1924, there appeared a notice to students taking 14A and 14B which would not have evoked cries of joy among the undergraduate student body: "In the first week and on such other occasions as seem desirable to the instructor, the class will also meet Saturday at 8." The regular meetings were Tuesdays and Thursdays at 8.[63] The reaction from students was swift. The reference to Saturday disappeared from the course description the following year.

Hatfield was still not free of administrative duties. In 1924-1925, he filled a term as chairman of the department of economics. And in 1927-1928, he served as acting dean of the College of Commerce (for which he received a salary supplement of $1,000), sandwiched between the terms of Stuart Daggett and Henry F. Grady.

In 1925-1926, Staehling offered a new, two-semester course, Advanced Accounting, which was an expansion of his course on Partnership Accounting. Advanced Accounting became a staple in the curriculum for students planning careers in accounting, and Staehling offered the course every year.

From 1923 to 1930, Hatfield's professorial salary was an unchanging $7,000. He and Carl Plehn were the two highest paid professors in the department. In 1923, both of their salaries had increased from $6,500 to $7,000, and Plehn received a further increase of $500 in 1926.

During the 1920s, Hatfield nurtured his interest, mentioned above, in the legal issues relating to concepts in accounting and finance. In 1923, for example, he gave a Master's student a thesis topic "which was of considerable interest to him as it dealt with the four terms: income, earnings, revenue, and profits.... He asked me to explore the legal, accounting, and economic literature then available [and] to assemble the various points of view."[64] In 1926, Hatfield wrote an introduction to a book by Prosper Reiter, Jr., on *Profits, Dividends and the Law* (New York: The Ronald Press Company). Reiter had been a student in Hatfield's Introduction to Accounting in 1913, with *Modern Accounting* as the textbook. Reiter recalled:

"His presentation of the subject was such that when it came time for me to write a thesis for my Juris Doctor degree, I had acquired an awareness of the importance of legal accounting; and it was with the encouragement and advice of Doc Hatfield that I embarked upon the preparation of 'Profits, Dividends and the Law'."[65] In fact, it was Hatfield who brought the book to the attention of Ronald Press, then the leading publisher of books related to accounting.[66] In correspondence, Hatfield had made many suggestions to Reiter on his use and interpretation of U.S. and U.K. court opinions.

Four years later, in 1930, Hatfield became an informal consultant to Henry Winthrop Ballantine (1880-1951), professor of law in the University's School of Jurisprudence, who had been charged by the Committee on Revision of the Corporation Laws of the State Bar of California with drafting the state's first modern corporation law.[67] Ballantine relied on Hatfield for advice on accounting concepts, such as assets, liabilities, capital, surplus and income, which would figure importantly in the proposed legislation. George S. Hills (1900-1980), a leading member of the New York Bar and author of *The Law of Accounting and Financial Statements* (Boston: Little, Brown and Company, 1957), who knew Ballantine and Hatfield personally, wrote in 1965 that "Ballantine had a very high regard for Hatfield and looked upon him as the leading accounting authority of his time. I shared that respect, and still do."[68]

PUBLICATION OF *ACCOUNTING* AND ITS RECEPTION

It was not long after he returned from Washington in 1919 that Hatfield began the process of revising *Modern Accounting*. In the fall of 1920, he engaged a shorthand specialist to take down his course lectures as the starting point for the revision of his book.[69] He faced a different kind of challenge from when he had written *Modern Accounting*, at a time when the literature was sparse and there existed no precedents upon which to draw. In his Preface to *Accounting*, which came out in 1927, he recounted some of the developments that had occurred since 1909, when *Modern Accounting* appeared:

> During that period more books have been written on the subject, and more serious study has been given to its scientific aspects, than in any other period of similar length, perhaps more than in the preceding centuries since Pacioli.
>
> Several causes have contributed to this progress in accounting. One of these is the increase in the number of large corporations, for as ownership and management become severed, the need of uniform and correct accounting procedure is imperative. The influence of the Interstate Commerce Commission, multiplied by the generally concurring state commissions, has been another potent factor. And the enactment of the Federal income tax law has, more than any other single event, emphasized the necessity of keeping accounts that will exhibit with approximate accuracy the annual income.[70]

He had, in fact, written reviews of several of the books that had come out since 1909: Robert H. Montgomery's *Auditing Theory and Practice* (Ronald Press, 1912), Arthur Lowes Dickinson's *Accounting Practice and Procedure* (Ronald Press, 1914), and Paton's *Accounting* (Macmillan, 1924). Montgomery, a founding partner in the accounting firm of Lybrand, Ross Bros. & Montgomery, became a leading figure in the American Institute of Accountants; Dickinson, an English chartered accountant, had been the architect of the American firm of Price, Waterhouse & Co.; and Paton, a professor at the University of Michigan, was fast becoming one of the intellectual leaders in U.S. accounting. Other works of note were Paton's *Accounting Theory* (Ronald Press, 1922), Earl A. Saliers' *Accountants' Handbook* (Ronald Press, 1923), and new textbooks by Paton and Russell A. Stevenson, Roy B. Kester, John R. Wildman, H. A. Finney, Saliers, and Paul-Joseph Esquerré, as well as revised editions of textbooks by Montgomery and William Morse Cole. Apart from Wildman and Montgomery, all of the foregoing authors were professors at U.S. universities. Wildman, who had taught at New York University and founded the AAUIA, left to become a partner in Haskins & Sells in 1918.[71]

In the spring of 1927, D. Appleton and Company published Hatfield's *Accounting: Its Principles and Problems*, which, with 472 pages of text, was one-third longer than *Modern Accounting*.[72] The organization of chapters followed the scheme in *Modern Accounting* but incorporated important changes. He dropped the two opening chapters on the Theory of Double Entry Bookkeeping and added chapters on the Consolidated Balance Sheet and the Interpretation of the Balance Sheet.

As in *Modern Accounting*, Hatfield did not intend to instruct students on proper accounting but instead to engage their intellect in a search for judgments that could best be defended by logic, consistency, and adherence to principle. Again, we see his use of Platonic dialectic to discourage shallow thought. Toward that end, he treats readers to an extensive survey of the accounting and law literature, and other sources of informed opinion and practical applications. Foreign references consume relatively less space than in *Modern Accounting*, because so many American books and articles had entered the literature since 1909. Prominent among the American authors cited by Hatfield were, by number of citations, Montgomery, Charles B. Couchman (a leading practitioner), Kester, Dickinson, Paton, Finney, Cole, Esquerré, and Stephen Gilman (the son of Stephen W. Gilman). The most frequently cited writers of books and articles published outside the United States were three prolific Englishmen, L.R. Dicksee, F.W. Pixley, and P.D. Leake; a Scot, George Lisle; and a German, H. Rehm, author of a 1903 treatise on the balance sheets of publicly held corporations. Hatfield profusely referenced the prescriptions of the Interstate Commerce Commission and the Federal Reserve Board's model balance sheet of 1917-1918. Throughout the book, he regularly mentioned court cases (114 of them, mostly American), statutes, and the financial and accounting practices of companies.[73] *Accounting* includes many more textual footnotes, often comparing and contrasting the discordant opinions in the literature.

Even more than in *Modern Accounting*, Hatfield criticized conservative practices that defied logic. Although he carried forward many of his judgments about accounting practice from his 1909 book, he seemed to be more confident of his ground in 1927: (1) he took a stronger stand in favor of the terminology Allowance (instead of Reserve) for Depreciation; (2) he assailed "cost or market, whichever is lower" for merchandise inventories as "confessedly illogical" (p. 99); (3) he favored showing the discount on notes payable as a deduction from the face value of the note instead of as an asset (contrary to the 1909 edition); and (4) he argued for grossing up the goodwill on consolidation to the 100-percent level to reflect the minority interest therein—a position not previously seen in the literature.[74] (See the Appendix to this chapter for a more detailed discussion of the contents of the book.)

In the preparation of the book, Hatfield became intrigued by the paradox that an investor buying $1 million of bonds at, say, 110 percent of their face value, and later another $1 million of the same bonds at 90 percent of face, would record a different aggregate amount of interest income each year than if he had instead acquired $2 million of the same bonds at face value. Since, he thought, the periodic amortization of the equal amounts of premium and discount by the effective interest method should have offsetting effects, why does such a difference emerge? He had been exchanging correspondence on the question with John B. Canning at Stanford. Hatfield exposed his paradox in *The Accounting Review*, and Canning replied with a mathematical generalization of Hatfield's paradox.[75]

Accounting remained in print until 1961, and it appears to have sold approximately 19,000 copies.[76] Scholars Book Co., of Lawrence, Kansas, a nonprofit publishing firm founded and run by Robert R. Sterling, an accounting professor at the University of Kansas, reissued the book in 1971 (to which I contributed a Foreword).

Hatfield dedicated *Accounting* "To R.M.H. in grateful acknowledgment of assistance rendered," an obvious reference to his second son, Robert Miller, who, though a graduate in electrical engineering, had been working as an accountant in New York City and apparently had helped in a small way with the book.[77] On June 18, a few months after publication of the book, a tragedy befell the Hatfield family: Robert, two months short of his 25th birthday, died of pneumonia. He had been married less than a year, and his wife Louise had given birth to Elizabeth Ann on May 24.[78] Henry Hatfield and his wife, then in Europe on a six-month sabbatical leave, immediately returned to the Robert Hatfield home in Dobbs Ferry, New York, a town 15 miles north of New York City. It was said that Robert's death was "the big sorrow" in Hatfield's life. Robert was like his father in appearance and build. Following Robert's death, the Henry Hatfields convinced Louise to bring her daughter to California, where Elizabeth (known as Betty) spent her early childhood years, summer vacations, and college years (she attended the University of California) in the Hatfield home on Le Conte Avenue. Louise, at the urging of the senior Hatfields, completed a degree in German at Berkeley and qualified as a teacher. After Louise received her degree, she and Betty returned to Dobbs Ferry.[79]

Accounting was a worthy successor to *Modern Accounting*. In a long review written for *The Accounting Review* (June 1927, pp. 189-193), Robert H. Montgomery detailed his areas of agreement and disagreement with Hatfield, and pronounced the book "a real treat." He added, "In addition to the pleasure of reading live comments on dry subjects, I have learned something new and my views regarding some old-fashioned theories are strengthened.... Perhaps the outstanding feature of the new edition is the attention given to other writers on accounting subjects, and to court and other authoritative decisions." Montgomery, in fact, was the authority most frequently cited by Hatfield.

Arthur W. Hanson of the Harvard Business School (*The American Economic Review*, December 1927, pp. 714-715) wrote, "in spite of its levity this is a profound and serious book written with a clarity which was surprising to several students who had struggled fruitlessly with some of the other well-known texts on the subject." J. Hugh Jackson (*The Journal of Accountancy*, October 1927, pp. 308-309), a professor at Stanford University's business school and shortly to become AAUIA president, wrote:

> Professor Hatfield has combined real scholarship with a vision and literary style unusual in the literature of accounting. This book may be considered a critical survey of existing literature on the principles of accounting; but it is more than that—it contains the gist of more than one hundred and thirty court decisions as they deal with accounting matters. Furthermore, numerous references to statutes, commission rulings, internal-revenue regulations, corporation reports, and so forth, make this, in the opinion of the present reviewer, the most important single book on accounting that has yet appeared.

Ten years later, Jackson added that *Accounting* "is in my opinion the most scholarly volume that has appeared in the literature of accounting. In subject-matter, in documentation, and in quality and clearness of expression it stands without an equal in the accounting field."[80]

Haskins & Sells' *Bulletin* (July 1927, pp. 55-56) praised Hatfield's book. The anonymous reviewer, probably John R. Wildman, noted that, 18 years after its publication, *Modern Accounting* had maintained "its high position in the literature of accounting" and merited "the frequent reference to this work as an 'accounting classic.'" The reviewer added, "The tolerant attitude which Professor Hatfield exhibits [in *Accounting*] toward differences of opinion is soothing when compared with arbitrary statements of others that the only correct procedure in a given instance is thus and so." The reviewer's conclusion was, "A volume of the character of Hatfield's *Accounting* is indeed a welcome addition to the literature of accounting."

In a lengthy, unsigned review, *The Economist* (June 18, 1927, p. 1290) reported that "Dr. Hatfield's new work, following his well-known 'Modern Accounting,' published in 1909, covers the whole field of accounting, and will be welcomed by all serious students of the subject."

The American Accountant published an unsigned review (probably written by Homer S. Pace, the editor, and owner of Pace Institute, now Pace University, a proprietary business school in New York City) which stated that, since its publication 18 years earlier, *Modern Accounting* "has always been resorted to as an authority." About *Accounting*, the reviewer said:

> Professor Hatfield has written an exceedingly intelligent work on accounting theory. It is not a book for the novice in accounting, nor is it a book to be used, as a text or otherwise, in teaching the mechanics of accounting. Rather, it is a serious marshaling of the theoretical phases of accounting....
>
> Professor Hatfield is at once tolerant and authoritative. He has made a scholarly contribution to accountancy which will be a credit to himself and to his profession.

In October 1928, the Grand Council of Beta Alpha Psi announced that its first annual Award of Merit, for the most outstanding contribution to the accounting literature for the year ended May 1, 1928, would be given to Henry Rand Hatfield for *Accounting: Its Principles and Problems*. The presentation ceremony was held on December 7, 1928 at a joint meeting of the California State Society of Certified Public Accountants and the Berkeley and UCLA chapters of Beta Alpha Psi, at the Engineers Club in San Francisco. Frederick W. Woodbridge, of the University of Southern California, represented the Grand Council, and John F. Forbes made a brief speech and presented the Beta Alpha Psi book award, in the form of a parchment scroll, to Hatfield.[81] A month later, an accounting magazine carried the following tribute to Hatfield by an officer of the fraternity:

> Without detracting in the least from the high merit of a number of other books of the year, it seems particularly fitting to express thus publicly an appreciation of this particular book, because in doing so one naturally thinks also of the man himself and of his work during the years past. He is not only dean of the faculties in his own university, but by common acclaim is dean of the teachers of accounting in this country as well. His "Modern Accounting" would in its day undoubtedly have brought its author a similar award had there been such a thing. As a scholar only this need be said of Dean Hatfield: he is practically the only American writer on accounting to show any evidence of a knowledge of continental European accounting literature, and one of the very first to recognize, and make use of the fact, that much of value and interest to students of accounting is to be found in the decisions of the law courts.
>
> The executive council of the fraternity is agreed that the award is well placed, and to judge by the expressed choice of a large number of practitioners and teachers as well, the selection accords with general opinion very well.[82]

Two conclusions emerge from the several reviews: first, that *Modern Accounting* had been a landmark in the literature and was widely acknowledged to be an authoritative work in the field, and second, that Hatfield's books exemplified scholarship in a field where academics were trying to earn the respect of their peers in other, more established disciplines, and where practitioners were seeking an intelligent understanding of the principles underlying their work. Sir Ronald Edwards, an influential theorist whose writings in the 1930s at the London School of Economics bridged accounting and economics, recalled that he had "a considerable regard for Professor Hatfield's work" when he moved into academic life in the mid-1930s. He made the following apt assessment of the nature of Hatfield's impact:

> I would judge that his impact on accounting literature and thought was more indirect than direct. It was the breadth of his interest and the scholarliness of his approach that exercised influence much more than the actual work that he did. In short, I would say that his effect on other writers may well have accounted for more than his own writing in the gradual broadening and deepening of accounting thought.[83]

In 1937, H.A. Finney, who was author of some of the most important U.S. textbooks from the 1920s to the 1950s, wrote to Hatfield (upon the latter's retirement): "In my sincere opinion, there is no other man to whom accountancy is so indebted for the raising of its standards to a level of professional scholarship [than you]."[84]

Accounting, like *Modern Accounting* before it, was extensively cited in the accounting literature. It has continued to be cited in recent decades. One can find references to *Accounting* in two research studies published in the 1960s under the auspices of the Accounting Principles Board,[85] in reference manuals published as late as 1970 and 1981,[86] and in accounting theory textbooks from the 1980s and 1990s.[87]

The book was also noticed outside the accounting literature. In *The Columbia Encyclopedia*, published in 1935, *Accounting* was the only published work cited in the lengthy entries on accounting and bookkeeping.[88] In his monumental treatise *The Valuation of Property*, James C. Bonbright quoted or cited *Accounting* in a dozen places.[89]

In 1940, Hatfield's publisher inquired whether he would prepare a revision. This matter is discussed in Chapter 4.

HATFIELD'S TEACHING PHILOSOPHY

Around 1928, shortly after *Accounting* was published, Hatfield read a paper, apparently to a class of his own students, in which he undertook to explain the approach adopted in his book. In the paper, he also defends his philosophy of teaching. In this never-published *apologia*, he responds to the question: why should an author pay so much attention to the views of others, rather than prescribe solutions of his own? Hatfield justified his tack as follows:

In the first place there is no recognized accounting arbiter. Opinions differ, terminology is uncrystallized, practice varies. Not only your text book but the so-called science of accounting is "a big mess." In the midst of divergent views why should an author interject his own views in a text intended for intelligent and semi-mature University students, who pine for opportunity to form their own opinions, who resent a dogmatic attitude, who proclaim that they want to learn, not to be taught? There has been too much dogmatism for so undeveloped a subject. Thus, for instance, many text books used to say "Fund can be used only to designate an asset, not as one of the divisions on the credit side of the balance sheet." But this was said despite the fact that our greatest corporation, the U.S. Steel Corporation, whose officers were presumably intelligent, and whose means were sufficient to enable them to hire the most competent auditors, persistently carried the item Sinking Fund as a credit item. On such matters as the use of "Allowance for Depreciation" instead of the phrase "Reserve for Depreciation" I feel free to express an opinion, an opinion which I believe has had some little effect on accounting practice. But as to whether premium is available for dividends, or as to whether appreciation of assets may be shown on the books, what better service can I do you, as students of the subject, than to call your attention to the absence of any generally accepted rule, to present to you the divergent and often discordant opinions of recognized writers and leave you to form your own opinion, in the hope that in time you may be able to do something to secure agreement and uniformity.

He then turned to the relevance of citations of overseas legal precedent, so liberally sprinkled throughout his book:

Are English decisions of significance to us? Read any volume of American law and see the dependence which our own courts place on English decisions. While the stream of law perhaps ripples as it passes from England to America it is, to a large extent, the same stream. Are we concerned with statutes of the continental countries? No, not in the sense of their having any legal significance to us. But in England and on the continent the practice of accounting has been much more specifically regulated than in our land. And there the framing of laws has not been haphazard or off-hand, but generally as the result of a careful examination by a select body of experts. Where absolute authority fails, surely it is advantageous to notice what is the carefully expressed opinion of a body of highly intelligent experts. And when you learn that Germany has one rule for valuing merchandise, and Austria another, and our income tax bureau three different rules, surely you are competent to decide which you think the more reasonable without accepting any dictum from this desk. If that attitude of mind does not appeal to you, your place is in the old type of commercial school, using the early editions of Williams & Rogers, which literally told in which line on which page a given entry is to be made, rather than in a University course on accounting.

BEGINNINGS OF ANOTHER TEXTBOOK

In 1928-1929, Hatfield agreed to do an elementary textbook with Thomas H. Sanders, of Harvard, and J. Hugh Jackson, who had joined the Stanford business school from Harvard in 1927. Both Sanders and Jackson had been under contract with Ginn and Company for such a book, and Selden C. Smith (1874-1939), a partner in Ginn and Company, had persuaded Hatfield to make it a trio. For some time, Hatfield had been looking for a suitable coauthor for such a book,[90] and he wrote: "Professor Jackson's views on the subject of accounting were so in harmony with my own, and I had so high an opinion of his ability, that I thought it would be desirable to secure his cooperation."[91] Selden Smith, based in San Francisco, had come to know Hatfield shortly after the latter's arrival in Berkeley in 1904, since Smith's wife and Ethel Hatfield had been sorority sisters at Wellesley College. After the 1906 earthquake, when the Smiths moved from San Francisco to Berkeley, the Hatfields and Smiths became even better acquainted. In 1925, the Hatfields' older son, John Glover, married Margaret Wyman, the Smiths' daughter. After the Hatfields' younger son, Robert Miller, died in June 1927, Selden Smith argued that Henry Hatfield should find a "money book" to help support Robert's widow and other financial burdens.[92] For a number of reasons, including Jackson's involvement with another textbook for Ginn and his appointment as dean of the Stanford business school in 1931, the group made little progress on the book until the late 1930s.

The Ginn book had two competitors for Hatfield's attention, as he explained in an October 6, 1927 letter to P. Kats, a Dutchman living in London who was a frequent author of articles on early bookkeeping history:

> I have made arrangements to devote considerable time during the next year to the writing of another book, but am in the unfortunate position of not knowing upon what subject to write. Three different works have been urged upon me in which I would be interested. These are an introductory textbook on accounting for use in bookkeeping classes in universities, a treatise on profits considered from the viewpoints of economics, law, and accounting, and third, the history of bookkeeping in collaboration with you. The second would be of more theoretical interest. The last named would fit in more with my own personal hobby, but seems to imply a terrible amount of work. So, standing between these three attractive fields, I am quite at a loss to know in which direction to drive. I only hope that I may come to a decision soon enough to be able to get to work promptly.[93]

In the end, the introductory textbook won out, and it was a loss to the literature that he did not try his hand at one of the other two.

ADDRESSES, ARTICLES, AND COMMENTARIES: 1927-1930

Hatfield addressed the annual meeting of the American Institute of Accountants on September 21, 1927, in Del Monte, California. The meeting celebrated the fortieth anniversary of the establishment of its predecessor body, the American Association of Public Accountants, yet the title of his address was "What is the Matter with Accounting?"[94] He began by offering congratulations for "the undeniable improvement in the standing and dignity of the profession which you so honorably represent" and for "indisputable evidences of life, vigor and hence of progress in the profession" (pp. 269, 270). But then he proceeded to compare accounting unfavorably with other scientific fields of endeavor. Recalling the difficulties he had encountered in making sense of the accounting literature when preparing the manuscript for *Accounting*, he took accounting practitioners to task for doing so little to build a sound theory. He criticized loose terminology, shallow and careless reasoning, and an apparent eagerness to avoid displeasing one's clients. In blunt language, he said:

> Accounting is something other than a set of clever devices for beating the income tax with the least damage to one's conscience, something more than a specious way of window-dressing whereby the best possible appearance is given to a somewhat undesirable stock of goods. It is a universal language of business.
>
> The prime requisite of a language is that it be understandable. There is a suspicion abroad that accounting as it exists today is not impeccable in this respect. Hartley Withers [a financial journalist] has said that "to most of the shareholders, [the balance-sheet] is about as comprehensible as a passage from Browning, translated into an unknown language" and speaks of it as an "impossible cryptogram with an esoteric meaning that is only revealed to an initiated caste, after much fasting and mortification" (pp. 270-271).[95]

Hatfield argued that accounting "needs above all else the formulation of sound theories, which can be crystallized into clear terminology" (p. 272). He aimed his sharpest criticism at "cost or market, whichever is lower," which, he said, was supported by "a ludicrously inappropriate argument [which is a] brilliant ... instance of flabby thinking" (p. 274). He challenged his practitioner audience to consider whether a balance sheet should be seen as "an exhibit of conditions at a given moment" or "a history of past events," and he posed several rhetorical questions: "Do you all know which view is correct? Do any of you consistently adhere to it? Will some one of you explain the proper view to the rest of us?" (pp. 274, 275).

On the vexed subject of depreciation, he said, "It is of only indirect credit to the profession that it could not put over the right view on a scientific matter until it became financially expedient so to do [i.e., when a tax deduction for depreciation was allowed]." He then added:

> I need not recall the interminable debate over the relative merits of straight-line and curved-line depreciation. Accountants, with rare impartiality, apply one system to one class of assets, another to other classes. It is somewhat as if one applied the Ptolemaic system to the motion of Mars, but regarded Jupiter as operating according to the Copernican system.
>
> More distressful and more pertinent to the present discussion is the nature of the arguments adduced in support of one or the other basis. These are often barren of any vestige of accounting theory. It may be said that the charge should be relatively low in the early years, not because depreciation is less, but because it "is inconvenient to burden the early years" with a heavy charge, or because such a charge would show an initial deficit. Is accounting a device to secure what is convenient, or to show what is real? Should accounting be twisted so as to conceal an initial deficit if one really exists, or should it show the facts? Even the physician does not always alter his diagnosis because it would be inconvenient for the patient just then to have an attack of smallpox. His duty as a scientist is to determine whether the disease is present. The accountant, if a scientist, should be concerned solely in what charges may properly be assigned to the current year as the effect of depreciation (pp. 275-276).

Even in his concluding remarks, he did not ease the pain of his lecture: "American accountants lead the world in technique. They probably also lead the world in the formulation of accounting doctrine. But the present need of the profession is a further development of sound theory rather than improved practice." Hatfield was perhaps the only accounting professor who could beard the lion in his den and escape unharmed. Indeed, 18 months later, no less an establishment figure than Robert H. Montgomery invited Hatfield to deliver a paper at an international congress he was organizing at the behest the Institute. Hatfield declined, owing to insufficient time in which to prepare a paper, but instead he offered to discuss a paper.[96] And in 1939, he was again invited to address the Institute's annual meeting when it was held on the West Coast, and he accepted.

In 1929, Hatfield spoke at two international congresses. Serving as one of the U.S. delegates to the International Congress on Commercial Education, held in Amsterdam on September 2-5, he delivered a descriptive paper on "Development in Education for Business during the Past 15 Years in the United States."[97] Of the congress, he said: "It was a polyglot meeting. It was interesting to notice there how the audience sat around and tried to look intelligent when someone spoke in English."[98] Then he hurried by airplane to London and by a fast steamer to New York City to discuss a paper at the International Congress on Accounting on September 11. He pronounced himself in "a somewhat dazed condition" from the trip, but not too dazed to take critical aim at a paper presented by no less than the president of the American Institute of Accountants, Frederick H. Hurdman, who had argued that the entirety of the amount paid in for no-par stock should be credited to Capital, and that it was "absurd" to credit a portion to Surplus. After prefacing his remarks with a characteristic disarming compliment ("I am supposed to talk on Mr. Hurdman's very excellent paper"), Hatfield began by firing a shot across the bow: "If it does not strike me as absurd, I know of no way in which to convince the person who says that it is absurd that he is wrong." He said he saw no reason why the incorporators of an enterprise could not announce that a portion of the amount contributed was being credited to Surplus, which could later be returned to the shareholders so long as full notice of the source were given to the public at large. He did not share Hurdman's view that Surplus could mean only the accumulated net profits from operations of the enterprise.[99]

In 1929, Hatfield was one of six academics invited to contribute to a "Symposium on Appreciation" directed by A.C. Littleton, at the University of Illinois, on behalf of the AAUIA's Committee on Research. The accounting treatment of appreciation had become a controversial issue in the 1920s, especially as numerous corporations were writing up their assets and the authorities were in disarray.[100] Several of Littleton's graduate students prepared a lengthy essay based on their reading of the literature, and they addressed a series of questions: What is Appreciation?, Is Appreciation Available for Dividends?, Should Appreciation be Brought into the Accounts?, How Can Appreciation be Treated in the Accounts?, and Is Appreciation a Depreciating Element? Several experts, such as Hatfield, were invited to comment on the student essay. The entire proceeding was published in the March 1930 issue of *The Accounting Review*.[101]

As might be expected, Hatfield criticized the terms set for the debate, including inept terminology (especially with respect to depreciation), questionable assumptions, improper phrasing of the concepts at issue, deficiencies in the exposition and argument, and above all, incantations of proper accounting practice that could not be supported by logic. Such statements by the students as "Accounting records, from the very nature of the case, cannot record value" (p. 6) offended Hatfield. He bridled at the students' assertion that "the usefulness of double entry bookkeeping for statement purposes" depends on its confinement to "the accumulation of recorded outlays" (p. 8). He delighted in ferreting out illogic. For example, he pointed out, "The objection to recording appreciation because it is a vague estimate applies just as truly to depreciation" (p. 33). Unlike Hatfield, whose instructional mission was to encourage students to think for themselves, Littleton, who was no less a scholar than Hatfield, had firm views on the internal logic of accounting. In his way, Hatfield focused on the logic of the argument about accounting and remained unconvinced that there were definitive answers to the questions posed in the students' essay. Yet, Littleton held established views on the attributes of the double-entry balance sheet (see his views at the end of the article, pp. 57-59),[102] which probably had been received favorably by his students. Hatfield's published remarks in the "Symposium" epitomized a clash of educational philosophies even more than of accounting philosophies.

While Hatfield, unlike Paton, was never an ardent exponent of current value accounting, he maintained an open mind with respect to departures from historical cost accounting.[103] In a book review published four years later, he wrote, "while I have not sworn allegiance to [the present value] school of thought, I can recognize that it deserves at least careful consideration."[104]

BOOK REVIEWS

Hatfield's dozen book reviews between 1920 and 1930 were unremarkable, apart from his paean to Paton and for early signs of his annoyance at authors' misstatements about the purport of depreciation accounting.

Even though he wrote that "there is perhaps no other accountant who equals [Paton] in keenness of insight, careful analysis and penetrative interpretation," Hatfield was not beyond caviling at Paton's practice, in *Accounting* (1924), of grouping liabilities and proprietorship under the head of "equities" (*The Journal of Accountancy*, November 1925, p. 389). He also adjudged Paton's preference for reckoning net income before subtracting interest—which was central to Paton's view that net income should be viewed as the return to all capital suppliers—to be "unnecessarily confusing" to those who were accustomed to interest being an expense. Hatfield chided, "one who had the originality to devise the term 'equities,' would surely have been able to think up some new term rather than to use an old term with a new meaning" (p. 390).

In his review of Frederick W. Woodbridge's *Elements of Accounting*, he showed irritation with dogmatic statements that were not shown to be rooted in principle. He wrote, "Without criticizing the author for repeating the stock dictum that 'no profits can be realized until the sale has taken place,' one could wish that some accountant would give a solid basis for this positive statement" (*The Journal of Accountancy*, February 1926, p. 152). He also corrected the author for attributing the term "trade debtors" to Kester. "This phrase," he wrote, "was used by both Lisle and Dicksee as early as 1903, and it is found in the examination of the British Institute [sic] of June, 1888." Who but Hatfield among American writers would have been a careful student of the British accounting literature?

In two of the reviews, Hatfield showed displeasure at authors' sloppy characterization of depreciation accounting, which continued to provoke him in the 1930s. Finally, in a speech titled "What They Say About Depreciation," delivered at the AAUIA's annual meeting in 1935, the association's elder statesman assailed his academic colleagues with a recitation of such errors that he found in their writings (see Chapter 4). In his review of R.G.H. Smails and C.E. Walker's *Accounting Principles and Practice* (the first Canadian accounting textbook), Hatfield wrote, "emphasis is repeatedly given to the statement that a reserve for depreciation is a means for retaining current assets with which the machine may be replaced, instead of being merely a recognition of consumed value" (*The Journal of Accountancy*, June 1927, p. 470). He was more lyrical when reproving Howard C. Greer (then the AAUIA secretary-treasurer) in a review of Greer's *How to Understand Accounting*:

> And, while grateful to the author for his satisfactory attitude in regard to depreciation, one grieves at being told that reserves for depreciation were formerly a retention of profits and only more recently have they changed their character and become offsets to assets. A Paul may at one time have been a persecutor of the saints. A Lucifer may at one time have held high rank among the heavenly hosts. But never, no, never could "a hole in the assets" have been, under any circumstances, a constituent part of profits (*The Accounting Review*, June 1928).

A SUMMARY OF HATFIELD'S CRITIQUE OF THE LITERATURE

Lack of logic and consistency, confusing use of terminology, and unprincipled reasoning recur as Hatfield's major concerns with the condition of the accounting literature. He believed that statements of recommended practice should be logically traceable to principles consistent with the mission of accounting, which was to present facts without fear or favor. Such statements should be consistent among themselves, and terminology should be chosen judiciously so as to avoid ambiguity and to promote clear thinking. As an example of his concern over the selection and use of terminology, Hatfield had difficulty understanding what writers meant by "realized profits":

> It is not always clear ... whether a writer considers that there are unrealized as well as realized profits, the latter only being of interest to the accountant, or whether there is no such thing as unrealized profit. If the latter is true the phrase realized profits is evidently tautological.
>
> Much of the discussion of realized profits is confused by an uncertainty as to whether the writer, perhaps a judge rendering a decision, means that profits are not in existence until realized, or that profits are not available for distribution unless they have been realized.[105]

He was also troubled by the insistence that profits could be shown only upon realization but that interest income could be accrued without realization:

> The denial that profit can exist without a sale and the simultaneous recognition of accruing interest as profit is another of the many inconsistencies in accounting practice. The exception in favor of accruing interest probably rests upon the idea that it is definitely calculable, its amount may be accurately determined. But if this is a satisfactory basis of differentiation, the rule for recognizing profits should be expressed in terms of calculability or certainty rather than made dependent upon the existence of a contract.[106]

Moreover, he could not abide the illogic of giving accounting recognition to value decreases, such as in "cost or market, whichever is lower," and not to value increases, which were known by the epithet, "unrealized appreciation." He praised Paton as having been "perhaps the pioneer in boldly coming out for consistent treatment of fluctuations in value as against the current, falsely-called conservative practice."[107] In a delightful footnote in *Accounting*, Hatfield wrote,

> The accountant transcends the conservatism of the proverb, "Do not count your chickens before they are hatched," saying, "Here are a lot of chickens already safely hatched, but for the love of Mike use discretion and don't count them all, for perhaps some will die."[108]

He also believed that a clear distinction should be made between principles and expedient solutions. In his review of J.M. Yang's *Goodwill and Other Intangibles*, Hatfield criticized the author's "indefiniteness as to the basis for refusing to allow a reappraisal of intangibles. Is this because they are intangible, or because those assets ordinarily called intangible are in many cases difficult of appraisal?" (*The Accounting Review*, December 1927, p. 410). Otherwise put, was the reason one of principle or practicability?

Hatfield believed that accounting should show the facts, whether pleasant or not. In the following passage, he found fault with a reason given by John R. Wildman and Weldon Powell in their *Capital Stock Without Par Value* (reviewed in the *California Law Review*, November 1929, pp. 101-103) as justification for charging organization expenses to the Capital Stock account:

> The naïve statement is made (page 74), "This procedure has the further advantage of keeping an unsightly and sometimes misleading item off the balance sheet," as if the criterion of a

> proper balance sheet is that like a woman's face it should be sightly rather than that, like the face of a clock, it should show the facts (p. 102).

These were the principles of discourse that Hatfield lived by. And this was his stately prose, free of clichés and fortified by pungent metaphors. In the 1930s, he began to publish poetry as well.

APPENDIX: SUMMARY OF HATFIELD'S *ACCOUNTING* (1927)

> The purpose of this Appendix is to summarize the distinctive features of *Accounting: Its Principles and Problems* (New York: D. Appleton and Company, 1927).

In the Preface, Hatfield identifies several causes that had contributed to progress in accounting since 1909, when he published *Modern Accounting*:

> One of these is the increase in the number of large corporations, for as ownership and management become severed, the need of uniform and correct accounting procedure is imperative. The influence of the Interstate Commerce Commission, multiplied by the generally concurring state commissions, has been another potent factor. And the enactment of the Federal income tax law has, more than any other single event, emphasized the necessity of keeping accounts that will exhibit with approximate accuracy the annual income (p. vii).

"In these circumstances," he adds, "it has seemed desirable, in revising *Modern Accounting*, practically to rewrite the entire book drawing upon the wealth of material which recent years have brought forth" (p. vii). Two notable additions to the roll of chapters dealt with the consolidated balance sheet and the interpretation of the balance sheet (note Hatfield's emphasis on the balance sheet, not on the financial statements). He dropped the two chapters on "The Theory of Double Entry Bookkeeping." Including the sample problems supplied at the end of the book, *Accounting* is one-and-a-half times the length of its predecessor. Probably at the suggestion of the publisher, Hatfield inserted many subheadings in *Accounting*.

Hatfield, ever the cautious scholar, was more comfortable as a commentator on the literature than as an advocate (as was Paton, for example), and the absence of an arbiter of proper practice encouraged him to scour the literature for precedents and the views of other writers. He offers the following reason for carrying forward this inductive approach from *Modern Accounting*:

> Although the science of accounting has made marked progress, it is still in a formative stage, and it were indeed a daring or foolhardy accountant who would attempt a categorical and dogmatic treatment of the subject. In accounting there is no person or academy whose pronouncement can be accepted as having unquestioned authority. Those who write on the subject must, in general, express opinions and formulate arguments rather than render decisions. Hence in this treatise there are presented the somewhat divergent, and at times perhaps contradictory,

> statements of recognized authorities. The student may thus get a broader view of the subject, and have a better opportunity to arrive at a reasoned conviction, than if the author had adopted the easier method of expounding only his personal views (p. viii).

Above all, *Accounting* is written in the dignified prose that one finds in all of Hatfield's writings.

Hatfield reports that he has examined "some hundreds of balance sheets" (p. 18), and at the end of Chapter I, he reproduces the balance sheets of 10 companies, together with five recommended formats.

In his first chapter, "Balance Sheet," Hatfield replaces the cumbersome Goods = Proprietorship equation (used in *Modern Accounting*), with Liabilities equaling Negative Goods, with the more familiar equation: Assets = Liabilities + Proprietorship. Sprague's dictum that the balance sheet is both the origin and the goal of all accounting is, Hatfield believes, a "slight exaggeration, as accounting has other aspects, but the balance sheet is certainly one of the goals of accounting" (p. 3).

Hatfield opines that the practice of English companies of showing assets in the right-hand column of the balance sheet, with liabilities and net worth in the left-hand column, "is a mild misfortune, but like the English custom of driving to the left, it must be recognized" (p. 5). With a smirk, he adds: "the accounting world in general is other-minded, without the disastrous wreckage which would mark the course of the Englishman who persisted in turning always to the left while driving on an American highway" (p. 5). This typical Hatfieldian humor is more evident in *Accounting* than in *Modern Accounting*.

There is a reference to "the well recognized convention, and one amply justified," of showing the inevitable decline in, say, a machine in a valuation or offset account, and he favors the terminology Allowance for Depreciation (and Allowance for Doubtful Accounts), the alternate term Reserve not being mentioned (pp. 9-10). Montgomery, in his review, also preferred this terminology.

Hatfield twice refers to the Federal Reserve Board's 1917-1918 recommendation on the format of the balance sheet (which is reproduced on pages 48-49). The impression is given that this has had much to do with companies changing their practice to list liabilities before, rather than after, proprietorship, and to display current items before, not after, fixed items in both the asset and liability sections (pp. 6, 12).

In *Accounting*, Hatfield continues to complain about vague and contradictory terminology. He finds it necessary to repeat verbatim a criticism from *Modern Accounting*:

> On the debit side [of the balance sheet] items representing losses or expenses may be confused with assets. On the other hand, the credit column contains such antipodal items as profits and depreciation—that is, those showing that there has been an increase in the net value of assets, and those indicating that the value of some of the assets has declined. Exactly the same term may be used to indicate these two categories, for both are frequently covered by what is called reserve (p. 23; p. 56 in *Modern Accounting*).

In his review, Montgomery agreed that, in practice, items are classified among the assets and liabilities that do not belong there.

On the subject of willful misrepresentation, Hatfield repeats, without alteration, his stern criticism from *Modern Accounting*. In these matters, apparently, he has noted no change in practice during the span of 18 years between books.

The annual reports of large corporations reproduced at the end of Chapter I vividly bring out the wide range of accounting treatments seen in practice. Examples include: something called "Undistributed Suspense Items" found in Assets; ample balances appearing in Reserves for Contingencies (enabling a facile smoothing of income); treasury stock shown as an asset; "Appreciation Surplus" on new discovery areas shown in the balance sheet of a petroleum company; Goodwill and other intangibles displayed at $1.00; and "Discount and Expenses on Capital Stocks" classified under Assets. Curiously, in the balance sheet recommended by the Federal Reserve Board, the book value of Goodwill is shown as a reduction in Net Worth.

In his discussion of "Assets and Their Valuation" in Chapter II, Hatfield states frankly that there is "a well-founded prejudice against goodwill, as an item in the balance sheet, based upon the fact that in many cases the value placed upon it is wildly extravagant and incorrect.... But the objection is not to the inclusion of goodwill, but to its overvaluation" (p. 65). His discussion of the inclusion of actually incurred interest among the costs of construction is virtually unchanged from *Modern Accounting*, but, perhaps suggestive of growing support for the custom in accounting circles,[109] his earlier observation that it was "gaining increasing legal sanction" now appears without the "legal" (p. 69).

In *Accounting*, Hatfield is more sensitive to the implications of asset valuation for profit measurement, perhaps reflecting the gradual increase in importance of the income statement during the 1920s, a decade of considerable stock market activity. One of his observations is as true today as it was in the 1920s: "much of the objection to showing appreciation of fixed assets is removed if such a showing is freed from the evil ordinarily accompanying it, that is a showing of a corresponding profit" (p. 78; also see pp. 284-285). Later, there is evidence why Hatfield's book can be a useful guide to the evolution of thought:[110]

> there are some daring and rigidly logical accountants who declare that the function of the balance sheet is to show actual values and that this should be done even where the present value of merchandise exceeds its cost. Foremost among such accountants are Paton, Stevenson, and Montgomery. The latter is less thoroughgoing in support of this doctrine and has apparently been influenced by the startling changes in price level which have accompanied the Great War (p. 284).

Hatfield's views on the unwisdom of the "absolute understatement" of asset values were carried forward from *Modern Accounting* (p. 80).

His recommendation that investments traded on a stock exchange be accounted for at market price (p. 90 in *Modern Accounting*) is repeated in *Accounting*

(p. 87). He also repeats the view that American accounting practice has not accepted the amortization of bond discount, as it is seen as unconservative (pp. 94-95). But he goes further, recommending that "the better practice is to adjust both premium and discount on the correct actuarial basis given above" (p. 95).

Under the head of "Mercantile Credits," Hatfield gives even stronger support for the terminology Allowance for Doubtful Accounts (in preference to Reserve) than he had done in 1909 (pp. 97-98).

In regard to merchandise inventories, Hatfield continues to believe that a "going concern" valuation requires the use of selling price. By 1927, however, he had become an outspoken critic of "cost or market, whichever is lower," characterizing it as "confessedly illogical" (p. 99). He argues that the use of selling price enables an assessment of the performance of a company's selling organization without being muddied by fluctuations in the market (p. 102). When there is an appreciation in selling price, Hatfield would credit the increment to Reserve Due to Marking up Inventory, which would be released to the Profit and Loss account or to Surplus at the time the goods are sold. A disastrous decline in value would be charged to Profit and Loss, as with "cost or market, whichever is lower" (pp. 103-104). Hence, Hatfield was not immune from the influence of conservatism when stating the amount of profit.

In Chapter IV, "Intangible Assets" (formerly "Immaterial Assets"), Hatfield repeats (pp. 112-113) the introductory remarks presented on pp. 108-109 of *Modern Accounting*. But in *Accounting*, he takes aim at recent gross overstatements of goodwill in corporation annual reports (pp. 115-116). Hatfield, always partial to irony, quotes Couchman's mocking advice to companies: "to put it briefly, if you can write it down, you need not; if you can not, you should!" (p. 123). In other respects, his treatment of goodwill in *Accounting* is essentially unchanged from that in *Modern Accounting*. "Deferred Assets" in *Modern Accounting* becomes "Deferred Charges" in *Accounting*, and in the latter work, he draws on cited authorities to suggest, cautiously to be sure, that prepayments of expenses relating to the near future "be listed among current or among working assets" (p. 127).

In Chapter V on "Depreciation: General Considerations," Hatfield repeats his dictum that all machinery is on an "irresistible march to the junk heap" (p. 130). He adds a section on the distinction between the accountant's concept of depreciation as a decline in value and the engineer's concept of efficiency, a discussion adapted from his critical review of Floy's *Valuation of Public Utility Properties* in 1913. "To take a homely illustration: a 'one-hoss shay' ran just as well in the last year of its life as it did in the first. The argument of the engineers would imply that no depreciation took place until the memorable moment when it utterly collapsed, but the account[ant] is correct in stating that there was a continuous decrease in value" (p. 132). To the accountant, efficiency is a matter of duration of service as well as its quantity in each period. Hatfield likens depreciation to the decline in the present value of an annuity.

In *Accounting*, Hatfield adds a section on misconceptions regarding depreciation, the first of which is that "it does not represent a sum of money" (p. 138). It is, quoting Cole, "a hole in the assets." Further, depreciation is not "something set aside from profits," as if to imply that "if there are no profits there can be no allowance for depreciation" (p. 138). Finally, "The allowance for depreciation is not inherently a provision for the replacement of an asset" (p. 139). "Whether the asset is to be replaced or not," he adds, "depends upon the policy of the proprietor." This discussion foreshadows his 1936 article "What They Say About Depreciation."

Hatfield observes: "Corporations are still apt to look upon the charge for depreciation as being an act of grace rather than of necessity and the allowance is frequently less in the lean than in the prosperous years." But, he adds, "the improvement since the first edition of this book in 1908 has been very marked" (p. 140). Why? He explains:

> At that time any recognition of depreciation was relatively uncommon in the accounts of American corporations and the relatively few companies which showed depreciation in prosperous years grew faint-hearted when business was poor [repeated from *Modern Accounting*]. But an examination of the balance sheets of corporations during the trying period following the Great War shows that many of them made charges for depreciation even though that resulted in a net deficit. This closer adherence to correct accounting principles was doubtless stimulated by the provisions of the income-tax law (p. 140).

When discussing obsolescence, Hatfield again refers to the income-tax incentive to show "all possible expenses," including a provision for obsolescence, which had been allowed by the Bureau of Internal Revenue (p. 147).

As in *Modern Accounting*, Hatfield complains about the recording of excessive depreciation, with the consequent creation of secret reserves (pp. 142-143).

There is more extensive coverage of depreciation methods than in *Modern Accounting*, with abundant citations to the supporters of the straight-line and annuity methods (pp. 157-158). Hatfield favored a "simultaneous apportioning of both repairs and depreciation between the years irrespective of the time when the expense [i.e., expenditure] is actually incurred" (p. 161).

In Chapters VII and VIII, both about "Capital Stock," Hatfield repeats from *Modern Accounting* his condemnation of the deliberate concealment of the discount on capital stock issued, by which the assets received are valued at an amount equal to the par value of the stock (pp. 207-208). The treatment of Capital Stock in *Modern Accounting* is, by and large, repeated in *Accounting*, but with updatings, a few new topics and more illustrative journal entries.

In Chapter IX, "Liabilities," Hatfield recommends that the discount on notes payable should be deducted from the face value of the discounted note (pp. 226-227, 230), thus reversing his recommendation in *Modern Accounting* (p. 188) that the discount should appear among the assets. In most other respects, Hatfield's treatment of liabilities in both books is similar, although, as in several other chapters, more journal entries are presented.

Hatfield repeats his view that, while the balance sheet is primarily of interest to the creditor, the profit and loss statement is chiefly of interest to the owner, though he continues to concede that "both are of importance alike to creditor and proprietor" (pp. 240-241). In Chapter X, "The Problem of Profits," Hatfield, apparently frustrated with the discord among authorities, writes:

> It is peculiar that while all business is carried on for the purpose of securing profits, while the distribution of profits is continually the subject of controversy in the courts, while the ascertainment of profits enters into the sum and substance of accounting and the nature of profits enters largely into discussions of every economist, the term is still vaguely and loosely used and without satisfactory definition by either economist, man of affairs, jurist or accountant (p. 241).

A major change in *Accounting* is the much looser link in Chapter X between the ascertainment of profits and the measure of dividends. In *Modern Accounting*, the two chapters on profits were filled with references to judicial determinations on allowable dividends. Issues relating to dividends are now treated in Chapters XI, "Dividends and Capital Losses," and XII, "Profits Available for Dividends."

Hatfield ponders "whether a writer [e.g., an accountant, a jurist, or an economist] considers that there are unrealized as well as realized profits, the latter only being of interest to the accountant, or whether there is no such thing as unrealized profit. If the latter is true the phrase realized profits is evidently tautological" (p. 251). He then observes:

> Much of the discussion of realized profits is confused by an uncertainty as to whether the writer, perhaps a judge rendering a decision, means that profits are not in existence until realized, or that profits are not available for distribution unless they have been realized (p. 251).

At the bottom of page 256 is the most famous Mike in the accounting literature. Pressed by his publisher to expand the index, Hatfield keyed "Mike, love of, 256" to the quotation in footnote 13 on page 256.[111]

When examining whether an unrealized increase in capital assets should be recognized as income, Hatfield could resist the temptation to interpose dividend availability as a criterion (p. 252). He concludes that "to consider both the increased receipts and the capitalization of the receipts as available for dividends to a certain extent is giving double recognition to a single factor" (p. 252). He uses the following example:

> An orchard of trees as it increases in growth from year to year undoubtedly becomes more valuable, but it is more valuable primarily because the larger trees yield a larger supply of fruit. The increasing yield is a cause of larger income. The increased value of the orchard as such is a reflection of this increased income but practically it is the crop income which is available as dividends and not the increased value of the orchard (p. 252).

He then points out that the "generally accepted view is that profits are realized when a sale has been made" (p. 255), which he prefers to interpret as the entering into of a contract that "gives the vendor an enforceable right against the purchaser" (p. 256). But, in a well-known bit of Hatfieldian wisdom, he comments on the apparent anomaly of recognizing the accrual of interest as profit:

> The denial that profit can exist without a sale and the simultaneous recognition of accruing interest as profit is another of the many inconsistencies in accounting practice. The exception in favor of accruing interest probably rests upon the idea that it is definitely calculable, its amount may be accurately determined. But if this is a satisfactory basis of differentiation, the rule for recognizing profits should be expressed in terms of calculability or certainty rather than made dependent upon the existence of a contract (p. 257).

The related subjects of surplus and reserves occupy two chapters, XIII and XIV, compared to a single fairly sizable chapter in *Modern Accounting*. One detects a greater strength of feeling in Hatfield's condemnation of the use of "Reserve" for accumulated depreciation. In *Modern Accounting*, he wrote that the use of "Reserve" for depreciation "is open to serious criticism" (p. 238). In *Accounting*, after noting that a committee of the American Institute of Accountants had approved the terminology, he writes that such usage "is still to be deplored" (p. 301). Hatfield was not unwilling to be critical of authority when it violates sound norms. Indeed, the Institute committee discouraged the use of "allowance" when referring to bad debts or depreciation. Montgomery agreed with Hatfield and expressed the hope that the Institute's report on terminology will be revised.

In *Accounting*, Hatfield devotes more space to classifying and describing the different classes of surplus (pp. 303-309). He states that "accountants generally agree" that appreciation of capital assets where there has been no sale should not be included in current profits, "but must be put in some surplus account, perhaps with a distinctive title indicating its peculiar source" (p. 305). That Hatfield does not give his own view on this practice suggests that he does not oppose it.

Hatfield dedicates more space to the distinction between reserves and reserve funds, but his discussion of secret reserves and the reserve for insurance in Chapter XIV is not much different from that in *Modern Accounting*.

In the new Chapter XXII on "Consolidated Balance Sheet," Hatfield illustrates the derivation of this comparatively recent financial statement. Of particular interest is his advocacy of imputing goodwill to the minority interest in a consolidation (pp. 447-448),[112] and his suggestion of a kind of "push-down" accounting (as it later came to be known) in the accounts of the majority-owned subsidiary (pp. 446-447). On pages 452-453, Hatfield argues that a Surplus balance in a newly acquired subsidiary should be matched by a "purely fictitious goodwill" of equal amount on the asset side of the consolidated balance sheet. Montgomery regarded such a balance sheet as "obviously wrong" and wondered why Hatfield, contrary to his usual practice, did not identify the authorities who support it.

In the new Chapter XXIII, "Interpretation of the Balance Sheet," Hatfield devotes several pages to the Statement of Sources and Dispositions of Funds, which was not mentioned in *Modern Accounting*. In commenting on the title of this new statement, he enjoys a metaphor:

> Professor Cole in the first edition of his *Accounts* uses the title "Where-Got-Gone" statement, but this has apparently been abandoned even by its author. It is a source of regret that a colorful term introduced into the drab literature of accounting should have fallen into disuse. But it hardly seems the function of this treatise to serve as an asylum for a foundling abandoned by its progenitor (p. 460n).

At the end of the book, probably at the suggestion of the publisher, Hatfield offers 63 pages of questions and problems, many of them drawn from David Friday's *Problems in Accounting*, professional examinations, and court cases.

NOTES

1. Letter to James Taft Hatfield, undated but probably written in August 1919.
2. *Annual Report of the President 1919-1920*, p. 327.
3. Letter to Hatfield from J.W. Edminson, president of the club, dated September 18, 1919.
4. E.T. Grether, "The College of Commerce: 1898-1943," *CalBusiness*, Winter 1985, p. 8.
5. Extract taken from a typescript of the resolution.
6. For example, in his address at the banquet on February 9, 1921, honoring both Hatfield as the retiring dean and Daggett as the incoming dean, Cross said that Hatfield was "a man beloved by all those who have been associated with him for many years past." Typescript of Cross's address in the Hatfield Papers, University of California, Berkeley.
7. Interview with Cross, July 23, 1964. Also: interviews with Merion Daggett (son of Stuart) and his wife, November 23, 1964; with Paul S. Taylor (former departmental colleague), March 23, 1965; with E.T. Grether, June 21, 1965; with Malcolm M. Davison, December 15, 1964; with Frank A. Waring (former student, Class of 1924), August 23, 1964; joint interview with Grether, Catharine Quire, and Maurice Moonitz, October 1964; and a letter to the author from Robert D. Calkins (former departmental colleague and dean of the College of Commerce from 1937 to 1940), dated June 29, 1965.
8. Interviews with Frank A. Waring, August 23, 1964, and with E.T. Grether, January 3, 1990. Probably not lost upon the members of the department was the way that Cross, hardly a religious man, got to Hatfield, the son of a Methodist minister.
9. See Douglas Young, "The Faculty Revolution at the University of California" (thesis submitted to Professor Walton Bean in January 1959), p. 28. (Available in the Bancroft Library of the University of California.)
10. Interview with Hildebrand, December 4, 1964. Hildebrand joined the Berkeley faculty in 1913.
11. Interview with the John G. Hatfields and E.T. Grethers, January 13, 1965.
12. See, for example, Verne A. Stadtman, *The University of California 1868-1968* (New York: McGraw-Hill Book Company, 1970), p. 252 (cited below as Stadtman); Verne A. Stadtman and the Centennial Publications Staff, *The Centennial Record of the University of California* (University of California, 1967), p. 264 (cited below as Stadtman *et al.*); and *Annual Report of the President of the University on behalf of the Regents to his Excellency the Governor of the State of California 1920-1921* (Berkeley, CA: University of California Press), pp. 7-11.

13. Stadtman, *op. cit.*, p. 251.

14. Raymond Walters, "Statistics of Registration in American Universities and Colleges, 1921," *School and Society*, Vol. XV, No. 373, February 18, 1922, p. 177. In his report two years earlier, Walters characterized the university's total number of persons in attendance of 36,904 as "prodigious." "Statistics of Registration of Thirty American Universities for 1920," *School and Society*, Vol. XIII, No. 318, January 29, 1921, p. 121.

15. See Stadtman *et al., op. cit.*, p. 273.

16. See Stadtman, *op. cit.*, pp. 251-252.

17. *Ibid.*, pp. 249-250.

18. These figures appear in the university's financial statements included in the *Annual Report of the President of University* for the years 1920-1921, 1921-1922, and 1922-1923.

19. In 1927, the Southern Branch was renamed the University of California at Los Angeles (UCLA). Stadtman, *op. cit.*, p. 234.

20. Hatfield's address is included among his unpublished papers in Chapter 7.

21. *Ibid.*, p. 253.

22. See Russell H. Fitzgibbon, *The Academic Senate of the University of California* (Office of the President, University of California, 1968), pp. 23-32; Stadtman, *op. cit.*, Chap. 16; William Warren Ferrier, *Origin and Development of the University of California* (Berkeley, CA: The Sather Gate Book Shop, 1930), pp. 522-526; and Ewald T. Grether, "Faculty Participation in University Government," *California Monthly*, April 1953, pp. 10-11, 39-40.

23. Letter to the author from Paton, dated April 9, 1974.

24. Maurice Moonitz, *History of Accounting at Berkeley* (Berkeley, CA: Schools of Business Administration, University of California, 1986), p. 16.

25. "The Paciolo Club," *Commercia*, Vol. II, No. 4, December 1921, p. 8. *Commercia* was the monthly organ of the College of Commerce, published by the Commerce Association from 1921 to 1927.

26. "Commerce Clippings," *Commercia*, Vol. VI, No. 1, September 1925, p. 8; Terry K. Sheldahl, *Beta Alpha Psi, from Alpha to Omega: Pursuing a Vision of Professional Education for Accountants 1919-1945* (New York: Garland Publishing, 1982), pp. 146-147; and Moonitz, *op. cit.*, pp. 21-22.

27. "Builders of the West—XCV," *Journal of Electricity and Western Industry*, Vol. 46, No. 4, February 15, 1921, p. 210. This quotation is a paraphrase by the interviewer.

28. Letter to sons John and Robert from Hatfield, dated June 2, 1921 (in collection of John S. Hatfield).

29. Oscar M. Voorhees, *The History of Phi Beta Kappa* (New York: Crown Publishers, 1945), pp. 326, 363. Joel H. Hildebrand recalls a remark Hatfield made when speaking at a dinner meeting of a Phi Beta Kappa chapter: "I now switch from Senatorial dotage to post-prandial anecdotage." Interview with Hildebrand, December 4, 1964.

30. Henry Rand Hatfield, Introductory Notes, in Charles E. Sprague, *The Philosophy of Accounts* (New York: The Ronald Press Company, fifth edition, 1922), p. xviii. This note is reprinted in Chapter 7.

31. *Ibid.*, p. xxi.

32. *Commercia*, Vol. IV, No. 1, September 1923, p. 8. South Hall, which dates from 1873, was the first building erected on the Berkeley campus.

33. *Sixty-fifth Annual Commencement, Monday, June 18, 1923, Northwestern University, Evanston, Illinois*, p. 5. Hatfield had received an A.B. degree from Northwestern in 1892. It is not known who promoted Hatfield for the honor. Whoever composed the citation misstated some of the facts. Although Hatfield's appointment at Berkeley was in the department of economics, his professorial title was always in accounting, not economics, and he had never served as dean of the Graduate Division (not School).

34. George A. Pettitt, *Berkeley: The Town and Gown of It* (Berkeley, CA: Howell-North Books, 1973), p. 95. Also see "The Berkeley Fire, September 17, 1923," compiled by Aubrey Boyd (n.d.).

35. Letter to the author from W.A. Paton, dated, June 28, 1965. Paton added: "Ira Cross told me that he went to a class when there was nothing but a trivial brush fire going miles north of his home. Before he could get home after this class his fine place and everything in it was completely destroyed." Paton's story was largely confirmed in an interview with Roland Abercrombie, June 29, 1965, but he had Hatfield standing on his porch, with a gun in each hand. Mrs. Lorraine T. Mitchell, a former student, writes that one of her memories was "of Dr. Hatfield standing on the roof of his home during the great fire in Berkeley and thereby preventing it from being destroyed in the back fire." Letter to the author dated September 27, 1964. Arthur Bolton, Jr., a next-door neighbor, recalls seeing the Hatfield boys, John and Rob, perched on the roof "trying to get the wooden shingles wet down" with a garden hose. Interview with Bolton, March 1, 1997.

36. Letter to James Taft Hatfield from Henry Rand Hatfield, dated September 29, 1923.

37. The version presented to the Berkeley Club has never been published, but "Historical Defense" is unquestionably the better of the two papers. "De Computis et Scripturis" is a typescript in the Hatfield files. "Historical Defense" is reprinted in Chapter 7.

38. The translation of the two Latin phrases is "justification of my life" and "everything unknown is something that causes wonderment," respectively.

39. "An Historical Defense of Bookkeeping," *The Journal of Accountancy*, Vol. XXXVII, No. 4, April 1924, p. 247. Hatfield used "dammed" in his Berkeley Club paper but "damned" in the typescript of his "Historical Defense" paper. "Dammed" was also used in two of the reprintings: in W.T. Baxter and Sidney Davidson, eds., *Studies in Accounting Theory* (London: Sweet & Maxwell, 1962), p. 7; and W.T. Baxter and Sidney Davidson, *Studies in Accounting* (London: The Institute of Chartered Accountants in England and Wales, 1977), p. 5. Curiously, W.T. Baxter's *Studies in Accounting* (London: Sweet & Maxwell, 1950), p. 7, used "damned."

40. "The Late Professor Henry Rand Hatfield," *Newsletter of the Association of University Teachers of Accounting*, No. 2, July 1949, p. 10.

41. Stephen A. Zeff, *The American Accounting Association—Its First 50 Years* (American Accounting Association, 1966; reprinted in 1991), p. 24 (p. 22 in the reprint). Greer called it "one of the most fascinating, entertaining and inspiring talks that I ever heard." He said that the accounting instructors at that time felt somewhat inferior to the economists, so Hatfield's talk resonated with his audience. Interview with Greer, October 1964.

42. Interview with Taylor, May 25, 1964.

43. Letter to the author from Littleton, dated May 22, 1964. With Hatfield's permission, Littleton included "Historical Defense," abridged and slightly rewritten, as the first chapter in his *Accounting Evolution to 1900* (New York: American Institute Publishing Co., 1933).

44. Letter to the author from Paton, dated June 28, 1965. By AAA, Paton is referring to the American Accounting Association, the name adopted by the AAUIA in 1935-1936.

45. A.W. Atwood, "Respectable Occupations," *The Saturday Evening Post*, April 16, 1927. What caused the delay from December 1923, when Hatfield gave his address, until April 1927, when the article appeared, is not known.

46. In Zeff, *loc. cit.*, the two-page picture immediately following the title page shows Hatfield at the head table during the banquet at the 1935 annual meeting. See pp. 38-41 (pp. 35-38 in the reprint), *ibid.*, for a discussion of what transpired at the 1935 meeting. A young instructor who was present at the 1935 banquet said, "though [Hatfield's] introductions were all extremely witty, many were so biting that I felt the past presidents being introduced must have been quite embarrassed." Letter to the author from Norman L. Burton, dated June 24, 1965.

47. An address with the same title, "Some Recreations of an Accountant," presented to the San Francisco Chapter of the California State Society of Certified Public Accountants on March 20, 1928, "proved to be very entertaining." Minute Book of the Chapter, June 1913 to May 1937, p. 42. Hatfield

later wrote that he "refused at that time [1927] to allow it to be printed, as I felt it was too much *infra dig*." Letter to Catharine DeMotte Greene from Hatfield, dated June 10, 1940.

48. See Zeff, *op. cit.*, pp. 34-35.

49. Interview with Kohler, June 23, 1964.

50. Letter to John R. Wildman, dated December 8, 1923, quoted in Zeff, *op. cit.*, p. 36; also see pp. 30-41.

51. *Ibid.*, p. 40.

52. *Ibid.*, p. 39.

53. Quotation from a letter to the author from William W. Cooper (who was a student of Kohler's and then an assistant to Kohler when the latter was a principal at Arthur Andersen & Co. and, later, when he was controller of the Tennessee Valley Authority), dated February 12, 1997.

54. *Publications of the American Association of University Instructors in Accounting*, Vol. IX, No. 2, December 1925, pp. 153-156.

55. Reported in *Commercia*, Vol. VI, No. 1, September 1925, p. 12.

56. "An Old English Work on Bookkeeping," *The Accountant*, July 11, 1925, p. 68.

57. "Pacioli's Summa," *The Accountant*, August 8, 1925, pp. 211-212.

58. "The Origin of the Term 'Balance Sheet'," *The Accountant*, August 14, 1926, p. 258.

59. "The Earliest Use in English of the Term Capital," *Quarterly Journal of Economics*, Vol. XL, No. 3, May 1926, pp. 547-548.

60. Minute Book of the Chapter, June 1913 to May 1937, p. 28. The date of the address was December 12.

61. "University Notes," *The Accounting Review*, Vol. II, No. 1, March 1927, p. 72.

62. Interview with Gulick, June 25, 1965. Gulick joined the faculty in 1926.

63. It has been suggested that the students, indeed, may have been thankful. Most large classes met on Mondays, Wednesdays, and Fridays, and Hatfield offered his principles course instead on Tuesdays, Thursdays, and often Saturdays, so as to help students distribute their weekly load of classes. Interview with Merion Daggett and his wife, November 23, 1964.

64. Letter to the author from Roy T. Culey, dated October 1, 1964.

65. Letter to the author from Reiter, dated September 9, 1964.

66. Copy of letter to Reiter from Lee Galloway, vice-president of Ronald Press (in the Hatfield files).

67. The Committee also recommended amendments to the California state constitution providing for limited liability for corporations. The constitution was so amended in 1930, and a General Corporation Law was passed the following year.

68. Letter to the author from Hills, dated September 7, 1965. Graham L. Sterling, Jr. (1904-1972), an attorney in a well-known Los Angeles firm who became an active member of the State Bar and coauthor (with Ballantine) of a treatise on California corporation law, confirms that Ballantine drew heavily on Hatfield. Interview with Sterling, December 30, 1964.

69. Telephone interview with Loda Mae Davis (who was the shorthand specialist), July 10, 1965. Then an undergraduate, she received her degree from the university in 1923.

70. Henry Rand Hatfield, *Accounting: Its Principles and Problems* (New York: D. Appleton and Company, 1927), p. vii. Also see Gary John Previts, *A Critical Evaluation of Comparative Financial Accounting Thought in America 1900 to 1920* (New York: Arno Press, 1980).

71. For further discussion of the major authors of the period, see John J. Kahle, *American Accountants and Their Contributions to Accounting Thought, 1900-1930* (New York: Garland Publishing, 1993). For a comprehensive directory of citations to published works during the period, see Harry C. Bentley and Ruth S. Leonard, *Bibliography of Works on Accounting by American Authors* (Boston: Harry C. Bentley, 1935), Vol. II.

72. Unlike *Modern Accounting*, which was translated into Japanese twice, *Accounting* was not published in Japanese. As far as I have been able to ascertain, *Accounting* was published only in English.

73. A comprehensive analysis of the sources cited by Hatfield may be found in Edward Hussey Binns, "The Influence of Henry Rand Hatfield," MBA Thesis (San Francisco State University, 1978), Chap. 5 and Appendices B-H.

74. In the 1940s, Moonitz extended Hatfield's analysis on the recognition of the minority interest in consolidated goodwill. See the discussion in R.G. Walker, *Consolidated Statements* (New York: Arno Press, 1978), pp. 350-353, as well as Maurice Moonitz, *The Entity Theory of Consolidated Statements* (American Accounting Association, 1944).

75. Henry Rand Hatfield, "An Accounting Paradox," *The Accounting Review*, Vol. III, No. 4, December 1928, pp. 342-344; and John B. Canning, "Hatfield's Paradox," *The Accounting Review*, Vol. IV, No. 2, June 1929, pp. 111-115.

76. This estimate is based on letters to the author from Helen Cohan, of Appleton-Century-Crofts, dated December 1, 1964 and January 11, 1965, and an inspection of royalty statements in Hatfield's files.

77. Interview with the John G. Hatfields and the E.T. Grethers, January 13, 1965, and with Arthur J. Goldberg (a teaching fellow at Berkeley who had Robert in class and knew him well), November 2, 1964, and a communication from Betty (Elizabeth Ann Hatfield) Werther, Robert's daughter, dated December 16, 1996.

78. Elizabeth (Hatfield) Glover and Dorothy (Boake) Young, *A Glover Family History* (Privately printed, 1984), p. 74. Robert was an ailing child who suffered from asthma.

79. Letter from Betty (Elizabeth Ann Hatfield) Werther, dated January 10, 1990, supplemented by a communication dated November 25, 1996.

80. Letter to Hatfield dated February 25, 1937 commemorating Hatfield's retirement from the University of California.

81. Sheldahl, *op. cit.*, pp. 429-449.

82. Quoted in "Award of Merit for Hatfield Book Should Stimulate Authors," *The American Accountant*, January 1929, pp. 28-29. The members of the final selection committee were the six men who constituted the Grand Council of the fraternity: A.C. Littleton, University of Illinois (president); Jacob B. Taylor, Ohio State University; William E. Cox, University of Washington; Woodbridge; H.D. McGirr, of Seattle; and Eric L. Kohler, of Chicago.

83. Letter to the author from Sir Ronald, dated November 30, 1964.

84. Letter dated March 1, 1937.

85. Robert T. Sprouse and Maurice Moonitz, *A Tentative Set of Broad Accounting Principles for Business Enterprises* (New York: American Institute of Certified Public Accountants, 1962); and George R. Catlett and Norman O. Olson, *Accounting for Goodwill* (New York: AICPA, 1968) These were published as Accounting Research Studies 3 and 10, respectively.

86. Rufus Wixon, Walter G. Kell, and Norton M. Bedford, eds., *Accountants' Handbook* (New York: The Ronald Press Company, fifth edition, 1970), p. A-6; and John C. Burton, Russell E. Palmer, and Robert S. Kay, eds., *Handbook of Accounting and Auditing* (Boston, MA: Warren, Gorham & Lamont, Inc., 1981), p. B-13.

87. See, for example, Eldon S. Hendriksen, *Accounting Theory* (Homewood, IL: Richard D. Irwin, Inc., fourth edition, 1982), pp. 48, 453; and Vernon Kam, *Accounting Theory* (New York: John Wiley & Sons, second edition, 1990), p. 244.

88. Clarke F. Ansley, editor in chief, *The Columbia Encyclopedia* (Morningside Heights, NY: Columbia University Press, 1935), pp. 11, 209.

89. James C. Bonbright, *The Valuation of Property* (New York: McGraw-Hill Book Company, 1937).

90. Hatfield began working on an elementary textbook in 1919-1920. Selden Smith had suggested to him that he coauthor with Fayette H. Elwell, of the University of Wisconsin, in succession to one of Elwell's books done with George W. Miner (which Hatfield had reviewed for Ginn and Company, the publisher). An obstacle was Hatfield's contract with D. Appleton and Company for a revision of *Modern Accounting*. It seems likely that the considerable time required to prepare a revi-

sion of *Modern Accounting*, which was hardly an elementary textbook, displaced any further work on a book for Ginn. Letter to Hatfield from Smith, dated January 14, 1920; and letter to Smith from Hatfield, dated February 10, 1920, together with sundry earlier correspondence.

91. Letter to S.C. Smith from Hatfield, dated December 14, 1929.

92. Interview with Mrs. John G. Hatfield, in 1964-1965. The market for Hatfield's *Accounting* was at the intermediate or advanced level of an accounting curriculum. The book that Selden Smith had in mind for Hatfield was at the elementary, or freshman, level, where the potential market would have been much larger.

93. This was one of many letters exchanged between Hatfield and Kats in the 1920s. The file of letters is included in the Hatfield collection in the Bancroft Library, University of California, Berkeley.

94. Henry Rand Hatfield, "What is the Matter with Accounting?" *The Journal of Accountancy*, Vol. XLIV, No. 4, October 1927, pp. 267-279. Page numbers in parentheses in this and the next two paragraphs refer to this article.

95. I have traced the source of this delectable quotation to Hartley Withers, *Stocks and Shares* (London: John Murray, second edition, 1917), pp. 120, 121.

96. Letter to Montgomery from Hatfield, dated April 12, 1929.

97. *Proceedings of the International Congress on Commercial Education*, Amsterdam, September 2-5, 1929 (Amsterdam, 1929), Part I, pp. 62-74. Hatfield was one of seven delegates chosen by the Secretary of State to represent the National Board of Education at the congress. It was reported that "many of his associates were surprised at his return with a full grown mustache." "Hatfield Will Resume Work at University," *The Daily Californian*, Vol. LXXXII, No. 26, September 20, 1929, p. 3.

98. *Proceedings*, International Congress on Accounting (New York, 1930), p. 1177.

99. *Ibid.*, pp. 1177-1179.

100. For a discussion, see R.G. Walker, "The SEC's Ban on Upward Asset Revaluations and the Disclosure of Current Values," *Abacus*, Vol. 28, No. 1, March 1992, pp. 4-7.

101. "A Symposium on Appreciation," *The Accounting Review*, Vol. V, No. 1, March 1930, pp. 1-59. The page numbers in parentheses in the next paragraph refer to this article.

102. Also see A.C. Littleton, "Value and Price in Accounting," *The Accounting Review*, Vol. IV, No. 3, September 1929, pp. 147-154.

103. For the record of Paton's advocacy, see Stephen A. Zeff, "Paton on the Effects of Changing Prices on Accounting 1916-55," in Stephen A. Zeff, Joel Demski, and Nicholas Dopuch, eds., *Essays in Honor of William A. Paton: Pioneer Accounting Theorist* (Ann Arbor, MI: Division of Research, Graduate School of Business Administration, University of Michigan, 1979), pp. 91-137.

104. Review of *Depreciation* in *The Journal of Accountancy*, Vol. 57, No. 5, May 1934, p. 387.

105. Hatfield, *Accounting*, *op. cit.*, p. 251.

106. *Ibid.*, p. 257.

107. Review of Paton's *Accounting* in *The Journal of Accountancy*, Vol. 40, No. 5, November 1925, p. 390.

108. Hatfield, *Accounting*, *op. cit.*, p. 256.

109. See, for example, Clinton H. Scovell, *Interest as a Cost* (New York: The Ronald Press Company, 1924).

110. For another such example, see his footnote 26 on page 77.

111. Anecdote provided by Jacob Viner in a letter to the author dated November 23, 1964. The anecdote was confirmed by Scott Dayton (a former Hatfield student) in a letter to the author dated March 15, 1965.

112. See R.G. Walker, *Consolidated Statements* (New York: Arno Press, 1978), pp. 350-353.

Chapter 4

The Final Active Years, 1930 to 1945

The final years of Hatfield's life included activities and interests that, when examined, more fully develop his personal and professional portrait. His continued interest in the history of bookkeeping revealed his belief in the value of classical education, as did his sustained view that accounting was not an academic discipline of the same intellectual stature as economics or law. His articles, presentations, and reviews of accounting textbooks and treatises similarly underscored his conservative value system, one that unrelentingly argued for adherence to sound theory rather than extant practice, which he found suspect as an arbiter of that very practice. Hatfield's value system never wavered: a commitment to ethical behavior and to accounting practices and terminology that were logical derivations of principle. He defended these values as one of the three authors of *A Statement of Accounting Principles*. Throughout, Hatfield dueled with ideas as a Socratic teacher. His output fully portrays the classical, Puritan shape of his mind and outlook.

> *Is the C.P.A. prepared to take a stand for accuracy in corporation accounts? May not C.P.A. stand for Conscience, Probity, Accuracy?... Stand therefore as a profession not merely for technical accuracy; be not content with the justification of business precedent but set a new standard; stand for high professional ideas; be uncompromising in demanding truth and as a result you will find the profession rise in dignity.*
>
> —Remarks to San Francisco CPAs, 1905-1906

1930-1945: EARLY BOOKKEEPING HISTORY AND SUNDRY WRITINGS

Continuing Interest in Bookkeeping History[1]

As part of his large intellectual curiosity in the history of bookkeeping, Hatfield became an accomplished bibliophile. Since at least 1924, he had been actively purchasing early tracts on bookkeeping both for his personal library and for the university's library. An anonymous benefactor contributed the funds for most of the purchases for the university library. That benefactor can now be identified as James K. Moffitt (1865-1955), a university graduate who was chairman of the board of the Crocker First National Bank of San Francisco, a long-time member of the university's Board of Regents, and an accomplished bookman himself.[2] In 1931 and again in 1939, Hatfield arranged exhibits of these rare books and manuscripts. The exhibit in September 1939 was held in connection with the annual meeting in San Francisco of the American Institute of Accountants, for which he composed the catalogue of works on display.[3] Then, in the early 1930s, Hatfield advised Walter Hausdorfer (1898-1970), librarian of Columbia University's School of Business library, including its Montgomery Library,[4] on the preparation of a "Bibliography of Accounting Texts (historical)," which, in the event, did not find a publisher until after Hausdorfer's death.[5]

Hatfield's interest in early bookkeeping history was apparently more as an antiquarian, stimulated by his classical studies in high school and college.[6] In addition to searching Europe for early works on bookkeeping, he wrote a number of short pieces, reviewed books on the subject, and carried on correspondence with Pieter Kats (1866-1941),[7] Cosmo Gordon (1886-1965),[8] Florence Edler, Raymond de Roover (1904-1972), and other kindred spirits, but he never published any substantial research on the subject. In correspondence, de Roover has written:

> [On the origins of double-entry bookkeeping] Hatfield never wrote anything of momentous importance or of great originality. He gave some publicity in [the United States] to the works of Besta and Penndorf. He also inspired and encouraged the endeavours of people like A. C. Littleton and myself.[9]

Hatfield's bibliophilic interest in early works on bookkeeping was perhaps best exemplified by his joint article with A.C. Littleton, "A Check-List of Early Bookkeeping Texts," published in *The Accounting Review* of September 1932. The article was a labor of love. The authors catalogued the bookkeeping textbooks published prior to 1850 that were held by one or more of nine university libraries, four society libraries, and four private collections, all in North America, and they identified which of the institutions held each item. The article was intended to supplement the catalogue of the extensive Montgomery Library at Columbia University. The success of Hatfield's indefatigable scouting for such books for the University of California library is evidenced by the many texts that, according to the article, were held in the university's collection. Of the 368 items listed in the catalogue, the University of California held 141, including important tracts by Flori, Gotlieb, Manzoni, Mellis, Pacioli, Pietra, Schreiber, Solórzano, and Tagliente.[10] Well behind Berkeley, in second position among the North American collections surveyed, was the Library of Congress with 93.

During the 1930s, Hatfield and Littleton exchanged numerous letters on antiquarian works that were available for purchase. Hatfield also corresponded regularly with Cosmo Gordon and other collectors.

In a two-page note, "The Early Use of 'Capital'," published in the November 1934 issue of the *Quarterly Journal of Economics*, Hatfield presented evidence that the term "'capital' was used by accountants sixty-four years before it appeared in other literature" (p. 163). Hence, to an assertion by Arthur Stone Dewing in his *The Financial Policy of Corporations*[11] that the accountant had appropriated "the economist's word 'capital'," Hatfield countered: "To the charge that accountants have in this instance committed the grievous offense of verbal larceny, I submit the above evidence to support the plea, 'not guilty'" (p. 163). The economist Jacob Viner has written that Hatfield's "articles on the history of the term 'capital' still have value."[12]

In "Accounting Trivia," a short piece in The Accounting Exchange section of *The Accounting Review*, published in September 1940, Hatfield ruminated on a number of bookkeeping customs that, in his view, had become anachronisms.

In his several reviews of treatises on early bookkeeping history, Hatfield showed his impatience with work that fell below his standard of detailed, precise, scholarly research, including: the faithfulness of translations and aptness of interpretations; the accuracy with which facts were rendered; and, above all, the completeness and freedom from error of a writer's bibliography. He was impressed by the novelty of descriptions or reproductions of previously inaccessible accounts and other records, and by fresh insights into the origin of terms and practices. Hatfield basked in the warmth of the historical scholarship he found in these books, but he was repelled by sloppiness and inattention to detail. He was so offended by the numerous mistakes he found in the first chapter of Wilmer L. Green's *History and Survey of Accountancy* (on which he reported in *The Journal of Accountancy*, April 1931) that he declined to read further and instead confined his report (not a review, he said) to a recital of many of the errors he found in only the one chapter. In an aside, Hatfield wrote that he was "personally more interested in the early history of bookkeeping than in the later developments of professional accounting" (p. 308).

Although Hatfield commended Edward Peragallo's *Origin and Evolution of Double Entry Bookkeeping*, which was a Columbia doctoral dissertation of which he was a reader (see below), he nonetheless noted several factual errors in his review of the book (*The Journal of Accountancy*, May 1939). Hatfield had sent Peragallo a list of *corrigenda* prior to publication and continued to do so by letter following appearance of the book. In his attentiveness to detail, as regards both published reviews and correspondence with authors, Hatfield had no peer in the accounting literature.

Hatfield had little but praise for R. Emmett Taylor's *No Royal Road: Luca Pacioli and His Times* (*The Accounting Review*, January 1943).[13] He wrote the author on November 9, 1942:

> With the exception of Chapter Six in regard to bookkeeping (which I read first of all, as it comes closest to my narrow academic interests), a subject with which Mrs. Hatfield refuses to

> be contaminated, we are reading the book aloud. It has opened to us a new vision, and we are finding it both enlightening, interesting and altogether delightful.

Reviews, Other Published Writing, and Correspondence

Reviews

Hatfield's punctilious dedication to sound scholarship, coupled with his beliefs about the principles to which accounting practice should adhere, can be seen in his published reviews of textbooks and treatises. During the 1930s and 1940s, he reviewed 19 books, all but four of which were for *The Journal of Accountancy*. Curiously, only one review appeared in *The Accounting Review*, the quarterly journal of the American Accounting Association, and it resulted from Hatfield's suggestion to the editor that he would be interested in reviewing the book. Reflecting his commitment to detail and accuracy, Hatfield read each book carefully, from front to back. He would often send an author a detailed list of queries and apparent errors. Even at the age of 77, he sent William A. Paton 14 pages of comments after reviewing Paton's *Advanced Accounting*!

In a review of both H.A. Finney's *Introduction to Principles of Accounting* and Frank Hatch Streightoff's *Advanced Accounting (The Journal of Accountancy*, December 1932), Hatfield found, not to his surprise, a substantial overlap of subjects covered by both books. Somewhat in despair, he wrote:

> Is there no agreement among instructors as to where these topics belong? It would be an interesting bit of research, for some zealous educationalist, to ascertain whether first and second year texts in German, in algebra, or in chemistry show more or less clearly marked delimitations than do similar works in accounting (p. 474).

Especially in *Advanced Accounting*, he found evidence that "accountants are still weak on theory" (p. 474). He also complained of inconsistencies of treatment from one topic to another, provoking a sarcastic observation:

> But why cavil at inconsistencies? Has accounting ever attempted to be consistent? It is to be hoped not, for otherwise the profession shows gross incompetence in carrying out its purposes, and incompetence is more disastrous than inconsistency. "With consistency," says Emerson, "a great soul has nothing to do." This should console accountants (p. 475).

Hatfield's review of *Twenty-five Years of Accounting Responsibility, 1911-1936* (*The Journal of Accountancy*, January 1937), an anthology of the writings of George O. May, is memorable for his recitation of beliefs and values that he shared with May, in which he underscored the importance he placed on ethical conduct by auditors:

> Among the substantive reasons for commending the work, the following may be mentioned:
>
> The emphasis which the author places on the fact that accounting is at best a record of opin-

> ion and judgment, and can not be considered a presentation of minutely and mathematically exact facts.
>
> The insistence on a high standard of professional integrity. This is all the more important because the statements to which the accountant certifies are incapable of objective verification and are reliable only so far as he is disinterested and honorable.
>
> The demand that the auditor should not merely avoid misstatements but should so frame his reports that the reasonably intelligent reader is not liable to draw wrong inferences therefrom.
>
> The author's objection to the establishing by statute or by commission of minute regulations of accounting procedure, as leading to lower, rather than higher, standards of accounting (p. 77).

The last of the these four opinions was one of Hatfield's few published utterances on how accounting standards should be set.

In a lengthy review of *University and College Accounting*, by Lloyd Morey, who was to become a leading authority on accounting for governments and educational institutions, Hatfield, from his work as dean of the faculties at Berkeley, had some firm ideas on the relevance of double-entry bookkeeping to such entities (*The Journal of Accountancy*, February 1931). He wrote:

> inasmuch as institutional accounting deals with funds (in the author's use of the term), with estimated income, and with appropriations, instead of with assets, liabilities and proprietorship, there is serious difficulty in adjusting it to the conventions of commercial accounting. This is not a criticism of the author, but rather shows the need of some new system of accounting calculated to deal with conditions not foreseen by the inventors of the Italian method (p. 145).

Indeed, he questioned whether the Italian method was even capable of coping with modern commercial enterprise:

> Systems of accounting [developed before Paciolo] ... served fairly well for the kind of business done in Germany in the fifteenth century. But with the expansion of commerce new needs arose and Italian accountants invented a method of keeping books better adapted to these needs. There is room to question whether this system, adequate to the commercial activities of the fifteenth century, is sufficient to present the relations of a twentieth-century corporation, with liabilities sometimes scarcely to be distinguished from proprietor's interest, or to present any adequate view of the value of a share of common stock, where there are many kinds of stock outstanding (p. 145).

In this reflection on the adequacy of double-entry bookkeeping, Hatfield almost seems ready to abandon the proprietary theory in favor of Paton's entity theory, under which liabilities and proprietorship are combined in a single classification labeled equities.[14]

Unhappily for us, Hatfield did not review John B. Canning's *The Economics of Accountancy* (Ronald Press, 1929). But, in a review of D R Scott's *The Cultural Significance of Accounts* (*The Journal of Accountancy*, September 1932), he did remark that Canning's work, as well as Scott's, were "flights previously untried." He added, "Pioneering aviators, even though failing to reach their goal deserve commendation for their efforts. So do these authors, whose works may serve as a stimulus to their successors" (p. 230). So he was sympathetic to their flights. But Hatfield seemed unable to judge Scott's idiosyncratic argument that accounting was on the way to supplanting the market as a control device. His review was uncharacteristically brief and inconclusive.

In his reviews of Streightoff's *Advanced Accounting* and of Willard J. Graham and Wilber G. Katz's *Accounting in Law Practice* (*The Journal of Accountancy*, February 1933), Hatfield repeated a point made in his *Accounting: Its Principles and Problems* (p. 443) on the valuation of goodwill upon the purchase of the stock of a subsidiary. In his review of the Streightoff book, he said, "There is the conventional inconsistency in assuming that a price paid for stock of a subsidiary in excess of the book value of its assets represents the cost of goodwill, when the price paid for the goodwill may easily be much less or much more than that excess" (p. 475). In the next sentence, he wrote, "There is the inconsistency, so beloved by many accountants, of showing only part of the goodwill, in the case of a consolidation of either firms or corporations, although there is no suggestion of showing only a similar proportion of the value of real estate." This suggestion that the goodwill associated with the interest of the outstanding shareholders (i.e., the minority interest) should be recognized in the consolidated balance sheet was close to his heart and was anticipated in his *Accounting* (p. 448).

Among all of the reviewers of Kenneth MacNeal's vituperative argument for the use of market values in financial statements, titled *Truth in Accounting*, Hatfield was the least dismissive of the author's argument and the most sympathetic toward his enterprise (Research Supplement No. 10 to *The Accountant*, January 1940). Hatfield wrote: "To this much-debated question the author contributes some good arguments.... Those interested in hearing one side ably presented will enjoy reading this book" (pp. 14, 15). But he expressed mild criticism of MacNeal's claim for a monopoly on "truth":

> he is somewhat ungenerous to those who hold the other view in that he repeatedly speaks of their statements as being untrue. It is just as truthful (whether as serviceable or not) to present a statement which professedly shows unamortized costs as it is to state estimated present value. One may prefer present value to original, or cost, value, but one is as much a fact as the other (p. 14).

Further, he found "a number of inaccuracies" in MacNeal's rendering of bookkeeping history and chided him for relying on a "crudely inaccurate book"[15] and thus for not being careful in his research for that section of his book. In October 1939, in the course of drafting his review, Hatfield wrote to MacNeal. In response to the latter's request, he sent him three pages, single-spaced, of *corrigenda* for the section on bookkeeping history. Hatfield and MacNeal continued to exchange friendly letters into the early 1940s. This was MacNeal's only correspondence with an accounting academic.[16]

Hatfield's review of Paton's *Advanced Accounting* (February 1942) was the last of more than two dozen of his reviews to appear in *The Journal of Accountancy*. Although he found fault in a number of areas, he concluded that "the treatment shows a mastery of accounting and a thoroughness by no means conventional" (p. 183). Based on his published and unpublished writings, Hatfield had a higher regard for Paton than any other contemporary accounting author.

Two Articles

Most of Hatfield's major published writings during the period 1930-1945 are discussed under topical headings elsewhere in this chapter. Two short articles published in the 1940s remain to be mentioned. The first, "An Accountant's Adventures in Wonderland," originally presented as "Some Recreations of an Accountant" at the 1927 annual meeting of the American Association of University Instructors in Accounting, was withheld from publication at that time because, as he later wrote, "I felt it was too much *infra dig*."[17] However, when Hatfield was induced to give a talk to the Los Angeles chapter of the California State Society of Certified Public Accountants on May 8, 1939, he dusted off his 1927 paper for the event. A year later, prodded by Howard S. Noble of UCLA, who had enjoyed the presentation in Los Angeles, Hatfield sent the paper to John L. Carey, managing editor of *The Journal of Accountancy*, for possible publication. The paper appeared in the December 1940 issue of the *Journal*. Making playful use of Lewis Carroll's "Alice's Adventures in Wonderland" and a few nursery rhymes, Hatfield illustrated a series of misconceptions of the role of interest in accounting reckonings.[18] The "Wonderland" article should be paired with his December 1928 *Accounting Review* article "An Accounting Paradox" as giving vent to issues involving the role of interest, which piqued his curiosity as he surveyed the literature in the preparation of the manuscript for *Accounting: Its Principles and Problems*.

On December 18, 1943, three weeks after his seventy-seventh birthday, Hatfield presented a brief paper, "Replacement and Book Value," at a one-day regional meeting of the American Accounting Association, held in Berkeley.[19] The paper, Hatfield's last, was published in the January 1944 issue of *The Accounting Review*. In the article, he argued that the book value of discarded fixed assets should not be a factor in decisions whether to replace the asset. He referred to letters he had received from "two [unnamed] outstanding authors, both leaders in the ranks of academic accountants" (p. 66) who defended the opposite view, and he asked his listeners and readers to register their views. The article evoked only one published reply, which supported his position.[20] In correspondence, Paton told Hatfield, "I agree one hundred per cent with your proposition that recorded figures do not in themselves represent objective facts. Some people seem to adopt this notion from time to time, but fortunately or unfortunately there is no tyranny of bookkeeping of this character."[21] One of the two unidentified "outstanding authors" was, indeed, Paton, who wrote in his letter to Hatfield, "I don't think you ought to be too timid about mentioning names. When we make blunders we ought to be spanked a bit."

Correspondence

A major portion of what we know about Hatfield emerges from surviving correspondence. He wrote a great many personal letters, which provide insight into his family and personal life. But his professional correspondence provides useful information for tracking his trajectory as an academic. Hatfield's output of letters was prodigious. His geographical isolation obliged him to depend on correspondence for the dialogue he so enjoyed with professional and academic colleagues. Yet, given the volume and character of this correspondence, even if he had been located closer to the academic and professional centers of the country, such as Chicago, New York City, or Boston, he would likely have remained the compulsive letter-writer he became as a young man. In both his lecturing and writing, he was forever collating and comparing the arguments advanced by authorities—academics, professionals, government agencies—for or against alternative accounting practices, and he would write the authorities themselves for a clarification of their views.

For example, during the 1930s and 1940s, Hatfield carried on an extensive correspondence with Howard S. Noble of UCLA; William A. Paton, at the University of Michigan; A.C. Littleton, at the University of Illinois; and John L. Carey, who was full-time secretary of the American Institute of Accountants and, from 1937 onward, managing editor of *The Journal of Accountancy*; among others.[22] As part of his correspondence with Noble (1893-1964), who was the senior accounting professor at UCLA, Hatfield (with the assistance of Catharine Greene) submitted, at Noble's request, many pages of detailed notes on the draft manuscripts of the 1935 and 1939 editions of Noble's revisions of James O. McKinsey's *Accounting Principles* (South-Western Publishing Company).

William A. Paton, as director of research of the American Accounting Association (AAA), was overseeing a writing project that A.C. Littleton was undertaking: a revision of the AAA executive committee's 1936 statement "A Tentative Statement of Accounting Principles Underlying Corporate Financial Statements." Paton wrote to Hatfield on March 31, 1937, "I am hoping that you can see your way clear to write something for the monograph concerning principles which Littleton is actively sponsoring." In the middle of mounting pressure to complete work on *A Statement of Accounting Principles*, which entailed the frequent exchange of memoranda and drafts with T.H. Sanders, Hatfield somehow found time to provide Littleton with an expression of his views on the "Tentative Statement," a searing criticism of its the logical structure, which he delivered at the AAA annual meeting in December 1937. (See the next major section for Hatfield's involvement in *A Statement of Accounting Principles* and for his critique of the "Tentative Statement.")

By the middle of 1937, Littleton was hard at work drafting the revision: expanding on the original, introducing more logical coherency, and distinguishing between principles and practices. He sent his drafts to Hatfield for reactions. During 1937 and 1938, Hatfield sent Littleton extensive comments on five chapters of his monograph. Hatfield later wrote:

> I read [Littleton's] preliminary draft, and frankly it was poor. Indeed it was so unsatisfactory to the Chairman of the Committee [charged with preparing an official revision of the "Tentative Statement"], Professor Paton, that he undertook to revise it. But that was a very difficult task. The result was such that the Committee was unwilling to sponsor it, merely agreeing to publish it not as a Committee report but as the product of Paton and Littleton as individuals.[23]

At the December 1938 AAA annual meeting, Littleton discussed the main points in his revision, without actually distributing copies to the audience. In addition to his editorial work on the rest of Littleton's monograph, Paton wrote Chapter VII, "Interpretation," a 37-page typescript that contemplated modifications of, and an expansion on, conventional practice.

Ironically, Paton and Littleton's *An Introduction to Corporate Accounting Standards*, published as Monograph No. 3 early in 1940 by the American Accounting Association, has had an immensely greater impact on the U.S. accounting literature than have the series of AAA principles statements, beginning with the "Tentative Statement" issued in 1936, with revisions published in 1941, 1948, and 1957. Unfortunately, the literature was deprived of a review by Hatfield of Paton and Littleton's monograph. In November 1939, when he was approached by John L. Carey to review the monograph for the *Journal*, Hatfield declined because of a fear that any negative criticism of the work might be seen, by Paton and others, as "the spiteful venting of a personal prejudice" in view of Paton's sharp criticism of *A Statement of Accounting Principles* in the *Journal* of March 1938.[24] When, on April 19, 1940, Carey invited Hatfield to contribute to a symposium of comments on the Paton and Littleton monograph in the June issue of the *Journal*, Hatfield declined again, this time owing to an attack of shingles which had invaded an eye. All that is known of his judgment of the monograph is the somewhat cryptic comment, conveyed in a letter to Carey dated November 15, 1939, that "Paton and Littleton's Statement ... is properly subject to very considerable criticism," which he amplified in a letter of December 8 to mean that "in some, perhaps many places, the opinions of the authors differ from those which I hold ... [but that] is far from saying that the thing is 'the bunk'."

In April 1941, Paton invited Hatfield to be a consulting editor for the section on Capital Stock in the third edition of the *Accountants' Handbook*, which Paton was editing for The Ronald Press Company. Hatfield accepted the assignment but declined to have "my name included in the list of advisors as the service which I might render in this matter does not entitle me to such distinction."[25] He rendered the service, and when the *Accountants' Handbook* was published in 1943, Hatfield's name was duly omitted from the list of Contributing and Consulting Editors.

1930-1937: ACTIVE YEARS TOWARD RETIREMENT

A New Course: Recent German Accounting Theory

Hatfield's all-encompassing classical mindset can also be seen in his interest in course development that ventured beyond the standard accounting curriculum. He had established his internationalist credentials in his textbooks and in his unpublished 1911 address, "Some Variations in Accounting Practice in England, France, Germany and the United States," but it is not known when he first acquired an interest in the writings of Eugen Schmalenbach and Fritz Schmidt, the two celebrated German theorists. In the spring semester of 1931, this interest became manifest, for Hatfield mounted a new graduate course titled Recent German Accounting Theory. It was a two-hour course and carried the following description:

> A study of the opposing schools of accounting theory, special attention being given to Schmalenbach's Dynamische Bilanz and Schmidt's Organische Tageswertbilanz.
>
> Prerequisite: a reading knowledge of German. The consent of the Instructor must be obtained before enrollment.[26]

Hatfield's requirement that students have a reading knowledge of German assured minuscule enrollments. He offered Recent German Accounting Theory again in the spring of 1932 and finally in the spring of 1935, following which it was dropped from the University *Register*.

Was Hatfield's course unique? One can hardly think of another American accounting academic who might have had the interest, let alone the knowledge, to offer such a course. Yet, Hatfield learned (probably from his brother James Taft) that an accounting professor at Grove City College, Grove City, Pennsylvania, offered a course on German and French accounting theory in the 1932 summer session at Northwestern University.[27] The instructor was Wilbur G. Collings, who held a doctorate from the Université de Lausanne. According to the *Accountants' Index*, Collings never published an article or book in the accounting literature. He was not a member of the American Association of University Instructors in Accounting (AAUIA) and was not known in accounting education circles. The description of Collings' course was as follows:

> *European Accounting Theory* (D12)   Credit to be arranged
> Dr. Collings.
> Prerequisite: Permission of instructor.

> The recent contributions of French and German writers to the literature of Accounting are critically and comparatively reviewed. The Schmalenbach-Schmidt controversy in Germany as to the merits of the "dynamic" and "organic" viewpoints in balance sheet construction will be examined. The methods developed by Schmalenbach and Mahlberg for coping with a depreciating currency are analyzed. Special emphasis will be devoted to the problems arising from periods of inflation and deflation, and to the methods of dealing with these problems, with reference to possible applications to American practice. The views of French writers, including Faure, Leger and Delavelle, are compared with those of German authors.
>
> Translated material will be available, so a reading knowledge of French or German is required only of those desiring extra credit for research work.[28]

Eight students completed the course, including Harry D. Kerrigan, who had previously completed a thesis for the Master of Science degree at Berkeley under Hatfield's supervision. As far as is known, the courses given by Hatfield and Collings were the only offerings in U.S. universities devoted to Continental European accounting theory,[29] and there is no evidence that the two men ever met or corresponded.

According to records supplied by the Registrar of the University of California, no students completed any of the three offerings of Hatfield's Recent German Accounting Theory, although one doctoral student, J. Fred Halterman, said that he took the course.[30] It is not known why Hatfield began giving the course in 1931, but it may have been in gestation since his half-year sabbatical leave in Europe in 1927, and it was perhaps given impetus by the Continental contacts he made at both international congresses he attended in 1929. At the New York congress on accounting, both Hermann Grossmann, rector of the Leipzig Handelshochschule (i.e., business school or commercial college), and Fritz Schmidt, the author of *Die organische Tageswertbilanz* (The Organic Current Value Balance Sheet) and professor at the Universität Frankfurt, delivered papers, and Hatfield met Schmidt.[31] Moreover, from the mid-1920s to the mid-1930s, U.S. journals evinced a considerable interest in German and French accounting. Much of the discussion focused on the accounting response to the postwar hyperinflation in those countries (especially Germany), mirroring the active debate in American accounting circles over whether the appreciation of asset values should be recognized in the accounts.[32] From 1929 to 1934, *The Accounting Review* carried as many as 16 articles on German and French accounting, including two written by Schmidt himself, as well as reviews of 23 books written in German, the two principal reviewers being Robert M. Weidenhammer of the University of Minnesota and A.C. Littleton of the University of Illinois. *The Journal of Accountancy* carried two articles by Henry W. Sweeney on German inflation accounting in 1927 and 1928, as well as two further articles on German accounting by other authors in 1931 and 1933.[33] By 1935, however, a sharp dropoff occurred in this interest, owing to the ominous political developments in Germany. In view of Hatfield's interest in the Schmalenbach and Schmidt schools of German accounting theory, it is puzzling that he never did any substantial writing on the subject.

During the spring quarter of 1931, Hatfield taught Accounting and Financial Problems of Management at Stanford's Graduate School of Business.[34] One supposes that the objective was to make some progress on his introductory textbook with J. Hugh Jackson and Thomas H. Sanders. Shortly after Hatfield's visit, however, Jackson became dean of the school, and not long afterwards he dropped out of the textbook project.

From 1930 until his retirement in 1937, Hatfield continued to offer Principles of Accounting, Advanced Accounting (retitled Unsettled Problems in Accounting in 1935), and Seminar in Accounting Problems. And he continued to attract nationally known accounting academics to the summer school. Fayette H. Elwell, of the University of Wisconsin, taught during the summer of 1930, followed in successive summers by William Morse Cole of Harvard University, Howard S. Noble of the University of California at Los Angeles, and Roy B. Kester of Columbia University. Elwell and Kester had been presidents of the AAUIA, and Noble was in line to become president in 1935.

During the first half of 1933, Hatfield was on sabbatical leave. On December 3, 1932, he and his wife sailed from San Francisco to New York by way of the Panama Canal and Havana. They then took a cruise to Italy and the eastern Mediterranean, where they toured Egypt, Palestine, Syria, Lebanon, and Turkey and then continued on to Greece, Venice, Germany (Munich and Frankfurt), Switzerland, Belgium, and Britain.[35] It was the most ambitious itinerary of their overseas trips. While in London, Hatfield was an AAUIA delegate to the Fourth International Congress on Accounting held on July 17-21, but of the leading German theorists, only Balduin Penndorf was present. Among the purposes of his trip was to continue to trace the early development of bookkeeping and to gather material for his course on Recent German Accounting Theory.

In 1930, Hatfield's salary was increased from $7,000 to $7,500, and thereafter until both Hatfield and Plehn became *emeritus* faculty in 1937, their salaries were the same. The university's salaries suffered during the Depression, and the salaries for the two declined to $7,309 for the academic years from 1933-1934 to 1935-1936. Then, in 1936-1937, their final year as professors on the active roll, their salaries were restored to $7,500. Others in the university were paid even more. For example, in 1932-1933, the highest-paid professors in a number of other departments received $8,000, $9,000, and even $10,000.

Ongoing Interest in Law and Accounting

The late 1920s and early 1930s were a time when the corporation laws of such important states as Delaware, Ohio, Michigan, Illinois, and Pennsylvania, as well as California, were overhauled. Numerous articles appeared in the law reviews and accounting journals on the new meanings of capital, surplus, and earnings, and their implications for the declaration of dividends. Hatfield himself contributed to this literature.

From 1930 onward, Hatfield was an informal consultant to Henry Winthrop Ballantine, a law professor in the university's School of Jurisprudence.[36] Ballantine had been charged with drafting the first modern corporation law in California, and he looked to Hatfield for advice on the meaning of the accounting terms that would appear in the draft legislation. The General Corporation Law (GCL) was passed in 1931 and amended in 1933,[37] but Ballantine and Hatfield continued to exchange memoranda on matters overlapping accounting and the law apparently into the 1940s. In his usual manner when researching a question, Hatfield scoured the accounting literature, made detailed notes of relevant passages in articles and books, and in not a few instances corresponded with the authors to clarify points. Yet, his work with Ballantine was frustrating. In 1936, Hatfield wrote, "Professor H.W. Ballantine ... has delved to a large extent in accounting matters. I find it very difficult, however, to find any common ground on which to discuss accounting matters with him."[38]

On November 1, 1932, Hatfield presented a paper on "The Accounting Features of the New California Corporation Law" to the San Francisco chapter of the California State Society of Certified Public Accountants.[39] His research also led to two articles. The first, "Accounting Principles and the Statutes," was a lengthy comment on an article by George S. Hills, a corporation lawyer whom Hatfield had met. In addition to making a few other points, Hatfield was critical of Hills for his use of inexact terminology: characterizing stated capital as an "amount of dollars" that cannot be "reduced" by a deficit and that, in certain circumstances, is capable of being "paid out."[40] In "Operating Deficit and Paid-in Surplus," Hatfield quoted from leading accountants in the United States, Germany (without translating the quotations), and England in support of the proposition, apparently rejected by others, that an operating deficit may be charged to paid-in surplus. He said as well that, as a consequence, "it is not unreasonable to argue that other expenses, which have resulted in an operating deficit, may ... be charged against paid-in surplus leaving any subsequent earnings available for dividends."[41] The article attracted considerable attention among members of the accounting staff of the Securities and Exchange Commission (SEC).[42]

Hatfield was apparently amazed at how little lawyers knew about accounting and found some of his exchanges with lawyers to be frustrating. In a review of *Accounting in Law Practice*, by Willard J. Graham and Wilber G. Katz (*The Journal of Accountancy*, February 1933), he wrote, "Lawyers look askance at the layman attempting to comprehend the arcana of their peculiar guild. Accountants, more generously, wish often that lawyers would learn some accounting" (p. 148). Hatfield expressed the hope that the book "succeeds in luring lawyers to study a subject they sorely need" (p. 149). In 1942, Hatfield gave the Dickinson Lecture on "Surplus and Dividends," which was a synthesis of his views on the interrelation between accounting and the law. The lecture is treated below.

Hatfield as a Creative Writer

Henry Hatfield may have been the first to publish both a poem and a fable in an accounting research journal. The poem, published in the December 1931 issue of *The Accounting Review*, was not signed, but it was by Hatfield. Titled "Meditations of a Student in Commerce 7, A Course in Advanced Accounting Theory (After reading 'The Raven')," the poem was written as an imitation of Poe's celebrated composition, and its message parodies accounting education. The student is depicted as being overwhelmed by the many authorities, routinely cited by Hatfield in his textbook and classes, whose views he expected them to learn. The final stanza goes as follows:

> Is there any rhyme or reason, any truth that we can seize on,
> Since the book that Fra Paciolo wrote in fourteen ninety-four,
> Books we've read in great profusion, but they all, without exclusion,
> Only add to our confusion, messing up accounting lore,
> English, French, Italian, German, only mess accounting lore,
> So does Hatfield, only more.

"A Fable for a Beginning Class in Accounting Some of Whose Members Objected to the Presentation of Alternative Methods" (Hatfield's full title), published in the September 1932 issue of *The Accounting Review*, imitates the Biblical parable to teach a lesson that Hatfield believed to be important in accounting education: accounting does not rely on one method any more than does football (or any other activity). In this "fable," a Young Man asks the Master to teach him "the Mysteries of Debit and Credit." The Master instructs: "Sometimes the Wise Men do this-and-that; and sometimes they do thus-and-so." But the Master is told by the Youth that "more than one thing at a time is too much for my limited Cranial Capacity." The Master then asks the Youth to explain the ways of football, and is informed that there is more than one kind of play. Thereupon, the lesson is revealed:

> Then the Master said, "Begone, thou Misleader of the Ignorant. I sought to learn how Foot-Ball is played. I would learn the one-and-only way and you have told me three ways and my mind is confused. If thou demandest that thou be told that there is only one way to toss a Debit-and-Credit, why tellest thou me there are three, and three-and-thirty, ways to toss a Foot-Ball? I will find me some one at a Coaching School who will tell me the one-and-only way and I shall be happy."
>
> But in this he spoke as in a Parable, in the vain Hope that he might perchance enlighten the Youth.

The final sentence, with its deliberate, almost awkward reference to the parable form, suggests that Hatfield was employing an even deeper irony in this didactic piece than a superficial reading suggests. Titling the parable "A Fable" may have been a subtle attempt to lampoon those accounting students who object to the presentation of alternative methods—more specifically, those who wish to avoid critical thought. From his classical education, Hatfield certainly knew the difference between a parable and a fable, a didactic narrative in which *animals* assume speaking roles. The allusion to a fable suggests that Hatfield was further questioning the intellectual competence of those who would reduce accounting to a series of mechanical processes disconnected from thought.

Hatfield wrote other poems that were not published. One poem, "Accounting," with the subtitle "Economics 14a" (the first half of his year-long Principles course), similarly attacks lazy students who see accounting as a mindless academic exercise:

Some trial-balance paper
  A place to write your name
Two rows of crooked figures
  Which add up just the same
Learning the foolish methods
  Of the Medieval Monk
Some call it Econ 14
  And others call it "bunk."

A debit and a credit,
  Some horses and a cow
Some losses and a profit
  A rule that tells you how
And all over ledger and journal
  A lot of foolish junk
Some call it double entry
  But others call it "bunk."

Paciolo's De Scripturis
  And Hatfield's hated book
Students taking their exes
  And passing by hook or crook
And dozens who lazy or stupid
  Are surely doomed to flunk
Goethe calls it "Schoenste Erfindung"
  But others call it "bunk."

"Meditations" and "A Fable" are reproduced in Chapter 7.

Hatfield Seeks Position with the New SEC

In September 1934, Hatfield wrote George O. May, the preeminent senior partner of Price, Waterhouse & Co. and the driving force in the American Institute of Accountants on matters relating to accounting and auditing, to volunteer to be considered for the position of consulting accountant at the Securities and Exchange Commission (SEC), which had come into existence on July 1. His letter, dated September 21, read as follows:

> The papers state that Mr. [Joseph P.] Kennedy's Committee on the Stock Exchange [i.e., the SEC] plans to have a consulting accountant. As you in times past twice honored me by considering me for a possible appointment, I make so bold as to ask whether you would be willing to suggest my name for that position. I presume that in view of your work in connection with the Institute's Committee on Cooperation of the Stock Exchanges you are in touch with Mr. Kennedy.
>
> Of course I am not a Certified Public Accountant and I recognize that this is a drawback. Perhaps it may be possibly in part offset by the fact that because I have not been a practicing Public Accountant I have had no entangling connections with any corporation whose securities are listed on the Stock Exchange.
>
> I do not know anything regarding the exact nature of the duties of the proposed consultant but in general a chance of doing some professional work of that kind appeals to me. If I should secure the position I presume I would have no difficulty in receiving a leave of absence from the University. The position, I am told, has already been offered to Mr. John F. Forbes and declined by him.
>
> I hope that you will not think I am unduly bold in writing you in this way, and of course I shall not in the slightest degree object if you do not see fit to mention me to Mr. Kennedy.

That Hatfield, at age 67, would be interested in such a demanding position, one that would remove him from academic life and his beloved Berkeley, suggests that his work at the university was losing its appeal. On the other hand, he had long been a critic of accounting practice, and the consulting position at the SEC would be a powerful base for promoting accounting reform. He had found his wartime assignments in Washington to be stimulating, and had written to his brother James, "My two months' work with the Advisory Tax Board was the most interesting thing I ever did, and I would have liked to stay longer."[43] The Board's task had been "to develop rules for the calculation of taxable income which were reasonably consistent with sound principles of accounting."[44] While not concerned with the rules of tax accounting, the SEC assignment would have involved developing norms and recommended practices and forms for the preparation and filing of companies' balance sheets and income statements with the Commission.

May's reply was not encouraging. In a letter to Hatfield dated September 28, he wrote:

> I participated in what was, perhaps, the first discussion between the Commission and outsiders regarding the appointment of a consulting accountant. One of the first questions raised was whether the appointee should be an accountant with wide practical experience, or one possessing primarily academic experience, and the sentiment inclined very decidedly to the former alternative. At the time, I suggested your name as being as good a selection as could be made from the academic field.[45]

As far as is known, Hatfield's inquiry went no further. During 1934 and 1935, Thomas H. Sanders, of the Harvard Business School, served as a special adviser to the SEC on the development of its forms and accounting regulations, commuting each week between Boston and Washington. It is not known whether his role was that of "consulting accountant."[46] As will be seen, in 1935 Hatfield joined Sanders in the preparation of a major report on accounting principles.

"What They Say About Depreciation": Hatfield Admonishes His Colleagues

The disquiet had been afflicting him since the early 1920s, and it had been intensifying since. Hatfield was irritated with the misstatements made about accounting for depreciation. In *Accounting: Its Principles and Problems*, he wrote, "it is necessary to discriminate between depreciation as a fact and depreciation as a term used in accounting."[47] In the accounting sense, he said, it does not represent a sum of money, it has no reference to profits, and it is not inherently a provision for replacing an asset. Hatfield's exposure of these misconceptions was indelibly etched in *Accounting*.[48] He repeated these criticisms in his series of commentaries in the "Symposium on Appreciation" in 1930. In 1931, he published a set of two exposés titled "How Can They Say Such Things?" in which he paraded a series of misstatements about depreciation, without identifying the offending authors. He concluded with the following lament:

> There is no intimation in the above that the author had an erroneous view of the nature of depreciation and profits, but if eminent accountants use language so loosely, how can one complain that the statements of lawyers and of judges concerning accounting matters are so often inaccurate?[49]

His intensified research into court opinions and articles by lawyers during the 1930s, spurred by Ballantine's request for advice, had heightened his previous concern to the level of annoyance.

At the International Congress on Accounting held in London in July 1933, he discussed a paper by the American practitioner and author A.S. Fedde on "Depreciation and Obsolescence," a subject, evidently, on which Hatfield was becoming known as a powerful critic. He complained that Fedde prescribed impossible roles for the depreciation charge: "to maintain the capital intact" and "to provide a reserve for replacement" and that Fedde tolerated as many as a half-dozen depreciation methods that are "contradictory in principle." Hatfield said:

> I am enough of an Hegelian at least to desire, when confronted by apparently contradictory principles, that an attempt be made to find some synthesis, which shows that while procedures may vary with differing conditions they all conform to one fundamental principle.
>
> There is no intimation of such a principle in this paper, and little hint of it in all the accounting literature.[50]

His exasperation was palpable.

His published review of *Depreciation*, a survey of legal and accounting problems prepared by the staff of the Public Service Commission of Wisconsin (*The Journal of Accountancy*, May 1934), was apparently the last straw. Almost the entirety of his lengthy review was a recitation of misstatements and misconceptions about the subject, yet it was written by a panel of experts.

In February 1935, AAUIA President Howard S. Noble invited Hatfield to present a paper at the next annual meeting. He accepted and advised Noble: "I give you full warning, however, that I have in mind the preparation of a paper which will attack everybody and probably make them all mad."[51] The result was "What They Say About Depreciation," published in the March 1936 issue of *The Accounting Review*. This article is reprinted in Chapter 7.

In his address, Hatfield spared few authorities. In all, he cited 44 offending works, almost all written by Americans. Most of the "household names" were there: Cole, Montgomery, Paton, Dickinson, Saliers, Sanders.[52] The essence of his complaint was as follows:

> Depreciation is a fact. It is a fact which evidently affects the financial status, or the operating results, or both, of the business enterprise. One seeks for no esoteric reason for recording the payment of cash, and its receipt, nor for the coincident emergence of loss or profit. But in the literature of depreciation, various alleged, but irrelevant, reasons for booking depreciation in its two-fold aspects are found. According to these, the booking is not made to record the facts but according to some, it is to "maintain" or to "provide" or to "replace" or to "reserve" or to "set aside" or as one of the most authoritative writers has it, lest "the investors be left at the end of the decade with no useful property" (pp. 20-21).

As in "How Can They Say Such Things?" Hatfield conceded that his criticism of the authors' language did not necessarily imply that they actually misunderstood the subject of depreciation (p. 26).[53]

After his recitation of misstatements, author by author, Hatfield said, "I do not claim my own writings to be free of these and similar inaccuracies, though modesty of course prevents quoting my own works." If there was a light moment in his fault-finding address, it was this convenient use of irony to excuse his supposed complicity.

Hatfield's Role in *A Statement of Accounting Principles*

Launching the Project

On May 14, 1935, Thomas H. Sanders (1885-1953), professor of accounting at the Harvard Business School,[54] airmailed Hatfield the following proposition:

> The Haskins & Sells Foundation is proposing that an independent committee of three persons, preferably of academic connections, be formed to conduct an investigation for the advancement of accounting principles. As you know, there is a feeling everywhere that accountants ought to do something of this sort or else principles will be forced upon us from without. They have been good enough to ask me to be Chairman, and I have said to them that I am very sympathetic to the project and hope it can be carried out. I understand that the Haskins & Sells Foundation would like to invite you to join the committee, and I am writing to say how very satisfactory it would be to me if you can accept.

Sanders proposed a further inducement:

> You will think primarily of the question of our joint book and of the time which may be required on this investigation. It seems to me that the studies we would make could not fail to be a valuable support to our book.

Sanders asked Hatfield whether he could attend a meeting on May 24 in New York City with John R. Wildman (1878-1938) of Haskins & Sells. Hatfield replied on May 16 that he "was very anxious" to attend the meeting. He was about to head east anyway, en route to Europe for a two-month trip.[55] Although time was short, Hatfield managed to make the meeting. On May 25, Sanders wrote as follows to Colonel Arthur H. Carter, senior partner of Haskins & Sells and chairman of the firm's foundation:

> Mr. Wildman has perhaps told you of the conversation which Professor Hatfield and I had with him, and of the fact that Professor Hatfield is distinctly interested in your project, provided his contribution can await his return from Europe early in August. On that subject I should like to say that in my judgment it is far more important to get Hatfield than it is to hurry the completion of the project.[56]

The project was Wildman's idea, and he had a high regard for Hatfield.[57] Wildman had been the founder and first president of the AAUIA, and had also been an accounting professor at New York University. Since 1918, he had been a partner in Haskins & Sells and was in charge of the firm's technical procedure. It was he who orchestrated the launching of the project.[58]

The mid-1930s were a tense period for the U.S. public accounting profession. The Securities and Exchange Commission (SEC) had been established in 1934, and a fear arose that, in the absence of authoritative advice from the accounting profession, the Commission would decide for itself which accounting principles were to be used in the financial reports filed with it by corporations. In December 1935, the SEC created an Office of the Chief Accountant, whose first occupant was Carman G. Blough.

Although, in its early actions, such as the *Northern States Power* decision in November 1934, the SEC signaled that it was willing to accept disclosure in lieu of ordering a registrant to change its accounting practice,[59] there were nonetheless apprehensions among professional accountants that the SEC might seek to impose some uniformity on accounting practice. In the December 1934 issue of *The Accounting Review*, Editor Kohler wrote, "Under the spell of rumored drastic regulations of the federal Securities and Exchange Commission, professional accountants are exhibiting a bad case of nerves" (p. 334). Sanders himself warned in the March 1935 issue of the *Review*:

> The work of the Securities and Exchange Commission is bound to have a vital influence in defining and giving effect to accounting principles.... It seems to be assumed that either

> accountants must speedily write their own principles in pretty definite terms, or the Commission will write them for us (p. 100).

He concluded: "The principles, practices, and literature of accounting must be advanced and developed to the point of being more definite, more helpful, to all the interested parties," and he recommended "friendly coöperation" between teachers and practitioners toward that end (p. 101).

About Sanders, Chatov wrote:

> An outspoken academic advocate of practitioner leadership in accounting theory was Harvard Professor Sanders, who, as might be expected, was held in high regard by the practitioners. In early 1935 Sanders was working [as a part-time consultant] within the SEC to help devise their reporting forms and procedures.[60]

Sanders was, therefore, a logical choice as chairman of the committee. Hatfield accepted, and William O. Douglas (1898-1980), a professor at Yale University Law School, was the third member appointed to the committee. The three committee members were to bill the foundation on a per diem basis. Hatfield's first billing rate was $50 per day.[61]

On June 16, 1935, the foundation distributed a mimeographed announcement of the "Study of Accounting Principles" and: (1) listed the items in the financial statements that Haskins & Sells analyzed in its annual survey of 500 published reports, (2) posed a series of questions for discussion, and (3) reproduced the official letter of invitation to Sanders[62] and invited interested parties "to submit a memorandum suggesting further topics, or questions, which have been found in your experience to be sufficiently perplexing to merit consideration by the committee." The announcement began with the following two paragraphs:

> The Foundation has arranged with a committee of three men from the universities of the country to make an independent and impartial study of the subject of accounting principles, with a view to developing, if possible, a body of such principles which will merit the approval of those competent to judge of their soundness, and thus attain to general acceptance. [the three committee members were then named]....
>
> The work of the committee will consist, in part, of seeking the views and opinions, with respect to accounting principles, of accounting officials of corporations, business executives, credit men, investment bankers, bank credit men, statisticians, prominent and experienced public accountants, teachers, practicing attorneys, government officials, national and state societies, etc.

Preparing the Report

Sanders and Douglas began their work in July 1935, with Hatfield joining in upon his return from Europe in August. In a memorandum to Hatfield and Douglas dated October 30, 1935, Sanders outlined the scope of the project and proposed the division of work, which included the following:[63]

As I understand it the assignment to our Committee stands as follows:

1. A statement on accounting principles as they apply to the published financial statements of corporations, and as determined from a study of the auditors' reports appended thereto. These accounting principles would presuppose that the underlying books of account would be so kept as to furnish the information and treatment specified in the principles. This I have always understood to be our primary assignment from the Haskins & Sells Foundation.

2. A study of accounting principles as they may be enacted into statutory law, in sections dealing with such matters as capital stock, surplus and reacquired shares. This section might include some discussion, together with model drafts of sections covering such points.

3. Accounting principles as they may be reflected in legal documents such as bond indentures, in their provisions for sinking funds, working capital, maintenance of current position, appropriation of income, and so on. This part also might take the form of drafts of model clauses for inclusion in such documents.

Items 2 and 3 have been suggested by Professor Douglas. Since he is a member of the Committee it seems to me very natural that we should undertake matters which without him we could not do anything like so well. I understand that Mr. Wildman, on behalf of the Foundation, concurs in this.

It will be natural that Professor Hatfield and I shall do most of Part 1, with Professor Douglas as reviewer. For Parts 2 and 3 we shall be dependent chiefly upon Professor Douglas for the primary drafting, with Professor Hatfield and myself supplying whatever assistance may be needed in accounting.

In a letter to Sanders dated November 14, the foundation reacted to Sanders' proposal for the committee's work. The letter, probably drafted by Wildman, underscored the foundation's desire that the committee lend authority to what was "accepted." A key paragraph in the letter was the following:

As we have viewed the situation, the pressing need of the profession of accountancy is for a body or code of accounting principles. The need arises by reason of the fact that in certain kinds of engagements accountants are required to express an opinion concerning the accounting principles followed by the clients as evidenced by their financial statements. In order, therefore, that this may be accomplished, it is necessary that accountants have some authoritative source to which they may turn for guidance in determining what are commonly accepted accounting principles. With a basis of that kind, accountants would be better enabled to judge how nearly in accordance with accepted accounting principles a given set of financial statements has been prepared.

Sanders kept Wildman informed of the committee's work on a regular basis.

In January 1936, Douglas was nominated and confirmed to serve on the SEC. He resigned from the committee shortly afterwards, but he asked to be kept informed of its progress. At Douglas' suggestion, Underhill Moore (1879-1949), also a professor at Yale Law School, was invited to join the committee, and his appointment took effect in March. This change in personnel did not affect the ongoing correspondence between Sanders and Hatfield on accounting issues, but Sanders, as chairman, needed time to integrate Moore into the project.

In a memorandum dated August 18, 1936, Sanders allocated specific drafting responsibilities and gave Hatfield the following subjects: intangibles (including goodwill), investments for control, reacquired shares, capital stock, surplus and reserves, contingent liabilities, the income statement (except for sales and cost of goods sold), dividends, and consolidated statements. In view of the general trend during the 1930s to give greater emphasis to the income statement over the balance sheet, it is interesting that, in his memorandum, Sanders listed the balance sheet assignments before those relating to the income statement, but in the *Statement*, the section on the income statement preceded that on the balance sheet.

The project proved to be an arduous assignment for Hatfield. At age 69 and separated by more than 3,000 miles from his two younger coauthors, he had to rely on correspondence when exchanging views, supplemented by infrequent train trips to the East Coast.[64] Moreover, Hatfield had no experience as a coauthor of such work. All of his published and unpublished papers on accounting principles and practice, as well as on bookkeeping history and on law as it applied to accounting, had been written alone and were composed in the language of a careful, punctilious scholar.[65]

But Hatfield participated as a full member in the work of the committee, and he made his points forcefully and persistently. He succeeded in moderating quite a number of Sanders' positions—for example, on the wisdom of conservatism. In his manner, he conducted an exhaustive review of the literature, in both accounting and law, made detailed notes on all that he read, and wrote lengthy letters to authors to clarify particular points. Sanders conducted most of the interviews of executives, leading accountants, and others.

A veritable blizzard of drafts, letters, and memoranda sailed between Hatfield and Sanders, who found that they disagreed on many matters. At one point, Hatfield wrote to Sanders, "I wish we were where we could talk matters over instead of employing the clumsy medium of correspondence." In a memorandum "Recollections of Henry Rand Hatfield" (reproduced in Chapter 7), Maurice Moonitz reports that Hatfield, in a moment of frustration, "came into the teaching assistants' room one day waving a sheaf of paper. 'Listen to this!' he said, and proceeded to read a definition of Prepaid Expenses, followed by one of Deferred Charges. 'Notice,' he said, 'the definition of Prepaid Expenses includes deferred charges and the one of Deferred Charges includes prepaid expenses. Both definitions are by Professor Sanders. What am I to do? I can't tell the man that *everything* he writes is wrong.'" In a letter dated December 23, 1936 to Paton, Hatfield wrote, "For Professor Sanders, I dare say, common or representative practice is good practice, but for me a thing which is clearly all wrong is not deserving of the label 'good' no matter how common." Hatfield's comment echoed his father's often reiterated views that "to innovate is not always to reform," that "truth cannot allow compromise," and that "what is popular may well violate our most fundamental principles."

Publication of the Report

The final version of the committee's report was transmitted to the foundation in November 1937 and was published as a monograph a few months later. In the minds of those at the foundation, two questions apparently arose. How would the foundation arrange for a wide distribution of the report, and would it be a violation of the ethical norm against advertising for the foundation to be shown as the publisher? Haskins & Sells was perhaps the most conservative of the major accounting firms on the matter of self-promotion.[66] At the same time, the Institute may have been looking for a vehicle for reasserting its preeminence in establishing accounting principles. A mutuality of interests must have been discovered, as Sanders wrote to Hatfield and Moore: "They [i.e., the Foundation] are pushing forward rapidly with preparations for publication. You may be interested to hear that they have been in contact with the American Institute, which has consented to bring out the report under its own auspices."[67] In January 1938, the Institute published the committee's report to the foundation, titled *A Statement of Accounting Principles*. It was distributed to its some 5,000 members and to other interested parties, and was placed on sale at a price of 75 cents. The Institute's executive committee would say only that the report was "a highly valuable contribution to the discussion of accounting principles" (Foreword).

Disputed Points in the Report

A Statement of Accounting Principles was a permissive document and was ribbed with compromise, especially between Sanders' and Hatfield's positions. Few alternative accounting practices, except those for which virtually no supporters existed among major accounting firms or large corporations (or so it would seem), were rejected. This outcome was not surprising in view of Wildman's charge to Sanders in his letter of November 14, 1935.[68] Principles were hard to find in the document, as the discussion concentrated on practices. Indeed, "principles" was defined in a way that made it little different than "recommended practice":

> The principles of accounting are, therefore, the more general propositions describing the procedure which should be followed in the making of records and the preparation of financial statements, if the functions enumerated are to be properly performed (p. 5).

Hatfield had difficulty with Sanders' definition of the term "principle." At one point, he even consulted a colleague in the Berkeley philosophy department on the meaning of the term. In a memorandum dated December 21, 1936, commenting on Sanders' draft of the front matter of the report, Hatfield (ever the critic) questioned Sanders' approach to deriving principles:

> There seems an implication that practice which "has persisted over long periods" is an indication of correct principles.
>
> I am almost inclined to make an exact negation of this, and say that the older the practice, the less likely it is to embody a correct principle. This may be because in earlier days very little attention was paid to matters of principle, and only in recent years has there been an effort to

> formulate and apply principles. This has been a progressive movement, with, it is hoped, a gradual reformulation approaching more nearly to the truth.... I would like to have the Haskins and Sells Commission appear as proponents of what Homer Pace calls "a better accountancy."
>
> This is not to deny, nor even to question, the importance of recognized practice. But the function of this Commission, as I argued in a memorandum sent you on May 19, 1936, is not to record what is the practice of 500 or 5000 corporations. That has been done by [the annual H&S survey of published reports]. It is to examine the question of accounting principles (pp. 3-4).

Like his father, Hatfield was less interested in sanctioning common practice than in arguing for what should be done.

In correspondence with Sanders, Hatfield argued that depreciation expense should appear in the operating section of the income statement, while Sanders preferred its inclusion in the nonoperating section. In its final report, the committee adopted a compromise, with which Hatfield must have concurred only grudgingly, allowing for an alternative presentation in which it was explicitly stated that operating costs were being shown exclusive of depreciation (pp. 33-34).

Hatfield much disliked the terminology "reserve for depreciation," but the committee swam with the current: "There is much to be said for [allowance for depreciation], but common practice has adhered to the older name" (p. 64).[69] The author of "What They Say About Depreciation" (published in March 1936, during the committee's deliberations) must have recoiled at paragraph (a) of the committee's statement on the "Purpose and Amount of Depreciation":

> There is much difference of opinion as to the purpose of the accounting provision for depreciation and, hence, much difference in practice as to the amount to be provided. On these questions the following observations are offered:
>
> (a) The main purpose of the accounting provision for depreciation is to allocate to the period a proper amount of operating expense. A further purpose is to maintain the capital intact (p. 31).

In addition to disapproving of the term "provision for depreciation," Hatfield had long been outspoken against the view that accounting for depreciation provided for the maintenance of capital. The best that he could do in paragraph (a) was to persuade Sanders to use two sentences instead of one. And the critic of Fedde's paper on "Depreciation and Obsolescence" at the International Congress in Accounting in 1933 could hardly have abided the abandonment of principle in paragraph (d):

> (d) It is agreed among accountants that the allocation of the total depreciation to the several fiscal periods should not be capricious, though there is no consensus as to the preferable method. In the United States the straight-line method commonly is used; in England the reducing-balance method. Until some agreement is reached, the use of either, or of any of several variant methods, may be considered good accounting practice (p. 32).

In *Accounting*, Hatfield had railed against the illogic of "cost or market, whichever is lower" for merchandise,[70] but the method nonetheless was endorsed by the committee as "the primary guide" (p. 73). Also in *Accounting*, he had argued that bond discount should be subtracted from the bond liability, and not shown as an asset. Yet, the committee concluded:

> The custom of carrying in the balance-sheet, as deferred charges, the balances arising from the issuance of long-term obligations at less than par, and from the expenses incurred in connection with such issues, is general and proper....
>
> The discount is in a sense an offset to the liability from which it arises, having the mathematical effect of reducing that liability to its present worth. But the practice is well established of showing the bond liability at its face value (p. 78).

The report also accepted as a "convention" in the preparation of balance sheets that "certain deferred charges to income, which are like assets only in that they are deferred charges, are listed on the assets side" (p. 57). Hatfield must have swallowed hard upon reading this tortured logic. One class of such "deferred charges" was the following:

> Impairment of net worth, particularly unusual or catastrophic losses which do not pertain to future operations but which the management decides to amortize gradually, instead of charging at once to current income or to surplus or absorbing as a reduction of capital stock (p. 57).

There could be no better example of an artificial leveling of profits. Hatfield had written in *Accounting* that such an item "is in no sense an asset, properly speaking not even a deferred charge" (p. 128).

Although the committee said that reacquired stock "is, strictly speaking, not an asset" and "should preferably be shown as a deduction from capital stock issued," it compromised its recommendation in the light of the figures presented in a survey of 500 balance sheets for the years 1933 to 1936 (p. 90). The survey showed that the number of companies classifying reacquired stock as an asset, while declining, was still significant. Not willing to be critical of current practice, the committee temporized thus: "It is unwise to make a fixed rule, however, since some circumstances seem to require, or at least to justify, its treatment as an asset" (p. 90). Hatfield would have preferred to show, by way of a footnote in the report, including citations, that "The majority of writers on accounting confirm the opinion that reacquired stock should not be listed as an asset." But this statement as well as his footnote were deleted.

Virtually all of the 22 pages of footnotes, comprising some 16 percent of the report, referred to court opinions, statutes, legal treatises, and the regulations of government agencies, all contributed by Moore. Only five citations alluded to the whole of the accounting literature: one to a survey of published reports by Mortimer B. Daniels (p. 132); three citing the views of senior partners of major accounting firms (Arthur E. Andersen, p. 117; Robert H. Montgomery, pp.

134-135; and Arthur Lowes Dickinson, p. 135); and only one to a textbook written by an academic (Roy B. Kester's *Advanced Accounting*, p. 129). Hatfield would have preferred to include citations of the opinions of accounting authorities on one or the other side of disputed accounting practices, but his efforts in this direction were not supported. Haskins & Sells had been making annual surveys of published reports since 1933, and these were provided to the committee as evidence of the degree of acceptance of particular accounting practices.[71]

Sanders took into account many of Hatfield's suggestions, especially on the tenor of the report and the use of terminology, and the resulting text was probably more cautiously and carefully phrased than would otherwise have been the case. Moreover, the committee concluded that, in the case of no-par stock, the amount of the consideration received therefor that should be credited to capital stock "is a matter for the determination of the management" (p. 88), a position that Hatfield had argued at the international congress in 1929. He succeeded in persuading the committee that the purchase of treasury shares "out of surplus" was a misleading construction (p. 91). But these were minor points. On most of the major substantive issues, Sanders, as chairman, prevailed. One suspects that Sanders was attuned to the sentiment within the foundation against an attempt by the committee to dislodge an established accounting practice from "general acceptance." Wildman and others in the foundation regularly read the committee's drafts and conveyed their reactions to Sanders.

Anson Herrick, a prominent San Francisco practitioner with whom Hatfield exchanged lengthy correspondence on accounting issues over the years and who was interviewed by Hatfield on behalf of the committee, has said that Hatfield had "as much to do with Sanders-Hatfield-Moore as I did."[72] In a letter sent in March 1938, Herrick wrote, "In point of fact I am quite sure that Professor Sanders and not Professor Hatfield bore the laboring oar for I am quite sure that, had Professor Hatfield led, some of the inconsistencies and other points which are open to criticism would not have appeared."[73]

Sanders the Pragmatist and Hatfield the Scholar could not have found their partnership to be an easy one. Sanders may have been too willing to accede to established practice, while Hatfield may have innocently believed that, in its deliberations, the committee would be concerned "not only with correct principles, but also with the niceties of formulation, the avoidance of vagueness, the respect due to the English language, with freedom from solecisms and adherence to logical consistency."[74] Hatfield was decidedly not comfortable as a source of *ex cathedra* pronouncements on proper practice. However, he held Harvard in awe, and Sanders was a determined chairman.

Others in Hatfield's position might have dissociated themselves from the *Statement*. Perhaps a younger Hatfield, more aggressive than in his later years and less impressed by the Harvard mystique, would have withdrawn as coauthor of a volume with which he was so fundamentally in disagreement. He may have believed, however, that half a loaf was better than none, and there always existed the prospect that he might persuade Sanders and Moore to his side in a revision. Yet, a man for whom correct expression and principled thinking were basic tenets could not have been at peace with himself as a signatory of the report.

Changing External Pressures

The committee's report was published in a rather different climate than that which had prevailed when it was appointed in 1935. In the June 1936 issue of *The Accounting Review*, the executive committee of the American Accounting Association (AAA, the newly adopted name of the AAUIA) published "A Tentative Statement of Accounting Principles Affecting Corporate Reports" as guidance to the Securities and Exchange Commission.[75] The principal authors of the statement were AAA president and *Review* editor Eric L. Kohler, William A. Paton, A.C. Littleton, Howard C. Greer, and Russell A. Stevenson.[76] Kohler had been publicly critical of the American Institute of Accountants for not taking the lead in defining accounting standards, and he called upon academics to fill the void.[77] The AAA's "Tentative Statement," a ringing endorsement of historical cost accounting, was the academic response.[78] A key passage was the following:

> The basic assumption made here is that a corporation's periodic financial statements should be continuously in accord with a single coordinated body of accounting theory, and that the purpose of the statements is the expression, in financial terms, of the utilization of the economic resources of the enterprise and the resultant changes in and position of the interests of creditors and investors. Accounting is thus not essentially a process of valuation, but the allocation of historical costs and revenues to the current and succeeding fiscal periods. Each of the following propositions embodies a corollary of this fundamental axiom (p. 188).

The 20 follow-on propositions were declarative statements of proper practice, dealing with costs and values, measurement of income, and capital surplus, but were not shown to be corollaries of the "fundamental axiom."

Carman G. Blough, the SEC chief accountant, praised the "Tentative Statement" as "a real contribution to the accounting profession."[79] But *The Journal of Accountancy* ignored it, and some within the AAA suspected that leading members of the Institute believed that "the teachers were trespassing on a preserve that belonged to practitioners."[80] It was a time of friction between leaders of the AAA and of the Institute.[81]

Also, the SEC chief accountant was stepping up the pressure on the profession. In a speech to the AAA annual meeting in December 1936, published in the March 1937 issue of *The Accounting Review*, Blough made it clear that the commission sought an authoritative statement of "generally accepted accounting principles," as well as a greater degree of uniformity of practice. He said:

> Almost daily, principles that for years I had thought were definitely accepted among the members of the profession are violated in a registration statement prepared by some accountant in

> whom I have high confidence. Indeed, an examination of hundreds of statements filed with our Commission almost leads one to the conclusion that aside from the simple rules of double entry bookkeeping, there are very few principles of accounting upon which the accountants of this country are in agreement.[82]

The AAA's "Tentative Statement" and Blough's address did not go unnoticed within Haskins & Sells. In a letter to Hatfield dated April 16, 1937, Sanders wrote:

> our friends in the Foundation ... are very much concerned by the amount of activity in accounting principles, as evidenced among other things by the recent issue of *The Accounting Review*, and the pronouncements of Mr. Blough of the S.E.C. They feel that it is somewhat urgent that we at least appear to be in the orchestra, even if we do not offer solos. Specifically, they were eager that we furnish them with a report in time for it to be issued in October. This would enable the accountants to consider it in connection with the annual closings.

Sanders proceeded to accelerate the pace of the committee's work, which meant that the lengthy and thoughtful exchanges of views between Hatfield and Sanders had to give way to difficult decision-making and the completion of the manuscript. Nonetheless, Sanders and Moore accepted virtually all of the last-minute changes that Hatfield recommended in the final draft of the report.

Published Reactions

Comments on *A Statement of Accounting Principles* were not long in coming. Within a scant two months, William A. Paton published a devastating criticism of the report. He began:

> In view of the distinguished authorship of this statement, I was expecting a report which would be outstanding in scholarly approach, in clarity of expression, and in sound and constructive formulation. Perhaps my hopes were unwarrantedly high. In any event, my general reaction to this statement, notwithstanding its many obvious merits, is one of keen disappointment.[83]

Paton disliked its lack of "substantive recommendations." He said, "In general, what the authors seem to be saying to business management is, 'Give the problem careful consideration and then do as you think best, subject to legal limitations'" (p. 196). He criticized the report for its "discouraging ambiguity and pussyfooting" over whether depreciation was an operating expense, and he wondered how the author of "What They Say About Depreciation" could be allied with such an equivocal position (p. 197). He devoted most of his article to reciting his objections to "cost or market, whichever is lower," which the committee had accepted as "the primary guide" for inventories. Paton pointed out that Hatfield, in *Accounting*, had "very effectively demonstrated" how "unsound and nonconservative" this method was (p. 201).

While several commentators responded, on balance, favorably to the report, others, like Paton, were negative. James L. Dohr, of Columbia University, said that he would have been even more critical than Paton.[84] Andrew Barr, of Yale University, agreed in general with Paton and believed that "A better title for their statement would have been *A Statement of Accounting Practices*, with a footnote referring to Professor Hatfield's book for a statement of principles."[85] Eric L. Kohler, who had recently presented the views of the AAA executive committee on the principles that should govern the preparation of consolidated financial statements, said, "the authors of *A Statement of Accounting Principles* have fragmentary and astonishingly naïve notions of consolidated statements."[86] In the annotated bibliography included in *An Introduction to Corporate Accounting Standards* (American Accounting Association, 1940) by Paton and A.C. Littleton, the *Statement* is dismissively characterized as "a summary of existing accounting practices and the present law of dividends" (p. 149). On the other side of the Atlantic, Ronald S. Edwards "found the report a disappointing piece of work" and would have liked to see an economist on the team of authors.[87]

Three later assessments are of interest. In 1964, Reed K. Storey wrote that the committee's "emphasis was on codification of accounting practice rather than on re-examination of individual practices. The result was largely uncritical acceptance of existing methods. The committee took the position that … the judgment of 'sound business management' determined appropriate accounting principles."[88] In 1967, Carman G. Blough, who had been the SEC's chief accountant when the *Statement* was published, wrote, "Without detracting from the great amount of work that went into the study and the comprehensive picture of what the accounting practices were, it must be said that the report did little, if anything, to narrow the areas of differences."[89] In 1979, Andrew Barr, who was a member of the SEC's accounting staff from 1938 to 1972, wrote that the report "was a useful inventory of then-current practice but it condoned some financial reporting practices which the SEC was finding unacceptable."[90]

Hatfield's Critique of the AAA's "Tentative Statement"

There may have been a tincture of vindictiveness in the tone of Paton's and Kohler's criticisms since, at the AAA's annual meeting held in December 1937, Hatfield had dissected the AAA executive committee's "Tentative Statement" and exposed cracks in its logical structure. His opening remarks would have immediately placed the AAA's leaders on guard:

> In this paper I am taking upon myself an ungracious and perhaps discreditable role—that of neglecting the substance of the *Tentative Statement* and limiting my comments to matters of form and expression, leaving to others the weightier matters of the law and confining myself to mint, anise and cummin. I have felt the ignominy of my position but have constructed a defense mechanism by rationalizing my conduct as follows:

> After all the American Accounting Association is largely an academic body. As such it is concerned in its semi-official enunciations not only with correct principles, but also with the niceties of formulation, the avoidance of vagueness, the respect due to the English language, with freedom from solecisms and adherence to logical consistency. So eminent a body should, like Caesar's wife, be free from ordinary frailties. Is this a sufficient alibi for my leaving to others the discussion of the substance of the report? I hope so.

He then undertook, with characteristic Hatfieldian verve, to expose defects in the arguments used by the AAA executive committee to support positions for or against particular accounting principles or practices. In particular, he zeroed in on the committee's "fundamental axiom" that accounting "is not essentially a process of valuation, but the allocation of historical costs and revenues to the current and succeeding fiscal periods."[91] "But what kind of an axiom is it," he asked, "when Wildman and Kester, and Dickinson and Schmidt and Canning deny its universality?" He also doubted that 10 of the 20 "corollaries" truly were corollaries.

Kohler and Paton were both members of the executive committee, the former having been the leader of the project. The AAA's officers had probably hoped that Hatfield, who was revered as the dean of accounting academics, would give added luster to the association's effort to play a leading role in establishing accounting principles. The warm glow from Hatfield's "Historical Defense" in 1923 could still be felt, and his "Some Recreations of an Accountant," presented to the AAUIA in 1927, had been entertaining. But at the 1935 and 1937 annual meetings of the AAUIA/AAA, Hatfield's adeptness as a critic was on display.

For unknown reasons, Hatfield's 1937 address, "A Critique of the Tentative Statement of Accounting Principles Underlying Corporate Reports," was not published at the time.[92] In 1941, Hatfield finally sent it to Editor Kohler, who declined to publish it on the ground that "a lot of water has gone over the dam since you read your paper, and I doubt very much whether you would maintain the same views today as you did then."[93] Hatfield was dumbfounded that Kohler could believe that he would submit a paper that did not represent his opinion, and he indignantly replied, "I wish you would do me the great personal favor of letting me know which of the opinions expressed ought to have been changed since 1937. In that case I will diligently reconsider them and see if I cannot revise them."[94] A misunderstanding existed between Hatfield and Kohler. Hatfield was unaware that the AAA executive committee had revised the "Tentative Statement" for publication in 1941. He had sent the paper to Kohler in 1941 because he had heard that the principles statement was to be discussed at the AAA's forthcoming annual meeting, not realizing what was to be discussed was a revised statement, not the 1936 statement.

A Reply to Paton

Sanders, Hatfield and Moore exchanged notes about whether to write a reply to Paton, and it was agreed that, after a time, they might write a summary statement in reply to any and all the comments and criticisms but that "we should not rush in to answer every individual criticism."[95] For his part, Hatfield wrote, "I am inclined to the opinion that it would be wiser and more dignified for the committee not to make a joint reply [to Paton]. We have shot our bolt."[96]

Four years later, Hatfield could no longer resist the opportunity to tweak Paton's nose. He wrote a lengthy letter to the *Journal* (October 1942, pp. 355-357) in which he criticized the use by an unnamed author "in an article in THE JOURNAL for March, 1938 (page 204)" of an arithmetical illustration to "prove" the superiority of "cost" over "cost or market, whichever is lower." Two months later, Paton replied with zest. After identifying himself as the culprit, he wrote:

> Why Professor Hatfield has waited four and a half years to show me up is something of a mystery. In view of his well earned reputation as an antiquarian it may be due to a conviction that nothing is worth reading until it has had a chance to ripen for at least four or five years I can't believe that it has taken him several years to ferret out the weakness in my example, and it's hard to believe that he's had the goods on me all this time and has simply been "playing possum."
>
> There's not much hope of rehabilitating anything Professor Hatfield has undertaken to demolish. The only thing to do in such circumstances is to admit error, pray for forgiveness, and promise to sin no more. Professor Hatfield's point is well taken; the example he refers to is purely hypothetical (which any reader would probably recognize) and is illustrative rather than demonstrative (December 1942, p. 541).

Hatfield wrote to Paton that his letter to the *Journal* had been inspired by his review of Paton's *Advanced Accounting*, published in February 1942, where Paton had used the same arithmetical illustration to prove the same point in his book.[97] None of the three authors of *A Statement of Accounting Principles* ever replied to Paton's substantive criticisms.

Impact of the Report

Moonitz wrote, "For all practical purposes, the report was ignored, both by practitioners and academicians, despite the fact that the report mirrored quite faithfully the best practices of the day."[98] Yet, evidence exists that the report was used to buttress current practice.[99] Although Storey observed that "The report seems to have had little direct impact at the time," he added, "The work was the first major building block in the structure of accounting principles, and it determined the form which this structure was to assume to a significant extent."[100]

A Statement of Accounting Principles has not been forgotten, as a sprinkling of citations to the report can be found in the authoritative literature as late as the 1970s and even later in accounting theory textbooks.[101] As noted below, swiftly moving events overtook the report, and by the end of 1938, the SEC and practitioners in the larger firms were instead looking to a committee of the American Institute of Accountants as the primary source of authoritative guidance on sound accounting practice.

Less than a year after publication, the Haskins & Sells Foundation and the three coauthors began to discuss whether to revise the committee's report. This matter is discussed in a later section.

An Unwilling Retirement

Hatfield turned 70 on November 27, 1936, and a retirement dinner for him and for Carl Plehn was held on April 30, 1937 at the International House on the campus. The university placed him on its retired list on July 1.

Hatfield was not ready to be put upon the shelf (as he put it), and he disliked the reclassification of his university status on the authority of calendar and clock. A year's retirement leave lay ahead, but he did not want it. In March, he wrote to Sanders, "I have an indefinitely protracted and personally undesired vacation after the fifteenth of May."[102] He pointed out to correspondents and, one supposes, to Berkeley colleagues, that he was not retiring. He was being retired.[103]

There were two surprises at the April 30th celebration. One was a booklet containing a handsome quarto reproduction of "An Historical Defense of Bookkeeping," together with the author's portrait and a list of his published writings. The booklet was planned by his admiring doctoral student Catharine DeMotte Greene[104] and financed by the Certified Public Accountants of San Francisco.[105] Hatfield was given a leather-bound copy. At the front of the booklet, one finds the following passage (with a suitable substitution) from Act II of Shakespeare's "Love's Labour's Lost":

> Another of these students at that time
> Was there with him, if I have heard a truth.
> "Hatfield" they call him; but a merrier man,
> Within the limit of becoming mirth,
> I never spent an hour's talk withal.
> His eye begets occasion for his wit,
> For every object that the one doth catch
> The other turns to a mirth-moving jest,
> Which his fair tongue, conceit's expositor,
> Delivers in such apt and gracious words
> That aged ears play truant at his tales,
> And younger hearings are quite ravished;
> So sweet and voluble is his discourse.

The second surprise was a bound volume of letters written by well-wishers. Among his academic colleagues at other universities who sent greetings were William A. Paton (Michigan), Thomas H. Sanders (Harvard), Roy B. Kester (Columbia), John T. Madden (New York University), John B. Canning (Stanford), William Morse Cole (Harvard), H.A. Finney (Northwestern) and J. Hugh Jackson (Stanford).

Henry and Ethel Hatfield in the late 1930s. In 1937, Hatfield had been made professor *emeritus* at the University of California.

The most distinguished of the letters was a warm and eloquent testimonial from Canning at Stanford. Although Canning and Hatfield were very different personalities and wrote along very different lines on accounting, they were both critics of conventional practice.[106] Canning held Hatfield in considerable regard, as is evident from the following passages from his letter (dated March 12, 1937):

> Even though you are a young fellow trying to get along it is high time some one spoke plainly to you. The fact is, you are an economist. I have been watching you for many years. Though you planted yourself years ago in a department of economics you have been putting it out to the world that you are a professor of accounting.
>
> * * *
>
> When I say you are an economist I mean it in a special, private sense. Disguised as a professor of accounting, you go prying into people's secrets. You peep into their account books. You ferret out the kind of things men use for information in their affairs. You stare rudely at their less than algebraic reasoning about simultaneous impossibilities.
>
> It would be bad enough if you had kept all this to yourself. But you did not. Ten years ago you published 474 pages of shameless gossip about it. You even called attention to the innumerable contradictions in it. This you excused by saying "The student may thus get a broader view of the subject...." You held out the solemn nonsense of judicial opinions, commission rulings, and statutory provisions so that anyone could see the intellectual sores and scar tissue. You referred to them as "these somewhat carefully prepared statements." You called the book *Accounting: Its Principles and Problems* instead of *Follies in Economic Behavior*. Problems, yes: but principles, no. Could anything be more unprincipled?
>
> * * *
>
> The things you have reported may be, for all I know, the frictional influences another kind of economist talks about. At any rate you have found grit that is often three times as big as the gear box.
>
> It is a grave thing, I know, to call a man an economist—even in trusted company. One must think twice: One must classify and qualify. But in any company of informed, hard minded realists one may, in candid truth, call you "economist *summa cum laude*."

One of the letters in the volume was from President Robert G. Sproul. Hatfield wrote to thank him for the friendly letter, and he took amusing advantage of a computational slip by Sproul to argue that his official retirement should be rescinded:

> Perhaps, when acknowledging a courtesy, I should not, in the same letter, bring up another matter but I nevertheless do so, saving time and stationery. There has been a shocking mistake made somewhere. I can submit documentary evidence that when I first came to the University of California I was still in my 38th year. I have the statement in your letter, and who shall question the word of the President of the University, that I have had the privilege of being a member of the faculty for 23 years. It is therefore merely a matter of common mathematics to figure that I am now 60 years old, and not 70. I trust that you will have no difficulty in convincing the Regents that they have made a mistake in putting me on the retirement list, and that the correction can be made so as to have the proper effect on the check which I expect to receive on August first of this year.[107]

Sproul's reply, if there was one, has not survived.

On the eve of Hatfield's retirement, a friend from town encountered him on the campus and said, "How do you do? I see by the *Berkeley Gazette* that the Regents made you an EE MER EYE TOOS [badly mispronouncing *emeritus*]. This is an honor you should have been given long ago!"[108]

Hatfield was one of the *emeritus* professors to be invited to continue teaching at the university at a fraction of his previous salary, a privilege extended to most retired faculty, and he accepted.[109] From 1937-1938 onward, including his retirement year, he was paid an annual salary of just under $4,000, in accordance with a university formula for compensating retired professors. His only obligation was to teach a small seminar, which he met once a week.

1937-1945: RETIREMENT IN NAME ONLY

Paton as a Possible Successor to Hatfield

The university secured William A. Paton as the Flood Foundation Professor of Accounting for the 1937-1938 academic year.[110] The economics department had hoped that Paton would be interested in succeeding Hatfield.[111] Paton taught the principles course as well as Hatfield's Unsettled Problems in Accounting, following Hatfield's habit of teaching the "first" and "last" accounting courses.[112]

As mentioned above, Hatfield held Paton in high regard. In a review of Paton's *Accounting*, which appeared in the November 1925 issue of *The Journal of Accountancy*, he said, "It is a pleasure to receive a new work on accounting by Professor Paton, for there is perhaps no other accountant who equals him in keenness of insight, careful analysis and penetrative interpretation" (*The Journal of Accountancy*, November 1925, p. 389). Sixteen years later, he repeated the earlier encomium and added, "This opinion is repeated and confirmed and should be emphasized" (*The Journal of Accountancy*, February 1942, p. 184).

Before Paton arrived, Hatfield had written to him, "I understand that you are at least coquetting with the idea of coming to the University of California for a year. If you make the right decision in that matter, would you be interested in coquetting with the idea of renting my furnished house for a year?"[113] He accepted, and William and Mary Paton and their two children stayed in the Hatfield house while the owners spent two months in Europe and the remainder of the year traveling and residing on the East Coast. Paton later wrote that he lamented the decision:

> [W]e foolishly rented Hatfield's house in 1937-1938—an attractive looking old place with nice redwoods in the yard. But we paid too much and had trouble keeping from freezing to death much of the time we were there. Apparently all the shingle and redwood homes of that vintage were built on the erroneous assumption that the Bay climate was such that practically nothing was required by way of stoves or furnaces. I wouldn't go through the experience again if the place were rent free.[114]

William A. Paton (left) and A.C. Littleton, two accounting professors whom Henry Hatfield held in the highest regard. Photograph was taken by the author in 1961. The University of California economics department recruited Paton as a one-year visitor in 1937-1938, after Hatfield had reached the mandatory retirement age, but Paton opted in 1938 to return to the University of Michigan rather than remain in Berkeley.

Hatfield was in Berkeley for short periods during Paton's visit.[115] Paton later recounted a hair-raising automobile trip to San Francisco, with Hatfield at the wheel:

> On one occasion he invited me to join him on a drive across the bay to a monthly meeting of the area CPA organization. No one had warned me that Hatfield was probably the worst driver in northern California if not in the entire U.S., and I was obliged to learn first-hand. We started out briskly on Le Conte Ave. toward the waterfront and before we'd traveled a half-mile I was uneasy. Henry Rand had a bad habit of keeping a foot on the clutch pedal, and pressing down a bit from time to time, mixing this with frequent variations in the pressure of his right foot on the throttle. The result was an erratic jerky pace, with no relation to corners or traffic conditions plus a considerable variation in the roar of the motor. Occasionally, again with no apparent relation to conditions, he put some pressure on the foot brake. But we finally made it across the Oakland bridge to downtown 'Frisco. Then came the real scare of the evening. We approached Market Street (if my recollection is correct) and on our left, as we came up to the tracks, a trolley car was approaching down the steep grade perhaps a quarter-mile away. There was plenty of time to cross, but my driver came to a full jolting stop, releasing the clutch and

applying the brake at the same instant. Then he took his foot off the brake and pressed down on the gas, with the clutch still out, with a resulting motor roar that was almost deafening. Our vehicle remained stationary, of course, and the streetcar continued to approach until the opportunity to cross safely was far gone. At this juncture, with the car perhaps 50 or 60 feet away, the noted Professor of Accounting, to my astonishment and horror, released the clutch, put on more gas and lurched ahead. The motorman clanged his bell furiously and put on his brakes sharply, but even so he missed the back end of our auto by not more than two feet. The sparks were really flying in the night air from the car wheels and the tracks. If there had been a cop around I'm sure my driver would have been arrested. The most amazing thing was that Henry didn't seem to be greatly perturbed by our close call. He made an uncomplimentary remark about careless motormen, and drove on coolly to our meeting place.... Friends on the faculty later informed me that Henry Hatfield had long been known as an incredibly absentminded and incompetent man behind the wheel of a car but had never—amazingly—been involved in a serious accident. All those in the know tried to avoid parking near his car on the campus, as he often bumped into the car ahead or behind him in parking, or in extricating his car, with unnecessary vigor.[116]

For personal reasons having nothing to do with Hatfield's house or driving habits, Paton decided to return to the University of Michigan after the year's visit.[117] Instead, he recommended Perry Mason (1899-1964), who was then an accounting professor at Antioch College, in Yellow Springs, Ohio, and had just completed his doctorate at the University of Michigan under Paton's supervision. Mason, who had written several articles, chiefly on depreciation,[118] accepted an appointment as associate professor of accounting and joined the department in 1938.

Hatfield's Only Accounting Doctoral Student at Berkeley

It has been a puzzle that Hatfield had only one doctoral student in accounting at Berkeley. Paton discussed this fact:

When I was teaching at Berkeley in 1937-1938, following Henry's retirement, I innocently remarked one day to Bob Calkins, chairman of the Department of Economics and also of the business ad[ministration] group, that California had been most fortunate in having such a man as Hatfield so long to stimulate graduate study at the doctoral level. Bob looked at me oddly and then explained that Henry had never pushed through a single candidate in accounting except Mrs. Greene (later Quire), and she didn't quite finish before he retired.[119]

Contrary to Paton's recollection, Catharine DeMotte Greene (1893-1978) defended her thesis on June 24, 1937, scarcely a week before the effective date of Hatfield's official retirement, thus enabling him to serve as chairman of her examining committee.[120] Her thesis was titled "The Dynamic Balance Sheet: A German Theory of Accounting."[121] A.C. Littleton, who happened to be in Berkeley at the time, attended the dissertation defense.[122]

For the next four years, Catharine Greene taught at the University of California, Mills College (in nearby Oakland), and Arizona State Teachers College, in Tempe, and then she returned to Berkeley in 1941. Hatfield regularly sought her advice on his writings and on books and manuscripts he was assessing, and they were in frequent communication.

She was Hatfield's sole disciple. As part of her doctoral preparation, she had taken Hatfield's seminar on accounting theory three times, as each time it treated a different topic. She said that Hatfield "dreaded" her doing the Ph.D. in accounting. He did not like telling people, face to face, that their work did not come up to his standards. But she persevered. She decided to study the German accounting theorists, especially the work of Eugen Schmalenbach, and she began preparing for the German language examination. Hatfield counseled that her proposed research would not be original. According to Moonitz, he "fought like a steer" against the topic of the German theorists.[123] He encouraged her to work for the Ph.D., but not in accounting. After she began her dissertation research, however, he was, she said, "of enormous help."[124] She dedicated her thesis to "H.R.H. the prince of counsellors."

Why was Hatfield so resistant to doctoral studies in accounting? Robert Gordon Sproul, president of the university from 1930 to 1958, believed that Hatfield feared embarrassment if a recommendation from him on the worthiness of an accounting doctoral thesis were to be rejected by the Graduate Council, which, he thought, did not regard accounting as an academic field."[125] Paul S. Taylor, a long-time departmental colleague, ventured the view that the department may not have been too receptive to a Ph.D. in accounting.[126] M.M. Knight, another departmental colleague, said that the requirements of the department were stiff, and anyone desiring to do a Ph.D. in accounting had to meet quite a few requirements in economics.[127] Charles C. Staehling, Hatfield's longtime junior colleague in accounting, said that the department was probably a little skeptical of a Ph.D. with a major in accounting, although no one came out and said so. But no one encouraged such a major, either.[128]

It was Hatfield, after all, in his famous "Historical Defense," who pronounced:

> accounting is, alas, only a pseudoscience.... its products are displayed neither in the salon nor in the national academy.... The humanists look down upon us as beings who dabble in the sordid figures of dollars and cents instead of toying with infinities and searching for the elusive soul of things; the scientists and technologists despise us as able only to record rather than to perform deeds.[129]

He wrote in his Preface to *Accounting*, "Although the science of accounting has made marked progress, it is still in a formative stage."[130] Twelve years later, in 1939, he wrote, "It is pleasing to think that accounting [has] become enough of a science to arouse interest in its history."[131] In the *apologia* for his approach to teaching, presented to a class of his students around 1928, he said, "There has been too much dogmatism [in accounting] for so undeveloped a subject." These beliefs alone might have given Hatfield pause as to whether accounting had matured as a proper subject for doctoral research. Maurice Moonitz reports that Hatfield told Catharine Greene that accounting was a poor field for Ph.D. research. Once you press on the subject, he is said to have told her, you will find that it is not accounting but is instead law, economics, and so forth.[132] According to Paul Taylor, Hatfield believed that, to do better in accounting, one should do a Ph.D. in economics (or in another established discipline) rather than in accounting.[133]

Hatfield did, however, supervise many master's theses, which he believed were appropriate for studying defined problem areas, such as intangible assets, inventory valuation, stock without par value, when is profit realized, the form and content of the income statement (or balance sheet). His sometimes pungent criticism in classes may have discouraged students from taking a doctorate with him,[134] and it may go some distance toward explaining why many of the master's theses he supervised were primarily descriptive, historical, or surveys of authoritative views, rather than normative. He encouraged such theses because they supplemented his own reading and raised questions about inconsistencies and anomalies in practice and in the literature that he enjoyed chasing down and exposing to criticism. To be sure, Hatfield himself was hardly a normative theorist.

Hatfield's master's students uniformly recall that he did not mark up a thesis with his comments. But if a point caught his eye, particularly a curious use of English or a misspelling, he would pounce. As an example, Charles W. Lamden remembers Hatfield's reaction to his use of "we" when presenting his own views. Hatfield scribbled, "Are you an editor or a man with a tapeworm?"[135] Hatfield also gave minimal direction to his master's students in writing their theses. He apparently wanted them to learn for themselves what the literature said.[136]

Evidently, Hatfield did believe that bookkeeping history was a fitting subject for doctoral study, since he accepted an appointment from Columbia University as a reader of Edward Peragallo's (1908-1990) doctoral dissertation, titled "Origin and Evolution of Double Entry Bookkeeping: A Study of Italian Practice from the Fourteenth Century." Hatfield was the only member of the examining committee with a knowledge of bookkeeping history, and he took part in the dissertation defense on February 9, 1938.[137] In 1943, he served on the doctoral committee for a thesis done in the Berkeley department of German, titled "A Study of the Fugger Financial Vocabulary, 1494-1525."[138]

In contrast to Hatfield's antipathy toward doctoral work in accounting, Paton at Michigan, Littleton at Illinois, and Roy B. Kester at Columbia (who had supervised Sweeney's celebrated thesis on "stabilized accounting") all had numbers of Ph.D. students in accounting during the 1930s. Paton and Kester also supervised accounting dissertations in the 1920s. At the University of Chicago, five doctoral theses in accounting were accepted between 1922 and 1937 on the recommendation of the business school,[139] and one accounting doctorate was awarded in 1929 (to John B. Canning) on the recommendation of the department of economics.

Catharine Greene may have been the first woman to complete a doctoral dissertation in accounting in the United States. She later wrote that Hatfield "was a firm believer that the profession of accounting should be open to such women as wished to enter it. In the late twenties and early thirties, he had a succession of women graduate students. Because of his interest, he conducted a sort of informal research among his accounting friends as to the opportunities for women. Periodically he brought back to us, with a certain whimsical regret at the foibles of male humanity, the results of his research."[140]

Hatfield's Attitude Toward Accounting Faculty Mix and Size

From 1912, when Lewis Lilly came to Berkeley, to 1937, when Hatfield retired from the active faculty, the number of full-time accounting faculty in the department of economics never exceeded two. When Lilly left in 1916, he was replaced by Charles C. Staehling. Except for the intersessions and summer sessions, when visitors did most of the teaching,[141] Hatfield recruited practitioners from the San Francisco accounting firms—beginning with John F. Forbes—to teach courses in which he and Staehling had little interest or competence, including:

Auditing
Public Utility Accounts
Cost Accounting
Governmental Accounts
Accounting for Extractive Industries

Hatfield would teach the "first" and "last" accounting courses: the two-semester Principles of Accounting sequence and the Seminar in Accounting Theory. Staehling offered the two-semester sequence in Advanced Accounting (including partnership accounting, on which he was preparing a book-length manuscript) as well as Accounting Systems, Analysis of Financial Statements, and Income Tax Procedure. Either because of lack of interest or for lack of time, Staehling stopped offering the income tax course after the 1925-1926 academic year. Curiously, the tax course—a staple in most accounting curricula—was dropped from the list of the department's accounting courses in 1933.

Hatfield's policy in regard to the size and mix of the accounting faculty was deliberate. In a 1978 interview, Lawrence L. Vance, who joined the Berkeley accounting faculty in 1941, provided some insight:

> The accounting faculty here at Berkeley used to be small, very small. I remember when Hatfield was in charge, the faculty waited for a chance to expand. Once he was away on a trip for a while, and the faculty voted in a full-time member! When Hatfield came back, he found out about it right away, of course. He killed it. He stopped the appointment.[142]

In the same interview, Vance said of Hatfield:

> He was sort of a philosopher, inclined to leave accounting to people in practice. Evidence: he used a lot of visiting instructors from San Francisco who were in practice. The build-up of the Berkeley accounting faculty occurred only after he retired.[143]

Indeed, not long after Perry Mason joined the department in 1938 as associate professor of accounting in succession to Hatfield, several full-time faculty with professorial rank were brought on board to offer courses in accounting: John G. Blocker (visitor, 1940-1941), Vance (1941), Leonard A. Doyle (1942), and Catharine DeMotte Greene (1943).[144] Greene doubled as assistant dean of women, and Doyle also gave work in applied economics. After 1940, all of the accounting coursework was taught by full-time faculty.

By contrast, at the University of Illinois in 1936-37 there were five full professors of accounting, two associate professors, and two assistant professors, all full-time.[145]

Hatfield was sensitive to the fact that he was not a CPA and that his experience in accounting was limited to having kept the books of the New York branch of a bond firm circa 1889-1890. His relationship with Staehling and the San Francisco practitioners (Forbes and the two younger colleagues in his firm) was comfortable, and Hatfield apparently had no desire to take on board another major player. Staehling was content to play "second fiddle" to Hatfield.

Montgomery as a Colleague-in-Arms

Hatfield was delighted to note that Robert H. Montgomery, the senior partner of Lybrand Ross Bros. & Montgomery, a noted author, and a professional leader, had declared his support for the terminology "allowance for depreciation" in the fourth edition of his widely respected treatise, *Auditing Theory and Practice* (New York: The Ronald Press Company, 1927). Montgomery had come a long way from his position in the first edition of his book, published in 1912, in which he tolerated the showing of "reserve for depreciation" among the liabilities.[146]

In the fifth edition, published in 1934, Montgomery strengthened his support for the "allowance" terminology. On November 19, 1935, Hatfield wrote to Montgomery that he had heard while in Chicago (probably from Eric Kohler, who was a member of the committee) that "you, as a member of the [Institute's] Committee on Terminology, were making a vigorous plea for the use of the term 'allowance for depreciation.' May I give you whatever moral support I am capable of in this most praiseworthy effort?" (In the committee's report, "reserve" won out.)

In 1938, Hatfield wrote to Montgomery that "now someone intimates to me that you are getting weak on the subject [of the term 'allowance'], perhaps reneging or recanting. If the latter is true I hope you are doing it with crossed fingers as Galileo did when he is said to have murmured, 'E pur si muove.'"[147] After Montgomery assured him that he was "more firm and more immovable than the Rock of Gibraltar" on "allowance," Hatfield was so joyful that he broke into verse:

> Your letter of July 8th was indeed a comfort to my soul. You are a rock in a weary land and a shelter in a time of storm. I am sorry there are not more practicing accountants who agree with

you. The position of Athenasius Contra Mundum is noble but awfully lonesome. But you are at least not entirely by yourself. I might liken you rather to Horatius at the Bridge. You recollect what Macauley wrote:

I with two more to help me
  Will hold the foe in play,
In yon strait path a thousand
  May well be stopped by three.
Now who will stand on either hand
  And keep the bridge with me?

Then out spake William Colius
  Proud Harvard man was he,
"Lo, I will stand at thy right hand,
  And keep the bridge with thee."
And out spake Hatfieldus,
  A Californian he,
"I will abide on thy left side,
  And keep the bridge with thee."[148]

Possible Revision of *A Statement of Accounting Principles*

In October 1938, less than a year after their manuscript had been submitted to the Haskins & Sells Foundation, Sanders, Hatfield and Moore were already discussing a possible revision of their *Statement*, and the foundation encouraged them to proceed. The sudden death in September 1938 of John R. Wildman, who, on behalf of the foundation, had planned and monitored the preparation of *Statement*, may have slowed their progress somewhat. On December 30, Sanders wrote to Hatfield that the representatives of the foundation "concur in the general idea of our committee that, while we should in the second edition make such changes as seem necessary, it was undesirable to rewrite the report to the extent of making it not recognizable as substantially the same thing as the first edition." In short, any revision should not be substantial.

In 1938-1939, however, the American Institute took several actions that had the effect of dooming any revision of the *Statement*. In September 1938, the Institute's council approved a proposal by its Committee on Accounting Procedure to enlarge the committee and establish a research department with paid assistants "for the purpose of preparing studies on particular questions, and ultimately formulating pronouncements on specific points which could be accepted as authoritative procedure by the entire profession."[149] In March 1939, the Institute announced that Sanders had agreed to become its director and coordinator of research, in charge of the new research department.[150] During most of the first half of 1939, moreover, Sanders was in Britain, giving lectures at the London School of Economics and examining developments in accounting there. Upon his return, he embarked on his duties at the Institute. He continued as a professor at Harvard and devoted as much as half of his time to the Institute. Clearly, by the

Institute's new initiative, the baton had been passed to the Committee on Accounting Procedure as the authoritative source of proper accounting practice.

In December 1939, Hatfield was still optimistic that the three coauthors would yet produce a revision of the *Statement*. He wrote that, although the work on the revision had been interrupted by Sanders' trip abroad, Sanders "sent to me last January some thirteen pages of suggested corrections covering ninety-three different items; and on January 29 I sent to both Sanders and Moore thirty-five pages covering one hundred and forty-five items."[151]

But Sanders, as chairman of the committee to prepare a revised *Statement*, found that this task conflicted with his new role at the Institute. The work of the Committee on Accounting Procedure, energetically directed by George O. May of Price, Waterhouse & Co., was to provide "substantial authoritative support" to the SEC on what constituted "generally accepted accounting principles." This was the first ongoing program by a professional accounting body anywhere in the world to establish proper accounting practice for companies and auditors, and the entire effort was undertaken to assure that the SEC itself would not dictate such practice.[152] How could a revised *Statement*, written jointly by the Institute's research director, an accounting academic, and a law academic somehow continue to be in the cards? The state of play had changed since 1937-1938. The SEC and the practitioner community now looked exclusively to the Institute's Committee on Accounting Procedure for leadership on accounting principles.

In May 1940, the Committee on Accounting Procedure created a subcommittee of three to make recommendations on a possible revision of the *Statement*. It was composed of Henry A. Horne (chairman) of Webster, Horne & Blanchard, New York City; Carman G. Blough of Arthur Andersen & Co., Chicago;[153] and Warren W. Nissley of Arthur Young & Company, New York City—all members of the parent committee. They recommended that the *Statement* be revised but, predictably, that it "should be drafted by the research department of the Institute, with collaboration by a small editorial group of members of the committee on accounting procedure, and with such reference to the original authors as this editorial group may deem necessary."[154] As Sanders put it in a letter to Hatfield, "The controlling factor in the situation as I see it is the general feeling within the committee that, if and when a revised edition is brought out, it will be brought out by the Institute and its contents will be well controlled and supervised by the committee."[155] Hatfield had hoped that he could somehow be involved in the revision, if only because of the considerable time he had already invested in the project, but Sanders counseled him that any such involvement was out of the question. In the end, no revision of the *Statement* appeared.[156]

The *Statement* was rarely mentioned in the Institute's utterances on accounting principles between 1939 and 1952. It was cited only once in the Committee on Accounting Procedure's 34 Accounting Research Bulletins and not at all in the eight reports issued by the Committee on Terminology. In the 30 statements published by the Institute's research department from 1940 to 1953, the *Statement* was cited only once, in 1942.

Hatfield's Address to the Institute's 1939 Annual Meeting

When the American Institute planned its 1939 annual meeting, to be held in September in San Francisco, Hatfield was again invited to give an address.[157] During the whole of 1939, the accounting profession was under the black cloud of the colossal McKesson & Robbins fraud,[158] and early in the year, the SEC had held extensive hearings on the auditing procedure used by the leading firms.[159] The SEC's report was awaited with no small amount of anxiety.[160] In June 1939, on the heels of the SEC's inquiry, *The Journal of Accountancy* printed "Extensions of Auditing Procedure," a set of reforms in auditing procedure recommended by the Institute's Special Committee on Auditing Procedure and approved by its council. In July, Hatfield was asked to give the opening address at a session devoted to a "Discussion of Auditing Procedure." The title proposed to him was "Review of Recent Developments in Auditing."[161] Hatfield's reaction to this title is not known, but he certainly had never professed a knowledge of auditing. On September 21, he spoke instead under the title "A Survey of Developments in Accounting."[162]

Hatfield's survey reviewed accounting developments since 1927, when he last addressed an Institute annual meeting. In that earlier address, he lectured his audience sternly for doing so little to develop a sound theory. He was less disapproving in his 1939 address, in which he reported detecting "at least some slight increase in the amount of consideration given to matters of theory" (p. 10). Recalling his struggle to overcome the heavy hand of accepted practice when drafting *A Statement of Accounting Principles* with Sanders and Moore, he emphasized the importance of using principles to shape practice. He counseled the profession, gently but firmly: define sound theory, have the courage of your convictions, and stop counting noses:

> The conflict between theory and practice is a false one, for practice to be sound should be related to sound theories. This is admitted by the practitioners in that almost all of their certificates state that in their opinion the accounts are "in accordance with accepted principles of accounting." It certainly behooves the profession, therefore, to know what a principle is, and what are the principles of accounting. (p. 5)
>
> * * *
>
> By some it is thought sufficient to find out what is done in published income statements and balance-sheets. (Whose balance-sheet is it?) On any point—valuation of assets, amortization of bond discount, showing of profits despite a previous operating deficit, etc.—the procedure is to tabulate the practice of many corporations, and swear by the results. This procedure rests on the dictum that
>
> ...spite of pride, in erring reason's spite
> One truth is clear: What ever is, is right. (p. 6)

* * *

> It is granted without even a mental reservation that rigid rules imposed on the profession by outside authority are inappropriate and harmful. But this does not mean that the profession should not have some ideas to which it desperately clings.
>
> Other professions are not so retiring and unassuming. Even in so inchoate a pseudo-science as medicine, the physician tells his patient where to get off, and sometimes he hits it right. Don't be so hypermodest. An inferiority complex, even in the presence of a great Captain of Industry, ill befits a C.P.A. (p. 10)

He welcomed the gradual recognition by writers that financial statements necessarily show estimates, opinions and guesses, not facts.[163] But at the same time, he advised the profession that there was "some danger in this attitude.... It may lead to 'loose and lavender language' or to what Professor Paton, I think less accurately, called 'damnable compromises'" (p. 9).

Hatfield was speaking at the end of a remarkable decade, which had begun in the wake of the stock market crash in October 1929. President Roosevelt's New Deal introduced the federal regulation of securities markets, including corporate financial reports, and created the SEC in 1934. The AAUIA transformed itself into the AAA and sought to have an impact on the SEC's accounting policies. And the American Institute, responding first to the New York Stock Exchange and, later in the decade, to the SEC, charged a succession of committees of leading accountants to publish their views on sound accounting practice. Notwithstanding all this activity, Hatfield found only small improvements in the accounting literature since 1927, and not all of them originated in America. As one might expect of Hatfield, developments in British and German accounting also occupied his attention.[164]

Hatfield's Support for Sweeney's "Stabilized Accounting"

When he reviewed Henry W. Sweeney's *Stabilized Accounting* in the December 1936 issue of *The Journal of Accountancy*, Hatfield wrote, "The treatment is scholarly and shows an intimate and intelligent acquaintance with a wide field of generally neglected literature in French and German" (p. 473). In an evident reference to A.C. Littleton's long and critical review of *Stabilized Accounting* in the September issue of *The Accounting Review*, Hatfield wrote that Sweeney's proposal "is one which accountants should not cavalierly dismiss on the ground that it is not 'orthodox accounting.' The profession should give careful attention to this work, and defer criticism of minor and unessential details until its main thesis has been grasped" (p. 474).

In Hatfield's critique of the AAA's "Tentative Statement" (which Littleton coauthored), presented in December 1937, he invoked Sweeney's work to complain that the committee had failed to differentiate "a particular change in price, and a change in the general price level due to inflation or deflation." Hatfield argued that changes in the general price level justify adoption of a "common unit in money." (Sweeney first presented his stabilized-accounting procedure in an article in *The Accounting Review* of June 1935, six months before the committee began drafting its "Tentative Statement." Eric Kohler, who chaired the drafting committee, was also editor of the *Review*, and Sweeney's theory had been presented in a series of articles in the *Review* since 1930. Hence, one could assume that the drafting committee was familiar with Sweeney's work.) It is evident that Hatfield was much impressed with Sweeney's theoretical argument.

It should be noted, however, that Hatfield showed sympathy as early as 1930 for an explicit accounting adjustment to reflect inflation, probably inspired by the writings of Schmalenbach.[165] Among his remarks in "A Symposium on Appreciation" (*The Accounting Review*, March 1930) was the following:

> If the dollar shrinks not by direct legislation but by gradual inflation, is there not some justification in holding that at a later day the more correct expression of the actual cost would be in terms of the then dollar equivalent to the former dollars paid out? (p. 14)

During the drafting of *A Statement of Accounting Principles*, Hatfield had urged Sanders and Moore to find some way of integrating Sweeney's proposal into their report, but the only fleeting mention of the point (in a section that was added at the eleventh hour upon the request of the foundation) was negative and defensive: "restatements of the money value of ... capital goods, and actual increases in them, are increases in capital in the narrow sense, and are not income" (p. 12).

In "A Survey of Developments in Accounting," Hatfield's paper presented to the Institute's annual meeting in September 1939, in which he was once again free to express his own views, he embraced Sweeney's theoretical argument thus:

> The discussion of the futility of accounting statements, when the purchasing power of the dollar fluctuates, as discussed in Sweeney's *Stabilized Accounting* [is evidence of progress since 1927]. The very accountants who proclaim the absurdity of adding disparate figures representing cost and present value have rather generally ignored the absurdity of adding dollars of different value. Sweeney's work is encouraging, whether or not his precise method of stabilizing is accepted as the correct one. (p. 10)

Hatfield's favorable assessment of Sweeney's theoretical argument is rarely mentioned.[166] Yet he was clearly one of Sweeney's most distinguished supporters.[167]

Elementary Accounting Textbook with Sanders and Burton, 1940

Before 1937, little progress was made on the elementary accounting textbook that Hatfield was to complete with J. Hugh Jackson and Thomas H. Sanders (see Chapter 3). Jackson had apparently withdrawn from the book by the middle of the 1930s, if only because of his heavy duties as dean of Stanford's Graduate School of Business. Sanders and Hatfield were, of course, heavily involved in the preparation of *A Statement of Accounting Principles* from 1935 to the end of 1937, and by then Hatfield was retired from Berkeley. Ginn and Company, the publisher, was becoming impatient.

Then, in August or September 1937, when Hatfield was traveling in Europe, Sanders invited Norman Lee Burton (1890-1976), an accounting professor at the University of Buffalo, to join the team, and he accepted.[168] Hatfield, who had never met Burton, agreed to the new arrangement reluctantly. Burton had received an M.B.A. from Harvard Business School in 1917, where he studied accounting under William Morse Cole, as did Sanders a few years later. Apparently, he came to Sanders' attention when Sanders reviewed his *Introduction to Cost Accounting* book in the Spring 1937 issue of the *Harvard Business Review*. A favorable recommendation from Cole likely played a role. In the spring of 1938, when the Hatfields were residing at the George Washington Inn, in Washington, D.C., during his year of enforced retirement leave, the three authors held their first conference.

Burton's recollection is that the first seven chapters and Chapters 15 (Special Features of Partnership Accounts), 17 (Surplus and Surplus Reserves), 19 (Offset Accounts for Depreciation and Bad Debts), and 21 (The Valuation of Assets) were to be written by Hatfield. The tally of chapters was to be 11 for Hatfield, nine for Sanders, and five for Burton, who was also to prepare the laboratory problems and practice sets. Hatfield, as usual, wanted to include copious footnotes, but Sanders and Burton objected. The book, *Accounting Principles and Practices: An Introductory Course*, was published by Ginn and Company in 1940. Hatfield was shown as the senior author, followed by Sanders and Burton. According to Burton, the book "was designed for a college's undergraduate school of business administration or for a one-year course in a college or department of liberal arts."[169]

Some of the differences between Sanders and Hatfield in *A Statement of Accounting Principles* found expression in the book. In Sanders' Chapter 16, "Special Features of Corporation Accounts," the Sanders-driven compromise positions in the *Statement* on the balance-sheet treatment of reacquired stock and bond discount reappeared. While Hatfield used Allowance for Depreciation and Allowance for Bad Debts in his Chapter 19, Sanders used Reserve for Doubtful Accounts and did not challenge the use of Reserve for Depreciation in his chapters. Anticipating this conflict, Hatfield wrote in Chapter 19, "Where, in deference to common practice, the term 'Reserve for Depreciation' is used elsewhere in this treatise, it is to be considered as synonymous with 'Allowance for Depreciation'" (p. 306).[170] In other respects, the book was representative of the class of elementary books then on the market.

A generally favorable review by Theodore Lang of New York University appeared in the December 1940 issue of *The Accounting Review*. A remark made by the reviewer in a positive vein may have been taken negatively by teachers in colleges, who preferred a procedural approach to the subject: "the authors have placed their reasoning on a high plane of what the accountant is trying to do rather

Henry Hatfield in the early 1940s. (Courtesy of the curator of the Bancroft Library, University of California.)

than merely detailing the rules" (p. 532). The book was not reviewed in *The Journal of Accountancy.*

In a review published in the British weekly magazine *The Accountant* (October 25, 1941), Stanley W. Rowland, a well-known author, London practitioner, and lecturer at the London School of Economics, adjudged it to be "an excellent example of a textbook conceived and executed on modern lines" (p. 245). He approved of the authors' point of view that "accounting is regarded, throughout, as the subject matter of intellectual contemplation rather than as a collection of cast iron traditional rules to be put into the memory and applied as specific cases arise." The latter approach typified most British textbooks of the period.

The initial printing was 5,000 copies. Poor sales meant that a second printing was not authorized. Burton attributed the weak reception to several factors: (1) the declining enrollments in classrooms owing to wartime conditions, (2) the publisher's lack of experience and ineffective sales promotion in the college market (Ginn's traditional market was high schools), (3) Hatfield's reputation for an approach to accounting theory that caused instructors at lower levels to fear that it might entail too much of a departure from familiar lines, and (4), as epitomized in one comment received by Burton, the book was "too highbrow and too well written." Hatfield would have enjoyed this final comment. The book went out of print in 1952.[171] It was certainly not the "money book" that Selden Smith had hoped it would be.

In a mirthful mood, Hatfield composed a satirical eulogy for the book, as follows:

> In the last decade or so there has been an appalling spate of accounting texts. A few of these are irretrievably bad, some are defective, incomplete, and in places illogical; all are unsatisfactory. The accounting world has, however, greeted with a paean of joy the announcement of a new book soon to appear. The enthusiasm is supported by two facts. It is to be issued by Ginn and Company, whose imprint is evidence and guarantee of supreme excellence (except in the case of Moore & Miner). And secondly there have co-operated in its writing the three most able and famous accountants in the United States, which means, as well, in the world. In it are united the classical scholasticism of Harvard and the exuberant vivacity of the Pacific Coast. In a word, it is written by accountants than whom there are no than whomers. No wonder then that from the Atlantic to the Pacific multitudes are awaiting its appearance with gladsome expectation which can not possibly be disappointed. It rivals Goldsmith in clarity of expression, in penetrating reasoning it reminds one of Socrates and Plato, in correct and elegant English it is like Walter Pater, but a Pater corrected by Fowler's Dictionary of English Usage and the discriminating judgment of the authors' secretaries.[172]

Honorary Doctorate from the University of California

At its Commencement ceremony on May 25, 1940, the University of California conferred an honorary Doctor of Laws (LL.D.) degree on Hatfield, with the following citation, which was read by Robert Gordon Sproul, president of the university:

> PROFESSOR OF ACCOUNTING IN THIS UNIVERSITY FOR MORE THAN THIRTY YEARS · ERSTWHILE DEAN, FIRST OF THE COLLEGE OF COMMERCE AND LATER OF THE UNIVERSITY · CONSTANT CHAMPION OF THE LOGICAL APPROACH, THE SANE VIEW, AND THE CLEAR DISCLOSURE OF THE ESSENTIAL FACTS OF GOODS AND PROPRIETORSHIP · DISCOVERER OF SCIENTIFIC PRINCIPLES AND SOUND PHILOSOPHY IN A FIELD OBSCURED BY DOGMA AND CONVENTION · ONE ABLE TO FIND LIFE AND EVEN HUMOR IN THE DUST OF LEDGERS

The honorary doctorate was Hatfield's second, the first having been awarded by his alma mater, Northwestern University, 17 years earlier.

Possible Revision of *Accounting*

In 1940, D. Appleton-Century Company invited Hatfield to consider revising his *Accounting: Its Principles and Problems*, published 13 years earlier. He advised the publisher that, in the light of the many developments that had occurred since 1927, "the entire work would have to be rewritten." In addition, he said, "I would hope to make it more distinctly an advanced text."[173] In June 1940, at the publisher's suggestion, he wrote to 16 teachers who had used the book, to obtain their suggestions for improvement. It seems that only three of the teachers replied, only one with any suggestions.

In a letter to Catharine Greene, he wrote, "I don't know whether to revise. With the spate of accounting texts which are appearing, I am afraid that at best it would be a labor of love and not of lucre, and I am not even sure that the revision of a textbook carries with it any soul exaltation." Yet, he added, "This is a question put in a purely tentative, noncommittal and unofficial way: would you be interested in collaborating in such a revision? Harry Kerrigan has written to me twice offering his services."[174] In the end, the revision was not carried forward.[175]

No manuscript of revised chapters has been found, but a graduate student in 1943-1944, who served as a teaching assistant in the Principles course, recalls,

> Shortly after I arrived in Berkeley, [Catharine Greene] and another person whose name escapes me had put together an elementary accounting text, and she had prevailed upon Dr. Hatfield to let his name be used as a co-author.... Mrs. Greene substituted her own text for elementary accounting in her classes. As the term progressed, and we teaching assistants came upon obvious errors in the text or problems, we would gleefully note them, and piously bring to Dr. Hatfield's notice the fact that we couldn't quite understand this matter in "his" book. Actually, we didn't do this very often, for he was such a dear, and so obviously distressed by errors in a book with his name on it. He ruefully admitted that he had had little or nothing to do with the preparation.[176]

This textbook with Hatfield's name on it is unknown and was perhaps never published commercially.[177]

Hatfield's Dickinson Lecture on "Surplus and Dividends" in 1942

On October 20, 1941, Wallace B. Donham, dean of the Harvard Business School, who had tried to move Hatfield to Harvard in 1919-1920, invited him to give the annual Dickinson Lecture in Accounting. Hatfield accepted the invitation, and in his follow-up letter of November 1, Donham mentioned Sanders' suggestion that Hatfield speak on "Accounting for Dividends." Sanders doubtless was influential in the approach to Hatfield.

W. Arnold Hosmer, an accounting professor at Harvard who was in charge of the Dickinson Lecture, wrote to Hatfield on November 18: "We thought of the subject of dividends because of your interest in that field and its historical background. There seems to be a trend at present away from a strictly legal interpretation and toward a broad accounting treatment." But Hatfield had hoped to choose from several topics, so Hosmer suggested three others in a letter of December 3:

The Legal Influence in Accounting
History of the Legal Influence in Depreciation Accounting
History of the Cost or Market Rule

Clearly, the fields marked out for Hatfield were history and the law, and his keen interest in depreciation and "cost of market, whichever is lower" was well known to Sanders. In the end, Hatfield chose "Surplus and Dividends."

The Dickinson Lectures in Accounting were begun in 1936 in remembrance of Sir Arthur Lowes Dickinson (1859-1935), who had been a partner in both the U.S. and U.K. firms of Price, Waterhouse & Co. (PW) as well as a leader of the profession in both countries. This was the first lecture series on accounting in the United States. Fifteen annual lectures were given at the Harvard Business School from 1936-1937 to 1954-1955, after which the series was discontinued.[178]

The first two lecturers were the senior partners of PW's U.S. and U.K. firms: George O. May and Sir Laurence Halsey. The third and fourth lecturers were William A. Paton of the University of Michigan and Walter A. Staub, a senior partner in Lybrand, Ross Bros. & Montgomery. Hatfield, fifth in the series, gave his lecture in two parts, on April 21 and 23, 1942. *Surplus and Dividends*, published in 1943 by Harvard University Press, would be his last major work.[179]

In the opening half of his lecture, on Surplus, Hatfield made two major points. First, paid-in surplus, which, he argued, should include the premium received on capital stock, should be shown separately from stated capital, as the latter is regarded as a buffer of protection for the creditors (pp. 7-15). Whether the premium on capital stock should be made a part of capital or surplus was a much-debated question. Some of those who favored its inclusion in capital, and thus not available as a measure for the declaration of dividends, argued that it would be "illogical" to distribute as a dividend a portion of the amount received from shareholders. Hatfield replied as follows:

> Whether it is illogical or not is not an accounting problem. Many financial transactions are illogical and foolish as, for instance, the financing of plant construction by the issuance of short-time notes or the paying of dividends which unduly reduce the cash on hand. The accountant is not concerned with the foolishness of a transaction but with whether the transaction took place. (pp. 11-12)

Second, under the heading of Charges to Surplus, Hatfield argued that corrections of errors made in prior periods should be reflected in a surplus account, not in the income statement (p. 23). Curiously, he adopted this latter position even though, in his lecture, he marshaled even stronger arguments in favor of taking errors through income (pp. 17-18). He seemed to be influenced by a 1937 decision of the Securities and Exchange Commission's chief accountant to prefer the use of earned surplus in such instances (p. 18), yet the issue facing the SEC was the choice between earned surplus and paid-in surplus, not between earned surplus and income. By the latter 1940s, however, the SEC's accounting staff favored the "clean surplus" approach, by which such adjustments should be taken through income, and in 1967 the Accounting Principles Board endorsed the position.[180]

Hatfield used his lecture to take a few licks at the AAA's "Tentative Statement," since *The Accounting Review* had refused to publish his critique (see above). On the subject of the treatment of write-downs, he made the "Tentative Statement" the butt of an amusing anecdote:

> The oft-quoted and dogmatically minded Tentative Statement would charge everything (and that includes the write-off of goodwill) to current income. There is, of course, the proviso that it must not distort the showing of current income, as if the charging of any item which does not belong in a given account does not distort it.
>
> I have a personal friend who gave a very elaborate reception at a San Francisco hotel. He received a bill which was even larger than the large amount he expected to be charged. Examination showed that the bookkeeper in making out the bill inadvertently added in the number of the room, 1571. Would the proponents of the Tentative Statement say, "Don't add in the room number if it distorts the total"? (p. 22)

Earlier in the lecture, he had derisively referred to the AAA position as "this corollary of a fundamental axiom" (p. 16).

Most of the lecture on Dividends dealt with the accounting treatment of appreciation of assets and the propriety of basing dividends on recorded appreciation, which had been topics of controversy since the 1920s. On the question of whether to record appreciation, he cited views covering the entire spectrum, from those who regarded it as blasphemy to those who thought it was a good idea if done properly. "Perhaps the strongest argument against showing appreciation," he said, "is that it 'savors of nonconservatism'" (p. 38). But then, with apparent approval, he quoted Montgomery's statement that "the so-called conservatism of the accountant hides understated values which it can never harm any one to know or hides overstated values which it would be useful to know" (p. 39). Hatfield was not impressed with the conservatism argument. He drew an analogy between recording appreciation in value and recording appreciation in a noninterest-bearing note receivable and said, "If it is legitimate to recognize the increase in value due to the approaching maturity, there needs to be some specific reason given for not recognizing some other increase in value, caused by industrial or market conditions" (p. 35). He rejected the argument that the note is predicated on a definite promise and therefore promises a certain result.

Finally, after hearing out both sides, he concluded:

> The conclusion is that appreciation may be recognized, with the obvious understanding that the appreciation must be genuine, objectively verified, and not arbitrarily done in order to make a "pretty balance sheet." (p. 43)

He would show the appreciation credit in a suitably labeled account in the surplus section, but apart from earned surplus.

Hatfield also contended that it was "an accounting absurdity" to interpret a dividend paid out of current-period profits, at a time when capital was impaired, as a distribution of profits (p. 26).

The subject of the lecture was not virgin ground for Hatfield. In both *Modern Accounting* (1909) and *Accounting* (1927), he had dealt extensively with such accounting and legal issues as capital, surplus, profits and dividends. In "A Symposium on Appreciation" (*The Accounting Review*, March 1930) and in his textbooks, he had commented at length on the appropriateness of booking appreciation and on its eligibility as a basis for the declaration of dividends.

Two reviews appeared. In *The Journal of Accountancy* (June 1943), George D. Bailey, a partner in Ernst & Ernst and a member of the American Institute's Committee on Accounting Procedure, wrote an admiring review. "No one in accountancy," he wrote, "is better fitted than Professor Hatfield to give us an analysis of the problems of surplus and the differences of thought existing thereon" (p. 551). He did not express disagreement with any of Hatfield's discussion.

In *The Accounting Review* (April 1944), George R. Husband of Wayne University, a Paton disciple, wrote a long and thoughtful review. True to his mentor, Husband commended Hatfield for his "disposal of the arguments frequently advanced against the recognition of appreciation" and added the argument that the appreciation credit should be made to "earned or income surplus" (p. 217). He took issue with Hatfield's unwillingness to regard a dividend covered by current-period profits, despite an accumulated operating deficit, as a distribution of profits. Husband preferred the "whole life" to the "fiscal period" view of the income statement and associated Hatfield's view with his antipathy toward the "clean surplus" view espoused in the AAA's "Tentative Statement" (pp. 217-218). Husband also found fault with Hatfield's analogy between appreciation in asset value and the increase in the carrying amount of a noninterest-bearing note receivable.

Husband's frustration with the confusing dispute over surplus and dividends in the literature led him to make the following statement:

> Accounting is caught between the law and economics. In all cases the decision, if at all possible, should be an accounting decision—not necessarily dictated by either law or economics. The accountant's task is to build his own structure. (p. 219)

Hatfield would have agreed with the first sentence but only partially with the rest. Economics and law, he believed, were the substantive underpinnings of accounting. While they may not "dictate" the terms of an accounting structure, their influence will and must be felt.

Surplus and Dividends does not seem to have left a major mark on the literature. By the early 1940s, interest in the interplay between legal and accounting definitions of capital and surplus, and their use in measuring dividend availability, had declined significantly from the level of the 1930s, chiefly because the number of corporate reorganizations and restructurings had subsided. In places where one might have expected to see references to Hatfield's lecture, it was seldom mentioned. Newlove and Garner's *Advanced Accounting*, which was exceptional among textbooks in the extent to which it cited the writings of others, made only one brief reference to *Surplus and Dividends* in its chapters on capital, surplus, and dividends.[181] It was also cited once in McLaren's *Annual Reports to Stockholders*.[182] But McLaren, a leading San Francisco practitioner and a 1914 graduate of the University of California, was undoubtedly a former student of Hatfield's. It was mentioned in May's *Financial Accounting*.[183] Worse, neither the fourth edition of the *Accountants' Handbook* nor Hills's encyclopedic *The Law of Accounting and Financial Statements* cited *Surplus and Dividends* at all.[184] That Hatfield's lecture appeared in a small book published by a university press instead of by Ronald Press or another commercial publisher of books on accounting may have limited its exposure to accounting practitioners and teachers, as well as lawyers.

Teaching during Retirement

Following his retirement leave in 1937-1938, Hatfield taught in each year until his health no longer permitted him to do so. He gave Unsettled Problems in Accounting in 1938-1939, and from the spring of 1939 to the winter of 1944-1945, he offered the Seminar in Accounting Theory in every term but two. During the term from October 1942 to February 1943, in the year following his Dickinson Lecture on "Surplus and Dividends," he even taught a course titled Legal Accounting in the School of Jurisprudence. The description of the course was as follows: "A study of accounting principles, with special reference to some divergent concepts in accounting and the law."[185] He used the elementary book he had written with Sanders and Burton as his textbook.[186] The course and Hatfield's involvement were probably arranged by Henry W. Ballantine.

In his advanced course and seminar, Hatfield would choose new materials for each term, just as, in his Principles course in earlier years, he would change the textbook every year or two as a new book appeared on the market. During the early 1940s, some of his major readings were *A Statement of Accounting Principles*, Paton and Littleton's *An Introduction to Corporate Accounting Standards*, and his Dickinson Lecture on Surplus and Dividends.

The offering of the seminar in the term running from October 1944 to February 1945 drew on still different materials. Samuel R. Hepworth, one of the students, wrote as follows:

> Our primary concern was exploring early accounting text books (late nineteenth and early twentieth century). I remember reading Pixley, Dicksee, Lisle, etc. Hatfield was perfectly alert,

> but, I suppose due to his advancing age, he was most concerned with finding fault, often in regard to rather minor points.[187]

Hatfield's professed objective as a teacher was to make students think for themselves. As he wrote in the late 1920s, he intended even his Principles course for "intelligent and semi-mature University students, who pine for opportunity to form their own opinions, who resent a dogmatic attitude, who proclaim that they want to learn, not to be taught." Several of Hatfield's teaching assistants (TAs) remarked that he would change the Principles textbook almost every year, in part to challenge the TAs to consider other ideas and in part so that the course would not become doctrinaire. He would deal with ideas in the lectures, and the practical work would be done in the labs. Judson E. Krueger, who was a student in Hatfield's Introduction in 1913 and later became a TA, said that Hatfield's lectures were often well over the students' heads. As a TA, even Krueger did not always comprehend Hatfield's lectures. For this reason, Krueger would give a lecture in the first part of his lab, to help the students understand Hatfield's ideas. Krueger believed that Hatfield wanted to inspire students to think, "rather than teach them anything." He said that Hatfield actually explained his purpose in just such words.[188] Another TA, Arthur A. Wender, recalled that "one thing Hatfield did with his students, especially the TAs: he made us think."[189]

A Life Ends

Hatfield's many files contain no correspondence dated later than the spring of 1944. Charles C. Staehling signed the instructor's grade report for Hatfield's seminar that began in February 1945. During that month Hatfield had suffered a stroke. As early as the previous fall, there were signs that his health was failing. His last attendance at the seminar was on March 4. He was confined to a rocking chair or to bed for the balance of the year, and was cared for, day and night, by nurses. By the fall of the year, he was incoherent except for brief periods. On October 3, his brother James Taft died at age 83 in Evanston, Illinois. Four weeks after his 79th birthday, on Christmas Day, Henry Rand Hatfield joined him.

Word spread fast in the community of accounting teachers. In the January 1946 issue of *The Accounting Review*, which was not given to publishing obituaries, the following notice appeared:

> Henry Rand Hatfield died on Christmas day at the age of 79. He held degrees from Northwestern University, University of Chicago and University of California; and since 1902 had taught at Berkeley. To a legion of friends he will always be Dean Hatfield. Officially he had been Dean of Commerce at Chicago and twice at Berkeley. Twice he was Dean of Faculties of the University of California, but unofficially he was Dean of Accounting Teachers everywhere.[190]

In May 1945, Elizabeth Ann (Betty) Hatfield, the daughter whom Henry Hatfield's deceased son Robert never knew, turned 18. As her grandfather would have wished, she returned to Berkeley the following fall to enroll in the University of California. Also, as both grandparents would have wished, she lived in the Hatfield home on Le Conte Avenue, where Ethel could look after her, during the four years of college. Betty graduated in May 1949 with a degree in political science and then left for graduate study at the Sorbonne. As Betty herself has observed, it was as if her grandmother had remained just long enough to ensure that Robert's daughter be cared for while an undergraduate at Berkeley.[191] Her mission completed, she was ready to join her husband. Ethel Adelia Hatfield died on October 26, 1949 at the age of 82.

POSTHUMOUS ELECTION TO THE ACCOUNTING HALL OF FAME

In 1951, Hatfield was elected to the Accounting Hall of Fame. The Hall had been established in 1950 by the department of accounting at the Ohio State University to honor "North Americans who have made outstanding contributions at any time to the field of accounting—public, private, governmental, or educational."[192] George O. May, Robert H. Montgomery, and William A. Paton were inducted as the first members. In 1951, Hatfield and the late Sir Arthur Lowes Dickinson were elected to membership. In the citation read at the election ceremony by Samuel J. Broad, a leading practitioner and chairman of the board of nominations, two comments stand out:

> [Hatfield's] major work was "Modern Accounting."... When it first appeared, this work shone like a bright light against a dull background, little accounting literature of note having appeared for some years....
>
> As an inspiring teacher, as a gifted author, and as one whose keen insight and independent thinking were a potent influence in the early development of accounting theory, the Board of Nominations is privileged to present for the Ohio State University Accounting Hall of Fame the name of Henry Rand Hatfield.[193]

The award was received on Hatfield's behalf by his successor at Berkeley, Perry Mason, who himself was elected to the Hall in 1964. Today, more than 60 members are enshrined in the Accounting Hall of Fame.[194]

NOTES

1. In Chapter 5, Basil Yamey, the distinguished historian of bookkeeping, offers a paper in which he surveys and assesses Hatfield's interests and work in this field.

2. Appropriately, his memorial at the university is the James K. Moffitt Undergraduate Library, which was opened in 1970.

3. Hatfield had the assistance of Christine Price, who was a member of the catalogue department of the university library, and was in charge of the rare books and of exhibits, and catalogued rare-book acquisitions. She wrote, "While I had no knowledge of [Professor Hatfield's] subject field,

as a bibliographer I appreciated his enthusiasm as a collector of rarities, and enjoyed the research demanded in the cataloguing of his acquisitions. After the Professor's retirement in 1937, he was able to concentrate on building up his collection, and Mr. [Harold L.] Leupp, University librarian, was cooperative and allowed the use of special funds for purchases." Letter to the author from Miss Price, dated December 14, 1964.

4. Robert H. Montgomery, one of the founding partners of Lybrand, Ross Bros. & Montgomery, was an avid collector of old works on bookkeeping, and in 1926 he donated his collection to Columbia University. See Chapter 23 in Robert H. Montgomery, *Fifty Years of Accountancy* (privately printed by The Ronald Press Company, 1939).

5. Letter to the author from Hausdorfer, dated March 9, 1965. Hausdorfer's manuscript, combined with his later work, was published as *Accounting Bibliography: Historical Approach*, edited by A. van Seventer (Palo Alto, CA: Bay Books, 1986). In his Preface, written in 1962, Hausdorfer acknowledged Hatfield's assistance.

6. An example of this antiquarian interest may be found in an extract from a letter written by Hatfield regarding a recent acquisition by the Montgomery Library at Columbia University, in *The American Accountant*, Vol. XVI, No. 7, July 1931, p. 207.

7. Kats was a Dutchman who worked in London as an accountant for the Royal Dutch Petroleum Company from the 1920s to 1931, when he returned to the Netherlands. As a hobby, he researched the contributions of Dutch merchants to the development of bookkeeping in the sixteenth, seventeenth, and eighteenth centuries. He published some nine articles on the subject in *The Accountant* and the *Maandblad voor het Boekhouden*. Letter to the author from Onko ten Have, dated July 26, 1965.

Kats also published one article each in *The Journal of Accountancy* (March and April 1929) and *The Accounting Review* (December 1930), which Hatfield had recommended to their respective editors. Hatfield's surviving correspondence file with Kats contains a frequent exchange of letters between 1926 and 1931. In 1927, Hatfield considered writing a book with Kats on the history of bookkeeping, but apparently no work was ever undertaken on the project.

8. Gordon, a Scot, was Librarian of the Institute of Chartered Accountants in England and Wales from 1933 to 1941 and for short periods in the 1910s and 1940s, and "can well be regarded as the co-founder—with F.W. Pixley, chairman of the Library Committee from 1893 to 1933—of the Institute's priceless collection of early books on accounting." *The Accountant*, May 29, 1965, p. 758. Hatfield corresponded with Gordon between 1933 and 1943. Gordon wrote that Hatfield "came to us at the Institute to see and consult our already rich collection of early books on bookkeeping, and our conversations were on bibliographical points in connection with these." Letter to the author from Gordon, dated October 1, 1964.

9. Letter to the author dated July 25, 1964.

10. B.S. Yamey wrote that, subsequent to publication of the article with Littleton, Hatfield acquired two very rare books for the University of California's collection: Symon Hübner's *Ein new Rechen - Büchen/auff allerley Kauffmanns-Rechnung* and the 1543 version of Ympyn's *Nouvelle Instruction*. Letter to the author from Yamey, dated March 18, 1997.

11. Hatfield's reference is to Arthur Stone Dewing, *The Financial Policy of Corporations* (New York: The Ronald Press Company, third revised edition, 1934), p. 468 (not p. 469, given in his article).

12. Letter to the author from Viner, dated November 23, 1964.

13. Writers on early bookkeeping history have disagreed whether the Franciscan friar's name is properly spelled "Pacioli" or "Paciolo." Hatfield preferred the latter. See the note on this spelling controversy in A.C. Littleton, *Accounting Evolution to 1900* (New York: American Institute Publishing Co., 1933), p. 76. A small literature is available on the subject: see Alfred V. Boursy, "The Name of Paciolo," *The Accounting Review*, Vol. XVIII, No. 3, July 1943, pp. 205-209; Raymond de Roover, "Paciolo or Pacioli?," *The Accounting Review*, Vol. XIX, No. 1, January 1944, pp. 68-69; and (the most extensive treatment) R. Emmett Taylor, "The Name of Pacioli," *The Accounting Review*, Vol. XIX, No. 1, January 1944, pp. 69-76.

14. Ironically, Paton had been reconsidering his initial enthusiasm for combining liabilities and owners' equity under the head of equities. In a letter to Hatfield dated March 4, 1943, Paton wrote, "Back in 1915 to 1920 when I was trying to find means of justifying the suggestion that there was an underlying similarity between all items on the right-hand side of the conventional balance sheet I undoubtedly overstated my case. As the years have gone by, I can see that my suggestion, while having some merit, was not as defensible as I originally thought."

15. Hatfield's reference was to Wilmer L. Green, *History and Survey of Accountancy* (Brooklyn, NY: Standard Text Press, 1930), which he had criticized in *The Journal of Accountancy* of April 1931.

16. For a discussion of MacNeal's book and its aftermath, see Stephen A. Zeff, "Truth in Accounting: The Ordeal of Kenneth MacNeal," *The Accounting Review*, Vol. LVII, No. 3, July 1982, pp. 528-553. In "An Historical Defence of Henry Rand Hatfield," *Abacus*, Vol. 16, No. 2, December 1980, pp. 151-157, M.J. Mumford claims that MacNeal misrepresented some of Hatfield's views and, indeed, that he plagiarized from Hatfield. In footnote 29, page 549 of the "Ordeal" article, the author agrees with Mumford's first claim but disagrees with the second.

17. Letter to Catharine DeMotte Greene from Hatfield, dated June 10, 1940.

18. In a lengthy letter to the *Journal*, George O. May, the doyen of the accounting profession who was then the chairman of the American Institute of Accountants' Committee on Accounting Procedure, replied, "It is a welcome relief to venture with an old friend into a wonderland in which bonds can be bought to yield ten per cent and the only riddles presented are homemade out of tricks of language and mathematics." He answered Hatfield's implied queries and posed a riddle of his own. "An Accountant's Adventure in Wonderland," *The Journal of Accountancy*, Vol. 71, No. 1, January 1941, pp. 72-73.

19. Wartime restrictions on Christmas travel, including congested hotels, forced cancellation of the AAA's 1942 and 1943 national meetings. Between June and December 1943, six regional meetings were held, and Berkeley was the meeting site on the West Coast. Perry Mason was in charge of the arrangements. See "Association Reports for the Year 1943," *The Accounting Review*, Vol. XIX, No. 2, April 1944, pp. 223-225, and Zeff, *The American Accounting Association—Its First 50 Years* (American Accounting Association, 1966), p. 64.

20. C.A. Ashley, "Replacement and Book Value," *The Accounting Review*, Vol. XIX, No. 3, July 1944, pp. 298-299.

21. Letter dated April 19, 1944. In addition, Hatfield received letters from Anson Herrick, of the CPA firm Lester Herrick and Herrick, San Francisco, and from W.H. Franklin, controller of Caterpillar Tractor Co., both expressing agreement with his thesis.

22. Although John B. Canning, at Stanford, and Hatfield, at Berkeley, worked at nearby campuses, their paths seldom crossed. Their only surviving correspondence is several letters from 1929-1930, mostly in regard to Hatfield's "Paradox" and the nature of "prepaid interest." These exchanges were usually initiated by Hatfield, who was Canning's elder by 18 years. In 1930, shortly after the publication of his *The Economics of Accountancy* (New York: The Ronald Press Company, 1929), Canning was a guest in Hatfield's seminar. Canning's active interest in accounting largely lapsed by the middle 1930s. See the author's article, "John B. Canning: A View of His Academic Career," *Abacus*, Vol. 36, No. 1, February 2000, pp. 4-39.

23. Letter to John L. Carey from Hatfield, dated December 8, 1939. Also see Zeff, *The American Accounting Association, op. cit.*, pp. 56-57.

24. Letter to Carey from Hatfield, dated November 15, 1939.

25. Letter to Paton from Hatfield, dated May 13, 1941.

26. *Register 1929-30, With Announcements for 1930-31*, Part II, p. 92. No syllabus has survived.

27. Hatfield's Scrapbook No. 14 contains a clipping, from an unknown source, apparently published in 1932, that gives a description of the course. Collings' surname was disclosed but the name of the university at which the course was offered was not given. In a letter to Howard S. Noble dated March 27, 1935, Hatfield wrote that a Professor W. Collings of Grove City College had offered the

course twice in the early 1930s at Northwestern University. The author is grateful to the Librarian at Grove City College and to the Archivist of Northwestern University for supplying additional details.

28. *Northwestern University Bulletin: The Summer Session 1932*, Vol. XXXII, No. 47, July 18, 1932, p. 119.

29. Collings offered a variation on European Accounting Theory in the 1934 summer session at Northwestern University. The 1934 course carried the title "The Effects of Alterations in the Monetary Unit on Financial Statements." Included in the course description was the following sentence: "This course aims to show how mild and radical inflation affects the financial accounts, how the problem was dealt with during the inflationary periods in Germany and France, and the possibilities of adapting those methods to American business practices." *Northwestern University Bulletin: Announcement of the 1934 Summer Session*, Vol. XXXIV, No. 27, March 12, 1934, p. 71. Fourteen students completed the course.

30. Halterman recalled that he took the course shortly after Hatfield had returned from a trip to Germany. Telephone interview with J. Fred Halterman, January 16, 1965.

In the announcement of his doctoral thesis examination in 1935, Halterman listed Econ 214, Recent German Accounting Theory, among the courses he had completed during his doctoral studies.

31. Schmidt's calling card appears in Hatfield's Scrapbook No. 13 (confirmed by Elizabeth Hatfield Glover in a letter to the author dated November 1965). In a letter dated May 21, 1933, Schmidt wrote to Hatfield, who was preparing to visit Frankfurt, that he wished to "renew this valuable acquaintance." (Hatfield Scrapbook, No. 9.) In a letter to Schmidt dated June 17, 1939, Hatfield referred to "your own courtesies to me in 1933." There is no evidence, however, that Hatfield and Schmidt (1882-1950) engaged in sustained correspondence. No contact between Hatfield and Schmalenbach (1873-1955) seems to have occurred. In a letter to the author dated January 12, 1965, Karl Hax (1901-1978; a Schmalenbach disciple), of the Johann Wolfgang Goethe-Universität in Frankfurt, wrote: "I asked Professor Theodor Beste, who was assistant of Prof. Eugen Schmalenbach between 1920 and 1926. He did not know Prof. Hatfield. The same information I received from Prof. Minz who was assistant of Prof. Schmalenbach from 1926 to 1932." As to Hatfield's visit to Germany in 1933, mentioned below, Hax wrote, in a letter to the author dated February 2, 1965, "Unfortunately Prof. Hatfield came in 1933 to Germany, at a period when the influence of the Betriebswirtschaftslehre was nearly cut off by the regime of the National-Sozialismus. After Hitler's assumption of power Prof. Schmalenbach laid down his lectureship." Rudolf Seyffert, in a letter to the author dated August 3, 1964, wrote that although he knew Schmalenbach and Balduin Penndorf personally, they never mentioned Hatfield to him. In a letter to the author dated February 7, 1965, Friedrich Henzel (1891-1984), an assistant to Schmidt for many years, wrote that he does not recall any visit by Hatfield.

32. For discussion of the theories propounded by Schmidt and Schmalenbach, see F.L. Clarke and G.W. Dean, "Schmidt's *Betriebswirtschaft* Theory," *Abacus*, Vol. 22, No. 2, September 1986, pp. 65-102; and O. Finley Graves, Graeme W. Dean, and Frank L. Clarke, *Schmalenbach's Dynamic Accounting and Price-level Adjustments: An Economic Consequences Explanation* (New York: Garland Publishing, 1989).

33. For reproductions of the articles by Sweeney and Schmidt, see Stephen A. Zeff, ed., *Asset Appreciation, Business Income and Price-Level Accounting: 1918-1935* (New York: Arno Press, 1976). Editor Eric L. Kohler of *The Accounting Review* said that during the late 1920s and early 1930s, several German writers eagerly sent manuscripts to the *Review* and other accounting and business journals published in English. A few, he said, even attended the annual meetings of the American Association of University Instructors in Accounting. *Ibid.*, "Introduction," fn. 18.

34. *Register for 1930-31*, Stanford University, p. 219; also, page 3520 of the minutes of the Stanford Board of Regents. The stipend was $1,200.

35. Numerous mementoes of the trip appear in Hatfield Scrapbook Nos. 14 and 15.

36. Note the acknowledgment to Hatfield in Henry Winthrop Ballantine, *California Corporation Laws* (Los Angeles, CA: Parker, Stone & Baird Co., 1932), p. viii of the Preface; and in Henry

Winthrop Ballantine, *Ballantine on Corporations* (Chicago: Callaghan and Company, revised edition, 1946), p. 527, fn. 2.

37. A provision in the GCL, as amended in 1933, that was one of the more progressive such provisions in state corporation laws, was the stipulation in Section 358, perhaps traceable to Hatfield's influence, that the balance sheet and statement of income or profit and loss to be sent to shareholders annually "shall be prepared in a form sanctioned by sound accounting practice for the particular kind of business carried on by the corporation." That was a time before "generally accepted accounting principles" came into use and even before any committee of the American Institute of Accountants began pronouncing its views on "accounting principles." It was, in all likelihood, an early attempt to set a kind of standard, albeit crude, for acceptable accounting practice.

38. Letter to T.H. Sanders from Hatfield, dated February 4, 1936.

39. Minute Book of the Chapter, June 1913 to May 1937, p. 82.

40. *The Journal of Accountancy*, Vol. LVIII, No. 2, August 1934, pp. 90-97.

41. *The Accounting Review*, Vol. IX, No. 3, September 1934, pp. 237-241 (quotation from p. 239).

42. As reported in a letter to Hatfield from C. Aubrey Smith, senior associate security analyst (an accounting professor on leave from the University of Texas) in the SEC's registration division, dated June 6, 1935.

43. Letter to James Taft Hatfield, undated but apparently written in August 1919.

44. C.W. DeMond, *Price, Waterhouse & Co. In America: A History of a Public Accounting Firm* (New York: Privately printed, 1951), pp. 133-134.

45. The two letters are in the George O. May Papers held by the Price Waterhouse Information Center, Price Waterhouse LLP, New York City, in the file "Securities and Exchange Commission, 1934 (2)."

46. In December 1935, the SEC appointed Carman G. Blough as its first chief accountant. Blough, a former academic who also had auditing and budgeting experience in state government, had joined the commission's staff in December 1934 as a financial analyst. For an insider's view of accounting developments in the early years of the Commission, see Carman G. Blough, "Development of Accounting Principles in the United States," in *Berkeley Symposium on the Foundations of Financial Accounting* (Berkeley, CA: Schools of Business Administration, University of California, 1967), pp. 1-14. See also Robert Chatov, *Corporate Financial Reporting: Public or Private Control?* (New York: The Free Press, 1975), Chaps. 7-8.

47. Henry Rand Hatfield, *Accounting: Its Principles and Problems* (New York: D. Appleton and Company, 1927), p. 137.

48. *Ibid.*, pp. 138-139.

49. *The American Accountant*, Vol. XVI, No. 2, February 1931, p. 50. The second installment appeared in the same journal, December 1931, p. 365.

50. "Discussion," *Fourth International Congress on Accounting 1933* (International Congress on Accounting, 1933), pp. 685-686.

51. Letter to Noble from Hatfield, dated February 19, 1935.

52. Five years later, in a published letter, Hatfield again criticized Saliers' characterization of depreciation. Henry Rand Hatfield, "Financial Aspects of Depreciation," *The Journal of Accountancy*, Vol. 69, No. 1, January 1940, pp. 48-49.

53. In a letter to Hatfield dated December 19, 1936, William A. Paton wrote, "I think you were rather charitable in saying or implying that the various writers you quoted knew better than they said. My feeling is that muddled written statements almost always show a muddled mental condition." Paton further asked, "why didn't you refer to the correct statement made by Perry Mason, one of my pet pupils, and published in the Accounting Review a few years ago as part of a symposium given at one of the meetings? It's the best brief statement on the subject in print."

54. Sanders was an Englishman whose surname was pronounced "Saunders." He received a Ph.D. from Harvard University in 1921.

55. During his time in London, Hatfield paid calls on Sir Josiah Stamp and P.D. Leake, among others. Hatfield and Leake exchanged letters off and on from 1935 to 1940, mostly on depreciation. Leake had written numerous articles but was best known for his books *Depreciation and Wasting Assets* and *Commercial Goodwill*, both of which went through several editions. In B.V. Carsberg, "The Contribution of P.D. Leake to the Theory of Goodwill Valuation," *Journal of Accounting Research*, Vol. 4, No. 1, Spring 1966, pp. 1-15, Hatfield's treatment of goodwill valuation in his *Modern Accounting* (New York: D. Appleton and Company, 1909) is included in Carsberg's review of the goodwill literature prior to 1914, when Leake first published his views on the subject.

56. Sanders wrote in his letter that Hatfield "raised the question of the desirability of having The American Institute and The American Society of Certified Public Accountants associated in some way with this undertaking. Since you also at the outset of our discussions referred to this possibility we all felt that it would be proper once more to bring it up for your consideration." Sanders strongly endorsed Hatfield's suggestion, which fitted in with the latter's long-held view that academics and the professional bodies should cooperate on a broad base. In mid-1935, the Institute and the Society, which was founded in 1921, were competitor organizations but were holding discussions for a possible merger, which was consummated in 1936. See John L. Carey, *The Rise of the Accounting Profession: From Technician to Professional, 1896-1936* (New York: American Institute of Certified Public Accountants, 1969), Chaps. 19 and 20. Evidently, Carter declined the suggestion, since the work of the committee was announced as a project of the Haskins & Sells Foundation alone.

57. Letters to the author from Arthur B. Foye, who was secretary of the foundation from its commencement in 1928, both dated October 1, 1964.

58. See Gary John Previts, *A Critical Evaluation of Comparative Financial Accounting Thought in America 1900 to 1920* (New York: Arno Press, 1980; originally written in 1972), p. 41.

59. See Joel Seligman, *The Transformation of Wall Street: A History of the Securities and Exchange Commission and Modern Corporate Finance* (Boston: Houghton Mifflin, 1982), pp. 113-114, 116-117, and 198-199.

60. Chatov, *op. cit.*, p. 112.

61. Memorandum to the foundation, dated March 11, 1936.

62. The entirety of this letter is reproduced in Thomas Henry Sanders, Henry Rand Hatfield, and Underhill Moore, *A Statement of Accounting Principles* (New York: American Institute of Accountants, 1938), pp. xi-xiv.

63. The committee papers supporting *A Statement of Accounting Principles* have never before been made public, and I therefore take this occasion to bring to light some of the internal discussions and points of disagreement, especially as they involved Hatfield. Included in Hatfield's files are many folders of correspondence relating to the project.

64. From August 1935, when Hatfield returned from Europe, until July 1937, shortly after he began a year's retirement leave from Berkeley, he appears to have traveled east only twice: in December 1935, when he spoke at the AAUIA's annual meeting in New York, and in August 1936. No meetings with Sanders and Moore were held on the West Coast. The major meeting occurred in July 1937. According to Sanders, "The committee was in practically continuous session from July 13 to July 24." Letter from Sanders to the Haskins & Sells Foundation, Inc., dated July 30, 1937.

Hatfield sailed for Europe on July 30 and returned to the United States in October, when he took up residence in the George Washington Inn, in Washington, D.C.

65. Hatfield's only previous coauthored work of any kind was "A Check-List of Early Bookkeeping Texts," with A.C. Littleton (*The Accounting Review*, September 1932), which was a compilation of bibliophilic data.

66. Haskins & Sells was, for example, the last of the Big Eight firms to allow copies of its internal house organ, *H&S Reports*, to circulate outside the firm, finally acceding to outsiders' requests for copies in the mid-1960s. The apparent concern was whether such a wider distribution would constitute advertising.

67. Letter dated December 11, 1937. In the letter, Sanders wrote that "Colonel Carter and Mr. Wildman expressed themselves as highly pleased with the report."

68. A copy of Wildman's letter was in Hatfield's files, so he must have been aware of what the foundation was hoping to receive. Nonetheless, Hatfield persisted with his arguments as if the committee were agreed that the report should contain only principled recommendations. Note in particular Hatfield's memorandum of December 21, 1936, below.

69. Sanders was impressed that C.A. Heiss, the comptroller of the American Telephone and Telegraph Company, one of those interviewed by the committee, did not like bond discount as an asset and very much preferred Reserve for Depreciation over Allowance for Depreciation.

70. *Accounting: Its Principles and Problems*, *op. cit.*, p. 99.

71. The survey results on the balance-sheet treatment of reacquired stock presented on page 90 of the report came from Haskins & Sells, although the firm's name was not mentioned as the source. Disclosure of the firm's name in this context might have been seen as an instance of unprofessional advertising.

72. Interview with Herrick, in 1965.

73. Letter to Henry W. Ballantine, dated March 2, 1938 (supplied by George S. Hills, to whom a copy was sent).

74. These were the standards against which he judged the AAA's "Tentative Statement" in an address given in 1937. By implication, these were the standards that governed his own work. The quoted passage is taken from his address.

75. A reprint of the statement was distributed under the slightly altered title "A Tentative Statement of Accounting Principles Underlying Corporate Financial Statements."

76. Kohler wrote Hatfield for his views on a near-final draft of the "Tentative Statement" in May 1936, and he submitted two pages of comments. But he was not one of its authors.

77. Kohler, *loc. cit.*, and "Standards Must Come," *The Accounting Review*, Vol. IX, No. 4, December 1934, pp. 334-336.

78. Kohler, Littleton, and Greer were dyed-in-the-wool defenders of historical cost accounting, and Paton, while very sympathetic to current values, was, at this stage in his career, wavering between the two extremes. See Stephen A. Zeff, "Paton on the Effects of Changing Prices on Accounting, 1916-55," in Stephen A. Zeff, Joel Demski, and Nicholas Dopuch, eds., *Essays in Honor of William A. Paton: Pioneer Accounting Theorist* (Ann Arbor, MI: Graduate School of Business Administration, University of Michigan, 1979), pp. 107-111.

79. Carman G. Blough, "The Need for Accounting Principles," *The Accounting Review*, Vol. XII, No. 1, March, 1937, p. 30.

80. Zeff, *The American Accounting Association*, *op. cit.*, p. 46. Another publication put out in 1936, *Examination of Financial Statements*, was the Institute's revision of an earlier bulletin that dealt primarily with auditing. However, the 1936 revision did include some comments on desirable accounting practice.

81. See *ibid.*, pp. 45-49.

82. Blough, "The Need for Accounting Principles," *op. cit.*, p. 31.

83. "Comments on 'A Statement of Accounting Principles'," *The Journal of Accountancy*, Vol. 65, No. 3, March 1938, p. 196. Ironically, Paton wrote the comment while he was living in Hatfield's house as a professor at Berkeley, while the owners were away on a year's leave of absence.

84. Comments on "A Statement of Accounting Principles," *The Journal of Accountancy*, Vol. 65, No. 4, April 1938, p. 316.

85. *Ibid.*, p. 318.

86. "Some Debated Issues on Consolidated Financial Statements," *Papers on Accounting Principles and Procedure*, presented at the 51st annual meeting of the American Institute of Accountants in 1938 (New York: AIA, 1939), p. 42.

87. *The Accountant*, Vol. XCIX, No. 3323, August 13, 1938, p. 226.

88. *The Search for Accounting Principles: Today's Problems in Perspective* (New York: AICPA, 1964), p. 29.

89. Blough, "Development of Accounting Principles in the United States," *op. cit.*, p. 7.

90. "Relations Between the Development of Accounting Principles and the Activities of the SEC," in William Cooper and Yuji Ijiri, eds., *Eric Louis Kohler: Accounting's Man of Principles* (Reston, VA: Reston Publishing, 1979), p. 46.

91. "A Tentative Statement of Accounting Principles Affecting Corporate Reports," *The Accounting Review*, Vol. XI, No. 2, June 1936, p. 188. Three years later, he referred to this "fundamental axiom" as a "categorical fulmination." Henry Rand Hatfield, "A Survey of Developments in Accounting," in *Papers on Auditing Procedure and Other Accounting Subjects*, presented at the 52nd annual meeting of the American Institute of Accountants in 1939 (New York: AIA, 1939), p. 7.

92. Indeed, Jacob B. Taylor, AAA president, wrote to Hatfield on January 3, 1938, suggesting that, if he had not already done so, Hatfield should send a copy of his paper to Editor Kohler for publication in the *Review*. (Hatfield Scrapbook No. 21.)

93. Letter to Hatfield from Kohler, dated February 14, 1941.

94. Letter to Kohler from Hatfield, dated February 24, 1941. There is no record of a reply from Kohler.

95. Letter to Moore from Sanders, dated February 28, 1938. In fact, the three authors of the *Statement* never did reply to the comments and criticisms.

96. Letter to Sanders, dated February 27, 1938.

97. Letter to Paton from Hatfield, dated December 28, 1942.

98. Maurice Moonitz, *Obtaining Agreement on Standards in the Accounting Profession* (Sarasota, FL: American Accounting Association, 1974), p. 13.

99. Previts and Merino have observed: "The study was used by some practitioners to justify existing practice. The correspondence file from [the Committee on Accounting Procedure's] early years and the annual meetings of the institute from 1937 to 1941 show that the study was cited by many as an authoritative source." Gary John Previts and Barbara Dubis Merino, *A History of Accounting in America* (New York: John Wiley & Sons, 1979), p. 262.

100. *Op. cit.*, pp. 30, 31. Storey may mean that the questionable practices condoned by the report may have become the target of the American Institute's Committee on Accounting Procedure and the SEC's accounting staff, since Storey remarks: "Most of the questionable practices that were in evidence in the report of Sanders, Hatfield, and Moore had completely disappeared by the late 1940's or early 1950's" (p. 48). Compare with Reed K. Storey, "The Framework of Financial Accounting Concepts and Standards," in D.R. Carmichael, Steven B. Lilien, and Martin Mellman, eds., *Accountants' Handbook* (New York: John Wiley & Sons, seventh edition, 1991), Chap. 1, p. 13.

101. See *Conceptual Framework for Financial Accounting and Reporting: Elements of Financial Statements and Their Measurement*, Discussion Memorandum (Stamford, CT: Financial Accounting Standards Board, 1976), Chap. 3. Also see Maurice Moonitz, *The Basic Postulates of Accounting* (New York: AICPA, 1961); Robert T. Sprouse and Maurice Moonitz, *A Tentative Set of Broad Accounting Principles for Business Enterprises* (New York: AICPA, 1962); and George R. Catlett and Norman O. Olson, *Accounting for Goodwill* (New York: AICPA, 1968). These were Accounting Research Studies 1, 3, and 10 in the series done under the auspices of the Accounting Principles Board. U.S. textbooks on accounting theory refer to the *Statement*. For example, Hendriksen and van Breda write, "For all its faults, this monograph is a fascinating repository of accounting practice at the time and an important source of data for positive research in accounting." Eldon S. Hendriksen and Michael F. van Breda, *Accounting Theory* (Homewood, IL: Richard D. Irwin, Inc., fifth edition, 1992), p. 99.

102. Letter dated March 25, 1937.

103. Frank G. Short, then a partner in the San Francisco office of Barrow, Wade, Guthrie & Co., said that Hatfield was still feeling pretty low about being retired almost six months later, when he attended the Fiftieth Anniversary Celebration of the American Institute of Accountants in New York

City in October, after returning from a two-month European trip with Ethel. Telephone interview with Short, December 13, 1964.

Hatfield wrote to A.P. Richardson, the retired editor of *The Journal of Accountancy* and author of its column "This Blessed Language" (which Hatfield admired) that, as regards retirement from Berkeley, "when I say 'I was retired' it shows that there was nothing voluntary on my part and that I was merely a victim of the Board of Regents and of old *tempus fugit*." Letter dated November 26, 1940.

104. Interview with Mary Gash (Hatfield's private secretary since 1934), December 14, 1964.

105. Letter to W.T. Baxter from Hatfield, dated December 8, 1938. It seems likely that Hatfield did not learn of Catharine Greene's role in planning the booklet even after the event, as his letters referring to the booklet do not mention anyone other than the CPA community.

106. Moonitz relates an anecdote that illustrates a difference in thinking between Hatfield and Canning, as well as Hatfield's humor. In his landmark *The Economics of Accountancy*, published by Ronald Press in 1929, Canning elaborately laid a central plank in his theory, the definition of an asset: "An asset is any future service in money or any future service convertible into money (except those services arising from contracts the two sides of which are proportionately unperformed) the beneficial interest in which is legally or equitably secured to some person or set of persons. Such a service is an asset only to that person or set of persons to whom it runs" (p. 22). He then wrote, "No definition substantially in this form is found in the literature." Alongside this latter passage, Hatfield scribbled in the margin, "Gott sei dank" (Thank God!). This anecdote is reported in Edward Hussey Binns, "The Influence of Henry Rand Hatfield," MBA Thesis (San Francisco State University, 1978), p. 9. For more on Canning, see the author's article, "John B. Canning: A View of His Academic Career," *Abacus*, Vol. 36, No. 1, February 2000, pp. 4-39.

107. Letter dated May 7, 1937 (Call No. CU 5, Hatfield file for 1937, in the Bancroft Library, University of California).

108. Interview with Joel H. Hildebrand, December 4, 1964.

109. Letter to the author from Robert D. Calkins (who was chairman of the department of economics and dean of the College of Commerce at the time), dated June 29, 1965.

110. Hatfield had tentatively proposed to spend the 1937-1938 academic year as a professor at the University of Michigan, but he later withdrew the proposal, saying: "I find now that matters have come up which would make it impossible for me to spend the year at Ann Arbor." Letter to Paton dated April 27, 1937. One suspects that his wife's aversion to cold weather may have played a part in the decision. Another factor may have been his need to be on the East Coast in order to work with Sanders both to finish the *Statement* and to make progress on their elementary accounting book.

111. Maurice Moonitz, *History of Accounting at Berkeley* (Berkeley, CA: Schools of Business Administration, University of California, 1986), p. 26; and letter to the author from Robert D. Calkins, dated June 29, 1965. Paton wrote, "I was engaged by President Bob Sproul to take over [Hatfield's] courses, and he went so far as to indicate that the post would be permanent if I wanted to stay on." Letter to the author from Paton, dated April 9, 1974.

112. Moonitz, *History*, *op. cit.*, p. 27.

113. Letter to Paton, dated March 16, 1937.

114. Letter to the author from Paton, dated June 28, 1965.

115. The Hatfields had planned to be abroad during the entire year of his retirement leave, but the need to complete work on *A Statement of Accounting Principles* obliged them to return to the United States in October. During most of the balance of the year, they resided in Washington, D.C. Letter to Paton from Hatfield, dated December 28, 1942.

116. Letter to the author from Paton, dated April 9, 1974. Mary Gash, Hatfield's secretary during the 1930s, recalled that Hatfield's car was frequently in the garage to have dents taken out of a fender. He would be driving along in deep thought, and he would run into something. Interview with Mary (Mrs. Robert) Gash, December 14, 1964. Illustrative of his absentmindedness was an occasion when he was having serious difficulty starting the car, which was parked in the front of South Hall, until his colleague Charles C. Staehling shouted from a window, "Say, Hatfield, what are you doing in my

car?" Anecdote related by Frank A. Waring (a former student and teaching assistant) in a memo dated July 2, 1964.

117. Although Paton believed that University of Michigan students were better than those at the University of California and was not pleased that the salary at Berkeley was lower than that at Ann Arbor, he might have stayed had his wife and children not longed to return to Michigan. Telephone interview with William A. Paton, Jr., November 25, 1996.

118. A condensation of Mason's dissertation was published in 1937 under the title *Principles of Public-Utility Depreciation*, as the first of the American Accounting Association's new series of monographs. Paton, as AAA director of research, had invited Hatfield to write a foreword to Mason's monograph, but he declined owing to his preoccupation with completing *A Statement of Accounting Principles*.

119. Letter to the author from Paton, dated June 28, 1965. Paton concluded, "One difficulty was that Hatfield became unduly absorbed with early European writers, especially the Germans, and lost interest in current problems of analysis and measurement." Catharine DeMotte Greene's thesis topic may have prompted this comment. But the thesis topic was her choice, not Hatfield's. In fact, the only evidence of Hatfield's being "absorbed with early European writers, especially the Germans," was in the breadth of his citations and references in *Modern Accounting* and *Accounting* and in the several scheduled offerings of his course on Recent German Accounting Theory in the early 1930s. He was much more "absorbed" with the early history of bookkeeping, collecting antiquarian tracts on bookkeeping, and the evolving relation between law and accounting than he ever was with the German accounting theorists Schmalenbach and Schmidt.

120. The other members of her committee were Robert D. Calkins, Ira B. Cross, Charles C. Staehling, and Max Radin (of the School of Jurisprudence). Her degree was a Ph.D. in economics. The year of 1929 given for the conferral of her degree in Moonitz, *History*, *op. cit.*, pp. 49 and 95 is in error; the correct year, 1937, is given in Moonitz, p. 25.

John Frederick Halterman, who is shown as having received a Berkeley doctorate in 1930 for a thesis on accounting (*ibid.*, p. 95), actually received his Berkeley doctorate in 1935 for a thesis titled "A Functional Analysis of the Cash Expenditures of the State of California, 1915-1934"; his committee was chaired by Malcolm M. Davisson, a finance professor. Hence, Catharine Greene was the first recipient of a Berkeley doctorate awarded for a thesis done in accounting.

121. The thesis was reprinted by Arno Press in 1980. It dealt primarily with the work of Eugen Schmalenbach and his disciple Ernst Walb.

122. Interview with Catharine D. Quire, July 6, 1964. Following the death of her husband, Ambrose Greene, she married Joseph Hayford Quire (Maurice Moonitz, Introduction to the Arno reprint of her dissertation, and correspondence with Catharine D. Quire). Both of her previous degrees were from the University of California: an A.B. in 1915 (she took Hatfield's Introduction to Accounting in 1912-1913) and an M.A. in 1929.

123. See Binns, *op. cit.*, p. 22.

124. Interview with Catharine D. Quire, July 6, 1964.

125. Interview with Sproul, January 15, 1965.

126. Interview with Taylor, March 23, 1965. Paul S. Taylor (1895-1984) was an economist. He joined the department in 1922 as an assistant professor after taking his M.A. and Ph.D. degrees at the university.

127. Interview with Knight, January 23, 1965.

128. Interview with Staehling, January 24, 1965.

129. "An Historical Defense of Bookkeeping," *The Journal of Accountancy*, Vol. XXXVII, No. 4, April 1924, p. 241.

130. *Op. cit.*, p. viii.

131. Henry Rand Hatfield, "A Survey of Developments in Accounting," in *Papers on Auditing Procedure and Other Accounting Subjects*, *op. cit.*, p. 5.

132. Interview with Moonitz, December 19, 1964.

133. Interview with Taylor, March 23, 1965.

134. Some credence is given to this view by Leonard A. Doyle, who joined the department in 1942. Interview, December 15, 1964.

135. Interview with Lamden, March 28, 1965.

136. Telephone interview with J. Fred Halterman, January 16, 1965. The Master of Science (M.S.) program in the department of economics was inaugurated in 1928.

137. Letter to the author from Edward Peragallo, dated September 19, 1989. Peragallo wrote that Hatfield "questioned me closely on my dissertation and suggested a number of changes be made, but generally approved of the work." Other readers of the dissertation included Roy B. Kester and Thomas W. Byrnes, both members of the Columbia accounting faculty. The degree was awarded on April 20, 1939. (Information supplied by the Registrar of Columbia University.) At that time, Columbia required publication of a thesis prior to awarding of the degree. The thesis was published in 1938 by the American Institute Publishing Company under the title *Origin and Evolution of Double Entry Bookkeeping*. The date of the dissertation defense is reported in the official notice, which is preserved in Hatfield Scrapbook No. 21.

138. The author was Ralph Alfred Brenninger, and Staehling also served on the committee. (Hatfield Scrapbook No. 24.)

139. In the United States, the first Ph.D. in Accountancy was given in 1939 by the University of Illinois, on recommendation of the department of accountancy. Previously, at Illinois and other universities, Ph.D. dissertations on accounting topics were formally awarded on the recommendation of the department of economics or the business school, and thus are variously classified in historical records as being in economics or business. In the new Illinois Ph.D. program, Littleton supervised no fewer than 12 theses completed between 1939 and 1943. See V.K. Zimmerman, "The Long Shadow of a Scholar," *The International Journal of Accounting Education and Research*, Vol. 2, No. 2, Spring 1967, p. 7.

The University of Michigan's business school has published a list of its Ph.D.s since 1935 (including the names of the supervisors), when the school began offering doctoral work. Paton supervised three of the school's theses between 1935 and 1942; he also had supervised accounting theses by Ju-Mei Yang (1926), Herbert F. Taggart (1928), George R. Husband (1932), Mortimer B. Daniels (1933), and Perry Mason (1938), all completed in the department of economics.

The doctoral information for the University of Chicago business school was taken from the school's *Announcements 1970-71*.

140. Catharine DeMotte Quire, "Pioneers in Accounting," *The Accounting Review*, Vol. XXII, No. 1, January 1947, p. 75.

141. From 1916 onward, Hatfield did not teach in the intersessions or summer sessions.

142. Interview with Vance on April 6, 1978, reported in Binns, *op. cit.*, p. 58. The quotation may not be entirely accurate, since Hatfield was not "in charge" after his retirement in 1937, and Vance did not arrive until in 1941. One suspects that Vance was citing the recollection of a colleague who was in the Berkeley economics department prior to 1937.

143. *Ibid.*

144. See Moonitz, *History*, *op. cit.*, pp. 29-33. Greene actually joined the department as an assistant professor in 1941, but she did not begin teaching the work in accounting until 1943. Also see the *General Catalogue for the Fall and Spring Terms* (Berkeley) for the years 1940-1941 through 1943-1944.

145. Norton M. Bedford, *A History of Accountancy at the University of Illinois at Urbana-Champaign* (Champaign, IL: Center for International Education and Research in Accounting, 1997), p. 112.

146. Robert H. Montgomery, *Auditing Theory and Practice* (New York: The Ronald Press Company, 1912), pp. 173-174. Hatfield reviewed Montgomery's book in *The Journal of Political Economy*, October 1913, p. 781. Although he showered the book with praise ("The primacy among treatises on auditing, which until the present has been held by Dicksee's work, now passes to Montgomery's

Auditing Theory and Practice"), Hatfield lamented that Montgomery "sanctions the placing of a reserve for depreciation among the liabilities."

147. Letter dated July 1, 1938.

148. Letter dated July 13, 1938. William Colius was a reference to William Morse Cole, who preferred "allowance" as early as 1908, in *Accounts, Their Construction and Interpretation* (Boston, MA: Houghton Mifflin), p. 85. Hatfield informed Montgomery that "in this case the noble three have some supporters behind them" and proceeded to cite 14 books whose authors favor "allowance."

149. "A Research Establishment," Editorial, *The Journal of Accountancy*, Vol. 67, No. 3, March 1939, p. 129.

150. *Ibid.*, pp. 129-130.

151. Letter to John L. Carey, dated December 8, 1939. Hatfield was trying to persuade the Institute not to reprint the *Statement* and instead await a revision.

152. See Stephen A. Zeff, *Forging Accounting Principles in Five Countries: A History and an Analysis of Trends* (Champaign, IL: Stipes Publishing Co., 1972), pp. 129-148.

153. In 1938, Blough had resigned as SEC chief accountant to join Arthur Andersen & Co.

154. "Report of the Subcommittee Appointed to Study 'A Statement of Accounting Principles' By T. H. Sanders, H. R. Hatfield, and U. Moore," *The Journal of Accountancy*, Vol. 71, No. 1, January 1941, p. 58. The subcommittee's report was adopted by the Committee on Accounting Procedure at its meeting on December 4, 1940.

155. Letter to Hatfield from Sanders, dated December 23, 1940. Sanders had sent Hatfield a copy of the subcommittee's report on November 26.

156. In 1959, the American Accounting Association reprinted the *Statement* at the suggestion of Maurice Moonitz, who was a vice president of the AAA in 1958. All of the costs of producing the reprint were borne by the Haskins & Sells Foundation. See Zeff, *The American Accounting Association, op. cit.*, p. 60.

157. As was made evident in Chapter 3, Hatfield was a favorite of the Institute. Even though he was not a CPA and, thus, not a member of the Institute, Hatfield attended the Institute's fiftieth anniversary celebration held in October 1937 in New York City. Robert H. Montgomery, who much admired Hatfield, was Institute president at the time.

158. See Charles Keats, *Magnificent Masquerade: The Strange Case of Dr. Coster and Mr. Musica* (New York: Funk & Wagnalls Company, Inc., 1964); Robert Shaplen, "The Metamorphosis of Philip Musica," *The New Yorker*, October 29, 1955; and "McKesson & Robbins: Its Fall and Rise," *Fortune*, March 1940, pp. 72ff.

159. See "Testimony of Expert Witnesses," *In the Matter of McKesson & Robbins, Inc.* (Washington, DC: United States Government Printing Office, September 1939).

160. The report finally appeared at the end of 1940. See "Report on Investigation," *In the Matter of McKesson & Robbins, Inc.* (Washington, DC: United States Government Printing Office, December 1940), and the SEC's *Accounting Series Release* No. 19 (December 5, 1940).

161. Letter to Hatfield from John L. Carey, Secretary of the Institute, dated July 5, 1939.

162. In *Papers on Auditing Procedure and Other Accounting Subjects, op. cit.*, pp. 5-11.

163. Forty-one years earlier, Hatfield quoted, with apparent approval, L.R. Dicksee's observation that "A Balance Sheet is not a statement of facts, but rather an expression of opinion." Hatfield, *Modern Accounting: Its Principles and Some of Its Problems* (New York: D. Appleton and Company, 1909), p. 55.

164. An unfortunate slip was his reference to "Rowland Edwards" (p. 7) when referring to Ronald S. Edwards of the London School of Economics (LSE). Unwittingly, Hatfield combined the names of Edwards and his LSE contemporary Stanley W. Rowland, who had taken violent exception to Edwards' writings on income measurement. In correspondence, Hatfield apologized to Edwards for the error. Edwards good-naturedly replied, "In point of fact, when I saw the article I was highly amused by your attempt to solve the dispute between my colleague and me by welding us together!" Letter dated August 1, 1940.

Chapter 5

Hatfield's Contributions

This chapter consists of two parts. The first summarizes Hatfield's accomplishments and characterizes his role in developing the youthful field of accounting. The second part consists of a commentary by Professor Basil S. Yamey, the distinguished accounting historian, on Hatfield's interests and work in the history of bookkeeping and accounting.

PART I

Accounting Textbooks

Of Henry Rand Hatfield's contributions to accounting, pride of place belongs to his pioneering textbook, *Modern Accounting: Its Principles and Some of Its Problems*, published in 1909.[1] Before the appearance of *Modern Accounting*, few U.S. and U.K. textbooks or supporting material were available for accounting courses in U.S. universities. A teacher had to choose from the following, arrayed by year of first publication:

	United Kingdom
1887	Garcke and Fells, *Factory Accounts*
1897	Dicksee, *Goodwill and Its Treatment in Accounts*
1898	Dawson, *The Accountant's Compendium*
1899	Lisle, *Accounting in Theory and Practice*
1903	Dicksee, *Advanced Accounting*
1903	Dicksee, *Depreciation, Reserves, and Reserve Funds*
1903/1904;1906/1907	Lisle (ed.), *Encyclopædia of Accounting* (8 vols.)
1908	Pixley, *Accountancy*
	United States
1908	Sprague, *The Philosophy of Accounts*
1908	Cole, *Accounts, Their Construction and Interpretation*

Note: This list omits works on bookkeeping, auditing, municipal accounts, and the accounts of trustees, liquidators, and receivers. Revised editions are not noted.

Henry Hatfield in a portrait photograph taken in the mid-1930s. In 1937, Hatfield was made professor *emeritus* at the University of California.

Table 5.1. Cole's *Accounts, Their Construction and Interpretation* (1908) v. Hatfield's *Modern Accounting* (1909): Outline of Chapters

Cole	*Hatfield*
Debit and credit	Principles of double entry bookkeeping
The fundamental books	ditto
The significance of particular accounts	The balance sheet
The trial balance, the statement, and the balance sheet	Assets and the principles of valuation
Labor-saving devices	The valuation of particular assets
The distinction between capital and revenue	Immaterial assets
The general principles of depreciation	Depreciation
The general characteristics and the interpretation of balance sheets	Capital stock
The general principles of cost accounting	ditto
The place of statistics in accounting	Liabilities
The relation of principal and interest in valuations	Profits
The general principles of capitalization	ditto
Railroad accounting	Surplus and reserves
Accounting in reorganizations	Sinking funds
Bank accounting	Trading, manufacturing, and income accounts
Trust accounting	Cost accounts
Accounting for insurance and for life tenures	Partnership accounts
Factory accounting	Statement of affairs and deficiency account
Municipal accounting	Technical improvements in accounting practice
Miscellaneous applications	
Auditing	

Hatfield wrote that, prior to the appearance of Sprague's book, "there were, indeed, few American texts which could lay any claim to scientific distinction.... In England the situation was scarcely better as regards theory."[2] Most of Sprague's book dealt more with the theory of bookkeeping than with the accounting issues facing those who prepared and used financial statements, although his explanations and interpretations were refreshingly modern.

Modern Accounting was the first American textbook or treatise to probe in depth the principles and practices relating to the preparation of financial statements, and it set a high standard for others to emulate. The comprehensiveness of its coverage, the ample respect it paid to accounting and legal authorities in the United States and overseas, and the author's balanced and perceptive treatment of each topic quickly established the book's reputation as an indispensable reference work for accounting practitioners. To consult Hatfield's *Modern Accounting* was to gain access to the best accounting thought: explained, interpreted, and sometimes criticized in the author's temperate prose. It was welcomed by accounting instructors as the first textbook at an advanced level that enlightened students on the principles underlying financial statements.

William Morse Cole's *Accounts, Their Construction and Interpretation* was the closest of previous American textbooks to Hatfield's *Modern Accounting* in terms of its treatment of the principles and practices in the preparation of financial statements. But, as is evident from Table 5.1, in which the chapter titles of the two books are compared, Hatfield's had by far the greater coverage. Apart from bookkeeping procedures and specialized applications, only six of Cole's 21 chapters (about one-third of the book) dealt with the principles and problems of preparing financial statements for general-purpose enterprise, while 13 of Hatfield's 19 chapters were devoted to these weighty matters. Cole, an assistant professor of accounting at the Harvard Business School, was concerned with the education of business managers, while Hatfield at Berkeley focused on educating future professional accountants. Moreover, while Cole's book was aimed at the introductory student, Hatfield's proceeded from a discussion of fundamentals to a sophisticated consideration of the most advanced and controversial topics in the field.

Modern Accounting stimulated interest in the field. No less a figure than William A. Paton has said that it played a role in his decision to pursue a career in academic accounting rather than economics.[3] Samuel J. Broad, a partner in Peat, Marwick, Mitchell & Co., who served as president of the American Institute of Accountants and as chairman of its Committee on Accounting Procedure, said of *Modern Accounting*: "When it first appeared, this work shone like a bright light against a dull background, little accounting literature of note having appeared for some years."[4] In 1937, upon Hatfield's retirement from the University of California, Geo. E. Frazer, a teacher, practitioner, and professional leader, wrote, "When I began the teaching of accounting at the University of Wisconsin in 1910 your text was the only worthwhile book then available for teaching."[5]

Hatfield's *Accounting: Its Principles and Problems*, the revision of *Modern Accounting* published in 1927, was an even more mature work, and it won the inaugural Beta Alpha Psi book prize. Yet by then other authors—Montgomery, Dickinson, Paton, Kester, Saliers, Esquerré, Finney, and Himmelblau, among others[6]—had launched a parade of textbooks and even a handbook; so Hatfield's contribution to the American literature, though substantial, was no longer without peer in coverage and depth of treatment. Yet, both *Modern Accounting* and *Accounting* set Hatfield apart from other textbook authors in two important respects: (1) his exhaustive and sensitive marshaling of the views of accounting authorities both in the United States and the United Kingdom, and (2) his thorough review of legal treatises, statutes, and court opinions not only in the United States and the United Kingdom but also on the European continent. When preparing both books, Hatfield made trips to Europe to expand his net of authoritative sources beyond the United States. Such an international quest for authoritative opinion remains unmatched among the authors of U.S. accounting textbooks published before or since.

Carl Thomas Devine, a preeminent accounting scholar, admired Hatfield's treatment of depreciation in *Accounting*. Thirty-six years after *Accounting* appeared, Devine wrote, "Hatfield's writings on depreciation were by far the most sophisticated in America at the time and are still more advanced than some treatments found in modern textbooks."[7]

Contributions to Journals

As a contributor to the periodical literature on accounting, however, Hatfield did not match the output of Paton, Littleton, May, or Kohler, four of his leading contemporaries.[8] He published 10 articles in English and one in German, of which three were major works of enduring value:[9]

"An Historical Defense of Bookkeeping," 1924
"What Is the Matter with Accounting?" 1927
"What They Say About Depreciation" 1935

Of all his writings, "An Historical Defense of Bookkeeping" is the most memorable. It amused and edified. And it struck a chord with his fellow accounting academics, who felt that their young field was demeaned by colleagues in other disciplines.

"Historical Defense" may have been the most admired accounting article in the English language during the first half of the twentieth century. Through numerous reprintings, it has stimulated interest in the study of accounting history both in the United States and Britain. Littleton acknowledged Hatfield's influence in the dedication to his landmark *Accounting Evolution to 1900*:[10]

TO
HENRY RAND HATFIELD
WHOSE
AN HISTORICAL DEFENSE OF BOOKKEEPING
PROVIDES THE INSPIRATION AND
MODEL FOR THIS BOOK

"Historical Defense" was ranked as a "classic" by Deinzer[11] and by Moonitz and Littleton,[12] and it was reprinted in both the United States and United Kingdom. When given as an address at the annual meeting of the American Association of University Instructors in Accounting (AAUIA) in 1923, it fired the interest of young accounting academics in building the field.

Hatfield also wrote two major, article-length papers on accounting that were not published during his lifetime:

"Some Variations in Accounting Practice in England, France, Germany and the United States," 1911 (published in 1966)

"A Critique of the Tentative Statement of Accounting Principles Underlying Corporate Reports," 1937

These five papers are reproduced in Chapter 7.

All five of his major papers, as well as his small book *Surplus and Dividends*, were read as addresses to gatherings of practitioners or academics. To Hatfield, apparently, the prospect of a spontaneous audience reaction to his papers motivated him to write. He was a performer. A man of catholic interests who enjoyed the intellectual dialogue at biweekly meetings of the university's literary clubs, he wrote and delivered 14 lengthy papers at such occasions; all but one treated subjects other than accounting. Of these 14, plus a paper he delivered in 1913 to high school teachers of bookkeeping titled "Some Heretical Views on the Method of Teaching Bookkeeping," only one was ever published: "An Historical Defense of Bookkeeping." Only two of the 15 were even submitted for publication. Unlike most of his accounting colleagues at other universities, whose intellectual output seemed to be confined to accounting, economics, or business administration, Hatfield indulged his intellectual curiosities in a variety of other areas (chiefly history and contemporary politics, with touches of philosophy, literature, and the classics), and he regularly used his sabbatical leaves to take world tours that inspired several of these nonaccounting papers. It is curious that, of the major papers written by Hatfield both in and out of accounting, the majority were never published. As I have suggested, Hatfield's papers were written primarily to be heard. Apparently, he did not have a compulsion that they be read.

Bookkeeping history fascinated him,[13] and his compilation of North American holdings,"A Check-List of Early Bookkeeping Texts" (1932), done jointly with Littleton, exhibited his passion as a bibliophile of historically significant works on bookkeeping. He spent much of his time, both in Berkeley and on foreign trips, in search of rare bookkeeping tracts for purchase by the University of California library. Hatfield also stocked the university's library with contemporary works. Mary E. Murphy, a close student of accounting academe and the profession, has written:

> Perhaps it is not too much to say that the best example of the work of a single individual in building up an all-inclusive library is that of the late Professor Henry Rand Hatfield at the University of California at Berkeley. The zeal which drove Professor Hatfield to seek out both rare and modern treatises in accounting in all parts of the world finds no parallels on other campuses.[14]

Hatfield was an inveterate reviewer of books, all of which he read from cover to cover, and not infrequently he sent the authors lengthy *corrigenda* for their private information. He was an unforgiving critic of those who used imprecise terminology or were guilty of illogical or uninformed argument. He was equally intolerant of misspellings and other inaccuracies. As Patti Mills has written:

> Although undogmatic in his own writings, Hatfield was less diffident as a critic.... In the numerous, elegantly written book reviews which he authored over the course of his life, he was always frank about what he considered the defects of an author's work.[15]

His own writings were crafted as if by a literary scholar: ribbed with classical allusions, ironic asides, and pungent wit. The best example of this style is found in "An Historical Defense of Bookkeeping." Because Hatfield's puckish demeanor and unquestioned erudition, he was in great demand both as a toastmaster and as an eulogist. He would always write out his remarks in advance of the event, and the few such orations that have survived are reproduced in Chapter 7.

Opposition to Doctoral Students in Accounting

Hatfield was not, however, a mentor of doctoral students. Unlike William A. Paton at the University of Michigan and A.C. Littleton at the University of Illinois, both of whom directed the work of many doctoral students, Hatfield did not believe that accounting was a proper field for doctoral study. He had but a single doctoral student—and he tried in vain to resist her entreaties to write on accounting. The student, Catharine D. Greene, who defended her thesis a week before Hatfield became *emeritus*, was 44 when she received her doctorate, and she did not publish any subsequent research. By contrast, the influence of Paton and Littleton has been felt not only in their own published writings and their professional service but also through the considerable work done by their many disciples, who became teachers, textbook authors, and researchers.

Current Value and General Price-Level Accounting

Paton and Littleton imprinted strong ideologies on the literature, but Hatfield did not. Paton favored an economics-based interpretation of accounting, and during most of his career he advocated recording current values in financial statements.[16] Littleton steadfastly held to the view that accounting should be rooted in an enterprise's transaction experience, and he opposed the recording of current values.[17] From the 1920s onward, the cost versus value controversy was debated intensely. Yet Hatfield recognized the centrality of value as early as 1911:

> The vital question in all accounting is the value which is to be placed on existing assets. That being determined, almost every other question is decided.[18]

But he was reluctant to take sides on the global question, as the following 1943 statement shows:

> Accounting ... is not concerned with material units—tons of ore, or barrels of oil—but with values, value being interpreted as an expression in monetary terms, either of the cost value or of the present market value, depending on whether one adheres to one or the other school of accounting theory.[19]

Yet, after surveying the arguments pro and con, he gave cautious approval to revaluing fixed assets so long as the increment were not credited to profit:

> Here it suffices to say that much of the objection to showing appreciation of fixed assets is removed if such a showing is freed from the evil ordinarily accompanying it, that is a showing of a corresponding profit. It would be little objectionable to indicate the increment in the value of land, if the balance sheet shows as the offsetting item, not Profit and Loss, nor Surplus, but a separate account distinctly labeled, say, Reserve for Appreciation in Value of Lands, or Surplus from Land Appreciation.[20]

He added the caveat that the appreciation must have substance behind it:

> The conclusion is that appreciation may be recognized, with the obvious understanding that the appreciation must be genuine, objectively verified, and not arbitrarily done in order to make a "pretty balance sheet."[21]

He counseled accountants not to use specious reasoning as justification to revalue certain classes of assets and not others as well.[22]

Eric L. Kohler, a close student of the literature and a staunch defender of historical cost, characterized Hatfield as a "mild enthusiast" for the use of current values.[23]

On general price-level accounting, Hatfield supported Henry W. Sweeney's theoretical argument for "stabilized accounting": the use of a common unit of money to reflect inflation or deflation in the financial statements.[24] Paton went further than Hatfield and even recommended Sweeney's restatement technique.[25] Littleton, on the other hand, was deeply skeptical of "stabilized accounting," which he believed would be confusing to readers and in the realm of the hypothetical—a departure from reality.[26] But because Hatfield's views on this question were uttered in two or three obscure corners in the accounting literature, few students of the literature are even aware of his position.[27] By contrast, Paton and Littleton wrote extensively on this question, and their divergent views have been widely noticed.[28]

Hence, on two such contentious issues as the use of current values and general price-level adjustments in the financial statements, Hatfield was a cautious progressive. Yet, the paucity and hedged character of his writings on these points failed to earn him a reputation as a participant in the debate.

An Internationalist

Hatfield was the first American accounting author to devote serious and continuing attention to the broad sweep of the contemporary literature overseas. To be sure, Robert H. Montgomery brought out an American edition of Dicksee's *Auditing* in 1905, but the first edition of Montgomery's *Auditing Theory and Practice* in 1912 contained comparatively few British references and none from other countries. Few American accounting writers paid any attention to the British literature, and even fewer—an outstanding exception being Henry W. Sweeney in the late 1920s and the 1930s—drew upon developments on the European continent. In the Preface to *Modern Accounting*, Hatfield offered the following reason for tapping the foreign literature:

> [In this book] considerable recourse has been had to other less obvious sources of information. These include the decisions of English and American courts, the commercial codes of Germany, France and Austria and the commentaries of the leading jurists of these countries. The legal provisions of the Continental countries are, of course, not binding on American practice. But they are of considerable significance in discussing the principles of accounting, for they embody the carefully expressed opinions of experts on many difficult problems.
>
> Such attention to foreign authorities is all the more necessary since in this country far too little attention has been given to matters of principle. American accounting is famed for short cuts and practical efficiency. At the same time the accounts of American corporations, until very recent years, have been replete with questionable practices, oftentimes vicious in principle and misleading in their results.[29]

Hatfield read several languages, and he had traveled to Europe twice before writing *Modern Accounting* in 1909 and preparing "Some Variations in Accounting Practice in England, France, Germany and the United States" for delivery in 1911 to the annual meeting of the American Association of Public Accountants. *Modern Accounting* and "Variations" (which Hatfield never offered for publication) were unequaled in their day as perceptive comparisons of the accounting traditions in the United States, the United Kingdom, and major countries on the European continent, drawing on the opinions of leading accounting and legal authorities and offering coherent explanations of the diverse practices he found in each. "Variations" was veritably a *tour de force*, especially when one considers the difficulty of locating source material for such a survey circa 1910-1911. His *Accounting*, published in 1927, was written in very much the same internationalist vein as *Modern Accounting*.

Hatfield's facility with languages could be jarring to his readers. In "Operating Deficit and Paid-in Surplus" (*The Accounting Review*, September 1934), when citing authorities on the other side of the proposition that charging "an operating deficit against paid-in surplus violates one of the fundamental principles of accounting," he presented five quotations from German authors without giving translations. At the end of his two chapters on Capital Stock in *Modern Accounting*—a textbook intended for undergraduate students—he directed readers to one work in French and two in German for "a more serious discussion of the principles involved."[30] In a speech to accounting practitioners, he interposed (without translating from the Latin): "Query: Is a sound principle one which is *vox et praeterea nihil*?"[31]

Hatfield believed that any review of authoritative writings should not be confined to one's own country or to one's own language. Of the 133 cited works in his end-of-chapter bibliographical notes in *Modern Accounting*, 82 were published in the United Kingdom, France, Germany, or Canada, of which 20 were written in French or German. By 1927, when *Accounting* appeared, the American accounting literature had expanded greatly, yet as many as 50 of the 176 items in his bibliographical notes were of foreign origin, of which 13 were in French or German. Hatfield continued to remind his readers that accounting thought and practice were not a product of American minds alone.

As an avowed internationalist, however, Hatfield failed to make any converts. Few American textbook authors cited other authorities, let alone overseas writings. The outstanding exception was George Hillis Newlove and S. Paul Garner's *Advanced Accounting* (Boston: D.C. Heath and Company, 1951), which cited the U.S. accounting and legal literatures extensively but shunned foreign sources. Leland L. Briggs, founder of *The Accountants Digest* (1935-1988), which contained reproductions and abridgments of accounting articles originally published elsewhere, began his quarterly journal "because I felt a need for foreign articles in my teaching of accounting and thought that others might be helped in their work by this material in easily available form."[32]

Hatfield's Discomfort as an Authority Figure

Although frequently cited as an authority, Hatfield himself disavowed such a role, except to puncture unprincipled argument and skewer inept and inconsistent use of terminology. When the literature was discordant, he declined to become the voice of ultimate authority, although he could have done so. Instead, he marshaled and examined the best intelligence the literature had to offer and served as arbiter of the logic and texture of the debate. From this stance, he provided the new field of accounting with its first model of scholarship assessment, a model more thorough than that practiced by the Modern Language Association at that time. In so doing, he helped to legitimize accounting as an academic field, though even he was not convinced that it deserved this status.

Hence, Hatfield reached his conclusions—always hedged with cautionary phrases—after consulting authorities. Who were Hatfield's authorities? Lawyers, yes, because he greatly esteemed law as a discipline. Court opinions and the regulations of government agencies, yes, because of their standing as the ultimate pronouncements in a society of laws. What of accountants? Throughout his career, Hatfield looked to practitioners, even more than academics, as the authorities on accounting theory and as a respected source on practices. That he himself was not a CPA and had never practiced as an accountant may have induced a certain restraint, but Hatfield's temperament as a punctilious (with Fowler,[33] he disliked the use of the word "meticulous" as praise) scholar drove him unendingly to search out the opinions of those whose views must be held in respect.

Hatfield performed in the literature as he did in the classroom. A disciple of Socratic teaching, he believed his mission was to stimulate thinking, not supply final answers. He invited academics and practitioners to join with him in a scrutiny of the accounting literature. In telling them what they did not want to hear, he challenged them to see the problems in their thinking and moved them to change their perspectives. As his presentations reveal, Hatfield always took exception to muddled thinking. Without stating what he believed the answers to be, he provided the guidelines for pursuing rational inquiry. In a sense, he seemed less interested in answers than in clear thinking. In "Moriturus Vos Saluto," his retirement speech to the Berkeley Club (reproduced in full in Chapter 7), he reflected on his "habit of mind":

> I look askance at any inconsistent mental attitude. I like straight-forward thinking. This is probably a defect. I have been greatly interested just now in reading a lecture by Lord Macmillan entitled "Two Ways of Thinking." These he illustrates by contrasting Scotland and England, represented respectively by the system of Roman Law and the system of Common Law. In the former case, the starting point is a principle, and all subsequent mental activities are bent on making actions and facts conform to the principle. In the other way of thinking, principles are, in general, ignored, or at least arrived at by a secondary process. The important thing is to observe present facts, and in one way or another an effort is made to find a practical, rather than a logical, way out of the muddle. Lord Macmillan considers that these two ways of thinking are fundamental and perhaps ineradicable. The best results might be secured if members of each group could at least appreciate the point of view of the other. If only one is adopted, it is probably that the habit of mind which relied upon principles is the more dangerous. I fear that to a large extent, I incline toward that way of thinking. I confess that my greatest impediment is that, in addition to laziness, procrastination, indecision, and inadequate intelligence—in addition to all these unqualifications, and more potent than any one, or than all taken together, has been an assumption that all other persons should act rationally, should be consistent in their conduct and logical in their thinking.

Thus, as the Socratic teacher, Hatfield measured his success not in the number of points he proved but in the illuminations he provided, the horizons he widened. He wanted to avoid the truth of things and focus instead on the truth about things—what he called "accounting principles"—instead of a jumble of "accepted practices" which rested on no set of conceptual foundations. Thus, he argued for principles instead of practices and showed that even principles were open to differing constructions by different writers. In positing principles—the truth about things—he assembled the best thinking in the literature to exercise the reader's or student's critical faculty. He defended his method in the Preface to *Accounting*:

> In accounting there is no person or academy whose pronouncement can be accepted as having unquestioned authority. Those who write on the subject must, in general, express opinions and formulate arguments rather than render decisions. Hence in this treatise there are presented the somewhat divergent, and at times perhaps contradictory, statements of recognized authorities. The student may thus get a broader view of the subject, and have a better opportunity to arrive at a reasoned conviction, than if the author had adopted the easier method of expounding only his personal views.[34]

Describing his philosophy of teaching, Hatfield justified his position as follows:

> In the midst of divergent views why should an author interject his own views in a text intended for intelligent and semi-mature University students, who pine for an opportunity to form their own opinions, who resent a dogmatic attitude, who proclaim that they want to learn, not to be taught? There has been too much dogmatism for so undeveloped a subject.

To be sure, Hatfield delighted in sparring with authors in his papers and with students in his classes. He would have been bored with accounting if the authorities had all been in agreement. He once wrote, "The most interesting feature of accounting is that there are so many points still open to discussion."[35] Ironically, however, while Hatfield's pedagogical methods—widening the vision of colleagues and students—worked to nurture clear thinking, Hatfield himself apparently did not anticipate that accounting would need authority within a decade following his death and that the "many points still open to discussion" would require closure.

Hatfield's recommended accounting practices were tucked away in his books and articles. Nonetheless, a persevering reader can detect firm views announced by Hatfield on a number of accounting practices. He took the following positions in *Accounting*, published in 1927:[36]

- The terminology Allowance (not Reserve) for Depreciation should be used;
- Any recognition of appreciation in the value of capital assets should preferably be credited to Capital Surplus;
- Discount on bonds payable should be shown as a subtraction from the par value, not as an asset;
- "Lower of cost or market" for merchandise is an illogical practice that deserves condemnation;
- Goodwill should be written off against earnings during the period of its calculated duration;
- The premium on capital stock issued should form part of Surplus, not stated capital; and
- When one corporation buys a majority interest in the capital stock of another and an amount of previously unrecognized goodwill is implied in the purchase price, the consolidated goodwill should be shown at the 100 percent level, with explicit recognition accorded the minority slice thereof.

But these views were dispensed in the context of his characteristically extensive sampling of the views of authorities on all sides of each question, and thus they might not have made a marked impression on most readers. Nonetheless, there is reason to believe that Hatfield's judgments, particularly his analyses of competing views on the many controversial questions he addressed, had an impact on the thinking of practitioners.

Hatfield's principal focus on the balance sheet, rather than on the income statement, while out of step with the changed thinking of the 1930s, was the approach eventually adopted by the Financial Accounting Standards Board in the 1970s. In this regard, Mills regarded Hatfield as "a prognosticator regarding accounting theory." She has written, "He saw that financial accounting derived its essential structure from the accounting equation and that income was fundamentally a creature of the balance sheet."[37]

Appeal to Practitioners

While Hatfield attended carefully to the views of accounting academics such as Paton and Kester, it is hardly surprising that, in *Accounting*, three of the four most frequently cited authors were leading practitioners: Montgomery, Couchman, and Dickinson. On a number of occasions, Hatfield urged practitioners to impart their wisdom on accounting theory and practice. In his address to the 1939 annual meeting of the American Institute of Accountants, he said:

> Is it not the function, the duty, the privilege of the accountant to consider the essential nature of accounting and to point out practices which should be changed? Who can do this better than the accountant, the independent accountant of whom we hear so often?[38]

A dozen years earlier, also in an address to an annual meeting of the Institute, Hatfield said:

> in the busy strife of professional life, in the problem of how to meet the task of serving the innumerable clients flocking to your office and each demanding immediate attention, you have somewhat neglected the higher task of developing a sound set of accounting theories.[39]

Hatfield did not shrink from criticizing accounting practitioners. He may have been alone among accounting academics in daring to lecture accounting practitioners, often in public forums, to improve the performance of their public role and especially not to be submissive to their clients. One of the best examples of this genre was his address to the annual meeting of the American Institute of Accountants in 1927. After referring to the "interminable debate" among accountants over the relative merits of straight-line versus curved-line depreciation, he said:[40]

> More distressful and more pertinent to the present discussion is the nature of the arguments adduced in support of one or the other basis. These are often barren of any vestige of accounting theory. It may be said that the charge should be relatively low in the early years, not because depreciation is less, but because it "is inconvenient to burden the early years" with a heavy charge, or because such a charge would show an initial deficit. Is accounting a device to secure what is convenient, or to show what is real? Should accounting be twisted so as to conceal an initial deficit if one really exists, or should it show the facts? (p. 276)

He reminded his audience:

> Accounting is something other than a set of clever devices for beating the income tax with the least damage to one's conscience, something more than a specious way of window-dressing whereby the best possible appearance is given to a somewhat undesirable stock of goods. It is a universal language of business (p. 270).

Even as early as 1905-1906, speaking to a group of San Francisco accounting practitioners, Hatfield pointedly reminded them of their public responsibility. After complaining that "there is no other country where such vicious principles of corporation accounting are countenanced as in the United States," he said, "Is the C.P.A. prepared to take a stand for accuracy in corporation accounts? May not C.P.A. stand for Conscience, Probity, Accuracy?" True to his father's teachings, he held himself and others to high ethical standards, and he was remorselessly critical of deceptive and misleading practices.

The Sanders, Hatfield, and Moore Monograph

Hatfield is remembered by many for the monograph *A Statement of Accounting Principles*, which he coauthored with Thomas H. Sanders and Underhill Moore. Yet it was the least representative of Hatfield's writings. The monograph was sponsored by the Haskins & Sells Foundation and published by the American Institute of Accountants in 1938. This was unquestionably Hatfield's most difficult writing assignment. He was separated from Sanders (at Harvard) and Moore (at Yale) by 3,000 miles, and all three authors were under pressure by the foundation to be permissive rather than restrictive in the accounting practices of which they approved. The nature of the project did not allow Hatfield the luxury of his usual thoughtful, balanced treatment of a subject, replete with footnotes to authoritative sources, since the goal of the writing assignment was to provide support for accounting practitioners in their dealings with the Securities and Exchange Commission. This project presented Hatfield with a profound conflict. On the one hand, he wanted to contribute to the improvement of accounting practice. But on the other, he was intellectually unwilling to offer himself as an authority.

The foundation pressed upon the authors its surveys of accounting practices used in company reports as sufficient ground for recommending a practice. But in an address to the American Institute of Accountants the year after the monograph was published, Hatfield bridled at the use of such an approach:

> By some it is thought sufficient to find out what is done in published income statements and balance-sheets.... This procedure rests on the dictum that
>
> "...spite of pride, in erring reason's spite
> One truth is clear: What ever is, is right."

> But there is a real difficulty here. Are all corporations, or all accountants, of equal significance? A Gallup poll shows which opinion on neutrality prevails, but unless you are a besotted adherent to the *vox populi, vox Dei* tradition, it does not show which is the proper opinion.... The accounting practices of a given moment are no proof of their validity.[41]

This was a time when the term "generally accepted accounting principles" was coming to mean practices whose widespread use by companies *ipso facto* earned them the mantle of approval.

Failure to Anticipate the Increasingly Important Role of Accounting

Even though Hatfield was actively engaged in preparing *A Statement of Accounting Principles*, he somehow failed to comprehend the important role that accounting was coming to play in corporate society. Other prominent members of the American Accounting Association, such as Kohler, Paton, Littleton, and Greer, understood this development. They realized that the accounting profession was being called upon to unite on a program to provide the government—specifically, the SEC—with authoritative guidance on sound accounting practice. *A Statement of Accounting Principles* was one element in this program. Another was "A Tentative Statement of Accounting Principles Underlying Corporate Reports," which was issued in June 1936 by the AAA's executive committee. At the AAA's annual meeting in December 1937, however, Hatfield—the respected elder among accounting academics—upbraided the authors of the "Tentative Statement" for expository defects in the document instead of addressing the weighty accounting issues it treated. As he said at the outset of his critique, instead of discussing the substance of the report, he would concentrate on "the niceties of formulation, the avoidance of vagueness, the respect due to the English language, with freedom from solecisms and adherence to logical consistency." In this respect, he allowed his instincts as a classical scholar to overwhelm the role he might have played in encouraging the AAA's effort with constructive and useful criticism of the substantive positions taken in the document. Apparently, no one encouraged him to submit the paper for publication in *The Accounting Review*, and one suspects that the authors of the "Tentative Statement" did not find his criticisms of the rhetoric to be apposite.

Hatfield as a Leading Figure in Academic and Professional Institutions

Hatfield was a pioneer in important academic and professional associations and was dean of two of the earliest business schools. He was a founder, in 1916, of the American Association of University Instructors in Accounting (AAUIA), and he was its president in 1919. He advocated a clear division of turf between the AAUIA and the American Institute of Accountants (Institute), the practitioners' body. Contrary to the views of most of the other early leaders of the AAUIA, he opposed efforts to broaden its mission beyond the province of accounting instruction. He felt that the AAUIA should not attempt to compete with the Institute. During his presidency, he was against the AAUIA's setting up its own journal, preferring instead that it cooperate with the Institute's *Journal of Accountancy*. In 1935, he spoke against the proposal to change the AAUIA's name to the American Accounting Association (AAA) and to add the following mission to its bylaws: "To develop accounting principles and standards, and to seek their endorsement, or adoption by business enterprises, public and private accountants, and governmental bodies." Hatfield regarded this activity as the preserve of the practitioners' organization, not of an organization of instructors.[42] Another proposed bylaw provision toward which Hatfield would have been cool was "To encourage and sponsor research in accounting and to publish or aid in the publication of the results of research." When Hatfield was president, "research" was not mentioned in the bylaws. He believed that the association should be concerned with the problems of the teacher, and this call for research would have been, in his eyes, too open-ended. (In the event, both the change in name and the new bylaws provisions were approved overwhelmingly by the membership.) It is likely that Hatfield's conservative views on the association's role did not endear him to its activist leaders in the 1920s and 1930s, especially Eric L. Kohler, the driving force in 1935-1936.[43] They may have felt that Hatfield was "out of touch" with the times.

Yet, as Mills has written, Hatfield had a "gift for prophecy":

> he correctly surmised that the AAA would abandon its focus on accounting education when it adopted a "research" emphasis beginning in the mid-1930s.... Almost sixty years later, the membership of the AAA, disillusioned by decades of research programmes and paradigms which yielded little by way of practice or pedagogy, have begun to renew their commitment to teaching.[44]

In his presidential address prepared for delivery at the AAUIA's annual meeting in 1919 (which was never published), Hatfield was probably the first leader of the AAUIA to anticipate another future development: schools of accounting. He wrote:

> In one respect accounting is in a peculiar, perhaps in an unfortunate position. It may be illustrated by comparing it with law. Courses in commercial law are given in Schools of Commerce, mining law in Schools of Mines, Roman law in Letters and Science, yet none of these courses train the lawyer. That is reserved for a professional School of Law. Similarly, Stevens Institute has some excellent lectures on accounting, our College of Agriculture gives a course in farm accounts, and any College of Commerce gives accounting. But in most universities there is no professional School of Accounting separate from the School of Business. Accounting, like law, is a profession, not a business. Schools of Business teach some law without becoming law schools. But for some reason professional teaching in accounting is relegated to Schools of Business, although it belongs there as little as professional law belongs in Commerce, Engineering or Agriculture.

Hatfield was also a leading figure during the early years of Beta Gamma Sigma, the national honorary society for business students, and of the American Association of Collegiate Schools of Business, the accrediting agency, beginning in the 1910s. In 1919, he became the only accounting professor ever elected vice-president of the American Economic Association, and from 1922 to 1928, he served as a senator of national Phi Beta Kappa. He was the first dean of the College of Commerce and Administration at the University of Chicago (1902-1904) and the second dean of the College of Commerce at the University of California (1909-1920). These were the first two university business schools, both founded in 1898, following the establishment of the Wharton School of Finance and Economy at the University of Pennsylvania in 1881. Both of his deanships carried only limited authority, since the real power in both universities resided in the academic departments, not in the colleges.

In 1910, Hatfield became the first honorary member of the California State Society of Certified Public Accountants. He frequently attended meetings of its San Francisco chapter, often bringing a graduate student as his guest. Shortly after coming to Berkeley in 1904, he had formed an alliance with John F. Forbes, a leading San Francisco practitioner who was to become the longtime chairman of the State Board of Accountancy. Their goal was to raise the standard of the young profession by developing a strong accounting curriculum at the University of California and by encouraging promising students to join its ranks. Although not a CPA, Hatfield believed that there should be a close tie between accounting teachers and the profession.

An Assessment

Unlike two of his leading contemporaries, Paton and John B. Canning, Hatfield was not an original thinker or a theorist. Both Paton and Canning formulated grand accounting theories,[45] but Hatfield did not. Another innovative thinker, Henry W. Sweeney, proposed a theory and set of practices for restating financial statements to take explicit account of inflation.[46] Hatfield was instead an annotator and critic of others' writings. In his most significant work, he was an archivist and scholar even more than a researcher: he digested, systematized, and instilled coherency in a dispersed and discordant literature for the benefit of practitioners, academic colleagues, and students. And, unlike almost all of his contemporaries, he wrote in an elegant prose with flashes of humor.

The only "theory" with which Hatfield is sometimes associated is the "proprietary theory," which has been contrasted with the "entity theory" identified with Paton.[47] Yet, Hatfield attributed scant importance to the difference between the two, and he never entered into a discussion of the two "theories."[48] His only comment even remotely related to this point appeared in a review of Paton's *Accounting*:

> To some it would seem that there is little significant difference between saying that the right-hand side of the balance-sheet contains two distinct categories, liabilities and proprietorship, and saying that it contains only equities, but these are divided into "two quite distinct elements."[49]

In research conducted almost 40 years ago, I concluded that the difference between the "proprietary theory" and the "entity theory" was greatly exaggerated.[50]

Hatfield was not a "driven" publisher of his major papers. As mentioned above, a significant fraction of his major papers—especially those on nonaccounting subjects—was not even offered for publication. He was more active in finding publication outlets for his short papers on subjects—digressions, really—that captured his fancy, typically on the use of terminology, facets of law related to accounting, intellectual puzzles, or some aspect of history. Ideas fascinated him, but if he could resolve a conundrum to his satisfaction through correspondence with academics and practitioners—and his correspondence was voluminous—he would not feel it necessary to break into print. It is disappointing that he made no significant contribution to the body of research on bookkeeping history or on German accounting theory, two subjects with which he was often associated.

It is not widely appreciated that, beyond the pieces that he published for his amusement, he very much wanted to make a mark on accounting practice. Accounting practices for which he could find no principled support troubled him. He lectured practitioners that they should be more attentive to the theory of their field, and he did not flinch from pointing out illogic and lack of principled reasoning in support of dubious practices, such as the use of "lower of cost or market" for merchandise inventory. Before the 1930s, he saw his textbook *Modern Accounting* (1909), which he revised as *Accounting* in 1927, as his major effort to improve accounting practice. When he composed a statement of his teaching philosophy in the late 1920s, he noted with some apparent pleasure that his opinion on the use of Allowance, instead of Reserve, for Depreciation was one "which I believe has had some little effect on accounting practice." In the 1930s, his desire to improve practice intensified. In 1934, at age 67, he unsuccessfully sought appointment as the accounting consultant (retitled chief accountant the following year) of the Securities and Exchange Commission. From 1935 to 1937, he was a keen and active coauthor of *A Statement of Accounting Principles*, sponsored by the Haskins & Sells Foundation, even though he seems to have been outvoted by Thomas H. Sanders and Underhill Moore, his two coauthors, on most of the important matters of style and substance. Nonetheless, in 1940, by then 73 and not in the best of health, he aggressively pushed for authority to prepare a second edition of the *Statement* (in which he might succeed in bringing his own approach to the fore), but it was not to be.

Perhaps because he was not a CPA and had never even taken a course in accounting, Hatfield did not promote himself as an authority on proper accounting practice. His recommendations, usually hedged in scholarly understatement, could be found in books and articles, but he did not accord them any prominence. Hatfield's extreme timidity in this regard is a major reason why his contributions to the literature are not better appreciated. He was an enlightened critic who was capable of advancing bold proposals for reform. An excellent example of such a proposal concerning the role of accounting in corporate society was his argument in March 1910 that:

> The most satisfactory remedy for financial misdeeds [perpetrated by powerful corporations] is ... the simple one of requiring publicity of accounts, with, of course, the implication that the accounts must be full and accurate. This not only remedies most of the abuses in the realm of finance, but even paves the way to prevent some of the other evils of modern corporations. Thus, for instance, the main evil of monopoly, that extortion is made possible, is less likely to be a permanent condition if the public is fully informed as to the exact rate of profits that are being made by the corporation on their actual investment. It is hardly conceivable that society will long endure an extortionate monopoly when once it knows the facts. But the actual conditions are so often concealed by a wrongful showing that the problem of restraint is made much more difficult.

This passage appeared in a modest paper that Hatfield presented to the Oakland chapter of the American Institute of Banking, but it was never published.[51] Hatfield's advocacy actually preceded by several years the establishment of the Federal Trade Commission, and it was some 16 years before the Harvard economist William Z. Ripley became celebrated for this and other reform proposals.[52] Three years after Hatfield's presentation, Louis D. Brandeis argued for better reporting of commissions and profits by investment bankers, uttering the famous dictum, "Publicity is justly commended as a remedy for social and industrial diseases. Sunlight is said to be the best of disinfectants; electric light the most efficient policeman."[53] Hatfield was a more progressive thinker than many believe, but his mindset as a classical scholar effectively suppressed this quality.

That Hatfield never pushed his best students on to the doctorate was a surprise and puzzlement to many. Although he supervised numerous Master of Science theses, mostly on practical accounting questions, he did not believe that accounting justified study and research at the doctoral level. In this, he could almost be grouped with those denigrators of the academic standing of accounting whom he sought to skewer in his famous "An Historical Defense of Bookkeeping." He began "Historical Defense" with the following passage:

> I am sure that all of us who teach accounting in the universities suffer from the implied contempt of our colleagues, who look upon accounting as an intruder, a Saul among the prophets, a pariah whose very presence detracts somewhat from the sanctity of the academic halls.[54]

But then he added, as if perhaps to signify his own inner doubts:

> It is true that we ourselves speak of the science of accounts, or of the art of accounting, even of the philosophy of accounts. But accounting is, alas, only a pseudoscience unrecognized by J. McKeen Cattell; its products are displayed neither in the salon nor in the national academy; one finds it discussed by neither realist, idealist nor phenomenalist. The humanists look down upon us as beings who dabble in the sordid figures of dollars and cents instead of toying with infinities and searching for the elusive soul of things; the scientists and technologists despise us as able only to record rather than to perform deeds.[55]

His Legacy

Hatfield's influence is better judged by the scholarliness he brought to accounting discussions than by the opinions he espoused. He was a classical scholar—indeed, a humanist—who, owing to experience in a banking house coupled with doctoral studies taken in political economy and political science, was tapped to coordinate the program of instruction in two of the early American business schools. He became the first full-time academic with professorial rank in the fledgling field of accounting. Recognizing that accounting and legal authorities were often in disagreement on accounting questions, he saw his mission as one of arraying and examining the views of the principal authorities, reviewing the practices commonly found in corporate reports, and then identifying the position that most accorded with principle. He proceeded as would a scholar. In 1971, upon the reissuance of Hatfield's *Accounting*, I wrote as follows:

> *Accounting* reveals an author whose mind is genuinely open to all ideas, however radical. To read Hatfield, especially his *Accounting*, is to be shaken loose from one's prejudices and preconceptions by an author whose objectivity and intellectual honesty are welcome antidotes to a literature replete with briefs and summary judgments. Hatfield approaches his subject as a student and beckons his reader to join in the quest....
>
> To Hatfield, the literature does not end at the water's edge. Fluent in German and French, he frequently compares U.S. practices and laws with those in France, Germany, Austria and Great Britain. He gently reminds us that accounting is not unique to America.
>
> It is not the volume or variety of quotations and references that make the work. What truly impresses the reader is Hatfield's deep understanding of the diverse literatures and authors from whom he borrows a pithy line here, a lengthy quote there. He traces an author's thinking through successive editions, pointing out ironies and inconsistencies. He juxtaposes apparently contradictory authorities, exposing curious anomalies to close examination. Above all, he demonstrates a comprehension and insight into domestic and foreign case law as it pertains to accounting that is exceptional for one who has not had the advantage of formal legal education....
>
> Hatfield does not dally with the routine. He heads straight for the topics most susceptible to debate. Authorities, though cited often, are not suffered gladly. No authority is spared, none is sacrosanct.[56]

Hatfield was sensitive to the low regard in which accounting was held by academics from other disciplines. Through his writings, he did much to establish the intellectual respectability of discourse in accounting. His method was to stimulate thinking rather than to codify accepted practice.

Mills provides a fitting tribute to Hatfield:

> To read Hatfield today, is to understand what accounting as a scholarly discipline has largely lost. Most contemporary accounting enquiry pales in comparison to the magnificent prose, the satirical wit, breadth of learning, and the intelligent discussion of critical issues displayed in Hatfield's work.[57]

PART II: HENRY RAND HATFIELD: HISTORIAN OF BOOKKEEPING AND ACCOUNTING BY BASIL S. YAMEY[58]

Henry Rand Hatfield had a vast and detailed knowledge of the early literature on bookkeeping and accounting. This is plainly evident from his book reviews alone. He reviewed virtually every book written in English on the history of accounting published during his lifetime, A.C. Littleton's *Accounting Evolution to 1900* (1933) being the important exception. Each review demonstrates his detailed knowledge, his feel for the subject, and the high value he placed on scholarly accuracy and thoroughness. In general, Hatfield's reviews, elegantly and clearly written, were designed to identify and praise the merits of the work reviewed, to encourage its author and yet to indicate shortcomings in the work, usually by pointing out errors in a kindly way. In some cases, he supplemented his published review by sending a further list of errors to the author or to the publisher. At the request of Kenneth MacNeal, author of *Truth in Accounting* (1939), Hatfield sent a long list of the "slips" he had found in the second chapter of the book, the chapter which deals with the history of accounting: "I pay you the very high compliment of taking you at your word when you said you would like to have me submit details regarding slips in your Chapter II."[59] He reviewed R. Emmett Taylor's *No Royal Road: Luca Pacioli and His Times* (1942), and in correspondence expressed some doubts of the author's rendering in English of certain phrases and terms in Pacioli's exposition of double-entry bookkeeping in the *Summa* of 1494. But he was generous in his praise of the book as a whole. The review includes the revelation that:

> my wife and I, neither of whom has been particularly interested in fifteenth century Italy, between us read the entire book aloud. And in these crowded days one does not take time to read aloud an historical treatise of 399 pages unless it possesses real interest and charm.

He regretted that he was unable to do justice to the broad scope and detail of Taylor's biographical study of Luca Pacioli.

Hatfield's natural geniality and generosity of spirit deserted him when he wrote the comprehensively adverse review of Wilmer L. Green's *History and Survey of*

Accountancy (1930). The flavor of the review comes through in the following extract:[60]

> However much allowance may be made for the recent style of impressionistic biography, when it comes to a matter-of-fact history of book-keeping, especially a history of the literature of the subject, it is fair to demand a high degree of accuracy, careful scholarship and scrupulous attention to bibliographical detail. The cited instances in which this history fails in these respects have been merely illustrative; many more could be given but are omitted out of respect to the patience of readers of The Journal.... There is still room for a comprehensive history of book-keeping.... It must be more accurate and trustworthy than the present treatise.

MacNeal, incidentally, had relied on Green's book.

Undoubtedly, Hatfield was the foremost historian of accounting of his generation in the English-speaking world. His knowledge of the early literature of the subject, especially, must have been remarkable. Yet his writings on the subject are disappointingly meager, and he did not leave to posterity any really significant work of synthesis or interpretation, or a general survey of the field or any major part of it. How is this to be explained? An answer to this question is attempted before turning to his actual achievement—for what he could have achieved greatly exceeded what he managed to achieve, an imbalance which has left us much the poorer.

The main explanation must be that Hatfield was a man of many interests. He was much in demand as a professor of accounting and a leading authority in his discipline. He was a busy man for whom the history of his subject was a side interest, although a beguiling side interest.

Pieter Kats, a Dutchman who worked in the oil trade in London, was an enthusiastic scholar who spent much of his limited spare time in the study of the history of bookkeeping and accounting. He published several important articles, in Dutch and English. He fell under Hatfield's spell, and a strong bond of friendship developed between the two men. They kept each other informed of new publications and new finds in the world of antiquarian books, and sent each other material relating to the early literature of bookkeeping. In 1927, Kats must have conceived the idea of a grand collaborative work. When Hatfield published his new book *Accounting*, Kats wrote to him hoping that "you might now be willing to collaborate in writing an outline of the history of book-keeping with special regard to developments in the U.S. Am. and the U.K." Kats also hoped to enlist the participation of Dr. Otto Bauer, who had published a book in Russian which "contains a lot which might be useful and I know that, since writing it, he has collected more data." Kats added, "Of course, you would have to be editor in chief and to instruct us as to what your collaborators would have to do with a view to the special needs of the American reader."[61] Kats had already spoken to a sympathetic publisher.

Hatfield replied six weeks later. He explained that he had "made arrangements to devote considerable time during the next year to the writing of another book," but that he was "in the unfortunate position of not knowing upon what subject to write." Three different works had been urged upon him "in which I would be interested." One was an introductory textbook on accounting; the second was "a treatise on profits considered from the viewpoints of economics, law, and accounting"; and the third was "the history of bookkeeping in collaboration with you [Kats]." The first, he wrote, would presumably be the most profitable, and the second "would be of more theoretical interest." The third "would fit in more with my own personal hobby, but seems to imply a terrible amount of work." He concluded: "standing between these attractive fields, I am quite at a loss to know in which direction to drive."[62] In fact, the second and third projects were not pursued. Hatfield the teacher won out against Hatfield the historian. It has been the misfortune of accounting history that those who were most capable of advancing the study of the subject have almost invariably been no more than part-time or casual laborers in this specialized field.

But Hatfield was far from idle in the pursuit of his "hobby." He was held in very high regard by many who sought and received his help. J.B. Geijsbeek, author of *Ancient Double-Entry Bookkeeping*,[63] acknowledged that Hatfield had "criticized the work"; and Hatfield reported that Geijsbeek had sent him his manuscript of the translation of Luca Pacioli's text.[64] This may help to explain why Hatfield did not review the Geijsbeek volume—the only book on Pacioli published in Hatfield's lifetime that he did not review. A.C. Littleton dedicated his *Accounting Evolution to 1900* to Hatfield. The dedication credited Hatfield's "An Historical Defense of Bookkeeping" with providing "the inspiration and model for this book." The first chapter is described as an "abridgment by permission" of Hatfield's "little classic." Edward Peragallo thanked Hatfield for his "reading and helpful criticisms of the manuscript" of his *Origin and Evolution of Double Entry Bookkeeping*,[65] although this did not stop Hatfield from reviewing it and sending its publisher a long list of "slips" found in the finished work. "Special credit" to Hatfield for his help and encouragement is also given in Walter Hausdorfer's *Accounting Bibliography*, which was completed in 1962 and published 24 years later, through the enterprise of Professor A. van Seventer.[66] Emmett Taylor wrote to Hatfield that he had thought about sending the draft of his chapter dealing with Pacioli on bookkeeping to Hatfield and Littleton "to run through the chapter for me." But he did not do so because he did not know either of them well enough.[67]

Hatfield devoted much time and energy to collecting old books on bookkeeping and accounting, principally on behalf of the library of the University of California at Berkeley. He was in contact with several antiquarian booksellers in Europe, and pursued his inquiries on his various travels abroad. He compared notes on difficult bibliographical questions with Kats and, in parallel with Kats's own tireless inquiries, searched for a copy of John Weddington's *Breffe Instruction*, published in Antwerp in 1567, the existence of which was known only through earlier bibliographical references. Their searches proved fruitless. A copy of the work was eventually located, after World War II, in the library of a theological college in Scotland.

Hatfield also carried on a lively correspondence with Cosmo Gordon, a classical scholar, bibliographer, and for many years the librarian of the Institute of Chartered Accountants in England and Wales. The two men met several times and became friends, with the Hatfields sending the Gordons parcels of tea during the war. Hatfield and Gordon were friendly competitors in the acquisition of rare books, and their correspondence is spiced with light-hearted exchanges.

When the Institute acquired a number of items concerning the South Sea Company from a London bookseller, Hatfield wrote to ask whether the Institute was "the odious competitor" who acquired them "before my order reached London? Is that the way to extend 'hands across the sea'?"[68] Some years later, a "local woman" offered Hatfield a book in German by Symon Hübner and asked him to "make a bid." He asked Gordon whether he had "ever run across it," and gave a short description of it. As to the woman owner, "I am not going to tell you who she is or how you can get hold of the book for your library until I have definitely found out that we can not obtain it."[69] Gordon replied:

> I suppose my cue in answer to your letter ... is to say that Symon Hübner's *Ein new Rechenbuchlein* 1567 is one of a common class of books, of little interest, and that probably several more copies will turn up in the course of the next few years or even months, that I certainly advise you to offer no more than a few dollars, say five, for it: but that if the "local woman" seems dissatisfied and you are willing to do her a favour *we* would probably offer a little more in order to acquire the book simply for the sake of completeness.

But he then went on to "give way" to his "natural impulse" and congratulate Hatfield on a very interesting find.[70] The university bought the book. The copy seems to be the only one to have survived. Gordon also recalled another episode. The Institute's library had two copies of an early Spanish book on bookkeeping, the *Compendio y breve instruction por tener Libros de Cuenta* of 1565. The library agreed to sell one copy to the University of California, leaving it to Gordon to set the price. There was no record of any recent sale, and each of the library's copies had been acquired as part of a larger lot. He asked for £20, and this was agreed. Shortly afterwards, another copy turned up and changed hands at a much lower price. Gordon learned of this from Hatfield, when they met by chance in Ely Cathedral. "What he said nearly took the roof off that ancient structure, but our friendship was not affected."[71]

Hatfield also became involved in two publishing projects during the interwar years. These plans came to nothing but took up time. The first project, probably inspired by Kats, was for a Dutch publisher to publish a volume that would include facsimiles of Jan Ympyn's *Nieuwe Instructie* of 1543 and the French version of the same date, supplemented by the text of the English version published in 1547. (At the time, the only known copy of the English book had been mislaid—it would be located in Moscow after World War II—and Kats proposed to print the transcription made by Dr. Bauer.) Hatfield actively supported this ambitious scheme, allowed his name to go forward as a patron, and sought to interest prospective buyers. He became somewhat disillusioned as a result of delays and silences. Nevertheless, a draft prospectus was printed, but shortly afterwards, the scheme was abandoned. The second scheme was for a newly formed American society, the Facsimile Text Society, to publish one or other of James Peele's books of 1553 and 1569. Kats again was enthusiastic, and Hatfield became involved. The society apparently decided to publish the shorter *Maner and Fourme* of 1553, and permission was obtained to reproduce the copy in the rare books collection of the Institute of Chartered Accountants in England and Wales. But nothing came of this project, either.

Another project, master-minded by Professor A.C. Littleton, was for an English translation of Dr. Bauer's book, published in Russian in 1911. Kats had drawn Littleton's attention to this work. Littleton was convinced of the importance of the book, found guarantors for the cost of translating it, and arranged for the text to be augmented by Bauer in light of his work since 1911. Hatfield apparently had not been consulted on this project; and, to judge from the conciliatory tone of a letter from Kats, he seems to have been upset by having been left out.[72] The translation, if completed, did not reach publication.

While the activities outlined above took up Hatfield's time and attention in the interwar years, it seems likely that he may also have been working on a book on the history of accounting or, at least, contemplating writing one. As no finished or unfinished manuscripts, or copies of letters by Hatfield making reference to it, have been found, it is uncertain whether Hatfield in fact did begin the study in question and how far he may have proceeded with it.

In November 1930, Kats wrote to Hatfield after an apparent silence of three years. After a few paragraphs on other matters, Kats asked: "Do you still entertain the idea of publishing one or more volumes on the history of book-keeping and accountancy?"[73] He added: "If so, I should be most happy if I could be privileged in collaborating in some way or other." A few months later, Kats wrote again. He told Hatfield that he had retired from business and planned to return to his native Holland. He again asked if Hatfield was "still cherishing the idea of writing a volume on bookkeeping history" and again expressed his interest in contributing "a part, be it ever so tiny."[74] About nine years later, Florence Edler de Roover, the distinguished historian and wife of Raymond de Roover, included this passage in a letter to Hatfield:[75]

> If you are working on your history of accounting, it may be that we have among our films material that you would like to use. We should be very glad to be of service to you.

Unfortunately, there are no copies of Hatfield's replies to these letters, and no indication in his papers of the scope of the work referred to by his two correspondents.

Another manuscript Hatfield may have been preparing was a new English translation of the section of Pacioli's *Summa* dealing with bookkeeping. It is known that Hatfield had reservations about the two English translations then available—Geijsbeek's of 1914 and Crivelli's of 1926.[76] It is known also that Hatfield wrote numerous letters to various scholars, ranging from Luigi Einaudi to Balduin Penndorf (whose German translation Hatfield admired and praised in a short review), asking for their opinions about the precise meanings of various troublesome phrases or passages in Pacioli. He also kept files of material on Pacioli's chapters and, as already noted, reviewed all new books on Pacioli except Geijsbeek's translation. It seems that Hatfield was deeply interested in, and perhaps obsessed by, Pacioli's pioneering exposition of the double-entry system. If so, a scholarly edition of a new English translation would have been a task that would have appealed strongly to Hatfield. Indeed, in a letter of February 1944, Florence Edler de Roover wrote:[77]

> Are you working on a new English translation of Pacioli? I hope so. In Atlantic City or somewhere else, you suggested that Raymond and I should do a new translation. I doubt whether we should ever get around to it, *but* we did have to translate cap. 24 for Raymond's dissertation on medieval banking in Bruges. We shall be very glad to send our version to you and the footnotes which explain things in it that puzzled Penndorf as well as other translators. It is the chapter dealing with banks in Venice etc.

I believe that Hatfield was well qualified to prepare a translation of the Pacioli text and to provide a scholarly elucidation of its difficult points, its significance, and its influence on later publications. Regrettably, neither he nor the de Roovers produced such a work. It is true that Hatfield himself wrote, "I am not an Italian scholar,"[78] and Raymond de Roover believed that "Hatfield was … handicapped by the lack of knowledge in foreign languages, especially Italian."[79] But it is clear from his reviews and, even more, from copies of his letters concerning errors in books he had reviewed, that Hatfield had studied the Pacioli text in the original with great care and understanding. He may well have had assistance from colleagues or friends who were fluent in Italian. He would have known how to use such assistance in getting to grips with the difficult, obscure, or occasional corrupt passages in the Pacioli text.

Hatfield quite clearly was not an idle man. His professional commitments and interests themselves are enough to explain why he did not produce a major study in the history of accounting, although it was a subject dear to him. But the high opportunity cost of engagement in such a study, and of seeing it through to the end, was perhaps not the only factor at work. It is likely that Hatfield may have been handicapped by his own insistence on accuracy and attention to detail, and by his realization that error was easy in a subject such as the history of accounting in which, by and large, so little careful and systematic work had been done on which he felt he could rely and build confidently. We may recall his remark, when approached by Kats about a collaborative work on the history of accounting, that it seemed "to imply a terrible amount of work." In his review of David Murray's *Chapters in the History of Bookkeeping, Accountancy & Commercial Arithmetic*

(1930), he refers feelingly to the evidence in it "of an appalling amount of research." Moreover, his own early experience in carrying out a research study may have been inhibiting.

In the study of the history of any discipline, the search for roots and first occurrences can be taken to extravagant lengths. Nevertheless, it is desirable to look for origins in order to construct reliable chronologies, to throw light on influences, and to chart the dissemination of ideas and practices. Hatfield was interested in this aspect of the development of bookkeeping and accounting. Thus—to take a minor example—in 1931 he drew attention to the fact that a "rhymed rule for making entries in the ledger" found in a manuscript essay "Upon the Italian Method of Book-Keeping...," dated 1716, could be traced to Richard Dafforne's *Merchants Mirrour* (1635), of which several editions were published in the seventeenth century.[80] In a later contribution, he showed that the trial balance was not first introduced in the literature by Pietra or Flori, as had been claimed, but "was fully described as early as 1494 in the earliest text on bookkeeping."[81]

Hatfield's first article on the history of accounting is "Zwei Pfadfinder" ("Two Pioneers") in the *Zeitschrift für Buchhaltung*, April 1909. Some 10 years earlier, the same journal had published an article by F. Hügli discussing the origin of the *Zweicontenreihen* theory of bookkeeping. Hügli claimed that the origination of this "now dominant theory" was due to two writers, G.D. Augspurg in Bremen and Georg Kurzbauer in Vienna, "whose works appeared almost simultaneously in the early 1850s" and who had thereby independently of each other discovered his theory of the double-entry system. Hatfield demonstrated, with ample quotations from their works, that two Americans, Thomas Jones and Benjamin Franklin Foster, had anticipated these two European authors, and that Jones could claim priority. The basis of the theory was the coexistence in the double-entry bookkeeping system of "but two distinct classes of accounts, which may be distinguished as follows; viz. – 1. Parts of property; – 2. Whole property" (in Foster's words), that is, assets and liabilities to third parties, and the proprietor's claims.

It appears that at some time between 1909, when his article was published, and 1928, Hatfield became aware that his two pioneers, in turn, had been anticipated by yet earlier writers. In fact, this realization must have occurred after 1922. In his "Introductory Notes" to the 1922 reissue of C.E. Sprague's *The Philosophy of Accounts*, Hatfield wrote:

> It is no detraction to the service rendered by Sprague that some of the points emphasized in "The Philosophy of Accounts" had been more or less fully brought out by an occasional writer in Italy, in Switzerland, in Germany, or by Thomas Jones in America.

He did not mention here the contributions by even earlier British writers. But by 1928, he had discovered anticipations of Jones's exposition of the logic of double entry in the books of Alexander Malcolm (1718), Hustcraft Stephens (1735), and F.W. Cronhelm (1818). Hatfield does not appear to have published anything about these authors. He did, however, give the relevant material to A.C. Littleton, who discussed them in an article published in July 1928.[82] Littleton wrote: "The quotations from Cronhelm, Stephens and Malcolm were generously contributed by Dean Henry R. Hatfield from among his notes."[83] Littleton properly also referred to Simon Stevin's writings early in the seventeenth century; but he was not aware of the major advance in the development of this explanation of the double-entry system made by Willem van Gezel in his *Kort Begryp* of 1681, nor of the later contribution by J.W. Fulton (1799).[84]

I believe that Hatfield was cautious by temperament. The fate of his work on the two pioneers may have helped to make him even more cautious in his study of the history of accounting and in his own writing in that field. But, whatever the reasons for his meager published output, we have not had for our instruction and delectation a major work from his pen. For delectable it would have been, as we know from his delightful "An Historical Defense of Bookkeeping" which, apart from its intrinsic interest, is undoubtedly the most frequently reprinted contribution in any language within the scope of Hatfield's "hobby." Hatfield referred to his "Defense" as a "skit which I read at a local club."[85] The "skit," together with his reviews and short papers and letters, constitute a body of work of lasting interest. Nevertheless, one can but agree with Raymond de Roover's assessment that "Hatfield never wrote anything of momentous importance or of great originality" in the history of accounting. De Roover did, however, acknowledge Hatfield's signal contribution in arousing interest in the history of accounting and in collecting a "marvelous collection of accounting treatises at the Library of the University of California." He also recalled Hatfield's personal kindness and generosity, and remembered Hatfield's chuckles on being addressed as "Reverend Sir" at their first meeting—de Roover had not appreciated the meaning of the term "Dean" as used in American academic circles.[86]

NOTES

1. A full list of Hatfield's publications is given in Chapter 8.
2. Henry Rand Hatfield, "Introductory Notes–IV," in Charles E. Sprague, *The Philosophy of Accounts* (New York: The Ronald Press Company, 1922), p. xvii.
3. Paton has made this statement in several places. See his Foreword to the Reissue, in Charles E. Sprague, *The Philosophy of Accounts* (Lawrence, KS: Scholars Book Co., 1972), p. iii. Also see William A. Paton, "Wandering into Accounting—Notes on [A] Writing Career," *The Accounting Historians Journal*, Vol. 5, No. 2, Fall 1978, p. 3.
4. Samuel J. Broad, "Presentation of Distinguished Accountants to the Accounting Hall of Fame," in *Proceedings of the Thirteenth Annual Institute on Accounting, May 18 and 19, 1951* (Columbus, OH: College of Commerce Conference Series Number C-75, The Ohio State University, n.d.), p. 85.
5. Letter to Hatfield dated February 15, 1937.
6. For brief biographies of these and other early accounting writers, see John J. Kahle, *American Accountants and Their Contributions to Accounting Thought, 1910-1930* (New York: Garland Publishing, 1993). Also see Gary John Previts, *A Critical Evaluation of Comparative Financial Account-*

ing Thought in America, 1900 to 1920 (New York: Arno Press, 1980) and the listings for the 1910s and 1920s in Harry C. Bentley and Ruth S. Leonard, *Bibliography of Works on Accounting by American Authors* (Boston, MA: Harry C. Bentley, 1935), Vol. II.

7. Carl Thomas Devine, *Readings in Accounting Theory* (Djakarta, Indonesia: Lembaga Penjelidikan Ekonomi Dan Masjarakat/Fakultas Ekonomi Universitas Indonesia, 1963), Vol. II, p. 173. Devine reprinted essentially all of Hatfield's Chapter 5, "Depreciation: General Considerations," from *Accounting*. I appreciate Sidney Davidson's bringing this quotation to my attention.

8. See, for example, James Don Edwards and Roland F. Salmonson, *Contributions of Four Accounting Pioneers: Kohler, Littleton, May, Paton* (East Lansing, MI: Bureau of Business and Economic Research, Michigan State University, 1961).

9. For publication particulars, see the list of Hatfield's published writings in Chapter 8.

10. A.C. Littleton, *Accounting Evolution to 1900* (New York: American Institute Publishing Co., 1933), p. v. Littleton's first chapter was an abridgment, with the author's permission, of "Historical Defense." The book was drawn from Littleton's doctoral dissertation, "The Historical Foundations of Modern Accounting," completed in 1931. See Kathryn Current Bruckner, *Littleton's Contribution to the Theory of Accountancy*, Research Monograph No. 62 (Atlanta, GA: School of Business Administration, Georgia State University, 1975), p. 253.

11. Harvey T. Deinzer, *Development of Accounting Thought* (New York: Holt, Rinehart and Winston, Inc., 1965), p. 4.

12. Maurice Moonitz and A.C. Littleton, eds., *Significant Accounting Essays* (Englewood Cliffs, NJ: Prentice-Hall, 1965), p. 3.

13. For a discussion of Hatfield's interests and work in bookkeeping history, see Part II of this chapter, written by Basil S. Yamey.

14. Mary E. Murphy, "Libraries for Students of Accounting," *The Accounting Review*, Vol. XXIII, No. 4, October 1948, p. 420.

15. Patti A. Mills, "Henry Rand Hatfield (1866-1945): 'Life and Humor in the Dust of Ledgers'," in John Richard Edwards, ed., *Twentieth-Century Accounting Thinkers* (London: Routledge, 1994), p. 298. Mills's essay on Hatfield is exceptionally well done.

16. See, for example, Stephen A. Zeff, "Paton on the Effects of Changing Prices on Accounting 1916-55," in Stephen A. Zeff, Joel Demski, and Nicholas Dopuch, eds., *Essays in Honor of William A. Paton: Pioneer Accounting Theorist* (Ann Arbor, MI: Division of Research, Graduate School of Business Administration, The University of Michigan, 1979), pp. 91-137.

17. See, for example, A.C. Littleton, *Structure of Accounting Theory*, Monograph No. 5 (American Accounting Association, 1953), and Bruckner, *loc. cit.*

18. Henry Rand Hatfield, "Some Variations in Accounting Practice in England, France, Germany and the United States" (written in 1911), *Journal of Accounting Research*, Vol. 4, No. 2, Autumn 1966, p. 175.

19. Henry Rand Hatfield, *Surplus and Dividends* (Boston: Harvard University Press, 1943), p. 37.

20. Henry Rand Hatfield, *Accounting: Its Principles and Problems* (New York: D. Appleton and Company, 1927), p. 78.

21. Hatfield, *Surplus and Dividends*, *op. cit.*, p. 43.

22. *Ibid.*, pp. 37-39.

23. Interview with Kohler, June 23, 1964.

24. See Henry W. Sweeney, *Stabilized Accounting* (New York: Harper & Brothers, 1936; reprinted in 1964 by Holt, Rinehart and Winston, Inc.), and Sweeney's articles in Stephen A. Zeff, ed., *Asset Appreciation, Business Income and Price-Level Accounting: 1918-1935* (New York: Arno Press, 1976).

25. See, for example, W.A. Paton, *Advanced Accounting* (New York: The Macmillan Company, 1941), Chap. XXXIII.

26. See, for example, Littleton's review of Sweeney's *Stabilized Accounting* in *The Accounting Review*, Vol. XI, No. 3, September 1936, pp. 297-298.

27. Even as close a student of Hatfield's views as Maurice Moonitz was, in conversation, taken by surprise at learning of Hatfield's support for Sweeney's theory.

28. For example, Hatfield is nowhere referenced in the 11-page bibliography in *Reporting the Financial Effects of Price-Level Changes*, Accounting Research Study No. 6 (New York: American Institute of Certified Public Accountants, 1963), pp. 254-264, while Paton and Littleton are represented by five and two works, respectively.

29. Henry Rand Hatfield, *Modern Accounting: Its Principles and Some of Its Problems* (New York: D. Appleton and Company, 1909), p. 7.

30. *Ibid.*, pp. 182-183.

31. Henry Rand Hatfield, "A Survey of Developments in Accounting," in *Papers on Auditing Procedure and Other Accounting Subjects*, presented at the 52nd annual meeting of the American Institute of Accountants (New York: AIA, 1939), p. 7.

32. Letter to the author from Briggs, undated but evidently written in early 1965.

33. H.W. Fowler, *A Dictionary of Modern English Usage* (London: Oxford University Press, 1926), pp. 353-354. Hatfield was addicted to Fowler.

34. Hatfield, *Accounting* (1927), *op. cit.*, p. viii.

35. Henry Rand Hatfield, review of Arthur Lowes Dickinson's *Accounting Practice and Procedure* in *The Journal of Accountancy*, Vol. XVIII, No. 6, December 1918, p. 482.

36. Also see Mills, *op. cit.*, pp. 300-304.

37. *Ibid.*, p. 305. For a discussion of the Financial Accounting Standards Board's shift to a balance sheet approach from the earlier income statement approach, see *Statement of Financial Accounting Concepts No. 6: Elements of Financial Statements* (Stamford, CT: FASB, 1985), and L. Todd Johnson and Reed K. Storey, *Recognition in Financial Statements: Underlying Concepts and Practical Conventions* (Stamford, CT: FASB, 1982).

38. Hatfield, "A Survey of Developments in Accounting," *op. cit.*, p. 6.

39. Henry Rand Hatfield, "What Is the Matter with Accounting?" *The Journal of Accountancy*, Vol. 44, No. 4, October 1927, p. 278.

40. Hatfield, "What Is the Matter with Accounting?" *loc. cit.*

41. Hatfield, "A Survey of Developments in Accounting," *op. cit.*, p. 6.

42. See Stephen A. Zeff, *The American Accounting Association—Its First 50 Years* (American Accounting Association, 1966), pp. 14-19, 38-41.

43. It is curious that, from 1928 to 1943, when Kohler was editor of *The Accounting Review*, he invited Hatfield to write only a single book review, and that came at Hatfield's suggestion. During the same time period, Hatfield, an avid reviewer, had 13 reviews published in the Institute's periodical, *The Journal of Accountancy*. Hatfield frequently exchanged friendly correspondence with John L. Carey, the *Journal*'s editor.

44. Mills, *op. cit.*, p. 305. For a discussion of the AAA's recent initiatives on accounting education, see Dale L. Flesher, *The Third-Quarter Century of the American Accounting Association 1966-1991* (AAA, 1991), Chaps. 6 and 7, and Gerhard G. Mueller and John K. Simmons, "Change in Accounting Education," *Issues in Accounting Education*, Vol. 4, No. 2, Fall 1989, pp. 247-251.

45. See William Andrew Paton, *Accounting Theory—With Special Reference to the Corporate Enterprise* (New York: The Ronald Press Company, 1922), and John B. Canning, *The Economics of Accountancy: A Critical Analysis of Accounting Theory* (New York: The Ronald Press Company, 1929).

46. See Henry W. Sweeney, *Stabilized Accounting* (New York: Harper & Brothers, 1936), and the nine articles by Sweeney in Stephen A. Zeff, ed., *Asset Appreciation, Business Income and Price-Level Accounting: 1918-1935* (New York: Arno Press, 1976).

47. See, for example, Gary John Previts and Barbara Dubis Merino, *A History of Accountancy in the United States: The Cultural Significance of Accounting* (Columbus, OH: Ohio State University Press, 1998), Chap. 5. Paton and Staubus preferred the more modest terminology "proprietary point of

view." See Paton, *Accounting Theory*, *op. cit.*, p. 52, and George J. Staubus, *A Theory of Accounting to Investors* (Berkeley: University of California Press, 1961), p. 24n.

48. In his "Recollections of Henry Rand Hatfield" (reproduced in an appendix to Chapter 7), Maurice Moonitz confirms that Hatfield regarded the difference between these two "theories" as "of minor consequence."

49. Henry Rand Hatfield, review of William A. Paton's *Accounting*, in *The Journal of Accountancy*, Vol. 40, No. 5, November 1925, p. 389.

50. Stephen Addam Zeff, *A Critical Examination of the Orientation Postulate in Accounting, with Particular Attention to its Historical Development* (New York: Arno Press, 1978). The manuscript was completed as a doctoral dissertation in 1961.

51. This paper is reproduced in Chapter 7, as an attachment to his 1918 paper on "Corporations and the Public." Moonitz, in his remarks on Hatfield's unpublished papers, also commends the progressiveness of Hatfield's position on the publicity of accounts.

52. William Z. Ripley, *Main Street and Wall Street* (Boston: Little, Brown, and Company, 1927), esp. Chap. VI, which had been published as an article in the September 1926 issue of *Atlantic Monthly*. To be sure, Ripley's proposals were much more extensively developed than Hatfield's.

53. Louis D. Brandeis, "What Publicity Can Do," *Harper's Weekly*, Vol. LVIII, No. 2974, December 20, 1913, p. 10. Also see Brandeis' *Other People's Money and How the Bankers Use It* (New York: Frederick A. Stokes, 1914), p. 92.

54. Henry Rand Hatfield, "An Historical Defense of Bookkeeping," *The Journal of Accountancy*, Vol. XXXVII, No. 4, April 1924, p. 241.

55. *Ibid.*

56. Stephen A. Zeff, Foreword to the Reissue of Henry Rand Hatfield, *Accounting: Its Principles and Problems* (Lawrence, KS: Scholars Book Co., 1971), unpaginated.

57. Mills, *op. cit.*, p. 305.

58. Professor emeritus of economics at the London School of Economics and Political Science. I provided Professor Yamey with the pertinent notes and correspondence from Hatfield's files.

59. Letter, Hatfield to MacNeal, November 17, 1939.

60. Hatfield's reviews are enumerated in the full list of Hatfield's publications at the end of this book; their place and date of publication are not always identified specifically in this part.

61. Letter, Kats to Hatfield, August 29, 1927.

62. Letter, Hatfield to Kats, October 6, 1927.

63. John B. Geijsbeek, *Ancient Double-Entry Bookkeeping* (Denver: The Author, 1914; reprinted in 1974 by Scholars Book Co.).

64. Letter, Hatfield to Taylor, November 5, 1942.

65. Edward Peragallo, *Origin and Evolution of Double Entry Bookkeeping* (New York: American Institute Publishing Company, 1938).

66. Walter Hausdorfer, *Accounting Bibliography: Historical Approach* (Palo Alto, CA: Bay Books, 1986). Hausdorfer's study includes a bibliography of bookkeeping texts as well as a bibliography of works on the history of bookkeeping. Hatfield wrote to Cosmo Gordon, "I have urged upon the American Institute of Accountants the publishing of the bibliography of the history. I have not heard whether my efforts have been fruitful or in vain." Letter, Hatfield to Gordon, June 24, 1942.

67. Letter, Taylor to Hatfield, November 12, 1942.

68. Letter, Hatfield to Gordon, December 13, 1935.

69. Letter, Hatfield to Gordon, May 22, 1940.

70. Letter, Gordon to Hatfield, June 19, 1940.

71. Letter, Gordon to Stephen A. Zeff, October 1, 1964.

72. Letter, Kats to Hatfield, September 2, 1930.

73. Letter, Kats to Hatfield, November 13, 1930.

74. Letter, Kats to Hatfield, April 21, 1931.

75. Letter, Edler to Hatfield, April 17, 1939.

76. Pacioli used an Italian proverb about the lawyer and the merchant in the fourth chapter of his bookkeeping text. Hatfield complimented Taylor on his translation of the passage: "The proverb states that more things are necessary to make a good merchant than to make a Doctor of laws." Hatfield continued: "I did my damndest to get him [Geijsbeek] to change his misleading translation, which reads: 'More bridges are necessary to make a good merchant than a lawyer can make.' But he is a Dutchman and would not budge despite all my efforts." Letter, Hatfield to Taylor, November 5, 1942.

77. Letter, Edler to Hatfield, February 13, 1944.

78. Letter, Hatfield to Taylor, November 5, 1942.

79. Letter, de Roover to Zeff, July 25, 1964.

80. See *The American Accountant*, July 1931, p. 207.

81. Letter, "Neither Pietra nor Flori," *The Journal of Accountancy*, February 1943, pp. 165-166. Hatfield also wrote two notes on the early use in English of the term "capital": *Quarterly Journal of Economics*, May 1926, pp. 547-548, and November 1934, pp. 162-163.

82. A.C. Littleton, "Pioneers of Accountancy," *The Certified Public Accountant*, July 1928, p. 201, fn. 5.

83. Hatfield had collected a large number of extracts from bookkeeping and accounting treatises. Most of these notes are in his own handwriting. Photocopying facilities had not yet been invented, and photostats were expensive. The extracts are remarkably accurate.

84. In a letter to Hatfield written on receipt of a copy of Littleton's article, Kats referred to the relevance of van Gezel's text. Letter, Kats to Hatfield, November 12, 1928.

85. Letter, Hatfield to Taylor, May 11, 1942.

86. Letter, de Roover to Zeff, July 25, 1964.

Chapter 6

The Personal Hatfield

The previous chapters have been a chronological study of the significant events and developments in the professional life of Henry Rand Hatfield, yet his biography would not be complete without an effort to draw a more detailed portrait of Hatfield as a person. Correctly portraying Hatfield is difficult. Both as an academic and a person, he emerges as a paradox of attitudes. William Morse Cole, in his review of *Modern Accounting*, perhaps best expressed the crux of the problem of defining Henry Rand Hatfield's contribution to accounting: "the author has given so much opinion of other people and so little of his own."[1] Accounting history remembers him as a dominant personality but a hesitant spokesman during the turbulent years in which corporate accounting came under federal regulation. As a person, he was forceful but restrained in his dealings with family, colleagues, and students. Thus, defining Hatfield's contribution to accounting requires defining him as a person, because the two sides of Hatfield are intertwined. Viewing Hatfield as a person gives us yet another perspective on Hatfield the professional—both his strengths and his curious reluctance to be a staunch advocate of the kind of accounting theory he saw as essential during the early decades of the twentieth century. His reticence on issues that affected accounting in his own time remain as puzzling as his lack of vision about what accounting, as a field, would become. Yet, when we analyze what we know about Hatfield as a person, we can speculate about his view of the discipline he helped shape.

Creating a biography that relies primarily on archival material has been necessarily dependent on extant information. In Hatfield's case, much of what is known about him, or what can be determined about him, emerges from his legacy as educator, author, colleague and his presence in the evolving association of accounting instructors. Clearly, the forceful quality of his personality during the emergence of accounting education shaped his reputation. While much of Hatfield's involvement in events during the emergence of modern accounting and collegiate business education can be found in the early twentieth-century accounting literature, a knowledge of his personal side requires reliance on surviving letters, interviews with two of his children and with his grandchildren, interviews with former colleagues and students, and letters written by other former colleagues and students whom I invited to describe Hatfield as they knew him. A portrait, although a shadowy one, of Hatfield as a person can be inferred from these sources. Ironically, in many respects, the portrait of Robert Miller Hatfield, drawn by James Taft Hatfield in his unpublished biography of their father,[2] provides a fitting framework for sketching Henry Rand Hatfield the person.

Hatfield, throughout his life, was intensely family-oriented. Henry and Ethel compiled 24 scrapbooks, which spanned the 48 years from 1897 to 1944.[3] The scrapbooks contain pictures of the family, movie reviews, announcements of lectures, theatre and concert programs, news clippings, and mementos of their foreign and domestic trips, particularly those during the years when the children were growing up. They contain pictures adjacent to handwritten descriptions of cities and sites visited during these trips. The care with which the scrapbooks were compiled suggests that the trips were highly valued by the entire family. Many postcards of scenic views are included, along with descriptions that explain how the specific site affected the family. Detailed notes from the Hatfield family's first trip to Europe in 1911, during which the most time was spent in London and Munich, provide sketches of the family's activities and of Hatfield's concern for his children, who fought a variety of illnesses throughout the trip. The trips, as recalled by Hatfield's daughter Elizabeth, were planned in conjunction with accounting meetings and study opportunities, but they also served to educate the Hatfield children.[4] Elizabeth wrote, "Usually long before the trip, planning began and books were read aloud on places to which travel was planned." Henry and Ethel would usually be accompanied by one or more of the children, together with Berkeley friends. Elizabeth recalled that, on one trip to Britain and Germany (apparently Henry and Ethel's favorite countries to visit), the morning would be devoted to:

> sight seeing, traveling or hours at the library of the Institute of Chartered Accountants or the library at the British Museum. Sundays there were Maude Royden or [Rev.] Studdert Kennedy to hear and Easter service in Salisbury Cathedral. If we traveled, lunch was often in or beside the car with apple, cheese, crackers, and chocolate, and a standard meal carried in the car. Time was taken out for tea most always. After dinner, there was walking about towns, or rowing on a castle-moat. Some purchases were made, handicraft work of the places visited, pieces of art, beautiful prints, many photographs and cards as of actors, buildings & scenery—and a suit made by a London tailor. Meeting accountants, economists, cousins, and friends from home were pleasant times. Concerts in evenings, theatre, festivals, and Himbeereis [raspberry ice cream] on a balcony overlooking the Leipzig Fair were enjoyed.[5]

HATFIELD IN 1898—THE MAN THROUGH HIS LETTERS

His Relationship to Ethel

Understanding Henry Hatfield the man must begin with his relationship to Ethel. Evidence suggests that Henry and Ethel were devoted to each other during the 47 years of their marriage. As grandson Henry Glover and son John G. Hatfield recall, Ethel never regretted giving up a career for marriage. She supported Henry in his work. Henry Glover stated that "they were a team; their personalities complemented each other,"[6] an observation that is supported by others who believed that Henry regarded Ethel as his best friend. Thus, it is perhaps appropriate that our first glimpses of "The Personal Hatfield" are found in letters he wrote to Ethel Glover, his fiancée, during a seven-month period in 1897-1998.

Henry and Ethel wrote to each other every day from December 1897 until June 1898, when they were married. This collection of letters, held by John S. Hatfield, Henry and Ethel's oldest grandson, provides our earliest view of Henry as a person and an emerging academic. While many are written with pen on whatever kind of paper Henry had available, most are typed. The letters contain valuable insights into Henry's views on academic issues and problems at Chicago, as well as his hopes and dreams for himself and Ethel. He was a newly minted Chicago Ph.D. in political economy and political science, teaching at Washington University in St. Louis, while Ethel was at Chicago completing her doctoral work in political science. During the time when these letters were written, we can see Henry's anxiety over whether he would be offered a position at Chicago. Having a teaching position that carried adequate salary was essential to their being able to marry during the summer of 1898. The letters, kept by Ethel through the years, always assured her of his love for her. As in his academic papers and speeches, his eloquence dominates. In a letter dated January 27, 1898, he avowed that she was also his best friend:

> In these later days when I am consumed with so ardent a love for you, I don't want you to forget that after all you are my best and dearest chum. That even if I were not passionately fond of you, I'd enjoy being with you, as I did enjoy being with you in the American Diplomatic History class. And that fact that we are too as love sick individuals as I know of, is not going to prevent us having lots of jolly times together, bicycling, rowing, working, going to concerts. (Cheap seats though you can bet.) It will be good, won't it my sweetheart chum.

Hatfield Anticipates His Appointment at Chicago

During this seven-month period, the letters repeatedly focused on his receiving an appointment at Chicago:

> But what is the use pretending that I am not counting on getting a favorable answer from Chicago and on getting married as soon as I can get your consent. Of course I am, and I am half-ecstatic at the prospect, half-terrified at the fear that I am to be disappointed (January 8, 1898).

Nearly every letter to Ethel expressed his concern for securing the position, his fears that J. Laurence Laughlin, the head of the department, would find "some better 'available' man" (January 20, 1898). The letters plunged from hope that he would find some kind of teaching position to fear and despondency that not hearing from "Uncle Larry" (with a firm offer) meant that he would not get the job. Henry worried about the propriety of writing follow-up letters, as he didn't want to appear too eager. By mid-January of 1898, he had given up and had accepted the decision—that he would not get the Chicago job—as God's will for his and Ethel's life: "They sing a hymn down at chapel which strikes me more favorably than many hymns do. It says: I ask not that for me the plan/ of good or ill be set aside/ But that the common lot of man/ Be nobly borne and glorified" (January 21, 1898). In another letter (undated), he wrote:

> The sermon was rather good. It was on the text: "in nothing be anxious; but in everything by prayer and supplication with thanksgiving let your requests be made known to God." I suppose it was rather appropriate, for you can well imagine I have been anxious this last week about the outcome at Chicago. As I wrote you last night, I think I have gotten back to a more normal state of mind. Not that I am any more confident of getting the job, but I have just quit worrying about it, and am trying to attend to other things as if Mr. Laughlin had not written me.

Hatfield's Emergence as an Academic

Henry's reasons for not pursuing an appointment at Northwestern also surfaced in one of his letters. At that point, he saw a return to Northwestern as his goal. Yet he was concerned about returning too soon, as he did not want to receive preferential treatment, based on his father's legacy at Northwestern. He also relished the challenge of proving himself with established scholars. Even in 1898, the pragmatic side of Henry's personality surfaced, as shown in a letter to Ethel:

> You say Chicago is a better stepping stone than Evanston. I said it would be a good stepping stone to Evanston. Well that is partly inbred in me, and it is hard to get it out. Of course I would like to [go to Evanston]. But I do agree with you that it would be more satisfactory in many ways to be in Chicago. I would always feel in Evanston that my personal pull with Dr. Sheppard and Mr. Crandon, and my relationship to my father had gotten me the place and that is not quite gratifying. And one does not do so well in his boyhood's home where everyone knows him as he does away. And if [The American University in] Washington ever amounts to anything, I am sure Chicago will be a much better recommendation than Evanston. And the work in Chicago is just what I want. Indeed when I saw many months ago a printed prospectus of the proposed College [of Commerce], I at once thought that was what I wanted. I am sure that my practical experience will fit me better for a somewhat practical course. And the opportunities in Chicago are all that one needs ask for. The mere fact of having to hold one's own against other men in the same department, is a help and a stimulus, which I would not have were I the sole economist at Evanston (January 7, 1898).

Henry's attention to detail, which would become one of his defining qualities as a scholar, surfaced in interesting ways in the 1898 letters. For example, he sent a sketch with an attached description of his room in St. Louis. In another letter, we can see his insistence on precision in the use of concepts, a topic that recurred in several of his speeches. He explained to Ethel that he might have to teach statistics at Chicago if he received the job he so dearly wanted to enable them to marry:

> Of course I do not know anything about Statistics. I never had a course in that, and personally do not see that statistics—as generally taught—is a science. Doubtless there is a legitimate science of statistics, taking in the methods of collecting, of making averages, of correcting errors, etc. and giving light on the methods in use in various countries and discussing the relative merits of the various sets of statistics. But to call instruction in statistical matter relating to various subjects the science of statistics is to me absurd. It would be akin to saying that having students read different things that were printed in books was the same thing as to give a course in typography (February 24, 1898).

Henry always thought of knowledge in traditional ways—studies were divided into arts and science—a trait that persisted throughout his career. He always enjoyed debating whether accounting was an art or a science.

Hatfield's Views of Ethel's Career Opportunities

Throughout the letters, we can see much discussion of Ethel's pending examinations and her doctoral thesis as well as Henry's pride in her accomplishments. (Her thesis was a study of the U.S. Interior Department.) He stated his expectation that she would work with him and have a career of her own. In one letter, he mentioned their coauthoring a book on civil government:

> I do not believe there is much use in attempting the Civil Government book, but I wrote them nevertheless, yesterday, asking for particulars. I told them that if I undertook it I would do it in collaboration with one of my associates who had taught the same subject at the University of Chicago. I did not mention your name. I thought I would better wait till I could speak of you as Doctor Glover (undated).

Henry deeply valued Ethel's academic achievement. He referred to her as the "Head Prof" in many letters and stated his belief that her education will enrich their marriage. Throughout these letters, his statements show that he valued her as his intellectual equal;

> What a wonderful thing love is, which can bring two people so close together. I am sure that I ought not to be impatient even for June, for I already have so rich a treasure in your love. And what a blessed thing it is that even taking a doctor's hood need not destroy the real woman's nature. Indeed I am almost inclined to believe that the higher education, when it comes to the right kind of a woman, makes her more womanly, more loving and more lovable, more satisfied with becoming a wife. Sometimes, of course, it works otherwise, but that surely is not always the case. I believe that you will be a good deal better wife than you could have been had you not had these years of college and university life. Don't you think so? And surely Miss Tunnicliffe, who was a typical college woman, is as domestic and as contented as you could ask. And I have not the shadow of a doubt that the happiest marriages are those made between people who have done similar work in college. At least to a college teacher, no other woman

> can make so satisfactory a wife—I do not mean merely so satisfactory a help mate—but so satisfactory a queen of his home (undated).

Always present, however, was the uncertainty surrounding the Chicago position:

> It really is to be your job as well as mine, and we are going to work together all our lives. I do not know how the prospect of working without getting credit or pay for it would appeal to an unregenerate mind ... but I am sure that it is attractive to you ... and I am sure that it is such better when the wife can join in the real work and not merely in the mechanical part like proof reading.... Won't it be nice to have the work itself of interest to both of us? It certainly is my idea of what a marriage ought to be. And I am sure that, as Mr. Browning said, the happiest marriages are of that type. The danger is that in making such a match there is a chance of merely going into a business partnership, instead of having the romance of real love. I fancy no one ... will question that we are deeply enough in love, and in as romantic a fashion, as anyone could ask (January 14, 1898).

In his letter of January 28, 1898 he asked if she felt badly about the possibility of not having a career. Apparently, Ethel had ambitions of becoming president of Wellesley College, her alma mater, although this may have been a tease.

> But tell me true, you are "human" are you not, and you do have "some feminine traits" do you not? And you do not feel very badly about the career. I do not object to your occasionally feeling a little regret that you cannot be my wife and President of Wellesley at the same time, but that is different from feeling as Mrs. Loeb's friend does. And there will be some room I am sure for you to use your rare scholarly gifts. I am sure we can do some work together, and perhaps both do as well, I certainly much better, than alone.

In a letter dated April 22, 1898, he again alluded to her dual role:

> I do want you to have opportunity to enjoy the things for which you are fitted, and I am sure you will be able to do it to some extent, although of course you will not be able to do any great and tremendous amount of independent and original contributions to knowledge. But I am sure that there are lots of young wives who do succeed in doing good work after marriage, and I think you will be one. You may not do very much, but I know you will have time for some intellectual work. And I really do not believe that you are gong to find the other irksome. After all, Ethel dear, you are a good deal of a woman, aren't you? And I fancy that the position of wife is going to be attractive to you in itself. Isn't that likely to be so? You do not misunderstand me, I am sure. All I mean is that, after all, making a home is not an ignoble occupation. I do not mean that to make a home one must be a drudge and not ever think of the old intellectual life. Indeed I think that it is necessary to keep that up, to some extent, in order to make a happy home, and I know our home is to be a happy one.

In other letters that he wrote before receiving the offer from Chicago, he suggested that she could tutor or do housework to help them financially after they married (for example, in a letter dated February 10, 1898).

Curiously, Ethel Glover never had a professional career. Yet, as granddaughter Betty Werther writes,

> Ethel was not only an iron support for Henry, her home, her children, her mother [who lived for a while in the Hatfield home], indeed her grandchildren. She was also a particularly active member of campus and community life, one of the most outstanding faculty wives. Her tea parties which, I remember, she began preparing days in advance, were acclaimed. To cite only the few examples of which I am aware besides church and Wellesley alumnae, she was very active in the University YWCA, Town and Gown and the AAUW [American Association of University Women]. She was also active in the DAR [Daughters of the American Revolution] until she resigned her membership (along with Eleanor Roosevelt) in protest when the organization forbade black contralto Marian Anderson to sing at Constitution Hall in Washington in 1939 (letter, January 15, 1999).

Ethel also was an honorary member of the Women's Faculty Club and a member of the League of Women Voters.

Grandson Henry Glover recalls his mother, Elizabeth Hatfield Glover, saying that Ethel was always quite content to support Henry and to serve as a sounding board for his ideas. As Henry Glover remembers, Elizabeth described the Hatfield house on Le Conte Avenue in Berkeley as a hive of social activity, with Ethel firmly in charge, but always in a quiet, organized way. It was regularly filled with guests and was well known for numerous receptions and dinner parties. Dinner was usually served not only to the family but also to guests (interview, January 1998). Because of Henry's administrative positions at Berkeley, both he and Ethel were immersed in the Berkeley social whirl, a fact that is evident in many of the family scrapbooks. Mementos and programs from parties, operas, plays, symphonies, formal speeches and lectures given by Henry, newspaper clippings noting the Hatfields' presence at university gatherings, and photos of Henry with local and state dignitaries all testify to the kind of life the family enjoyed. It was certainly not one that would have allowed Ethel to pursue her own academic interests.

Hatfield's Early Religious Views

The letters also show that Henry attended church regularly on Sunday and occasionally on Wednesday night. In many letters, Henry, always the critical thinker, commented on the sermon he had heard the previous Sunday, carefully restating the sermon and its theme, and then giving his objective assessment. In these passages, we can see the beginnings of his later mindset, the probing quality of his analysis and his belief in the viability of his faith:

> You would not complain of his discourse, as you do of those of Dr. Ratcliff, on the score of being commonplace. His sermon this morning was an apotheosis of doubt, one might say. He read a lesson, from Emerson possibly, as to the necessity when doubt comes of cleaving to the principles of morality. "Even if there is no God it is better to be generous than to be selfish, to be chaste than to be licentious, to be truthful than to be dishonest, to be brave than to be cowardly." And he added that by such cleaving to the assured facts, the doubt might disappear. The sermon was based on the cry of Jesus: "My God, my God, why hast thou forsaken me!" It showed, says Dr. Cave, that to him came doubt. That an orthodox person would say that Jesus

> at that time was an atheist, an infidel. Of course, the lesson was that we should take Him for an example, and when doubt comes, as it surely will, we must cleave to our conscience, even if we cannot see that God is good. He illustrated it by the story of the King (who was it) at the battle of Cressy, who refused to succor his son, preferring to let him win his own spurs. So we may be left alone, to fight our own battles, without God's assistance or presence.
>
> There was a good deal of the polemical in the sermon. Why is it that "liberal" preachers are so often that way. Perhaps it is inevitable. But it would seem more consistent if they were not. I fancy his own experience entered into his discourse considerably. He was formerly an orthodox minister, and he had a son who went very bad. He was passionately fond of him, and it nearly broke his heart. After a long struggle with himself he came out as a liberal of the most advanced type. Several times he spoke in the sermon of the relations between a father and a son, I think from a full heart. And several times he spoke of the way in which the present salt of the earth (meaning the members of his church) were abused by orthodox people with what seemed to me to be a little bitterness.
>
> The sermon was short, thoughtful, polished if not eloquent, and rather improving. One might possibly question the justification of the doubting and distrusting of the goodness of God, of which he almost seemed to boast.... Well dearie, even though we do have disappointments we will try not to lose faith in the protecting kindness that is around us. And I am sure that the richness of our mutual love will make it easier for us to realize the nature of the Divine love (January 23, 1898).

The letters, written when Henry was 31, show that he both exhibited and rejected his father's value system. His commitment to Protestant ethics never wavered. His analyses of sermons were always objective, and several letters suggest that he had moved away from the fervid Methodism of his father. In his letter of February 2, 1898, he wrote:

> Dear heart, I fairly hate at times the hollowness and mockery of the formalism which stands in place of real religion, I fear, in my heart. You I am sure can help me to get the real spirit; you have already helped me by having loved me, by having showed me your own pure heart. You will help me more during this coming year, will you not, dearest? There is not another person on earth to whom I speak thus.

In another letter, he told Ethel:

> What do you think I did this evening. I went around to the church for a while to a prayer meeting. I used to go quite frequently the first year I was here, but have not been at all since I came back (undated).

Ethel was apparently more confident of his getting the Chicago position than he was. Allusions to going to church and to Scripture surfaced frequently during the months before the final offer arrived, in early May of 1898. Henry sought solace and relief from his anxiety in his religious experience, which he always applied to his and Ethel's situation.

Henry remarked in several letters about alcohol and tobacco, which were both anathema to his father. The quality of Henry's remarks seems to suggest that he did not consider the use of alcohol and tobacco to be as evil as did his father. Interviews with Henry Hatfield's grandchildren and former students reveal that he never used tobacco, even during the years in which he and Ethel were engulfed in the bustle of social activities at Berkeley. But his views on alcohol were less pronounced than those held by his father. While he did not consume alcohol, he did not condemn those who did. Even in 1898, he voiced concern over the "inconsistencies" in his views relating to the use of both. He told Ethel that he took whiskey and hot water for his cold: "Do you think that a person who is as particular as I am about beer and wine does wrong, I mean is he inconsistent, in taking whiskey and hot water under such circumstances?" (undated) Yet, he felt that his refusal to consume alcohol in public was a personal issue. In a letter to Ethel dated March 19, 1898, he described having dinner with a family named Zeublin:

> I had a rather stupid time at the Zeublins. I reached there about 10:15. Mr. Brooks, a Mr. Stern, and Mr. and Mrs. Dwight Perkins were there. Perkins is an architect and a great friend of Whitney. You may have heard of him. Mrs. P. is a kind of an aesthete, very charming I guess, but inclined to be dogmatic. We had oysters, veal loaf, olives, and bread to eat. Beer and coffee to drink. I took water. The first thing Mrs. P. asked me was whether it was taste or principle, which struck me as not very good manners.

In another letter, dated January 16, 1898, he commented, with irony:

> What do you think of this scheme? That I shall take to smoking, I have not decided about drinking, so that when we get married there will be something for me to give up. It would be doubly advantageous for people should say of me, as they do of Smith, "How nice it was of him to stop smoking to please his wife," and besides it would give me an opportunity to economize, so that matrimony will not seem so extravagant. This suggestion somewhat resembles Whitney's and also Mark Twain's, but it was formulated independently of the latter. He suggests, you know, that smoking is a great blessing because you can cure practically any disease by swearing off from tobacco. I await your instructions.

Hatfield's Attitude Toward Teaching

In addition to revealing a portrait of Henry and Ethel's relationship and of his attitudes prior to their marriage in June 1898, the letters supply valuable insights into events and Henry's own inclinations that led him to select accounting as his academic field. For example, during his time at Washington University, he taught a variety of courses—psychology, economic theory, descriptive economics, and money. At that time in his career, he was grateful for any teaching opportunity but did not enjoy psychology, preferring instead courses of a "practical" nature. Shortly before he received Laughlin's tentative offer in February, he was concerned that he might have to remain at St. Louis, if that were even possible. He was not sure that he could do so:

> Well, do not get discouraged, sweetheart, we are going to get something somewhere. Nothing very exciting, so far today. Only one class, Psychology. Mr. Snow intimated that I might make the announcement for Psychology to cover a year instead of a term. I wanted to see the chan-

> cellor before doing that. I do not want to bind myself to teach Psy. unless that is necessary to keeping my job or to getting a raise.... I will have a class in Advanced Economics next term, and one in Money (January 5, 1898).

In his letter of January 9, 1898 he commented again:

> Mr. Snow did not mention Pol. Sci.... I do not want to offend Snow, by seeming to be trying to drive him out of part of his work. I will teach Psychology or any old thing next year, if by so doing I can get a raise ... but I do not hanker after Psychology.

Then, in a letter of January 13, 1898 he showed his uncertainty about what to do about his employment situation:

> Would it be advisable to write to Mr. Laughlin and find whether there is any prospect of learning our fate before next term begins [February 1]. I have to start in a week from Monday on the new work and I have not the least idea whether I ought to try to give three courses or only two. It is very aggravating. Yet I do not know about writing him. To tell the truth I am so anxious to get the place that I distrust my judgment on anything in any way connected with it.

The months of anxiety over whether he would receive the offer, which would determine if they could marry during the summer of 1898, tried his patience. Shortly before the offer finally came from Chicago, he expressed his agitation at not yet receiving a firm offer. When the offer finally came on February 24, he was not ecstatic at the tentativeness of it. In a hurriedly handwritten note, he remarked:

> This has just come. I have not replied yet. Will probably write this afternoon saying I would "consider" a proposition if made at once. I hate this kind of letter. Why can't they ever make a clean definite offer at Chicago, instead of fiddling around. Of course this would be only $4200 for the three years instead of $4500. But we surely could get along. We could use the fund for 2 years and you could do some tutoring and I can do some "sealfin" on loans in Chicago which I cannot here.

Yet, despite the frustration that surfaced in the letters, being separated from Ethel, and not knowing about his future, Henry had a self-effacing quality that his students and colleagues would later recall. Conscious of his own limitations and never arrogant, he expressed his concern that he would be successful enough for Ethel, whose intellectual prowess he deeply admired and which drove him to excel. He was quick to admit his absent-mindedness (letter dated January 19, 1898) and also wrote, "And I know that if any thing can ever help me conquer my indolence and general shiftlessness it will be the faith that you have in me, and the stimulus that you can give me" (January 11, 1898).

Why Henry chose accounting as his field remains a puzzle, even after he was happily employed at Chicago. He was tapped by Laughlin to teach Commercial Geography (letter dated April 2, 1900), and he wrote Ethel, who was in Washington (with her parents) shortly after giving birth to John Glover, about the possibility of their going to Germany to "study up" to prepare to teach the course. He told

Ethel that the course would be included in Political Science. Because it would be a growing field, he believed, based on Laughlin's recommendation, it "would be a good thing for me to take up" (April 3, 1900).

Two years earlier, while he was still in St. Louis, accounting appeared in one of his letters to Ethel:

> Then I went to the library and began working on bibliography for next year. I began on the section containing works on business, Commerce, etc. and started to go right through. I do not mean that I am reading all the books, but I am finding out what there is on the subject. This will help me both on the course on Industry and on the Accounts course (March 11, 1898).

Thus, his entry into the teaching of accounting apparently occurred as with other courses. The opportunity arose, and he took it. Henry's habit of surveying the literature before teaching was thus one that became evident early in his career.

Before he began his career at Chicago, he had taught a variety of courses and explored how each fit in with his interests. As he commented to Ethel in a letter dated March 11, 1898:

> Did I tell you that the first time I heard of the college of Commerce etc., way last Spring, when I saw a preliminary announcement of it in Laughlin's office, I immediately said to myself, "That's what I want." And really, as far as I can see, it is exactly the kind of work I would choose, if I had my choice of all kinds. It has enough of the practical element, it comes into direct enough contact with real people, it seems to me to have sufficient justification for being ... and this is just what suits me.

In a letter dated March 3, 1898, he explained that he was interested in the Industries course, even though he knew nothing about it. He noted that he was thinking of a course on "the History of Political Parties, taking up the platforms and showing especially the economic questions involved and how they affected politics, and how, on the other hand, political exigencies have determined economic policy.... Of course I have a general knowledge of the attitude toward the tariff and the Bank. And we could work it up together and have fun doing it."

The letters also allude to his teaching correspondence courses. He apparently taught Modern Industries by correspondence and considered offering accounting by correspondence: "If I ever give Accounting etc. I'll offer that by correspondence too. It might be popular among some clerks etc. and it would lend itself first rate to correspondence" (March 24, 1899).

His use of Socratic teaching methods, remembered by his students and colleagues, was set fairly early. Former students recall that Hatfield wanted students to think, to find the fallacies in their own reasoning, to defend their position—that he wanted to stimulate discussion but not impose his point of view on the class. This approach, which would be vintage Hatfield by the 1920s, clearly surfaces in one of the 1898 letters in which he describes how he will teach his economics courses:

> And I shall speak of the Money course. If I can get anyone to take that, only admitting those who are also taking the course in Ec. 2, I intend to make it very matter of fact and practical. I expect to give them the questions asked by the Monetary Commission and try to get them to form opinions on each of the questions asked. I do not design to answer the questions at all, but to give them some of the matter necessary to discuss the problems. It is surprising how they form opinions without knowing anything about the facts. They are all violently opposed to silver, except one fellow, Cave (undated).

Hatfield's love of historical accounting also became manifest in this collection of letters. In a letter dated April 30, 1900, he discussed his idea of an accounting museum and that Laughlin supported the idea: "I am very sure I can get a good many contributions of specimens from various houses, and L. says that at any time he might then get some one also to give money." Many of Hatfield's former students recalled his discussion of accounting history in his courses. In his statement recommending the establishment of the Hatfield Chair at Berkeley in 1964, Frank A. Waring referred to Hatfield's great interest in accounting history texts and treatises:

> Hatfield also is responsible for the distinguished collection of books and other items in the field of accounting and accounting history housed at the University of California. He acquired these items partly from his own personal funds and partly from contributions he was able to obtain from sympathetic professional accountants and other business friends in San Francisco and elsewhere. This collection is still a mecca for scholars from around the world who are interested in the earlier developments in the field (memorandum, July 2, 1964).

Then, in a letter to Ethel dated March 2, 1898, which he wrote after receiving a letter from Laughlin commenting on the courses he might teach at Chicago, Henry discussed his perception of his academic strengths and interests. Even at this point in his career, he was more partial to history than accounting:

> The perfectly awful list of courses he [Laughlin] suggested rather staggers me. If he thinks he is going to scare me off, so as to make room for "the best man available" he will be fooled. I'll make a bluff and teach Sanscrit if it is necessary, but of course that will mean an awful lot of work. I do wish I could ask your advice about things but I will have seen Uncle Larry before this reaches you, so I can't. I can try the Industries course all right, and Co-operation does not scare me. I do not know a thing about either of them but never mind. But annuities does appall me. You should have seen Chaplin hoot at the idea of my teaching anything about annuities. Engler told him I could do it all right, though it would be no fun. I'll do my best to persuade him to give me one easy and decent course. I think he ought to. And then comes Prof. Judson. If I cannot get him to give me something respectable instead of Law, well, I'll teach the law, that's all, bad'cess to them. You see I'm getting mad, and something is bound to happen. I'm going in a few minutes with T.F.C. to visit one of his law classes which meets at 5. B.W. If I have to teach that, there are two courses at that hour which I will take. They meet different days. One is on Partnership, so it is on Agency and the other on Commercial Paper. They will be of help. But you may be sure I will strike the Dean for Civil Gov. or something easy if I can. I thought some of proposing a course in the History of Political Parties, taking up the platforms and showing especially the economic questions involved and how they affected politics, and how, on the other hand, political exigencies have determined economic policy. Don't you think

> that would be a rather useful course and not a very difficult one to work up. Of course I have a general knowledge of the attitude toward the tariff and the Bank. And we could work it up together and have fun doing it....
>
> Say it would be a joke if Larry should "turn" me down because I do not know anything about Statistics, or about higher mathematics involved in annuities? But I do not think he will try, and we will not let him if he does. A person who has faked it through Psychology will dare anything.

Finally, at the end of May, 1898, Henry received the coveted offer from Chicago. His letter to Ethel dated May 30, commenting on Laughlin's offer letter and reacting to his initial teaching assignments, provides insight into the state of business education at Chicago:

> Well, Well, what do you think of this? I have at last heard from Uncle Larry [Laughlin] and this is what he says.... "My dear Mr. Hatfield, I have your telegram. Come as soon as you can. I can see you Friday—but not in the p.m. or on Saturday. Think over these courses: 1. Processes of Leading Industries. 2. Commercial Arithmetic. (Exchange, Annuities, Bond-tables, etc.) 3. Statistics (Gen Course, 1 Quar.) or Co-operation. In Pol. Sci. I hope they will have you give European and American Commercial Law; and possibly Commercial Geography. But that is not to say. Sincerely yours, J. Laurence Laughlin."
>
> Did you ever hear of a lay out like that. I don't know a blooming thing about a single one of them. The first is not bad. I rather thought he would want that. You know he spoke to me about it last Summer, having magic lantern pictures and all that. I'll have to work it all up, but it is not uninteresting. I'll begin right away going through the shoe factories and the brewery here. They are probably the biggest in the country. But fancy that second! Who would want to study that. What a thrilling course. Getting pretty close to a business college too. The Co-operation will be interesting. I do not know but that I would prefer Statistics to #2 [Commercial Arithmetic]. And look at the Pol. Sci. What in the world do you know about them?

He concluded the letter by stating:

> I do like the practical character of the work, and I believe there will be a field for doing really valuable work. Perhaps I can get in touch with business men, better than some, and that will be an ambition worth some effort. These subjects are dry, but then we will have to make them interesting and I believe there is more in the function of a teacher of undergraduates than the mere courses. Is that very old fashioned and un-scholarly?

Hatfield added a postscript to this letter to the effect that he was disappointed that he would be teaching arithmetic and geography after having taught psychology and ethics at St. Louis.

Hatfield's Attitude Toward His Family

This collection of letters, which Henry wrote to Ethel nearly every day for seven months, not only provides precious evidence of his early academic concerns and his relationship to Ethel but also yields insight into his relations with the Hatfield family in Evanston. His father, Rev. Dr. Robert M. Hatfield, had died in

1891, and his mother, Elizabeth, was not in good health. Comments about her health intermix with observations about other family members: Henry characterized his sister Emily as "flighty," his brother James and brother-in-law S.A. Kean as difficult, and Maude (James's wife) as lacking in common sense. He felt that Ethel would have been a better match for James, whom Henry admired for his scholarly acumen. Henry blamed James for Maude's lack of "good common sense" (May 3, 1898). Henry felt that, because he [i.e., Henry] was easier to get along with than either S.A. or James, he was "too good natured, too easy going ever to amount to anything." Again and again, he states his admiration for Ethel's "hard sense."

Hatfield's Views of His Experience with S.A. Kean & Co.

Comments scattered throughout Hatfield's speeches as well as in these letters make it clear that his experience with the banking firm of S.A. Kean & Co. made an indelible impression on him. He recognized that S.A., his sister Anna's husband, was a difficult person, but he told Ethel in the letter of May 5, 1898 that S.A. had not been dishonest in the failure of his company. His comments to Ethel are the only personal insights we have about the bank failure. He—and apparently his mother, too—was concerned about Anna's welfare. Henry wrote to Ethel:

> I never knew anyone who did get along well with S.A. One instance will do. I went to work for him in Sept. 1885 and quit in Dec. 1890. In that time every one of the employees, and his partner too, had left him, and I sent in my definite resignation a month before. I merely held on temporarily so as to accommodate him during the pressure caused by the Baring failure. When you recollect that of all positions bank clerks generally stay the longest you can see that that is significant.

Henry then recalled that, even in the good years, people left the bank because they could not get along with S.A.:

> I often wonder why [Anna] married him. I fancy that she was a little dazzled.... Well, I am mighty sorry for her.
>
> Did mother make any remarks to you about S.A.? Or what do you know of her "attitude." It is funny sometimes how she gets me up in her room, shuts the door, and then frees herself. Not that she gets mad, she never does that. And her favorite name for him is "Loyola." But really I do not mean to abuse him. I am tremendously sorry for him. He has had a hard disappointing life. I know, absolutely, that he was perfectly honest in a business in which that is saying a great deal. And yet you will have to hunt with a rake to find anyone in Chicago, not intimately acquainted with him and his affairs, who does not think that he has a pile hidden away which he stole from his depositors.

The incident further suggests Henry's gentle, forgiving nature toward family and his desire not to be too hard on people, a quality noted by many of his former students and colleagues. Yet, more than 45 years after the event, the experience with

S.A. arose again, in his valedictory speech "Moriturus Vos Saluto," given at the Berkeley Club on April 29, 1937. In the opening segment of this presentation, he demarcated the major turning points in his life. He recounted his experience with Kean as an important rite of passage:

> In the life of anyone who has lived to maturity, there have been a number of such changes.... Aside from these physical changes, there are others, as when one ceases to be a student and becomes an active man of affairs; when he ends the chrysalis stage of bachelorhood and begins the brightness and joy of matrimony. In my own case, I count the ending of a business career of several years when I returned to finish my college course as the end of an old life and the beginning of a new one. And, less markedly, the transition from the status of student to that of member of the faculty seems like a death and a resurrection.

Several paragraphs later, in assessing his experiences in the university, he noted:

> What are the reactions of one coming from a little experience in the world of business to academic life? Perhaps the first experience was that of disillusionment and a growing appreciation of the fact that, after all, academicians are not so very different from the business man. I thought, in my innocence, that faculty members walked by the pure light of reason, that they were guided exclusively by intellect and not by emotion. I knew that the business man was not always rational, for I remembered a banker boasting of the superiority of his clan over economists, "for economists," said he, "rely only on theory, while we business men rely on solid facts." But a little examination showed that he was a more rigid theorist than any economist I had ever known, the only essential difference being that the business man's theory was the fallacious kind based purely on *post hoc propter hoc.*

Hatfield as Seen in Later Letters

A number of letters written later—these were also kept by Ethel Hatfield along with the 1897-1898 group—show Henry's loving concern for Robert Hatfield, who was the most lively of the three Hatfield children. Two pictures of Robert and his motorcycle can be found in one of the scrapbooks. Robert suffered from asthma as a child, a condition that worried Henry. Despite poor health throughout his childhood, Robert apparently attempted to ignore his asthma, which led to his death of pneumonia in 1927 at age 24. In a letter to Robert dated June 2, 1921, Henry chided sons John and Robert, who at that time were 21 and 18 years of age, respectively, for their life style:

> Well you certainly are having a wild life. What with convict camps, and old man Sancho, and rifles, and tires, and mud, and deserts, even Tuolume and Dick the Bandit must seem like a Sunday school picnic. Come now, tell up, just how did you feel when you were 30 miles from grub, and short of gas? Did you have any thoughts of walking the 30 miles on an empty stomach? And did you reckon that you would eat your shoes first or try to live on sage brush?
>
> * * *
>
> I have one suggestion—you ought to have sent us a postal card just before your departure from Round Mountain. It would not have been much trouble, and would have saved some consider-

> able days uncertainty as where in the world you were. Remember you are two (2) Hatfields. [signed] HRH

THE LATER HATFIELD—PERSPECTIVES OF COLLEAGUES AND STUDENTS

Hatfield the Socratic: The Eternal "Why?"

An attempt to sketch the personal side of Henry Hatfield the teacher and colleague relies heavily on the memories of former students and others who knew Hatfield at Berkeley.[7] Their recollections enable us to depict the human side of Hatfield, what he was like as a teacher and a colleague. The characteristics that students most consistently remember was his questioning, probing mind and his demand that students think. He was always asking questions. This quality is evident in a number of reminiscences from different perspectives. For example, Harry D. Kerrigan, a lifelong accounting academic who studied under Hatfield for his B.S. and M.S. degrees in the late 1920s, recalled that "Hatfield was an intellectual who tolerated details only as unavoidable vehicles for getting things done practically. He was at his best in the realm of ideas.... He was a logician, a student, and encourager of ideas" (letter, July 31, 1964). James S. Reece, chief of the Division of Audit and Financial Review for the U.S. Department of the Interior's Bureau of Reclamation, who wrote a master's thesis under Hatfield in 1929, echoed this image:

> The keen mind and quick wit that gained himself so much popularity as an after-dinner speaker, were projected into his lecture and seminar periods to the benefit and delight of his students. In my particular case, when engaged in the preparation of a thesis, his assistance with the accounting research involved was both interesting and effective. Through knowledgeable discussion he would highlight the points requiring attention and lay them bare in a manner that generated both incentive and interest to pursue them to a final conclusion. In graduate school seminars he had a thought provoking way all his own to develop a subject to a point where the students gradually picked up the threads to carry forward a stimulated discussion of the many technical facets so painstakingly developed (letter, September 14, 1964).

Judson E. Krueger, a San Francisco practitioner and part-time teaching assistant during the 1920s and 1930s, remembered that Hatfield "liked to discuss and argue.... He enjoyed the mental stimulus of arguing." Krueger was not sure that Hatfield actually liked accounting, as he would move away from accounting and into esoteric subjects during his seminar. "He wanted to inspire people to think rather than to teach them anything." Students received good grades if they presented their positions logically. Krueger added:

> In Hatfield's Advanced course, he said he wouldn't lecture, but he asked some questions: What is the connection between A and B? We could see no relation. In fact, that was Hatfield's

point—he wanted the students to see that it was a foolish question. He tore into the students for not having the courage of their convictions to say so. He believed that the most important thing for a college instructor is to teach students to think. They will learn what they need to know in private business and accounting (paraphrased from an interview, October 19, 1964).

Frank A. Waring, Hatfield's student in the early 1920s (who completed M.A. and Ph.D. degrees at Berkeley in 1930 and 1932, respectively), proposed the establishment of a Hatfield Chair at Berkeley in July 1964. (At that time, the university did not entertain such requests, so the effort failed.) In arguing for the chair, Waring described Hatfield's teaching methods in a similar way:

> His graduate seminars possessed to a very special degree the quality of "live" interest. Graduate students were induced to embark on "voyages of discovery" in their examination of standard and contemporary works dealing with theory and practice. Although encouraged to develop individual initiative and thought, there was always, as one former student expressed it, "the guiding hand usually gloved in velvet which often took the form of brilliant but gentle wit. We felt we were reading independent undirected judgments. We even felt we had reached new ideas or analyses. And we certainly participated with enthusiasm." Graduate students under Hatfield gained a respect for scholarliness in thought and expression (memorandum, July 2, 1964).

H.F. Freeman, Class of '30, another former student, echoed this view:

> As the most significant characteristic which distinguishes Professor Hatfield from other faculty members with whom I was associated, I would call attention to his insistence that a student develop an independent viewpoint in the subject matter area. He had no patience with reasoning which was merely based on statements made by alleged authorities in the field of accounting. He rejected the concept that there are certain inviolable principles of accounting which a student could absorb by reading a text book (letter, September 3, 1964).

J. Henry Schweich, who wrote a master's thesis under Hatfield in 1926, noted:

> He never criticized a statement but by the time he had asked three questions the student discovered his own errors.... He tried to develop creativity in the student and the graduate teaching fellow.... His conception of a satisfactory master's thesis was that it contain a degree of originality and demonstrate the ability to do analytical thinking. Also if a previous book in the field had been written, a sufficient differentiation was necessary.... He was the kind of inspiring leader that you never forget and rarely find. Brilliant but humble and keenly interested in developing young people. He made you think and no idea or statement was handled superficially (letter, August 18, 1964).

Gordon J. Miller, who was deputy business vice-president of the University of Utah, took Hatfield's seminar in the spring of 1941. He later wrote:

> I believe Professor Hatfield used us as guinea pigs on which to try out his ideas on accounting principles. I am certain he did not wholly agree with all that was published and felt that it represented a start. Professor Hatfield had the unique ability of stimulating students in scholarly pursuits. He was always kindly, but could make you feel embarrassed if you failed to research

> carefully some part of the assignment. He had a deep interest in his students and was always interested in contributing to their development. In the seminars I had he never lectured, merely posed questions to open a discussion. He was a master at probing so that the student would extend himself to the limit of his capabilities. He gave you the impression that he was a fellow student looking for answers just as you were (letter, July 2, 1965).

J. Fred Halterman, who received a Ph.D. in finance from Berkeley in 1935 and who completed an M.S. thesis under Hatfield in 1931, similarly noted that Hatfield gave minimal direction on a master's thesis, leaving it, in large measure, up to the writer. He apparently wanted the writer to learn what the literature said (telephone interview, January 16, 1965).

In the advanced course, Hatfield took particular delight in criticizing the more traditional views of students, implying that they were hidebound. Michael N. Chetkovich, a student in Hatfield's seminar in 1940, became the national managing partner of Haskins & Sells and served as chairman of the American Institute of Certified Public Accountants in 1976-1977. He remembers that Hatfield would get into a philosophic area, "get you to develop your own position, get you to crawl out on a limb, and then gently saw you off" (telephone interview, January 26, 1965).

Harry R. Buttimer, Jr., a student in Hatfield's seminar during the fall of 1943, summarized Hatfield's method:

> He acted as a catalyst. He allowed a person to slip and find the fallacy of his reasoning. He had no plan of which we were aware about presenting his views. The seminar was held in his study at home. Hatfield had pictures of famous accountants (including Paciolo) on his paneled wall. He was very caustic in his treatment of people in the group. It was to make sure that you were on your toes. You would need to defend your position. I recall that someone quoted Hatfield. He was very quick to say that that is one thing we don't do in this seminar. He was inclined to treat other authorities the same way as he treated himself. At times, the students deliberately disagreed in order to bring him out. But he was slippery. Mentally, he was fantastically alert (paraphrased from an interview, January 18, 1965).

Erudition Cloaked in Humor, Satire, and Wit

Hatfield's keen penchant for spying error in language or thought was legendary. He relished erudition and explorations into the ways in which language was used. Catharine D. Quire, Hatfield's lone doctoral student and a veritable disciple of the man she venerated, said that he deeply disliked the pretentious and the fuzzy: "His great respect for the beauty and flexibility of pure English, *Oxford Dictionary* English and the English of Fowler's *Modern English Usage*, enriched our discussions."[8] Harry Kerrigan also observed that Hatfield "fussed with public law statutes mainly because he found the material beautifully classified, and, in judges' pronouncements, magnificent use of the English language and such attractive (or careful) applications of 'equity' to the parties at interest." Charles C. Staehling, Hatfield's junior accounting colleague for more than 20 years, believed that legal cases interested him in two ways: "both for support and as something to shoot at" (interview, January 24, 1965). No idea or fact or philosophy was beyond the realm of discussion. As Leonard A. Doyle, who joined the Berkeley accounting faculty in 1942, recalled:

> Hatfield held a weekly luncheon at the faculty club for those teaching accounting. It seemed to be more a vehicle for the display of his erudition. He would prepare thoroughly. He was one of a small number of his generation who could be said to be literate, and he enjoyed the exhibition of this capacity (paraphrased from an interview, December 15, 1964).

Robert D. Calkins was chairman of the Berkeley economics department in the 1930s and later became dean of the Columbia University business school and president of the Brookings Institution. He came to know Hatfield well. Calkins recalled:

> Dr. Hatfield had intellectual friendships more than personal, emotional friendships with his colleagues. For example, I well recall that he and Professor Max Radin in the Law School would, upon encountering one another on campus, launch immediately into some discourse on the Bible, or Greek literature, or medieval law, or the early history of accounting, or some such topic....
>
> I recall one dinner at his home at which we were the guests along with Professor Radin. During dinner Hatfield quoted the Bible, Radin contested the accuracy of his quotation, and the evening was spent in one of the most lively and interesting discussions I ever heard on the history of the Bible and the meaning of certain passages in Hebrew, Greek and the English St. James version. Hatfield had a remarkable memory, as did Radin, and a great capacity to quote from those things which had interested him (letter, February 19, 1964).

Radin, according to Charles A. Gulick, Jr., one of the economists in the department, was light years away from Hatfield in social and economic views, yet they had a very special relationship. Gulick recalled that Hatfield and Radin wrote each other notes in Latin in which the messages contained subtle errors in grammar for the other to correct (telephone interview, June 20, 1965). In a memorandum, Frank Waring commented in a similar vein:

> Henry Rand Hatfield was more than an eminent scholar of accounting, he was a cultured human being with an amazing breadth of knowledge and interest. He read Latin as readily as English and wrote in their own tongue to his academic friends in Greece. He was fluent in German and French and had a working knowledge of Italian and Spanish. His command of foreign languages increased his appreciation of the correct usage of his own, and many a graduate student found an unanticipated by-product of an accounting seminar to be the improvement of his English (memorandum, July 2, 1964).

Hatfield was a keen reader of A.P. Richardson's column "This Blessed Language," which appeared from 1939 to 1944 in *The Journal Accountancy*. He had dealt with Richardson for many years during the latter's long tenure (1911-1936) as editor of the *Journal*. Richardson, it was said, "displayed in his editorials and essays breadth and depth of erudition in such varied disciplines as law, literature and accountancy";[9] and he and Hatfield apparently formed a mutual admiration society. In a column in 1939, Richardson printed an extract from a letter from Hatfield, describing the author (without naming him) as "one of the most brilliant members of the great profession of teachers."[10] Hatfield had written to complain of an "-ate" that he disliked:

> I ask as a personal favor that you never use the word "evaluate" in my hearing. I know this is a somewhat discreditable idiosyncrasy, but, just as some people are allergic to ragweed pollen and others to strawberries, so am I to that word which I will not even pronounce in this dictation. It has a worse effect on me than did Liza Doolittle's use of "bloody" on her hearers. It makes me sick at my stomach and gives me a pain in my neck.[11]

Hatfield's command of language, as well as his erudition, became the foundation for his wit, for which he was well known. As Doyle also recalled:

> Bus tours would stop at the campus, on Oxford Street. The guide would say, "You see before you one of the best groves of eucalyptus trees in the country, with a great number of varieties." Hatfield, in the vicinity, would interpose, "Ladies and gentlemen: this is a university professor of which there are several varieties and many hundred on this campus," as he embarrassed the colleague with him (paraphrased from an interview, December 15, 1964).

Frank Waring observed that there was a "pixie" quality about Hatfield's humor. It was never unkind, but it was often pointed. For example:

> Professor Cole of Harvard, with whom Hatfield did not always agree, accepted an invitation to lecture at Berkeley during a summer session. As part of the hospitality extended to the visitor, Hatfield drove him to Yosemite. En route he said to his guest, "Cole, isn't it strange? You and I have so much in common—we both regularly attend church; neither one of us smokes or drinks; we are both academicians—and yet one of us is such a rotten accountant" (memorandum, July 2, 1964).

Hatfield was in great demand as an after-dinner speaker because of his wit and sense of fun, his graciousness, and the deftness with which he could amuse in mock seriousness. As Dennis B. Wheeler, Class of '22, recalled, "Mrs. Hatfield always came and sat next to him. The two of them were a working cooperative pair. She would continually pass him little notes reminding him of quick comebacks. He would then keep the audience in hilarious uproar with his quick wit" (letter, March 27, 1965). Always kindly in his concern for people, he nevertheless disliked pretense and used wit with dexterity. As Waring explained:

> On one occasion when he was Dean of the Faculties he agreed to preside over a dinner at which a Bishop of the Methodist Church was to be one of the speakers. The Bishop was dignified, austere and very conscious of his position. Hatfield began his introduction by saying, "I did not mind presenting to you the Dean of Men, or even the President of the University, delicate as that assignment might be. But I confess that I was troubled by the task of introducing a Bishop.

I was the son of a Methodist Minister and when a Bishop came to visit in my father's house it was a time of awe and solemnity. What should I call him? Should I say Your Grace, Your Eminence, or Your Holiness? How should I address him? Recently, however, a student solved the problem for me. He came to me, the Dean of the Faculties, and he didn't say Dean; he didn't say Professor; he didn't even say Doctor. He just said, "say Prof., listen." Hatfield turned quickly to the pompous Bishop saying, "Say, Bish., listen," and his audience roared with delight (memorandum, July 2, 1964).

An excerpt from a speech on "accounting for woman," published in 1927, illustrates his ability to use puns and verbal irony in his orations:

Now why is it that weak, timid woman who will show such bravery rushing into a burning building or defying a raging tiger to save her child, nevertheless, run shrieking in terror when a mouse approaches. The only explanation is, there is no accounting for woman. This does not seem to apply in this circle. As I sat here, I tried to figure it out; there is no accounting for her—is she for accounting?

I wonder what we should do with woman in accounting. I try to see where she belongs. In the first place, I am puzzled as to which side of the balance sheet she belongs. I have often heard that woman was man's chief asset or greatest treasure, but I have known many a man who has found her quite a liability. If she is an asset, what kind of asset? I suppose this side of Reno she is a fixed asset; up there I don't know what she is—circulating, I guess.

Then you turn to the other side of the balance sheet and it is even worse. Of course, she is capital, generally preferred, never common. I have often heard of a woman belonging in bonds of matrimony—I have heard of womanly reserve. Kipling tells us of a million surplus Maggies. She doesn't belong in depreciation, I am sure. I don't know what to do with her. I suppose you might say that in her early years she is often called cash; when she gets engaged she goes into the appropriation account; when she gets married she is in the allotment account; when she becomes a happy mother we put her in dividends, and when she dies we put her into real estate.[12]

Punctilious Scholar, Kindly Teacher

Other testimony of former accounting students at Berkeley presents a similar picture, one depicting Hatfield as a Socratic teacher whose sensitivity to the use of language and logic marked his teaching and his approach to accounting: he posed questions, not with answers in mind but with the sole purpose of making students think. John A. Ferguson, Class of '15, was one of Hatfield's students and recalled him as a "lovable, wonderful man, who was a wonderful teacher":

He had an unruly head of red hair, was decidedly informal (in contrast to Carl Plehn and especially Adolph Miller), knew all the students, and was approachable. He was inclined to present both sides. Hatfield and Lilly [a junior faculty member] would argue during a class. Hatfield always took the other side. He wasn't argumentative to the point of keeping you from thinking. There was nothing vicious about the man (paraphrased from an interview, October 2, 1964).

One of Hatfield's students from the early 1930s, who was also an assistant who made out file cards to classify his huge library of accounting books, characterized him thus:

> a person of warmth, charity; never one to offend or to make one feel inadequate; one who made suggestions, even if they be adverse, always with a twinkle in his eye and a smile on his lips. Having associated with Professor Hatfield off and on over four years (1930-1934), I can hardly forget this medium-sized man with his thinnish reddish hair, freckled countenance, small, peering, beady eyes, the sandy reddish mustache, the slight twitch in one shoulder (which one, I forget), and his hands thrust into his pockets as he talked with me (Edwin Pendleton, Class of '32, memorandum of November 1964).

Merrell W. Skeels, who took Hatfield's seminar in the 1930s and also served as his teaching assistant, stated that his most vivid recollection of Hatfield was "his practice of leading the unwary down the primrose path by getting them to agree with him in a particular position and then reversing his stand and cutting down the arguments he had just previously been expounding" (letter, July 20, 1965). Arthur A. Wender, a teaching assistant in 1925-1926, stated that "Hatfield liked to kid Staehling, who was somewhat fixed in his thinking. Hatfield was quick to challenge people who asserted a confident knowledge. In class, Hatfield would ask a student for opinions on a subject and then proceed to take the other side and challenge the student" (paraphrased from an interview, January 26, 1965).

Staehling remembered how thoroughly Hatfield immersed himself in teaching the introductory course in accounting. "He would leave his lecture hall looking like he was working in a flour mill" (interview, January 24, 1965). In the 1910s, Lewis Lilly, an accounting instructor, would spot Hatfield following his lecture and say, "Come here, chief," and brush the chalk off Hatfield's blue suit (interview, Mrs. Lewis Lilly, January 25, 1965).

Hatfield shined in the seminar, which apparently was his favorite forum. In fact, one student from the late 1920s, Malcolm M. Devore, who became an executive office partner in Haskins & Sells, found Hatfield to be disappointing as a lecturer. He wrote:

> I consider him to be one of the driest lecturers I ever heard but, on the other hand, one of the most interesting writers whose works I have ever read. To me he had the faculty of making his thoughts come alive in the written word but he did not possess the same faculty in the spoken word—at least of the lecture variety (letter, June 22, 1965).

Hatfield's wit, kindness, but commitment to correct logic, language, and thinking were intertwined. James E. Tannahill, who wrote an M.S. thesis under Hatfield in 1933 and later became a partner in Haskins & Sells, recalled, "His seminars were conducted with the utmost informality; the students were expected to do most of the talking. He only interrupted to effect a correction of either ideas or expression, or both" (letter, October 17, 1964). In 1927-1928, Robert M. Douglas was a reader of examinations for Hatfield's 14 A-B elementary accounting course. He remembered:

> It was customary for the readers and teaching fellows to convene in the basement of old South Hall in the evening where Dr. Hatfield would review several papers with us in order to estab-

> lish a uniform grading pattern for the solutions submitted by the students to the various problems. It became my habit to bring some peanuts, popcorn and a few bottles of pop which we would open up after an hour or so of this intense indoctrination. Dr. Hatfield enjoyed these periods of jovial relaxation immensely as did all the rest of us and it became standard procedure for that academic year at least (letter, April 15, 1965).

Edna Jaffee, who took Hatfield's seminar for three successive terms in 1943-1944, recounted:

> I do not remember a text being used, but rather that Dr. Hatfield tossed out problems in accounting theory which various members of the group would have to research in the library. He himself brought various books and periodicals to the seminars, and would read statements on accounting theory or practice and then ask for comments from specific members of the group. I do not know that he followed any particular curriculum—I think his purpose was more to teach us to think. "Miss Cox, do you agree with that statement, and why?" While Miss Cox was still floundering around with that one, or as soon as she paused for breath, he would continue, "How would you have treated the situation, Mr. Jackson?"...
>
> Despite his advanced years, and despite the fact that we were presumably the cream of the accounting students, his mind moved so rapidly that he was always away ahead of us, dissecting our ideas and those of the authors, pointing out the fallacies in arguments, and suggesting sensible solutions. One of the bright boys ... once calculated the minimum number of students necessary for comfort in a Hatfield seminar. I think he decided there must be at least six, or otherwise one had no time to catch a mental breath between Dr. Hatfield's piercing questions (letter, July 9, 1965).

Hatfield—quixotic and demanding, though gracious and kindly—dealt with students as individuals. Students remember him as "a gentle human being" (Edwin Pendleton, Class of '32, memorandum of November 1964) who had a quick wit and enjoyed argument and verbal jousts when these led to a better understanding of the issues. As Catherine M. Laughren wrote, "I remember Dr. Hatfield as a kindly and very approachable man, and I think I got more from his human values than from his technical ones.... Whenever I went back for counsel, he was generous in time and interest" (letter, August 14, 1964). Holden S. Sanford stated:

> The course I took from Dr. Hatfield, Economic Theory of Accounting [in the early 1940s], stands out now in my memory, not so much from what I learned in the course as the fortunate and pleasant association with Professor Hatfield.
>
> * * *
>
> I felt that Dr. Hatfield was more interested in the academic and theoretical aspects of accounting than its more practical side. He appeared more interested in developing teachers of accounting than Certified Public Accountants (letter, July 23, 1965).

E. Cary Brown, professor of economics at the Massachusetts Institute of Technology, was a student at Berkeley in the 1930s. Although he did not study under Hatfield, he was Staehling's teaching assistant. He recounted the following anecdote about dinner at the Hatfields:

> I can recall one evening when Professor Hatfield and his wife had some of us undergraduates over for dinner and talk.... The evening was a charming one in which the Hatfields put several nervous undergraduates at ease and completely captivated them. Hatfield was a disarming conversationalist, carried his great scholarship lightly, always young in his ability to consider a new idea, and tolerant of any point of view. He loved to toy with ideas, and his constructive skepticism was stimulating. The evening was also memorable because it was, I believe, the *only* one I ever spent in the home of a faculty member as an undergraduate (letter, August 4, 1965).

Many letters from former students suggest that Hatfield was often relentless in his criticism of sloppy thinking, yet he disliked confronting students with criticism. He wanted them to think, yet his teaching was never separated from his awareness of his students as individuals. Holden Sanford related the following recollection of the Hatfield seminar:

> We met at Dr. Hatfield's house. It was one of the few older homes north of campus not destroyed by the Berkeley fire ... it reflected the quiet charm that went with a man who spent his life in teaching, in reflection, and who had reached what appeared to be a happy and satisfied maturity.
>
> The classroom was his library—a fairly large room upstairs and to one side of his living room. All four walls were lined solidly from top to bottom with books; mainly accounting, but much about all subjects was covered. I even believe there were a few detective stories, as we discussed some prominent men who read these as a diversion.
>
> The middle of the room was taken up by a "U" shaped table. The professor sat in the middle of the "U" while his students pushed books aside for working space.
>
> * * *
>
> As a basis for the course, we used *An Introduction to Corporate Accounting Standards* by Paton and Littleton. He recommended (never assigned or ordered) quite a bit of outside reading by various accounting writers. There was also a long term paper submitted which he constructively criticized with suggestions for further study and changes.
>
> * * *
>
> On the whole it was a discussion course, with Dr. Hatfield starting arguments, if we didn't. These arguments covered everything from the definition of profit, which seems to vary for each accountant (and is different from income) to consolidated balance sheets.
>
> Class was from 7:30 to 9:30 P.M. Regularly, about 9:15, Mrs. Hatfield would call from downstairs, "I think you have worked long enough, Doctor. I am sure your young men would like some chocolate," or it would be postum and, on the warmer evenings, punch or iced tea—cookies always (letter, July 23, 1965).

The Absent-minded Professor

Hatfield was renowned not only for his quick wit, charm, and felicity as a master of ceremonies but also for his forgetfulness. As Holden Sanford recalled:

> Dr. Hatfield invited us and our wives for dinner in lieu of the last class meeting. When we arrived, it was obvious from the bustling around by Dr. & Mrs. Hatfield that dinner was not ready. We later learned from Mrs. Hatfield, that around 4:30 P.M. (we arrived at 6:00 P.M.), Dr. Hatfield had asked if the preparation for dinner was in order. It was not. He had forgotten to mention the invitation at all previously. Mrs. Hatfield was accustomed to this, and we had a very good and pleasant chicken dinner, cooked by Mrs. Hatfield, although a little late (letter, July 23, 1965).

Cary Brown recalled:

> Hatfield's absent mindedness was always a topic of conversation. I remember a Beta Gamma Sigma banquet at which he was to be the main speaker. We went through the dinner, still no speaker. Finally, frantic phone calls routed him out of bed. With apologies he showed up, considerably overdue, and captivated us with his modest and fascinating account of the economic and statistical work he carried on during World War I (letter, August 4, 1965).

Mary (Mrs. Robert) Gash, Hatfield's secretary in the 1930s, remembered that he was absent-minded and frequently left his keys inside his locked office on the third floor of the library. A notoriously bad driver, his car seemed to be always in the garage for repairs, as he would be driving by himself, thinking, and run into something (interview, December 14, 1964). Charles Staehling, Hatfield's junior colleague, recalled that "he would walk home when he had driven to school in the morning" (January 24, 1965). M.M. Knight, an economist colleague, recounted: "Once he was to go to a party. Instead, he undressed and went to bed. Mrs. Hatfield had to get him out of bed and to the party" (paraphrased from an interview, January 23, 1965).

Frank Waring shared this recollection:

> Hatfield had all of the characteristics of the perfect professor, including that of absent mindedness. The legends are legion, but many of them have a basis in fact. As Dean of the Faculties he appeared at an official formal dinner in San Francisco correctly attired—almost—to welcome a new Ambassador from Japan. He had dressed early, but had slipped into a jacket to read. Time flew by and he suddenly discovered that only minutes remained to make transportation connections. Hurriedly slipping into a top coat, he rushed for his train and thus arrived in San Francisco in a lounging jacket. When he was called upon to speak, he explained what had happened to the obvious delight of everyone present. On another occasion he was having serious difficulty starting his car which was parked in front of South Hall until Professor Staehling shouted from the window, "Say, Hatfield, what are you doing in my car." At still another time, when asked why he had failed to appear as principal speaker at the initiation banquet of Beta Gamma Sigma, he exclaimed, "Oh, that explains everything. Last night I parked my car in front of the house and then went up stairs to change for the banquet, but instead put on my pajamas and went to bed. That is why the police impounded my car for parking all night on the street. I couldn't imagine why I hadn't put it in the garage" (memorandum, July 2, 1964).

Hatfield's driving habits were the source of many anecdotes, including the one by William A. Paton recounted in Chapter 4. Cary Brown similarly recalled:

Henry Hatfield at the desk in his study of his Berkeley home. Photograph was taken in about 1914. It was in this study that Hatfield conducted his theory seminar in the years following his retirement in 1937.

> Still another time his white-faced teaching fellows returned from giving the final exam. Apparently, while Hatfield was driving up Telegraph Avenue after the exam on the way to South Hall, someone had propounded a question to him. The car bore down unswervingly on Sather Gate, the entrance to which then had steel posts planted firmly across it. At the last moment the paralyzed assistants realized a loud warning was necessary, and the car was braked just in time to avoid damage to University property and staff (letter, August 4, 1965).

The Hatfield Home on Le Conte Avenue

Dr. Otto H. Houser and his wife, who lived in the Hatfield home during 1932 when the Hatfields were traveling abroad, described the house:

> The appointments in the house were complete. Everything was immaculate and orderly. The yard was idyllic. A circle of redwoods—berry bushes—fruit trees—flowers of many kinds—these were ours for the use. I recall the apricot tree that lay flat like a vine against the garage. Utility and art combined to convey the character of the man (letter, July 3, 1965).

The Le Conte address was designed in 1908 by the renowned architect Julia Morgan according to Hatfield's tastes, and it is today known as the Henry Hatfield House. In April 1996, it was one of 17 North Berkeley properties included in a house tour by the Berkeley Architectural Heritage Association.

Gordon Miller, the business officer at the University of Utah and also an accounting professor, reported: "I believe I prepared the last tax return [Hatfield] filed." Miller, a student in Hatfield's seminar in 1941, provided a word picture of the Hatfield home and of the Hatfields' graciousness and civility that is worth quoting in detail:

> I have met many of the great names in the academic field. In most instances their lustre dims as you get to know them. By that I mean they take on characteristics of the ordinary rather than the exceptional. However, I do not believe one could come in contact with Professor Hatfield without being cognizant of the fact that here was a great intellect, a warm personality and a great teacher....
>
> I believe that I was in the last seminar which Professor Hatfield taught. The seminar was held each Monday evening from 7:30 to 9:00 in his home north of the Berkeley campus. Professor Hatfield lived in one of those beautiful multi-story old homes north of the campus. It had several fireplaces, inasmuch as this was the only way of heating at the time it was built. On the landing, up one flight of stairs, was a beautiful study; it had warm redwood paneling on the walls and they were lined with book shelves and books. Most of the library consisted of historical and scholarly works on accounting, but there was a substantial collection of mystery stories. Professor Hatfield loved murder mysteries. Promptly at 7:30 each Monday evening three graduate students met in that study for a year. We always had the feeling that this seminar was the most important thing in Professor Hatfield's life. Promptly at 9:00 we adjourned to the living room downstairs and the Hatfields' maid would wheel out the coffee table with coffee, milk and sweet rolls or other pastries. I cannot remember a single instance when Professor Hatfield failed to meet this seminar. I recall one time he had a ranking British official as his house guest. He still held the seminar. Normally we sat in the living room and chatted for about an hour with Professor and Mrs. Hatfield. If he had house guests they, of course, entered in the discussion (letter, July 2, 1965).

This picture accords with that presented earlier by Holden Sanford, another of Hatfield's last seminar students.

Edna Jaffee, also a student enrolled in Hatfield's last seminar, commented on the high regard in which the Hatfields held students, as if they were no different than faculty colleagues:

> At least once, and I think possibly once a term, the Hatfields had a dinner party for the accounting assistants. Mrs. Hatfield was quite as well preserved as her husband, and they had a pleasant, tastefully furnished home on the Berkeley hillside near the campus. I remember a lovely semi-formal dinner which impressed all of us. Dr. Hatfield always treated his students with old-world courtesy, and nowhere was it more evident than in his own home (letter, July 9, 1965).

Vera Mae Twist, the departmental secretary, recalled that when the Hatfields entertained, which seemed often, they always had something planned (interview, July 1, 1965). It might be an evening of bridge, anagrams, or identifying quotations, or a wide-ranging conversation about almost anything that interested their guests. Malcolm M. Davisson, a departmental colleague, recalled that Hatfield always won, hands down, at the word games (interview, December 15, 1964).

Betty Werther, who regularly visited her grandparents' home on Le Conte following the death of her father, Robert, in 1927, contributed a very personal recollection:

> Myriad magic trips with HRH at the wheel—Muir woods, petrified forest, Yosemite, Asilomar, HRH reading aloud during dinner—and, above all, the rare complicity and total harmony between my grandparents. A single word from Henry would set comets sparkling from Ethel's eyes—to the very end....
>
> I remember the incredible plants grandfather would bring home from the botanists on campus, countless new species like loganberries which we were sometimes the first to taste and judge. Then there was a particularly exotic tree called an acacia pendulum which caused every passer-by to stop and gape (letter, January 10, 1990).

A Trail of Anecdotes

Stories abound about Henry Hatfield's absent-mindedness, his idiosyncrasies, his thoughtfulness, and his humor and wit. To many, he was an unforgettable personality.

John Ferguson recalled an episode from 1912-1913: "One day when Dr. Hatfield was lecturing, I fell asleep. Dr. Hatfield picked up a piece of chalk and hit me on the forehead and woke me up. He kept right on lecturing as though nothing had happened" (memorandum, October 1964). Hatfield's son John related a similar tale concerning "a one o'clock class on a warm afternoon when a student in the front row fell asleep with his mouth open. Without a word Father picked up a short piece of chalk from the blackboard and threw it into the student's open mouth. He said he had never seen a more surprised look on anyone's face."[13]

In 1926, when J. Hugh Jackson was appointed professor of accounting at Stanford University at a very large salary, Hatfield remarked, "Now a man can marry for love and teach for money" (J. Henry Schweich, letter of August 18, 1964).

DeWitt Alexander, a partner in Peat, Marwick, Mitchell & Co. in San Francisco, related a tale from World War I: Hatfield was hiking in Marin County and accidentally wandered onto Federal property, which was guarded. The guard challenged him, and Hatfield immediately broke into a torrent of German and scared the guard half to death! (interview, December 11, 1964).

Charles A. Gulick, Jr., a departmental colleague, recounted an incident at a dinner party in the Hatfield home: Hatfield, dressed in a tuxedo, greeted the arriving guests, who were clad in business suits. He thereupon dashed upstairs to put on a dark suit. Then M.M. Knight, another colleague in the department, arrived in a tux. Hatfield then went upstairs to put on his tux again. Only about a third of the men among the some 14 guests were in tuxes (interview, June 25, 1965).

Maurice Moonitz recalled Hatfield's wrath when New Deal politics invaded the academic sanctuary:

> When Wesley Clair Mitchell came to Berkeley to deliver a public lecture, Hattie presided, resplendent in tuxedo and black tie. A few weeks before the lecture, a group of student wheelers-and-dealers had persuaded the local chapter of Phi Beta Kappa to make General Hugh Johnson an honorary member. Johnson was then head of the National Recovery Administration (NRA). At some time earlier in his career he had been assigned to Berkeley, probably in connection with the campus ROTC program. In his spare time, the General attended classes at the Law School and earned high grades. The politically motivated move by Phi Beta Kappa outraged many on campus, especially a staunch foe of the New Deal like Hatfield. So, as the large audience [at the lecture] quieted down, HRH rose in all his dignity, walking to the podium, put his hands on his hips, and said, loudly and clearly, "This is not the occasion for initiating General Hugh 'Iron Pants' Johnson into Phi Beta Kappa! We are here for a more important matter."[14]

Paul S. Taylor, one of Hatfield's longtime departmental colleagues, recalled that Hatfield would come into 119 South Hall, where all the faculty had their desks, and utter some statement or raise some question that was à propos of nothing at all. "It was a shocker. It was not slapstick. He had an intellectual, refined sense of humor" (paraphrased from an interview, March 23, 1965). Others recounted similar occurrences.

Mary Gash, Hatfield's onetime secretary, recalled that he would walk across the campus with arms behind his back, snapping his finger nails. When he came into his office, he would open a floodgate of words, having composed the letter while walking (interview, December 14, 1964). She said that following another professor's visit to Hatfield's cubbyhole on the third floor of Doe Library, the visitor mistakenly walked off with Hatfield's coat instead of his own. When he returned to get his own, Hatfield remarked, "I admire your taste more than your honesty." She also said that Hatfield had a hot temper. After dictating a strong letter, he would then soften it and say, "Butter wouldn't melt in the mouth of the man who said that, would it?"

One student recalled Hatfield's unconventional "gift" to his students:

> One of Hatfield's little pleasantries was not to appear for lecture one day out of each semester, but never to let students know what day it would be. So we went to class and waited breathlessly for the ten minutes to pass by, at which time, if the professor did not appear, students could make a headlong rush to the door and to "freedom" for the period. Whenever this occurred, Hatfield, with a benign smile, would tell us that this was his "trick" for the semester (Edwin Pendleton, memorandum of November 1964).

In what was then a man's world, Hatfield nonetheless believed that women should be encouraged to embark on professional careers. Catharine Quire said that he was "one of the battlers" for women going into accounting (interview, July 6, 1964). He was displeased that Beta Gamma Sigma, the national honorary fraternity in the field of business, was limited to men. During his tenure as the fraternity's grand vice-president, from 1913 to 1922, he worked to have this limitation removed, without success. But at Berkeley, he promoted the formation of a women's honorary society in the College of Commerce[15] which, in 1920, affiliated with Gamma Epsilon Pi, a national honor society in business for women only. Finally, in 1932, Beta Gamma Sigma approved women as members, and it merged with Gamma Epsilon Pi the following year.[16]

Hatfield valued and honored the women in his life. Every year on October 22, Emily Huntington's birthday—she had joined the departmental faculty in 1928—an unsigned card, which she knew was from Hatfield, appeared on her desk. Hatfield, she said, was a "warm, gentle spirit, and was thoughtful of people" (paraphrased from an interview, December 8, 1964). Others recalled that he would bring violets to Miss Huntington on her birthday and would send daffodils to his wife, with a note.[17] He would conquer his forgetfulness by remembering to bring a flower every day to Vera Mae Twist, the departmental secretary from the mid-1920s onward.[18] Hatfield and Jessica Peixotto, Berkeley's first woman full professor, got on famously even though their political views were poles apart. He was fond of Peixotto, one of the early social economists, whom he liked to call "the Little Sister of the Poor." He contributed an admiring portrait of her to a volume marking her retirement:

> There have been, and perhaps still are, some benighted males who have the delusion that high intellectual attainments and a life of professional and public service are incompatible with what used to be considered the essential feminine attributes. Homage should therefore be paid to one who combines all the intellectual qualities of the dowdiest of bluestockings with the distinction and charm of the polished hostess and the gracious lady.[19]

Many recall Hatfield as an avid reader of detective stories. Catharine Quire recalled that he liked the works of Dorothy L. Sayers and "usually he had the solution by the middle" (interview, July 6, 1964). Friends urged him to write detective fiction. The Canadian humorist Stephen Leacock was another of this favorite authors.

Son John recalled his father's gift of some of his extensive collection of detective novels to a worthy cause: "One time when visiting a student who was temporarily confined in the University hospital he was dismayed to find that the only reading material available was *Pollyanna*. He immediately selected about 100 of his best mystery stories and donated them to the hospital."[20]

Hatfield's other hobbies included travel, keeping a catalogue of movie reviews, and books—he was a voracious reader. A member of the Sierra Club, he loved hiking and camping in the hills and the high country. While not one who played sports, he was known to excel at shuffleboard on Atlantic crossings. Among his favorite games were Russian bank (a version of double solitaire) and Chinese checkers. Sitting in his Morris chair, he enjoyed reading stories to neighborhood children (interviews with Arthur Bolton, Jr., March 1, 1997, and with Hatfield's grandchildren, January 24, 1999).

In the 1930s and 1940s, Hatfield wrote frequent letters to the popular radio program "Information, Please," in the hope of stumping the panel of experts on historical, literary, scientific, or other kinds of trivia. In one letter, he questioned a ruling by Clifton Fadiman, the host, on a stumper from the previous broadcast, and he adjured Fadiman to make a public apology for "the misinformation which you have thus spread over hundreds of thousands of admiring listeners" (letter to Fadiman, August 15, 1940). After Hatfield died in December 1945, one of his submissions triumphed, and Ethel received a set of encyclopedias as the prize.

Devotion to Church

Even though his brother James became a Unitarian and smoked, Henry Hatfield remained a staunch Methodist. As Otto Houser recalled:

> As a churchman, Dr. Hatfield was a stalwart. He held no office while I served [as minister at] Trinity Methodist Church those five years, though he had been an official in one capacity or another in previous years. He said that he wanted to make room for the younger men. Yet he was always in his place for worship Sunday after Sunday. He was a kind of "elder statesman," never formulating church policies but always consulted for the wisdom he possessed. Never lavish in compliment he yet would back his minister with such words of appreciation as "we're glad for a good minister." That may have been a bit on the generous side yet it showed the kindly heart that beat behind a rather gruff exterior.
>
> * * *
>
> I recall this solidly constructive and reserved man with many thoughts of thankfulness. For I felt at home with him not because he splashed outside himself but because he never withheld the values he had when one needed to lean on them (letter, July 3, 1965).

The three children of John Glover and Margaret Hatfield remember that Henry Hatfield never smoked, danced, or took alcohol. Even their father John, who smoked two packs a day, never lit up in the Henry Hatfield home. It was only once, when James Taft Hatfield came to visit, that smoking was seen in the Hatfield home on Le Conte (interview, January 24, 1999). The Henry Hatfields refused to subscribe to a Sunday newspaper because they did not want the delivery boys to work on the Sabbath.

Frank Waring assessed Hatfield in the same way that Carl Van Doren judged Benjamin Franklin:

> [quoting from Van Doren] "Mind and will, talent and art, strength and ease, wit and grace met in him as if nature had been lavish and happy when he was shaped.... Whoever learns about his deeds remembers longest the man who did them. And sometimes, with his marvellous range, in spite of his personal tang, he seems to have been more than any single man: a harmonious human multitude" (memorandum, July 2, 1964).

HATFIELD AND THE DEVELOPMENT OF ACCOUNTING

The 1898 letters show that Hatfield wanted a position in the College of Commerce at Chicago because he felt an affinity for the practical nature of the work. Because of his experience with the banking firm of S.A. Kean & Co., he was called upon to prepare and develop the business courses. He was scheduled to teach a course in "Railway Accounts, Exchanges, etc." during the autumn quarter of 1898, his first as an instructor at Chicago, but the course was canceled. During the winter of 1900-1901, Hatfield took a three-month tour of major European business schools but spent most of his time at the Handelshochschule (business school) at Leipzig. It was apparently in Leipzig that he discovered an interest in bookkeeping and its history. As a result of this tour, he offered his first accounting course in 1902, and repeated it the following winter. He continued to teach a wide range of other courses as well, and he served as the College's first dean in 1902-1904. It was to develop the coursework in accounting that Hatfield heeded the call from the University of California in 1904. At Berkeley, he was appointed associate professor of accounting, thus becoming the first full-time U.S. accounting academic with a professorial title. He remained a professor of accounting until his death in 1945.

Hatfield's Paradoxical Stance on Accounting

Despite his teaching commitment to accounting, his ambivalence toward accounting as an academic field remains the most puzzling and difficult aspect of his life and work to assess. In an important sense, his view of accounting remains a paradox, one that has clouded and even diminished his impact on the field. Like many paradoxes, understanding requires a review of his position, including his thought from several perspectives.

As a young man returning to college after five years with the banking firm of S.A. Kean & Co., he noted, with realism, the assiduous attention to detail required of the bookkeeper, which would become his defining characteristic as an accounting scholar:

> The book-keeper learns persistence and the power of all-absorbing attention, and finds in his formidable ledgers the same satisfaction and the same training gained from college mathematics.... This persistency is not gained so well in college. We puzzle for awhile over an obscure construction.... In a bank there is no relative importance in mistakes. The difference must be found and the amount is absolutely unessential....
>
> I have shown that the discipline received in a banking office is such as to train and develop the faculties most needed in future life. And this is becoming known by many, so that it is no uncommon thing for young men to take a course of a few years in a city bank who have no purpose or desire to make that their life's work.[21]

However, in 1920, after returning from service on the War Industries Board, he extolled the value of a traditional, broad education to prepare individuals for situations in which flexibility of thought was required.[22] In 1923, he argued for accounting as a discipline worthy of respect ("An Historical Defense of Bookkeeping"), yet he did not recognize it as worthy of doctoral research, believing that issues appropriate for dissertations would ultimately be aspects of economics or law, not accounting. He stymied the growth of the accounting department throughout his years at Berkeley, refusing to add full-time faculty. He wanted practitioners, whom he admired—as well as Staehling, a solid technician—to teach most of the accounting courses, except for the first and last courses—the two-semester Principles of Accounting sequence and the Seminar in Accounting Theory—which Hatfield reserved for himself. He believed that accounting students could best learn practice following graduation by way of on-the-job training in accounting firms.

University study, he often asserted, should focus on traditional liberal arts education. He apparently did not believe that accounting taught the same kind of thinking skills that were learned in traditional liberal arts studies. In his paper on the War Industries Board, he supported the view of E.F. Gay that decision making should be based on the fullest knowledge obtainable and not on the businessman's "hunch." In the conclusion of the paper, he used his experience with the board to argue for the merits of general education:

> With the exception of strictly technical and engineering work, men seemed to be selected rather on the basis of general training and ability. If the war was at all well managed, the experience should be something of an argument against specialized, and in favor of general cultural education.[23]

Similarly, in 1922, in a speech delivered to the Charter Day Assembly at the Southern Branch of the University of California, he argued that general education was ultimately practical because it developed right methods of thinking:

> By moderation in fees, by simplicity of its life, by the nature of its curriculum, it must be truly a school for the people, not a club for aristocrats. But there is perhaps a greater danger that in the anxiety to escape snobbery the University drift into the commonplace and the mediocre. Steadfastly must the friends of a State University see to it that it is not forced into too narrow an interpretation of vocational training. It must not, in response to a false demand, waste the time of faculty and students in matters of lesser moment, which are falsely called practical. It must ever be borne in mind that the function of the university is not inculcation of practical facts, nor in mere training in dexterity of hand, or eye or mind, but in giving insight into fundamental matters, in stimulating the spirit of independent research, in training in right methods of thinking, in opening the mind of the youth to higher things—and these things are, of all things, the most practical.[24]

We may be able to understand Hatfield's Socratic, yet incongruous, approach toward accounting—a perspective which is quixotic by modern standards—by recalling that, throughout his life, he remained the classical scholar. As Judson Krueger noted, he was not sure that Hatfield actually liked accounting because he spent so much time in his course discussing esoteric subjects instead (interview, October 17, 1964). Leonard A. Doyle, a colleague who joined the Berkeley accounting faculty in 1942, believed that "[William A.] Paton was much more concerned with accounting and its nature in society than was Hatfield" (paraphrased from an interview, December 15, 1964). Content to examine the world he inherited and the world in which he lived, Hatfield challenged his students to examine current issues by the same set of values espoused in liberal education. He asked endless questions: no topic was exempt from his probing queries. He targeted topics of critical importance in accounting principles and practice, and he examined them in fastidious detail; he demarcated areas through precise, often scathing questions; but he never undertook research with the goal of marking and then defining the new territory that lay beyond the questions he asked.

Henry Rand Hatfield—A Classical Educator and Humanist

While Hatfield steadfastly advocated scholarship and appropriate academic (classical) preparation, he was not himself a prolific writer or publisher of major articles on accounting, as discussed earlier. He published only three of the five major papers he wrote on accounting. The corpus of his work shows that he was content to examine the contributions of others, critically assess their ideas, and shape his criticism into questions which he left to others to answer: the same technique he used as a teacher. Lawrence L. Vance, who joined the Berkeley accounting faculty in 1941, provided an astute assessment of Hatfield: "He was sort of a philosopher, inclined to leave accounting to people in practice."[25] Despite his visionary arguments for the integrity of the financial statements and his insistence that only logical, consistent, and principled reasoning be the arbiter of proper accounting practice, he contributed little to the advancement of theory that would allow accounting to grow and develop. As always, he remained content to examine, question, and critique the contributions of others.

As a scholar, he kept alive a variety of classically oriented interests, such as the history of accounting and German accounting theory. His own published work was more broadly informed and sensitive to the evolving literature than that of any of his contemporaries. But, in a literature that he criticized as narrow, often self-serving, and inattentive to principle, he made no effort to remedy this deficiency by attracting budding scholars to doctoral study in accounting and thus perpetuate his internationalism and Socratic method of inquiry.

Hatfield's strength as a teacher—his ability to question, probe, and push students to their intellectual limits—was also his Nemesis. Because accounting lacked philosophical richness, he could not see it as worthy of serious study. He chose to focus on developing students' thought processes and believed that all things practical could be learned on the job. He was attracted to accounting, as he himself said, because it admitted of so many unanswered questions. To Hatfield is owed major praise for his clarification of the issues on which accounting emerged in the first half of the twentieth century. But this valued clarification did not progress to the next stage of laying the groundwork for the continued development of the field, including the development of doctoral students to support the effort.

As a classicist, Hatfield believed that truth and language were equal, that language could contain truth. His carefully crafted speeches can be seen as an attempt to capture the essence of the matter about which he was speaking. In his 1937 speech "A Critique of the Tentative Statement of Accounting Principles Underlying Corporate Reports," he began by saying that he would limit his comments to "matters of form and expression, leaving to others the weightier matters of the law and confining myself to mint, anise and cumin." However, his acrid attack—which describes 10 classes of deficiency in the Statement—illustrates his view that language cannot be separated from content, that the text had to contain precise meaning:

> Another instance of inconsistency is when it is said "assets in use or ultimately to be marketed" (thus covering plant as well as merchandise) should be reduced to "such amounts as may reasonably be expected to be recoverable in the course of future operations." (page 10) Probably the Committee does not mean this. They should not say what they do not mean. The value of an article is not what it will bring at some future day. The present value of a future good is the discounted value of the sum, not the sum itself. But it seems strange to set up future recoverable values in a document which proclaims "cost not value." Canning is consistent (whether correct or not is immaterial) in his argument regarding asset values to which reference has already been made. But he does not say he is following a theory of cost.

Hatfield also was unforgiving of illogical analysis. Point 5 in his attack illustrates his profound impatience with inconsistent argument:

> V. Certain adjustments are criticized because they are in accordance with "expected business development." (page 9) And this is the same section of the report which says "assets in use or ultimately to be marketed" should have as carrying value "such amounts as may reasonably be expected to be recoverable in the course of future operations." (page 10)
>
> Great Scot! "expected business developments" ruled out of consideration, and "recoverable in the course of future operations" set up as a criterion!
>
> One often hears that this is a mad world in which we now live. But isn't there still consistency and logic to be found in even the American Accounting Association?

Ironically, in focusing solely on the deficiencies in language and in the thread of logic, Hatfield failed to give any credence to the forward-looking mission that motivated the association's leaders to draft and promote the Statement. He was respected as the elder statesman among accounting academics, and his failure to comprehend the significance of the association's daring initiative keenly disappointed his younger colleagues.

Perhaps the impetus behind Hatfield's perspective resides in the influence of his mentors at Chicago, Thorstein Veblen and J. Laurence Laughlin, whose views he echoed. Hatfield exemplified Veblen's ability to articulate scathing criticism while incorporating Laughlin's ability to survey and then understand a given topic. Two additional examples of Hatfield's ability to be critical of an audience without giving offense were his two addresses to annual meetings of the American Institute of Accountants: "What Is the Matter with Accounting?" (1927, reproduced in Chapter 7) and "A Survey of Developments in Accounting" (1939).

Reflecting his Methodist background, Hatfield was ever the advocate for education as critical to the success of a democratic society. Hatfield saw education as critical to economic salvation, but the education he suggested was always more classical then practical. Perhaps his greatest contribution came from his exemplary books, which showed how scholarship should be applied to understanding. Yet his scholarly contribution, his strength, also became his weakness—principally, his failure to see what accounting could and needed to become.

Much of Hatfield's reputation likely stemmed from his ability to use language powerfully and memorably. As his essays suggest, he enjoyed language, the sound of it. He enjoyed juxtaposing the common with the recondite, the familiar with the arcane:

> When I came to Berkeley, the unpaved streets were thick with dust. The dust was full of fleas. The fleas were endowed with malignant mordacity which made life something of a burden to the non-immunized tenderfoot.... There was at that time no proper restaurant in Berkeley, and now, as one walks along a single block on Telegraph Avenue, one finds nine places which offer sybaritic repasts including hot dogs and Eskimo Pies.
>
> * * *
>
> But I deny that I am a pessimist, and I am by no means an atribilious dyspeptic ("Moriturus Vos Saluto").

These semantic juxtapositions served no rhetorical purpose in the larger purpose of the essay. Yet, they showed a writer who believed in the power of the spoken word and saw illumination through contrast.

Hatfield's training in classical rhetoric permeates all he wrote, but the fact that his comparatively small number of major articles were given as speeches suggests that he enjoyed public addresses, which gave him the opportunity to edify and even amuse a live audience. The loose structure of many of his speeches suggests that Hatfield was thinking aloud as he wrote. Even in speeches in which he approached his topic with a philosophical tone, his style still retains a conversational quality, one that is preserved in his textbook *Accounting*.

His ability to explore the nuances of meaning also manifests his classical perspective. Unlike many modern scholars, Hatfield believed that text could and should contain all meaning, that truth was univocal, that agreement on facts and the meaning of facts and the principles underlying those facts was possible. In a speech given to the Berkeley Club in 1942 ("Of 'Loose and Lavender Language'"), he stated his case for accuracy in language, and his examples remind us of the stance he took with colleagues and with students throughout his career. Hatfield would have had no patience with the modern view that what a statement means is relative. In building and arguing for his perspective, although via Socratic means, he believed that his view of the world was correct. Persuading

Henry and Ethel, with son John and his family, in about 1940. From left, standing: John and Sara Ellen (Sally); sitting: Ethel, John's wife Margaret (with Emily on her lap), Henry, and John. (A Hatfield family tree appears as an appendix to Chapter 6.)

others of the accuracy of his view, leading them to explore his view of things through skilled use of language, and establishing a template for assessing the quality of current thought became the heart and soul of his argumentation, the effectiveness of which defines his legacy.

APPENDIX

Henry Rand Hatfield's and Ethel Adelia (Glover) Hatfield's Parents, Siblings, and Children and Grandchildren (First Generation Only)

Parents

Robert Miller Hatfield (1819-1891) married Elizabeth Ann Taft (1824-1903) in 1843
John J. Glover (1835-1914) married Mary Ellen Williams (1843-1931) in 1866

Henry and His Siblings

Elizabeth Ann (1844-1846)
Robert Miller (1846-1847)
Marcus Patten (1849-1909) married Harriet Augusta Harris in 1876
Anna Rebecca (1851-1931) married Samuel Axtell Kean in 1871
Mary Imogene (1854-1858)
William Woodbury (1856-1861)
Emily Marcia (1860-1928) married William T. Hobart in 1882
James Taft (1862-1945) married Maude Hillingsworth Wilson in 1890; married Ann Estelle Caraway in 1910
Henry Rand (1866-1945) married Ethel Adelia Glover (1867-1949) in 1898
(Four other children died young)

Ethel and Her Sibling

Ethel Adelia (1867-1949) married Henry Rand Hatfield (1866-1945) in 1898
Mabel Stanley (1872-1946) married Franklin Paine Mall (1862-1917) in 1895

Children and Grandchildren

John Glover (1900-1980)
- married Margaret Wyman Smith (1900-1982) in 1925
  - Sara Ellen (Sally) (born 1926)
    - married Edgar Hamilton Chappell in 1948

John Selden (born 1930)
married Carol Terminsen in 1964
Emily Taft (born 1935)
married Gordon Alan Benner in 1959

Robert Miller (1902-1927)
married Louise Marie Kindervatter (1899-1975) in 1926
Elizabeth Ann (Betty) (born 1927)
married Gilbert Azancot in 1953
married Maurice Werther in 1963

Elizabeth (1904-1989)
married Charles Arthur Glover (1890-1973), a second cousin, in 1931
Amy Louise (born 1932)
married Thomas Squire in 1954
married Leonard Roemer in 1978
Henry Hatfield (born 1935)
married Jo Helen Peterson in 1960

Principal sources: Abraham Hatfield (compiler), *The Hatfields of Westchester* (New York Genealogical and Biographical Society, 1935), and Elizabeth (Hatfield) Glover and Dorothy (Boake) Young, *A Glover Family History: Descendants of Amos and Ann Katherine (Smith) Holmes Glover* (privately published, 1984), supplemented with other sources.

NOTES

1. William Morse Cole, review of Hatfield's *Modern Accounting: Its Principles and Some of Its Problems* in *Journal of Political Economy*, Vol. 17, No. 9, November 1909, p. 647.
2. James Taft Hatfield, "Robert Miller Hatfield" (unpublished manuscript, 1938), 46 pages, on deposit in the Northwestern University Archives.
3. Henry and Ethel died in 1945 and 1949, respectively. Two of their children, Elizabeth Hatfield Glover and John Glover Hatfield, divided the scrapbooks between them. Today, Henry Hatfield Glover, Elizabeth's son, possesses nine of them. The remaining 15 were donated by John Hatfield to the University of California, Berkeley, where they were eventually deposited in the university's Bancroft Library.
4. A limited family tree, "Henry Rand Hatfield's and Ethel Adelia (Glover) Hatfield's Parents, Siblings, and Children and Grandchildren (First Generation Only)," is included as an Appendix to this chapter.
5. Letter to the author dated December 1, 1965. Maude Royden was active in the Women's Movement.
6. Interview with Henry Hatfield Glover, Columbus, Ohio, January 1998. Henry Glover is the son of Elizabeth Hatfield Glover, Henry Rand Hatfield's daughter.

7. The recollections that follow are, in the main, excerpts from interviews and letters from a number of Hatfield's former graduate and undergraduate students at Berkeley from the 1910s to the 1940s as well as from former colleagues.

8. "Reminiscences about Henry Rand Hatfield," 3 pp., undated.

9. Michael T. O'Neill, ed., *A.P. Richardson: The Ethics of a Humanist* (New York: Arno Press, 1980), p. 3.

10. A.P. Richardson, "This Blessed Language," *The Journal of Accountancy*, Vol. 68, No. 5, November 1939, p. 350.

11. *Ibid.*

12. Henry Rand Hatfield, excerpt from an untitled speech reproduced in *The Auditor* (published by the San Francisco Institute of Accountancy), September 1927, Vol. I, No. 12, p. 3.

13. John G. Hatfield, "Recollections About Father," *The Accounting Historians Journal*, Vol. 4, No. 1, Spring 1977, p. 15.

14. Maurice Moonitz, "Recollections of Henry Rand Hatfield," which is reproduced in Chapter 7.

15. Letter to the author from Catherine Laughren, dated August 14, 1964.

16. See Fayette H. Elwell, *The First 50 Years of Beta Gamma Sigma* (Homewood, IL: Richard D. Irwin, Inc., 1963), Chap. 8.

17. Interview with Mr. and Mrs. John G. Hatfield, Dean and Mrs. E.T. Grether, and Mr. and Mrs. Peter Blos, January 13, 1965.

18. Interview with Vera Mae Twist, July 1, 1965.

19. Henry Rand Hatfield, "Jessica Blanche Peixotto," *Essays in Social Economics in Honor of Jessica Blanche Peixotto* (Berkeley, CA: University of California Press, 1935), p. 14. For more on Peixotto, see Mary E. Cookingham, "Social Economists and Reform: Berkeley, 1906-1961," *History of Political Economy*, Vol. 19, No. 1, Spring 1987, pp. 47-65.

20. John G. Hatfield, *op. cit.*, pp. 14-15.

21. Henry Rand Hatfield, "The Bank Clerk," *The Northwestern*, Vol. XI, No. 21, September 25, 1891, p. 267.

22. See his unpublished paper "Experiences with the War Industries Board," which is reproduced in Chapter 7.

23. *Ibid.*

24. This speech, "The State University and the Body Politic: The Southern Branch of the University of California," is reproduced in Chapter 7.

25. Quoted from an interview with Vance on April 6, 1978, conducted by Edward Hussey Binns and reported in his MBA thesis, "The Influence of Henry Rand Hatfield" (San Francisco State University, May 1978), p. 58.

Chapter 7
Hatfield's Papers

Throughout his career, Hatfield gave numerous presentations in a wide variety of professional and academic settings. Many of the presentations, which he prepared as complete essays prior to delivery, were never published. Both in his oral presentations and published writings, Hatfield demonstrated his command of classical rhetoric. The purpose of this chapter is to exhibit a number of Hatfield's papers, both unpublished and published, that illustrate his interests, his personal and professional values, his experiences, his views of events of his time, and, above all, the deftness of his expository style.

This chapter contains a selection of Henry Rand Hatfield's unpublished and published papers. His unpublished papers provide additional insight into his personality—his values and perspectives, and his attitudes toward accounting, accounting education, and business and world events.

The 23 unpublished papers that survive—which I found in his files that had been preserved at the University of California—provide examples of Hatfield in a wide range of roles: as toastmaster, eulogist, polemicist, and classical essayist. Fortunately for us, at all of his scheduled appearances, whether as toastmaster, eulogist, or presenter of a formal paper, Hatfield read from prepared texts. In some instances, the texts discovered in his files were handwritten, while others were typed.

The entire chronology of Hatfield's unpublished papers follows (those presented to the Berkeley Club are marked BC), all of which I have edited:

Remarks to a Group of San Francisco CPAs, c. 1905-1906
"The Study of Economic History," probably delivered sometime between 1900 and 1920
Paper on Corporations, 1910
"Business Efficiency as a University Ideal," 1912
"Some Heretical Views on the Method of Teaching Bookkeeping," 1913
Eulogy at the Funeral of Ramon Pohli, an undergraduate student, 1913

Remarks upon the Inauguration of Henry Suzzallo as President of the University of Washington, 1916
A Meeting on the North Side of Berkeley, c. 1917-1918
"Corporations and the Public," 1918
Presidential Address to the 4th Annual Meeting of the American Association of University Instructors in Accounting, 1919
"Experiences with the War Industries Board," c. 1920 (BC)
A Reply to the Paper on "Profits" by E. R. A. Seligman, c. 1920
"The State University and the Body Politic: The Southern Branch of the University of California," 1922
"De Computis et Scripturis," 1923 (BC)[1]
"Cui Lumen Ademptum," 1925 (BC)[2]
Eulogy at the Funeral of Solomon Blum, a department colleague, 1926
"Parliament and the Trade Unions," 1927 (BC)
"The Inner Workings of a Pool," 1931 (BC)
"Germany of the Present Day," 1933 (BC)
"George Washington and Doctor Craik," 1934 (BC)
"Moriturus Vos Saluto," 1937 (BC)
"A Critique of the Tentative Statement of Accounting Principles Underlying Corporate Reports," 1937
"Of 'Loose and Lavender Language'," 1942 (BC)

This chapter contains 13 of his unpublished papers and several that were previously published. Each paper has been selected because it illustrates a particular facet of Hatfield's perspective, presentation skills, or stance on some aspect of accounting or accounting education. Every paper exemplifies Hatfield's training in classical rhetoric. His skilled use of rhetorical strategy—by which he matched his technique with the topic and occasion—defines the effectiveness of his presentation.

When reading Hatfield's unpublished papers, one must be cognizant that, except for his critique of the "Tentative Statement," none was written for publication. Especially for those read to the Berkeley Club, an intimate gathering of Berkeley scholars and friends, the occasional flippant or unguarded remark, or casual reference, should be judged in the context in which the paper was to be read.

As these essays illustrate, throughout his career, Hatfield built argument through logical analysis (*logos*) and the power of his own character (*ethos*), but never by purely emotional appeal (*pathos*). His writings stand as monuments to classical structure, reasoned analysis, and pungent, pristine style.

The papers are divided into three classes:

1. Unpublished short papers that richly illustrate Hatfield's singing prose;
2. Unpublished longer papers that reflect his views on accounting and other topics as well as looking back on his experiences; and

3. The most noteworthy among his previously published writings.

Each paper is preceded by an explanatory note.[3] The paragraphs of most papers have been numbered to enable readers to key the explanatory comments with pertinent passages in the text. The chapter concludes with two appendices. One contains a series of comments by Maurice Moonitz on Hatfield's unpublished papers. Moonitz was a former student of Hatfield's and author of *History of Accounting at Berkeley* (Berkeley: Schools of Business Administration, University of California, 1986). The second appendix contains further recollections of Hatfield by Moonitz.

UNPUBLISHED SHORT PAPERS

Remarks to a Group of San Francisco CPAs, c. 1905-1906

Hatfield gave this paper sometime during his first or second year after joining the Berkeley faculty. The presentation, which was likely arranged by John F. Forbes, a leader of the San Francisco certified public accountants, has been dated by Hatfield's reference to the *Heppenheimer* case, which was decided in April 1905. Forbes was greatly concerned about certain unethical practices of some CPAs. In this paper, Hatfield challenges CPAs to aspire to high professional standards. His tone echoes his father's sermon style in its pungent presentation of his position.

In presenting his argument, Hatfield used a direct, succinct style to convey his unwavering belief in the importance of ethics in accounting. His attitude shows his disapproval of inflated valuations of assets and his insistence on the priority that ethics should command in all facets of accounting practice.

From a rhetorical perspective, this essay exemplifies what classical rhetoric calls *deliberative* discourse. Hatfield was attempting to persuade his audience to accept his point of view. As defined in classical rhetoric, which Hatfield would have studied as an undergraduate student at Northwestern, the *deliberative* discourse argues for what is good or advantageous. Hatfield showed that his position was both good and expedient—that high ethical standards would lead to the public good and increase the public's respect for the accounting profession. This speech follows standard classical essay structure, as it contains:

¶ 1: Introduction (*exordium*);
¶ 1-2: Statement of the case under discussion (*narratio*);

¶ 1: Outline of the points in the argument (*divisio*);
¶ 3-7: Proof of the case (*confirmatio*) and refutation, where he counters objections (*refutatio*); and
¶ 8-10: Conclusion (*peroratio*).

The introduction announces two points, which Hatfield develops in Paragraphs 2-7, followed by his conclusion, Paragraphs 8-10, in which he reinforces his thesis. In the opening paragraph, Hatfield ingratiates himself with his audience by emphasizing the positive aspects of the accounting profession. He uses the classical "introduction preparatory" by tactfully suggesting that he will concisely explain the needs of this sacred profession. Hatfield announces that he will discuss two points—his position and supporting ideas (*logos*). However, before he introduces his argument, he does a masterful job of establishing his credibility as a speaker: he states that he is an outsider and humbly asks permission to state his view that, while accounting is producing many clients, the general public does not perceive the importance of the profession. Note that Hatfield, while he will attack the ethics of the profession in the essay, begins by praising the profession and lamenting that the public does not appreciate it as much as it should. As all of Hatfield's essays illustrate, he was a master at building *ethos*—ingratiating himself with his audience and establishing his credibility to deal with the topic. In this essay, he builds his own trustworthiness with the audience by emphasizing his commitment to accounting.

Paragraphs 2-4 address the first point—the need to educate the public about the necessity of independent auditing.

Paragraphs 5-7 address the second point—the importance of the accounting profession establishing the highest ethical standards.

Paragraphs 8-10 form the conclusion, in which he restates his position—the importance of ethical practice in all aspects of accounting. Paragraph 8 shows Hatfield's view that the liberal arts education provides a major impetus in the development of character and citizenship, a value embedded in classical education theory that would permeate several of his other addresses.

Hatfield's management of style is best exemplified in Paragraph 6, which contains the climax of his argument. The paragraph develops inductively, building to the final two sentences, which present his stance in a pungent aphoristic sentence phrased as a rhetorical question: "Is the C.P.A. prepared to take a stand for accuracy in corporation accounts? May not C.P.A. stand for Conscience, Probity, Accuracy?" As a concise example of an efficiently presented and argued position, this essay is unsurpassed in the collection of Hatfield's addresses. It shows his education in classical rhetoric.

[1] It is a pleasure for me, a member of one of the oldest, to greet your representatives of the youngest of the learned professions for, despite its youth, accountancy is already so advanced that none may be admitted to your ranks without a severe initiation and a lengthy apprenticeship, and your calling is considered so sacred that some, at least, would legally prohibit the exercise of any of its foundations by those not within the cult. May I, as an outsider, yet one who to some extent shares in your labors without hope of gaining you the higher documents—speak a few words on the needs of this new profession. I will mention only two, for the time is short.

[2] First the business public needs to be educated to the necessity of calling in public accountants to do independent auditing. So much progress has been made in recent years that it seems almost needless to mention this need. There may have been a time when the public accountant sat alone—relieving his solitude with tobacco and solitaire while he waited for the clients to appear. Now you are doubtless troubled with a too-importunate string of clients, your ante rooms bear the motto "standing room only," your [entryways] are hedged about with railings and door keepers to keep the eager crowd at bay. But while so much progress has been made, still the American public is not awake to the importance of your profession.

[3] Birmingham, England, of about the same population as San Francisco, has 249 Chartered and 75 Incorporated Accountants. I do not know how many public accountants live in San Francisco. I understand that there are some in other parts of the state and that Sacramento, for instance, is so important a center for accounting as to claim two-fifths of the membership of the State Board of Accountancy, but the whole State, including San Francisco, Sacramento and Fresno contains only half a hundred public accountants. Is there no proof that the public does not realize the importance of the profession?

[4] How can the public be educated? It is difficult to say. The University is doing what it can, and at least every graduate of the college of commerce has the importance of accounting impressed on him, and arguments are presented to these future business men showing the importance of consulting the expert accountant. My other suggestions are purely negative. They are: 1). Unprofessional advertising is not the best way of inspiring general confidence in the value of professional attainments and 2). Legislation such as that proposed in Ohio is in my mind distinctly detrimental and partakes more of the nature of Trade union restrictions than of professional conduct. It is correct in principle to prohibit the use of the title C. P. A. by those who have not won it, and to prevent the use of other initials intended to mislead; but a law preventing one from doing expert work in examining accounts who is not a C. P. A. seems to me impossible to enforce, illogical in principle, resting on a false analogy and almost a confession of weakness in the part of the profession itself.

[5] The second need of the profession is the establishing of the highest possible standard for its members. I plead not merely for technical dexterity in the investigation of accounts and the detection of frauds; not merely for knowledge derived from prolonged study of the principles of accounting and the legal and economic factors inherent thereto; not merely for a high standard of personal probity which will make men willing to intrust to the accountant their intimate business secrets, nor the high code of professional ethics which should reflect this character. The profession should claim all these, but much more.

[6] I am thinking rather of the public role which you must occupy and the high standard which you should set in that respect. Let me mention a single illustration. The most important problem before the public is the regulation of corporations. There are many sides to this problem but most of them center about the finances, the questions of investment and of profits. In a word, they are questions of accounting. But there is no other country where such vicious principles of corporation accounting are countenanced as in the United States. In proof of this, look at the text book on corporation accounting recommended by N.Y.C.P.A. This explicitly states that there is no objection (I quote the words literally) to listing the assets acquired by stock purchase at twice their actual value. In the English and German texts there is no hint that any one ever thought of such an improper course, except perhaps where the author is referring to confessedly fraudulent manipulations. Is the C.P.A. prepared to take a stand for accuracy in corporation accounts? May not C.P.A. stand for Conscience, Probity, Accuracy?

[7] Our laws are becoming somewhat more clear. Doubtless you are familiar with the recently published decision in *C, receiver v. Heppenheimer*[4] (where the highest court in New Jersey—New Jersey the home of inflated corporations—held responsible those who purchased various plants by issuing stock whose par value exceeded the actual value of the assets acquired. Stock dividends in general give me no alarm, water is a useful hygienic fluid; over-capitalization in itself is a peccadillo, but the moment that a plant is set down at a conscious overvaluation, or a non-existent good will is classed as an asset, we have a crime committed against the principles of accounting. Purge the business community of such faults and you have done a public service of inestimable value and have by the very act solved most of the problems of corporation control. Stand therefore as a profession not merely for technical accuracy; be not content with the justification of business precedent but set a new standard; stand for high professional ideals; be uncompromising in demanding truth and as a result you will find the profession rise in dignity.

[8] I said there were two things to be done: to educate the public and to raise the standard of the profession. But there is really only one thing: raise the professional standard—stand for something more than fees, and the public will see the advantage in any enterprise of having the certificate of the educated, the honest, the impartial public Accountant.

[9] The University can also do something. We can furnish you young men of good character and careful training who have already learned the essentials in the theory of accounting and in the principles of law and need only the practical training to be found in your offices. Such material will be the best recruits to the profession, and in the instruction given in the University, what ever else may be lacking there will at least be found an effort to emphasize the eternal importance of using accounting to preserve and not to hide the truth.

[10] And because I believe that the gentlemen gathered about this board do stand for these high ideals, it has given me greater pleasure to be with you and to offer to you any cooperation within my power to help give to accountancy the dignity which is its due.

Eulogy at the Funeral of Ramon Pohli, an Undergraduate Student, 1913

The collection of unpublished papers contains two eulogies. The first is an eulogy given at the funeral of an undergraduate student whom Hatfield taught at Berkeley. These two speeches exemplify Hatfield's ability to deliver what classical rhetoric calls the *epideictic*—or declamatory, ceremonial, or panegyrical—oratory, which honors a person or an event. In this kind of oratory, the speaker is preoccupied not with persuading the audience but with pleasing or inspiring it. Epideictic oratory is the most literary form of discourse. To praise the individual in elegaic form, the orator chooses a different stance than that selected in persuasive or argumentative discourse. Both of these eulogies exemplify elevated diction that is formal and elegant; sentence structures are crafted to produce a stately rhythm that embodies graceful praise.

In all his papers, Hatfield never used emotional appeal *(pathos)*. When he spoke, he argued for ideas. Despite the elegaic occasions for which he wrote these pieces, both eulogies illustrate Hatfield's ability to praise and honor through restrained presentation emotion.

Austin Ramon Pohli, Class of 1914, was killed in a hiking accident in Yosemite Valley on May 20, 1913. The *Daily Californian* reported: "Pohli was making his way across Snow creek when he accidentally slipped into the stream and was carried to instant death over the five hundred foot falls a short distance below.... Pohli's tragic death stopped short a college career of unusual achievement. He was a member of Golden Bear and Winged Helmet. As manager of several English Club productions he was actively identified with that organization. He had also just completed a year as manager of the Occident and had been elected manager of the Pelican for the coming year. He was a member of the Psi Upsilon fraternity " (August 15, 1913, p. 8).

The eulogy develops inductively, and Paragraph 5, the final paragraph, exemplifies Hatfield's ability to craft elegant praise and the inevitable need, in a panegyric elegy, to honor the individual while reflecting on the mysteries of death.

[1] In a large university it is but rarely that the instructor can gain any clear impression of the individual student. The constantly shifting personnel of the classroom, meeting together only two or three score times and then breaking up into new groups and combinations, gives to the instructor a kaleidoscopic view of the student body as a whole, but makes difficult that personal contact which used to count for so much. But occasionally appears a student who stands out among and above his fellows, and it is contact with these that makes the life of the teacher really worth while. Such one was Ramon Pohli.

[2] In January of last year, he first enrolled in one of my classes. Striking in appearance, polished in demeanor, brilliant in scholarship, he, above any of his classmates won his instructor's interest, respect and friendship.

[3] There are few in whom the qualities which appeal to the students and those which delight the teacher were so admirably combined as in Ramon Pohli. Deservedly popular with his associates was he, untiring in his service for the welfare of the student body, genial yet strong and self respecting, modest yet masterful. But at the same time he appealed to the instructor by an attitude of intelligent interest in his work and a scholarship which went deeper than high marks. A teacher could ask no greater pleasure than to have a class composed exclusively of such as he.

[4] In one way and another the associations so pleasantly begun were strengthened and deepened in the year just closed, during which he attended four of my classes. Always shall I remember him, seated generally in the front row, keen and alert, contributing materially to the success of the work by voluntarily bringing in outside matters which he thought would be of interest, scholarly but not pedantic, helpful but unobtrusive, deferential but frank, an ideal student.

[5] It is not for me to attempt the philosophy which would justify the ways of God to man. All that I can do is to pay the last tribute of friendship and to stand aghast at the tragedy of what seems to our dull eyes an unfulfilled career. For today we cannot, as is the wont on such occasions, recount the fruitions of a well-rounded life. Our very words of well deserved praise but add to our grief that powers such as his are prevented from grasping the prizes so near at hand. Of no student have I more confidently predicted life's richest success. In character and temperament, in training and personality, in power to deal with intellectual problems and in the rare power to deal wisely with one's fellowmen, Ramon Pohli gave every earnest of a brilliant career. And yet the successes and achievements of his young manhood have their merit and their reward no less truly then those of the forum and the market place. No life however long, no career however richly crowned with honors can gain a higher income than this: He fulfilled with credit

all the duties which fell to his hand. And that praise already belongs in fullest measure to him whom we respect, love and mourn.

Eulogy at the Funeral of Solomon Blum, a Department Colleague, 1926

> Solomon Blum, born in 1883, died on January 14, 1926 of tuberculosis. He was a professor of economics in Berkeley's department of economics. As he usually did in his presentations, Hatfield establishes *ethos* by opening his speech with sentences designed to build community with the audience. He then uses three sentences (Paragraphs 2, 3, and 4) structured in parallel to set the tone of the eulogy. The remaining paragraphs present an elegant, restrained valediction. The language is formal until the last paragraph, which combines the familiar with a final, elegant assessment and tribute.

[1] It is a solemn and seemly custom to gather, as we have today to pay honor to the memory of one who has left us. But I need not, as is so often done, make this an occasion for any extended review of his achievements or portrayal of his merits. We are a little group of friends and close associates who need not be told of the life of Solomon Blum, but who wish merely to join in all expression of a common bereavement, to unite in a common tribute of honor and affection.

[2] As a friend, perhaps the first of our group to make his acquaintance, I pay tribute to a friendship unmarred by any infelicities, made warm by the genuine and real sweetness of his character.

[3] As a member of the department I honor the memory of a colleague wise in counsel, loyal to his associates, masterly teacher, endeared alike to students and faculty.

[4] As a member of the broader fellowship of scholars I honor one who has left a true monument of his learning, who could treat of controversial matters with an absence of dogmatism, whose scholastic researches were made comely by literary grace and made vital by a humane spirit. We all rejoiced when the President acknowledged his achievement by the unusual, and perhaps unique honor of promoting to the highest academic rank one who was not in active service.

[5] It is not my part to attempt the philosophy which would justify the ways of God to man. All that I can do is to pay this last tribute of friendship and to stand aghast at to what to our dull eyes seems so tragic an ending to a career at once so promising and so fruitful. But what further achievements could add to the real dignity of a life such as his. If ever one played a man's part in this world it was Solomon Blum. Against overwhelming odds he accomplished that which puts the rest of us to shame. In weakness and infirmity he persistently carried on his work, in discouragement and disappointment repeated again and again he showed, not the hard and rebellious spirit of one whose head was bloody but unbowed, but the equally heroic and more difficult attitude of a serene and smiling fall undaunted

and yet unembittered. Shall I say that his life is an inspiration to us all? Yes, were it not that it seems so far beyond our powers that we are dismayed at the thought of imitation.

[6] We who were close to Solomon Blum would that we could say something to those bound to him by those more sacred and intimate ties. But even we, associates who honored and loved him, could not, without impertinence presume to enter into the grief of that inner circle. We can only repeat that

> "The truest token
> Of sympathy is silence, and when the heart is broken
> The dearest words of friendship are those that are unspoken."

[7] Farewell, Blummy, my true friend, loyal associate, brilliant scholar, noble, brave realman heroic. We mourn your departure, but we rejoice to have known and therefore to have loved you.

Remarks upon the Inauguration of Henry Suzzallo as President of the University of Washington, 1916

Hatfield, as many of his former students and colleagues recall, was in great demand as a toastmaster. As Maurice Moonitz comments, here Hatfield was representing the University of California in his capacity as acting dean of the faculties. This speech illustrates his expertise in another type of ceremonial or *epideictic* oratory. Many of Hatfield's speeches, like this one, indicate that he was always ready to amuse as well as intrigue his audience by selecting unique illustrations that conveyed his position.

Paragraphs 1-2: He begins with the introduction paradoxical, designed to intrigue listeners by approaching his topic, a commentary upon the inauguration, from an oblique perspective. Hatfield then moves into dramatic irony: he describes the football game between the University of Washington and the University of California (whose mascot is the Golden Bear) as an epic battle.

Paragraphs 3-4: He suddenly shifts into a narration leading to verbal irony on the word "chair."

Paragraph 5: Hatfield shifts again to war imagery, combat between the great universities. He praises the lesser universities stretching between Berkeley and Seattle before leaving humor behind and voicing an elegant, lofty paean on the occasion. From humor to hymn of praise, Hatfield shows his dexterity in shifting both tone and style. As in most of his speeches, Hatfield enjoyed combining wit and praise, the formal with the familiar, the lofty with the colloquial. This speech effectively illustrates Hatfield's command of sentence variety and his ability to use irony in the design of supporting illustrations.

Hatfield wrote this script on the back of stationery of the New Washington Hotel, Seattle; apparently, it was composed shortly before delivery.

[1] Ungracious though it may seem, I had considerable hesitancy in making this, my first visit to your university, to your city, to your state. There was uneasiness as to my exact role at this celebration. Unfortunately, or fortunately, I was unable to attend an event which took place in Berkeley last November.[5] From the accounts of eye witnesses, accounts perhaps exaggerated and incorrect, it seems that there came down from the north a horde, valiant as Vikings, stalwart as the Goths, irresistible as Thor himself. Despite sacrificial fires burned on our Grecian altar, and stranger vigils kept beside our hallside, the fairest flower of California classical culture went down before that horde, and the place thereof knew it no more.

[2] In my childhood, I saw a huge painting of the triumph of Germanicus in which the arrogant conqueror sat in state while before him were paraded his vanquished foes. For thirty-five years, my mind has kept the picture of that procession, many clad in gay colors, blue, and red, and gold, with garments of strange cut and headgear quaint and outlandish. Toward the end of the procession came a captive and dejected bear. Could it be that California was to be led before you northerners as a symbol of your victory, that the bear in the picture was to be the erstwhile rampant Golden Bear.

[3] My position on today's program was also puzzling. Not alone that a mere dean should be sandwiched between two presidents, but that I should have a place in what seemed a purely family matter. Yesterday many outlanders spoke. Today I appear with those who are part of the educational system of Washington. Do you consider that since last November, California has not only been conquered but also benevolently assimilated? Do you, as do the cannibal warriors, first defeat your foes and then absorb them into your system?

[4] But when I reached here, my forebodings ceased. Not foes but friends, not barbarians but brothers, dwellers in a delectable land, the one spot in which a Berkeleyan feels in danger of slightly fracturing the Tenth Commandment. So charmed was I with the surroundings that when the President of the Board of Regents suggested that the guests should remain here, my heart quickened within me. But if it is permissible to criticize the hospitality of a host, I would remind the Regents that, where I was brought up, the most rudimentary etiquette demands that when one asks a guest to stay awhile, he shall forthwith offer him a chair. Now, there are a number of academic chairs which in a pinch I would try to occupy, but strain my ears to uttermost I heard none offered, nor any mention of the emolument thereunto appertaining.

[5] Much has been said of the new athletic union between Washington and California. But it is not the factitious ties of athletics that unite the two universities; the bonds between us reach far beyond the agreement made last summer. British and Scotch soldiers at the front engage in occasional athletic contests. But surely it is no such petty thing which will forever bind the hearts of these comrades in arms, but the devotion to a great common cause. So with us there is more than the friendly rivalry of the striped field to bind us together. The two universities, regiments in a united army, standing in the trenches at the front of the continent, are bound by the closest of ties, a responsibility borne together.

[6] In emphasizing the ties which bind our two universities, there is no intention to ignore the other institutions on the coast, the distinguished representatives of which are your honored guests. We are all one family, including our little baby sister at Portland, still too coy to play with her neighbors, the grand dame of Palo Alto bedecked with the jewels of art and architecture so becoming to her stately charms, and our less-heralded sisters, scattered through the three states, poorer mayhap in the world's goods, but rich in religious fervor and steadfast in devotion to churchly ideals. These may well speak for themselves.

[7] Nor would it be seemly for any of us to make vainglorious boast of numbers, or of the building of stately, and yet more stately, incursions for the academic soul. But rather should we search our souls lest being more richly endowed, our greater opportunity prove our greater condemnation.

[8] And so California sends greetings to her great sister in the north. A state institution wise beyond provincialism, educational, not political, who, having passed the perils of youth, has surely found herself. We congratulate you. In one year you have taken victory from California and from Columbia have taken Suzzallo. Auspicious act in a prohibition state to choose one whose name can be pronounced only by those indubitably sober.

[9] Congratulations to you students one and all, from seniors whose diplomas are the first to be given by the new President, down to freshmen, first to reap full benefit from his beneficent guidance. You who can so successfully support athletics stand together, I conjure you, in support of Henry Suzzallo, who in things academic is your new captain, your new coach, your new mascot, your new presage of success. Remember that many a perfectly good president has been spoiled by indifference and disloyalty. Stand with and behind him, confirming and strengthening him in all goodness, pardoning his offenses (for even on inauguration day we may admit that, after all, presidents are human), that you and he may together walk in the academic way everlasting. California wishes you well. Fellow workers, not rivals, friends brought but the closer together by the mimic antagonism of athletics, co-laborers in the work of the Pacific Coast, each bearing the responsibilities placed on it by an empirical commonwealth. California and Washington must ever rejoice each in the other's advancement. And so, on this, the brightest day of all your history, in behalf of the President, the faculty and the students of the University of California, I do indeed wish you well. May God bless you.

Presidential Address at the 4th Annual Meeting of the American Association of University Instructors in Accounting, 1919

Hatfield was president of the American Association of University Instructors in Accounting in 1919. In the report of the Association's annual meeting on December 29-30, 1919, published in the proceedings volume following the meeting, there is no reference to Hatfield's presidential address. However, it is likely that he did give it.

In this address, Hatfield was perhaps the first to suggest a professional School of Accounting. While he did not see the establishment of such a school as imperative, he added: "But imperative it is to distinguish the instruction in accounting appropriate for the prospective business man, and that suited to train one for the C.P.A."

The presentation shows us what Hatfield considered the important issues in accounting education. He reflects, rather sardonically, on the remnants of Paciolo's tract on double-entry bookkeeping, particularly that his methods were still slavishly followed in contemporary accounting textbooks, although no reason existed for those traditions to be kept. Hatfield, as he did in most of his addresses, challenged his audience to think, rather than simply accept, what was happening in current practice: When should accounting be taught? Where should it be taught? How should it be taught? Why should publication and research be valued?

This speech represents another example of *deliberative* oratory in which he states his position and also argues—attempts to persuade listeners—to agree with him. Hatfield, in this presentation, has much information that he wishes to cover. Thus, his paragraphs are not well developed. He skips lightly over each topic in a highly conversational style that does not develop any point.

The script for this address was found scrawled on the back of several sheets of the association's stationery.

[1] The papers presented to this conference have been so many and so scholarly that it seems superfluous for the retiring president to attempt to be learned, or to do more than suggest the problems which affect us as an *organized* body of instructors in accounting. Our very name implies that our interest is primarily in instruction, rather than in practice.

[2] Accounting as a subject for university instruction occupies a peculiar position. Despite the fact that it was presumably taught in a university four and a quarter centuries ago, its position in American universities is so recent that one of our own still qualified members can claim to have given the first accounting course that was offered at Harvard.

[3] As compared with teachers of law, of the classics, of mathematics, teachers of accounting are greatly disadvantaged in that while attempting to teach accounting to hordes of university students we have not, as have the teachers of the elder disciplines, any well-considered scheme for the What, the When, and the How of such instruction.

[4] The function of this organization, at least at present, is not to formulate any scheme of propaedeutics. But it is up to us to hear, as we have heard at this conference, of the experiences of those attacking a common problem in diverse manners, and by the interchange of experience and opinion, to make each of us more confident and efficient.

[5] The problem of *what* to include in university instruction is fundamental, and still debatable. At the very outset comes the question of *bookkeeping* as something inferior and preliminary to accounting.

[6] In passing, I might interject my opinion that the distinction, while possibly a real one, is as yet undefined. It cannot be, as one prominent writer has asserted, that accounting is correct, or rational, or scientific, while bookkeeping may be the reverse of these. It can scarcely be a distinction that one relates merely to the mechanical technic, the other to the substance, for form and substance are not thus to be separated. But from Boston to Los Angeles I find, under one name or another, instruction given in the veriest elements of bookkeeping, while at the same time, argument is made, that because of the crowding of our Universities all elementary subjects, languages, mathematics, and physics should be relegated to secondary schools. It is well for our association to consider this question.

[7] In addition to this fundamental aspect of the *What*, we should consider whether we, in the Universities, are to emphasize the general principles or the more highly elaborated detail of specialized technique. Whether we are to prepare students to pass technical examinations given by State Boards, or to eschew that, as serving of a cramming school, and put the instruction on a scientific basis.

[8] In one respect accounting is in a peculiar, perhaps in an unfortunate position. It may be illustrated by comparing it with law. Courses in commercial law are given in Schools of Commerce, mining law in Schools of Mines, Roman law in Letters and Science, yet none of these courses train the lawyer. That is reserved for a professional School of Law. Similarly, Stevens Institute has some excellent lectures on accounting, our College of Agriculture gives a course in farm accounts, and any College of Commerce gives accounting. But in most universities, there is no professional School of Accounting separate from the School of Business. Accounting, like law, is a profession, not a business. Schools of Business teach some law without becoming law schools. But for some reason professional teaching in accounting is relegated to Schools of Business, although it belongs there as little as professional law belongs in Commerce, Engineering or Agriculture.

[9] The establishment of separate schools is by no means imperative. The professional accountant may be trained in a school labeled Commerce, just as, in

Europe, science is taught by the Faculty of Philosophy. But imperative it is to distinguish the instruction in accounting appropriate for the prospective business man, and that suited to train one for the C.P.A. Both may rest on the same foundation, but they differ as widely as do the Redwood and the Madrone, both springing from the same soil.

[10] Let us provide the most thoroughgoing professional training, but let us not think that such a course is suited to the needs of most of our students who are to be business and not professional men.

[11] *When* is accounting instruction to be given? One finds in American universities that the beginning of such work ranges from freshman (in Illinois) to the first graduate year (at Harvard), while courses of advanced accounting frequently appear in the high school curriculum. This is a question which we should freely discuss.

[12] And *how* is accounting to be taught? That, as in most studies, is a question of prime significance in the introductory course, whether called bookkeeping or accounting. Strangely enough, of all subjects taught in the schools, not excepting theology, bookkeeping is most subject to the thrall of antiquated custom. Row Fogo has called attention to the way in which even bookkeeping technic has blindly followed rules, for no reason save that it was so prescribed in that quaint old XV century book. We don't light our fires, or shave our faces, or write our letters as Paciolo did. But still we date our Ledgers differently than our Journals, still we write "Balance" in our ledgers although there is no longer a Balance account. Just because a back-number Dago Geezer did so before Columbus discovered America. Trifling yet highly significant is one most remarkable survival. Paciolo, piously inclined, interjected many moral aphorisms in his text. When telling about the Journal, he exhorts the reader to hear Mass, and in the discussion of bills of exchange he inculcates giving of alms. This has continued in unbroken line down to the present. One current book has at the bottom of each page a sentiment which would do credit to any Italian monk. I opened at random and read, "The use of character is to be a shield against calumny." In other texts used today, I find, "Excellence in any line can be attained only by painstaking, persistent effort," and again, "Perfection is made up of trifles, but perfection itself is no trifle." Algebra was first published in this same work of Paciolo, but while Algebraic texts no longer disseminate moral counsel, bookkeeping texts do. Surely the following, found in the leading American text, "Take pride in being accurate. Do not be content with doing a thing nearly right, do it exactly right," applies even more to the multiplication table than to the Journal. Yet it causes no surprise to find it in the leading American bookkeeping text, although it is never found in an Arithmetic.

[13] Some strange spell has surrounded bookkeeping. It follows old models, it repeats old rules, it reiterates meaningless formulas, like a classical saint mumbling the sacred names of Buddha, while lost in contemplating the esoteric significance of his own navel.

[14] Van Cleve, in his refreshingly iconoclastic work, says, "I have never seen a textbook [on bookkeeping] which gave any indication whatever that its author had even the remotest conception of the principles on which the act is based." Much is to be said on that side but some think his statement extreme. But it surely behooves our association not to ignore the past, but seriously to question each tradition of bookkeeping, and, if not Bolshevists, at least become Progressives.

[15] As instructors, presumably we have allied interests not to be overlooked. Among these are to be mentioned:

A. Our relationship to other organizations.

[16] The chief of these are the A.E.A. [American Economic Association] and the National C. T. [Commercial Teachers'] Federation, both of which are now in session in Chicago. Then, too, the Institute of Accountants, and the Association of University Schools of Business. All of these are dealing with the same problems. The closest possible cooperation is to be sought.

B. Publication

[17] The interests of accounting are greater even than the interests of teachers of accounting. There should be some significant publication in which all interested would cooperate—public accountants, teachers, economists. Such a publication would be expensive. It needs the widest backing. Splitting up the field produces several weak organs. It is worth an effort to make one good national publication.

C. Research

[18] Our best hope to be successful teachers is to stimulate scholarly research. Fundamental problems are awaiting solutions.

UNPUBLISHED LONGER PAPERS

"Some Heretical Views on the Method of Teaching Bookkeeping," 1913

The Regents of the University of California adopted a policy to use the campus' department of education to upgrade the teaching in the secondary schools of the State. (President's Report for 1908-1910, pp. 23-25). Hatfield participated by teaching courses on bookkeeping in the summer sessions. In at least one instance, he used a visitor to teach the course—James O. McKinsey (1920), then at the University of Chicago.

This is one of only two of the unpublished longer papers that deal explicitly with bookkeeping or accounting. The second is the critique of the 1937 statement on accounting principles, which is included later in this chapter. In this first paper, Hatfield moves directly to the point—that accounting has changed since Paciolo, but bookkeeping textbooks do not reflect that (Paragraphs 2-6). After a series of examples, in Paragraph 7, he summarizes the position he is defending—that bookkeeping texts do not explain what they advocate. In Paragraph 13, he articulates a theme repeated in his later work. For example, in speaking of the textbooks used at the time, he states, "All alike err grievously in that there is no connection between the explanations which they give, and the work they are attempting to do."

Hatfield was well known for his interest in the history of accounting. In many of his essays, his knowledge of early accounting surfaces. Like the preceding essay, this one challenges contemporary accounting educators to consider many of the traditions established by Paciolo and whether they need to be maintained in textbooks (Paragraphs 3-5). As he always did, Hatfield criticizes blind adherence to tradition and points out that much of what confuses students should be eliminated from bookkeeping texts (Paragraph 6). He incisively analyzes weaknesses he found in current books (Paragraphs 7-25). In assessing the weaknesses of bookkeeping textbooks, he presents his own position on how bookkeeping should be taught, a position that would eliminate confusion in terminology while helping students understand what they were doing, the driving rationale behind his recommended changes. In the remainder of the essay, Hatfield uses rich analogies to illuminate his points (Paragraphs 13, 15).

Almost four decades later, Hatfield returned to this theme in a brief article, "Accounting Trivia," published in the September 1940 issue of *The Accounting Review*.

[1] The first text book on bookkeeping was published in 1494. For long, it remained almost the only text. This is so because the numerous books which appeared in the years thereafter were mostly very close copies of Paciolo, even copying errors, although most of the copiers concealed their indebtedness and put out their works as being original productions. Thus, through Paciolo's own work, and through plagiarizations thereof, and through the translations of plagiarizations, the whole business world was captured by a system of bookkeeping expounded by an Italian monk, who was a professor of Moral Philosophy, teaching Mathematics in the University of Milan.

[2] Now a good many things have happened since 1494. Most treatises of that time are decidedly out of date. The peculiar thing about bookkeeping is that a good many practices continue merely because they were found in the original text of 1494, without any other excuse or justification. Thus, as Row Fogo remarks, ledgers generally bear the date at the side, while journals are dated in the middle of the page, without any shadow of reason except that Paciolo did so more than four hundred years ago. America shows more freedom, but it is only of very recent years that bookkeepers have dared to omit "To" and "By" in ledger entries,

a matter which, to Paciolo, seemed very important, but which certainly had no real significance. So, too, the entering of the name of the account in which the counter entry is made, has continued down to our memory, and it is only the daredevil Americans who have ventured to break away from that hoary tradition.

[3] Some things we still cling to. Thus, the writing of the word Balance when an account is being closed at the end of the year, at one time meant something, but means nothing now. Then every account outstanding when the books were closed was actually transferred to a ledger account called the Balance Account, a practice still found in Continental ledgers. Balance appeared as an item in A's account just as Bills Receivable, Notes Receivable or Cash appeared there. They all indicated the name of the counter account in which the other side of the entry was posted. But we, who no longer have a balance account, and no longer indicate in the ledger the place where the counter entry actually appears, still put down Balance, still consider it insanity or blasphemy to intimate that a ledger account might be ruled off and the excess debits indicated without making an equal footing appear in the debit and credit columns of the account.

[4] Another peculiarity found in Paciolo and his successors has strangely survived. That is the practice of using a bookkeeping text as a means of inculcating moral or religious principles. Bookkeeping texts, and the journals and ledgers themselves, were highly moral works in the olden days. Thus, Brown says of Paciolo, "he tells his readers to post their journals and to hear mass, or he stops short in the middle of some explanation of bills of exchange to inculcate the giving of alms. Never on any account, he warns us, must a new book be commenced without the glorious sign of the cross 'before which every enemy flees and the powers of evil deservedly tremble!'" Similarly, one of his plagiarizers in 1543 opens the journal with a prayer, and when a profit is shown "Right across the book there is written in large letters: 'Honour and praise to the Almighty God who has granted me these things.'" (Brown, 129-130) And Petri, in 1588, when he closes his model ledger, ends it with these words, "Thus is this my book balanced and compared, wherefor to the Almighty and eternal God be all praise, honour and glory. Amen." (Brown, 134)

[5] Have you ever noticed a similar tendency in bookkeeping works of today? One of the most popular texts now used has printed at the bottom of every page sentiments which would do credit to an Italian monk. I opened at random and read, "Language is the close fitting dress of thought," and opposite it, "The use of character is to be a shield against calumny." From the most used books in this state, I cull the following gems, one from each text:

> "No matter how smart you are, do not for a moment think that your native ability, however great, will compensate for the want of patient care and FAITHFUL WORK." (Lyon, p. 7)

> "Excellence in any line can be attained only by painstaking persistent effort." (M. & M., 231)

And in the one most of all used:

"Remember, perfection is made up of trifles but perfection itself is no trifle." (W. & R., 4.)

[6] Now, think for a minute what is involved in this. Did any of you ever see a high school algebra text, or a chemistry text, with moral apothegms as foot notes, or even a multiplication table which said, as does one most popular work in bookkeeping: "Take pride in being accurate. Do not be content with doing a thing nearly right, but do it exactly right." (W. & R., 4.)

[7] Why do I mention these trivialities? Because they are indicative of the attitude toward bookkeeping, and the far-reaching tendency to accept what has been customary in such books from the time of Paciolo, only here and there breaking loose and really thinking what we are doing. This is particularly true in regard to the discussion of bookkeeping theory. Despite his mathematical bent, Paciolo was not a theoretician. He described with painstaking care the details of bookkeeping technique. But the theoretical or explanatory side he ignored. And the same tendency has continued till today. That is to say, most of the texts in common use today are notoriously weak in matters of bookkeeping principle. One is tempted almost to accept the absurdly extreme statement of a somewhat unbalanced writer whose recent book states: "I have never seen a text book which gave any indication whatever that its author had even the remotest conception of the principles upon which the art is based. In their descriptions of double entry bookkeeping many of the text books are very successful, and most of them are fairly so; but in their attempts to explain it all of them, that I have ever read, are absolute failures."

[8] This is most apparent in reference to the crucial matter in bookkeeping—the determination of Debit and Credit. Let us see how this is handled by text books in common use in the high schools of this state. Of the five works most used on the Coast, two attempt a single rule for Debit and Credit. These are not couched in identical terms, and they do not on the face seem to be identical in meaning. They both are, I think, demonstrably false. One might say confessedly false, for while the rules are laid down as a general principle, neither author sticks to the formula consistently, and in one case, way at the end of the book, in an appendix, after the harm has been done, the General Principle or Rule is expressed in quite different terms from the way in which it is expressed in the earlier part of the work way back on page 16. In one of these works, the rule laid down is to debit that which is received by the business, in the other the rule is to debit that which costs value. The former is the most common formula for bookkeeping entries, by those who attempt a single rule. The objections to it are clear:

(a) To the unsophisticated, it is nonsense. This is most apparent in regard to credits. Inventory is credited to Merchandise account. Is the inventory something that the business has given out? The unsophisticated would say it was the only part of the merchandise which had not been given out. When merchandise is bought on credit, has the business given anything? It would look as if it was the seller gave, not the business. But most clearly of all, only some perverted form of mental operation can regard a destruction of property by fire, or abstraction of cash by a thief, as having anything whatever to do with a receipt by the business, and yet something must be debited.

(b) The author does not follow his rule logically. He explains a charge to accounts receivable as showing that someone "became indebted," not in terms of the business having received. Interest is debited, he says, "because it cost something," when he should have said because the business "received" something.

(c) It fails altogether to explain the meaning of the Proprietor's Capital Account. For, surely, nothing has been given out by the business. The only possible way in which such a conception could pass any muster is by regarding the Proprietor's Capital as a liability, which of course it is not.

[9] The formula that Debits represent costs and Credits represent value produced is somewhat similar. The credit to Cash, say, when money is stolen, is certainly not, in any reasonable sense, a case of value produced.

[10] The trouble with both of these is that they attempt a single explanation of things which are not the same, and cannot be explained by a single rule. This was well expressed by Jones many years ago as follows:

> The terms debit and credit have proved a stumbling-block to every person who has undertaken to explain the system of double-entry. These terms are used merely to distinguish the left from the right hand side of an account in the ledger; while authors and teachers attempt to preserve their ordinary meaning by showing that all items in the debit columns are in some way indebted to the concern, and vice versa. Now, the debit items of one account are a collection of purchases; of another, losses; of another, receipts; of another, bills redeemed; of another, liabilities. The debit side of Stock shows the merchant's liabilities at the time of opening the books; on the contrary, the debit side of a personal account shows what that person owes to the concern. The debit side of Bills Payable shows liabilities in the shape of bills; but the credit side of Bills Receivable shows the amount of bills disposed of. The debit side of Cash shows the amount of cash received; but the debit side of Profit and Loss shows losses. In each class of accounts, the debit items are different in their nature; and one debit is like another no further than as it belongs to the left-hand column of the account. But even if we could point out some hidden relation of owing in each debit entry, we should only be luring the learner from the investigation of principles, by employing his ingenuity on a series of conundrums, not one of which can throw light on the next, the whole being dependent upon an arbitrary use of words.

[11] The next two texts give a double explanation of debit and credit. This is an improvement, for the rule laid down is not quite so inconsistent. It sometimes works. But even though the rule is workable, not much more can be said in favor of the theoretical merits of these works. One of them brags, somewhat gratuitously, that no time is wasted in unnecessary theorizing, and its first instruction is "Do just as you are told to do." Furthermore, a rule of general application which must immediately be followed by eighteen other rules seems to lack somewhat of

adequacy, and to be somewhat confusing. When one learns in algebra that the multiplication of like signs produces +, but that the multiplication of unlike signs produces –, he does not have to follow it up with eighteen or with eight rules. Either the first so-called General Rule belies its name, or the latter rules are superfluous.

[12] And the fifth book gives three explanations. These are in most cases adequate, though even they fail when it comes to such matters as reserve accounts, nor does the author even refer to his three general principles when he comes to explain when a reserve account should be debited and credited.

[13] But what has been thus far said touches only the surface objection to the texts in common use. One book may be better than another in the adequacy of the rule of thumb employed. All alike err grievously in that there is no connection between the explanations which they give, and the work they are attempting to do. Let us take one of the books, which will serve as type of all in this respect. It starts out, in the second line of the text, with the statement that the object of bookkeeping is to show the profits and losses, and to exhibit the assets and liabilities. This statement is nearly, though not quite, correct. But the formula, once expressed, apparently has nothing to do with subsequent events. It resembles, not remotely, a political platform which states that the party is endeavoring to secure some great reform, but the party apparently is satisfied with the platform and devotes itself thereafter to jobs and spoils. It expresses its purposes in one set of terms, but its activities all in another set of terms, quite incommensurable.

[14] If the pupil is trying to keep a record of how much in assets he has, and what losses he has suffered, how comes it that he is made to express everything in terms of goings and comings, of costs and productions. And then when the time comes for closing the ledger, what a marvelous transformation there is. He has an account labeled Proprietor in which certain givings-out by the business are on one side, and, on the other, certain receipts (both sadly confusing, for a debit to the Proprietor's account makes a strange sort of a receipt by the business) and behold the drawing of six lines—"Be sure, children, to draw them with red ink, and to hold the pen carefully between the thumb and fingers or perhaps the magic transformation will not take place"—and this record of receivings and givings becomes a statement of how much the proprietor is worth. A whole set of accounts, which for a year had dealt solely with receivers and givers, or with costs and yields, becomes transformed without explanation or logical connection into a list of assets, another list of liabilities, and a statement of how much the proprietor is worth.

[15] In this, I think, lies the real difficulty of practically all American bookkeeping. There is no attempt to show the pupil what he is trying to do, and why he does it. There may be alleged principles, or rules, or theories, but these all have no connection with what is the real purpose or the real result of the bookkeeping process. Even though there were no inconsistencies in the theories of bookkeeping, even though the explanations or rules for debit and credit did really cover all the entries

to be made in the book, that is of little avail so long as explanations are in one language and purposes in another. It is too much like the grading of universities according to the prowess of a score or two of football players. There might be a perfectly consistent system of classification, but it would not have anything at all to do with the purpose of universities. It leads almost inevitably to such a statement as that the fundamental principle of bookkeeping is that the debits equal the credits.

[16] Who cares whether debits equal credits or not? What good is a list of debits and a list of credits such as is found in a trial balance of footings? Are we to hire a dozen clerks to work twelve months to support the glorious principle of "Every debit has a credit," or that more atrocious formula, "Equal debits and equal credits"? Why, of course not! But it may well be worth the expense to keep records which will enlighten us on the question of what are our assets and what our liabilities, what was our capital at the beginning of the year and how and how much have we added thereto.

[17] The main point of the method here advocated is that the pupil is taught to regard business transactions with reference to the way in which they really affect the proprietor, and not in accordance with some mere formula of comings and goings. According to the underlying theory, double-entry bookkeeping is double, not because there are two columns in an account, nor because every debit has a credit, nor because there are two entries for each transaction, but because it attempts to make two parallel sets of records, leading to a double portrayal of essential facts. First, it portrays in such detail as is needed all the items that go to make up the assets and the liabilities, and secondly it portrays the status of the net wealth of the proprietor, including therein the original wealth with which he began business, and any subsequent changes, whether accretions or subtractions. It portrays these two sets of accounts and shows that there is always an equation between them. The assets minus the liabilities must ever equal the original capital plus or minus the profit and loss.

[18] The keeping of such records has an obvious value. The listing of receivers, received things, and costs, all as debits, has no significance in itself, indicates no purpose of the labors, has no apparent value. Let the pupil start from the beginning with an idea of what he is really attempting to do, let him decide every puzzle with reference to that which he is attempting, and bookkeeping will cease to be a meaningless jumble of rules and become a most valuable discipline. To be sure, there are difficulties in teaching bookkeeping, no matter what system is followed. But is it not better to face the difficulties clearly, recognize them for what they are, and down them in a good logical fight, than to putter around with the applications of mere rules of thumb which have no reference to the real problems?

[19] The ideal way of teaching bookkeeping, I believe, is to begin neither with the journal nor with the isolated ledger account (which is the alternative generally discussed), but to begin with the balance sheet, or, if you prefer, with the statement of affairs. Have you ever read Dunbar's little book on banking? In one chap-

ter, he takes up bank accounts, starting with an initial balance sheet, giving a list of transactions, and showing, at once, how these affect the balance sheet, or, in other words, how certain transactions affect the assets and liabilities, and how they increase or decrease profits. The book is generally read by students who know absolutely nothing of bookkeeping, who could not tell a debit from a wheelbarrow, and yet such students have little or no difficulty in recording the changes made by the transactions, even though the transactions deal with discounts, drafts, premiums, and other matters ordinarily supposed to be of some complexity. On the other hand, I have known students who have spent a year in studying bookkeeping to go entirely to pieces when asked to record discounts, that not having been included in their exercises, or having escaped their memory.

[20] The purpose of bookkeeping is to record changes in assets, liabilities, and proprietorship. Very well, let's to work and see from the beginning how transactions do affect these categories, and one has a logical basis for the bookkeeping operations. The first exercises must be vastly simple so as not to confuse the pupil, but a complete system of bookkeeping may be comprised in a set of three accounts, and surely that is not too complex for the high school student. Let us begin, then, as does Dunbar with a simple balance sheet which shows: Assets = Liabilities + Capital, and show how it would be altered by a given limited set of transactions. Soon appears the inconvenience of altering figures in a balance sheet, especially where more than one change is wrought in a given item. Inevitably, perhaps at the pupils' initiative, there will come the suggestion that changes can best be recorded by arranging the various items of a balance sheet in a series of parallel columns, so that additions and subtractions can be recorded seriatim. The ideal form of bookkeeping is thus introduced, that is, a columnar book, combining the description of the transaction and the appropriate classified entry in some account. This is virtually the columnar journal-cash book, but applied in such a way that there is a column for every ledger account—a simple matter in the beginning exercises.

[21] Thus far, all has been clear, simple, and, as the prayer book puts it, easily to be understanded of the people. Of course, the student knows that if cash has been paid out he must subtract a sum from the cash previously on hand. He does not need any rule to tell him that if someone pays him $10 in cash, that he must add that amount to his cash, and that he must also add it to an account which indicates how much he is worth, or if separation is made between original Capital and Profit and Loss, that he must add $10 to the column in which he indicates the gains which he has made.

[22] But now comes the one difficult point in bookkeeping. It is something like the table of nines in the multiplication table, something really difficult, but something which, I am told, really can be learned. And that is merely the fact that, by a curious convention, when one wants to add a sum to an asset account it is placed in the left of the two columns into which that account is divided. But that if a sum is to be added to liabilities or to proprietorship the sum is placed in the right-hand

column. This resembles learning that in this country the driver turns to the right, but in England to the left. Now is that a very terrible thing to learn? Yes, in some respects it is. But it can be done. Of course, it implies that one must know whether a given account represents an asset or a profit. But, for goodness sakes, what is the use of a boy keeping a set of books if he does not know what is the difference in meaning between an asset and a profit? What is the use of his running an account called cash unless he knows that it indicates a peculiar kind of a thing which he possesses, and that it does not mean expense? Doubtless the system I am advocating is more difficult to teach than a rule of thumb whereby an entry is made in the journal merely because Mr. Profit & Loss sitting off somewhere on top of a pile of ashes is conceived of as receiving something when the store burns down. But is there an advantage in having a boy make a journal entry when he does not understand what it really means, and when he does not see just how it affects that for which all bookkeeping exists—the balance sheet?

[23] After some exercises in this ideal kind of bookkeeping, it becomes manifest that it is not applicable, in its entirety, for a very extended set of accounts, and that columnar bookkeeping becomes unwieldy when it gets to comprising five or ten thousand accounts. Before that is reached, the pupil sees that the same system of accounts is maintained by cutting up his columnar sheet, and placing the several accounts one on top of the others, instead of side by side—and then we have a ledger. Have we been a long time reaching this place? Perhaps, but each step in the way has been taken because he has seen where he wants to go, and how to get there, and not because he reads a sign board bearing the inscription "Rule 997, this item is to be entered on the third line of the left-hand column of the second account on page 43."

[24] And then comes the journal, now not a matter of difficulty. For if the pupil understands that a certain transaction would result in the addition to an asset called Cash, and if his God-given memory is sufficiently strong to enable him to remember the only thing in bookkeeping which he has to remember by brute force, he realizes at once that an entry must be made in the left-hand column of the asset account called Cash. If he knows this fact, he will have no difficulty in putting down on paper instructions indicating the entries that he has already decided must be made in the ledger—and such instructions constitute the journal. So far as the principles of bookkeeping are concerned, the journal is a somewhat unessential book, just as it is one little used in actual practice. But it has value as a class-room tool, serving to indicate what the pupil proposes to do to the ledger, without taking time to thumb over the pages and make the actual entries.

[25] I need not try your patience by continuing to show the development of the subject, and how one can proceed step by step until the most complicated entries are mastered.

[26] I have called these suggestions heretical, and doubtless they so appear to you. But it is not a schism which I have myself started. You will find that the substance of this method of attack was clearly brought out by an American who pub-

lished a work in 1838, three-quarters of a century ago. And today it is clearly recognized in Germany as a competing system even by those who do not use it. Professor Schär of the Commercial University in Berlin, formerly of the Technical School at Basle, has done more than anyone else to make it well known, although in this he has been greatly aided by Hügli, formerly government accountant of Berne, but unfortunately no longer living. The main features are also developed by Charles E. Sprague, the most original of American authorities on accounting, whose active life as President of a New York bank and professor of accounting at New York University was ended about a year ago.[6]

"Corporations and the Public," 1918

Including an Earlier Paper on Corporations, 1910

In these two papers, written in 1910 and 1918, Hatfield articulates his knowledge of economic history and forms of business organization (partnerships and corporations). He combines this knowledge with his firm belief in the benefits to be derived from a competitive system, subject to limited controls by government. In the 1910 paper, he brings accounting to the fore as a remedy for the "financial misdeeds" that had occurred and might recur, by requiring "publicity of accounts." Thus, Hatfield was well ahead of Ripley in calling for greater financial transparency by corporations.[7] However, Hatfield never championed his recommendations, a characteristic which was likely his greatest weakness as a major figure in accounting. Thus, the 1918 paper omits the plea for "publicity of accounts." The 1918 paper was scheduled for presentation at the Kosmos Club but was never presented. Available evidence suggests that the earlier paper on corporations was presented March 17, 1910 at the Oakland Chapter of the American Institute of Banking. The following notes refer solely to the 1918 paper.

This is an excellent paper that embodies a concise discussion of the history of the corporation and illustrates Hatfield's usual tendency to approach topics from their historical roots. He traces the history of the corporation, and reviews three classes of objections to corporations, before describing and then assessing a host of unethical practices that had emerged during the evolution of the corporation. He never excoriates corporations but, with dispassioned objectivity, incisively surveys the problems emerging from the modern U.S. corporation.

A well-structured example of deliberative oratory, "Corporations and the Public" follows the pattern of classical argument that we saw exemplified in "Remarks to a Group of San Francisco CPAs."

Paragraphs 1-3: Introduction. The theses (end of Paragraph 3) are stated as questions which the remaining paragraphs explore.

Paragraph 4: *Narratio*: Succinct answers to the questions posed, with answers based on the history of the corproration beginning in Italy in the 14th and 15th centuries.

Paragraphs 4-6: History of the corporation.

Paragraphs 7-12: *Confirmatio*: Statement of problems of the corporation, stemming from its roots.

Paragraphs 13-17: *Confutatio:*. Refutation of the objections to corporations.

Paragraphs 17-32: Analysis of the refutation arguments.

Paragraphs 33-34: Summation and Conclusion.

"Corporations and the Public"

[1] While corporations existed in earlier centuries, even back to the days of ancient Rome, the corporation problem is distinctly a matter not merely of modern times but even of the last seventy-five years. Even so late as 1776, corporations were so unimportant in the business world that Adam Smith, generally an exceedingly keen interpreter of current affairs, said that the corporation could never compete with the individual proprietor, except in a very limited number of enterprises where the business carried on is extremely simple. These were banks, water companies, insurance companies. That railroads should be added to this list was apparent as soon as they appeared. Somewhat later, manufacturing establishments drifted into corporate form, but the taking over of retail stores by corporations was almost unknown until forty years ago. But now, practically every sort of an enterprise is conducted by corporations apparently more satisfactorily than by individuals or partnerships. Surely, times have changed.

[2] The stock explanation of this remarkable growth is that corporations possess three marked advantages, and these advantages, as they are conventionally described, are immortality, limited liability, and the bringing together of large amounts of capital made up of many relatively small contributions. As you are all familiar with this hackneyed statement, I need not trespass on your time by expounding upon it in the fashion so natural to an academician. I need not even argue that the first advantage, immortality, is ill-phrased, and that the bringing together of many contributions is not a third advantage, but a result of the two factors first mentioned.

[3] But, granting the three advantages mentioned to be salient characteristics of the modern corporation, it may be worthwhile to examine why these obvious advantages possessed by the corporation did not sooner cause the substitution of the corporate form in business. If limited liability is so important an advantage, why was the device not sooner hit upon? Why did not some earlier age recognize the real advantage of a definite life to the business organization, why did not this

simple means of bringing together the scattered units of loanable capital to the benefit of all concerned make a place for itself in the medieval world? Was not mankind anxious to avail itself of opportunities for gain, even before the advent of James B. Dill or Barney Barnato?

[4] The answer is that the corporation was not a device created out of the void but a natural outcome of changed conditions in the world. The corporation came when it did, and as it did, because a new world needed a new form of business organization. This is true even if we go back to an earlier age and consider the first appearance of corporations on any considerable scale—considerable, though insignificant, as compared with the manifestations of recent years. This was in the days of the Italian Republics of the XIV and XV centuries. Corporations, the establishment of public credit, banks, and double-entry bookkeeping were all efflorescences of that remarkable period. But they all appeared as they did because that was pre-eminently a period of new commercial activity, of traffics and discoveries, of the compass, of new trade routes, of opening up of a new world. The medieval corporation appeared at that time in response to the demand for instruments adequate to carry on the new business activities. Similarly, the more modern manifestation of the instinct for incorporation appeared when it did because it too was necessary for carrying on new forms of business activity thitherto unknown in the commercial world.

[5] With the exception of the Great War, perhaps the greatest change in the world as a whole which has ever been brought about was due to that series of events commonly known as the Industrial Revolution, events which occurred toward the end of the eighteenth, and which began to work out their fruits in the nineteenth, century. The American Revolution, important though it was, not only to our prejudiced and patriotic minds but to the whole world, was insignificant compared with the changes wrought by the Industrial Revolution. The world which until then had jogged on for some three hundred years with a monotonous steadiness suddenly took on new life. Almost simultaneously, several of the most important inventions of history were made. These related to new methods of manufacturing iron, the introduction of the steam engine as a motive power, and the series of inventions having to do with machine production of textiles. Coal, iron, steam, machinery—these were the battalions with which the Industrial Revolution conquered the sluggish world, and, for good or ill, the world has thereby been made anew. These changes meant production on a large scale, they meant the factory system thitherto existing only in embryo, they meant machinery, they meant worldwide markets and industry on a large scale, they meant capitalism. Then, for the first time, it was found that much capital must be invested, because then, for the first time, elaborate machinery and costly plants were necessary in production. Permanent investments, such as the railroad, displaced the temporary equipment that previously had been used by the teamster. Is it not clearly seen how well the characteristics of the corporation fitted in with these new requirements? Immortality, or at least permanence, became necessary so soon as great enterprises

involving permanent capital became necessary: limited liability became essential to the gathering together of enough capital for carrying on the new businesses in the new fashion. The corporation came into its present dominance because it alone was fitted to the new world brought about by the inventions of the Industrial Revolution. Steam, machinery, the corporation are all parts of the same whole; none could adequately be used without the others.

[6] Among the greatest of inventions, then, is the business corporation. It may have been used for good or for ill, but its efficiency is now indisputable; it is an organic part of our body politic. One might as well grumble at having a stomach as at having corporations: both are indispensable. Certain institutions of modern life might perhaps be suddenly removed without great loss, just as one occasionally sacrifices his vermiform appendix. But the corporation, like the stomach, is here to stay.

[7] It is curious, however, to notice the illogical attitude of the public toward corporations. Instead of glorying in the greatness of this modern invention, as we glory in the telephone and the airship, or instead of merely taking it for granted, as we accept potatoes and sugar as necessaries without considering that once they were unknown, the present-day newspaper and the present-day politician look upon the work of man's hand and find it bad.

[8] This was forcibly brought to my mind some years ago in an incident which you may recollect, even though it may not have impressed you at the time. A political campaign was on, and someone, I know not now whether his name was Jones or Smith, or whether he was Republican or Democrat, placarded the fences with glaring posters which read somewhat as follows, "The Corporations are opposed to Smith for Assessor." The inference was clear. Whatever the corporations oppose is what the people want. Corporations are so inherently and incorrigibly vicious that our only motto is "Vote against them." Patrick Henry, you remember, said he had only one lamp by which his feet were guided, and that was the lamp of experience. The modern statesman's only lamp and guide is more simple, and does not necessitate rummaging the pages of history. All he asks is to know what the corporations want, and he straightway sets himself, at least ostensibly, to do exactly the opposite.

[9] One cannot take up a paper, serious or comic, without seeing some headline, cartoon, squib, editorial or article in some way portraying the evil of corporations. Why is it that civilization takes so little pride in its great invention; why is it, if corporations are so inherently vicious, that society continues to have them, for they are absolutely the creation of law, and would have no existence without legal sanction? Surely the public, Frankenstein-like, seems to have used its creative genius to produce a monster which, once in existence, seems only to plague its magician creator.

[10] One can find almost every crime in the calendar, and then some, charged against the corporation. If one attempts out of the discordant array to bring some order, the complaints can mostly be classified under three heads. The corporation

is envied because it is an aggregation of wealth; it is feared because of certain monopolistic features; it is hated because it has occasioned speculative misadventures. These may be spoken of as the objections of the Democrat, of the Consumer, and of the Lamb. There is much good reason in the first objection, especially in a democracy such as ours. As Sumner has so clearly shown in his life of Jackson, wealth is essentially and irretrievably obnoxious to pure democracy. Its existence denies the principles on which democracy rests; its continuance gives the lie to Democracy's most cherished dogma; it threatens openly or insidiously to substitute another form of rule for that of King Demos. Naturally, then, an institution which makes more possible, and more obtrusive, the aggregation of wealth incurs the hostility of the public. It is true that there has been much loose thinking and foolish talking in reference to the accumulation of wealth in corporate control. The figures given almost always refer to the par value of the securities, something only vaguely related to the wealth involved. The U.S. Steel Corporation, when first established, was always spoken of as the Billion Dollar Corporation, regardless of the patent fact that the entire enterprise was valued by that keen and impersonal appraiser, the stock exchange, at less than half that figure. Or tabulations were prepared, designed to show the overwhelming amount of corporate wealth in which were listed and added the stock issued by the holding company, and the stock of the subsidiary corporation thus acquired—leading to duplication and, in many cases, to even higher multiplication of the actual wealth. But crude and unscientific, hysterical and unsound though most of the statements have been, it remains true that the chief advantage possessed by the corporation is at the same time its chief offense.

[11] The second objection, resting on monopolistic features of corporations, does not apply to all corporations, though the unthinking public often speaks as though corporation and monopoly were synonymous terms. "The Corporation Problem," "The Corporation Evil," "The attitude of the President towards the corporations" are phrases often used, and generally in cases where the monopoly element is the main feature. It is, of course, true that almost all monopolies, or even quasi-monopolies, are controlled by corporations. This is true whether one refers to natural monopolies, such as municipal franchises, or those which have been created by the magnitude of the business, such as some of the modern trusts are at least popularly supposed to possess. It is, of course, not necessary to decry the existence of monopoly nor profitable to attempt its justification. But monopoly is not dependent on corporate organization; it acts in that form merely because of the greater convenience. Human ingenuity would still find ways to forestall the market, to make corners, to crowd out competition, to act the hog, even though corporations were unknown.

[12] The last class of criticisms rests on certain features of speculation in corporation stocks. So much stock has been floated at an exorbitant figure, so much rigging and thimble rigging of the market has occurred, so many lambs have been shorn, so many margins have been lost, so many dividends are passed, so many

bonds, even, are defaulted, that the public, especially if the public has itself been taking flyers, comes to hate the whole institution. Who can lose at craps without questioning whether the dice are loaded?

[13] It is, however, erroneous to assume that the abuses of corporation finance are more flagrant now than in earlier days, although that statement has frequently been made. So early as 1855, the New York Railroad Commission complained of lack of qualifications of railroad directors, and charged them with "prostituting their trust to promote their own private interests." The early railroad stocks were more generally speculative than at present. Harlem sold as high as 190 and fell to 65 within six weeks. Poor has stated that, for the first twenty years, 1828-1847, even the best located roads were run at a loss. Railroad stock in the earlier days was fully as speculative as were the early industrials seventy-five years later. Speculative fluctuations are inevitable in any new class of undertakings. While railroads were new, no one could accurately estimate earnings; investors were misled by extravagant prospectuses. As the conditions of railroad success became better known, speculation sought a more congenial medium, and found it in the securities of the great industrials, so prominent at the end of the century. No one could calculate with accuracy just what would be the effect of the consolidation of the steel plants of the country, and hence the U.S. Steel Corporation furnished a matter on which opinions could differ, on which wagers could be made. But the abuses of corporation finance are no more pronounced now than in the earlier days of railroad promotion, even though the sums involved are somewhat larger. A more striking difference appears in reference to bank stock. The stocks of the two great central federal banks were the subject of wildest speculation. In 1817 and 1818, this went to the length of stock-jobbing by the directors of the bank in the stock of their own institution, including the grossest misuse of the bank's funds in order to carry the purchases of stock made by the directors. In these days, one scarcely expects to find such abuses by bank officials.

[14] Innumerable are the plans suggested for improving corporations or for mitigating their baleful effects. The nature of the reforms varies with the reformer's viewpoint, whether he is a democrat, or a consumer, or a lamb. On the extreme left are such proposals as that of the arch-democrat of the nineteenth century, the peerless prophet of the Platte, who urged that corporations should be limited in size, so that no one organization could possess more than a stated maximum of wealth, and thus plutocracy's power, just as Germany's, could be curtailed by limiting the size of its armies.

[15] But most of the proposals have looked more toward the protection of the consumer by regulation of prices, thinking thus to check the extortion which might otherwise be practiced by a monopolistic corporation.

[16] These efforts were directed first toward public utilities rather than toward ordinary industrial corporations. This was both natural and logical for two reasons. Public utilities, by their very nature, tend to become monopolies, competition being extravagant and generally only temporary; and in the second place

because public utilities, being regarded as especial beneficiaries of the bounty of the state, having received peculiar privileges, particularly the right of eminent domain, may properly be held to stricter account than the ordinary business enterprise.

[17] It is beyond the scope of this paper to recount the history of the development of the regulation of public utilities. The history has been one of steady expansion, both in scope and in content. Beginning with the regulation of railroads, it has spread to include electric roads, water, gas, and electric companies, hydro-electric power companies, telephones, express, and sleeping car companies. Beginning in a timid way in Massachusetts, taken up by the Interstate Commerce Commission, copied and extended by the numerous state railroad and utility commissions, it has gone through the stages of investigation, of advice, of redressing wrongs, arriving at the present position of initiating and determining rates. One and apparently only one restraining influence has been felt in this process, and that is the attitude of the courts, holding that the rates must be high enough to allow a "fair return."

[18] But this ruling, instead of being the solution, is only the stating of the problem and has given rise to a bitter and interminable controversy. There are many minor phases to the dispute as to rate regulation, but, in the main, the whole contest has centered on the question as whether the original cost of the plant should be taken as the sum on which the fair return is to be allowed.

[19] Commissions and courts, engineers, economists and accountants have participated in this discussion, but, unfortunately, in most of the discussion there has been no determination of the guiding principle, or what Allison calls the over-theory, by which the question is to be settled.

[20] Most of the writers have somewhat naïvely assumed that equity was the determining principle. Thus, Whitten, in his elaborate, scholarly and exhaustive treatise on the valuation of public utilities, arguing in favor of the cost value as the proper base for rate fixing, states:

> The corporation devoted a certain amount of money to a public use and is equitably as much entitled to a fair return on that investment, provided the business can be made to earn it, as though it had actually loaned that amount to the public. It is the actual investment or sacrifice on the part of the company that is entitled to consideration.

[21] Consider for a moment the absurdities of this argument. In the first place, sacrifice is not in itself a basis for remuneration. One may labor and sweat in body and soul, but, unless something of service is produced, the labor is vanity. In the second place, the argument viciously begs the question by comparing the investment in a public utility to a direct loan. Conceivably, the transaction might rather resemble a lease with revaluations at stated intervals. No one questions the equity of such a lease, even though the rental paid in the later years is altogether out of proportion to the original value contributed by the landlord. Doubtless, if the cap-

italist's investment in a public utility were like a loan, return should be like interest; but it is a bald and gratuitous assumption that it resembles a loan rather than a lease, and, in the third place, Whitten's argument that the investment must be treated as resembling a loan to the public is entirely emasculated and made absurd by the final modifying clause, "It is equitably as much entitled to a fair return on that investment as though it had actually loaned that amount to the public, *provided* the business can be made to earn it." It is a strange conception of equity between borrower and lender to make the obligation of the debtor turn upon whether he did or did not make a profitable and wise investment of the sum borrowed. In my opinion, equity is an insufficient criterion of a system of rate regulation.

[22] But I cannot believe that the already invested enterprises are the more important element in arriving at a proper treatment of public utilities. Vast though the investments are in railroads, in electric companies and the like, they are a small part of the vaster sums about to be invested as the country and the world develop. New fields will appear, new enterprises will be undertaken, and perhaps more and more of those will be looked upon as public utilities. Mines and forests are already considered as partaking of the same character; the distribution of milk and other food supplies is already said to be a public utility; the future utilization of the trackless ways of the air, the shackling for mankind of the boundless possibilities of radio activity, and other inventions as yet undiscovered, as undreamt of now as the airplane and wireless were a few years ago, all these mean the development of new public utilities on a scale so vast that the present investments will be relatively insignificant.

[23] For these new investments, the question of equity is not determinant. Not determinant, for any arrangement may be equitable if entered into with intelligent consent of both parties. One may make a lease for a long period at a specified rate on the cost price of the property, or one may make a lease calling for a fixed percentage of future value to be determined at certain fixed intervals. Presumably, the rate of income in the latter case will be lower than the former, for the general assumption will be that property will increase in value. But one cannot say that it is either more or less equitable to rent at 6 percent of the present value than at 4 percent of the value, to be appraised each ten years. It is neither more nor less equitable to allow to one investor a residual share of indeterminate profits than to allow to another a definite rate of interest on the sum loaned. I doubt even that it is more equitable to sell liberty bonds at a stated price, than to sell, as foreign governments have often done, a lottery ticket for a dollar, which may bring in a capital prize of 100,000 but in all likelihood will yield nothing. Assuming intelligence, discretion, and freedom of contract, any arrangement made between the state and capitalists as to the future regulation of rates may be perfectly equitable, for the differences in attractiveness, or the differences in possible gains, will all be reflected and adjusted in the terms of the contract itself.

[24] While equity is negligible merely because it may theoretically be obtained under any agreed-upon system, the other effects of regulation need most careful consideration. Of these, two may be considered: the effect on the distribution of risk, and its relation to future technical progress.

[25] No new enterprise can be undertaken without a risk of failure. Never can a Columbus fare westward of the pillars of Hercules, never can a Langley experiment in the sky, never can inventions be tried out, or works of high emprise essayed, without a chance of great loss, an ineluctable and tremendous risk of failure. Allison, brilliant writer on utilities, says:

> The true aim of regulation is to bring about eventually a condition where so far as possible, all risk and all speculation will be removed from the enterprise.

But this is a vain fantasy. One person or another may bear the risk, but the risk is unavoidable. In times past, this risk has been ordinarily undertaken by the investor. If new undertakings are still to be carried on by private capital, either the investor must be induced to take the risk by what seems a satisfactory chance of unusual gain, or someone else may assure to the investor a definite income, himself assuming the risk.

[26] If, then, in fixing rates, they are fixed so low as not to allow a possibility of unusual gain, there must either be a guarantee of normal minimum return, or new enterprises will not be undertaken. Either the public must bear the risk, or it must forego the possible advantage to be derived from successful ventures in new fields.

[27] I do not presume to maintain that the state is a poorer judge of the desirability of new undertakings than is the private capitalist.

[28] Private capitalists have indeed often made a sorry mess of it. They have built and torn up again an Ocean Shore railroad; they have a monument of inefficiency at Orinda Park road; they have partly dug and left to tropic destruction an immensely costly Panama Canal; they have paralleled railroad tracks through wildernesses, and found that even parallel lines meet in the bankruptcy court; they have dug mines where no gold is found; they have drilled oil wells which yielded only salt water; they have planted out figs where not even thistles would grow; they have been adventurous with the money of others, unwise, foolhardy, dishonest. Perhaps a sober-minded governmental agency would make fewer mistakes; I express no opinion on that subject.

[29] The second point I wish to make is less obvious, and has been less frequently discussed. And that is that, in determining whether rates should be based on original cost, there should be considered the effect on the utilization of new processes, which might tend to reduce the cost of the commodity handled by the public utility.

[30] The investor makes an investment expecting a fair return on the cost. But improvements in technology arise. A more effective plant can be erected in later

years at half the price. In ordinary competitive enterprises, some new capitalist would see the opportunity, would adopt the new methods, would produce and sell the commodity at half the former price. The first investor might perhaps lose the larger part of his investment, but the public, or at least the body of consumers, would profit by the lower cost of the commodity. But in a public utility such competition is generally not feasible. Should the rates nevertheless be kept up to yield a return on the original cost, the consumer profits nothing by the advance in the arts.

[31] The fixing of rates on the basis of original cost is to be considered not merely, as Whitten suggests, as an equitable payment for a virtual loan, but it must be considered in the light of its being a possible bar to securing the advantages ordinarily gained by competition, the giving to consumers of the benefit derived from cheapened methods of production.

[32] One thing must be borne in mind. It is impossible (and might even be inequitable) to allow the capitalist to bear the loss of many unsuccessful enterprises, and then balk at allowing offsetting gains in one successful venture. That would be akin to refusing to pay insurance to one who had paid only a few premiums, because it would represent an inordinate profit. Such a policy would be a death blow to insurance policies. Or it would be akin to denying to the holder of the successful lottery ticket the payment of the capital prize, because the gain on that one ticket was inordinate, disregarding the fact that the purchaser had perhaps spent a fortune on other unsuccessful tickets.

[33] I attempt no solution of the problem of regulating the rates of utilities. The monopolistic character of such enterprises makes some regulation necessary and beneficial. But I hope that Dr. Rowell will find some underlying principle, some over-theory, and that in searching for such a principle he will go behind considerations of mere equity, and will work out some formula (with that same deftness with which he works out those marvelous and intricate paper designs) by which can be determined how one or the other basis of rate making will throughout future years secure the desirable initiative of new enterprise, will properly distribute losses between the investor and the public, and will allow the consumer to profit by the progress of invention.

[34] My prolixity has left me little time for one other aspect of the public toward the corporation, that prompted by the abuses of frenzied finance. Less has been done, though much has been said on that subject. Only recently have the various utility commissions entered the field, and perhaps these have looked more toward preventing the public from paying income on unwise investment than toward protecting the investor from his own folly and the promoter's fraud. But in very recent years, the so-called Blue Sky laws have been passed in many of the states, designed to protect the investor. Much good has been accomplished by such regulations, but it is a difficult endeavor and one not free from real danger. Patent fraud can be detected and, in a measure, prevented. But no commissioner of corporations is competent to determine whether an honestly established corporation

will be economically profitable. There is some danger that the certificate of good character will be interpreted as an official recommendation of the investment, and that I consider dangerous and harmful. The statement formerly printed on food containers, "Guaranteed under the Pure Food and Drug Act," doubtless sold many adulterated goods, for almost everyone thought that it implied a government guarantee of the contents, when it really meant nothing of the kind. The Blue Sky laws will accomplish something well worth doing, but here again either legitimate but wildly speculative enterprises will be hampered, or there will be a danger that people will falsely suppose that the legitimate speculation is a safe venture. Other much-lauded devices to prevent speculative abuses, prominent among which is the much vaunted reform of removing the dollar sign from the share of stock, is, in my mind, a rather puerile device which, while harmless in itself, accomplishes nothing. As a panacea, it is like other patent medicines.

[35] To sum up: The corporation is one of the great achievements of the human, ranking with steam and electricity as aid to industry. It came to the world in response to the peculiar needs of the time, and has done valiant service in making possible the improvements of modern time. But the public looks askance at this great invention, for the democrat fears the power of agglomerated wealth, the consumer feels that he suffers from the extortion of monopolies (which he illogically identifies with corporations), and the poor sucker repines over the wildcat stock which he was induced to buy. Accordingly, many attempts have been made to remedy or prevent the evils or abuses. Primarily, this has taken the form of attempting to prevent extortion—principally in the case of public utilities. While these attempts have concerned themselves principally with a consideration of equitable treatment of investments already made, a really sound basis of public regulation must consider the effect of rate fixing on new enterprises, on the bearing of risks, on the enjoyment of the fruits of invention. And while fraudulent financing is properly a subject of legislative action, it cannot altogether protect the foolish investor from the process by which the fool and his money are soon parted.

Earlier Paper on Corporations, 1910

The advantages in the corporate form of business organization are generally stated to be threefold: immortality, limited liability, the bringing together of small amounts of capital. In the ordinary partnership, business is interrupted; it may even be that the firm will be dissolved in case of the death of one of the partners. The corporation goes on its way even though the entire body of stockholders should all be simultaneously killed by a sudden earthquake. The old phraseology is now rather misleading. Corporations now are seldom actually perpetual. The law may require all charters to be limited to twenty or fifty years. At present, this first merit of corporations would better be called a "definitely prolonged period of life." But even in the weaker form of expression it may easily be seen how important this limited immortality is for business requiring a large amount of invested capital.

The second merit of the corporation is limited liability (even in California where, in contrast to other states, the stockholder may be compelled to pay corporation debts without any absolute limit, he still can be compelled to pay only his proportionate share of the debts.) In a partnership, any one member of the firm may be compelled to pay the entire amount of the firm's debts no matter how large the debts nor how small his proportion of the firm's capital. Without doubt, the principle of limited liability has been the chief source of the advantage to be found in the corporation.

The third feature generally mentioned, that the corporation serves to unite small capitals, is important although it is not altogether a separate advantage, distinct from those already mentioned. True, the corporation does serve to unite and make more serviceable small portions of capital which, without such an instrument, could not be made available for industrial investment. But the fact that individual capitalists are willing to entrust their small sums to the management of the corporation is in itself the result of the other two features, the prolonged and definitely delimited life and the limited liability of the corporation.

The remedies suggested for corporation evils depend on the particular class of evils in the reformer's mind. Some extremists, who view with the greatest dismay the mere aggregation of wealth, have recommended the outright prohibition of corporations with more than a given limited capital, or the removal of limited liability, which in most cases would make capitalists unwilling to take a share in any excessively large aggregation.

Those who fear the monopolistic feature of corporate activity naturally recommend various measures which would make competition possible or which would limit the extortion possible under monopoly. More interesting, however, are the reforms suggested by those who wish to restrain the financial activities of corporations. Foremost among these are proposals to regulate the issue and sale of stock. The prevention of stock watering, a term vague and undefined, yet currently assumed to be a crying evil even by those who cannot define it, is sought by various devices. In most cases the issue of watered stock is already prohibited by law. This is done by requiring—as is the case even with that foster mother or wet nurse of most of the trusts, New Jersey, where there is so much water in the stock that it keeps all the region around Newark and Jersey City a perpetual mosquito breeding swamp—that stock may not legally be issued save for full value received. But while this doctrine is well established, unfortunately it is most difficult of application. Most of the stock of the large corporations is issued not for cash but in exchange for property purchased or services rendered by promoters or inventors. Naturally, it is a difficult matter to determine just what is the value of an extended plant for which stock is issued. Two men may disagree as to the value of a simple corner lot, and differ with perfect honesty, and with apparently equally good grounds for their varying beliefs. How absolutely impossible is it, then, to determine just what value should be affixed to a plant comprising perhaps scores of buildings, ore deposits in Michigan, coal mines in Pennsylvania, lime quarries in Indiana, railroads, steamships—a vast assortment of property whose real value it is impossible to state. In such cases, the courts have ordinarily accepted the judgment of the directors of the company as to the value. So far has that principle carried that in one case where a railroad cost $2,000 to construct, and had been purchased by a promoter for $15,000, the court held that its sale to a corporation for $3,800,000 in securities was not on the face a fraudulent transaction. Sometimes, however, the laws go a little further. Thus, in England and in some of our states, the law compels the promoter to give a full and explicit statement as to the exact property to be received for shares, and without requiring any authoritative statement of value either by the promoter himself or by an impartial board: attempts to put the investor in possession of the facts which will enable him to form his own opinion. Connecticut goes further, requiring the directors to state in writing their deliberate opinion that the property is worth the amount of stock given in exchange. They are liable for fraud in valuation. More drastic still are the regulations enacted in regard to certain corporations in Massachusetts, where, before the securities can be issued, the property must be examined by a state board, without whose sanction the transaction cannot be completed.

Financial control also takes the form of regulating dividends. The most universal rule in this matter is that no dividends may be paid that have not been earned. This well-recognized rule of law is designed primarily to protect the creditor of the corporation against loss due to the directors paying back to the stockholders their original contributions, in the guise of paying dividends. Incidentally, the prohibition of unearned dividends works also to the protection of investors. The payment of such dividends would create the impression that the stock was really profitable, and thus enable the directors to sell to outsiders at a great overvaluation. This, for instance, took place in the early history of the Union Pacific.

The restriction on dividends sometimes takes the form of limiting the amount of dividends that may be paid, requiring that any earnings in excess shall either be spent in improving the service, as in the case of a railroad, or be paid to the state in lieu of taxes. Other practices in regard to dividends which are sometimes regulated by law are the prohibition found against paying dividends out of borrowed money, and against paying out as dividends any profits which have not actually been received in cash, even though they may have been actually earned. (This restriction is found in the California Bank Law, and is entirely illogical in principle, however conservative and worthy the motives which led to enactment of that provision may have been.)

The prohibition of paying dividends in stock is very frequently found, a prohibition which rests rather on prejudice than on reason. Another way of regulating the finances of a corporation is by a public regulation of the prices which it may charge, thus directly and positively placing a restriction on the profits which it may earn. This is, of course, especially common in the case of railroads and other public service corporations. The extension of the same rule has, however, been urged in respect to any corporation having a virtual monopoly on its products or services.

The most satisfactory remedy for financial misdeeds is, however, the simple one of requiring publicity of accounts, with, of course, the implication that the accounts must be full and accurate. This not only remedies most of the abuses in the realm of finance, but even paves the way to prevent some of the other evils of modern corporations. Thus, for instance, the main evil of monopoly, that extortion is made possible, is less likely to be a permanent condition if the public is fully informed as to the exact rate of profits that are being made by the corporation on their actual investment. It is hardly conceivable that society will long endure an extortionate monopoly when once it knows the facts. But the actual conditions are so often concealed by a wrongful showing that the problem of restraint is made much more difficult.

The cheating of investors, and all the ills of stock-jobbing, would, however, soon be removed were full and accurate accounts published. The incidental forms of stock-jobbing would then become of little significance. The issuing of watered stock, for instance, would be of little or no significance if the accounts showed the correct value of the property and the fact that the stock really was issued in excess. Stock dividends are of little moment one way or the other if only the accounts are not distorted so as to allow unearned dividends to be paid.

It is true that there is one element necessary in addition to the publicity of accounts, and that is the ability of the public to understand the published accounts. Fortunately, there is evidence that advance is being made along that line. Without exaggerating the importance of universities, it is at least significant that all the leading universities, including even conservative Harvard, now give instruction in accounting, designed not so much for those who expect themselves to become accountants, but to enlighten the ordinary business man and the investor as to the meaning and interpretation of accounts. Thus, Professor Cole of Harvard has issued a most admirable book entitled *Accounts, Their Construction and Interpretation* [1908] for business men and students of affairs. Similarly, Mr. E.E. Garrison has issued a little work bearing the significant title, *Accounting Every Business Man Should Know* [1909]. With progress along this line, publicity seems the most vital reform to be brought about. Demand absolute truth in accounts so far as that is possible, take such measures as may be necessary to secure such truth, either by impartial supervision or by penalties rigidly enforced for false statements, and the dear public, so tenderly coddled in some ways by our legislatures, may pretty safely be left to look out for itself. (Some of the aims and methods of such proper accounting I hope to discuss at our next meeting.)

"Experiences with the War Industries Board," c. 1920

This paper, presented to the Berkeley Club around 1920, was prepared after Hatfield returned to Berkeley following his service as director of the Division of Planning and Statistics of the War Industries Board, in Washington. The presentation provides extensive information about his activities on the board, the work of other members of the board, and the goals of the board in general. It also provides insight into Hatfield's views, which he emphasized in other speeches, that a general cultural education best prepared individuals for whatever work they would be required to do (Paragraph 45). His admiration for the women who contributed to the war effort (Paragraphs 30, 35) illustrates his unflagging support for opportunities for women. The paper also conveys Hatfield's unswerving belief in the value of decisions based on analytical thinking, a perspective noted by former students and colleagues.

[1] The War Industries Board, as a separate organization, was established by executive order on May 28, 1918. Five somewhat similar bodies were established to assist in carrying on the war. These were the Fuel Administration, the Food Administration, the War Trade Board, which primarily regulated exports, the U. S. Shipping Board, which dealt more with imports and had control of the construction and operation of ships, and the War Industries Board which controlled the production of all commodities, other than food and fuel, which were of importance in the prosecution of the war. These boards, especially the last three, worked in close operation.

[2] I must forego any attempt to describe in detail the organization of the Board. The Board proper consisted of nine members, but legally these acted only in a co-operative and advisory capacity, for the charter explicitly stated, "the ultimate decision of all questions, except the determination of prices, should always rest with the chairman." In actual operation the organization consisted, therefore, of Bernard M. Baruch, a series of some fifty commodity sections, and a smaller number of Divisions of more general character.

[3] When Mr. Baruch was appointed chairman, the public questioned the wisdom of the selection. To put the control of all industries in the hands of a man who had not been concerned with any industry, to give more than dictatorial power to one known chiefly as a shrewd, successful, and (in the opinion of some) not too scrupulous operator in Wall Street, to entrust a stupendous organization to one whose business had been free of any organization, seemed, indeed, a venturesome procedure.

[4] But there is little dissent from the opinion that the selection was a happy one. To be sure, organization, in the narrow sense, was sadly lacking. The man whose business was such that, on coming to Washington, he needed only to put on his silk hat and close his desk, continued to show indifference to organization. He was quite likely to refer some inquiry to whomever happened to be in his office when the inquiry was received, even though he had previously appointed officials specifically charged with the administration of that particular subject

matter. But it would be picayunish to criticize for lack of organization one who made the thing work. Masterful, dignified, urbane, quick of decision, unflinching in purpose, above all skillful in selecting men and unstinting in the support given to his lieutenants, he was one of the distinct successes of war-time Washington.

[5] The bulk of the work of the War Industries Board was done by the several commodity sections, of which there were about fifty. These dealt, each with some commodity or group of commodities, as, for instance, the Automotive Products section, the Brass tubing section, the Chain section, and so on down the alphabet, to tobacco, wool and yarn. Each of these was controlled by a chief, a dollar-a-year man, a businessman, directly concerned with the industry. The sections were the seat of administrative authority, regulating the industry, summoning representatives to Washington in conference, directing production, allotting orders, assigning raw material, ruling the industry in such a way as to secure the product desired for war purposes. The men in control of these sections were generally of high ability, and, so far as any rumor goes, of quite unquestioned probity. There was Everett Morss, son of Harvard, nervous, excitable, wiry, full of quaint conceits, fertile in imagination, vigorous in action and expression, flamboyantly profane in language. There was Charles McDowell of Nitrates, a Chicagoan, an Adonis in figure, a Brummel in dress, a Chesterfield in manners, the only one in the staff of fifteen hundred who was reputed to have a private bath in his office. There was Russell Hubbard of Paint and Pigments, cultured Philadelphian, who, when called to the War Industries Board, came to Washington against his physician's orders, and, overworking in an ovenlike office during that awful August, gave up his life to his country as surely as did those in the Argonne. Manly in bearing, dignified yet lovable, a rare combination of strength and gentleness. In marked contrast there was J.H. Replogle of Steel, he of newspaper notoriety who like Schwab had been an operator in the mills, but had suddenly gained wealth and fame by single handedly buying out the Cambria plant. Brusque, bull-necked, intolerant of suggestions, stentorian voiced, yet apparently the man in the right place, controlling the entire destinies of that greatest of war necessities, steel. But it is impossible to go through the list of half a hundred. It was a remarkable aggregation of self-sacrificing, untiring, patriotic, broad-minded men, association with whom, even to one privileged to associate with the Berkeley Club, proved a stimulus, and an education.

[6] In addition to Barney Baruch and the Commodity Sections, the War Industries Board was made up of a series of more general divisions, dealing with certain activities common to all commodities. The most important of these general divisions were the Conservation Division, the Priorities Division, the Requirements Division, the Division of Planning and Statistics, and the Price Fixing Committee.

[7] Of these divisions, the Priorities was, in some respects, the most active and important. Its function was to see to it that the resources of the country were so apportioned as to secure the most efficient prosecution of the war. It determined what industries were most important, and decided the sequence in which manu-

facturers or producers of raw material should fill orders. This involved an immense amount of detail, and the personnel of the division was larger than that of any other. Myriads of applications were received asking for priority certificates. Thus, for example, a manufacturer of iron beds would ask that he be given a priority certificate so that his order for so many tons of tubing should be given priority by the manufacturer of tubing.

[8] In the latter part of the war, the work of this division expanded along another line. In August, matters began to be more urgent. The Steel Section finally awoke to the fact that the hopeful statistics which it had previously prepared were glaringly inaccurate. At about the same time, the program for a larger army made it evident that still greater supplies would be needed. In the confidential weekly meetings of the commodity chiefs, there was an air of depression, almost of panic. (Incidentally, I may say that ordinary air, of the atmospheric variety, was almost absent from that crowded and stifling committee room. One of my keenest memories of Washington is the intolerable suffocation in those weekly meetings. The room was packed and without ventilation, the afternoon sun beating down on the shell-like temporary structure. Indeed, my immediate superior promised, though the promise is still unfulfilled, to raise my salary because I had to attend those meetings. But this is a digression.) When estimates were made that, aside from any civilian uses of steel (and the country could not forego all such), there would be a deficit of seven million tons of steel in filling the mere requirements for war purposes, the dismay became almost despair. Should the promised shipments of steel to Japan be stopped, will it be necessary to lessen the production of ships, must the construction of new ways be abandoned, is it really necessary to make so many shells, is there also a shortage of pig iron, how large is the stock of steel hidden in warehouses? For a while, everyone agonized over such questions, and, especially for the statisticians, night seemed no longer to be considered a time for sleep, and Sunday lost its old character as a day of rest. It may be true that the poet "lisped in numbers for the numbers came." But the numbers with which the statisticians deal have not that happy-come-lucky disposition, and it is only with infinite pains that they are summoned. If it is not literally true that "such come only through fasting and prayer," it is certainly true that frequently they came only after fasting and prolonged vigils.

[9] At this time, the President ordered an investigation of the savings that might be secured through the elimination of non-essentials, and the committee which undertook this work was so nearly the same as the Priorities Division that in some of the meetings it was not always certain in which capacity it was acting. Known first as the Non-essential Committee, then as the Curtailment Committee, and still later as the Industrial Adjustment Committee, it came to be known, in select circles, as the Snickersnee Committee, because of the way in which industry after industry was summoned before it, each in turn being beheaded, or halved, or quartered in a single stroke. The chairman was Judge Parker, a Southern gentleman, a genial soul, exuding benignity from every pore and fairly beaming with benevo-

lence. Yet he could wield the snickersnee with the gusto of a Turk, and often turned the committee room into a shambles. In the early days, the slaughter was limited mainly to industries which consumed large quantities of iron or steel. First, automobiles, then metal beds, then elevators were attacked. But soon the list became more general. The production of all sorts of commodities was violently curtailed, from the baby carriage of infancy to the burial casket of age, pocket knives and pianos, the steels of milady's corset and the metal tops of bottled drinks, stoves and electric heaters, clothes wringers and sporting goods. One industry after another was ordered to cut its product 25, 30, even up to 66⅔ percent. As the work went on, the committee became more ruthless and oftentimes even amusing. Thus, in one meeting, Judge Parker ordered a cut in the production of sewing machines, stating that, in war time, women must forego such luxuries as sewing machines, and the few tons of steel used for watch springs were said to be, after all, something worth saving. I remember one meeting in which some very minor products—one of them was steel dies—were considered. The amount of steel in these seemed inconsiderable, but Mr. Woolley of Chicago waived aside my scruples with what became a formula, almost a ritualistic response. Having estimated the weight of a six-inch shell, he would say, "one hundred and twenty-five tons does not seem much, but it would make five hundred shells and perhaps one of those shells would be the last one necessary to destroy the last German fortress," and so with each changing item of possible saving. The committee was approaching the position that, not merely steel and fuel, but labor as well, must be cut off from non-war production. Thus, confectionery, chewing gum, and soft drinks were already reduced, and, had the armistice not come when it did, it is likely that a general order would have been issued cutting off labor from all occupations deemed not necessary for war needs.

[10] The Conservation Section did its work somewhat more logically and, in my opinion, much more efficiently. Its aim was not to curtail production, but to eliminate waste in production. Its most striking service was in showing manufacturers how their products could be made more economically, or how less-needed materials could be substituted. Instead of reducing the number of metal beds, it reduced the number of sizes and patterns, eliminated ornamentation, reduced the size of tubes and angle bars. Trunks were produced in fewer styles and patterns, sole leather was being eliminated, metal corners and other appurtenances reduced in number and weight. Instead of seventeen hundred varieties of hotel china, only three hundred and thirty were allowed. Zinc was substituted for aluminum in kodaks, composition for metal in automobile license plates, and five-thousand five-hundred varieties of rubber footwear were eliminated.

[11] The admirable work of this section was under the direction of A.W. Shaw, publisher of *System*—a business man, it is true, but one somewhat tinged with academic qualities, for he had organized much of the work of the Harvard Graduate School of Business Administration, and for a time himself lectured there. Mr. Shaw was inclined to believe that there was no necessity to economize on labor as

such, that the country did not, as many supposed, face a general shortage of labor. His argument was that, while there was a tremendous new demand for the production of war material, and a depletion of the ranks of labor through the draft, this was more than offset by the conversion of pre-war industries into war activities (as where a watch factory devoted itself to the manufacture of time fuses), by the cutting off of demand for luxuries both by voluntary abstention in order to buy liberty bonds and by the natural effect of high prices, and by the entering into industry of the vast number of women, previously industrially idle. Whether he was correct in this opinion is not determined. Our own Professor Daggett was, at the time of the armistice, engaged in a most interesting investigation along this line. He had not gone much farther than to make a preliminary survey of a few industries with a view to ascertaining whether it would be possible to obtain convincing statistics along these lines. Naturally, the armistice put a damper even on his love for research. The subject, however, demands further investigation by statisticians. Surely, nothing would be more fruitful than a knowledge of the precise effect of war on industry, nothing could be more valuable in determining governmental policies in the untoward event of war again breaking out.

[12] The Requirements Division was a failure. Its function was to ascertain the supplies required for war purposes, including the needs of army, navy, Marine Corps, railroad administration, shipping board, Red Cross, and other essential war agencies. All such agencies were supposed to submit to the Requirements Division detailed statements of their future needs. But, from the first, difficulty was experienced in obtaining these figures. The army, being the largest consumer of war goods, was generally the storm center. The desideratum was a schedule of requirements expressed in terms of the individual soldier, so that it would be a simple matter of a multiplying machine to determine the additional requirements of each article caused by an increase in the personnel of the army. But at first the army had no such figures, nor was there any uniformity in the method of making estimates. According to a statement made to me by General Hugh S. Johnson, known to many of you, and whose phenomenal rise from Lieutenant to Brigadier General doubtless excited your surprise and admiration, there were at least seven different branches of the army which made entirely separate estimates, without any uniformity of method, and often expressed in incommensurate terms. He attempted to secure some system and order, but, according to his statement (which was made after the war was over, and therefore I presume was not a privileged communication), his efforts were frowned upon, and he was given to understand that his function (as Director of the Division of Purchases) was to buy what he was told to buy, not to attempt to introduce system into the formulation of requirements. Very wild estimates were frequently made. One of them, run to earth by W.C. Mitchell, related to the requirements for leather. The number of halters asked for, when translated into the number for each mule, would have implied that the army mule was more than a Cerberus, almost a hydra. So, too, with shoes, the estimates of both these items far exceeding the needs actually experienced by the

British Army during that very war. The proof of the inaccuracy thus brought out by one "of those damned professors" (I assure the Berkeley Club that my manuscript has inverted commas around those offensive words) was so conclusive that the stated requirements were duly modified.

[13] The estimates of requirements were much belated in reaching the War Industries Board. Many of the important schedules for the year beginning July 1, 1918, did not reach the Board until November of that year; some had not then arrived. The statement of requirements and the request for permission to make specific purchases (the "Clearance," as it was called in War Industries Board jargon) were frequently received after the goods had already been purchased by the army.

[14] The greatest difficulty was in respect of the so-called "conversion factor." A requirement for a harness had to be converted into a requirement for so many feet of various kinds of leather, and this into terms of hides. The conversion of requirements into terms of component parts, then into terms of raw materials, in many cases was vastly complicated. I will not attempt to analyze what the production of an airplane signifies. But even so minute a thing as the speck of platinum needed in the magneto was significant, and had to be combined with demands for platinum by the medical corps, in wireless service, in transport service, and elsewhere, for at that time platinum was so scarce that every known ounce was catalogued, and none could be sold without permission of the War Industries Board. But even more complicated requirements were presented, as, for instance, for a "train unit," fully equipped with the various machine shops, repair shops, machines, tools and supplies.

[15] It should be borne in mind that the army had a task of infinite difficulty. It is by no means easy to convert even a dynamo into all its constituent parts. It can be done only by experts, and the task presents some of the characteristics of an infinite regression. But the failure to have such statements was a serious, incalculably serious, impediment to the functioning of the War Industries Board.

[16] I come last to the division in which I was particularly concerned, the Division of Planning and Statistics, the second largest of the War Industries Board. But its work has little of interest to you who did not share in its labors. To us, there was much, not merely of interest, but of fascination and of artistic satisfaction. My entering the work was a little peculiar and may be mentioned as somewhat typical of much of war work. I left Berkeley, having been called to the Shipping Board, to work under W.C. Mitchell in scientific work for which my studies in accounting seemed to fit me. When I reached Washington, I was set to work with the War Industries Board, nominally over, instead of under, Mitchell, and in purely administrative rather than academic work, being called Director of the Division of Planning and Statistics. The work was not in itself alluring, for there were many difficulties connected with the reorganization and expansion of a disrupted organization. But it was not easy to refuse a war task, especially when presented by E.F. Gay.

[17] Gay had, previously, organized the statistical work of the Shipping Board, with such eminent success that he was asked to supervise also the statistical work of the War Trade Board, the War Industries Board, and later the Central Bureau of Planning and Statistics. Tower of Chicago, Swanson, Dean of Commerce of Northwestern, and myself were respectively made directors of the statistical work of the three boards, each acting under the direction of Gay. In this way, the fullest co-operation was secured in the work of the three boards, to the great benefit of the service. It was one of my chiefest pleasures to be brought into such close contact with Gay of whom (since he has just become editor of the *New York Post* and hence is not even a Presidential possibility) I can now speak without suspicion of being his campaign manager. Mr. Gay's whole attitude was that action should be based on the fullest knowledge obtainable and not on the business man's "hunch." His instructions were, "Get all the facts that can possibly be gathered within the time limit, and then use a hunch for the rest." A born administrator, indefatigable in work, inspiring to his associates, fearless, outspoken yet diplomatic, he became a real force in Washington.

[18] The Division of Planning and Statistics was itself divided into several sections, such as the Price Section, the Commodities Section, and the Editorial Section. Its function was primarily to gather information for any subdivision of the War Industries Board, though it very often assisted other governmental agencies, such as the Federal Trade Commission, the Department of State, and, of course, the army.

[19] The most satisfactory part of the work was in reference to Price Statistics, for which there was a special section conducted by W.C. Mitchell. His job, like that of a bishop, was a "nice, clean, decent job," academic in its nature, dealing generally with available records. Mitchell is the leading authority on price statistics, and you need not be told that his task was executed with superlative excellence. With a large force of assistants, he prepared many series of price statistics and charts, in most instances for submission to the Price Fixing Committee. When the armistice came, the section undertook an even more comprehensive general survey of prices during war time which was crystallized in a series of fifty-seven reports now coming off the government press. These constitute the most comprehensive piece of price statistics ever attempted.

[20] More interesting in a way were the special investigations made to meet some emergency. The first one undertaken by the Division is typical. It attempted to learn the amount of castor oil used for each of the various purposes to which that protean liquid is put. The air service found castor oil the best lubricant for airplane engines. The supply was somewhat limited, but, before commandeering the entire supply, the general staff desired to learn how important the other uses were, and how much might be saved if substitutes could be found for certain of these uses. At that time, there was no one in the United States, or elsewhere, who could answer the question. How much was produced and how much was imported was known. How it was used was a new inquiry. It was necessary, therefore, to go

back to the original producers or importers, find from them the jobbers to whom they sold, obtain the lists of customers from the jobbers, and so on until definite information was reached or intelligent guesses could be made. I cite this merely as an example of the kind of tasks attempted, and to give an idea of the appeal which such an investigation makes to the hunting instinct still surviving in the soul of the statistician.

[21] At another time, the army gave orders that in the future all army uniforms should contain a certain proportion of shoddy. This at once affected the rag market, and woolen rags formerly selling at about two cents a pound jumped, I believe, to about sixteen cents. This, of course, could not be tolerated, and the Division of Planning and Statistics was asked to make a statistical investigation of the rag market. It was a surprise to me to learn that the rag market is one of the most highly organized markets in the country. It is divided into a hierarchy of different divisions, beginning with the familiar rag picker, and ending with the magnate who sells the sorted and graded rags. In this hierarchy, there are, I believe, four grades quite as distinct as are the solicitors and the barristers of the English bar. It was also a surprise to learn that rags are not merely rags, but are graded, not into a score or so as is cotton or grain, but into over three hundred distinct grades, each having a duly recognized, but constantly fluctuating price. This investigation was turned over to a slip of a girl, graduate of Bryn Mawr, with much statistical training and experience, who up to then was working on the statistics of wool. Before long, she had twenty statisticians and clerks working under her, and the rag-lady was gathering the information necessary for any intelligent effort to regulate the industry, when the armistice interfered with the full fruition of her toil and skill.

[22] I merely mention the investigation of soft drinks carried on by Professor Wildman, head of economics at Stanford; and of Automobiles, of Non-essential Industries, of the effects of curtailments on industry, of the general effect of war on industry, of the possible effects of a Thrift Campaign, all supervised by Professor Daggett.

[23] One of the intolerable things which grew up in war time was the unlimited number of questionnaires sent to manufacturers. Apparently every governmental agency used its spare moments in sending out questionnaires. Frequently, these covered the same ground, yet with sufficient variation to make it impossible for the manufacturer to use the same figures for two reports, as, for instance, in one case he must report all employees under sixteen, in another all under eighteen. Furthermore, the framing of a questionnaire is a special art, and those prepared by amateurs frequently proved worthless, and a revised edition was sent to the overburdened manufacturer. In many factories, special bureaus had to be established merely to answer government questionnaires—one factory had a force of twenty in such a bureau. One company, because of having accepted a contract for about six hundred dollars, found it necessary to fill out a questionnaire the preparation of which involved a cost of over two thousand dollars. Yet these questionnaires

had to be answered. In one case where the benignant Judge Parker thought, somewhat unfairly, that there had been undue delay in replying to an inquiry regarding sporting arms, I was ordered to telegraph each manufacturer that, unless immediate replies were received, his supply of fuel, raw materials and transportation would straightway be cut off. I feel it safe, at this time and distance, to confess that the telegram I actually sent was so emasculated that its progenitor would never have recognized it as his progeny.

[24] The abuse became so great that a separate section was organized in the Division of Planning and Statistics which first offered to assist any subdivision of the War Industries Board which planned to send out questionnaires. In October, an order was issued by Mr. Baruch that all questionnaires sent out by any part of the Board must go through this section. Having thus centralized the questionnaires of the War Industries Board, steps were being taken to secure uniformity and co-operation between all governmental agencies. This was a more difficult task and was not yet accomplished on the fateful eleventh day of November.

[25] Our work certainly did not lack variety. It is literally true that, like the walrus, the Division of Planning and Statistics spoke of many things, of shoes and ships and sealing wax, and cabbages—even though kings were outside our jurisdiction.

[26] To show somewhat the diversity of activities which fell to my lot, I quote a sentence written at the time, enumerating the activities of a single day: "I am learning to be as wise as serpents and as harmless as doves. In addition to the regular conferences and other routine matters, I today conciliated Colonel H., called down the Requirements Division for a fool thing done by one of their men, appeased the Chemical Division for that same fool act, crawled before the Miscellaneous Section for sending out a questionnaire without consulting the chief, jollied Dr. W. who is being tempted to go into other statistical work with the lure of a uniform and gold maple leaves, hired a new expert, promised Guylee to do everything he wanted but persuaded him he did not really want what he thought he did, and incidentally learned all that could be learned about whiting." On that day, the thermometer was up to a hundred, and I, a red headed man, spent most of my energy acting as peace-maker regarding matters of which I was personally innocent. It was indeed the life!!

[27] Finally came the time when peace was first whispered, then spoken of, then planned for. The early mentioning of peace was thought to be harmful because it inevitably had a deterrent effect on the work of the Board. The President's message to Prince Max took much zest out of the work, and, before the end of October, interest in war activities was distinctly declining. It was hard to get the manufacturers of shoes, for instance, to plan for the manufacturing campaign of 1920 when it was felt that peace might come at any day. The first official action recognizing the possibility of peace was on November 5, when we were directed to prepare statistics which might be useful at the peace table.

[28] In connection with this work, there occurred so characteristic an episode that I must refer to it. The statistical divisions were practically merged in the preparation of a great series of charts and huge statistical sheets covering all the commodities which perhaps might be considered at the Peace Table. By dint of unstinting labors, including meal-less days, restless Sundays and sleepless nights, the material was delivered at the day and hour specified, and a special messenger was deputed to take it to New York to catch a steamer. But that very evening, plans were changed: the reports were to be taken abroad by a new commission which could not leave for two weeks. And so the labor had much of it to be done over, for that which was the best obtainable in the shorter space of time could be much improved, especially in the matter of form. But, oh, if only the latter date could have been known at the beginning. There followed another series of vigils, resulting in the preparation of a report of eight volumes, issued in photostatic form, a most limited edition of only six copies, one of the most expensive publications ever prepared. While all the boards co-operated, the immediate task of getting out the edition fell to my own division, and I shall never forget the strenuous and devoted work of those having it in charge. It had to be delivered to Major Dulles at 8:30 of a certain morning. It was finished at some hour the night before, and the weary but exultant workers betook themselves to Child's, whose all night feature was to war workers frequently like the shadow of a rock in a weary land. Would that someone would properly celebrate Child's, feeder of the hungry, recourse of the poor, winner of the war. There was a time when I might have blushed to mention that proletarian resort in your presence. But on my first visit I met Professor Jameson, another time I sat next to an officer whom I had last seen at an Olympic Club dinner, on a third occasion I sat opposite Max Thelen. The social status of Child's is established.

[29] The coming of the armistice was in a way depressing. Particularly was this noticeable in the case of Gay. He was one who had worked unceasingly, shouldering any responsibility, shunning no man's criticism, courting no one's approval. Others of us felt discouraged at times. I know that I resigned twice myself, and Swanson of War Trade did so every few weeks. But Gay was always composed, reliant, apparently free from the weakness either of exultation or depression. But when the armistice came, he too fell into the Slough of Despond. In part it was due to the removal of the intoxicating stimulant of war work, in part, as Dennison told him, it was merely the result of the thwarted instinct of workmanship. And that was doubtless true. After months of strenuous endeavor, things were straightening out. Within two weeks before the armistice, two distinct victories had been won in the cause of intelligent administration. In a hard-fought battle, the Shipping Board had consented to handle certain matters purely from the point of view of war policy, and, after many struggles, the Secretary of War had at last issued an order definitely placing the army records at the disposition of the Division of Planning and Statistics. The era of unsatisfactory work seemed ended, the opportunity for which Gay, and those associated with him, had longed and worked and

prayed seemed already realized, and then came that wretched armistice. Unfinished work on hand, into which every atom of energy had been put in the expectation that it might, when finished, advantage the government, became worthless junk which no one wished to complete. No one enjoys looking back on fruitless toil, and it is no wonder that depression came to all.

[30] Already I tire you with details interesting to the participants, but dry to you outsiders, prosaic to those who were in active service. May I, however, add some general impressions of Washington and its war work. The first was that of the morning and evening processions on the way to and from office. I had never before been an office-holder, but, in former years, I had spent much time in Washington. The contrast was most marked, not merely in the numbers which transformed Washington from a sleepy village to a crowded city, but also in the character of the persons. No longer a rather sad array of aged veterans or of professional office-holders, whose life and initiative had been killed by the dreary routine of a government job, but an army of women, young and ambitious, keen eyed, wide awake, enthusiastic, inspired, the best that America had, each zealous to do her bit. Thus, in my own division there were, among others, a woman professor of mathematics, a sister of a Justice of the Supreme Court, and a prominent society girl of Washington, daughter of a Navy officer, who, after taking a day off, returned as the bride of another. But there were no traditional clock watchers, there was none of the time service rendered by political henchmen. One bright girl from the University of California was typical, though fortunately extreme. She worked all day in the Red Cross, and then worked on a night shift in the War Risk Insurance Board, rosy, fresh, claiming to have gained twelve pounds in the process. One particular type of girl, though not very numerous, was much in evidence in the restaurants. I can best describe her as the girl graduate who reads the *New Republic* through large shell-rimmed spectacles, while she smokes cigarettes, not so much in a manner savoring of personal indulgence as with the air of one determinedly standing up for her convictions.

[31] A second impression was of the devotion, the patriotism, the forgetfulness of the dollar, on the part of the average business man. I refer not merely to the dollar-a-year man, but to the representatives of the industries who were called to Washington to confer with the War Industries Board. Never did they seem reluctant to put up with any restrictions which would advantage the government. They would, of course, try to show how their particular industry was serving government needs, that, for instance, the manufacturers of composition roofing ought to be allowed to put special nails in each roll of roofing, because the use of such roofing, instead of making a drain on steel, actually saved it so many more nails being required for shingles. But where it appeared that a cutting down of the industry would help the government, there was, to my knowledge, never a word of complaint, or objection, never even a plea for leniency. One day I chanced to hear the long-distance telephone message given by a business man, a member of the board. He was speaking not as an official of the board, but as the manager of

his own factory out in Illinois to which he was talking. The burden of his remarks was that the factory must turn out two hundred artillery wheels a day. I could not hear the man in Illinois, but could infer somewhat of his excuses and explanations. Lumber was hard to find, "flu" was prevalent, costs were high, difficulties of one kind and another were faced. Never did I hear more forceful and direct statements made. If lumber was scarce, send out men with axes and have them steal every hickory tree within reach; the wheels must be turned out; I don't care a damn what they cost; let the company go bust if necessary, but those wheels must be supplied, etc., etc. This, I think, was typical. Public, not private interests; war, not business; government, not stockholders; patriotism, not dollars, was the attitude of the business man as he showed up in the War Industries Board.

[32] It was due to this attitude of the business interests, rather than to its own qualities, that the War Industries Board proved so successful. To be sure, the board had power to enforce its orders. In one case, a manufacturer was fined $75,000 for disregarding priority orders. Another instance of coercion occurred in respect of an owner who came to the chief of the Cotton Linters Section complaining of the low price which the government proposed to pay for linters, and rather defied the section to make him sell. Mr. James, a perfectly gigantic mass of flesh, yet with all the suavity of the Southern, told him he did not have to sell if he did not want to. But, he added, "Of course, if you do not sell you cannot ship elsewhere, for no transportation will be furnished either on land or sea; you cannot use them in manufacture, for no fuel will be furnished you, and the banks will refuse to extend the credit by which you are carrying them." With a most engaging smile, Mr. James said to me, "The man came back the next day and said he would be good."

[33] While means of coercion thus were not lacking, the effective force was the spirit of loyal co-operation rather than official mandate. Dr. Clark recently called our attention to the fact that the rationing of food in the United States, where it was practically a voluntary matter, was much more effective than in Germany, where it was prescribed by law. So in regard to industries. It was voluntary compliance with suggested measures rather than the urge of a cracking whip that brought success. It was in part due to this condition that the War Industries Board melted away almost while the armistice was being signed. Some thought control ought to continue through the period of reconstruction. Perhaps a keener insight saw that, with the cessation of arms, industry would at once become restive, would no longer practice self discipline, and that coercion would be difficult, and indeed impossible.

[34] A third impression was of the omnipresence of the professor. On the face, this was flattering to my profession, though on closer thought the inference was not so clear. I remember when in college, six of the baseball team at Northwestern were members of Phi Kappa Psi. Those of us who were Betas did not interpret this as showing some one-to-one correlation between Phi Kappa Psi and ability to play ball, but rather linked it up with the fact that the captain of the ball team was him-

self a member of that fraternity. It is quite conceivable that, with a professor for President, important positions were filled with men of his caste. (I apologize if any of you think I am slamming the profession.) But it remains to be proved that these positions were well filled. I remember the complaisance with which one Commodity Chief told me how the administration was going to absolute chaos until business men were brought down to take the place of those professors. The Dean of Commerce at Northwestern tells the following on himself. He was coming out of a committee meeting in which they had decided to prohibit the importation of human hair. One interested in the business entered into converse with him, knowing neither who he was nor what part he had had in making the rule. He said such a fool rule could only have been made by some damned professor who probably supposed that human hair was imported to make wigs, when really it was used as filter cloth in making linseed oil, a war necessity. And Swanson admitted to me that the man had correctly diagnosed the situation.

[35] On another occasion, a special committee composed of college professors was studying a detailed list of commodities to determine which were non-essential. The list of cotton manufactures was being read when the item "corset laces" appeared. Straightway spoke forth a distinguished professor from Pennsylvania (a married man, by the way), saying: "Corset laces certainly are not essential. They can just as well wear them without any trimming." When I was told this, I immediately requested a bright woman graduate of the University of California to serve on the committee.

[36] Everywhere the professor and his kin were present. It seemed at times as if most of the war work was transacted at the Cosmos Club. My own impression is that much of it was well done, some superlatively well. The professor showed more poise and even more practicality than the hard-headed practical man of affairs. The latter was more apt to go off on unfounded rumors, and baseless conclusions. Fact was needed in this war, not fancy, and the trained scholar stuck somewhat closer to fact than the intuitional business man.

[37] Outstanding among college professors was Lincoln Hutchinson, who, despite his calling, did practically the work of a section chief. While not officially head of the Tin Section, he not only became the great authority on the statistics of tin, but was a potent factor in regulating affairs.

[38] A characteristic incident occurred in connection with a tin mine in one of the southern states. Because of a dispute between two litigants, it was lying idle and had not been worked, I believe, for about thirty years. Hutchinson tried in vain to secure an amicable working adjustment between the litigants. Failing in this, he succeeded in having the mine taken over by the government, made an arrangement that one of the litigants should operate it, paying rental into the probate court to be held by the court pending the decision as to which contestant was entitled to the rent so paid. So important were the services rendered by Hutchinson that when it was decided that there should be an international, not merely a

national, regulation of tin, he was one sent over to London to perfect such an arrangement.

[39] A fourth most vivid impression was the confusion and rush of it all. Several different bodies all attempting the same thing. Everyone impatient of delay, and finding it easier to start a new bureau than to rely on the information gathered by several similar bureaus already in existence. Centralized bureaus established to combine the work of others and prevent duplication, the result often being merely the addition of another duplicating wheel. One was impressed with the pity of it all—everyone was overworked, conditions of work were not favorable, there was much work not done at all, and workers were scarce—and yet on every hand duplication of effort, unnecessary interference with business through multiplication of reports and interviews, and lamentable waste of paper when the paper section cried for conservation.

[40] The rush of the work was at once a charm and a despair. My first task is typical. It was to prepare an elaborate report on the production, consumption and requirements of all the leading commodities. This was to be sent to a conference in London, and must be finished in two days in order to catch a steamer. It is true that, when nearly done, notice was sent that thirty-six hours more time could be taken, but that was more an aggravation than a blessing. An eighty-page report was sent on time. Imperfect, of course, but, as Dennison said, a damn sight better than other reports sent at the same time. This is not self praise, for the work was done by members of the staff, not by myself.

[41] Similarly, Wildman prepared a report on soft drinks in four days; Daggett had little longer for automobiles. Finished work could not be done. The criterion of success was not the completeness of the report, but whether the report was the best that could be prepared and contained all the information which could be gathered in the time limit.

[42] Of course, the army was a trial. It had thrust upon it duties to which it was unaccustomed, and for which it was unprepared. Being the army, it naturally thought that it should run the war in all its aspects, and attempted, even at that late date, to install the system which had been tried and rejected by England before we entered the war, of giving control of matters civilian, as well as matters military, to the army. The army organization, with its military etiquette, rank, and red-tape was incompatible with the best results in ordinary affairs. Even within the statistical division of the General Staff, there was so much friction that some branches would hardly communicate their findings to other branches of the same division.

[43] It was a distinct revelation to my civilian mind to learn that army orders were not always obeyed. I have seen formal orders directing that certain statistical reports should be regularly sent to a given army officer. But though this order was issued in the summer, it was still unaccomplished in November. General Goethals gave other orders that certain officers detailed to co-operate with the Commodity Sections of the War Industries Board should actually be on the job, keeping desks in the War Industries Board building, and that, if necessary, they would be

relieved of any conflicting duties. This was hailed with delight by the officials of the War Industries Board, thinking at last real co-operation would be secured. Only in very few of the fifty sections were the orders carried out.

[44] Apparent extravagance was one of the features of war-time Washington. Every clerk in the War Industries Board building had a wickedly expensive oak desk, telegrams were sent lavishly and needlessly, forms were printed one hundred thousand at a time and never used, reports reproduced by the expensive photostat process were in evidence everywhere—and yet, I am not sure that the extravagance was culpable. It was so much more important to have them done in the cheapest possible manner. Information was so much more important than dollars that some carelessness in matters of detail is excusable. As was said, "If we can stop the war ten minute sooner, almost any extra expense will be justified."

[45] Another striking fact was that so few men seemed to be assigned to work corresponding to their previous training. With the exception of strictly technical and engineering work, men seemed to be selected rather on the basis of general training and ability. If the war was at all well managed, the experience should be something of an argument against specialized, and in favor of general cultural education. A college dean was assistant secretary of war, a Wall Street operator controlled industry, a miner regulated food, a Texas judge curtailed manufactures, a college president administered fuel, the editor of a provincial paper ruled exports, and a manufacturer of pneumatic tools was autocrat over our imports. I even met a professor of English in the University of Manila who, at the time, was functioning as expert on the exportation of electrical machinery to Argentina.

[46] As I look back on the year at Washington, there is much that was unsatisfactory. Factors to be mentioned are the pressure under which most of the work was done, a certain lack of co-operation between different governmental agencies, especially between the army and civilian bodies, the fact that everyone's nerves were much stretched and somewhat jangled, that offense was taken when none was intended, that those charged with a given task did not always receive full support from members of the board, that one was hampered by ludicrous notions of secrecy. Altogether, work in Washington, especially with the official thermometer registering 112, was such that, only in the sense in which Guatamozin used the words, could one have said, "And I, do I lie upon a bed of roses?" My stock admonition to members of the Division of Planning and Statistics was that if one looked only on the impediments to satisfactory work one would either resign or go crazy in twenty-four hours. But when one really got into the game, regarding the difficulties only as one regards the hazards and bunkers in golf, when one could ignore jangled nerves, whether one's own or another's, and realize that the game was to do all that could be done with conditions as they were—why, then, the work became infinitely fascinating, the rush was an added charm, the difficulties, like the difficult crags of the Sierra, became the very essence of enjoyment. We tame civilians missed the thrill of active service, but I believe we all feel that even our experience in Washington was something we would not have

missed, and I am sure I speak for Daggett, as well as myself, in expressing our deepest gratitude to those of our colleagues who, generously taking over much of the burden of our university work, made it possible for us to be in Washington.

"The State University and the Body Politic: The Southern Branch of the University of California," 1922

This paper exemplifies Hatfield's skill in developing the traditional expository essay, on this occasion to honor the Southern Branch of the University of California, in Los Angeles. In his capacity as dean of the faculties, Hatfield presented this paper at the Charter Day Assembly, on March 23, 1922, at the University's Southern Branch. On July 24, 1919, Los Angeles State Normal School had become the Southern Branch. The Branch was renamed the University of California at Los Angeles (UCLA) on February 1, 1927.

The paper opens with an *exordium* in which he compliments Los Angeles by linking the city to Thor, the god of thunder. In many of his essays, Hatfield revealed his classical education by allusions to Greek myth, often in an attempt to show that current issues could be approached according to classical paradigms. Paragraphs 1-6 form the introduction in which Hatfield sets the stage for developing his thesis, stated in Paragraph 6, to explain the requirements of contemporary higher education. He then surveys the history of education, through Egypt, Greece, early Western Europe, England, and now in modern democracies, where education, he notes, has become essential. He argues that the modern university requires financial freedom, the fullest intellectual freedom, and freedom from the bondage of excessive drudgery that would stifle the creativity of faculty.

¶ 1-6: *Exordium* and introduction;
¶ 6: Thesis;
¶ 7: Financial freedom;
¶ 8: Intellectual freedom;
¶ 9: Dangers of censorship; and
¶ 10: Bondage of routine.

In the remaining paragraphs, Hatfield calls for democratic rather than aristocratic education and reveals his paradoxical stance on accounting, a perspective that would pervade his teaching and shape his approach toward the development of the accounting program at Berkeley (Paragraphs 11-12). The *preroratio* and conclusion comprise Paragraphs 23-26.

The essay provides a concise statement of Hatfield's philosophy of higher education, his belief in classical education as the most practical education because it teaches students how to think, and his rationale for academic freedom in an age in which tenure was unknown. In his final point, he argues that reverence for the past must not nullify the need for the modern state to change and to recognize that need. Ironically, in warning against reverence for the past, Hatfield did not see that his own view that classical education provided adequate education for all students betrayed his own inability to see and acknowledge the need for change in higher education curriculum, particularly business education.

From a stylistic perspective, Hatfield uses a number of coherence devices to develop his thesis—particularly, the opening sentences of each paragraph. In most paragraphs, the opening sentences state the topic of the paragraph, often serving as a transition to link the previous paragraph to the one that follows.

¶ 7: Discussion of financial freedom for faculty;
¶ 8: Links this idea with the need for fullest intellectual freedom; and
¶ 11: Announces freedom from deadening routine, and concludes the paragraph with a restatement of the three freedoms: financial, intellectual, and from bondage to a machine-like routine.

[1] Los Angeles, smiled upon by Nature, enriched, not by the barren gold mines, but by the ever replenishing gold of its groves, and by its inexhaustible and revivifying golden sunlight, has been even more richly endowed by its peculiar citizenry, a gathering together from all the states, of those who had somewhat of the initiative without the crudeness of the pioneers of '49—a people mature, successful, combining experience and adventure—a people of ideals and of hopes.

[2] In such a surrounding attention to education was inevitable, and within, or close to this wonder city there appeared a host of colleges—Southern California, Occidental, Throop, Pomona—all reflecting credit on the communities which established them, all rendering high service to those within their influence.

[3] But less than three years ago, there appeared in Los Angeles an intruder, for the State University, for half a century confined to the North, began to lead a double life. Unsatisfied with its domestic establishment among the Berkeley fogs, it came to this more genial clime, and said: "Here, I will make, at least, one of my homes." It was as if Thor, or some other of the mist-enveloped Gods of the Northland, had suddenly moved down to sunny Greece, and begun at once to flirt with the muses of Parnassus.

[4] I do not ask why the University, staid and senile, should have taken this surprising step. A half million people in Los Angeles can give reasons why any person, individual or institutional, should migrate to this city, of which one cannot

speak without seriously encroaching upon his stock of superlatives. But why, I ask, should Los Angeles desire another college—for, I may as well admit that even muses are not always unduly coy, and that the newcomer did not come altogether without invitation, but felt assured of a hearty welcome. Were not the institutions native to the South sufficient to her needs—institutions which were part of the very life of the community, sanctified by the devotion of their founders, imbued with a spirit of true religion in which a State institution can with difficulty share, grown into conformity with the spirit of your own people (a spirit, in many respects, alien to that inherited from the Argonauts of the North). Why, I ask, should Los Angeles desire another institution of learning? Why pick out the State University as a desirable addition to the intellectual life? What is there that a State institution could contribute to your already ample endowment?

[5] This is a question hard to answer. Perhaps the answer can be arrived at only indirectly by considering the relation between the University and the State, by considering what services it can render, and on the other hand, the claims which it can make on the people of the state for support and sympathy—the reciprocal rights and obligations.

[6] It would be an affront to an audience composed in so large a part of professional educators, should I attempt to instruct you in any of the details of the history of education. But I may, without impertinence, recall to you some few features, for the sake of using them as pegs on which to hang the thread of my discourse. Even without being professional educators, everyone knows, for everyone has read Wells's *Outline*, that education on a general scale is a recent institution. We hear much of the lore of Egypt, of the skill of her engineers, of the early knowledge of astronomy, of the libraries and schools, even half-believed hints of a transcendent lore dealing with things mystical, uncanny and awful. Yet we know that in Egypt, despite all this, education did not reach the masses, and that the educated few were a class by themselves, joined in a mystic and exclusive cult.

[7] We are more at home in the learning of classical lands, and we still long for the Augustan Age, for the golden age of Pericles. We still go back to Greece for our most significant buildings, still do we grope in attempts to master Greek Philosophy, still, after all these centuries, do we find our culture resting essentially on that of Greece. But we are told that Greek education could reach only to a limited aristocracy, and that teaching and the carrying on of literary and philosophical activities was, in part, the function of mere slaves, bred for that purpose, somewhat as hunters and canaries are bred to rival Pegasus and Euterpe.

[8] We know still more of the revival of learning in western Europe, and academic nomenclature, and academic garb, traced back to the great medieval universities of England. Still, there are many who think that the most appropriate housing of our universities is that modeled upon, or copied from, the halls and colleges of Oxford and Cambridge. Yet we are told that both these institutions were the universities of the rich—that they were part of the machinery of aristocracy;

that they became the educational preserve of the nobility and gentry; that the classical training characteristic of England was the education of an aristocratic leisured class, who had not to earn their living.

[9] A later development of education in England seemed more general and more popular. But this came when it was found that the wise use of machinery demanded a type of mind superior to that of the drudge, who was valued because his arms could wield a hoe, or his back could bear a burden. And education, so far as it became popular, was rather limited to what the upper classes thought an artisan ought to know, not that which an intelligent democracy would itself elect to learn.

[10] Throughout most of its history, we find education tied to slavery, to patronage, to aristocracy, to making men more valuable to their employers. "It was limited," says Wells, "to the idea of capturing young clever people for the service of their betters, and popular education, in any broad sense, was regarded, by the upper and middle classes, with hostility as a mischievous thing."

[11] But with the growth of the democratic state, education became, at least theoretically, the essential thing. Without education, and widespread education at that, the Democracy must fall of its own weight, or explode in the fires of revolution, leaving only the blackened ruins of a State. Even with this idea of education, it was for a time left to private endowment, was still a prerogative of a chosen few. The State University, with doors wide open, with education practically free, offered not as a benefaction from the rich, but as a right and duty, established and paid for by the people themselves, ushered in a new era in higher education: A new era still in its infancy. An educational movement, dazzling in its promises, surprising in its audacity, imperfect in its achievement, inchoate as yet in its organization—but, with all its faults, the hope of society, the earnest of progress, the last resort and salvation (if such there be) for perplexed and bewildered mankind.

[12] Surely then, it is not to be wondered at, that your community should welcome the State University. Even though you were richly supplied with other colleges, surely you too could appreciate the advantage of having such an institution, rich in possibilities, and unique in purpose, as a part of your community life.

[13] Now, while almost all things transplanted to your soil have thrived and flourished, we should inquire what are the conditions necessary to the welfare of the new importation, what soil does it need, how shall it be valued and cultivated, that it may bring forth abundant fruit in its season?

[14] In the first place, it must be ever kept in mind that a State University stands for the newer ideal of education; that the old Grecian notion that a teacher and a philosopher might still be a slave; that he differed little from the later type of court fool, displaying his wits for the amusement and for the exaltation of his kingly patron, is no longer appropriate. Whether the old verse—"To rule the free, one must himself be free"—is true or not, it is undoubtedly true of one who is to teach the free. This implies several things. The most obvious is that the teacher, unlike the slave, must receive an adequate compensation for his labors, a compensation,

not necessarily equal to that which men of equal ability might gain in commercial pursuits, but one which, after making due allowance for the spiritual compensations of teaching, and the attractiveness of the work itself, is at least commensurate thereto. A compensation which should make the professor free from undue worrying as to his future, free from the necessity of doing hack outside work in order to pay grocery bills, free from the distracting cares of poverty which tend so much to limit the flights of imagination and to impede the successful accomplishment of sustained intellectual endeavor.

[15] It is, however, not merely, perhaps not chiefly, financial freedom which is needed by a State University. More important still is that the University should in all its activities have the fullest intellectual freedom. Unfortunately, this is a matter fraught with especial danger to State Universities; but a matter in which, be it said, to the everlasting glory of the State of California, our own University has been singularly blessed. I know the danger and the temptation of a young democracy to lose faith in itself, and think it must interfere with academic freedom. In many of our states, that has been a constant peril, oftentimes a realized and overwhelming disaster. As you value the integrity of scientific effort; as you believe in truth itself, and have a religious faith that truth is indeed the all-conqueror; as you hope for progress instead of stagnation; as you wish to avoid the shame of being one who stones the prophets, who suppresses and stultifies Galileo, or who crucifies the incarnate Truth himself—shun, I adjure you, any attempt to censor the statements made by the sincere scholar, no matter how wrong you may think them. Sometimes, of course, the scholar will err, and err grievously, lamentably, even asininely. But that is an evil soon corrected; some other wiser and saner one will disclose the error, which will hasten to hide its discomfited head. But a censored or suppressed error becomes a danger point; like concealed infection, it tends to spread through all the body politic, poisoning and life destroying. And censoring and suppression, while it can not destroy a truth, may delay progress, and will, inevitably, destroy the censor. Despite the efforts of censors, the world still does move, and the name of Galileo still lives, but the names of his persecutors are shrouded in an oblivion that is kindly only in that it prevents obloquy.

[16] The attempt to censor or to muzzle academic freedom comes from many directions. The capitalist fears that certain statements will destroy the order to which he is habituated, and perhaps while with an awful sacrilege, he masquerades in the pontifical robes of Americanism, 100, or 99.44 percent pure, he becomes essentially un-American, by attempting to destroy free speech, and by becoming apostate to the American idea that truth will prevail. Or the attack may come from the other wing, and the laborer may think that certain statements must be suppressed because they tend to support the present capitalist system and to militate against the interests of the working man. Or, again, the attack may come, curiously and inconsistently, from the press, which, for some reason or other, demands that the University shall be denied that freedom of expression which has been conceded to the press, and has much more frequently been abused by the

press than it ever has by the professor. Or the demand may come from ecclesiastical sources, insisting, as has recently been reported in Kentucky, that the legislature prohibit certain obnoxious tenets.

[17] I have no quarrel with restraints, which may have been necessary in time of war. War is monstrous, unnatural, subversive. Of course, it is accompanied with horrors, with sufferings, with evils. And among these evils, especially in democracies, is the inevitable result that the cherished institution of free speech will, and must, be interfered with. If the circumstances of war are such that patriotic citizens are willing to forfeit their property and to lose, if need be, their limbs and their lives, certainly they may, without protest, be willing to lose somewhat of their cherished birthright of free speech and free thought. We need not worry so much over these evils, when they are incidental to the horrid emergency of war, but we must be jealous of any encroachment in time of peace.

[18] A third bondage from which the University should be free is the bondage of deadening, initiative-destroying routine. One who spends too many hours in the classroom, one who spends too much time correcting exercises, one who wastes too many days in committee meetings and administrative routine, cannot have the buoyancy, the inspiration, the enthusiasm necessary for the really successful teacher, or the really great scientist. Bagehot, the English economist and essayist, said that he never went into a large establishment and found the head always busy, that he did not know that there was something wrong. And if the manager of a commercial establishment needs what Thoreau calls a wide halo of ease and leisure, much more is that true of the one who is devoting his energies to the more refined intellectual activities of the teacher and the scholar. You must then assure financial freedom, intellectual freedom, and freedom from bondage to a machine-like routine.

[19] We saw a moment ago that the older education tended to be aristocratic. Surely a State University must avoid this evil. By moderation in fees, by simplicity of its life, by the nature of its curriculum, it must be truly a school for the people, not a club for aristocrats. But there is perhaps a greater danger that in the anxiety to escape snobbery the University drift into the commonplace and the mediocre. Steadfastly must the friends of a State University see to it that it is not forced into too narrow an interpretation of vocational training. It must not, in response to a false demand, waste the time of faculty and students in matters of lesser moment, which are falsely called practical. It must ever be borne in mind that the function of the university is not inculcation of practical facts, nor in mere training in dexterity of hand, or eye or mind, but in giving insight into fundamental matters, in stimulating the spirit of independent research, in training in right methods of thinking, in opening the mind of the youth to higher things—and these things are, of all things, the most practical.

[20] When I was a student at the University of Chicago, a young newspaper man used to stop off at the University to attend an early class before he went to his downtown office. Years passed, the young man has risen in business and political

importance, and is known throughout the world as the former president of the National City Bank of New York. After he had risen to eminence, he one day sought out the professor whose classes he used to attend, and said to him: "If I seem to have any advantage over the average New York banker, I want to say that I consider it as due to the training in economics which I received in your classes in Chicago. And, if you tell this to your students, add that what was of value was not the practical, but the theoretical matters." Whether you are members of the faculty, or citizen supporters of the university, resist, I beg you, any tendency to overemphasize the obviously practical. I am myself a professor of accounting, and have for long been intimately concerned with commercial education, but even from my philistine view point, if a choice has to be made, mathematics is more important than accounting, literature is more important than stenography, philosophy than business practice, economic theory than foreign trade.

[21] One of the significant facts, and it may possibly be also a lesson, derived from war time experience in Washington was that so many important positions were filled by persons of broad general education, but with no special technical training for their particular jobs. A college dean was assistant secretary of War, a Wall Street operator controlled industry, a miner regulated food, a Texas judge curtailed manufactures, a college president administered fuel, the editor of a provincial paper ruled over exports, and a manufacturer of pneumatic tools was autocrat over our imports. If the war was at all well managed, the experience may well be an argument against highly specialized and in favor of general cultural education.

[22] In the desire to escape the aristocratic tendencies of earlier universities, there is also danger of subordinating the University to the inconsidered behests of popular clamor. In a state where immediate democracy is so evident, where referendum and initiative, and constitutional amendments are so much to the fore, the University must see to it that its activities, its curriculum, its mode of expression is not determined by popular vote, but by the University itself. I recognize the right of the voters to determine that for which the taxes are to be spent, I admit that a State University must keep in touch with the people, that it must in a word be democratic, not aristocratic. But democracy does not necessarily mean direction by the incompetent. If it is true, as Sumner states, that "democracy affirms that men are, may be, ought to be, were born, or were created equal ... facts to the contrary notwithstanding," it may nevertheless recognize differentiation of functions. Even the Soviet government of Russia relies upon a conservative professor for advice and guidance in things economic.

[23] The modern State University must then be free; it must be democratic; in addition, it must stand for service to the State. But here too lies a danger. Training for citizenship is doubtless an essential, if not the prime duty of a State University. This does not mean merely a cheap form of Americanism. The trained citizen is not one who has been drilled merely in patriotic ritual, not one who has been misled into a belief in the infinite superiority of all things American to all things else,

not one who has been persuaded that an attempt to better things American is unpatriotic.

[24] Training for citizenship means so training one that, first, he may perform some useful function in the society to which he belongs, second, that he will bring to the infinitely difficult problems of modern society a mind equipped with a knowledge of all pertinent past experience, and competent to interpret such experience, and, third, that he be able to discriminate between that of our inheritance to which he should cling with all the fervor of devoted loyalty, and that which, because it is perhaps an outgrown good, demands an equally patriotic effort to change. I do indeed believe in the motto, "Our country right or wrong," but in the sense that our very loyalty and patriotism, which makes our country an object of supreme devotion, by that very devotion demands that we do what is to be done to better our country. It is the intensity of love for his invalid wife that leads the husband to attempt her cure. His marriage vow, which proclaimed her his wife "in sickness or in health," leads to no such sentimentalism that he does not wish any change in the object of his love.

[25] The three essentials of a successful university, then, are that it stand for freedom, for democracy, for service. Can such an institution maintain itself in such a State as ours? The task is more difficult than in the case of an endowed institution. Especially difficult is it just now. War emotions and the strain on nerves due to war have not altogether subsided. Dissatisfaction with present-day conditions on the one hand, and fear of corruption from the propaganda of foreign revolutionaries on the other, cause intolerance toward the expression of views obnoxious to one or the other side, and create an atmosphere peculiarly disturbing to academic life. The position of the state university just now is unusually difficult, if not precarious. Its welfare can be assured only by watchfulness and devotion.

[26] While the University is an institution supported by the entire State, the success of this branch depends in large part on the local environment. Los Angeles, not content with bringing to its doors the imprisoned lightning and streams of living water, has brought also a great University—source, too, of a refreshment, of illumination and of power. But having done this, it has created an obligation to live up to its new adornment. One may with perfect self-respect, wear khaki, flannel shirts, overalls, or even cords. But one may not wear these at the same time that he carries a great solitaire diamond. Diamonds demand of their wearer not only clean hands, but as well, artistic and elegant clothing, or the very incongruity shrieks and cries aloud to Heaven. As the host sees to it that all is seemly for the distinguished guest; as the acolyte seeks by purgations and vigils to prepare his soul for the imminence of his deity—so a community should make sure that its garb and behavior are worthy of the dignity of a University. Can Los Angeles furnish the proper environment for an institution devoted to freedom of thought, to love of truth, to high endeavors, free from commercialism, to idealism, purged from taint of selfish interests? Even a stranger, like myself, needs but to look

around him to know the answer. And because of my faith in this city of dreams and of accomplishments, I rejoice that in addition to its magnificent natural environment, in addition to your achievement of material success, you, too, have sought the higher things; and have brought into your crowded and perhaps feverish life, the Southern Branch of the University of California.

"A Professor Looks at Germany," 1933

Hatfield enjoyed trips abroad throughout his life, and Germany and England were his favorite countries to visit. He used the trips abroad to educate his children, to scout for early tracts on bookkeeping, and to gather knowledge for use in his teaching, textbook writing and research. This paper, originally titled "Germany of the Present Day," was presented to the Berkeley Club on September 7, 1933. The paper is, as Hatfield writes, "a record of impressions," but it does not purport to be a "scientific portrayal of economic and political facts." However, given Hatfield's life-long commitment to questioning all facts and encouraging others to avoid accepting events and theories at face value, his inability to comprehend the import of what he saw occurring in Germany is surprising. Given his knowledge of history, his sensitivity to the meaning of history and culture, and his interest in the relationship of culture to accounting, his objective rendering of the mounting anti-Semiticism is contrary to his usual astute analysis of culture. The final two sections, *Prognostications* and *Apologia*, seem strained in their effort to avoid analysis.

Withal, this is a compelling account of conditions during mid-1933 in Hitler's Germany, as viewed by an American visitor who was fluent in the language.

It is to be hoped that the Academic Senate will not be officially informed that one of its members is apparently attempting to describe conditions in Germany after a sojourn of only a little more than two months in that most perplexing land. To do that would imply a lack of an appropriate scientific sense, which ought to lead to senatorial discredit. But my face may, perhaps, be saved by stating that the breach of academic propriety is, as said, only "apparent." I do not profess to state what the conditions are. I speak only of the impressions made on a temporary sojourner. This is not a study of German politics, or of economic conditions. It is a record of impressions. Anyone may with propriety record his own impressions. The result, as in the case of Freudian analysis, may be merely a rather disgraceful revelation of one's own peculiar mental activities. As such, it may have some slight validity; but it is not a scientific portrayal of economic and political facts.

Being of ministerial parentage, I naturally divide my paper into six heads, namely: Observations, Impressions, Interpretations, Comparisons, Prognostications, and Apologia. The evening being still young, these six heads will be taken up in orderly sequence.

I. Observations

The sight which first impresses one is of endless processions, flags, and swastikas, and, on every side, of the displacement of the old banners of Bavaria and Munich which used to fly from the flag poles in front of the Feldherrnhalle by the black, white, and red of the Empire and by the Hitler banner. Processions of Hitler youth, of Stahlhelm, of the S.A., of girls' organizations of various kinds marching continually, and joining in monster gatherings in some public square. Some of the processions are of those who are being taken out to do work on the roads or other construction, but in regard to most of them, one wonders when they can do any work when so much of their time is spent in ceaseless parading. The marching is enlivened by military bands, by girls with banjoes and violins, and by the singing of "Deutschland über Alles" and the Horst-wessel-lied. As a woman observer says:

> I felt at the same time gay and ashamed of this Babbitry. For Babbitts they are, beuniformed, bebadged, saluting, strutting; Babbitts getting a whack at the world. It is the triumph of baiting: Communist-baiting, Jew-baiting, free-thought-baiting, newspaper-baiting, sex-baiting ("Let's clean up Germany!"), and superior-person-baiting (that above all).

The boycott I did not personally see, as I arrived in Germany ten days too late. Perhaps the boycott was of a milder character in Munich than elsewhere, where, so far as I could learn, it was a rather tame affair. It was for only a single day. That day was Saturday, when many of the stores would normally be closed for the afternoon, and, being on Saturday, it was on a day when all proper Jewish store-keepers should have been closed altogether.

When I arrived in Munich, a number, but by no means the majority of the stores, proclaimed their Aryan character by a sign "Deutsches Geschäft." This seemed to be particularly true in the case of merchants whose names might seem to indicate Jewish blood. Thus, a Rosenberg, if he could honestly do so, would be very apt to proclaim that his was a Deutsches Geschäft, while one whose name might be von Klenze would not feel this necessary.

The bonfire at which objectionable books were burned took place on May 10. It was preceded by a meeting held at the University where an address was given to the students, who at about ten o'clock marched in varied regalia to the light of torches, men and women together, through the streets to the Königsplatz. To the large assemblage there gathered, a rather absurd speech was delievered by Schemm, the Bavarian minister of education. It was not, as some of the papers would lead one to believe, an effort to rid the city of pernicious literature. The number of volumes burned was insignificant. It was a symbolic ceremony somewhat more serious than the cremation of Trig which used to be customary at American universities. Perhaps it can be likened to Luther's burning of the Papal Bull, certainly merely a symbol of detestation for the object that was burned. Similarly, the students expressed by outward and visible sign their disapprobation of works which they thought had a dangerous influence. The books which were banned and burned were not primarily books by Jewish authors but books that were condemned because of their doctrine. Of course, the works of Marx and other socialistic writers were included. "All Quiet on the Western Front" was objected to because it seemed to throw contempt upon the military activities and, as was formally stated, because it degraded the purity of the German language. Feuchtwanger's *Success* was burned because it was thought to throw ridicule upon the earlier activities of Hitler, although the author in his preface somewhat untruthfully denied that he was portraying any actual characters. The works of Mann that were burned were not his novels but some of his political writings, and so on generally throughout the list, including the works of Upton Sinclair, Helen Keller's *Why I Became a Socialist*, and some of the works of Fosdick.

The activities of the University students, aside from the spectacular and rather harmless *auto da fé*, were impressive to any observer. Most noticeable was the large placard, perhaps three by two feet, displayed upon the bulletin board of the University. This, while issued by the students rather than by the faculty or other officials of the University, bore at least the stamped approval permitting its display on the official bulletin board. It was printed in large type and with the brightest of red ink, and bore the title, "Gegen den undeutschen Geist." It was signed by the "studentenschaft," or the associated student body. I did not copy all of the twelve sections of this notice, but give you a free translation of some of the more significant sections.

4. Our most dangerous opponent is the Jew, and he who is subservient to him.
5. The Jew can think only in a Jewish manner. If he writes German, he lies. The German who writes German but thinks in an un-German manner is a traitor. The student who speaks and writes in an un-German manner is fundamentally thoughtless and unfaithful to his task.
7. We will regard the Jews as foreigners and we will treat the national feeling seriously. We therefore demand from the censor:
   - Jewish works to appear in the Hebrew language. If they are issued in German, they must be designated as translations.
   - The severest measures against the misuse of German (deutsche Schrift).
   - German is only for the use of Germans.The un-German spirit to be eradicated from public libraries.
9. We demand from German students the will and the ability to maintain the German language in its purity.
10. We demand from the German students the will and the ability to overcome the Jewish intellectualism and the liberal tendencies associated with it in the spiritual life of the Germans.

11. We demand the selection of students and professors with reference to the soundness of their thinking in accordance with the true German spirit.

It was to this pronouncement that Dr. Kohlrausch, Rector of the University of Berlin, took exception. He strenuously objected to the students arrogating to themselves the right to make such an announcement, and demanded its withdrawal. But the Prussian Minister of Education refused to back Kohlrausch, and, accordingly, a few days later, he resigned the rectorate.

In some cases, the activities of the students were of a more direct character. Even rather late in the semester, the president of the student body appeared in one of the lecture rooms in Munich and informed the class that, as the professor was not a proper character to instruct German youth, he would not give any more lectures. This action was apparently taken entirely by the students. It must, however, have had at least the tacit approval of the University authorities.

The status of the universities in this great upheaval is of peculiar interest. We have so long looked upon the German universities as the stronghold of academic freedom that it is something of a shock to find the lectures of the professors and their publications subject to such strict censorship. It is obviously something of a shock to the Germans themselves, both to those who are members of the faculty and to others outside the universities who have been concerned with educational matters. A defense must be set up to justify to their own minds this reversal of a long-established policy. A public evening lecture was given at the University of Munich by Professor Baeumler of Berlin on the tasks of the university. In this, he argued that the university, while fostering and encouraging the scientific spirit, must get away from the early idea of science as being something impersonal and disinterested. He defined science as being not an activity of the intellect but of the spirit, and conceived the spirit as something active and effective in us, not merely as the thinking faculty. Knowledge, says he, is neutral; science and spirit are specifically masculine. The error of our times consists not in making the spirit scientific but in despiritualizing science:

> The German student body should be more than a bringing together of groups of experts (Fachschaften). It must have a special relation to the state; it must be a factor in the state. This is to be realized only when the system of national education is accomplished in the soldierlike spirit of the S.A. Over the new university must stand not "Der Wissenschaft und Erziehung" but "Dem gebildeten Wissenschaftler" (Baeumler, May 31, 1933).

The excuse for the dismissal or side-tracking of professors was that they were definitely corrupting the German youth, instilling in their minds radical and communistic ideas or, at least, ideas not in harmony with the development of a supreme unified German state. It was not true as stated in some of the papers that the dismissed German professors were prohibited from leaving the country, nor were they exiled. As you know, several are now in this country. Some, though dismissed from their posts, still remain in Germany.

I give for what it is worth a statement which came to me apparently through very reliable channels but reaching me as perhaps fourth-hand news. It was that when one of the highest Nazi officials under Hitler was asked about this general movement against university professors-deemed-undesirable, the official stated that it had gone too far, but that at present the authorities could not oppose the students. When asked what would be the outcome, it is said that he expressed the opinion that nothing could be done just at present but that in the course of time and somewhat gradually the discharged professors would be reinstated. As Ripley says, "Believe it or not."

Certain phases of the Nazi movement have a distinctly humorous or absurd aspect. Thus, one paper was punished because it stated that General Balbo, the Italian aeronaut, was a baptized Jew. Whether the report was true or not, it does not seem to be a very serious offense. Again, one can hardly take seriously the action of excluding Jews from taking part in official tennis tournaments, or in chess matches, or even in joining an association for rabbit breeding. Even more petty seems the action of the German government in retaliation for the Austrian administration's objections to Nazi-ism, in laying a fee of 1000 marks for the visa of any German citizen who wished to cross the Austrian border.

It is amusing to note that German sportsmen were urged to visit the mountain regions of the Tyrol for winter sports, a region which was described as having been stolen from them (although it had belonged to Austria, not to Germany) by the Italians. Thus, Germans were urged to visit the territory belonging to a former enemy for the sake of skiing, but virtually prohibited from attending the great musical festival held at Salzburg in the domain of Germany's former ally. A little later, no Austrian was allowed to go over the German section of the direct road from Salzburg to Innsbruck unless he could show a card of membership in the Nazi party. This action compelled a detour of some sixty miles, greatly lengthening the distance between Salzburg and Innsbruck.

Perhaps there is something a little amusing also in the recent provisions regarding candidates taking examinations for admission to the bar. After having passed a written examination, for the three weeks intervening before the verbal test is taken, the candidates are compelled to go to a camp under Nazi leadership. In this camp, books are barred, as are tobacco and alcohol. The day begins with gymnasium at 6:15, includes four hours of field exercises, four-and-a-half hours of lectures about team sports and other matters, and ends at 9:00. It is said that this is designed to make sure that the lawyers of the future will all be faithful servants of the revolution and free from political heresy, but it is difficult to see how the prohibition of books, tobacco and alcohol for three weeks will gain this desirable end.

The most astounding of my observations was that the young women were letting their hair grow, had discontinued the use of lipstick, and had to a very large extent abandoned smoking. When asked why the reactionary attitude, the reply was, "Mr. Hitler does not approve of women with short hair, or those who use lip stick and tobacco." Did ever any dictator successfully buck up against women's fashions; or, if so, did he ever come out victor; or, if victor, did he succeed by peaceful means? In face of such an unprecedented achievement, one may surely join in the acclaim, Heil, Hitler!!!

The making of new crimes is another striking phenomenon. Some of these have already been mentioned. To these may be added the law which provides a severe penalty for any who publicly treat the swastika, the symbol of the national movement, in any way which will lessen reverence for it. The discovery of new crimes includes also the case of a Stahlhelm officer arrested for a casual remark made while drinking beer with fellow officers. It was stated that he said that he would fight against brown murder just as he had fought against red murder for fourteen years. The court stated that, while the witnesses could not affirm that he had made such a remark, it did not necessarily follow that he had not made it, and as he had placed the brown front and the red front on a level, his remark was likely to injure the national-socialist movement seriously. In another instance, a bank clerk was sentenced because of having ostentatiously refused to raise his arm in the Hitler salute when the Horst-wessel song was sung at a public meeting. The court made it clear that the Hitler salute had become a symbol of the entire German nation.

Again, it having been noticed that officials, clerks, and workers have made in conversations with other persons "remarks calculated to arouse distrust and dissatisfaction with the administration's measures," the Prussian premier issued a notice that such persons should be designated "grousers" and considered disguised Marxists. Not only is the making of such remarks made a criminal matter, but the failure upon the part of those hearing such remarks to report the names to the premier is to be considered a declaration of solidarity with wire-pullers and agitators.

Very serious penalties are prescribed for anyone who starts a new political party. And finally, Premier Goering prescribes the death penalty in all cases where the dignity and existence of the State is imperiled by the so-called atrocity propaganda.

Perhaps the most objectionable action has been the taking of reprisals upon members of the family of persons disapproved of by the government. A striking instance is the arrest of relatives of Scheidemann, the former German Chancellor, because the latter was supposed to have written an article published in *The New York Times*, but which he denied having written. Again, in Thuringia the wife and daughter of a former mayor were taken as hostages to secure silence on the part of the exiled official. A recent order provides that every member of the family of a convicted person living in the same household forfeits all public benefits and claims on the Reich, state, or municipality. (*Manchester Guardian*, July 28, p. 64)

Another criticizable action was the praise heaped upon the assassins of Rathenau, the former German Foreign Minister, at the time of the dedication of a monument to them. They were described as heroes who removed the tyrant "and instead of slavery, cowardice and submission, planted the flag of courage and the manly deed in the shame of their times." Another speaker praised them for not having been able to bear that "a racial alien man, representative of international high finance, should guide Germany's destiny."

II. Impressions

The outstanding impression is the wonderful enthusiasm apparently pervading the entire population. As Enid Bagnold states:

> there is a wave of emotion running through the people which is like a religious revival. It is unexplainable in any other way. Hitler has his programme; but if you ask a true-blue Nazi what it is that makes Nazi-ism he all but cannot tell you. "It is a feeling ... it is an emotion"—this particular man touched his breast. He was a big importer and exporter. "It is not a question of my English, in speaking to you. I cannot even explain it in German to my brothers-in-law, for instance, who are Catholics. To begin with, it is the most wonderful sense of comradeship. And then again it is a reinstatement of self-respect. It is to be again a great nation. Ah, I feel free!"
>
> Even the anti-Nazis admit that Hitler is a sincere man. To the Nazis he is almost divine. I don't exaggerate when I say I have seen business men blink with something like tears when they speak of him.
>
> "We will submit to anything" [said one German]. "To lack of freedom, to loss of fortune—for the movement. I myself as an exporter and importer suffer terribly over the expulsion of the Jews and the breaking of my relationships in foreign countries. But if I were ruined I would bear it. For the movement. And he looked fierce enough and true enough and moved enough to be sincere.[8]

A second impression is of a new *unity* throughout Germany. This is surprising when contrasted with the former somewhat aloof attitude of Bavaria. I recall, some years ago before the World War, a conversation with a very intelligent Bavarian woman, a member of a noble family connected by marriage with the Austrian Emperor. She even stated that, in case of a new war, she would prefer to have Bavaria side with France rather than with Prussia. Her attitude, perhaps characteristic of many high-born Bavarians, was one of almost open hostility to Prussia and its hegemony in the empire. Now Bavaria is deprived of the right even of choosing its own president, but apparently all is accepted as working for Unity.

A third impression was one of hopefulness as to the future. It is quite likely that this was a reaction from the depths of despair in which the people had been sunk. It was perhaps in the nature of forlorn hope, but still it seemed that hope was still springing eternal in the German breast.

III. Interpretations

The German attitude toward Jews. It seems to me that this is to be explained in several ways. There is, in the first place, a long, deep-seated racial antipathy. It is true that there are many, some even in our own University, who deny that there is any such thing as a Jewish race. But whether from a scientific anthropological viewpoint this is true or not, it is certain that throughout many centuries and at the present time in almost every part of the world there is a feeling more or less openly expressed and more or less violent in its character against the Jew as a Jew, and this feeling, I think, must be taken into consideration as something distinct from other causal elements.

In the second place, hostility toward the Jew is in part due to the identification of Jews with communists. Of course, no one claims that all Jews are communists, but it has been felt that so many of the communists are Jews that it is wise to consider the terms almost synonymous. The prominence of Jews in the Russian revolution, and the fact that many Jews with communistic ideas have come into Germany from Russia and Galicia, have increased this tendency.

A third element is doubtless the economic rivalry. It seems strange that, as Dr. Hamilton has said, 65 million Germans should feel themselves submerged and shocked by a 570-thousand Jewish minority, and, having no hope of the Germans winning the battle by intellectual weapons, must resort to physical force. But undoubtedly the Jews have had an influence in business, the professions, music, and drama far out of proportion to their relative numbers, and this the Germans bitterly resent.

Finally, it is thought by some and apparently with some reason, that the campaign against the Jews has been fostered by the authorities as a piece of political strategy. Germany was composed of many discordant and disunited factions, and the number of political parties was astonishingly great and prevented any concerted governmental policy. Hitler desired above all things to secure unity, and some think that he realized that there is no stronger cementing bond than to find a common object of hate. He had, of course, preached hostility to the Jews from the beginning of his career. As far back as 1927, I heard him give a speech in which his main emphasis was that of hostility against the objectionable and dangerous Jew.

So, various elements explain the wide-spread anti-Jewish feeling. Again quoting Enid Bagnold:

> The business man hates them because he has been worked up to believe that the Jews financed Communism in order to divide and rule and threaten him. The uncomplicated German woman (with her mate) hates them because they represent sophistication, night life, the threat against the hearth. The young Nazi's emotion, faced with a Jew, boils; it does not like the knowledge, the age, in the Jewish eye.

One must speak of atrocities, but with some caution. Were the reports of startling or catastrophic events ever correct? I recall that in 1906 my friends in the East read that Berkeley was entirely engulfed by a tidal wave; my residence in which I still live was on paper destroyed by the Berkeley fire, and in every battle the reported losses are generally ten times too great. So, on general principles I doubt the literal correctness of the statements of atrocities. I cannot accept without question the statement of one of my sober colleagues that "the accounts of atrocities are all true." When I read in *The Nation*, "Whatever so-called atrocity tales you may have read are all absolutely true," I ask, with Pilate, "What is truth?" When Mr. Untermyer writes: "Nothing that has seeped through to you begins to tell a fraction of the frightful story of fiendish torture, cruelty and persecution," I begin to question the arithmetical accuracy of the statement. When I read the highly vouched-for report of one Pierre van Paasche:

> There is no precedent in history for the terror that rages in Germany today. The frightful blood-baths of medieval St. Batholomew's and the Sicilian Vespers pale in comparison with the horrors that are being perpetrated today on defenseless human beings by the fiendish hands of Nazi-ism. (*Atlanta Constitution*, April 5, 1933)

I am tempted even to make a categorical denial.

When I read, as I have read, that Jews have been eliminated from the professions, I recollect that I, and later another American professor, were sent by our landlord, himself an ardent Hitlerite, to a Jewish physician; when I read that the proscribed books are banished from the bookstores, I recall seeing the works of Thomas Mann, and even Marx's *Kapital* displayed in neighboring shops; when I am told that business establishments, owned by Jews, are closed, I testify that the department stores of Tietz and Oberpollinger were doing business in Munich, and I can submit a receipted bill to show that Baer was still selling books at his elegant stores in Frankfurt. Indeed, my motto, instead of being "Credo quia impossible," is rather, in so far as to any specific report, "It may be so: but I ha' my doots."

As to a fundamental interpretation of the Nazi movement. It seems to me that Trotsky's view, expressed in the October number of *The Atlantic*, is sound. Hitler, or those furnishing the brains behind him, desire above all things to build a strong state which would enable them to right what they consider the injustices and hardships of the Versailles treaty. In order to build up such a powerful Germany, it is necessary to have at least the moral support of England, and to be sure that England will side with Germany rather than with France, whose friendship is not to be dreamed of. To secure this, the Nazis hold up the bugbear of Russian sovietism and the fear of its over-running the western world. Germany wishes to appear as the main bulwark against the inundation of communistic ideas. If it can play that role, England, it is thought, would be friendly toward Germany. And Trotsky thus interprets the Nazi policy not as being a form of madness, but a carefully calculated plan designed to alienate England from France and secure a rapproachement between England and Germany.

How is the striking unity in Germany to be interpreted? Germany has generally been characterized by "particularismus," but just now the boundaries between the states have been practically wiped out, the antagonism between employer and employee has, at least according to official statements, disappeared, the numerous political parties have all been disbanded and merged into one, the several protestant churches are at least united, and various social organizations are in the process of being absorbed into one Nazi group. How has this come about? Probably it is in part due to the feeling that it was a case of either this or chaos. An American woman married to a German nobleman is quoted by Dr. Hamilton as saying:

> Think what the people have been through in the last nineteen years. Our young people saw no hope for themselves, no chance for a satisfying life, for pride in work and success, and now they think the great leader has come, they believe in him passionately and are ready to follow him anywhere!

She also quotes a young clergyman of fine type as saying:

> Hitlerism is the last hope of the despairing people. We cannot be sure of success—maybe it is not perfect, but it is a way out, and let us try it; there is only ruin on the path we have been following.

While almost all classes are at least upon the surface united in the support of the present government, there are still different groups of supporters. First come those who are whole-hearted believers in the movement, the followers of Hitler who were behind him before he had obtained power or even when he was regarded as a criminal. The young men of the country to a large extent belong in this class. And it is they who are most evident in their manifestations of enthusiastic support. The second group are perhaps somewhat halfhearted. These are the ones who are not real believers in some of the Nazi doctrines, but they know no other hope and are willing to lend loyal support to the movement, at least until they find that it too is unavailing. A retired German professor is quoted as saying:

> It is the young that have made the revolution; and now we must not do or say anything that will hurt it, we must hope that it will succeed, and if we do not like the new world that they are building, well, it is they who must live in it, our day is over.

A professor still in service expressed himself somewhat guardedly in conversation with me. He had not originally been a Nazi; he did not approve of all of their policies, but professed willingness to support it for the present.

A third group must exist, although its membership is not ascertainable. These are those who fear or detest the activities of the Nazis, who feel that their actions are in many cases brutal and wrong, but have not the courage or the fool-hardiness to come out against them. Naturally, these do not express themselves in public. In this connection, it is interesting to note that there are still a very few who dare to criticize the present government. Count Reventlow has spoken with surprising frankness. If he is not unique, he is certainly very exceptional. It is interesting and gratifying to note that an American, Dr. Sherwood Eddy, has shown unusual courage in bluntly speaking his opinion in a lecture given under the Carl Schurz Foundation. In this, he lamented their denial of justice and liberty, and bluntly said they would fail unless they changed their course. The speech was received peaceably but was not reproduced in the German papers.

One more interpretation of the movement seems in place. It is essentially and confessedly anti-democratic. Captain Goering, who is thought by some to be the real brains of the Nazi party, and to have selected Hitler as a figurehead merely because his personal magnetism secures the support of countless Germans, says:

> [Nazis] were and would remain the mortal foes of the democratic doctrine of majorities, and with the death of this doctrine Parliament was finished. (*Times*, 7/11/33, p. 13)

The change in the fundamental structure of Prussia embodies, in the Prussian Council of State, the Nazi doctrine of personality and leadership as against the:

> "anonymous doctrine which elevates the cowardice of figures to domination" [says Goering]. Its members, though invested with the powers almost of regional dictators in their districts will at the most be able to recommend discussion in the Council; there will be no voting, for that would be "a sin against the National-Socialist spirit." (*Times*, July 11, 1933, p. 13)

> The Hitlerist State is founded on the principle of "leadership" or of "responsibility from the bottom upwards," as against the democratic principle by which the Government is responsible to Parliament and Parliament to the electorate; the Nazi storm trooper is responsible only to his storm troop leader, the storm troop leader to his superior officer, and so on, up to Herr Hitler, above whom is the President. (*Times*, July 13, 1933, p. 13)[9]

IV. Comparisons

It is very natural to indulge in bitter criticism of the policies and activities of the Nazi government. The newspapers of America have yielded to this temptation. Without in any way appearing as an advocate of the present régime, it seems appropriate and fair to make some comparisons. In general, one fact should be borne in mind which is usually overlooked in current discussions. That is, that there has been a real revolution in Germany. As Sherwood Eddy said in the speech referred to above, we must expect atrocities in time of war or revolution. It is true that there have been no armed forces contending on a field of battle, but the revolution is no less real and the use of violence was inevitable; it is entitled to whatever condonation may properly be given to violence in any sort of war.

As regards the treatment of the Jews, it should be noted that, whether rightly or wrongly, the Jews are looked upon as foes of the German nation. If, in a time of war, any individual or group of individuals is correctly or incorrectly thought to be an enemy, God pity him. The criticism of the attitude of the government toward Jews is more properly directed at a senseless and unintelligent opinion of the Jews rather than as against the treatment based upon this opinion. Of course, as the Germans have pointed out, much to our displeasure, our own skirts are not entirely clean in regard to the treatment of minorities. I remember a visit to San Francisco which I made in 1893. Denis Kearny reappeared after semi-oblivion and delivered an address on the steps of the Mint, an address of course directed against the Chinese. The diatribes against the Jews in Germany were matched by the utterances of our own demagogue, and I think it is safe to say that, for many years, as long as the Chinese were considered a distinct menace to our civilization, the treatment accorded to them savored of the brutalities of which we hear in Germany.

Similarly, during the period of the Great War, there was hostility shown against the minority who were supposed to be a dangerous threat to the public welfare. This even extended in cases to those who were perfectly loyal and actively supporting the government if they happened to have a German name. I remember a striking instance. I was asked by a government official in San Francisco to recommend two students who might serve him as private secretaries or assistants. One of these was a thorough-going American but had a German name. The official, a highly intelligent and thoroughly humane person, said that he could not employ him because of his name. I am happy to say that, after some discussion, he changed his attitude and received satisfactory service from the appointee. There is not very much difference between refusing appointment to a person whose grandfather was a German and restricting the activities of one whose grandmother was a Jew. Either action is illogical and unreasoning if it has no basis aside from ancestry. Furthermore, the treatment of so-called radicals since the war makes an interesting comparison with what has taken place in Germany. In Germany, many people have been shut up in concentration camps or confined in prison. In our own country, a small minority, who, because of the smallness of their numbers and because of the difference in the general situation, are far less dangerous than are the communists in Germany, have also been sentenced under the anti-syndicalist law. If Germany punishes for lack of respect to the swastika, we should remember that one of the grave accusations against Anita Whitney, who indeed was not confined in prison but who by all the laws ought to have been, was that the draping of the American flag when she delivered an address in Oakland did not show proper respect for that emblem of personal liberty.

The burning of books was a foolish performance, perhaps, as some think, damaging rather than beneficial to the Nazi cause, for even some Germans realized the absurdity of the performance and regretted that it make the German people something of a laughing-stock. However, I have heard of a similar attitude on the part of Mayor W.H. Thompson of Chicago, advocating that all British works should be banned from the libraries and schools and consigned to the flames.

The brief boycott, which perhaps in some places is still operative, may possibly find a counterpart in this country in regard to those, if there should be such, who show themselves enemies of the public welfare by refusing to cooperate with the National Recovery Administration. We are not to have a boycott in this country, but are to show preference to those displaying the Blue Eagle. In Germany, it was frankly declared a boycott, but there, too, the boycott was in part secured by designating certain establishments as "Deutsches Geschäft" rather than labeling the other Jewish institutions.

Finally, while recognizing fully the difference in purpose of the Nazi government and our own government's activities at the present time, it is to be noticed that both call for overwhelming and enthusiastic popular support. In general, it is to be hoped that such support will in this country be given freely. In Germany, this has been the case. The recalcitrant members of the community are really very few. In this country, Henry Ford seems to be the only member of the opposition party. In both countries, there is a symbol of the popular movement, in one case the swastika and in the other the blue eagle. In both cases, this symbol is to be treated with reverential respect. Disrespect to the swastika is legally made an offense. In this country, we have no law on the matter, but the daily paper recently stated that General Johnson has prohibited a public official from calling a new prize dahlia "NRA." Parallelism, while not exact, is at least significant.

V. Prognostications

I am not the seventh son of a seventh son, nor was I born with a caul over my head. I am merely an accountant and no longer a theoretical economist. It is the latter group who in recent years have essayed to prophesy future events and to predict the end of depressions and other matters. May the Lord have mercy on them for some of the statements they have made. I am not encouraged by their efforts to try the rôle of prophet, and therefore I have no prognostications to make as to what is to be the outcome of the Nazi movement.

VI. Apologia

Lastly, my brethren, comes the epilogue in the form of an apologia. I feel perfectly sure that, at least, some of you will misinterpret my remarks and say dreadful things about me. I know further that people while giving ready credence to cock-and-bull stories, place no reliance on personal disavowals. Nevertheless, though realizing that any disclaimer will be considered as self-incrimination I solemnly declare that whatever I may have said, I am not a Nazi, I disbelieve in their doctrines and loathe and abhor their practices, and I have never yet, nor do I intend ever in the future, to torture any Jew.

"Moriturus Vos Saluto," 1937

Hatfield gave this paper, "I, who am about to die, salute you," as his valedictory speech to the Berkeley Club, on April 29, 1937. Of all his presentations, this one provides the most revealing insights into Hatfield as a person. It is his best example of the use of the classical essay, as a vehicle for surveying his career at Berkeley. Throughout the essay, Hatfield plays with language, showing his skill with rhetorical schemes and his enjoyment in combining arcane diction with the commonplace in the same sentence.

The essay is the most valuable of all of his unpublished papers in showing the experiences at Berkeley that, to him, illustrated issues and human behavior that were worthy of discussion. He twice mentions his experience with the banking firm of S.A. Kean & Co. (Paragraphs 2 and 16), an episode that apparently affected him deeply and may have a factor leading him, in so many of his essays, to question the ethics of American business.

The essay also shows the influence of his Methodist heritage, his classical education, his pragmatism, his amused acceptance of human foibles, his penchant for sardonic humor, his views on faculty responsibilities, and his assessment of the weaknesses in higher education. In style and presentation, the essay is elegant, amusing, stylistically rich, and descriptive of Hatfield's values and perspectives.

Hatfield's retirement was involuntary, decreed to occur at age 70 by the rules of the University's Board of Regents.

[1] Death, in the opinion alike of Pauline theologians, of transmigrationists, of followers of Conan Doyle and Oliver Lodge, does not mean an end so much as a beginning. It resembles the term commencement in the life of a student. The similes which have been used, such as "That which thou sowest is not quickened except it die," and the analogy of the caterpillar which, by ceasing to be a caterpillar, becomes a butterfly, changing thereby its environments, its activity, its entire character, are familiar to all.

[2] In the life of anyone who has lived to maturity, there have been a number of such changes. He has had more than the traditional nine lives of a cat. The infant ceases to be an infant and becomes a child. The time comes when one puts away childish things and becomes a man. Aside from these *physical* changes, there are others, as when one ceases to be a student and becomes an active man of affairs; when he ends the chrysalis stage of bachelorhood and begins the brightness and joy of matrimony. In my own case, I count the ending of a business career of several years when I returned to finish my college course as the end of an old life and the beginning of a new one. And, less markedly, the transition from the status of student to that of member of the faculty seems like a death and a resurrection.

[3] I am not, therefore, appearing before you tonight to announce my intended suicide, nor, despite the fact that for many years I have been ineligible as a candidate for insurance, am I predicting a speedy demise. But I am facing with such equanimity and composure as I can muster the ending of an academic career which began a little over 43 years ago, or, at least, the ending of a life in this one institution of 33 years. Surely, then, it seems not altogether inappropriate that I who am thus about to die should indeed salute you.

[4] There are two traditions regarding one's attitude at the time of death: One is that the prospective corpse hastily reviews all of his past life, presumably with special emphasis upon his misdeeds. But I am not here to make a public confession. A recent account of the Oxford Groups says that even that organization has decided that it was a mistake to emphasize public confessions which, experience showed often, led to a state of spiritual pride.

[5] The other traditional attitude is one which looks not to the past, but toward the future. As an old hymn expresses it:

> My thoughts on awful subjects roll,
> Damnation and the dead
> What horrors seize the guilty soul
> Upon the dying bed.

[6] My attitude, however, partakes, to a slight degree, of both of these traditions:

> The present only toucheth thee:
> But och! I backward cast my e'e
> On prospects drear!
> An' forward though I canna see,
> I guess an' fear!

[7] You must not expect me to fulfill another tradition, and await my bursting forth into a wonderful swan song, for that tradition is purely mythical and both swan and I cannot, at the moment of death, transcend the habits of a mute and inarticulate lifetime. Certainly I shall not even attempt anything in that line.

[8] Equally mythical is the tradition that in the act of dying there comes an apocalyptic vision and, if one can catch the last whispers of the dying man, they will be fraught with words of wisdom. But of course that is all the bunk. It has sometimes been assumed that the reputed last words of the dying Goethe carried with them some mystical message, but really when he called out "Mehr Licht" all that he meant to say was, "Pull up the blinds." So you must not expect, in these my last words, to find aught of wisdom. All that I shall attempt is a brief retrospect and a still briefer prospect appropriate to the change, which, to the academic man, is indeed his great climacteric: when he ceases to be an active member of the faculty and becomes merely a Professor Emeritus. In doing this I hope I shall not make a display of senile pessimism, but at worst merely exhibit the garrulity of age. Reminiscence is, I suppose, always an indication that one is himself a has-been.

[9] There have been many changes since first I came to Berkeley. When I was preparing to move, I looked in the census and saw that the population of Berkeley was 13,214, a pleasant suburban community, it seemed to me, after the noise and the bustle of Chicago, infested with elevated trains, factory chimneys and stock-

yard odors. I do not know the exact population at the present date. You all know that it is now a city. If I can not say with Augustus, "I found a city of brick and left one of marble," I can say that I found a village of shingles and I am leaving a city of stucco. I found bungalows and am leaving apartment houses. When I came to Berkeley, the unpaved streets were thick with dust. The dust was full of fleas. The fleas were endowed with malignant mordacity which made life something of a burden to the non-immunized tenderfoot. I found at that time that many of the residents obtained water by means of windmills erected in their back yards, and heated it by means of sun heaters erected on the southern slopes of their roofs. Now, of course, we assuage our thirsts through Mokelumne and obtain heat through the P. G. & E. There was at that time no proper restaurant in Berkeley, and now, as one walks along a single block on Telegraph Avenue, one finds nine places which offer sybaritic repasts including hot dogs and Eskimo Pies. (This number was correct yesterday. Very likely it has changed over night.) There was no real hotel in Berkeley; one had to put up temporarily in a hotel in Oakland. Even Cloyne Court, that genial haven for mature gentlewomen, was only building. And one did his shopping in Oakland or in San Francisco, because of the then inadequacy of Berkeley shops. But why should I indulge in my relatively brief reminiscences? I must appear the veriest parvenu before such pioneers as Richardson and Hart. To tell them of early experiences is not unlike the experience of the man who lost his life in the Johnstown flood of 1889. It is said that when he found himself in Heaven, he immediately proceeded to buttonhole each saint whom he met on the golden streets, and inflicted on him a thrilling tale of the catastrophe, telling in excited language how the wall of water came down the valley carrying all before it. After doing this on one occasion, he said to a bystander, "Who is that boorish old guy with the long beard over there? I told him all my exciting adventures in the Johnstown flood, and all he said was, 'Oh, Hell,' and turned on his heel and walked away." "That man," replied the more experienced saint, "was Noah."

[10] One naturally expected that life in a small academic town will be serene and placid, but in the years which I have been here, there have been a number of exciting catastrophes—earthquake, fire, sword, and pestilence. These sound like the four horsemen of the Apocalypse, and to them might be added revolution. Each of these catastrophes was accompanied by an outburst of hysteria, oftentimes of a somewhat humorous nature. I recall one instance following the great earthquake. A neighbor of mine, a colleague, an enormous man, tall and with unusually broad shoulders, paraded through the quiet of Benvenue Avenue carrying on his shoulders the toy .22 rifle of his small boy, and, ringing my doorbell, politely ordered me to turn on my porch light. The contrast between this enormous man and the toy gun, and the absurdity of his sentry patrol made it difficult to keep a sober face. I recall, too, that the citizens of Berkeley organized as a relief committee, took money which was sent from a generous East to the victims of the earthquake and fire, and used it to hire people to patrol our streets and protect us

against an imagined, but non-existent, danger. And I remember, too, the depths of despair to which the head of one of the university's departments fell, when, indulging in a Jeremiad, he predicted that the University would never recover from the catastrophe but at least he felt that he could make a living, and planned to go to Louisiana where he could use his knowledge of Roman Law. Fortunately the University was not so soon deprived of his services.

[11] The second catastrophe was the outbreak of Bubonic Plague in San Francisco, accompanied by hysterical repercussions in the Faculty Club. I recall that I posted upon the bulletin board in the Club a statement put out by an official commission to the effect that experience in India showed that there is little danger of infection for those who live under reasonably hygienic conditions. I thought that this message would be consoling to the panicky residents of the Club. It was amusing to find that in this very center of academic life—the *cor cordum* [heart of hearts] of the University—the residents could not bear to hear the truth. My placard was vehemently torn from the bulletin board, and for a time I feared that I might be expelled, if not tarred and feathered.

[12] The period of the sword, too, was characterized by hysteria, but how can that be otherwise when war is on and people lose their reason? I recall particularly the activities of the Sons of Nathan Hale, a patriotic group of youth whose pleasure it was to save Berkeley from the Huns. Among the other activities, a student kept watch all night at the top of the Campanile, and duly reported that he had seen mysterious signaling by lights from the Berkeley hills. The signaling was, in fact, merely the bobbing of a lantern carried by a wayfarer tramping along a trail. I recall, too, the violent objection made by one, himself an alien, to a member of our department, having in his hand an issue of *The Nation*, and his formal protest against the Faculty Club's having upon its shelves copies of that and of other periodicals of which he did not approve. I recall the warning—almost a threat—given to a former member of the Berkeley Club, Mr. Warren Gregory, because, in a fireside talk which he gave in his home, he stated that during his experience with the Belgian Relief Commission he himself had not personally seen children whose hands were cut off. I suppose that those who remonstrated with him thought that if he had not seen such things, he ought to have, or at least he ought to keep his mouth shut. Vernon Kellogg, under whom Gregory had served in the Belgian Relief, told me later that he, himself, had made the statement a dozen times. But the patriotism of Berkeley could not stand it.

[13] I recall, though it gives me pain to do so, the treatment given to a Professor of German, excusable perhaps at the time because of the hysteria, but inexcusable in the later refusal to retract a sentence given upon unreliable and self-refuted testimony. I recall, too—again with infinite pain—the opprobrium heaped upon our beloved president who, on his return from Washington, reported that the commissioners who had come from England said that they were practically at the end of their resources, and would be defeated if the United States did not quickly come

to aid. Exactly the same statement has been made in print by Admiral Sims, but in the period of war hysteria, it was imputed a crime to speak the truth.

[14] And there was the fire—not the San Francisco fire of 1906—but the great Berkeley fire of 1923. Perhaps the most amusing incident then was when some self-appointed guardians of public welfare appeared at the house of Mr. Aronovici and warned him to get out as they were about to dynamite his house to prevent the spread of the fire. The amusing element is that the house was entirely built of concrete—floors, roof, walls, and even some of the interior furniture, such as book cases—and many of the neighbors had brought their treasures to this house as the only safe place. Wisely, Mr. Aronovici brandished a pistol and said he would shoot the first person who attempted to blow up the house, and the house is still standing.

[15] Should I add to these events the revolution of 1920 when, by a strange mob psychology, the members of the Faculty went clamoring for an additional uncongenial and unremunerated burden, a Youth Revolt against age, a demand that the younger members of the University faculty should be appointed to positions of responsibility—on the whole a beneficial move which has worked well, but not without its humorous aspects. One of these is found in the census which I took a few years ago which showed that, at that date, those who had been appointed as younger men to supersede the antiquated incumbents—those one-time youths, who were still holding office, had an average age three-and-one-half years greater than the average age of those whom they dispossessed.

[16] What are the reactions of one coming from a little experience in the world of business to academic life? Perhaps the first experience was that of disillusionment and a growing appreciation of the fact that, after all, academicians are not so very different from the business man. I thought, in my innocence, that faculty members walked by the pure light of reason, that they were guided exclusively by intellect and not by emotion. I knew that the business man was not always rational, for I remembered a banker boasting of the superiority of his clan over economists, "For economists," said he, "rely only on theory, while we business men rely on solid facts." But a little examination showed that he was a more rigid theorist than any economist I had ever known, the only essential difference being that the business man's theory was the fallacious kind based purely on *post hoc propter hoc*. I thought that nothing irrational would be found in academic circles, but I found that one of the most brilliant and famous scientists in all his dealings, except those in his laboratory, was swayed by prejudice and emotion. In his own field he was a genius and a model thinking machine. Outside of his *Fach* [field of expertise] he was a mere human being.

[17] Dare I say it? I found that university life was not altogether free of a sort of graft—graft, indeed, which had no element of personal gain, graft which was done with the best of motives, graft which doubtless redounded to the welfare of the University. I give but a single instance. The head of a department admitted that, not being able to secure the services of a particular stenographer at the hourly

rate granted by the University, he made out his payroll in such a way that he put down twelve hours' work when only eight hours' had been rendered, thus raising the rate from 50¢ to 75¢ an hour. In political procedure, such a process is known as padding the payroll and is supposed to be a prerogative of corrupt politicians. In the university, what shall we call it? Let us say, an effort to secure results beneficial to the university despite stupid rules made by a dictatorial administration?

[18] In the university I found, too, what is akin to nationalism in international politics. By this I mean a centering of interest in one's own department rather than in the university as a whole, the feeling that the department in a certain sense is a unit against which all other departments are hostile aggressors. And when budget time comes, one's own unit must be aggrandized even though it be at the expense of the general welfare.

[19] I have been amused, or perhaps somewhat shocked, at the assumption of superiority on the part of academic people. This was particularly noticeable during the war when a serious protest was made against the draft being applied to members of the scientific departments (poor economists, of course, did not count). The idea expressed to me in person, and with great emphasis, was that the scientist was so much more valuable a man than his neighbor that he ought not to be called upon to endure the risks of war. I am perfectly willing to admit that a trained scientist is a more valuable member of society than, let us say, an acrobat or an accountant, but when it comes to demanding that a man offer up his life for his country, the inestimable sacrifice involved is so great that all other differences sink into insignificance. It is indeed noble to risk one's life for one's country—it is noble to risk one's life to save another human being—but it is base and ignoble to demand that someone else should offer up his life in order that one may continue to teach. It is too much like the man during the Civil War whose patriotism went to the length of his being willing to sacrifice all his wife's relatives for the sake of his country.

[20] Another characteristic of university life is that in these circles individualism has gone mad. Of course, all college professors are individualists and all persons, academic or otherwise, have, especially since the war, rejoiced in the evasion of rules. I do not object so much to revolt against rules laid down by regents, or presidents, or deans, or librarians, by outside dictators, or by arbitrary legislators, but it does strike me as rather amusing that an intelligent body of academicians, after they make their own rules, feel a conscientious duty to disobey them. The academic senate boasts of being a self-governing body even to the extent of demanding, in the revolution of 1920, that it should have an elective instead of an *ex officio* chairman. This self-determining senate made the rule that there should be no smoking in the library building. Now I am not either favoring or objecting to the rule. A similar rule applying not only to the library, but to the other buildings at Columbia, was in force while I was temporarily on the staff there, and it was scrupulously obeyed. I seem to remember that in Columbia, the rule was made by some administrative authority. In this institution, it was made

by the senate itself. Walk into the library at any time and see to what extent it is observed.

[21] The individualistic spirit has manifested itself from time to time by making a factitious distinction between what it calls the administration, meaning thereby the deans, and the faculty. Not once, but often, one has heard in the meetings of the senate a contrast drawn as if these two sets of individuals were separate. As every dean is a member of the faculty and generally actively engaged in teaching as well as in administration, the attempt to set one class against the other or to establish that there are two different classes is certainly peculiar. I even recall a pronouncement made in the senate by perhaps the most distinguished member of the faculty that the president of the University should have no interest in educational policy.

[22] Individualism shows its madness also in the perverted ideal of academic freedom. The idea of academic freedom is a valuable one, and dear to every academician. It was adopted largely from the German universities, where it probably never existed in any extreme form. Only in Itellyou [sic] does it really exist. A perversion of the idea has at many times appeared in the form that when the regents hire a professor to teach music, he should at his own pleasure have the privilege of abandoning music and teaching apiculture or oto-rhino-laryngology without any injurious effect upon his salary.

[23] I do not know whether it is an exhibition of individualism gone mad or rather an emergence of a guild spirit that is found in the distorted idea of qualifications for an academic position. A university professor should be a productive scholar. To base promotion almost exclusively upon printed pages without too much regard to the merits of the published matter is an unfortunate attitude not altogether absent in faculty circles. It is especially unfortunate if the lack of published work offsets other more significant accomplishments. Is the writing of a book on foreign trade a better basis for recognition than the making of seventeen trade agreements with foreign countries? Is it better to write about things than to do them?

[24] Similarly, overemphasis upon the possession of a doctor's degree as a requisite for receiving an appointment as an instructor is a mistake. It might be rational to provide that no one should be given the task of teaching who had not received the doctor's degree. I do not say that this is a sound proposition. But it is at least an arguable one. We do not wish to have the students inefficiently taught by an untrained man, but the rule as actually applied permits the instruction to be given by one who has not had the supposedly necessary training, insisting only that he be called "assistant," or "lecturer," and not "instructor," as if his unfitness to teach were altered by the title which he bears. Another effect of this academic attitude, which is found in a much more extreme form at the University of California than at almost any other college or university, is to cause the ambitious teacher to obtain by hook or crook some sort of a doctor's degree, whether it has any reference to his academic activities or not. If the obtaining of the doctor's

degree means anything, it is that it is perhaps not a guarantee, but at least *prima facie* evidence, that the person has shown ability and originality in his particular field. But when it is held that one is better qualified to teach music by taking a doctor's degree in history, or that one becomes better fitted to teach physical education by taking a degree in philosophy, it seems a strangely irrational attitude.

[25] The second attitude of one entering on a new life is as expressed above:

> Forward though I canna see
> I guess an' fear!

So now I pass from reminiscence to prospect. To me it seems that the general outlook is that we are headed straight towards unlimited inflation and national bankruptcy. I hope that even Professor Stratton will accept the statement that I am not prophesying that this will take place. I do not even say that it is likely to take place. I do not say that it is the necessary culmination of the course we are now pursuing. A skier, sliding down a steep slope which ends in an abrupt precipice, is surely headed toward destruction. But he may, in the nick of time, skillfully execute a Christiana and thus escape. But even so, in its execution he may save his life but break a leg or two in so doing. The public might inaugurate a sit-down strike and refuse to go any further along the road which we have been traversing in the direction towards which we are heading. This is certainly conceivable, for the human mind is capable of retracing steps, but we have to remember:

> ...facilis descensus Auerno;
> ...sed reuocare gradum superasque euadere ad auras,
> hoc opus, hic labor est.[10]

[26] I look askance at any inconsistent and self-contradictory mental attitude. I like straight-forward thinking. This is probably a defect. I have been greatly interested just now in reading a lecture by Lord Macmillan entitled "Two Ways of Thinking." These he illustrates by contrasting Scotland and England, represented respectively by the system of Roman Law and the system of Common Law. In the former case, the starting point is a principle, and all subsequent mental activities are bent on making actions and facts conform to the principle. In the other way of thinking, principles are, in general, ignored, or at least arrived at by a secondary process. The important thing is to observe present facts, and in one way or another an effort is made to find a practical, rather than a logical, way out of the muddle. Lord Macmillan considers that these two ways of thinking are fundamental and perhaps ineradicable. The best results might be secured if members of each group could at least appreciate the point of view of the other. If only one is adopted, it is probable that the habit of mind which relies upon principles is the more dangerous. I fear that to a large extent, I incline toward that way of thinking. I confess that my greatest impediment is that, in addition to laziness, procrastination, indecision, and inadequate intelligence—in addition to all these unqualifications, and

more potent than any one, or than all taken together, has been an assumption that all other persons should act rationally, should be consistent in their conduct and logical in their thinking.

[27] With that type of mind, it is natural that the present illogical jumble in economics and politics is particularly distressing. It would be more satisfactory either to cling to the principle of private property or to come out whole-heartedly in favor of a communistic system. And here I remark, parenthetically, that if Professor Stratton reports that I am an advocate of communism, I shall sue him for slander. I do not think that the welfare of mankind would be promoted by a communistic system. That is a purely economic question which should not be discussed in ethical or religious terms, and the word communism in its proper economic sense has, of course, no necessary connection with the exiling of Trotsky, the abolition of God, or the purging of the communistic party in Russia.

[28] At the present time, no one knows just what are our ideals, what our policy, if we have any such.

[29] The recent interesting discussion of the sit-down strike is perhaps in point. Much has been said about the property right which the worker has in his job. The fundamental error is a confusion between property right and a contractual right. This may be illustrated by the case of a rented house. Under present law, the property holder owns the house. It is his property. But if he has rented it for a definite term, he may not tear it down, he may not evict the tenant, he may not raise the rent, he may not enter the house and sleep in the parlor during the period for which he has rented it. On the other hand, the tenant, in a certain sense, owns the house. I would consider it a perfectly proper use of language, as well as a highly appreciated courtesy, if one of you should say to me, "Come up to my house for dinner tomorrow night." The language would be equally appropriate whether the house in which one lives is secured by a warranty deed, or merely by a lease. But while the tenant may speak of his house, he cannot use it as a sweatshop, nor turn it into a cheap boarding house; he can not insist on having the rental reduced during the term of the contract, nor can he insist that for one year's rent he may have its exclusive use for two years.

[30] And so with wages contracts. The worker has a right to demand the fulfillment of the contract, but he has no right to demand that while the contract lasts he should receive a higher rate of wages or be allowed to lessen the stipulated services.

[31] To one who likes to rest upon principles, it would in itself be consistent to have the workers own the factories, or, without owning them, to run them, as was attempted by the labor organizations in Italy before the advent of Mussolini. But this horrible hodgepodge of property rights which are recognized and denied, of an organization at once capitalistic and communistic, of the denial of any right to profits at the same time that profit inducements are offered on every hand, this seems to the Scottish type of mind, of which Lord Macmillan spoke, to constitute a situation the sight of which, to quote William James's friend:

> made him sick
> like the sight of the horrible motion of a mass
> of maggots in their carrion bed.

Perhaps in this my thoughts:

> Do take a sober coloring from an eye
> That hath kept watch o'er man's mortality.

But I deny that I am a pessimist, and I am by no means an atrabilious dyspeptic.

[32] So far, despite the fact that I have at least ostensibly been a teacher since January 4, 1894, I have said nothing of education. "Shall not the hand of the dyer be subdued to what it works in?" At the preceding meeting of this club, Professor Hart discoursed learnedly upon the future of education. I leave that to him, and will only briefly touch upon the impression that past education has made upon me.

[33] The general and sweeping indictment, perhaps unsound just because of these qualities, is that university education is insincere and ineffective. It is insincere in that the college curricula insist upon prerequisites that are in no sense necessary for the following course. It is inconsistent in that when the student enters a following course, the fact of his having been equipped by a prerequisite is generally ignored. This is, of course, not true in many cases, but lamentably so in others. An illustration in point is the requirement in the College of Commerce that a student shall have had a course dealing with the mathematics of investments. Generally speaking, when the student goes into an advanced course, the application of the subject matter of Mathematics 2 is either evaded, or the instructor in the higher course laboriously, and less competently, repeats the instruction given in the lower division.

[34] That college education is to a large extent inefficient is particularly noticeable in regard to the foreign languages. I am not here indicting instruction in foreign languages because the student does not acquire a ready facility in speaking. That is of little moment. But there is no use in one's studying French or German if no ability to use it is thereby acquired. It is safe to say that in many, perhaps in a majority, of upper division courses, the student is relieved of any necessity to read works in other than English, although he has fulfilled all the foreign language requirements. The attitude of Professor Thorstein Veblen, when I was a graduate student at the University of Chicago, is commendable. One of my fellow students, who is now an outstanding member of the faculty of the University of Pennsylvania, was asked to report on a French author. The student confided to me that he had never studied a word of French, and was quite at sea. As I happened to be on rather intimate terms with Veblen, even though he was my instructor, I told him of the dilemma, and said that I did not see how a report could be made by one not knowing the language. To this he replied, in his characteristic drawl, "I don't know that I'm responsible for that." What was the result? The student secured the services of a fascinating young co-ed who translated the work with him. As a

result of this irregular procedure, he passed an examination for a reading knowledge of French which gave him a Fellowship at Pennsylvania, and he crowned it by marrying the co-ed. *Haec fabula docet*: I don't know just what.

[35] The educational system at present seems unsatisfactory in the practically unlimited enrollment. There seems to be an idea that every citizen has an inalienable right to a college education, just as he has a right to a job or a right to free speech, which in this club is construed as a right to talk for more than the five-minute limit. I suppose all of us admit that our over-crowded classrooms are an impediment to good work, that many students are here who are receiving no benefit adequate to the expense involved, that many of them would be individually benefited by some other occupation. Yet we do nothing about it, and, at least apparently, boast every time that the registration statistics show an increase in attendance.

[36] It also seems an inefficient procedure to grant free tuition under certain circumstances to residents of other states. To furnish instruction to a student is not only an expensive matter, but when the number of students is increased, the larger classes are a detriment to each individual enrolled therein. My own attitude would be that if Michigan is willing to furnish free tuition, we should heartily wish them Godspeed, and rejoice whenever they relieve us of the burden of educating any person. On the contrary, we and other universities are engaged in a wild competition, both by advertising and by offering subsidies to induce people to come to Berkeley in order that they may be an additional burden on our educational system. To me, this doesn't make sense.

[37] Despite the scriptural injunction: "Say not thou, What is the cause that the former days were better than these?" it is a common attitude to speak of general decay as a characteristic of our times. One hears that the Senate no longer contains a Webster, an Evarts, or a Calhoun, but in recent years we have had Huey Long and Tom Heflin, with Borah as the best specimen. We hear that Washington, Adams and Jefferson have not been followed by presidents of equal distinction, but that we have had such non-entities as Pierce, Arthur and Harding. Of course, it is admitted that there may be an exception, and that in the present incumbent of the White House we have the one transcendent genius who outshines all his precursors. But generally speaking, both in the Senate and in the Presidential chair, the standard of excellence is thought to have declined. I would not say the same thing about our University. There are those who point back to the good old days of the Le Contes and Moses, but surely even after Plehn and myself are put on the shelf, there still will be as great men, or greater, than any of their illustrious predecessors—men as great, and, of course, more of them. Although, with the great expansion in the University and its faculty, I would not venture to say whether the percentage of great men is as high as it may have been at one time. But who can look around at a meeting of the academic senate without a glow of pride? Medals galore, if not exposed on their bosoms, recline in their bureau drawers or in the pockets of its members. The crimson rosette of the Legion of Honor flashes from

the lapels of more than one. Members of the faculty have been admitted to the Academy and the Royal Astronomical Society, and to Skull and Keys, or have been made president of the local Rotary Club. And while modesty should check my tongue, it does not, and I boast of having been the only living man who was a president of Berkeley Mothers' Club.

[38] Impressions have been recorded relating to the state of the Universe and the University of the State. I now turn to this exalted body in which, for 21 years, I have been honored by membership. It would be pleasant to utter words of high praise of the Berkeley Club, but I recall that praise to the face is open disgrace, and in your presence:

> A solemn reverence checks my song
> And praise sits silent on my tongue.

[39] But there is no inhibition against paying brief tribute to some of those who have been colleagues in the Club, but who have joined:

> the choir invisible
> Of those immortal dead who live again
> In minds made better by their presence.

There was Moses, leonine, profound scholar, sympathetic leader, whose competence combined the mastery of three different departments, a professor who, long before the days of the New Deal, served as a Government official, and was even efficient in his service, one whose comprehensive view literally "observed mankind from China to Peru."

[40] Shall I speak of Bradley, whom all held in real affection, whose perfect diction and keen analysis made his papers and his comments so marked a contribution to the meetings of the Club. I recall my first attendance as a visitor, and his clear, incisive comments have stayed in my memory for considerably more than a score of years. Nor can I forget the delightful experience of being his companion in a packtrain trip in the Sierra, where he showed that he possessed, in addition to his knowledge of Siamese archaeology and his appreciation of English literature, an astounding knowledge of nature and a love of its beauties. To him I pay homage.

[41] Of Howison, the great philosopher, not long in the Club after my admission, it would be almost an impertinence for one who is a mere bookkeeper to venture even to render honor. In reverence and sincere humility, I leave to you, who knew him better, the placing of a wreath in his memory. And what beautiful scraps he used to stage with Fred Torrey!

[42] There was Earl, a strange combination of practical man of affairs and a deeply religious mystic, Friend of the Club whose skill made him purveyor of those marvelous duck dinners, above all a devoted and unselfish friend of the University. Even the one who suffered most at his hands expressed in private conver-

sation with me unqualified appreciation of Earl's loyalty to, and labors for, the University. To me, as well as to others in our group, a fraternity brother and friend. Though differing from him in most matters of opinion, and opposed to some of his policies, he who was always addressed as "Hatty" now pays friendly tribute to the memory of Guy.

[43] Torrey was to me a closer personal friend and associate than any of those previously mentioned. But it is as a member of the Club, not merely as a beloved friend, that I mention his name. Rare combination—who else was at once an authority on such diverse subjects as coleoptera, birds of the Sierra, evolutionary theory, literature, and, of course, art? Most devoted to the Club, despite the competition of alluring attractions, never missing a meeting, until the advance agent of his last and only enemy placed an impediment on his steps, and a halting finger on his lips. But up to the very end of his last tragic year, maintaining his interest in the papers read at the Club which were often submitted to him. We all miss him.

[44] I would like to do more than merely mention him who has so recently left us. The memory of Pillsbury's departure is too fresh, and our appreciation of him will be so much more adequately presented in the Club's formal memorial, that I forbear further comment.

[45] But the Berkeley Club is not a thing of the past. It still lacks seven years of reaching that age when, along with other antiques, it must be placed upon the shelf.

[46] Praise to your face has already been banned. So if comment on the present-day Club is to be made, it must partake of the nature of criticism. Not unfriendly criticism in any sense. Perhaps not criticism at all, merely suggestions. These will be limited to two matters:

[47] The enforced discussion of papers, in which each member is called upon, in turn, seems to me a mistake. Although I was brought up in the practices of the Methodist Class meeting, I like better the idea of the old Quaker meeting, where no one is called upon, but each waits until the spirit really moves him. I have always liked the phrase: "Having nothing to say, he said it." But I prefer it in the literal sense, not with the idea that one in that dilemma nevertheless kept on talking. If each one must willy-nilly comment on a paper, it often results in empty or platitudinous compliments which are occasionally indulged in although supposed to be contrary to the traditions of the Berkeley Club. Violent criticism would be more entertaining than the repeated phrase, "I greatly enjoyed the paper."

[48] The present effusion is not such as to provoke thought, or to arouse discussion. But if the chairman unwisely goes around the circle, I am at least giving you vastly greater opportunity for censure than for praise.

[49] The most refreshing comment which has come to me in regard to my work is as follows: A young accountant was given a copy of my first book which, while not so planned, came to him on Christmas day. Opening the package, he commented, as he read the title: "Hatfield's *Modern Accounting*. Well, if that isn't a

hell of a Christmas present!" In a few minutes, this paper will be in your hands. Do your darnedest.

[50] The second suggestion is heretical, it is *lése majesté*, it is almost blasphemy. It is that the meetings are too frequent. Once a month would be better than once each fortnight. Frequent meetings were very desirable in 1873. But back there Berkeley had no Symphony concerts, no University Orchestra, no movies, no Little Theater, no Oakland Forum, no Hitchcock lectures, no Sather lectures, no Faculty Research, or Weinstock or Foerster lectures, no Faculty Club dances, no Rotary, or Lions, or Kiwanis. It did have one institution which the Secretary of this Club, soon after his coming, was urged to join in the following words: "You really ought to join the Druids; it is so nice to have some way of spending your evenings." Do you feel the necessity of such an outlet?

[51] The effect of too frequent meetings, I believe, lessens attendance. If some competing attraction comes on the meeting night, any member less devoted than were Torrey and Pillsbury is inclined to say, "I hate to miss the Berkeley Club tonight, but there will be another in only two weeks." If held at longer intervals, one would be less inclined to play hookey. And perhaps the recent regrettable declination of membership would not have been made had membership implied absence from the family circle only once a month instead of each fourteen days. If this be treason, make the most of it.

[52] This paper was entitled *Moriturus Vos Saluto*. But you were not asked here either to bewail my demise, nor riotously to celebrate an Irish wake. The felicitations, so commonly given by saying "Now you will be free to do what you want" are inappropriate. I have been doing just that ever since I began to teach. Even more inappropriate are the words of Charles Wesley:

> Weep not for a brother deceased
> [Your] loss is his infinite gain
> A soul out of prison released
> And freed from his [faculty] chain.

[53] It was wrong to quote:

> backward do I cast my e'e
> On prospects drear.

The prospects, or more puristically, the retrospect, of 33 years are not drear, but on the contrary very *dear*.

> The thought of our past years in me doth breed
> Perpetual benediction.

It is good to be here.

[54] I go to the land entitled Emeritas from which one never returns to an academic Cathedra. To the land where blue books cease from troubling and the registrar gives us rest. Where committees are unknown, and deans do not longer make one afraid. But think not that the change is altogether longed for. The transition from one form of life to another is the great adventure, but it is neither a dread calamity nor a joyful release. Perhaps, rather, a change of the harness by which Pegasus is hitched to the cart. The old harness has chafed in places, but through long custom these places have become callous and no longer painful, for:

> Our torments also may in length of time
> Become our elements.

Will the new harness bear more lightly, who can tell? As I make this parting salutation to you, all I can say to myself is:

> In years foregone was all not well
> Still lovelier life awaits thee, fear not thou.

[55] So I toast Plehn as well as myself, and include Richardson also, in the somewhat ribald words of the old song sung by British officers during the plague:

> Here's to those who are dying
> And hurrah for the next who dies!

[56] My paper began with a familiar Latin quotation. It closes by linking it with one equally trite, but equally appropriate:

> *Moriturus vos saluto*

and

> *De mortuis nil nisi bonum.*[11]

"A Critique of the Tentative Statement of Accounting Principles Underlying Corporate Reports," 1937

> This paper was read at the 22nd annual meeting of the American Accounting Association, on December 29, 1937. Hatfield did not get round to submitting the paper to *The Accounting Review* until 1941, but editor Eric L. Kohler decided against publication because, he said, a revision of the 1936 "Tentative Statement" was shortly to appear. Even though the 1941 version did not differ significantly from the original, Kohler probably believed that Hatfield's critique was not constructive or useful.

Despite its weaknesses in addressing the substantive accounting issues in the "Tentative Statement," this presentation illustrates Hatfield's sustained dislike of language that was used imprecisely. As many of his former students remembered, he believed that clear writing was inextricable from clear thinking. Hatfield justifies (Paragraphs 1-2) the approach he takes in discussing the statement: the language was so vague and illogical that these omissions needed analysis before the substance of the report could be considered. The presentation exudes a strident, although conversational, tone in attacking what he considers to be major problems in meaning based on imprecise language. Hatfield's irritation is palpable, although humorous.

While his criticism becomes more strident as the essay progresses, Hatfield, as he always did in beginning an essay that would evolve into an attack, ingratiates himself with his audience. He adopts a self-effacing tone in stating that he will leave to others "the weightier matters of the law," while he confines his remarks "to mint, anise and cummin." Ultimately, however, he argues that, without accurate use of language, the statement has little worth, a position that demolishes his reverence for the "weighter matters" stated in the opening paragraph.

[1] In this paper I am taking upon myself an ungracious and perhaps discreditable role—that of neglecting the substance of the "Tentative Statement" and limiting my comments to matters of form and expression, leaving to others the weightier matters of the law and confining myself to mint, anise and cumin. I have felt the ignominy of my position but have constructed a defense mechanism by rationalizing my conduct as follows:

[2] After all, the American Accounting Association is largely an academic body. As such it is concerned in its semi-official enunciations not only with correct principles, but also with the niceties of formulation, the avoidance of vagueness, the respect due to the English language, with freedom from solecisms and adherence to logical consistency. So eminent a body should, like Caesar's wife, be free from ordinary frailties. Is this a sufficient alibi for my leaving to others the discussion of the substance of the report? I hope so.

[3] I. My first criticism is that the report begins with a criminal assault on the English language. It essays to present a fundamental axiom, followed by twenty propositions, "each of which," I quote, "embodies a corollary of this fundamental axiom."

[4] It annoys me when a discussion of some phase of accounting begins with reference to dictionary definitions. Accountants have their own peculiar jargon on which the dictionary throws little light. But "axiom" and "corollary" are not technical accounting terms. In vain I search the Institute's report on accounting terminology, in vain the indexes of accounting texts, or the pages of Lisle's

Encyclopedia for these terms. They belong to the spheres of philosophy and mathematics. If an accountant uses them there is a moral obligation to pay some attention to their accepted meaning.

[5] Is there doubt as to the meaning of "axiom"? Is it not "a self-evident truth," a proposition whose truth is so evident that no reasoning or demonstration can make it plainer, an established principle which is universally received, such as "a thing cannot at the same time be and not be"?

[6] Now this alleged axiom, and it is not merely an axiom but a fundamental axiom (if one knows the difference), is that accounting essentially is not a process of valuation but the allocation of historical costs. Is this self-evident? Does it need no demonstration? Is it universally received?

[7] But one John R. Wildman, the first president of the Association, and R.B. Kester, whose acumen and perspicacity none can gainsay, and A.L. Dickinson, whom no one ever accused of being so moronic as to deny a fundamental axiom, all state (the quotations will be furnished on request; enclose a self-addressed, stamped envelope) that it is wise and proper at times to substitute appraised values for historical costs.

[8] And what about Professor Fritz Schmidt, putative head of the Frankfort School of Accounting Theory, whose whole structure of accounting rests on the proposition that all assets should be recorded at their then market value—not at some anterior cost. And there is Canning, whose stimulating *Economics of Accountancy* says that all the items in the balance sheet should appear at the discounted value of the services or disservices which they will yield. And finally, in a recent survey of corporation balance sheets only eighty-seven percent stated distinctly that the property was valued on the basis of cost. Not for a moment am I arguing that accounting should not rest on a cost basis. But what kind of an axiom is it when Wildman, and Kester, and Dickinson and Schmidt and Canning deny its universality?

[9] And what of these twenty corollaries of this somewhat temperamental axiom? A corollary, says the *New Oxford Dictionary*, is "in geometry a proposition appended to another which has been demonstrated and following immediately from it, without new proof; hence, generally an immediate inference, deduction, consequence." I will not argue about all these so-called corollaries, but will discuss only one as an example. The ninth proposition states that the income account should be divided into two sections. Suppose one were so foolish as to dispute the fundamental axiom, would he not still want a sub-division of the income statement? Such an accounting device is entirely independent of whether accounts represent present values or historical costs. It cannot in any sense be considered a derivative of the fundamental axiom.

[10] I have refrained from citing other propositions which are statements of recommended procedure and are not corollaries of the main thesis. But I ask you seriously to consider whether propositions 6, 8, 10, 12, 13, 14, 16, 17, 18, and 19 are not wrongly labeled corollaries.

[11] Instead of repeating the trite but eminently pertinent quotation from Humpty Dumpty regarding the meaning of words, I quote a somewhat less familiar authority, Mr. Dooley. In his description of expert testimony in the Luetgert case, he reports the expert as testifying:

> I made lab'ratory experiments in an i'r'n basin with bichloride of gool, which I will call soup stock, an' coal tar, which I will call i'r'n filings. I then packed it in ice which I will call glue, an' rock-salt which I will call fried eggs an' obtained a dark queer solution which is a cure f'r freckles which I will call antimony, or doughnuts or anny thing I blamed please.

Somewhat similarly, the Committee on Principles might almost say:

> I put in a much disputed dictum which I will call a fundamental axiom, then I added twenty unrelated statements which I call corollaries an' obtained a dark queer solution of accounting problems which I will call a Tentative Statement, which is a cure for all accounting difficulties, which I will call rules, or principles, or a hodge-podge of unrelated values of no explicable significance, or anny thing I blamed please.

[12] II. In the second place, I charge the report with treason. Treason in that having sworn allegiance to a great principle (it is immaterial whether it was an axiom or not) it later does not prove loyal in its allegiance. If that be not treason, make the most of it.

[13] Emerson, indeed, says, "A foolish consistency is the hobgoblin of little minds." But facing the obloquy of showing myself one of the little-minded, I do think that a formal, much labored, often revised document emanating from a learned body should try to avoid inconsistent statements.

[14] How far does the report cling to its position that accounting is not a process of valuation? It falls down when it has recourse to market value of inventories.

[15] There is a strong argument, made by one of our own members, that the cost or market rule is really an application of amortizing original cost. But nevertheless, the process is one of valuation, not of the application of "an intelligible formula."

[16] This point may be clarified by a simple illustration. An annuity of $100 a year, running 20 years, is bought for $1147 (1146.99) at which price it yields 6%. At the end of ten years, a calculation would show that of the $1000 received in installments, $589 represented interest at 6% on the amount invested and $411 was a reduction of the capital. The annuity would then be listed at $736. That is, the original cost of $1147 has been partially amortized, $411 being allocated to the preceding ten years, $736 held as applicable to the future. This is a proper allocation of historical costs "measured," as the report says, "according to an intelligible formula" and is not essentially a process of valuation. Very good.

[17] But suppose that at the end of ten years, the current rate of income has risen to 7 percent and the credit standing of the company issuing the annuity is so lowered that its promises are heavily discounted. If in such case an estimate is made

that the annuity is now worth only $400, the mark down for the preceding period of ten years would be $1147 – $400, or $747.

[18] In the first case a calculation is made of how much of the cost of the annuity has been paid off, and the remaining cost is carried over. In the second, the process is reversed. A value, bearing no predeterminable ratio to the cost, is ascertained by outside means. And having determined the present value, the allocation of cost is entirely dependent thereon. This is a valuation, in contrast to an actuarial, process. In one case, cost is the base, from which the other figures are derived. In the second one, appraisal is the base, from which amortization of cost is derived. The first method, by one or another intelligible formula, is ordinarily applied in depreciation. The second method is used whenever the lower market price is substituted for the price paid for merchandise.

[19] But again the dogma regarding cost is shattered by the statement in corollary 2, that cost is measured "by the fair market value of property acquired in exchange for securities." Surely that is not cost in any sense. If the securities issued are shares of a new corporation, they have no value in themselves. It is not cost that is ascertained, but a value of acquired assets learned from outside sources. Here we have a process of valuation pure and simple.

[20] Another instance of inconsistency is when it is said "assets in use or ultimately to be marketed" (thus covering plant as well as merchandise) should be reduced to "such amounts as may reasonably be expected to be recoverable in the course of future operations." (page 10)[12] Probably the Committee does not mean this. They should not say what they do not mean. The value of an article is not what it will bring at some future day. The present value of a future good is the discounted value of the sum, not the sum itself. But it seems strange to set up future recoverable values in a document which proclaims "cost not value." Canning is consistent (whether correct or not is immaterial) in his argument regarding asset values to which reference has already been made. But he does not say he is following a theory of cost.

[21] Again, the paragraph immediately following the rejection of valuation starts out "The accountant's valuation"; the next following paragraph contains the phrase "fair market value of property acquired"; the summary says "the foregoing paragraphs ... provide a ... basis for asset valuation procedure." (page 9)

[22] Another instance where subsequent statements do not agree with the basic statement occurs in connection with income. The report states that "Accounting is ... the allocation of historical costs and revenues to the current and succeeding fiscal periods." (page 7)

[23] Now allocation means a proper allocation. To charge an expense solely connected with 1940 to 1941 and 1942 is not allocation in any but the crudest etymological sense.

[24] But on page 13 the report, in so many words, sanctions as one alternative treatment, the showing of "charges or credits to the current period of losses or gains which actually apply to earlier periods." On the same page it is stated that

the income statement should contain adjustments to allow for gains or losses not strictly applicable to the current period.

[25] May I put in a word of personal defense? I am not here arguing as to whether expenses which really occurred in 1940, but were not booked until 1941, should or should not appear in the income statement of the latter year. But I do contend, and as strongly as possible, that a report which starts with the fundamental axiom that accounting is the allocation of historical costs to the current and succeeding fiscal periods is not true to its dogma when it openly includes in a given income statement items not so allocable. It is a sound objection to the language of the report that it confuses a change taking place *during* a given period and the *recognition* and *recording* in a given period of a change which took place previously. Whether depreciation was recorded in 1940 or not, it was then that it took place. The correction in 1941 of the omission is not recording a change which took place in 1941, except in the utterly futile sense that anything which is recorded in a given year changes the record. But surely accountants are discussing changes in income, and assets, and not merely changes of balances written in a ledger.

[26] Perhaps the report justifies itself by stating (page 9) that principles should be applied with flexibility. This is somewhat akin to the rule in *The Lost Horizon* that moderation should be applied to all things including chastity. But principles in a science are stubborn things. Applications may be flexible. But flexibility does not extend to clearly contradictory statements.

[27] III. A third charge in the indictment of the report is that it uses language which is vague and violates the injunction to write so that he who runs may read.

[28] Specifications under this charge include the following matters:

[29] 1. The report puts the showing of financial condition as a prime object of accounting, but nowhere explains what the term means. Some earlier accountants seem to mean by the term, an exhibit of the relative position of assets, and liabilities, leading up to the 2:1 rule, and the Acid Test. That is a possible concept if accounting is showing present values. But it does not apply in a system which rejects present values, and considers costs. If current liabilities are $100,000 and current assets are readily realizable at $200,000, so far as the 2:1 rule is of any significance, this does give some sort of a picture of a financial condition. But if these same assets are listed on the balance sheet at only $100,000, because that was the original cost, what is the financial position exhibited? The committee should explain.

[30] 2. The report speaks in Corollary 1 of a rule for the valuation of "physical assets." Does the term "physical assets" include merchandise? And does the rule that part of the cost should be written off to reflect expired usefulness apply only to physical assets? Does the committee disapprove of amortizing a leasehold, or a definitely limited franchise, or a terminable annuity? But is any one of these a physical asset?

[31] Corollary 5 seems to identify, although not conclusively, physical and fixed assets. In ordinarily accepted accounting jargon, the terms are not synonymous. Physical assets include merchandise but not a leasehold. Fixed assets include a long term leasehold but exclude merchandise.

[32] 3. What does the report mean when it says the gross amount of an obligation should be shown in the balance sheet?

[33] If I were discussing the substance rather than the form of the report, I might express approval of the doctrine involved, despite its general non-acceptance by the profession.

[34] If three notes are issued, each due in one year:

One for $1060 without interest
One for $1000 with interest at 6%, payable at maturity
One for $1000 with an additional interest note for $60

the borrower should, if 6% is the ruling rate, receive the same amount, $1000. The report holds that the first note should be shown at the gross amount of the obligation, that is $1060. Should the second and third notes be similarly shown at the gross amount of the obligation, which is identical with that of the first note?

[35] 4. The verbal distinction between cost and value is out of place in a scientific document. Value is defined, not by Webster but by a committee of Certified Public Accountants, as "the attributed worth of anything expressed in money." Any figure, appearing in the balance sheet or in the ledger, expressed in dollars, is thus, obviously, a "value." The distinction which the report is trying to make is not between value and non-value, but between cost-value and present market- or replacement-value.

[36] IV. The report is inconsistent and illogical in its discussion of the effect on accounts of changes in the general price level, a matter which Mr. Sweeney has treated in a masterly and scholarly manner.

[37] But I am permitted to criticize the committee for failing to differentiate a particular change in price, and a change in the general price level due to inflation or deflation. Because of particular economic conditions, such as an abnormal war demand, or the opening of new mines, a quantity of copper which cost $200 might later be worth $400 or $100. Such a change may perhaps legitimately be ignored in accounts because it does not affect cost. But if that which cost $200 is now quoted at $400, not because of change in copper but because $400 at the later date is the equivalent of $200 of the old dollars, the situation is different. The dollars appearing in the Cash account, and represented by the receivables and payables are present-day dollars.

[38] The argument is made that to regard such price changes is to reduce accounts to a "hodge-podge of unrelated values of no explicable significance." (page 9)

[39] An analogy is found in a different measuring unit. Suppose a grain elevator contains 100,000 bushels of wheat, bought when a bushel was legally 60 pounds. Later the bushel is legally reduced to 30 pounds, and 200,000 such bushels are added to the stock on hand. Would it not be "hodge-podge of unrelated values" to report that the wheat on hand amounted to 300,000 bushels? Should it not be expressed either at 200,000 bushels old style, or 400,000 bushels new style, or as 12,000,000 pounds of wheat? Must not units added together be similar in content? Why does the attempt to introduce a common unit in money differ from using some common unit for wheat?

[40] Furthermore, "recognition" of the changed content of the dollar does not imply a substitution of present for cost value. It attempts merely to express the *cost* of different units in a common unit. If two machines were bought, one for $10,000 and the other, at a time when the dollar had depreciated 50 percent, for $20,000, it would be meaningless to say the two cost $30,000. Thirty thousand what? The confusion is the same as in the expression of the stock of wheat. If 10,000 old dollars are added to 20,000 new dollars, the total is mathematically unsound. An attempt to express the cost of all articles in the same monetary unit is not an abandonment of the cost basis.

[41] The dogma that significant changes in price do not take place in a single generation is surely false. How great the change should be to demand recognition may be debatable. But there is little sense in requiring the showing of two percent depreciation on a building and ruling out, as immaterial, changes in the value of money of 50, 40 or 30 percent.

[42] Even were it true (which it isn't) that significant changes in price level cover a generation, it is amusing to advance that as an argument against their recognition in a document which properly attempts to apportion slowly moving forces—such as depreciation—to annual, or in some cases, to monthly periods.

[43] Again, an "ordinary change" in price levels is to be rejected in a report which in its advocacy of "cost or market" does not recognize *ordinary* change in price.

[44] V. Certain adjustments are criticized because they are in accordance with "expected business development." (page 9) And this in the same section of the report which says "assets in use or ultimately to be marketed" should have as carrying value "such amounts as may reasonably be expected to be recoverable in the course of future operations." (page 10)

[45] Great Scot! "expected business developments" ruled out of consideration, and "recoverable in the course of future operations" set up as a criterion!

[46] One often hears that this is a mad world in which we now live. But isn't there still consistency and logic to be found in even the American Accounting Association?

[47] There is a story of a man, on a winter journey, who was joined by a fire-breathing dragon. The man did not like the new comrade, but knew not how to be rid of him. They stopped at an inn. When the man blew on his soup, "Why

do you do that?" asked the Dragon. "To cool my soup," said the man. "But," said the Dragon, "a while ago you blew on your fingers to warm them, now you blow on your soup to cool it. I can understand warming things by blowing on them. That is simple. But I cannot fathom one who can blow both hot and cold. I am afraid of such a combination." And he quit the man's company, greatly to the latter's relief.

[48] I, too, am awe-inspired, and much afraid when an accountant both rejects and adopts an estimate of future business development. But though afraid, I hope still to retain the companionship of those who blow both hot and cold.

[49] VI. I charge the report with a double standard, something which the Women's Party holds most objectionable. This appears in regard to what are actual occurrences.

[50] Recognition of a change in price is apparently not a consistent record of "actual occurrences." (page 9) But is the amount charged for depreciation in a given year an "*actual occurrence*"? Depreciation has undoubtedly occurred, but its amount no one knows. And even with an "intelligible formula" whatever formula is used, the two factors, life of the asset and residual value, involve some estimate of future events.

[51] Is not the charge for obsolescence even more a matter of guesswork, yet such a charge is advocated? (page 8)

[52] Is the allowance for bad debts an "actual occurrence"?

[53] As compared with these, a change in price established by published quotations is related, so far as actuality is concerned, as a hippopotamus to Conan Doyle's Ektoplasm.

[54] VII. I charge the report with libelous disparagement of the ability of accountants.

[55] The report says, "It would seem to be beyond the ability of the accountant to establish the propriety of some new (how come new?—Paciolo used it in 1494) basis of valuation which has no relation to past outlays or experience of the business or industry." (page 10) And this is in the same report which substitutes the lower market price which certainly has "no relation to past outlay." Again, I insist that the rule of cost or market, whichever is lower, is not a calculation of unamortized cost but a value not even related by marriage or adoption to past outlays—except in the absurdly literal sense that any arithmetical figure has a percentual relation to every other one.

[56] VIII. I charge the report with inhumanity in that it gives a stone to those who want bread.

[57] Much talk is there of capital gains. But the poor beggar who wants to know when a gain is a capital gain is put off with the statement that "the income statement should show realized capital gains." (Corollary 9)

[58] The probate courts have consistently distinguished between capital gains and income. Is a capital gain income, or isn't it? If it is not income, why should it

be put in the income account? One longs for enlightenment from an authoritative source.

[59] And when is a capital loss realized? The report says: "Reduce the carrying value of assets in use (which surely includes factory site and building) to such amount as may reasonably be expected to be recoverable in the course of future operations." (page 10) Has this loss been realized or is it to be realized in the course of future operations? And is the rule for determining whether a *loss* is realized different from that which tells whether a *gain* is realized? This is not implying any objection to including unrealized losses and excluding unrealized gains.

[60] IX. An interesting statement appears on page 16, where reference is made to the principles of accounting as restricting procedures which are "not in accord with good accounting and finance." How are accounting principles dependent on good finance? Is the accountant to ignore, or to report, transactions which are not good finance? It may well be bad finance to use short term notes to obtain funds to construct a building, it may be bad finance to pay a dividend although undoubtedly there is abundant earned surplus, if the cash disbursed as a dividend is vitally necessary to pay a debt due the next day. But if these acts of bad finance are done, the accountant has no choice. His function is to show what took place: to ascertain profits and to classify rightly the several assets and liabilities. Even if a dividend is paid when there are no profits whatever, the principles of accounting say merely that the accountant must show the dividend was paid, and that the capital has been impaired thereby. The principles of accounting have nothing more to do with good finance than they have with the bleaching of the stenographer's hair, or the hue of her nails. Indeed *the* (not *a*) fundamental axiom of accounting is to give as correct an account of what has taken place as is possible. In fewer words, to tell the truth about the operations of a business.

[61] X. Two random queries:

Are costs ever diminished, or are they more immutable than the pyramids? (Corollary 3)

Why should a purely "present" value basis of accounting such as advocated by Canning and by Schmidt "reflect uncertain and inconsistent financial policies"? (page 10) The picture of present values does not necessarily reflect financial policies at all; the policies need not have been at all *uncertain*, and a strict adherence to present values might indeed be carried out with the most perfect *consistency*. Why support one theory of accounting by attributing to some other theory effect and defects not thereto adherent? Even an erroneous theory may have some good points.

PREVIOUSLY PUBLISHED PAPERS

"Some Variations in Accounting Practice in England, France, Germany and the United States," *Journal of Accounting Research*, Vol. 4, No. 2, Autumn 1966, pp. 169-182.

This paper, which Hatfield delivered to a meeting in 1911 but never submitted for publication, was finally published in 1966, when I brought it to the attention of David Green, Jr., editor of the *Journal of Accounting Research.* It represents the first study in the English language that compares the accounting practices of several major countries. Hatfield gathered his data on two trips to Europe, one in 1900, while he was at the University of Chicago, and the second in 1907, when he was on leave from the University of California, during which he also spent time in New York City. A comparative study of this kind, conducted at a time when so little reliable information about accounting practices and their institutional origins was accessible outside of a country, amply testifies to Hatfield's resourcefulness and pertinacity. It also relied heavily on his ability to read German and French, language skills that few other accounting writers in the English language literature at that time would have possessed. An additional introductory note appears at the front of the article. This article is reproduced by permission of the *Journal of Accounting Research.*[13]

Some Variations in Accounting Practice in England, France, Germany and the United States*

HENRY RAND HATFIELD†

Henry Rand Hatfield (1866–1945) was a pioneer in collegiate accounting education in the United States. He received a Ph.D. in political economy and political science in 1897 from the University of Chicago, and in 1898 joined the Chicago faculty. He became the first dean of the College of Commerce and Administration at the University of Chicago in 1902 and offered an accounting course in 1901–02 and 1902–03, based in part on a three-month tour of Colleges of Commerce in France and Germany in 1899–1900, where, at the University of Leipzig, he met and became influenced by Johann Friedrich Schär. In 1904, he moved to the University of California, beginning a long tenure in the College of Commerce as associate professor, then, professor of accounting.

In 1911, the American Association of Public Accountants (predecessor of the American Institute of Certified Public Accountants) held its annual convention in San Francisco, and Hatfield was asked to present a paper. Unlike most of his contemporaries, Hatfield eschewed the dogmatic approach in favor of critical surveys of what legal and accounting authorities had written. He chose as his topic the accounting practices in England, France, Germany, and the United States, evidently believing that the collective wisdom of practitioners and writers in these countries might profitably be used as authoritative guidance in the United States. In 1911, the accounting literature in this country was small indeed.

Hatfield discovered Simon's treatise during his European trip in 1899–1900, and it is probable that he found the identically titled work by Rehm shortly after it was

* This paper was prepared for presentation before the annual meeting of the American Association of Public Accountants, at San Francisco, on September 20, 1911. The author having been absent on leave at the time, the paper was read by George R. Webster, of the California State Society of Certified Public Accountants. As far as is known, it has never been published or circulated generally. The original manuscript has been slightly edited, to correct mispellings, to improve punctuation, to implement the author's own pencilled alterations (where intelligible), and to bring older spellings into agreement with current practice.

† Professor of Accounting, 1904–1937, University of California (Berkeley).

published, in 1903. Since he was unable to be present for the A.A.P.A. meeting, the paper was read by another. It has never been published or referred to in the accounting literature, and was recently found, together with several other unpublished papers, in Hatfield's files at the University of California, Berkeley. In point of chronology, the paper is Hatfield's first article-length manuscript on accounting which survives. It followed publication of his *Modern Accounting* by two years, antedated "An Historical Defense of Bookkeeping" by thirteen, and was one of Hatfield's few literary efforts during the fifteen-year period between these two better-known works. In the context of the currently expanding interest in international accounting, the paper represents a rare source of insight into comparative accounting practices 55 years ago. It is reproduced with permission from the Hatfield Papers, Schools of Business Administration, University of California, Berkeley.—STEPHEN A. ZEFF

To make such a comparison as is called for by the title of this paper implies first of all, exact knowledge as to what is the accounting practice of any particular country. But who can with confidence describe even the practice of American railways in regard to showing sinking fund transaction. One road differs from another in this respect and who can say which represents the best, or even the typical American practice? Or, in American practice, what is meant by the term "Reserve Fund," or what rate of depreciation is the customary one? So vague is accounting terminology, so unsettled is accounting practice, so unhampered are the idiosyncracies of accountants that it would take a high degree of assurance for one to assert that he knew the rules of accounting practice, even in his own country.

The same difficulty is found in studying the methods in vogue in foreign countries. In some of them there is a little less self-initiative, in some respects there may be a greater uniformity, but it is indeed difficult to determine whether some peculiar form met in foreign accounts is typical of differences between foreign and American methods, or whether it represents merely such a particular variation as might as well be found by comparing different American accounts.

Furthermore it is to be recognized that foreign and American accounting methods are, at heart, one. Accounting in all the modern world has developed from the same simple beginnings. Paciolo's *Tractatus*, either in the original or in translations or adaptations, spread through all Europe, and everywhere is the basis upon which modern accounting rests. One speaks in accounting literature of Italian, of American, of German bookkeeping. But Italian bookkeeping is not at all limited to Italy, American bookkeeping, at least as the term is used abroad, did not even originate in America, and German bookkeeping differs only in unessential details from the other systems.

Recognizing then fully the difficulty, or even the impossibility, of adequately discussing the subject, it may still be possible to bring forward a few points in which differences are found and to compare some variations in the accounting methods prevalent in the several countries.

The first point on which one can with some confidence speak, is that in European countries, there has, at least to the present time, been a more definite effort made to regulate accounting practice by direct legislation.

On this point the United States, in very recent years, has made some marked progress, of which the most noteworthy step has been the minute regulations prescribed by the Interstate Commerce Commission. But in general, accounting has been neglected, perhaps not altogether to its injury, by legislation. But in Europe, especially on the continent, bookkeeping methods, like so many other industrial activities, have been distinctly regulated by the government. Thus, it is almost universally the custom in countries all around the world to prescribe by law that merchants, as well as corporations, must keep accounts. Except in the Spanish-speaking countries, it is not distinctly specified that books must be kept in double entry, but the provision found in German law that the books must be kept according to the principles of "*ordnungsmässige*" bookkeeping, and the law, common to the other European countries, that the accounts must include a balance sheet and a statement of profit and loss, are by some thought to imply, that at least so far as concerns corporations, the keeping of double-entry books is not merely a matter of common practice, but is as well an obligation under the law.

German law provides further that the books of account must be bound with consecutively numbered pages, free from lacunae, erasures and alterations.[1] England makes no such requirement. France[2] and other continental countries, however, have similar requirements so far as relates to consecutive numbering and uninterrupted records. In France, Belgium and Switzerland, but not in Germany, there is provision for having the main books of accounts inspected and viséed by a public official, who certifies that the book is the recognized account book and that it contains such a number of pages. This provision, it is interesting to note, goes back almost unchanged to the very beginning of bookkeeping, the method being fully described in the seventh chapter of Paciolo's treatise.

The provisions relating to the use of bound books, with consecutive and uninterrupted records, and even those providing for the authentification of books of accounts have, perhaps not necessarily, had an impeding effect on the introduction of loose leaf forms in bookkeeping, although even in Europe this modern improvement is growing somewhat in favor.

The next step in the regulation of bookkeeping is the specifications as to the particular books which are to be kept, or the specific accounts which are to be framed. Almost all countries, with the exception of Germany, England and the United States, distinctly provide that there must at least be kept a chronologically arranged book of original entry called a journal or day-book. This may be kept in approved double entry form, but generally that is not specifically required, and it may follow the model of the old *memorial* current in the very beginning of bookkeeping. Of the more than twenty-five countries having such a provision, almost all follow rather slavishly the provision of the French Code, which, indeed, has set the

[1] *D. H. G. B.* § 43.

[2] *Code de Commerce*, Article 10.

standard for most of the continental regulation of accounting practice. The Code reads in part "Every merchant is bound to keep a day-book (*livre journal*) which shall exhibit, day by day, the debts due to or payable by him, his business transactions, and negotiations, the acceptance or endorsement of bills, and generally all that he receives or pays on any account whatever, and that shall show month by month, the sums used for the expenses of his household; the above being irrespective of other books generally used in business, but which are not obligatory."[3]

This provision, says Stern, on the face requires that every transaction should be entered in a single book. But this insistence on a single book of original entry, honored though it may be by the doctrine first laid down by Paciolo, and confirmed by *Ordonnance of 1673*, from which the Code has borrowed freely, is but seldom observed in actual French practice.[4] The absurdity of attempting to conduct modern books, on the model which served well enough in the primitive conditions of the 15th century, has been formally objected to by French accountants, whose official congress demanded a modification of this article of the Code. But so far the change demanded has not been made.

In addition to the daybook, almost every nation except the United States requires that an annual inventory be prepared. The provisions in this respect are almost identical; an annual balance sheet also is required in some thirty countries, in most of which the requirement applying to individual traders as well as to corporations.

Less uniform are the requirements in reference to the form of the balance sheet, and the conditions of its publication. Legislation has generally contented itself with prescribing a balance sheet, without laying down rules as to the form in which it shall be made out. Indeed, when the question was distinctly raised by the French commission of 1902 it was finally decided that the better policy was merely to demand publicity without prescribing forms. Similar action was taken in Belgium. But a somewhat close approximation to a uniform balance sheet is found in the well-known model located in Table A of the English Company's Act of 1862. While this form has been somewhat followed by accountants, it was never compulsory, and in the revision of 1906 it was dropped from the Table. It is not necessary to dwell upon the peculiar nature of this commonly accepted English form, for the divergence which it shows from the practice of other countries, in placing the liabilities on the left side, has been commented upon, favorably or unfavorably by every writer on accounting. Nor is it necessary to emphasize the peculiarities of another form of balance sheet used in England, the so-called double account balance sheet, applicable to parliamentary companies and familiar in the reports of English railroads. The separation in such balance sheets of the capital assets and liabilities from the other accounts has been much criticized and has led to some perhaps unnecessary infer-

[3] Article 8.

[4] R. Stern, *Buchhaltungs Lexikon* (1904), 275.

ences as to the treatment of a decline in value of the fixed plant. The double account form is almost unknown outside of England, the only instances of its use in this country which I have noticed, being found in the accounts of the Atchison, Topeka & Santa Fe Railway and in those of the Mexican International Railroad. Except, however, in the implications drawn from the form, and the effect which it may have had, in leading the English accountants to disregard losses of fixed capital, the variation between the double account balance sheet and the conventional form is of very little significance.

In this country the legal provisions in regard to balance sheets are few and generally limited in character. Massachusetts has indeed published a model balance sheet, and specific forms are required of national banks and of railroads. In the latter, as laid down by the Interstate Commerce Commission, there is a greater amount of detail and a more strenuous effort to secure a scientific and intelligible exposé of the status of the company, than is attempted by the legislation, or attained by the ordinary practices of any other country. So much may not be said of the form prescribed for national banks, yet even these compare favorably with the statements published by either the Bank of France or the Bank of England. The former being rather confused in arrangement and the latter woefully deficient in details.

Another rather important variation rests upon the principle of German law that the balance sheet is in large part designed to indicate the amount of profit available for dividend. In England, and probably also in the United States, the balance sheet seems designed rather to assure the interested creditor of the solvency of the concern. This is particularly true in case of banks in this country where neither in the balance sheet nor in any other published statement is there any indication whatever of the earnings of the bank. But the German balance sheet must show not merely the balance of the undivided profits, but by law must, and in practice actually does, exhibit the net earnings of the year; and within the limits of the balance sheet itself is indicated the proposed allocation of profits, so much to reserve, so much as tantième to directors, so much as dividends, and so much carried over to the new account. A balance sheet thus prepared does not exhibit the exact status of affairs after the final adjusting entries have been made, so it is not unusual to offer two balance sheets, one indicating total net profits with an indication of their proposed allocation, the other showing the condition of the accounts after such a distribution shall have been made.

Of greater moment in the comparison of usage in the different countries is the fact that in orderliness and clearness of statement the balance sheets prepared in England and on the continent do not rank as highly as those prepared by the leading corporations in this country. In some respects foreign balance sheets may be more accurate, and they may excel in some minor detail mentioned below, but so far as the grouping of items, the arrangement so as to make an easy comparison of related categories, e.g., the familiar juxtaposition of Current Assets and Current Liabilities, American balance sheets are superior to those of England, France or Germany.

Further difference in legal regulation is found in regard to the publication of the balance sheets of corporations. In both Germany and France the balance sheet must be presented to the stockholders at their annual meeting, in England limited companies must file an annual balance sheet with the registrar. While not absolutely required to send copies to the several shareholders, yet Table A and most of the articles adopted by companies do provide for submitting the balance sheet to the annual meeting, and as well for sending them to the registered members. Belgium, though in general copying closely the French Code, goes further in requiring that the annual balance sheet shall not merely be accessible before the annual meeting but shall be sent together with the profit and loss statement to the shareholders and afterwards published. In this country, with rare exceptions, there is no legal requirement for securing publicity of the balance sheet. In part this lack of legal requirement is remedied by the rules of the New York Stock Exchange.

One other general requirement in Germany and France is in contrast to the practice in England and the United States. In the former countries (as is indeed true of most continental countries) the directors must furnish to the shareholders a profit and loss account as well as the balance sheet. It is true that in this country the railroads are compelled to publish an income and profit and loss account, and both here and in England many companies, not required by law, do publish similar statements. But it is evident that there is no general requirement of American companies to make public a profit and loss account. This is most strikingly brought into contrast in the statements published by banks. Detailed though they are, there is never any indication even of the net profits of the year. Sometimes this may be estimated by comparing the balance of surplus and undivided profits of two years and adding the dividends paid in the meantime. But this is indirect, unsatisfactory, and often misleading. In marked contrast are the statements of German banks. These regularly exhibit not merely the balance of the income but also the separate items entering into it, showing as credits, for instance exchange account, interest, commissions on securities, commission on coupons, rental of building; and on the debit side, general expenses, depreciation on inventory, depreciation on accounts current, etc. The leading English banks less satisfactorily exhibit the gross profits and the expenses of the business, or, in other cases merely the net profits, together with unusual charges, and the allocation of the profits, but without indicating the various sources from which the several items of gain have accrued. One may search in vain for information regarding American banks similar to that furnished in Europe. This seems curious when one reflects on the details furnished by American railroads. Doubtless it would seem undesirable to the bankers of this country to furnish such information, on the ground that it might excite competition. Yet there seems no logical reason why the information regarding the operation of banks should not be as minute as that published by the railroads. The banks, perhaps even more than the railroads, perform a public function, for the issuing of currency is historically an attribute of sovereignty, while from time immemorial furnishing transportation has been a private industry. In other respects the regulation of banks, the restriction on their business, the supervision of their activities, has been more marked than is the case with railways. But in no instance, not even during the life of either of the great monopolistic Banks of the United States, has there been any publication of the profits earned by the banks.

We have considered the divergent attitude of the laws in the leading nations regarding accounting forms and procedure. While certain differences have been noted, it should be borne in mind that custom varies less than the laws. Thus while one country may require double entry bookkeeping and another have no such requirement, yet in practice both will alike use that system of accounting. But in some cases a substantive difference in practice exists. Probably the most striking of these differences in actual practice are those already alluded to, *viz.*, in the continental countries there is a more widespread publication of the details of profit and loss, and in America there is considerable superiority in orderly arrangement of the fundamental statement, the balance sheet.

Turning now from the question of form to the more vital point of substance some differences in accounting practice may be noticed, most of which depend on legal enactment, but some of which have arisen merely from business custom.

The vital question in all accounting is the value which is to be placed on existing assets. That being determined, almost every other question is decided, although, in some cases, there may arise a question as to whether an excess of assets is available for distribution as dividends. Yet in both English and American law there has been almost no attention given to the question of valuation. England does, it is true, require in the Companies Acts that the accounts shall be "full and fair" or "a true and correct" view of the status of the company, and in the United States there is, as well, obligation that accounts rendered shall be correct. But as to what is correct, as to what principles should be observed in estimating values, our statutes are generally silent, and the dicta of the courts have been conflicting, confusing, and often irrational. In this respect Germany excels the other countries in definiteness and in comprehensiveness of legislation, some of the laws applying to all corporations, while in other countries, as is particularly true of Switzerland, and to some extent the United States, the rules that are laid down apply only to a particular class of corporations, the railroads. In Germany the general rule is that all assets and debts are to be set down at the value which they possess at the time of the balance sheet. This is to be interpreted, however, in the light of the following provisions: 1. Securities and commodities which have a publicly quoted price are to be listed at that price when it is below the cost price. But when the quoted price exceeds the cost price the latter is to prevail. 2. Other articles are not to be valued above their cost price. 3. Fixed assets may be valued at cost irrespective of change in market price, regard, however, being had to depreciation. 4. Costs of organization and administration are not to be listed as assets.[5] No other country has laws of general application attempting to regulate these matters.

Some of the more important kinds of assets may be briefly considered in respect to actual practice. All accountants incline to the view that fixed assets are to be carried at an unchanged price, save as influenced by depreciation in their use value.

In all countries custom has sanctioned the carrying of plant purchased by securities at the par value of the securities thus issued. Abuse in this matter has probably been greater in the United States than in other countries, although recent events in England seem to furnish a counterpart for almost any abuse on this side of the ocean. But while Germany has been more conservative in this respect, as is clearly indicated by the quoted price of industrial securities, many of which command a premium, yet even in that country it is apparently not merely customary, but even obligatory to list such purchases at the par value of the securities issued, this being true even when the stock is clearly issued at a discount.[6] On the other hand there is a growing tendency in this country to prevent an overvaluation of plant in this fashion, as is clearly indicated in the restrictive regulations of the various public service commissions and of the Interstate Commerce Commission. France, however, does not always permit the construction account of a railroad to show all of the actual cost, for if that exceeds the amount authorized by the state, the excess, although an actual capital expenditure, must appear as a charge against revenue.[7] A curious custom has, however, arisen in Germany. Where it is estimated that a plant will cost a given sum and securities are issued to that amount, any saving in cost of construction is treated not as diminishing the value of the plant, but as creating a surplus. This absurdity which would be universally condemned in this country, was not only customary in earlier days, but even received the sanction of the Prussian ministry.[8] A somewhat similar variation is found in cases where German corporations have provided by capital issues not only for the cost of construction of the plant but for a sum to be used as actual working capital. By a stupid misuse of terms in the Code[9] it has been considered necessary to show such a sum as a reserve on the credit side of the balance sheet necessitating either listing the plant at the full

[5] *D. H. G. B.*, Article 40.

[6] H. V. Simon, *Die Bilanzen der Aktiengesellschaften* (1899), 376; H. Rehm, *Die Bilanzen der Aktiengesellschaften* (1903), 706.

[7] Sakolski, in *Quarterly Journal of Economics*, XXIV, 493.

[8] Simon, *op. cit.*, 121, 37.

[9] *D. H. G. B.*, 261, 5.

amount of the capital stock, only part of which was invested therein, or inserting some purely fictitious and arbitrary asset. Somewhat reversed is the position regarding contributions made to the company by promoters or other interested persons. In this country these are generally credited as if constituting a surplus, perhaps under the misleading title of "working capital." But while this too has been done in many cases in Germany, it is held to be counter to the law, and the Swiss law even explicitly states that "the cost of construction and equipment covered by subventions *à fonds perdu* may not be charged to construction account." This attitude, while perhaps convenient as a rule affecting the price at which a railroad is to be taken over by the state, is not in essence a correct method of valuing the plant, and is, furthermore, contrary to both practice and legal interpretation in England and America.

German custom seems to be steadfastly opposed to marking up the value of the fixed assets, even as an offset to a previous excessive depreciation. Simon states that, in many thousand balance sheets examined by him, he finds no case where fixed assets have been thus marked up. But such an action is justified in England, and is not unknown in American practice, as for instance by the Excelsior Water and Mining Company, in which instance the action was subsequently sanctioned by the Supreme Court of California.

Closely allied to the problem of valuing assets is that of depreciation. On this matter both the law and the practice of the continental countries is in advance of England. Still more do they transcend American accounting practice, for until the recent rulings of the Interstate Commerce Commission, which are still fragmentary and inconsistent, there was almost no clear expression, in statute book or court decision, of the necessity of depreciation. Moreover, practice as shown in corporation accounts was as unsatisfactory as the laws. The provisions of the German Code, already cited, definitely prescribe depreciation, and an examination of published balance sheets shows that depreciation is reckoned by almost every German company, including banks as well as industrial corporations. In contrast with the rules of the Interstate Commerce Commission, the Prussian railways require provision for renewal, not only of all equipment, but also for ties and rails. In this country, depreciation is likely to be dependent on large profits, and to be omitted in lean years. In Germany even when there is a net loss, the companies almost invariably show a depreciation charge.[10] But even in Germany there is apt to be greater liberality when profits are high; and such a procedure in Switzerland is even sanctioned by law.

In England, depreciation is less consistent. Some, as Sakolski, have claimed that the "double account balance sheet does not permit the writing-off of depreciation and abandoned assets acquired through capital expenditure." [11] In practice it is doubtless true that the loss of capital assets has

[10] See annual statements published in Neumann's, *Tabellen*.

[11] *Quarterly Journal of Economics*, XXIV, 481.

generally been ignored in English balance sheets. But it should be noted that even in the decision given in the case which has been most relied on as justifying the disregard of capital losses, Justice Lindley was careful to state: "It is obvious that capital lost must not appear in the accounts as still existing intact; the accounts must show the truth and not be misleading or fraudulent."[12] The double account form of balance sheet certainly encourages the neglect of depreciation; that it either practically or legally compels such neglect is surely to be questioned.

The treatment of plant discarded because of obsolescence resembles depreciation. In the United States, companies such as street railways and water companies have frequently failed to take any recognition of the outgrown pipes or of the antiquated equipment discarded for newer models. Thus the Census Bureau openly criticizes the failure to charge off the capital lost by the replacement of horse and cable, by electric roads. This criticism doubtless conforms to advanced professional opinion, but corporation practice has lagged somewhat behind. But in France abandoned property of railways is generally charged off.[13] In Germany, however, the custom is similar to that in this country, the abandoned portions, as well as the new, being included in the assets. A distinction, however, is drawn between property displaced by innovations, or improvements, and that destroyed by use or accident. Thus an old station, though torn down to give place to a new one, the temporary structure used during the alterations, and the new station are, with Simon's approval,[14] all included in the assets of a German railroad. But a building which accidentally fell down must be charged off. Surely this furnishes a proper stimulus to provide fit accommodations without waiting until the old structure actually falls on the patrons' heads; and might with some reason be recommended to certain American railroads. In England, custom and authority are divided on the proper treatment of superseded plant,[15] but Swiss law requires writing-off all abandoned plant.[16]

The listing of securities whose market price has declined, at the original cost less only the proper amortization, is in this country generally discountenanced, especially so in the case of banks and insurance companies. In Germany the question is somewhat uncertain, for while law prescribes that listed securities be taken at the quoted price when that is below cost, it also provides that assets for permanent holding may be valued at cost irrespective of market price. Accordingly, the bank for Oriental Railways holds its railroad securities at cost despite shrinkage, agreeing therein with the English decision in the case of the Commercial and General Trust. But despite this decision English banks at the present time quite generally take account of the present low price of British consols. Thus at the last annual

[12] L. R. [1894] 2 Ch. 267.

[13] Sakolski, *op. cit.*, p. 494.

[14] *Die Bilanzen der Aktiengesellschaften*, 372.

[15] *Cf.* the interesting decision in *Cox v. Edinburgh and District Tramways Co. Lim.*, 6 S. L. T. 63.

[16] Law 27 Mar. 1896 Art 6.

meeting of the Capital and Counties Bank, $500,000 was taken from the reserve and $200,000 from the year's profit in order to mark the consols down to 80, the directors calling attention to the fact that in 1910, thirty-two of the leading banks had written-off more than $10,000,000 to cover the decline in the market value of securities held by them. But French companies go far in considering securities as permanent rather than circulating assets, government securities being generally maintained at cost despite subsequent decline in market price.[17]

Organization expenses are in Germany specifically excluded from the list of assets. As a consequence the promoter generally pays such out of his own pocket, taking the stock at par, and then places the stock with the ultimate holders at a premium sufficient to reimburse his outlay. But the law, inconsistently, does not prohibit the inclusion of organization expenses as part of the cost of construction, drawing the line only at showing them openly in the balance sheet. A differentiation is further made between expenses of establishing the company and those of organizing the plant. France allows organization expenses among the assets but requires a rapid amortization. But in practice French companies often include in organization expenses items which do not properly belong there.[18] In England and the United States the inclusion of organization expenses in the cost of plant is common, with less uniformity in regard to writing-off such items.

Interest paid during the period of construction somewhat resembles the costs of organization. It is practically universal to allow such payments to be counted among the costs of construction and hence to appear among the permanent assets, and even in this country such treatment has been specifically allowed by the Interstate Commerce Commission. But in both England and Germany a further step is taken which is not permitted in France or in the United States. While dividends are not ordinarily permissible where there are no profits, and the contract to pay a fixed dividend is not binding, yet in both English and German law[19] there is provision made allowing, in certain circumstances, interest in lieu of dividends, to be paid to shareholders during the period of construction. Such payments, as is interest on bonds, are added to the cost of construction. The practice of England and Germany is logically consistent, for it admits that the real cost of a completed plant includes not merely the immediate payments for construction, but, as well, reimbursement for capital necessarily idle during a long period of time. If the purpose of accounting is to determine a real cost upon which a fair return is to be allowed by rate regulation, there can surely be no ground for regarding the accidental circumstance under which the capital is secured. The objection to the logical method is a precautionary one. Its purpose is to oppose the dangerous tendency to show an unrealized gain by the simple process of marking-up assets.

---

[17] Simon, *op. cit.*, 332.

[18] *Bulletin de l'Institut International de Statistique*, XIV, 2, p. 173.

[19] *Companies (Consolidation) Act*, 1908, Sec. 91; *D. H. G. B.*, 215.

Goodwill is probably more overvalued in this country than abroad, and its writing-off is relatively infrequent. In Germany, however, it is not uncommon for prosperous industrial companies to write-off their goodwill in periods running from three to fifteen years. English companies, like American, are less inclined to write-off goodwill, and in this are supported by the courts and by many accounting authorities.

England took the advanced step in 1889, in the now famous decision in the Lee case, that exploitation of wasting assets, such as a mine, need not be regarded in determining profits available for dividends. In the United States the same view has been authoritatively accepted, at least by the courts, and France goes even further in not permitting the writing-off of such assets.[20] But Germany clings to the older view and requires that as exploitation proceeds, the exhaustion be shown, and only the net profits may legally be divided.

Discount on securities issued in England, France and Germany is customarily placed elsewhere than in profit and loss. In the accounts of German railways it either appears as a permanent asset not being amortized, or is added to the construction account. German industrials sometimes treat discount as a permanent asset, sometimes write it off in arbitrary instalments, with a more recent tendency to charge off at once against surplus. In this country it is recognized that a regular amortization is most legitimate, but in many instances it is more rigorously treated.

Premium on stock is variously treated. In England it is perfectly legal to use such premium to pay dividends, and this is occasionally done. But in Germany corporations may not do so.[21] France agrees with England in regarding premiums as available for dividends. But in all these countries alike, conservative custom looks askance at increasing profits by including premiums therein.

It is a delicate task to attempt to characterize the accounting systems of the different countries or to make comparisons which might seem invidious. It is, however, obvious, that Germany and France, with greater definiteness, attempt to regulate accounting procedure by statutory provisions, France being more particular in the details of bookkeeping form, Germany being much more definite in the enunciation of certain important accounting principles. On the other hand, England, where, with few exceptions concerning forms for particular enterprises, rules for accounting procedure are not enacted, does require that all company accounts shall be audited, the auditors to be appointed in the interest of the shareholders and to report to the annual meeting.

In this country we have been accustomed to look to England rather than to the continent for accounting inspiration. When one attends a gathering of public accountants, his first thought is that he has been transported to England, his second, after his ears catch the pleasing "burr", that he is

[20] Simon, *op. cit.*, 381.
[21] *D. H. G. B.*, 262.2.

north of the Tweed. Our system of certifying public accountants is based on English models, and the examination questions are frequently cribbed from those set in London. The works of Pixley, and Dicksee, of Mathewson, of Garcke and Fells, of Lisle, and Dawson are standard authorities. Yet at one time Pixley himself stated that the standard of bookkeeping among commercial people is far higher on the continent of Europe than in the United Kingdom.[22]

Continental bookkeeping is more methodical, more cumbrous, more tenacious of inherited forms than British, and much more so than American. Time must indeed hang heavy on the hands of the continental bookkeeper, if one is to judge by the elaborateness of entry, the duplication of records, the time-consuming methods of closing books.

The more advanced work in accounting in Germany and France, if one is to judge at all by published treatises, has generally been done by jurists, as for instance Rehm and Simon in Germany, Rousseau and Bastide in France, and enters into minute discussion of the verbal niceties of the law. But in England the best work has been done by chartered accountants, and bears particularly on the work and the responsibilities of the auditor. In England, moreover, cost accounting appeared earlier and has been more scientific than on the continent.

And as to America? Here is to be found accounting almost unregulated either by statutes or by courts. No authority recognized, almost every abuse apparently sanctioned by the practice of prominent if not always reputable concerns. Yet throughout all there is an exhibition of American adaptability and inventiveness. So successful have American accountants been in devising forms suited to the desired ends that on the continent any bookkeeping device recognized as having peculiar merit and originality is, irrespective of its actual origin, apt to be called "American" bookkeeping.[23] Particularly advanced has been the development, in the United States, of cost accounting, and this may properly be spoken of as the great characteristic contribution which the present generation has made to the science of accounting. As on the continent one looks to jurists, and in England to chartered accountants, in this country it is perhaps to engineers that one looks for the greatest stimulus and inspiration in accounting progress; for in large part the development of cost accounting is due to the initiative of engineers, although the public accountant has greatly contributed to its development.

In education for accountants the United States has its peculiar field. Here has preeminently flourished the business college. Once the object of deserved ridicule because of crudeness and superficiality, it has spread a knowledge of bookkeeping throughout the country, and, while doing this, has raised its own standard, almost without assistance from professional organizations or higher educational institutions. More recently have ap-

---

[22] *Accountant*, XVI, 135.

[23] C. P. Kheil, *Ueber amerikanische Buchhaltung*.

peared colleges of commerce and technical schools for training the public accountant. Founded though these are on European models, and in some instances, perhaps, at first harmed by too slavish an imitation, they are, I believe, superior in their particular field to their foreign prototypes. Under their influence there is appearing a new literature of accounting, and the dreary and apparently interminable succession of bookkeeping texts, for long all that appeared in this country, has been broken by the appearance of such scientific treatises as those of Sprague and of Cole.

The new activity in regard to the examination and certification of public accountants is a new powerful force in the development of accounting methods, as is the work of the American Association and of its subordinate state organization. And finally the recent action of the Interstate Commerce Commission, and of the various Public Utility Commissions, and the necessity of more exact accounting as a basis for income and corporation taxes, and for regulation of railroad rates and of monopoly charges, give earnest that America will soon, if it does not already, hold chief place as the exponent of exact and scientific methods of accounting.

Introductory Note to the fifth edition of *The Philosophy of Accounts*, by Charles E. Sprague. New York: The Ronald Press Company, 1922, pp. xvii-xxi.

Hatfield was a great admirer of Sprague's fresh and undoctrinaire presentation of double-entry bookkeeping in its relation to a company's financial statements. When Sprague's famous series of 12 articles titled "The Philosophy of Accounts," originally published in *The Journal of Accountancy* in 1907-1908 and as a book in 1908, was posthumously published in a fifth edition in 1922 by Ronald Press, Hatfield was invited to write an introductory note, a task he undertook with relish. Of the four authors of the introductory notes, Hatfield was the only one who had not known Sprague personally.

IV

For a hundred and fifty years after the time of Paciolo's "Summa," little was written in a serious way on the theory of double-entry bookkeeping. It is true that many works on double-entry bookkeeping were published, but almost all of them were mere handbooks, serviceable in drilling the student in the art of bookkeeping, but barren of theory. Paciolo's work itself, vastly important though it has been, is a book of practical directions, telling how books are to be posted, how to check back a ledger, how to enter an inventory—even how to mark the book with the sign of the cross—but paying no attention to theoretical matters. For generations little was written that was at best more than a half-concealed plagiarism of Paciolo. Even in later times there has been a surprising adherence to tradition, and rules and forms, directions and explanations have from writer to writer followed the precedent set in earlier years. In general, the literature of bookkeeping is a dreary succession of banal directions, showing little originality, little systematic thinking.

This is particularly true in America. When Sprague's "The Philosophy of Accounts" appeared in 1906, there were, indeed, few American texts which could lay any claim to scientific distinction. There were many texts written primarily for commercial schools, there were some sets of intelligent answers to accounting problems, there were one or two books dealing with some phase of corporation accounting, there were a few excellent works, among them Sprague's own "Accountancy of Investment," dealing with some limited field of accounting, but one may search in vain for any general treatise dealing with the theory of accounts.

In England the situation was scarcely better as regards theory. Even the masters of accounting, honored alike on both sides of the Atlantic, were blind followers of tradition in regard to the theory of bookkeeping, as may be instanced by quoting from one, perhaps the acknowledged leader of them all, who, in explaining a simple balance sheet, says "The owner is creditor of the business for £1,000," and within the compass of the same paragraph, following a time-worn but inexcusable tradition, states that the proprietor's capital is the excess of assets over the liabilities.

If, then, one wishes to appraise the value of Sprague's contribution, consideration must be given to the paucity of valid theory in the current textbooks of his day. It is the contrast between "The Philosophy of Accounts" and what went before that gives significance to the work.

Primarily, praise is due to the successful effort made to give a sane presentation of the fundamental principles of double-entry bookkeeping. The approach to bookkeeping, in earlier authors, was generally through the transaction. The isolated journal entry was regarded as the central fact in bookkeeping. The equivalence between debit and credit was treated as its fundamental principle. But that is formal. Double-entry bookkeeping might exist, with practically all its benefits to business, without debits or credits. Sprague shows that the bookkeeper is not interested in a mere game of matching debits and credits, but that he is concerned in preserving an accurate record of assets, of liabilities, and of the changing proprietorship. He presents to the student an explanation of technique which relates itself to an obviously desirable end: knowledge of the status and the progress of the business, grouping all around the balance sheet, "the groundwork of all accountancy, the origin and the terminus of every account."

Because of this method of handling the subject there is an avoidance of the previously well-nigh universal futility of framing some universal rule for determining debits and credits. This persistent attempt of earlier writers has generally led to confusion and absurdity. The favorite formula was: Debit what the business receives. But it requires considerable mental gymnastics to apply this formula, when, for instance, the student is faced with the problem of booking a loss by fire. The naïve thinker has difficulty in discovering the thing received, although the sophisticated student of bookkeeping rules, posits an imaginary person, called "Profit and Loss," or "Loss by Fire," seated on a pile of ashes, who receives the burned property, and him he debits. In most bookkeeping texts the attempt at a single rule leads ultimately, not merely to gymnastics and confusion but to contradiction and absurdity. But Sprague has emphasized the fact that debit means addition in one class of account and subtraction in the other two classes. From this he shows that in each of the nine possible combinations occurring in bookkeeping entries, a debit always is accompanied by a corresponding credit—a convenient check on accuracy rather than a principle. And the result is not merely a rule-of-thumb, not merely a clear and correct statement, but an explanation which is expressed in terms significant to the desired result of all bookkeeping. The older explanation trained the student to look upon entries in the books as a series of records of receivings and of givings, not always clear as to whether the recipient was an abstract "business," or the person named at the top of the account. After working through a month or a year, recording esoteric receipts which apparently have nothing to do with business interests, the student performed a mysterious process called "closing the books" (accompanied with certain cabalistic marks, always in red ink, or the magic would not work), and behold, instead of a simple record of receivings and givings there appear "Assets," "Liabilities," and "Net Worth." Sprague avoids this fantastic approach to bookkeeping. Entries are made because every business man desires a record of assets, liabilities, and proprietorship, and, the conventions by which positive and negative items are recorded being explained, the whole process becomes rationalized and intelligible.

A third service rendered to accounting theory is the abandonment of the conventional classification of accounts. This most frequently was a division into personal and impersonal accounts. But in almost every case (there are a few exceptions) personal accounts included both accounts receivable and capital, which are altogether dissimilar; and impersonal accounts included profit and loss and notes receivable which also are dissimilar. Accounts receivable and notes receivable, which in many respects are almost identical, on the other hand are separated, as are also the proprietor's capital and profit and loss, although they are so much akin that once each year they blend and merge one into the other. Sprague makes a simple logical division, one group containing the assets and liabilities, the other containing capital and profit and loss. He thus substitutes systematic treatment for a classification which was made up on one hand of meaningless and unreal distinctions, and on the other of a grouping together of categories which should be kept separate.

Mention may also be made of Sprague's refreshing freedom from the trammels of convention so prevalent in accounting. For decades bookkeepers continued to use "to" and "by" when the two-column journal made them unnecessary. The day book, now happily discarded, continued, as Row Fogo has shown, long after the necessity which existed in the days of Paciolo had disappeared. Even in this somewhat careless age, moral maxims still appear in many a bookkeeping text, in a way foreign to any other scientific writings, merely because the first treatise was written by a Franciscan monk who interlarded his text with warnings against sloth, and inculcation of attendance at mass. It is then really refreshing to find independence of tradition in a work on accounts. Sprague tells us that the record in the stubs of a check book is a real account; that the arrangement of accounts and of books may be indefinitely varied, that the ordinary form of ledger account may at times advantageously be abandoned. He has done much to introduce flexibility and sense in place of subservience to convention.

These are some of the things which make "The Philosophy of

Accounts" noticeable. As to the influence which the book has had on subsequent writers, one has only to examine the treatises which have appeared since 1906. These show clearly the influence of Sprague's teaching. They may differ in detail; the author in some instances may even unduly emphasize what he considers a radical variation from Sprague's formula, but the resemblance is greater than the differences. The sanity and clarity introduced into accounting literature by Sprague is inestimable in its value, imperishable in its influence.

It is no detraction to the service rendered by Sprague that some of the points emphasized in "The Philosophy of Accounts" had been more or less fully brought out by an occasional writer in Italy, in Switzerland, in Germany, or by Thomas Jones in America. Most of these writers were little known or have been more than half-forgotten. They had little effect in raising the standard of bookkeeping texts. It remained for Sprague to present a well-rounded treatise, which marks a real step in advance in American accounting literature.

While this article is by prescription limited to a consideration of matters of accounting theory, and another and more competent pen is dealing with the more personal aspects, the writer cannot forbear paying a personal tribute to Colonel Sprague. Man of affairs and of books, original in modes of thought, urbane in demeanor, cosmopolitan in interest, high type of the scholar in business—from across the continent may this expression of homage be added to the contribution of those whose association was closer, but whose respect is no more profound.

HENRY RAND HATFIELD

The University of California,
March 10, 1922.

"An Historical Defense of Bookkeeping," originally published in *The Journal of Accountancy*, Vol. 37, No. 4, April 1924, pp. 65-75.

This is Hatfield's most famous article. Having presented an early version to the Berkeley Club, he restyled it for delivery to the 8th annual meeting of the American Association of University Instructors in Accounting on December 29, 1923 in Columbus, Ohio. Hatfield's wit and verve are evident throughout. In arguing for the respectability of accounting, he touched a nerve, as the accounting academics in his audience had often felt the sting of condescension from economists and colleagues in other departments in their home universities. "Historical Defense" was the most celebrated accounting article in the English language during the first half of the century, and it was reprinted numerous times both in the United States and the United Kingdom. The version of Hatfield's paper reproduced here is the one prepared by his colleagues and friends upon the occasion of his (involuntary) retirement in 1937. In this version, minor errors in the earlier published versions were corrected.

AN HISTORICAL DEFENSE OF BOOKKEEPING

BY HENRY RAND HATFIELD

A PAPER READ BEFORE THE
AMERICAN ASSOCIATION OF UNIVERSITY INSTRUCTORS
IN ACCOUNTING, DECEMBER 29, 1923
REPUBLISHED BY FRIENDS AND COLLEAGUES
ON THE OCCASION OF THE AUTHOR'S RETIREMENT
FROM ACTIVE TEACHING
AT THE UNIVERSITY OF CALIFORNIA
MAY 15, 1937

Another of these students at that time
Was there with him, if I have heard a truth.
"Hatfield" they call him; but a merrier man,
Within the limit of becoming mirth,
I never spent an hour's talk withal.
His eye begets occasion for his wit,
For every object that the one doth catch
The other turns to a mirth-moving jest,
Which his fair tongue, conceit's expositor,
Delivers in such apt and gracious words
That aged ears play truant at his tales,
And younger hearings are quite ravished;
So sweet and voluble is his discourse.

LOVE'S LABOUR'S LOST—ACT II

I AM SURE that all of us who teach accounting in the universities suffer from the implied contempt of our colleagues, who look upon accounting as an intruder, a Saul among the prophets, a pariah whose very presence detracts somewhat from the sanctity of the academic halls. It is true that we ourselves speak of the science of accounts, or of the art of accounting, even of the philosophy of accounts. But accounting is, alas, only a pseudoscience unrecognized by J. McKeen Cattell; its products are displayed neither in the salon nor in the national academy; one finds it discussed by neither realist, idealist nor phenomenalist. The humanists look down upon us as beings who dabble in the sordid figures of dollars and cents instead of toying with infinities and searching for the elusive soul of things; the scientists and technologists despise us as able only to record rather than to perform deeds.

We suffer perhaps in silence, even, as Carlyle says, "consuming our own choler as some chimneys consume their own smoke," perhaps in public denying that we suffer at all, but here—in a meeting not of accountants, but of university instructors in accounting—we can admit among ourselves that at times this academic attitude does get under our skins.

The contempt for accounting is not limited to university circles, but is well-nigh universal. It is evidenced by ignorance of the subject, by condescension toward its devotees, by their exclusion from polite literature.

And how abysmal that ignorance! I give two instances. The university speaker who said, "If you do so and so your ledger [speaking figuratively, of course] will show a debit balance." Would he have spoken of an equation with unequal members? And the distinguished writer in the October *Atlantic,* thesaurus of culture, supposedly barred to academic solecisms, who says, "In most sections of America the fact that a man or woman has been divorced . . . is something to be set down . . . on the debit side of the account," ignorant that likely as not a debit (as for instance in the bank account) means the imputation of additional value—which I take it is quite contrary to what Mrs. Gerould intended.

But the contempt for accounting is even more clearly shown by a constantly repeated phrase, a phrase which of all phrases is to me the most exacerbating—because of the combination of ignorance and supercilious condescension. This phrase, which I could quote from uncounted sources, is: "That is a mere bookkeeping entry." One might as well say, "That is a mere algebraic equation," or "That is a mere statement of discovered fact," or, "That is the formulation of a mere axiom." Mere truth, mere fact, mere sanctity, mere virtue. Do you wonder that I lose my temper every time I see the phrase? Of course one may make a misstatement in bookkeeping, just as one may lie either in Greek or in German: But that merits some adjective more invidious than "mere."

And remember how accounting has been slighted in literature. The public eye has generally, both in history and in fiction, been turned on the man on horseback, but nevertheless at times there comes upon the stage a more prosaic figure. Great masterpieces have grouped themselves about a scholar as Faust, about a carpenter as Adam Bede, about a manufacturer as in *Les Miserables,* about a sailor as Robinson Crusoe, about courtesans, thieves and beggars beyond recital. Even a horse and a dog have been made the heroes in *Black Beauty* and in *Rab and His Friends.* But never, so far as I recollect, has a bookkeeper been made the hero of novel, play or poem. The bookkeeper is not even honored by being made a noteworthy villain.

Long ago Sir Roger de Coverley assumed that "little that is truly noble can be expected from one who is ever poring on his cashbook or balancing his accounts." Literature has maintained this attitude ever since, and the bookkeeper has reached his apogee in the gentle and pathetic figure of Tim Clerkenwell. Compare him for a moment with the military hero. The latter appears mounted on a horse, leading, to the music of bugle and drum, his martial columns in charges against the foe, brandishing a reeking sword, and wearing on his brow the victor's wreath of laurel. The bookkeeper too is mounted, but on a quadrupedal stool, he too marshals columns, but of figures to the accompaniment of a clicking Burroughs, his charges are those on the debit side of the ledger, his brow is encircled but by a green eye shade, he brandishes only the humble rival of the sword, guiltless doubtless of his country's blood, and incarnadined only with Carter's cardinal ink.

But it is not good for a man's soul always to suffer under the inferiority complex. Let us no longer bear in humility the lash of contumely. Let us face our contemners, be they classicists, philosophers or scientists.

"No matter if he is a houn',
They gotta quit kicking my dog aroun'."

Let us boldly raise the question whether accounting, the late claimant for recognition as a profession, is not entitled to some respect, or must it consort with crystal-gazing, sociology, chiropractic, pedagogy and palm-reading.

Three elements, if not conclusively proving, at least presumptively establish, respectability. These are, first, parentage and lineage; second, the company one keeps; and, third, the services which one renders the community. Let us examine accounting in these aspects.

Without raising the question as to accounting in antiquity, we look upon the Franciscan monk Paciolo as the father of modern accounting, as his *Summa,* published in 1494, which was the first printed work dealing with algebra, also contained the first text on bookkeeping, a slender tractate entitled *De Computis et Scripturis.*

Not much can be said of Paciolo,* aside from his writings, but his academic credentials are flawless. He was an important if not a great mathematician. His first appointment to teach in a university was at Perugia. In less than a year his request for an increase of salary was granted. The reason stated in the official records has a singularly modern sound. It reads: "because he has already taught for two months and has shown himself to be a man of highest learning, and because it appears that he manifestly can not live on such a meagre stipend." Again in less than six months he was promoted, this time with a more permanent tenure as well as increase of salary. Soon afterward he left the university, probably devoting himself to the study of philosophy and theology. He returned to Perugia in 1487, and while he had previously signed himself "Brother Luke," in his later writings he was wont to describe himself as a "humble professor of sacred theology." He held many other university positions, at various times teaching at Naples, at Pisa, at Florence and at Bologna. He ended his career with his highest honor, for in 1514 Pope Leo X appointed him professor of mathematics in the *Sapienza* at Rome, a position in the "university of the highest standing in all Christendom."

In 1496 he was called to Milan by the reigning duke, Ludovico il Moro, whose court was a center of light and learning, and to be established there was a signal honor. Adams in China, Hollander in Porto Rico, Bogart in

* H. Staigmüller, "Lucas Paciuolo, eine biographische Skizze," in *Zeitschrift für Mathematik und Physik,* Bd. 34, Historisch-literarische Abtheilung, pp. 81–102, 121–128.

Persia, Paciolo in Milan—all indications of deserved recognition of professorial eminence—all doubtless to be kept in mind for at least 427 years.

At Milan, Paciolo was brought into contact with many prominent persons, the most significant being Leonardo da Vinci, perhaps the most eminent man of his day. Between the two there grew up an intimate friendship. Da Vinci himself tells that he hastened to buy a copy of Paciolo's *Summa* as it came off the press, and he collaborated with Paciolo on a later book, the *Divina Proportione,* for which Paciolo furnished the text and Da Vinci the illustrations. Honor indeed for a university professor! Would not the most eminent mathematician of today rejoice if the greatest man of his time, say Roosevelt or Henry Ford, had hastened to buy one of his treatises (even though it contained the adventitious attraction of some chapters on bookkeeping)? Would not even one so eminent as William James have been flattered if in his psychology the somatic reactions of the emotions could have been illustrated by the master hand of the creator of Mutt and Jeff!

I need not outline to you the nature of Paciolo's treatise, with which you are familiar, at least through Geijsbeek's somewhat paraphrastic translation. Have any of you not read this you will be interested in it, not merely as a piece of technical literature, but because of its quaintness of expression, its naïve attention to detail, its exuberance of piety, its flavor of mediævalism.

It is seldom the case that a first book on a subject has so dominated its literature as was the case with Paciolo's *De Computis et Scripturis.* It is nearly true to say that for a hundred years the texts appearing in England, France, Germany, Italy and the low countries were "at the best revisions of Paciolo, at the worst servile transcriptions without even the courtesy of referring to the original author." But further than that many little matters of bookkeeping technique were followed for at least four centuries, merely because they were inculcated by Paciolo, persisting like buttons on our coat sleeves, long after their significance had disappeared. I need not mention these to you, but may I refer to a peculiar instance relating rather to a matter of general form?

Whether it was because of his churchly connections or because it conformed to the customs of his day, Paciolo's book is replete with gems of moral and religious advice. I know not how it may be in the higher branches, such as sociology or Americanization—but in the elementary text-books, such as algebra or chemistry, we do not today find the thread of the discourse interrupted by bits of proverbial philosophy or moral exhortation. But in bookkeeping this has continued down until today. I might cite instances from many of the high school texts used today, from practically all used so lately as ten years ago. But let me take a single extreme example. Soule's book is still in vogue in this country. At the foot of nearly every one of his 749 pages, he has a line quite in keeping with Paciolo. The statement in the earlier writer, "Who does nothing makes no mistakes, who makes not mistakes learns nothing," is matched by Soule's "Our greatest glory is not in never falling but in rising every time we fall." "It costs more to make a good merchant than to make a doctor of laws," is matched with "Experience is not a free school, we all pay for our tuition." But even a fifteenth-century monk can not rise quite to the level of the twentieth-century practical American who tells us "The only amaranthine flower on earth is virtue, the only lasting treasure truth." Bookkeeping was spread throughout the world by a series of plagiarisms and imitations of Paciolo. The habit of imitation became so fixed that in bookkeeping it has persisted throughout the centuries, and even the foibles of Brother Luke are reproduced in the treatises of today.

Let those who vaunt the superior merits of other disciplines remember that this first presentation made by Paciolo was not crude and incorrect but contains the essentials of bookkeeping as we know it today, despite the fact that it was written at a time when chemistry partook of the vagaries of alchemy, biology was a weird collection of errors, and medicine had more in common with the medicine man than it has even today. It may be well to see how this discipline—I do not venture to call it science—compares in its antiquity with the more arrogant natural sciences. In neither case do I go back to the feeble beginnings and adumbrations of learning but compare the position of bookkeeping, as it was first formulated in print by a university professor, with the formulation of natural sciences—not by some dim groper in far-off antiquity—but by the first vice-president of Harvard College. A comparison, thus made, is, I am sure, more than generous to the natural sciences, despite their illiberal attitude toward the social sciences with which, in general, they admit of no kinship.

Charles Morton, who, like Paciolo, was at once distinguished teacher and cleric, was brought to Harvard from England almost two hundred years after Paciolo had formulated bookkeeping. If not professor, he was at least made vice-president, and his work on science was used as a text-book in the college.*

But he explained the problem of the migration of birds by saying that each autumn they flew to the moon, 200,000 miles distant, a two months' journey, and in his text-book, earthquakes are explained as follows: "They come from choking up of wind below, fermenting, bursting out, causing trembling and strokes." Or dropping into verse:

> *"In subterranean caverns winds do frolic*
> *When Mother Earth is troubled with the colic."*

How marked a contrast to the teachings of the geologist at the University of California. It is told that when he appeared in court as an expert witness, the opposing lawyer foolishly attempting to ridicule his pretension of knowledge, said: "And do you pretend to know what is going on in the bowels of the earth?" To this the geologist replied: "I do not know that the earth has any bowels."

Only two hundred years ago science—in the leading American college—was a futile and ludicrous display of ignorance. More than four hundred years ago, in the very first book published on the subject, bookkeeping was outlined in a form which still prevails around the entire world. Can not bookkeeping claim an honorable and ancient lineage? Is it indeed an upstart as compared with geology, and chemistry, and landscape gardening, and social psychology, and business English, and olericulture, and otorhino-laryngology, and other cherished subjects of the university curriculum? Founded, like San Francisco, by a follower of St. Francis of Assisi, cradled in mathematics with algebra as a twin, established under the ægis of a great university—surely this is an origin sufficiently academic to give respectability to this our "houn' dog." Perhaps I should adopt the language appropriate to the kennel and speak of bookkeeping as having been sired four hundred years ago by a monk, and today damned by thousands of university students, and yet, despite cer-

* Authority for the following statements is found in Meriwether, *Our Continental Curriculum*, pp. 188 ff.

tain questions which the frivolous might raise to a celibate paternity and the extremely puzzling biological enigma of such a multiple maternity, bookkeeping is thoroughly respectable.

But many a house founded by a great man has degenerated and the descendants have been of quite inferior clay. Has the later entourage of bookkeeping been made up of a fair number of respectable persons?

The second book on bookkeeping was also written by a man of distinction, Grammateus or Schreiber. He, like Paciolo, combined algebra and bookkeeping, and his book, dated 1518, was the first work published in Germany dealing with either of these subjects. On the authority of Cantor, he stands, as a mathematician, unquestionably in the front rank of his time.

Almost immediately following Grammateus was Jerome Cardan, that picturesque scrapegrace and brilliant scholar, astrologer, physician, scientist, mathematician, professor of medicine first at Pavia, later at Bologna. He, too, wrote a book combining algebra and bookkeeping. This work, says Richard Garnett, marks an era in the history of mathematics, being the first in which the principle of cubic equations was fully explained. Everett says it is one of the most valuable contributions to the literature of algebra. As a physician he was so eminent that he was called to Scotland, no mean journey in those days, to attend an archbishop; he was famous enough as an astrologer to visit the court of Edward VI to cast the king's nativity. But his chief claim to distinction is his general scientific attitude, so far in advance of his times. Says Garnett: "Alike intellectually and morally, Cardan is one of the most interesting personages connected with the revival of science in Europe. He possessed the true scientific spirit in perfection. As a mathematician he effected most important advances, and to complete the catalogue of his accomplishments he is no contemptible poet." And to add picturesqueness to his career he became involved in difficulties, was addicted to gaming, imprisoned for debt, banished from Milan, was later deposed from his professorship, imprisoned, released, prohibited from further teaching, but spent his latter years in Rome as a pensioner of the pope.

Out of the first six writers three are thus seen to be men of eminent distinction—in fields other than that of bookkeeping, as judged by persons who are not themselves particularly interested in bookkeeping. Surely the early days—if not the unknown origin of bookkeeping—are sufficiently respectable so that we need not be ashamed.

Extending somewhat the field of survey we find that Brown lists only 150 names of writers on bookkeeping before 1800. But even the reduced list of those who have reputations in fields other than bookkeeping is too long to repeat in detail. These are not a group of narrow specialists. One finds there authorities on algebra (as is to be expected), on navigation, on optics, a commissioner to settle the foreign exchange, the author of the French code of 1763 (who not only had this great code named after him, the Code Savary, but is perhaps even more distinguished by having had seventeen children who also bore his name), astronomers, a French grammarian, an authority on gunpowder and the historian of the Baptist church. To find these names in the *Encyclopædia Britannica* one does not look under accounting or bookkeeping—these articles are scant and unsatisfactory and both contain misstatements concerning the history of the subject—but under the following rubrics: algebra, camera obscura, deaf and dumb, earth figure, fortification and siege craft, gravitation, infinitesimal calculus, insurance, logarithms, mathematical tables, Napier, and navigation.

Perhaps I may be pardoned if I mention more specifically three of the names. There is Simon Stevin. Cantor styles him a Dutch mathematician, but says his claims to fame are varied. He invented a horseless carriage which worked, he was first to solve some problems regarding polyhedra, he proved the law of equilibrium on an inclined plane, he discoverd the hydrostatic paradox, he explained the tides by the moon, he devised new forms of fortification, was many times public officer, a soldier and statesman, and the first to introduce decimals. Yet he thought it well worth while, in 1602, to write an extended treatise on bookkeeping for the express purpose of training his royal pupil, the prince of Orange.

There was Charles Hutton, a colliery boy, who became teacher of mathematics at eighteen and later professor at the royal academy at Woolwich, fellow and foreign secretary of the Royal Society (three others in the brief list were also fellows of that distinguished body), perhaps most famous for his computation of the density of the earth, an achievement recognized by Laplace and said by various competent critics to show ingenious and important methods, which can hardly be improved upon, author too of a work on conic sections said by Montucla to be a model of precision and clarity, receiver of the Copley medal for his paper on gunpowder, and doctor of laws of Edinburgh. And yet this man, who could weigh the earth as in a balance, condescended to write a text-book on bookkeeping, a subject which many think worthy the attention only of writing masters and proprietors of business colleges.

There was Robert Hamilton, who after some years' experience as a banker, betook himself to teaching, and was professor first of natural philosophy and later of mathematics at Aberdeen; famed, however, more as an economist, for it was he who exposed the economic fallacies of Pitt's policy of the sinking fund. Yet this man, banker, merchant, mathematician, capable of confuting England's master statesman, thought it not beneath his dignity also to write on bookkeeping.

I have limited this survey to writers before 1800. I will mention only two persons since then. Augustus De Morgan, whose eminence needs no description, was so far interested in bookkeeping that one of the best elementary books ever written on the subject acknowledges that it is based on the suggestions of De Morgan. And finally Arthur Cayley, who thirty years ago turned aside from his duties as professor of mathematics at Cambridge long enough to write a most excellent work, entitled *The Principles of Double-entry Bookkeeping*.

I have cited illustrious men who have written on bookkeeping rather than illustrious writers on bookkeeping. I did this merely to establish the argument that bookkeeping is a subject worthy the attention of men of ability—not to be relegated to the ordinary business college.

But not all who have attempted to write on the subject have succeeded. He may, like Grammateus, stand high as a mathematician, and yet, as a writer on bookkeeping "deserve no praise beyond that of being the first German who ventured to write on that difficult subject," producing a book, which Row Fogo says is "so confused that it is extremely improbable that he himself knew much about what he was attempting to teach." He may, like Cardan, show originality and genius in science, yet as a writer on bookkeeping be worse than banal. He may, like Collins, hold an honorable position in the Royal Society, yet produce a work on bookkeeping which receives no particular mention by the historian of the subject. He may, like Hamilton, deserve the encomium of McCullough, that he succeeded in the impossible task of opening the mind of the British public on an economic question, and yet have the *Encyclopædia Britannica* say that his work on bookkeeping is now forgotten. A man of distinction may write on bookkeeping; his work in that line is not necessarily distinguished. Would it be fair to say that it takes a peculiar genius to make a success in that subject?

The third presumptive evidence of respectability is that one performs some important service in the world. Can this be said of accounting? Perhaps this can best be answered by showing that bookkeeping appeared, not as a chance phenomenon, but distinctly in response to a world need. This is true not only of the days of Paciolo, but, as I hope to show, of that more important, almost present-day, revival.

It is not without significance that bookkeeping appeared at the end of the fifteenth century, nor that its birthplace was in the Italian republics. We all know of the marvelous awakening of that period, and particularly of the sudden expansion of commerce. Sieveking, one of the few historians who has paid attention to the subject, says that bookkeeping arose as a direct result of the establishment of partnerships on a large scale, a feature of the expanding commerce.

But bookkeeping dozed for several centuries, and it was not until just about four hundred years after Paciolo's book, that a startling awakening took place. New works in unheard-of abundance and of a new quality began to appear, and again the universities seriously undertook instruction in a subject which had fallen into academic disrepute.

Why this new prominence in a subject taught before 1500? The answer is so obvious that I offend by explanation. The end of the nineteenth, even more than the end of the fifteenth century, was marked by a most extraordinary expansion of business. Then was the period of the organization of the great corporations (ordinarily called trusts), a phenomenon common to America, England and Germany. Then came that new appearance, the billion-dollar corporation, and just then—not a curious coincidence but a necessary response—accountants woke up. Garcke and Fells started the list of works on cost-accounts, Pixley first and then Dicksee began their voluminous writings dealing with the more refined problems of corporation accounts, England chartered the Institute of Chartered Accountants, New York set the example, since followed by every American state, of granting the title of "certified public accountant," the adding machine was invented, logarithms were placed beside the ledger, books were written, conventions were held, accounting was.

In part the new significance of accounting is due to subdivision of ownership and the severance of ownership and control so characteristic of the corporate form of business organization. If the substitution of a small partnership for the individual trader called for improvement in bookkeeping methods, how much more was improvement needed when the partnership was displaced by the corporation with its owners numbered by the tens of thousands.

But still more significant has been the great investment of fixed capital characteristic of modern production and made possible by the organization of corporations. The use of fixed capital on a large scale increases incalculably the difficulty of determining the profits earned in any given year. Paciolo made no serious effort to do this. Business in his day was a congeries of disconnected ventures. A ship went here, a caravan there, a joint venture was undertaken with Messer Juan Antonio in French wool, and a flyer was taken in *ginger michini*. As these ventures fell in, the profit gained in the completed transaction was ascertained, somewhat roughly, it is true, but fairly satisfactorily. But no attempt was made to deal with unfinished operations.

But today business is a continuum. Machinery serves for many years, the factory building stands for a generation, the railroad is built to last forever. The industrial process is made up of a never-ending stream of raw materials, goods in process and finished commodities. Expenses are incurred in common and not like the expenses of a caravan solely in connection with one parcel of goods. But man is strangely agricultural in his tradition, even though society has become industrial. Time was when the recurring cycle of the year was of immense significance to him, for seedtime and harvest each came in connection with the course of the earth around the sun. And man still thinks that he must reckon results in terms of the accidental period involved in such a circuit. We demand to know how much a concern makes in a year. We must know, because the reciprocal rights of preferred and common stockholders may be altogether changed, depending on whether profit is to be attributed to the month of December or to the following January. We must know in order to satisfy the demands of the income-tax collector. And so accountants are asked to perform the hopeless task of taking this economic continuum, of chopping it up into arbitrary and meaningless lengths called a year and apportioning to each such year a proper part of the cost of a building which will last fifty years, of a machine which will be used for twenty years, of a blast furnace which will last ten, and of a stock of coal bought in December which will all be consumed before spring again appears.

Progress in the science seems slow. There stand out, however, two contributions of present-day accountants, one of practical, the other of theoretical importance. The first, made by America, consists of innumerable little devices for saving work in the handling of great masses of figures. Cumbersome and needless forms, surviving as tradition from the past centuries in England, and still more on the continent, have been discarded in America and new forms have been introduced by which results can be obtained with less labor. The other contribution has been the attempt to ascertain the exact cost of producing objects or parts of objects or for carrying on processes in continuous manufacture. Manufacturers now must know not only what it costs to make a machine but what is the cost of each separate wheel, pinion and screw in that machine; what is the cost not merely of a yard of cloth, but of carding, of roving, of spinning, of weaving, of dyeing, of finishing, of selling that yard of cloth. This has has been the characteristic scientific contribution of recent years.

Progress is being made. What better evidence is there than that even lawyers and courts are coming to appreciate that there are such things as accounting principles? No longer is it possible for the supreme court of the United States to declare that "the public . . . rarely ever take into account the depreciation of the building in which the business is carried on."* Never again, I believe, will the supreme court of California repeat the statement regarding depreciation:† "The theory is . . . that a sum should be set aside to be handed to the stockholders upon the sad occasion of the company's demise, as an alleviating salve to their sorrow, but such a thing is all wrong. The theory can not be tolerated for a moment that such a fund is to be stowed away to make glad the hearts of the stockholders."

I have tried to remove the stigma attached to accounting by showing that in its origin it is respectable, nay even academic; that despite its pres-

* *Eyster* v. *Centennial Board of Finance*, 94 U. S. 503. † *San Diego Water Co.* v. *San Diego*, 118 Cal. 556.

ent disrepute it has from time to time attracted the attention of men of unquestioned intellectual attainment; that it justifies itself in that it has arisen to meet a social need. Its functions are to locate responsibility, to prevent fraud, to guide industry, to determine equities, to solve the all-essential conundrum of business: "What are my profits?"; to facilitate the government in its fiscal operations, to guide the business manager in the attempt to secure efficiency. Are not these efforts worthy of any man's attention? And so I close this paper with quotation from men whom all must respect: Scott, the romanticist, declared the profession of accounting "respectable"; Goethe, the universal genius, speaks of bookkeeping as "one of the fairest inventions of the human mind," and Cayley, scientist beyond question, even more significantly declared "Bookkeeping is one of the two perfect sciences." With these I rest the defense of my houn'dog.

"What Is the Matter with Accounting?" *The Journal of Accountancy*, Vol. XLIV, No. 4, October 1927, pp. 267-279.

This is the best example of Hatfield lecturing accounting practitioners for their failure to develop a sound theory and clear terminology. To prove the point, he presents instances of specious, inconsistent, and even spurious arguments commonly given in support of accounting practices, and adds, "These are often barren of any vestige of accounting theory." Hatfield delivered the paper to the annual meeting of the American Institute of Accountants on September 21, 1927 in Del Monte, California. Earlier in the year, he had published the revision of his textbook *Accounting: Its Principles and Problems*, and his address to the Institute's annual meeting reflected his frustration when cutting through the thicket of the accounting literature in order to discover the principles, if any there were, underlying accounting practice.

Preprinted from the JOURNAL OF ACCOUNTANCY, October, 1927

What Is the Matter with Accounting?*

BY HENRY RAND HATFIELD

Some there are who have made bold to exalt accounting because of its antiquity and to draw invidious comparisons with the natural sciences. These boast that the essentials of accounting had already been developed at a time when medicine, and biology, and chemistry were still a mass of fantastic superstitions.

Writers who dwell on the long existence of correct accounting methods are prone to exalt the science as representing the old nobility among a horde of upstarts, and to assume that its age is a testimonial of its dignity and worth. But may not these very facts bear a different interpretation? Accounting was well established while other sciences were undeveloped. Is that to say that in four hundred years the natural sciences have made tremendous advances, that alchemy has changed into chemistry, astrology into astronomy, and the medicine man has become a bacteriologist, but that accounting alone boasts of its past, and with more than British conservatism refuses to budge? Antiquity in this case may mean petrifaction; early maturity may mean senile decrepitude; the symbol of the accountant may perhaps be an Egyptian mummy, which was the same four thousand years ago as it is today.

The introduction of bookkeeping was not an isolated phenomenon, but part of a general awakening, when men's minds, after centuries of stagnation and slumber, in a measure broke from the traditions of the past and began to think along new lines. But in other sciences this awakening, or this renaissance, was only a beginning. Is it conceivable that accounting alone came forth in a nearly finished form that needed no improvement?

But perhaps accounting has in reality progressed despite the assertions of its protagonists. It was indeed claimed, more than two hundred years ago, that accounting had reached a state of perfection, and that "without a fault nothing can be rescinded from or added to it." Yet, strangely enough, almost every subsequent textbook has claimed to be a new or improved system and that what went before was practically worthless.

*Address delivered at the annual meeting of the American Institute of Accountants, Del Monte, California, September 21, 1927.

Let us turn from such vague claims of advance and ask for details and specifications. Have substantial discoveries been made in the science of accounting as in other fields of human knowledge?

Yes, says Holland, speaking for the seventeenth century, for my great scholar Stevin, who advanced mathematics through his invention of the decimal system, did also introduce—the compound journal entry.

Yes, says England, for I place beside the name of James Watt, who in the next century invented the steam engine, that of Edward Thomas Jones, whose work was protected by patent and lauded by the governor of the Bank of England as an entirely new system of accounting.

Yes, says Italy, for the nineteenth century saw not merely the dazzling discoveries of Marconi, but the introduction by Cerboni of a really new system superior to double entry and adopted by the Italian government.

Yes, says America, in this latest era, I place on the scroll of fame, alongside the achievement of aviation, the introduction of—loose-leaf ledgers.

A rather sorry list of achievements. Compound entries are but poor rivals to so momentous an invention as the decimal system. Jones' heralded invention is one which those of you who know of it at all remember only as a curiosity. Logismography, despite certain merits, has in fifty years declined rather than expanded. And the loose-leaf system, while a more generally accepted improvement, is, forsooth, at best but a somewhat petty technical device which in no way affects the general principles of accounting.

It would, however, be unfair not to recognize evidences of progress. Three of these are prominent. The unprecedented outflow of serious scientific literature is a hopeful sign. This is so recent that some of you remember its beginning. In England one may take Dicksee and Pixley as the pioneers in this field, and these are both still active accountants; in this country the beginnings were with Sprague, whom many of you knew, and Cole, whom all delight to honor. It were invidious to mention other names. Most of you see a prominent author of accounting literature every time you look in your mirror.

Another bit of evidence exists in the fact that again, after some centuries of neglect, practically all universities in America, and

What Is the Matter with Accounting?

some abroad, are giving serious attention to instruction in accounting. I should hesitate, being an academically inclined person, to mention this before a group of professional accountants. The man who does often condemns him who teaches. But I am emboldened by the fact that my fellow speaker, the sometime president of this organization, is at the same time one of those academic guys, and that many others of your members are in the same boat.

A third evidence of progress is the undeniable improvement in the standing and dignity of the profession which you so honorably represent. Your opinion is sought not only in the ordinary course of business but by the government when it frames new laws, when it needs to wage a war, when it has the vastly more difficult task of arranging for the payment for a war already lost and won. You would not now be represented in the councils of the nation and of the world, if the science had not materially progressed.

It may even be possible to list some specific points in which present-day accounting excels that of former times. The most striking, though to me by no means the most interesting, has been the general improvement in technique, to which America has contributed so much. The problem of modern accounting is to deal with the myriad transactions of big business. Volta's first generation of an electric current was, indeed, the really significant step in advance in the study of electricity; but today the problem is not how to make a laboratory spark, but how to conduct, and control, and utilize, the power of a million horses over a tenuous copper wire. So with bookkeeping, the handling of transactions in enormous numbers is a real problem, not faced in past centuries, but wonderfully achieved today.

In addition I would mention three achievements, one of practical, one of pedagogical, one of theoretical interest. The first is the development of cost accounting (due to engineers rather than to professional accountants, but still an achievement in the science). This I consider the typical contribution of the present generation.

The second is the substitution, for the idea that bookkeeping is in essence a mere matching of debits and credits, of the view that its significant aspect is its striving to present the equation: assets = liabilities + proprietorship. The name of the honored and lamented Sprague stands prominent in this movement. But it was formulated long before his day, and can be traced back to German, American and English writers—for more than a hundred years. But the general adoption of the so-called balance-sheet approach in place of the purely journal method is a recent matter. Paciolo and his immediate successors give no hint of it.

The third point is the effort to introduce some unity into accounting theory instead of regarding its phenomena as diverse. For long it was generally considered that the investment of capital was in marked opposition to the payment of an expense. This view was crystallized in the phrase "capital expenditure or charge against revenue." It assumed that these two were radically different in nature, and one must never be confounded with the other. Today one sees a continuous gradation, land, building, machinery, raw material, expense of labor—each one of a series, each differing only as to length of the service which it renders, each paid for with the view of getting all possible use out of it in the productive process. The development of this point of view is, I believe, a real achievement in accounting theory—one not dreamt of in earlier centuries.

I find real cause for congratulation (I can not say pride, for, alas, I am not one of you) in these indisputable evidences of life, vigor and hence of progress in the profession. It may be ungracious, but perhaps for your souls' good, if my congratulations are tempered by raising the question as to what the science, or profession, lacks. In what is it weak? Where has it failed?

To do this, it is first necessary to ask what is, in fine, the purpose or nature of accounting. It is one of the technical languages wherein the facts of business are expressed. In this it is a twin sister to statistics, which expresses a different set of business facts through a different medium. It is, as it were, the distinction between the French of diplomacy and law Latin, languages at one time indispensable to government functions, each used in a restricted field, each with a separate vocabulary. Accounting is something other than a set of clever devices for beating the income tax with the least damage to one's conscience, something more than a specious way of window-dressing whereby the best possible appearance is given to a somewhat undesirable stock of goods. It is a universal language of business.

The prime requisite of a language is that it be understandable. There is a suspicion abroad that accounting as it exists today is not impeccable in this respect. Hartley Withers has said that "to most of the shareholders, [the balance-sheet] is about as comprehensible as a passage from Browning, translated into an unknown language" and speaks of it as an "impossible cryptogram with an esoteric meaning that is only revealed to an initiated caste, after much fasting and mortification."

Perhaps this criticism is somewhat unfair. The fluent lucidity of Xenophon, of Cicero and of Goldsmith is wasted on one who does not know the languages in which these wrote. Mr. Withers' inability to grasp all the beauties of the annual report of the Steel Corporation may possibly betray his own illiteracy rather than any lack of lucidity on the part of the Steel Corporation or the distinguished accountants who act as its auditors.

In order to be understandable a language must possess a clearly defined terminology, and the lack of this is the chief defect of accounting. As in economics, no new vocabulary has been adopted (I trust I do no injustice to my colleagues who have adopted "equities" in place of "proprietorship and liabilities" or have devised the really picturesque term, "where-got-gone statement"), but the ordinary language of the market place has been used in senses the market place knew not of, and in senses varying with different accountants.

Accounting is almost the only science (with the exception of economics, if that be a science) which is deficient in this respect. Physics may not know the ultimate nature of electricity, but progress has been made in describing its manifestations. When one speaks quantitatively of its various aspects there is no lack of definiteness, and ohms, volts and amperes are standard around the world. The nature of matter may be unknown to the chemist, but the formulas H_2O and C_2H_6O can never be confused, even though, before Volstead, the substances may have been mixed. But it is different with accounting terms, even with those of greatest significance.

This is manifest in respect of the more interesting and important of the two phases of accounting—that relating to the increase of wealth taking place during a fiscal period. Income subject to the federal income tax is indeed a fairly definite term, although, in many cases, a more appropriate rubric would be "the amount which we expect to get away with at the revenue office." But other aspects of the increment during the year are more significant than the amount taxable. Business is not run for the purpose of paying taxes, but for the purpose of making profits (call this by some other term if you wish), and there should be no uncertainty in defining the term, no unavoidable vagueness in expressing the best possible guess at the amount.

But one finds a state of actual confusion in this fundamental matter. Net earnings, net income, gross profits, profits, net profits? I have tried for years to find the proper term to be used and the exact connotation of each of the terms just quoted. I have appealed to academic writers, both economists and accountants, and I find only confusion. I have turned to the courts, and found in their decisions a confusion overwhelmingly ludicrous. If one sees the word "profits" in a textbook he has no idea of its content until he carefully studies the context. Even then he may still be left in doubt. It is as if one picked up a book and read a single word spelled "d-a-m-i-t." Until he learned whether the book were German or English he could neither pronounce the word, nor know whether it was an inoffensive conjunction or a mildly profane expletive.

So I turn to you, the recognized organization of the ablest group of professional accountants in the world. I turn to you who use the terms every day of your lives. I turn to you, as I would turn to the chemists for the meaning of ethyl alcohol, or as I would turn to engineers to learn what is the meaning of horse-power. I look through formal published statements, and I find that what one of you calls "net income" another calls "profits." I find that by some "income" is a comprehensive term including profits and also other items; by others "profits" is the more inclusive term, from which, certain deductions having been made, "income" remains. I find that a perfectly respectable, nay, an outstanding, accountant approves of a statement in which "net income" represents a remainder after subtracting interest on bonds, while another outstanding, nay, even perfectly respectable, accountant sanctions the use of the same term where interest is not deducted. Does one chemist describe water as a combination of one atom of oxygen with two of hydrogen, while another thinks it legitimate to use the same term for a combination from which one of the atoms of hydrogen is omitted? Does one engineer use a formula in which π is multiplied by the square of R, while another using the same formula omits the exponent of R?

Accounting, however, needs something more than a definite nomenclature. It needs above all else the formulation of sound theories, which can be crystallized into clear terminology.

What Is the Matter with Accounting?

Progress in the other sciences has for its milestones a series of formulated theories, comprehensive and significant. Astronomy was not content with calling the stars by name, but has developed a law of gravity which, starting with a falling apple, gives a rule applicable to suns and spheres remote beyond human comprehension, and which made it possible to posit a still invisible planet. Chemistry has developed theories which, permeating all matter, solve the mysteries of the infinitesimal. Like astronomy, it too was able to predict the existence of missing elements, as yet undiscovered in the laboratory. Biology found the theory of evolution, which embraces the immeasurable expanses of time and makes a continuum of all life in all ages.

But accounting is a laggard. Its great problems (I refer to matters even more significant than that bone of contention, whether in certain places the ink used should be black or red) are not only unsettled but their surface has scarcely been scratched. Some of these may be mentioned in sequence.

Accounting primarily deals with imputed values and records the changes therein. Can progress be made without formulating some theory as to what value is proper for accounting purposes?

There is, indeed, rather general agreement that in the first instance a newly acquired asset is valued at cost. But as to any theory, underlying and supporting this rule, there is general silence. A statement found in a thesis which your own association has crowned with your noblest laurels asserts, "We deny that a given object can have a value to its owner in excess of cost." I am in doubt as to just what the author meant, but surely you and the author alike must agree that what he says evidently is not true.

There are undoubtedly some practical advantages in preferring costs to guesses, but I have still to find any adequate theory or scientific hypothesis which supports the opinion just quoted. Accountants in this respect rely on reiteration in lieu of argument.

In the more difficult problem as to the basis for revaluing assets at the close of a fiscal period, the lack of sound theory is as great, the divergence in practice appalling. On this matter accountants (and for purposes of criticism only, I make bold to include myself among accountants), on this matter we accountants have been—or, more correctly, are—illogical, inconsistent and vacillating. We have arbitrarily laid down different rules for different classes of assets; we have promulgated the phrase "cost or market, whichever is lower", supporting it by a ludicrously inappropriate argument; we have for years strenuously advocated a given rule, only to make a complete *volte face*, when the effects of the great war made a continuance of such a policy unpleasing to one's clients.

The arguments adduced in favor of valuing at cost or market, whichever is lower, are so brilliant an instance of flabby thinking as to deserve some further attention. The stock argument is that such a procedure is justified on the ground that it is conservative. But if conservative treatment is desirable, if, as Neymarck says, accounting is good to the extent that values are underestimated, the rule of cost or market, whichever is lower, is illogical and unsatisfactory. It permits a commodity, which was purchased at the top of the market for $2.00, to be valued at the full present market quotation, say $1.95, but forbids that an article purchased for $1.00 and now risen to $2.00 be valued at even $1.20, although that is 40 per cent. below the actual market. Surely, if conservatism is the goal, it would be more effectively secured by saying that merchandise should always be valued at market less a margin for safety, even though in some cases that represented a marking-up. It is this sort of slipshod theoretical discussion of accounting problems which does little justice to the intelligence of the profession and raises doubts as to the distance which it has traveled since its mediæval beginnings.

Somewhat similar is the problem of the balance-sheet. Accountants agree with Sprague's felicitous statement that the balance-sheet is the starting point and the goal of all accounting procedure. If the balance-sheet is so important, should there be any uncertainty as to its nature and purpose? I speak not now of divergencies of opinion and practice as to insignificant matters of technique, such as the sequence and subdivisions of assets, or whether an item should appear as an addition or as a subtraction from the *contra* side. There should be agreement as to its essential character. But some hold that a balance-sheet is an exhibit of conditions at a given moment—when the clock strikes twelve at the end of a fiscal year. Others assert that the balance-sheet is a history of past events, showing what has been contributed to the concern and how the funds so received have been employed. In one conception, capital funds unwisely invested, "sunk and gone" to use a famous phrase, are no longer existent and hence have no place in a "cross section" of the concern of today. From the other viewpoint, the investment in an unproductive plant is a historical fact, and adequately explains the use made of contributed capital. Do you all know which view is correct? Do any of you consistently adhere to it? Will some one of you explain the proper view to the rest of us?

Depreciation is another matter on which your science has been laggard, although by no means absolutely paralyzed. Substantial progress has been made, but there are still those who speak of depreciation in unscientific terms. Not infrequently statements are prepared in which a given sum is stated as "amount available for depreciation and dividends." Such a confusion of unlike things should not be tolerated by a profession of the standing of yours. It is as though wages and overhead were subtracted from sales and the remainder labeled "amount available for replacement of raw materials and dividends."

Again, there are still those who, both in their practice and in their writings, not infrequently speak of depreciation as a reserve, something held back, or as a deduction from profits. But depreciation is something gone, not something kept; it is, as Cole so cleverly said, a "hole in the assets," and a hole is a difficult thing to hold in any position. Ever to speak of depreciation as a deduction from profits is a glaring error. It is not merely the survival of a form of expression, as when even an astronomer speaks of the sun rising, for even if you accountants know better, the average business man still thinks of depreciation as something other than it is. Or, at least, he did until the internal-revenue bureau allowed a deduction for depreciation. It is of only indirect credit to the profession that it could not put over the right view on a scientific matter until it became financially expedient so to do. If the average business man has wrong conceptions of accounting principles, the profession cannot be considered efficient. Even the medical profession did not rest easy until it convinced mankind that the proper treatment of epilepsy was not by means designed to exorcise a devil, and that a horse chestnut in the pocket is unreliable as a prophylactic against rheumatism.

Accountants do indeed agree that if a machine wears out in ten years its cost must somehow be distributed as a charge during those years. But there is no agreement whatever as to the proportion of the amount to be allotted to each particular year. I need not recall the interminable debate over the relative merits of straight-line and curved-line depreciation. Accountants, with rare impartiality, apply one system to one class of assets, another to other classes. It is somewhat as if one applied the Ptolemaic system to the motion of Mars, but regarded Jupiter as operating according to the Copernican system.

More distressful and more pertinent to the present discussion is the nature of the arguments adduced in support of one or the other basis. These are often barren of any vestige of accounting theory. It may be said that the charge should be relatively low in the early years, not because depreciation is less, but because it "is inconvenient to burden the early years" with a heavy charge, or because such a charge would show an initial deficit. Is accounting a device to secure what is convenient, or to show what is real? Should accounting be twisted so as to conceal an initial deficit if one really exists, or should it show the facts? Even the physician does not always alter his diagnosis because it would be inconvenient for the patient just then to have an attack of smallpox. His duty as a scientist is to determine whether that disease is present. The accountant, if a scientist, should be concerned solely in what charges may properly be assigned to the current year, as the effect of depreciation.

Sometimes a specious theoretical basis is indeed brought forth, namely, that the straight-line method is preferable to a curved-line method, because the former alone charges the actual cost. Here I argue neither for nor against a particular procedure, but merely assert that accounting in this case shows a crudely unscientific attitude. Whether a straight-line method is preferable or not is subject to discussion. But whatever merits it may have —and these may consist in the virtues of simplicity, ease of application, and understandability—the one thing that is certain and should be unquestioned is that the straight-line method does not charge off each year the amount actually paid for that year's service rendered.

This may be established by assuming that A rents property for two years at an annual rental of $104.76 to be paid in advance on January first each year. The contract is made in December, 1927, but the lease does not begin until January 1, 1928. Just before that date the owner suggests to the prospective tenant that he pay rental for both years on January 1, 1928, instead of paying it in two equal annual instalments. The tenant is perfectly willing to do so, provided proper adjustment can be made. Obviously, unless interest for him is at the rate of 0 per cent., he will not pay $209.52. Assuming a rate of 10 per cent., he would be justified in paying just $200. This is made up of the $104.76 in any case due and payable January 1, 1928, and $95.24, the value as of that date of $104.76 payable a year later. If then he pays $200 for two years' rental, the actual amount paid for the first year is not, as is assumed in the argument under criticism, one-half of the amount paid for two years, but a larger sum. When the interest rate is unknown, the only statement that can be made with confidence is that the amount actually paid for the first year is not the total price divided by the number of years of service.

Even in its progress, accounting has been hampered by careless reasoning. Two instances are in point. The first relates to municipal accounts. The increasing use of a municipal balance-sheet, due to the campaign inaugurated some twenty years ago, has everywhere been hailed as a real improvement. But, unfortunately, it was apparently assumed that the customary form of double-entry balance-sheet, invaluable to a corporation, should be used by a municipality. A spur being a good thing for quickening the speed of a horse, therefore let us use spurs to accelerate our automobiles, forgetful that a pneumatic tire is a quite different thing from a horse's flanks. Only after some years was it recognized that the characteristic of a corporation balance-sheet—the easy comparison of liabilities with the assets protecting them—does not at all apply to a municipality. With little exaggeration it may be said that municipal debt is, in reality, secured by the value of all the assets within the city walls save those which belong to the city and are listed in the municipal balance-sheet.

While modifications of the balance-sheet are now made, municipal accountants generally continue to employ the forms of double-entry bookkeeping. Is it an impossible hope that there is among you some genius who will invent a new form of accounting, particularly suited to governmental accounts? One can not foretell its nature, any more that those whose plodding backs built the pyramids could foretell the exact nature of Watt's invention which was to lift man's burdens, nor than the runner from Marathon, who exhausted himself in hastening the news to Athens, could tell how in future ages news would be brought without runner, without even a road, through the pathless ether. Cerboni attempted a new system, in logismography, but without notable success. But I long for the appearance of the genius who shall transcend tradition and devise a system of municipal accounting as superior, for that purpose, to double entry, as the latter excels the accounting procedure of Menher and Grammateus. Will not the candidate for this honor kindly raise his hand?

The second instance of imperfect progress is found in the consolidated balance-sheet. This anomalous document is a balance-sheet of a non-existent entity; it combines the debts of one corporation with the assets of another legally distinct corporation; it lists indiscriminately assets which belong to a given corporation with those which do not. It is something new, distinctly American in origin. But the consolidated balance-sheet serves a purpose. The task before you accountants is to agree on the rules for playing this new game. If in this country we play American football instead of Rugby we at least agree on the rules for Americans to follow. But eminent accountants still disagree on such significant matters as the treatment in the consolidated balance-sheet of a pre-existing surplus of a subsidiary company and the value to be attached to the shares of non-consenting stockholders. It is not strange, therefore, that in England there has been much recent discussion as to the legitimacy of this American device. One would similarly question football if umpires were uncertain whether the game consisted in forcing the ball over the opponents' goal or in seeing how long the fullback could maintain his balance while sitting on the ball. You have devised a new and valuable form. It is your task to perfect it.

My argument has been that notwithstanding the excessive claims of its admirers, accounting really is not a mummy, but is alive and growing. Progress it has indeed made, but nevertheless deficiencies appear, several of which have been mentioned. If I am to sum these matters up, it would be by saying that in the busy strife of professional life, in the problem of how to meet the task of serving the innumerable clients flocking to your office and each demanding immediate attention, you have somewhat neglected the higher task of developing a sound set of accounting theories. With the necessary attention to the anise and cummin you have, perforce, neglected the weightier matters of the law. After all, advancement in any service comes most often from the

What Is the Matter with Accounting?

consideration of abstract problems. Pupin made long-distance telephony possible because of research which he carried on in regard to the amplification of waves before there ever was a telephone; the greatest improvements in medicine were brought about by studies of test tubes rather than by diagnosing individuals; the great dye industries are the outgrowth of experiments in chemical laboratories rather than in factories.

American accountants lead the world in technique. They probably also lead the world in the formulation of accounting doctrine. But the present need of the profession is a further development of sound theory rather than improved practice.

"Meditations of a Student in Commerce 7, A Course in Advanced Accounting Theory (After reading 'The Raven')," *The Accounting Review*, Vol. VI, No. 4, December 1931, p. 307, and "A Fable," *The Accounting Review*, Vol. VII, No. 3, September 1932, p. 175.

These two snippets display Hatfield's sense of fun. Yet, the points he drives home are central to his style of teaching: that sound thinking about accounting practice requires comparing the views of leading authorities and, thus, becoming familiar with the relative merits of alternative approaches. Hatfield eschewed the all-too-common instructional practice of teaching rules to be memorized. He wanted students to think for themselves after consulting articles, books, court opinions, and regulations. Hatfield served, in effect, as their reference librarian. Probably because "Meditations" named several of his colleagues at other universities, as well as Hatfield himself, he had it published anonymously.

"What They Say About Depreciation," *The Accounting Review*, Vol. XI, No. 1, March 1936, pp. 18-26.

In this paper, which he read to the annual meeting of the American Association of University Instructors in Accounting on December 27, 1935 in New York City, Hatfield took many of his colleagues to task for their use of careless language when referring to accounting for depreciation. He seldom missed an opportunity to censure the inept use of terminology, and this paper gave vent to his growing disquiet with sloppy references to depreciation. In the announcement for the annual meeting, Hatfield's topic was given as "Theories of Depreciation" at a session shared with William Morse Cole, A.C. Littleton, and William A. Paton. Those in attendance would therefore have been taken aback at the presentation they actually heard.

MEDITATIONS OF A STUDENT IN COMMERCE 7, A COURSE IN ADVANCED ACCOUNTING THEORY

(After reading "The Raven")

Once at seven-thirty p.m., weary as the tired b.m.
Over many a punk and rotten volume of accounting lore,
There I nodded, nearly snoring, for it was so awful boring,
Sitting there so long a-poring, poring over books of yore.
"'Tis a waste of time," I muttered, "poring over books of yore,
Waste of time, and nothing more."

Soon a sound my ears was paining, 'twas the voice of one complaining,
Little knowledge they were gaining and it made the prof. feel sore.
"You will never get your M.A.s, if you waste your youthful heydays,
You will never be C.P.A.s, if you do not study more,
Small returns you'll get on pay-days, if you do not study more
You'll be dubs and nothing more."

"Is it true that all the rest-er you misfits have not read Kester,
A. Lowes Dickinson, McKenzie, Finney, Jenkinson, and Ror-
em, Van Cleave, or even Pixley, and the famous L. R. Dicksee?
All you loafers make me sick, Sec! for these writers I adore,
Great and famous are these writers, writers whom I do adore,
You'll get D's, and nothing more."

"Mr. Smith, if you've read Paton, what is it, that he is great on?
What's the curious, quaint, and novel great hypostasis he stands for?
Is it not found in the saying that the balance sheet's arraying
Only two groups is displaying, only two, not three or four,
Only Equities and Assets, that makes two, not three or four?"
Smith said "Yeah," and nothing more.

Then they came to study Canning, rather more than they were planning,
Mr. Brown grew thin and pallid, swamped by philosophic lore.
Long they pondered on the saying, "That there may be a prepaying
Of one's rent, there's no gainsaying, but not interest," so he swore.
"'Tis not interest but an offset to a debt," he roundly swore,
"Just an offset, nothing more."

Profit, Profit, thing of evil, Profit still, though from the Devil,
By the Heaven that bends above us, and the Science I adore,
Tell this soul, in search of knowledge, if you learned it when in college,
Harvard School, or Business College, what's its meaning, I implore!
Has it any earthly meaning, tell me, tell me, I implore
Tell me that, if nothing more?

Then methought the class grew denser, Esquerré they could not censor;
Could not even think the thoughts that they had often thought before.
Cried the prof., "I swear by Heaven, you're unfit for Commerce 7
Minds of dough, you need the leaven, given you in Commerce 4*
Little kindergarten lessons, taught to you in Commerce 4,
You are fit for nothing more."

Is there any rhyme or reason, any truth that we can seize on,
Since the book that Fra Paciolo wrote in fourteen ninety-four,
Books we've read in great profusion, but they all, without exclusion,
Only add to our confusion, messing up accounting lore,
English, French, Italian, German, only mess accounting lore,
So does Hatfield, only more.

* An introductory course in bookkeeping.

A FABLE*

HENRY R. HATFIELD

NOW there came a Young Man saying: "Master, thou art learned in the Mysteries of Debit and Credit. Teach me, I pray thee, for I am told that the Science is passing fair and maketh him to rejoice who is versed therein." And the Master taught him from the Scriptures as they were written aforetime by the Fathers. And he said unto the Youth: "Sometimes the Wise Men do this-and-that; and sometimes they do thus-and-so."

And the Youth waxed wroth and replied: "Tell me not varied ways, for a multiplicity of Instruction burdeneth my Soul. Tell me rather: 'Do this and not that'; for I would learn the one and only way to do a thing. For then I shall learn without Labor; and in Nights of Leisure shall I delight my Soul. And when the great Day of Judgment cometh, it will be unto me a Snap. But more than one thing at a time is too much for my limited Cranial Capacity."

And on the last day of the week the Master said unto the Youth: "Take me, I pray thee, to the great Assembly whence cometh the tumult and the shouting; and explain to me the Game which is played there. For it is great, and full of glory, but its Mysteries are unknown to me."

And the Youth took him gladly and explained to the Master how the Game is played, saying, "Behold the Ball lyeth in the center of the Field, and one runneth and kicketh the Ball so that it soars aloft and afar." And the Master said, "Now I see how the Game is played, well is it called Foot-Ball." But, anon, the Youth said, "Behold and see, for one throweth the Ball forward with his Hands; and another catcheth the Ball and runneth with it clasped to his Bosom." And the Master was perplexed, but he replied, "Yeah, I see." And a third time the Youth said, "Now the Ball will neither be kicked, nor will one fleet of foot run therewith, but it is given to a Giant, who will buck-the-center for a one-yard Gain."

Then the Master said, "Begone, thou Misleader of the Ignorant. I sought to learn how Foot-Ball is played. I would learn the one-and-only way and you have told me three ways and my mind is confused. If thou demandest that thou be told that there is only one way to toss a Debit-and-Credit, why tellest thou me there are three, and three-and-thirty, ways to toss a Foot-Ball? I will find me some one at a Coaching School who will tell me the one-and-only way and I shall be happy."

But in this he spoke as in a Parable, in the vain Hope that he might perchance enlighten the Youth.

---

* For a beginning class in Accounting, some of whose members object to the presentation of alternative methods.

WHAT THEY SAY ABOUT DEPRECIATION

Henry R. Hatfield

This is an assembly of instructors. While many of you have the advantage over me of being also practicing accountants, in this meeting we all should primarily be interested in the teaching of accounting rather than in its practice. I shall therefore make no reference to published balance sheets and income statements nor to the form and content of the auditor's certificate. I shall examine solely what the textbooks and other treatises on accounting have to say in regard to depreciation assuming that what is contained in these books approximately represents what is taught in our classes.

This is an association of *university* instructors and therefore I may properly assume that we all cherish high standards; that as university men we are interested in the nicety of expression; that even correct ideas do not satisfy us if they are concealed by vague verbiage; and that we stand firmly for clear thinking, for logical consistency, and for lucid exposition.

Unfortunately the standard in accounting literature has been relatively low. Let me cite a single extreme, but probably not unique, example taken from a textbook which has had very wide use throughout the country. On a single page this stated that assets equaled liabilities and also that proprietorship is equal to the difference between the assets and liabilities. On reading this, unless it is accepted blindly as being somewhat in accord with traditional statements, one must ask whether the author was incapable of straight thinking or was he culpably careless in the presentation of his thought. Whichever may be the answer, surely as university instructors we must deplore such an example of what Professor Willett has called "loose and lavender language."

It would seem as if by this time the subject should have been pretty well threshed out. To be sure it is frequently said that only recently has there been a proper recognition of depreciation as a factor in accounting. Certainly until relatively few years ago very many American corporations made no reference to depreciation in their published reports. So late as 1906 when the Interstate Commerce Commission required that depreciation be reckoned on certain railroad property, it was so much of an innovation that many high railway officials vigorously opposed it. But the recognition of depreciation is not limited to the present century. Professor Littleton calls attention to the first specific exposition of the proper handling of depreciation in accounts which he has found. This is in the textbook by Inglis published in 1861. Probably many of you have received from the University of Michigan a reproduction of accounts showing depreciation taken from the textbook by Monteage, published nearly two hundred years earlier, that is, in 1675; but again that indefatigable researcher in the history of accounting calls attention to *pro forma* accounts appearing in the textbook by Mellis, published in 1588. While there may be some question as to whether these accounts actually represent the handling of depreciation in the now accepted sense, there is at least a possibility that such is the case. But long before this, in 1408, the books of Francesco di Marco da Prato (according to Penndorf) show an unquestionable allowance for depreciation. But even a more extended leap backwards may be made to Vitruvius' work on architecture in which he lays down the rule that in valuing a masonry wall, one-eightieth of its cost should be deducted for each year it has stood, this resting on the assumption that such a wall has a life of 80 years. Here we have a very clear recognition not only of depreciation but an acceptance of a straightline method.[1]

Despite the nearly twenty centuries since Vitruvius wrote, accountants are not of one voice on the subject, nor have they all learned to make satisfactory exposition. In this paper I shall attempt to show what recognized writers have actually said, and to draw attention to what seem to me to be inconsistencies, contradictions, and confusion.

Should I seem too critical, may I plead that it is only the printed word which is criticized. I am sure that the writers in most of the cases would refuse to abide by the letter of their statements. Sometimes it is merely a case of failing to state an implied proviso or exception, sometimes the slipping in of a conventional phrase, whose long acceptance has obscured its ineptness. And finally, I am sure that the criticized passages do not imply a lack of understanding. Of this I am sure for I have myself committed all the things[2] of which I complain, and who am I to say I have not intelligence and understanding?

One difficulty in discussing depreciation is in distinguishing between the fact of depreciation and the recording of the fact in the accounts.

The fact is itself a physical or economic phenomenon. There is almost universal agreement that a physical asset does, in the process of use, wear out, at least to the extent of making its continued use uneconomical. The economic phenomenon which may be correlative with the physical phenomenon, but may often-times be independent thereof, is that with continued use of a physical asset the services which it renders tend to become exhausted. Hence, in the absence of disturbing outside influences, the lessened number of service units which the asset remains capable of yielding are of less value than were the larger number originally embodied in the asset.

Accounting does not concern itself with the actual wearing out of an object.[3] But in so far as the wearing out of an asset, or the exhaustion of its potential services affects the value to be ascribed to the asset by the going concern, accounting is called upon to make some record of such changes. To take ridiculously simple illustrations: if the friction involved in its use actually wears out the substance of a brake lining, so that after the car has run 20,000 miles it is no longer serviceable, it is obvious that a lining which has lasted for fifteen thousand miles is of less service value than one which has run only 5,000. Or, taking a case where physical wear is not the significant factor, if machinery is erected at a mine, in such circumstances as to make removal uneconomical, that machinery, when the mine is half exhausted, will have the power of rendering a smaller number of service units than when it was first installed. It is immaterial that the brake lining may perhaps stop the car as quickly on the fifteenthousandth mile as on any preceding mile; it is immaterial that the machinery is in no sense half worn out. In the absence of price fluctuations, no one would willingly give as much for an asset whose supply of service units is partly exhausted as he would for that asset with undiminished fertility. When half of the contents of a barrel of oil has been extracted, no

[1] For this I am indebted to Mr. H. E. Hale in his "What Is Depreciation?" in the *Railway Age*, Vol. 86, p. 403 (Feb. 16, 1929).

[2] I wish to modify the statement originally made. I confess committing some of the errors, but not all of them. Decidedly not all.

[3] Occasionally an accountant uses an expression which on the face implies that accounting records changes in the asset rather than changes in the value attached to the asset. Thus C. Bowman and A. Percy state (*Principles of Bookkeeping and Business*, N. Y., 1927, p. 53) that "Depreciation represents that portion of the asset consumed in operating the business." But this probably is an inept expression rather than an indication of a difference of opinion.

one (again with proviso of there being no change in price) will give as much for it as he would have given for the barrel when it was full. The same of course applies to the services which may be said to be barreled up in some physical asset.

The fact of depreciation is admitted by all. Inevitably the service value of any fixed asset (with some few possible exceptions) decreases with continued use. One need quote only the statement in "Accounting Terminology": "Depreciation is loss in physical or functional value due primarily and chiefly to ordinary wear and tear."

Having recognized that the service units to be rendered by a machine diminish during its service life, the real accounting problem is how is this fact to be recorded in the books. This is a problem in the technic of accounting and should be kept distinct from the physical or economic fact previously mentioned. Yet the same term "depreciation" is used now to mean the one, now the other thing. This confusion is found not merely as between the writings of different authors, but as well in the texts of the individual authors. Some clear examples of such confusion are the following.

"Depreciation" says one eminent writer "means the consumption in production processes of a preliminary outlay in such [fixed tangible] assets as make production possible" but in the same article he says: "depreciation is to maintain the capital intact."[4]

Waiving for the present the question as to the legitimacy of the latter statement in itself, how in the name of all accountants from Luca Paciolo to Fritz Schmidt can "consumption" ever maintain capital? Capital may be maintained despite consumption but to consume is *not* to maintain. The first phrase evidently relates to the physical fact. The second gives an alleged result of making a certain booking of the fact.

Another writer says "Depreciation . . . is an impairment of value" and on the very next page, "Depreciation cares for that portion of a plant . . . consumed."[5] Again waiving the appropriateness of the latter statement *per se*, it is surely the case that when he mentions "impairment" he is referring to the physical or economic fact; when he says it "cares for" he is referring to the bookkeeping entry. Yet he uses the same term for both, apparently unmindful of the confusion of thought involved therein.

Another, most recent writer, must be referring to different things when he speaks on two contiguous pages of depreciation as a *decrease in value* due to wear and tear and as the periodic *retrieval of value*.[6] I care not whether one or the other is the proper statement. Both cannot describe the same phenomenon.

Again, in a widely used text, recently revised, it is stated, again on consecutive pages, that depreciation is an "exhaustion of capital assets" and that it is the means of "reserving out of earnings" etc.[7] Did exhaustion of assets ever reserve anything out of anything? The second phrase relates to the supposed effect of making a given entry, the first clearly describes a purely physical phenomenon.

But criticism of accounting literature is not limited to the confusion of the fact of depreciation with its recording in accounts. Even in the technic of booking, the peculiar province of the accountant, one finds confusion and inconsistency.

One would suppose that those writing texts inculcating the principles (if such there be) of accounting, would not feel the need of any defense mechanism, would not attempt any artificial rationalization for so reasonable a procedure as recording depreciation. Depreciation is a fact. It is a fact which evidently affects the financial status, or the operating results, or both, of the business enterprise. One seeks for no esoteric reason for recording the payment of cash, and its receipt, nor for the coincident emergence of loss or profit. But in the literature of depreciation, various alleged, but irrelevant, reasons for booking depreciation in its two-fold aspect are found. According

[4] Fedde, A. S., *International Congress on Accounting* (1933), pp. 656 and 675.

[5] Racine, S. F., *Accounting Principles* (1917), pp. 131, 132.

[6] Burtchett, F. F., *Corporation Finance* (N. Y., 1934), pp. 591, 592.

[7] Bell, W. H., and Powelson, J. A., *Auditing* (N. Y., 1932), pp. 229, 228.

to these, the booking is not made to record the facts but according to some, it is to "maintain" or to "provide" or to "replace" or to "reserve" or to "set aside" or as one of the most authoritative writers has it, lest "the investors be left at the end of the decade with no useful property."

No writer, so far as I have observed, has ever said that when fuel is consumed, a record must be made in order to provide for something in the future, nor to replace the consumed fuel, nor to set aside something else in place of the fuel, nor so that the investors will not be left with no fuel on hand. Without exception, one is told to record the consumption of fuel in order to show that there is less fuel on hand than previously, and that a coincident and equivalent expense has been incurred. The function of accounting is to record all the recognized events which enter into the operations (in the broader sense) of the concern. Why, then, this peculiar and irrational urge to find other justification for recording depreciation than is required for recording the consumption of fuel? The accountant's sole and supreme obligation to tell the truth applies to both. If this is done, no other justification is needed.

One who for many years has lectured on accounting to classes of previously unenlightened beginners cannot even in this place break the habits to which he is so accustomed. Shall not the dyer's hand be subdued to what it works in? Therefore I cannot refrain from stating that in recording depreciation there must be a debit and a credit—a statement which to your ears is startling only because of its triteness, but it serves as a guide to further discussion.

The debit is ordinarily to an account called simply Depreciation. As to the nature of this entry there is comparative agreement. The most generally accepted view is that it represents an operating cost. I have listed some twenty-five writers who in no uncertain terms make this statement. Many of these elucidate further by saying that it is just as much a cost of operating as is consumption of fuel or any other of the items universally listed under operating costs.

There are others (I have listed three),[8] who describe the charge to depreciation as representing a cost, not specifying it as an *operating* cost. Similarly depreciation is said to be "losses actually incurred."[9] Another eminent writer says it is "a loss, a definitely experienced loss."[10] If, indeed, the *actual* loss is not known, it is "the *estimated* loss from the wearing out of the assets,"[11] or, again, it is the "loss or expense resulting in a reduction in the value of an asset."[12]

Only two writers are noted who at least superficially present a different opinion. Professor Canning, in his truly illuminating book, says "Depreciation is not an expense in and of itself, it is the outlay for the depreciating object that is the primary expense."[13] I do not myself like this statement but it need not be discussed here. For whether it is the payment or the gradual consumption that constitutes the expense, in either case the annual charge to depreciation represents an expense allocated to that period.

The other statement is that "depreciation of assets is merely an expression of values . . . that have reproduced themselves."[14] It is probably unnecessary to tarry over this lone voice of dissonance. *Athanasius contra mundum* was a noble figure. But, while standing by one's opinion in the face of all the world may indicate a noble character, it does not guarantee that the opinion held is correct. Besides, the disagreement is probably more a difference in the form of statement than in the attitude of mind. To this writer apparently all "expenses of operation" are "values which have reproduced them-

[8] Klein, Joseph J., *Students Handbook of Accounting* (N. Y., 1915), p. 76. Leake, P. D., *Depreciation and Wasting Assets* (London, 1912), p. 33. Moore, K. A. E., and Moore, Michael, *Company Accounts and Balance Sheets* (London, 1931), p. 62.

[9] Dickinson, A. L., *Accounting Practice and Procedure* (N. Y., 1914), p. 45.

[10] Dewing, A. S., *Financial Policy of Corporations*. 3rd ed. (N. Y., 1934), p. 562.

[11] Sanders, T. H., *Industrial Accounting* (N. Y., 1929), p. 146.

[12] Sunley, W. T., and Pinkerton, P. W., *Corporation Accounting* (N. Y., 1931), p. 174.

[13] Canning, J. B., *Economics of Accountancy* (N. Y., 1929), p. 129.

[14] Castenholz, W. B., *A Solution to the Appreciation Problem* (Chicago, 1931), p. 65.

selves" so that the statement regarding depreciation does not exclude it from operating costs.

With this consensus regarding the nature of the debit entry (when one debits Depreciation and credits Allowance (or Reserve) for Depreciation) it is a great surprise to find such disagreement as to the meaning of the credit side of the entry. When it is said that the debit indicates the expense, or loss, due to the using up of part of the value of the machine, it is difficult to understand how anyone can logically say that the credit account represents anything other than the reduction in value[15] which has been the occasion of the loss or expense. Many authors not only understand this, but possess (what is not always an accompaniment of clear understanding) the ability clearly to express the correct idea.

I have again listed more than twenty-five writers, by no means an exhaustive list, who thus interpret the meaning of the credit item. It is not necessary to quote these; they run from Sprague and Cole, the first scientific American texts, down to the very latest treatise just off the press, that of McKinsey and Noble. But it is interesting and somewhat appalling to note the dissentients. Or perhaps it were better to say "to note the dissonance" for it is what they say rather than their well-concealed thoughts that trouble us.

1. Mention may be made first of what is perhaps the most appalling group of writers. These are they who say, not that the allowance for depreciation represents a deduction from the amount debited to machinery, but that the credit balance in the allowance account implies an equivalent amount of cash. The following examples are given:

> The whole object of providing for depreciation is to save up money to meet a known future expenditure.[16]

> Inasmuch as the charge to Depreciation Expense involves neither a concurrent expenditure of cash (or other current assets) nor the assumption of a liability, there will be a sum of cash (or other current assets) equal to the amount so charged . . . .[17]

> Depreciation . . . does not mean a thing unless expressed in cash reserves.[18]

> [If $90 depreciation is charged each year for 10 years] the utility would have on hand the sum of $900.[19]

These statements are taken from recognized authorities, of highest standing. They knew better. Two of the four have elsewhere made a correct statement. But it is fair in this somewhat dialectic discussion before a group of academic men, to take the words as they read. For it is the printed word which confronts the beginning student. The statements made are clearly unsatisfactory in two respects. First there is omitted the essential proviso that the business has not run at a net loss. You all know that operating deficits do occur. In some cases the amount charged to depreciation may have been larger than the deficit for the year. If there had been no charge to depreciation there would have been no deficit. In such a case there is no other asset corresponding to the allowance unless you call the deficit an asset, which Heaven forbid! The second defect is that even if cash came in, in sufficient amount, there is no reason for assuming that there will be an accumulating amount of cash keeping pace with the accumulating allowance. Is any intelligent manager likely to withhold for 10 years,—is any manager, intelligent or not, going to withhold for 50 years, cash equalling the growing allowance? Will he not use it to pay debts or to extend the plant, so that when the asset is abandoned after half a century's use, there will *not* be a sum of cash on hand equal to the value consumed? Why then say there will be? Even though you cross your fingers while saying it. The student reading the text sees the author's words, not his fingers.

2. Closely akin to this is the view ex-

---

[15] Value as here used presumably refers to the unabsorbed cost, without reference to current market prices.

[16] Dicksee, L. R., *Auditing*. 13th ed. (London, 1924), p. 155.

[17] Paton, W. A., and Stevenson, R. A., *Principles of Accounting* (Ann Arbor, 1916), p. 144.

[18] Allen, T. H., "Depreciation as It Applies to Physical Properties." *The Certified Public Accountant* (Jan., 1936), p. 10.

[19] Wisconsin Public Service Commission. *Depreciation; A Review of Legal and Accounting Problems* (Madison, 1933), p. 23.

pressed by writers that while not necessarily implying an amount of *cash* on hand, the allowance for depreciation does imply the existence of a fund composed of current assets. Such are: "The sole function of a depreciation reserve or allowance . . . is to prevent the impairment of its capital invested in physical assets and to provide a fund for the replacement of such assets . . . .[20]

In passing, is it not strange that the *sole* function consists of two unrelated acts? And how can the provision of a fund prevent the impairment of the physical assets? Isn't such impairment inevitable as the asset wears out? Again: "Depreciation reserves [are] a fund to be used in cases of the wasting of fixed assets, such as wear and tear . . . ."[21]

Another: "The fund . . . created [by setting up a Reserve for Depreciation]."[22]

3. Without using either of the terms "cash" or "fund," a similar idea is expressed in the following:

> [Depreciation] reserves are amounts set aside out of earnings . . . bookkeeping entries setting aside each year an amount . . . .[23]
>
> the amount to be set aside [for depreciation][24]
>
> a common practice is regularly to set aside sums called depreciation or replacement charges.[25]

The same general attitude is shown by those who assert that the allowance for depreciation shows that some other asset has been substituted for the consumed value of the depreciating asset. For examples:

> Depreciation is the periodic retrieval from current incomes of the value . . . .[26]
>
> The reserve for depreciation measures the expired portion of the original cost of the assets and also indicates that the loss has been covered out of the gross income of the business.[27]
>
> the amounts . . . which are from time to time written off or recovered out of gross income as provision for depreciation . . . .[28]
>
> Depreciation . . . is merely an expression of values in one form that have reproduced themselves in other forms.[29]

Perhaps it seems hypercritical and pernickity to object to a statement merely because a proviso which some might consider obvious, has not been stated. But if we prate of the science of accounting, are we not to be held to scientific accuracy of statement? When we read in algebra $(a+b)\times(a-b)=a^2-b^2$, we assume it is universally true. Its truth does not depend on *a* being smaller than *b*. No such proviso being stated, we assume there is none.

When one says that the allowance for depreciation shows that other equivalent assets have replaced the consumed value of the fixed asset, the statement is not universally true. It is true only when expenses are not greater than earnings. If the algebraic equation depends on the relative value of *a* and *b* the proviso must be stated or algebra is no science. The analogy I think holds. The authors I have quoted did not state the proviso. *Very* few writers do so.

4. Another group of incorrect expressions is the following: Accepting the doctrine that the booking of depreciation is an attempt to ascribe to each period the appropriate amount representing the consumption of cost logically allocable to that period, expressions are nevertheless used as follows:

"*Eventual* loss,"[30] "*expected* losses,"[31] "*anticipated* losses,"[32] "to meet a known *future* expenditure,"[33] "shrinkage from depreciation etc. may be *anticipated* . . . by setting

[20] Bowker, W. T., "Obsolescence." *American Appraisal Co.* (1923), p. 3.

[21] Coles, A. C., *Company Accounts* (N. Y., 1920), p. 221.

[22] Dewing, A. S., *The Financial Policy of Corporations.* 2nd ed. (N. Y., 1926), p. 461.

[23] Wall, A., and Duning, R. W., *Ratio Analysis of Financial Statements* (N. Y., 1928), p. 71.

[24] Montgomery, R. H., *Auditing—Theory and Practice.* 4th ed. (N. Y., 1927), p. 683.

[25] Mosher, A. W., "Depreciation Based on Unit Cost." *Journal of Accountancy,* 52: 29 (July, 1931).

[26] Burtchett, F. F., *Corporation Finance* (N. Y., 1934), p. 591.

[27] Sanders, T. H., *Industrial Accounting* (N. Y., 1929), p. 146.

[28] United States. Department of Commerce. Business Advisory and Planning Council. *Reports to Stockholders* (Wash., 1934), p. 17.

[29] Castenholz, W. B., *Solution to the Appreciation Problem* (Chicago, 1931), p. 65.

[30] Howitt, H. G., *International Congress on Accounting* (1933), p. 626.

[31] Goggin, W. J., and Toner, J. V., *Accounting Principles and Procedure* (Boston, 1930), p. 265.

[32] Racine, S. F., *Accounting Principles* (Seattle, 1923), p. 214.

[33] Dicksee, L. R., *Auditing.* 13th ed. (London, 1924), p. 155.

up a reserve,"[34] "Net loss occasioned by retirements."[35]

In all these expressions the implication is that the loss is not one which has already occurred, but one which is bound to, or may possibly, occur in the future. This certainly does not harmonize with the idea that the attempt is being made to record what has been consumed during the current fiscal period. Similar in thought, although expressed in different terms, are the following:

Charging depreciation and crediting depreciation reserves provides for the recovery of an original stated outlay . . . .[36]

Depreciation is charged off for the purpose of providing an allowance . . . for the purpose of replacing the plant facilities when they are worn out or become obsolete.[37]

Provision for the replacement of the depreciated assets . . . .[38]

. . . the amount which the depreciation reserve should contain in order to make provision, through operating expense charges for the net loss occasioned by retirements.[39]

5. Other authors look upon the Reserve for Depreciation not as a negative item to be subtracted from the value attached to the machine but as a positive force that does something.

The sole function of a depreciation reserve or allowance . . . is *to prevent* the impairment of its capital.[40]

The amount of capital invested in the asset is *to be kept* at its original amount *through the credit* to the depreciation reserve.[41]

A depreciation reserve account is one set up . . . for the ultimate *replacement* of property.[42]

the systematic provision from year to year of an adequate sum to cover the depreciation of wasting assets . . . and thus *to provide* for their renewal. . . .[43]

The capital sum *to be replaced* by depreciation allowance.[44]

6. A sixth misconception, or more charitably, a sixth misleading expression, concerns the relation of the allowance for depreciation to profits despite the consensus that the debit indicates an expense or loss.

"Reserve accounts," says one, "are created for the purpose of showing on the *credit side of the accounts* the amount of profits required to be set aside . . . ; and on the debit side the actual loss from depreciation. . . .[45]

And this although on the same page it is said that the balance of the reserve for depreciation account shows the amount by which the cost (or the depreciating asset) has diminished by reason of the estimated wear and tear and efflux of time.

the depreciation reserve is set up to measure the true value of the asset . . . and also to withhold from free profits amounts which will be required in a subsequent period for replacement.[46]

a provision out of profits to the extent of cost[47]

the reserve account therefore represents profits withheld from capital.[48]

7. Other writers misled by the objectionable phrase "Reserve for Depreciation" look upon the credit entry as a "means of reserving out of earnings"[49] or as another most distinguished member of our Association puts it: "In providing depreciation there is a reserving or withholding from gross in-

[34] Belding, A. G., *Accounts and Accounting Practice* (N. Y., 1918), p. 173.

[35] Wisconsin Public Service Commission. *Depreciation; A Review of Legal and Accounting Problems* (Madison, 1933), p. 64.

[36] Castenholz, W. B., "The Accountant and Changing Monetary Values." ACCOUNTING REVIEW, 6: 283 (Dec., 1931).

[37] Frank, T. B., "Depreciation Accounting in the Machine Tool Industry." *N. A. C. A. Bull.*, 9: 1398. (No. 24, sec. I.) (Aug. 15, 1928.)

[38] Reitell, C., and Van Sickle, C., *Cost Finding for Engineers* (N. Y., 1930), p. 106.

[39] Wisconsin Public Service Commission. *Depreciation; A Review of Legal and Accounting Problems* (Madison, 1933), p. 64.

[40] Bowker, W. T., "Obsolescence." *American Appraisal Co.* (1923), p. 3.

[41] Lawrence, W. B., *Cost Accounting* (N. Y., 1931), p. 308.

[42] Bernard, R. J., "Depreciation and Depreciation Reserves." *American Accountant*, 15: 305 (July, 1930).

[43] Dicksee, L. R., *Depreciation, Reserves, and Reserve Funds* (London, 1912), p. 72.

[44] Grimes, J. A., "The Income Tax—Depletion and Depreciation." ACCOUNTING REVIEW, 3: 175 (June, 1928).

[45] Bentley, H. C., *The Science of Accounts* (N. Y., 1911), p. 149.

[46] Russell, F. C., and Hurdman, F. H., *Accounting Principles* (N. Y., 1924), p. 205.

[47] Fedde, A. S., "Depreciation and Obsolescence." *International Congress on Accounting* (1933), p. 667.

[48] Goggin, W. J., and Toner, J. V., *Accounting Principles and Procedure* (Boston, 1930), p. 265.

[49] Bell, W. H., and Powelson, J. A., *Auditing* (N. Y., 1924), p. 228.

come. . . ."[60] I ask you all and particularly do I ask him, who in the discussion to follow is expected to lambaste and excoriate this paper: Is an entry showing a diminution of value a means of doing anything except showing that diminution, or how can a mere bookkeeping entry withhold anything?

8. Some writers state that the Allowance, or Reserve, for Depreciation represents a "liability for the ultimate retirement of the plant. . . ."[61] I recognize the high authority, and pay respect to the ability and acumen of these authors. But if a credit to the Allowance for Depreciation is an alternative to a direct credit to the Machinery Account, how can it also show a liability, no matter how tenuous, transcendental, or esoteric a connotation may be attached to the accounting term "liability"?

The statement that the Allowance represents a liability is coupled with one which explicitly says that the debit indicates "as much a cost of operations as are current payroll and material expenditures . . . ."[62] An expense according to current accounting theory can occur only with the following alternative accompaniments. An expense may arise when an asset is diminished as when material is consumed, or cash is paid out. Or expense occurs when, without other changes, a new liability is created, e.g., when interest payable, or unpaid wages accrue. But there cannot be both a $1000 diminishment of assets, and a $1000 increase of liabilities with an expense of only $1000. Wages expense of $1000 cannot be a corollary of $1000 paid for wages and also of $1000 accrued payroll. It just simply can't be.

Say if you like (personally I do not like) that the credit to reserve shows a liability. But if you insist on this interpretation you have thereby abandoned any indication that the service value of the asset has diminished. Is that good accounting? But whatever you do, do not say that the credit indicates both A− and L+.

Shades of Luca Paciolo who combined in a single volume the first printed treatise on both algebra and bookkeeping! May we thy undutiful disciples ever remember that the two are related. May it be forgiven us when we say $-1000P = -1000A + 1000L$, for it is neither good bookkeeping, nor good algebra, nor good barnyard arithmetic!

9. The following quotation is from the most comprehensive book on depreciation. The author states:

> if the manufacturer omits depreciation costs he merely delays recovering the loss until some later period.[53]

Time limits compel the excision of my discussion of this. I merely suggest:

(1) Recovery does not depend on a bookkeeping entry but on the amount of earnings.
(2) There is no assurance of even a postponed recovery, and
(3) the statement that a loss is *ever* recovered is at least debatable.

A final quotation from an accountant and professor of accounting, who stands so high in the hierarchy of the profession that when we mention his name we do so with the bated breath of reverence. He stated that an allowance for depreciation is an allocation of cost, and, not indeed on the same page, but some 20 pages later (yet one ought to remember for at least 20 pages what he himself has written) headed a paragraph in heavy faced type "Investment of Depreciation Allowances."[54] I have heard of those who proposed to pay a dividend or even to run a government, out of a deficit but I cannot understand through what investment banker one invests an "allocation of cost."

To sum up:

1. There is confusion of the *fact* of deprecia-

[60] Sanders, T. H., *Industrial Accounting* (N. Y., 1929), p. 146.

[61] United States. Department of Commerce. Business Advisory and Planning Council. *Reports to Stockholders* (Wash., 1934), p. 18. Ball, T. F., "Can the Authorities Get Together on Depreciation?" *Public Utilities Fortnightly*, 13: 6: 347 (March, 1934). Similarly: Cole, W. M., *Accounts—Their Construction and Interpretation* (Boston, 1908), p. 83.

[62] United States. Department of Commerce. Business Advisory and Planning Council. *Reports to Stockholders* (Wash., 1934), p. 17.

[53] Saliers, E. A., *Depreciation—Principles and Applications* (N. Y., 1922), p. 111.

[54] Montgomery, R. H., *Auditing—Theory and Practice*. 4th ed. (N. Y., 1927), p. 698.

tion and the consequent accounting therefor.

2. There is agreement that in booking depreciation the debit represents a cost or expense due to the consumption of service value. This is fundamental to any theory of depreciation.
3. In regard to the credit various expressions are inconsistent with the above theorem. Among these are the following statements regarding the allowance:
   (1) that it implies cash on hand
   (2) that it implies a fund, not necessarily cash
   (3) that it implies the possession of other equivalent assets, although not necessarily impounded in a fund
   (4) that it relates to a future contingency, not to an already incurred expense
   (5) that it is not a negative quantity but an active force
   (6) that it is part of profits
   (7) that it shows a reservation
   (8) that it shows a liability
   (9) that it recovers a loss.

This all seems irreconcilable with the thesis that depreciation is the loss in value due chiefly to wear and tear.

I do not impugn the intelligence of any author, even myself, who has made these or similar statements. I merely criticize the language used. I do not deny that in the very works from which I have quoted, there are other passages which clearly prove that the author had the correct understanding. I merely deplore the presence in these works of conflicting statements, which must confuse the beginning student. I do not claim my own writings to be free of these and similar inaccuracies, though modesty of course prevents quoting my own works. All we like sheep have gone astray, following in the beaten track of tradition.

APPENDIX A: "THE UNPUBLISHED PAPERS"

by Maurice Moonitz

"The most liberal course I ever had at college was introductory accounting at Berkeley taught by Henry Rand Hatfield." So stated Thomas Henry Carroll, who had a distinguished career as an academic (Harvard, Syracuse, North Carolina), as a dean (Syracuse, North Carolina), as a university president (George Washington), and as an associate director and vice president of The Ford Foundation.

When I first heard the statement quoted above, I felt that Tom Carroll exaggerated a bit, but after reading the previously unpublished papers of Hatfield, I can understand his enthusiasm. They range over a large expense of knowledge and reflect the ideas and opinions of a person who was "liberal" in the best meaning of the term.

These papers shed light on certain aspects of Hatfield's background, character, and attitudes that are difficult if not impossible to glean from his more formal published books and journal articles. For one thing, with the exception of his "Critique of the Tentative Statement of Accounting Principles Underlying Corporate Reports," they were not written for publication. Many of them were composed for presentation to relatively small groups of friends and colleagues, such as the members of the Kosmos and the Berkeley Clubs at the University of California. Furthermore, the topics addressed were, with one or two exceptions, concerned with issues other than accounting. As a result, they assist us greatly in seeing Henry Rand Hatfield as a whole person.

Hatfield's *religious background* is clearly etched in these papers. His father was a Methodist minister, so he was conversant from childhood with the Bible, with the moral precepts of an organized religion, and with the contents of the prayer books used by his father. The influence of the Bible, especially the King James version, is marked in Hatfield's English style. Even when he is discussing something not directly related to faith or morals, the feel, in many places, is that of the historical Books of the Old Testament. Another phase of his English style is found in his figures of speech, such as "institutions ... sanctified by the devotion of their founders, imbued with a spirit of true religion" and "as the acolyte seeks by purgations and vigils to prepare his soul for the imminence of his diety." Both of these quotations come from a completely nonreligious paper, "The State University and the Body Politic...."

The influence of his early religious training is shown by an incident at Berkeley. Hatfield was discussing his *Modern Accounting* (1909) with a group of us. He stopped at one point, somewhat bemused, to tell us that one of the reviewers of that book had praised it for "its high moral tone." He smiled and said that he was somewhat surprised at that comment; he was not aware that the book had any tone, moral or otherwise. This comment of Hatfield's was not uttered from modesty; he was genuinely unaware of this element in much of his work.

Another influence which comes through is his *classical background.* Hatfield was conversant with Greek and Latin. He knew Greek mythology. He knew and used Latin quotations from various sources; they crop up in many places in these papers.

The influence of Thorstein Veblen comes from Hatfield's days at the University of Chicago. Veblen was a faculty member, about 10 years older than Hatfield. Their friendship covered both Hatfield's student days and his tenure on the Chicago faculty. The following excerpt from the article on Veblen in *The New Columbia Encyclopedia* (1975) captures the essence of the influence he wielded:

> Veblen was able to dissect social and economic institutions and to analyze their psychological bases, thus laying the foundation for the school of institutional economics. His dry, involved, satiric style enabled Veblen to coin famous phrases, such as "conspicuous consumption."

Particularly in his earlier work, Hatfield's style was certainly "involved," with a tendency to use long, unusual words in place of those more colloquial at the time.

In at least three of the unpublished papers, Hatfield exhibits considerable *skill as a journalist*—the paper on the "War Industries Board" (1920); on "Parliament and the Trade Unions" (1927), in which he reports on the aftermath of the 1926 General Strike in Britain; and the 1933 paper, "A Professor Looks at Germany," Hatfield, in these papers, is objective and even-handed. Almost to a fault, he gives people the benefit of the doubt, of being "fair-minded."

The preceding forces contributed to making Hatfield an "enlightened conservative." He consistently espoused individual freedom and a highly competitive economic system, but he was not blinded thereby to the talent and sincerity of those whose views differed from his. His deep respect for Veblen and for Wesley Clair Mitchell reflects this trait, even though both were not in agreement with him on political, or on economic issues. It also shows in the early (1910, 1918) papers on "Corporations and the Public" and in the 1927 paper on "Parliament and the Trade Unions." Indeed, in the later paper, I feel that he has correctly identified his own deeply felt beliefs when he states, "But, with all these admissions, I still am inclined to think the action ill-advised. *But opinions on such matters are less a result of logic than of temperament.* And I, who *temperamentally* am more akin to the Liberals than to either Tory or Labour party, seem to agree with Grey and Reading (i.e., Liberals) rather than with either Hogg (i.e., Tory) or Jones (i.e., Labour)" (emphasis added).

What emerges for me is a picture of Hatfield as a man who knew his worth, who felt secure in what he was doing, and who had a set of values to which he could refer. And he loved teaching. When he was told, upon his retirement in 1937, "Now you will be free to do what you want," he replied, "But I have been doing that since I began to teach."

Now, to the papers themselves. I list them below, each with a brief commentary. A good place to start reading is the 1937 paper "Moriturus Vos Saluto;" it gives the most comprehensive view of Hatfield, by Hatfield. The best single piece, in my view, is the short 1916 paper he gave at the University of Washington. It is a paper he obviously enjoyed writing and giving.

"The Study of Economic History," c. 1900-1920

This paper reflects the influence of Hatfield's contacts with Thorstein Veblen at Chicago, as well as his stint at Washington University, where he taught Economic History. This paper is an excellent illustration of his penchant to: (1) get behind appearances to substance, and (2) to relate "research" or "study" to human problems.

Toward the end of this paper, he voices his strong distaste for "legal tender" (inconvertible currency). This distaste is restated more vigorously some 35 years later in "George Washington and Dr. Craik."

"Business Efficiency as a University Ideal," 1912

A good paper, full of zip, in which Hatfield sides with an "outsider" in his criticism of university habits. The influence of Veblen is evident here in the dissection of a "hallowed institution," like academe, and the use of unusual and long words.

Re Veblen: Sometime between 1934 and 1937, Hatfield regaled a group of teaching assistants at Berkeley with a true story about Veblen. At Chicago, Veblen was noted as a "walking encyclopedia" who knew the answers to *everything*. If you asked him who held the world's record for the 100-yard dash, Veblen would reply, slowly, "Well, I'm not sure I know. I don't usually follow that sort of thing. But I think that if you checked, you'd find the record is 10.2 seconds, held by John Doe who set it in 1886 at a meet in Podunk, Minnesota." Of course, when they checked, they found that Veblen was right in every detail. So Hatfield and a group of his colleagues set out to trap Veblen. They asked him: "What is the difference between a teepee and a wigwam?" (The questioners thought there was no difference.) Veblen replied: "I'm not sure there is any difference. But if you check, I think you'll find that the teepee is used by Great Plains Indians and the wigwam by the Algonquian Indians, and they are constructed differently." Of course, Veblen was right, even to the use of buffalo hides by one group and tree bark by the other.

"Some Heretical Views on the Method of Teaching Bookkeeping," 1913

Hatfield's interest in bookkeeping: The Regents of the University of California adopted a policy to use the campus Department of Education to upgrade the teaching in the secondary schools of the state (*President's Report for 1908-1910*, pp. 23-25). Hatfield participated by teaching courses on bookkeeping in the summer sessions. In at least one instance, he used a visitor to teach the course—he was James O. McKinsey (1920), then at the University of Chicago.

This is one of only two of these formerly unpublished papers that deal explicitly with accounting and its subdivisions. (The other is the critique of the 1936 Statement of the American Accounting Association's executive committee.)

In this early paper, Hatfield sets forth some themes that run through his later work. For example, in speaking of the texts used at the time, he states, "All alike err grievously in that there is no connection between the explanations which they give, and the work they are attempting to do." And, shortly after, "There is no attempt to show the public what he is trying to do, and why he does it."

Remarks upon the Inauguration of Henry Suzzallo as President of the University of Washington, 1916

A little gem. It exhibits Hatfield at his best as a toastmaster, an accomplished speaker who knows the appeal of brief remarks. He uses the victory of Washington over California at football in 1915 to allude to Vikings, Goths, Thor, and Germanicus. From art, he recalls the picture of Germanicus reviewing his vanquished foes, including a "captive dejected bear." (Berkeley's sports symbol is the Golden Bear.) He combines this with a pun, in his comment on the invitation for him to stay a few days but no "chair" is offered. And then, in a serious close, he pays his respects to all the institutions of higher learning in the three Pacific Coast States.

"Corporations and the Public," 1918 and 1910

In the 1918 paper, Hatfield brings together his knowledge of economic history and of forms of business associations (e.g., partnerships, corporations), and his firm belief in the benefits to be derived from a competitive system, subject to limited controls by government. In the earlier (1910) paper, he brings accounting to center stage as a remedy for the "financing misdeeds" that have occurred and may recur, by requiring "publicity of accounts." Thus, he was at least a decade ahead of the proposals in the late 1920s and early 1930s for "publicity of accounts" in response to corporate excesses. But, as far as I know, he never built on this solid recommendation. For example, his 1918 paper leaves out the plea for "publicity of accounts."

A Reply to the Paper on "Profits" by E.R.A. Seligman, 1920

This is not a good paper. It is easy to see why he did not publish it, because it violates one of his own precepts—his discussion does not address itself to Seligman's paper. Instead, it attempts to show why accountants have a more difficult time than economists in defining "profits." (One of my friends in Mathematical Statistics, Michel Loève, used the term "sacred monsters" to describe the great leaders in the field of mathematics. This paper indicates that even as "sacred" a monster as Hatfield, in the field of accounting, can have feet of clay.)

"Experiences with the War Industries Board," 1920

A strong paper. Hatfield served as a Director of the Division of Planning and Statistics of the War Industries Board, where he had an excellent view of what was going on. Noteworthy to me is his recital of the relationship between the military and the civilian in procurement activities. He becomes almost rhapsodic in his praise of the contributions of business leaders brought to Washington. In a nutshell, he demonstrates that "central planning" not only works under certain circumstances, but is essential. Contrast this paper with one written about 15 years later, in which he castigates the New Deal from pillar to post ("George Washington and Dr. Craik," 1934). In the latter paper, Hatfield does not seem to understand that in the crisis of the Great Depression, the business leaders who performed so well during World War I balked at and resisted every attempt to prevent a true social and economic collapse, a threat that was not present in the 1917-1918 period.

"The State University and the Body Politic...," 1922

A strong paper, well-reasoned, well-balanced, focused on the underlying essentials.

"The Scholar's View of War," c. 1926

A thoughtful piece, written with passion. Compare this with Hatfield's paper on Germany (1933) and the one on "loose and lavender language" (1942) where he seems to have forgotten his own awareness of the fact that, in times of stress, governments lie so skillfully that it is impossible to separate the truth from the illusions.

"Parliament and the Trade Unions," 1927

An excellent paper, written in an even-handed manner. A first-rate report and analysis of the way that the British Parliament, dominated by the Conservative party (the Tories), reacted to the 1926 General Strike. From his vantage point as a "Liberal," Hatfield is able to make a dispassionate report of the strengths and weaknesses of the dominant parties (Conservative and Labour) and their spokesmen.

"A Professor Looks at Germany," 1933

A fascinating paper that reflects the views in the early 1930s of many intellectuals outside Germany. Hitler is already in power and moving relentlessly against his enemies within Germany, but "fair-minded people," like Hatfield, refused to believe that Hitler was a monster, the embodiment of evil. This paper will repay careful reading.

Here, again, he ignores his own post-World War I paper in which he correctly assessed the effects of the outright lies and slanted partial truths from governments "in time of war."

"George Washington and Doctor Craik," 1934

When George Washington was seriously ill, his doctors, led by Dr. Craik, bled him several times. And so, the Father of Our Country died. When our country was seriously ill during the Great Depression, the "doctors," led by Franklin D. Roosevelt, were systematically bleeding the "patient" to death. This is the gist of the paper. It contains some cogent criticism of the New Deal but few or no constructive proposals. Hatfield pays no attention to the total ineptitude of the conservatives, headed by President Hoover, whose only remedy seemed to be to reassure us that "prosperity was just around the corner," and who thought that the revolution was here when the Bonus marchers camped across from the White House.

"A Critique of the Tentative Statement of Accounting Principles Underlying Corporate Reports," 1937

Unlike most of the other papers in this set, this one is about accounting, straight on. This paper properly reflects Hatfield's views, as set forth in the articles and monographs published during his lifetime. It is a good paper, originally intended for publication, but he delayed too long in submitting it to a journal.

"Moriturus Vos Saluto," 1937

The title is a variation on the Roman gladiators' salute before entering combat—"Hail, Caesar! We who are about to die salute you!" The paper closes with another bit of Latin, which, freely translated says, "Of the dead, (speak) nothing but good."

The occasion for the paper must have been his impending retirement (June 30, 1937), at age 70. In it, Hatfield reminisces, recalling major events during his tenure at Berkeley. He offers a few views of the future. It is a revealing paper, worth reading.

"Of 'Loose and Lavender Language'," 1942

To me, this is not a welcome paper. Written when Hatfield was 75, it lacks the bite, the wit, and the verve of his earlier output. Its form is also somewhat rambling, but that can be overlooked because: (1) it was not written for publication, and (2) it was presented to a group (the Berkeley Club) that knew what was behind it. Still and all, I feel sorry that Hatfield had aged so quickly—he sounds querulous. Instead of an argument on the merits of his "opponents'" position, he takes refuge in an attack on their use of "loose and lavender" language, a valid point of weakness but hardly an important target. What we have here is a talent, previously original and creative, reduced to using the form that had stood him so well in the past without the substance. One is reminded of an author, a poet, or a composer who has run out of ideas but can still exhibit the technical skills developed over the years.

"The Hatfieldiad" by Max Radin, Professor of Law, Boalt Hall School of Law, Berkeley; Brother of Paul Radin, Professor of Anthropology, Berkeley

Max Radin, like Hatfield, was versed in the classics. The two enjoyed each other's company and had many spirited exchanges. One of them occurred during the Doctor's Oral of Catharine (Greene) Quire. Catharine relaxed for about 20 minutes during the exam while Radin and Hatfield discussed one of the questions posed to her.

This item was written on the occasion of Hatfield's retirement, or later. See "Canto the Third," third line from the end, "till he emerited" (i.e., 1937); also "Canto the Sixth," third line, "active or retired."

APPENDIX B: "RECOLLECTIONS OF HENRY RAND HATFIELD"

by Maurice Moonitz

I knew Henry Hatfield personally from 1934 until his death in 1945. Our first direct contact was in his seminar in accounting theory at Berkeley, where I was in the Ph.D. program of the Department of Economics. The announced topic of Hatfield's seminar was "depreciation." At the beginning of the course, I was puzzled at the narrowness of the topic. After all, we could cover that topic in about three weeks. What were we going to do the rest of the semester? Under Hatfield's guidance, however, we did plunge into "depreciation," but by pressing below the surface, we covered most of the important variables in the accounting problem. Lesson No. 1—It matters little where you start in any field. Press hard and deep enough, and you will cover the field.

The details of that course escaped me many years ago, but I do remember vividly the readings and discussions in the field of public utilities. To this day, I am convinced that the discussion of depreciation is handled much better in the public utility literature than in the general accounting sources.

In one of Hatfield's seminars, Professor William A. Paton of the University of Michigan was a guest speaker. Paton was on a trip to the Pacific Coast and was spending a few days in Berkeley. At the time, Hatfield was in his late 60s, Paton in his mid-40s. The total group in attendance was small, not more than a dozen persons in the seminar room. Paton was standing at the front of the room, giving his remarks. Hatfield was sitting at the rear, his attention focused on the visitor. Characteristically, Hatfield would listen, then shrug his shoulders. Paton was understandably nervous, and stopped once or twice to see if Hatfield was going to make a comment. But Hattie just smiled at Paton and said, "Go on! Go on!"

A few years later, in 1937, Hatfield retired and Paton came to Berkeley as a visitor to see if he would accept a position as Hatfield's successor. Hatfield was a dyed-in-the-wool "proprietary" theorist, whereas Paton was the principal architect of the newer "equity" theory and a stern critic of the older emphasis on the owners of an enterprise to the relative neglect of the long-term creditors. To Hatfield, however, this difference was of minor consequence. He recognized Paton's outstanding qualities, and that was what mattered. This same quality in Hatfield was made evident to me in his high regard for scholars such as Thorstein Veblen and Wesley Clair Mitchell, whose political views were certainly at odds with his own.

Ruth Lubin and I were married in the fall of 1934. Once we got settled in our apartment, we invited my fellow graduate students and the accounting faculty to an "open house." Hatfield and his wife were the only faculty to come. Before long, the two of them were leading the festivities. Hattie himself went on the attack, addressing the obligatory question to me, "How did you ever get such a lovely young lady to marry you?" Hattie and his wife then settled down to tell us of their years at the University of Chicago, where they had met as fellow-students. Hattie even told us of the poems he had written to Ethel Adelia Glover (later his wife). She nodded assent with a pleased expression on her face.

Several other incidents occur to me, unrelated to the courses I took. Catharine (Greene) Quire was completing her dissertation under Hatfield on German accounting theory and was teaching part-time. Hatfield, Quire, and I would get together often for a meal at an off-campus coffee shop and some extended discussion of whatever we were working on at the time. Another way in which Hatfield would get to know his graduate students better was to take one of them each month to a meeting of the San Francisco chapter of the California State Society of CPAs. This necessitated traveling together by public transportation from Berkeley to San Francisco, including a trip across the Bay on a ferry boat. He took me to the meeting at which John F. Forbes of Haskins & Sells, and President of the American Institute, was the speaker. Forbes was accompanied by John L. Carey, who had just joined the Institute's staff. This practice of Hattie's not only provided an occasion for informal conversation but emphasized his belief that accounting academics should keep in touch with the profession and take part in its activities, even though, as in his own case, he had never practiced as a professional accountant.

Another close association with Hatfield revolved around my interest in consolidated financial statements. He was on the committee that supervised my master's thesis (on consolidations) and later (after his retirement) assisted me greatly in connection with the monograph *The Entity Theory of Consolidated Statements.* He read the preliminary draft of the monograph and spent a great deal of time and energy on it, both through personal conferences and detailed written comments. Two typical Hatfield comments come to mind—when he heard that I was doing a thesis on consolidations, he confronted me in a group and asked, "Are you the one who is going to straighten out that area?" Later when, he had completed his reading of the first draft of the monograph, he told me that at numerous points he thought he had me in an error or oversight but, he said, "I turned the page, and there you had covered the point!"

While I was on the faculty at the University of Santa Clara (1937-1942) and later at Stanford (1942-1944), he and I corresponded frequently. He was the initiator, posing some point with which he had difficulty and asking for my reaction. That correspondence disappeared from my files years ago, but, as an example, I recall one letter in which he described what was, to him, an anomaly in the compound-interest tables. I replied as well as I could. He acknowledged the promptness with which I responded, quoting a bit of Latin: "Bis dat, qui cito dat" (He gives twice who gives promptly).

Hatfield was in great demand as a toastmaster or after-dinner speaker. When Wesley Clair Mitchell came to Berkeley to deliver a public lecture, Hattie presided, resplendent in tuxedo and black tie. A few weeks before the lecture, a group of student wheelers-and-dealers had persuaded the local chapter of Phi Beta Kappa to make General Hugh Johnson an honorary member. Johnson was then the head of the National Recovery Administration (NRA). At some time earlier in his career, he had been assigned to Berkeley, probably in connection with the campus ROTC program. In his spare time, the general attended classes at the Law School and earned high grades. The politically motivated move by Phi Beta Kappa outraged many on campus, especially a staunch foe of the New Deal like Hatfield. So, as the large audience quieted down, Hatfield rose in all his dignity, walked to the podium, put his hands on his hips, and said, loudly and clearly, "This is *not* the occasion for initiating General Hugh "Iron Pants" Johnson into Phi Beta Kappa! We are here for a more important matter."

In the 1936 presidential election, Governor Alf Landon of Kansas ran on the Republican ticket against Franklin D. Roosevelt. The *Literary Digest*, a leading weekly magazine of the time, conducted a poll of names gathered from telephone directories (hardly an appropriate pool from which to get a cross-section of voters, because most people then did not have a telephone). At any rate, those polled favored Landon to win the election. In an office pool, I followed the "experts" and bet 10 cents on Landon to win. Roosevelt swept to victory in a landslide; I lost my 10 cents; the *Literary Digest* slowly faded from the scene. Hatfield came into the teaching assistants' room the day after the election to bemoan the fate of the country. One of my colleagues told him that Moonitz had bet on Landon to win. Hattie looked at me as though he was seeing me for the first time and said, "You did?" I nodded assent. He pulled his coin purse out of his pocket and counted out five pennies and a nickel. He gave them to me, telling me that he was so happy that *someone* had his head on straight! I never had the courage to tell him that in fact I was no supporter of Landon.

About the same time, Hattie came into the teaching assistants' room just after returning from a trip to New York. He looked stunned, unbelieving. He told us that at a meeting in the Wall Street district, he had heard talk of a plot to use force to overthrow the government headed by FDR. A retired general, whose name he mentioned, stood ready to lead the coup. Hatfield told us he had been sure they were joking, so he smiled and gave a little laugh, but he was shocked to learn that they were in earnest.

During the late 1930s, Hatfield was engaged in a joint project with Professor Sanders of Harvard. Hatfield came into the teaching assistants' room one day waving a sheet of paper. "Listen to this!" he said, and proceeded to read a definition of Prepaid Expenses, followed by one of Deferred Charges. "Notice," he said, "the definition of Prepaid Expenses includes deferred charges and the one of Deferred Charges includes prepaid expenses. Both definitions are by Professor Sanders. What am I to do? I can't tell the man that *everything* he writes is wrong."

In 1944, the Federal Power Commission and the Montana Public Service Commission held joint hearings in Butte, Montana, on the extent to which the assets of the Montana Power Company contained "water" under the rules laid down by the FPC. Most of the leading accountants (e.g., W.A. Paton and T.H. Sanders) testified as expert witnesses. Hatfield was also asked to appear. I happened to be in the teaching assistants' room when Hattie came in and said, "A hundred dollars a day and expenses—a hundred dollars a day and expenses, just for saying the things I have been teaching and preaching all my life—and my doctor says I can't go!"

I do not remember why his doctor wouldn't let him travel to Montana, but he died about a year later. The last time I saw him was at his home just north of the Berkeley campus. He was seated in a rocking chair, wrapped in a blanket, obviously ill, without any energy, but with the mustache still properly trimmed and the faint, quizzical smile on his face.

NOTES

1. Hatfield revised this paper for presentation, under the title "An Historical Defense of Bookkeeping" to the annual meeting of the American Association of University Instructors of Accounting in December 1923.

2. Hatfield presented a paper titled "The Scholar's View of War" at the installation of the Phi Beta Kappa Chapter at Occidental College, Los Angeles, on May 12, 1926. It was an abridged version of "Cui Lumen Ademptum," which has not survived.

3. The comments on Hatfield's use of rhetoric have been prepared by Elizabeth Tebeaux, for which the author is most grateful.

4. The case was decided on April 3, 1905 in equity court and is cited as 69 NJ EQ 36.

5. Hatfield is referring to the Big Game played on November 6, 1915, at which the University of Washington football team defeated the University of California's team, 72-0.

6. Hatfield's references are to: R. Brown, *A History of Accounting and Accountants* (Edinburgh: T.C. & E.C. Jack, 1905), for which Row Fogo wrote Chapters V and VI; W.H. Lyon, *Capitalization: A Book on Corporation Finance* (Boston: Houghton Mifflin, 1912); J.H. Moore and G.W. Miner, *Bookkeeping* (Boston: Ginn and Company, first published 1912); L.L. Williams and F.E. Rogers. *Theoretical and Practical Book-keeping* (Rochester, NY, first published 1882). For the Moore/Miner and Williams/Rogers works, it is not clear which edition is being cited.

7. See William Z. Ripley, *Main Street and Wall Street* (Boston: Little, Brown, and Company, 1927), especially Chapter VI. Ripley had first exposed his reform proposal in an article appearing in the September 1926 issue of *Atlantic Monthly*.

8. The source of these quotations, and the one that follows, is Enid Bagnold's article, "With the Nazis—Ten Days in Germany: The New Revivalism," in *The Times* of June 2, 1933. Several discrepancies in Hatfield's rendering of the extracts have been corrected.

9. These three extracts are from two articles filed by correspondents of *The Times*: "Check to Nazi Extremism—'German Revolution Finished'—Cabinet's Order" (July 11, 1933) and "New Trainer for Nazi Leaders" (July 13, 1933). Several discrepancies in Hatfield's rendering of the extracts have been corrected.

10. The passage is from Virgil, *Aeneid*, Book VI, lines 126-129:

> ...the descent to the Underworld is easy;
> ...but to retrace one's steps and come out to the upper air–
> that is a task, that is a struggle.

11. This line translates: "From the dead, nothing but good comes."

12. Page references are to the pamphlet reprint of the statement in *The Accounting Review* of June 1936.

13. The credit line, for copyright purposes, is: Henry Rand Hatfield. "Some Variations in Accounting Practice in England, France, Germany, and the United States," *Journal of Accounting Research*, vol. 6, no. 2 (Autumn 1966), pp. 169-182. Reprinted with permission of the Institute of Professional Accounting, Graduate School of Business, University of Chicago.

Chapter 8

List of Hatfield's Publications

BOOKS

Lectures on Commerce, editor. Chicago: University of Chicago Press, 1904; republished in 1905 under the title *American Commerce and Finance*.

Modern Accounting: Its Principles and Some of Its Problems. New York: D. Appleton and Company, 1909; reissued in 1976 by Arno Press, New York.

Accounting: Its Principles and Problems. New York: D. Appleton and Company, 1927; reissued in 1971 by Scholars Book Co., Lawrence, KS.

A Statement of Accounting Principles, with Thomas H. Sanders and Underhill Moore. New York: American Institute of Accountants, 1938; reprinted in 1959 by the American Accounting Association.

Accounting Principles and Practices, with Thomas H. Sanders and Norman L. Burton. New York: Ginn and Company, 1940.

Surplus and Dividends. Cambridge, MA: Harvard University Press, 1943; reprinted in *Selected Dickinson Lectures in Accounting, 1936-1952*, edited by Zeff. New York: Arno Press, 1978.

ARTICLES

"The Chicago Trust Conference." *Journal of Political Economy*, December 1899, pp. 1-18.

"Zwei Pfadfinder." *Zeitschrift für Buchhaltung*, April 1909, pp. 80-86. (An English translation appears in *The Accounting Historians Journal*, Spring 1977, pp. 2-8.)

"Some Neglected Phases of Accounting." *Electric Railway Journal*, October 16, 1915, pp. 799-802.

"An Historical Defense of Bookkeeping." *Papers and Proceedings of the Eighth Annual Meeting, The American Association of University Instructors in Accounting* [in Columbus, Ohio, 1923], Vol. VIII, No. 1, June 1924, pp. 65-75. Reprinted: in *The Journal of Accountancy*, April 1924, pp. 1-13; as a booklet in recognition of the author's retirement from the University of California, May 15, 1937; as A.R.A. Reprint No. 2 of The Accounting Research Association, 1939; in Baxter, *Studies in Accounting*, London: Sweet & Maxwell, 1950, pp. 1-12; in *The Illinois CPA*, June 1953, pp. 33-42; in Baxter and Davidson, *Studies in Accounting Theory*, London: Sweet & Maxwell, 1962, pp. 1-13; in Moonitz and Littleton, *Significant Accounting Essays*, Englewood Cliffs, NJ: Prentice-Hall, 1965, pp. 3-13; in Chatfield, *Contemporary Studies in the Evolution of Accounting Thought*, Belmont, CA: Dickenson Publishing, 1968, pp. 1-11; and in Baxter and Davidson, *Studies in Accounting*, London: The Institute of Chartered Accountants in England and Wales, 1977, pp. 1-10. Reprinted in abridged format in Littleton, *Accounting Evolution to 1900*, New York: American Institute Publishing Co., 1933, pp. 3-11.

"What Is the Matter with Accounting?" *The Journal of Accountancy*, October 1927, pp. 267-279; reprinted in *The Canadian Chartered Accountant*, January 1928, pp. 213-225; in *Licentiate in Accountancy*, January 1928, pp. 237-248; and in *Financial Accounting Theory: Issues and Controversies*, by Zeff and Keller, New York: McGraw-Hill Book Company, 1964, pp. 353-361.

"Development in Education for Business during the Past Fifteen Years in the United States." *Proceedings, International Congress on Commercial Education*, Amsterdam, 1929, pp. 62-74.

"A Check-List of Early Bookkeeping Texts," with A.C. Littleton. *The Accounting Review*, September 1932, pp. 194-206; reprinted in *Readings on Accounting Development*, by Garner and Hughes, New York: Arno Press, 1978.

"Accounting Principles and the Statutes." *The Journal of Accountancy*, August 1934, pp. 90-97.

"Operating Deficit and Paid-in Surplus." *The Accounting Review*, September 1934, pp. 237-241.

"What They Say About Depreciation." *The Accounting Review*, March 1936, pp. 18-26; reprinted in *Studies in Accounting*, by Baxter, London: Sweet & Maxwell, 1950, pp. 337-350; abstracted in *The Accountants Digest*, September 1936, pp. 31-32.

"A Survey of Developments in Accounting." *Papers on Auditing Procedure and Other Accounting Subjects*, The American Institute of Accountants, 1939, pp. 5-11.

"An Accountant's Adventures in Wonderland." *The Journal of Accountancy*, December 1940, pp. 527-532.

"Some Variations in Accounting Practice in England, France, Germany and the United States." *Journal of Accounting Research*, Autumn 1966, pp. 169-182 (published posthumously; written and presented in 1911).

DISCUSSION COMMENTS, NOTES, CORRESPONDENCE, AND OTHER SHORT PIECES

"Paper Money for War Expenses." *Student Life* (Washington University), May 1898, pp. 5-9.

"The Taylor-White Process for Tool Steel." *Journal of Political Economy*, September 1900, pp. 538-539.

Note on the University of Göttingen, *The Nation*, Vol. 72, No. 1860, February 21, 1901, pp. 158-159 (unsigned).

Installments in the series "Commerce of the Twentieth Century," *The Record-Herald's* Current Topics Club (Papers by Experts and Specialists, Seven Courses of Study), *The Chicago Record-Herald*:

III. New Industries, July 9, 1901, p. 7

XIII. War and Commerce, September 17, 1901, p. 7

XIII. The Commercial Development of Germany, September 24, 1901, p. 7

"Sir C. Furness's Ship-Building" (Correspondence). *The Nation*, Vol. 74, No. 1912, February 20, 1902, p. 149 (unsigned).

Discussion in *Convention of Educators and Business Men for the Discussion of Higher Commercial Education*, held under the auspices of the Michigan Political Science Association, February 5-7, 1903, Ann Arbor, Michigan, pp. 177-186.

Discussion of "The Management of the Surplus Reserve," by Edward S. Meade, in *Papers and Proceedings of the Sixteenth Annual Meeting, American Economic Association, December 29-31, 1903*. American Economic Association/Macmillan, May 1904, Third Series, V, No. 2, Part II, pp. 272-277.

"From San Francisco." *The Evening Post* (New York), December 31, 1913, Annual Financial Review section, p. 12 (unsigned).

Introductory Note to the reissue of *The Philosophy of Accounts*, by Sprague. New York: The Ronald Press Company, 1922, pp. xvii-xxi.

"University of California," in "Who Should Instruct Engineering Students?" *Engineering Education*, February 1922, pp. 266-267.

"An Old English Work on Bookkeeping" (Correspondence). *The Accountant*, July 11, 1925, p. 68.

"Pacioli's Summa" (Correspondence). *The Accountant*, August 8, 1925, pp. 211-212.

Introduction to *Profits, Dividends and the Law*, by Reiter. New York: The Ronald Press Company, 1926, pp. ix-xi.

"What is Business? Can It be Taught?" *Proceedings of the Stanford Conference on Business Education*, Stanford University, CA: Stanford University Press, 1926, pp. 138-144.

"Balance Sheet Value of Investments" (Correspondence). *The Accountant*, January 2, 1926, pp. 21-22.

"In Defense of George Washington" (Correspondence). *The Literary Digest International Book Review*, February 1926, p. 272.

"The Earliest Use in English of the Term Capital." *Quarterly Journal of Economics*, May 1926, pp. 547-548.

"The Origin of the Term 'Balance Sheet'" (Correspondence). *The Accountant*, August 14, 1926, p. 258.

["Accounting for Woman"]. *The Auditor* (published by the San Francisco Institute of Accountancy), September 1927, p. 3.

"An Accounting Paradox." *The Accounting Review*, December 1928, pp. 342-344.

Discussion Comments in *Proceedings, International Congress on Accounting, 1929*, International Congress on Accounting, 1930, pp. 1177-1179.

Comments in "A Symposium on Appreciation." *The Accounting Review*, March 1930, pp. 12-14, 26-27, 33-34, 53-54.

"Meditations of a Student in Commerce 7, A Course in Advanced Accounting Theory (After reading 'The Raven')." *The Accounting Review*, December 1931, p. 307 (unsigned); reprinted in *The Accounting Sampler: An Introduction*, by Burns and Hendrickson, New York: McGraw-Hill Book Company, 1967, pp. 3-4.

"How Can They Say Such Things?" *The American Accountant*, February 1931, p. 50.

(Extracts from Hatfield letter included in article) "Montgomery Library Acquisition Arouses Interesting Comment by Professor Hatfield." *The American Accountant*, July 1931, p. 207.

"How Can They Say Such Things?—II." *The American Accountant*, December 1931, p. 365.

"A Fable." *The Accounting Review*, September 1932, p. 175.

"The Early Use of Capital." *Quarterly Journal of Economics*, November 1934, pp. 162-163.

"Jessica Blanche Peixotto." *Essays in Social Economics in Honor of Jessica Blanche Peixotto*, Berkeley, CA: University of California Press, 1935, pp. 5-14.

(Extract from Hatfield letter included in article) "Early University Education in Accountancy," by Jeremiah Lockwood. *The Accounting Review*, June 1938, pp. 134, 138.

"Financial Aspects of Depreciation." *The Journal of Accountancy*, January 1940, pp. 48-49.

"Accounting Trivia." *The Accounting Review*, September 1940, pp. 417-419; reprinted in *Readings on Accounting Development*, by Garner and Hughes, New York: Arno Press, 1978.

"Accounting Boners" (Correspondence). *The Journal of Accountancy*, April 1942, p. 355.

"On the Unreliability of Arithmetic" (Correspondence). *The Journal of Accountancy*, October 1942, pp. 355-357.

"Neither Pietra nor Flori" (Correspondence). *The Journal of Accountancy*, February 1943, pp. 165-166.

"Replacement and Book Value." *The Accounting Review*, January 1944, pp. 66-67; reprinted in *The Accountants Digest*, June 1944, pp. 262-263.

REVIEWS

Donisthorpe, *Law in a Free State*. *Journal of Political Economy*, June 1895, pp. 381-383.

Norman, *Norman's Universal Cambist. A Ready Reckoner of the World's Foreign and Colonial Exchanges of Seven Monetary and Currency Intermediaries*; and Norman, *The World's Exchanges in 1898. A Reckoner of Foreign and Colonial Exchanges. Journal of Political Economy*, March 1899, pp. 280-284.

Brooks, *Cotton: Its Uses, Varieties, Fiber Structure, Cultivation, and Preparation for the Market and as an Article of Commerce, also the Manufacture of Cotton-Seed Oil, Cotton-Seed Meal, and Fertilizers, With Especial Reference to Cotton Growing, Ginning, and Oil Pressing in the United States*; and Wilkinson, *The Story of the Cotton Plant. Journal of Political Economy*, June 1899, pp. 416-417.

Marot, *A Handbook of Labor Literature; Being a Classified and Annotated List of the More Important Books and Pamphlets in the English Language. Journal of Political Economy*, June 1899, p. 420.

Baker, *Monopolies and The People. Journal of Political Economy*, March 1900, pp. 271-274.

Jones, *Economic Crises. Journal of Political Economy*, December 1900, pp. 135-137.

Petrenz, *Die Entwickelung der Arbeitsteilung im Leipziger Gewerbe von 1751 bis 1890. Journal of Political Economy*, March 1902, p. 309.

Clow, *Introduction to the Study of Commerce. Journal of Political Economy*, March 1902, pp. 310-311.

Cleveland, *Funds and Their Uses: A Book Describing the Methods, Instruments and Institutions Employed in Modern Financial Transactions*; and Pratt, *The Work of Wall Street. Journal of Political Economy*, March 1903, pp. 326-327.

Meade, *Trust Finance: A Study of the Genesis, Organization, and Management of Industrial Combinations. Journal of Political Economy*, December 1903, pp. 156-160.

Campbell, *Insurance and Crime. Journal of Political Economy*, March 1904, p. 301.

Chisholm, *Handbook of Commercial Geography*; Trotter, *The Geography of Commerce: A Text Book*; Redway, *Commercial Geography: A Book for High Schools, Commercial Courses and Business Colleges*; and Lyde, *A Short Commercial Geography. Journal of Political Economy*, March 1905, pp. 285-287.

Official Record of the Proceedings of the Congress of Accountants, held at the World's Fair, Saint Louis, September 26th, 27th and 28th, 1904. Kritische Blätter für die gesamten Sozialwissenschaften - Bibliographisch-kritisches Zentralorgan, April 1905, pp. 215-216.

Sprague, *The Philosophy of Accounts. The Journal of Accountancy*, November 1908, pp. 67-69.

Nixon, *Accounting and Banking. The Journal of Accountancy*, November 1908, pp. 69-70.

Garrison, *Accounting Every Business Man Should Know. The Journal of Accountancy*, August 1910, p. 305.

Moxey, *Accounting Systems*; Walton (Part I: Auditing) and Gilman (Part II: Cost Accounts), *Auditing and Cost Accounts. Journal of Political Economy*, July 1912, pp. 858-861.

Lyon, *Capitalization. The Journal of Accountancy*, July 1913, pp. 86-87.

Van Cleve, *Principles of Double-entry Bookkeeping. The Journal of Accountancy*, August 1913, pp. 162-164.

Montgomery, *Auditing Theory and Practice. Journal of Political Economy*, October 1913, p. 781.

Floy, *Valuation of Public Utility Properties*; Foster, *Engineering Valuation of Public Utilities and Factories*; and Whitten, *Valuation of Public Service Corporations. Political Science Quarterly*, December 1913, pp. 669-675.

Dicksee, *Bookkeeping for Accountant Students. The Journal of Accountancy*, June 1914, p. 475.

Turner, *The Repayment of Local and Other Loans, Sinking Funds. Journal of Political Economy*, November 1914, pp. 913-916.

Dickinson, *Accounting Practice and Procedure. The Journal of Accountancy*, December 1914, pp. 480-482.

Gerstenberg, *Materials of Corporation Finance. The American Economic Review*, March 1916, pp. 138-139.

Gerstenberg, *Financial Organization and Management of Business. The American Economic Review*, March 1925, pp. 112-114.
McKinsey, *Managerial Accounting. The Journal of Accountancy*, May 1925, pp. 432-433.
Paton, *Accounting. The Journal of Accountancy*, November 1925, pp. 389-390.
Crivelli, *An Original Translation of the Treatise on Double-entry Book-keeping by Frater Lucas Pacioli. Publications of the American Association of University Instructors in Accounting*, December 1925, pp. 153-156; also a brief review in *The Journal of Accountancy*, January 1926, p. 74.
Woodbridge, *Elements of Accounting. The Journal of Accountancy*, February 1926, pp. 152-153.
Smails and Walker, *Accounting Principles and Practice. The Journal of Accountancy*, June 1927, p. 470.
Yang, *Goodwill and Other Intangibles. The Accounting Review*, December 1927, pp. 409-411.
Greer, *How to Understand Accounting. The Accounting Review*, June 1928, pp. 210-212.
Baldwin, *Accounting for Value as Well as Original Cost. The Accounting Review*, June 1928, pp. 218-219.
Schmaltz, *Bilanz- und Betriebsanalyse in Amerika. The Journal of Accountancy*, June 1928, p. 474.
Wildman and Powell, *Capital Stock Without Par Value. The California Law Review*, November 1929, pp. 101-103.
Murray, *Chapters in the History of Bookkeeping, Accountancy & Commercial Arithmetic. The Journal of Accountancy*, July 1930, pp. 63-64.
Morey, *University and College Accounting. The Journal of Accountancy*, February 1931, pp. 144-146.
Green, *History and Survey of Accountancy. The Journal of Accountancy*, April 1931, pp. 308-309.
Eldridge, *The Evolution of the Science of Bookkeeping. The Journal of Accountancy*, September 1931, p. 224.
Sunley and Pinkerton, *Corporation Accounting. ABA Journal*, December 1931, p. 817.
Scott, *The Cultural Significance of Accounts. The Journal of Accountancy*, September 1932, p. 230.
Greeley, *Law for Laymen. The Journal of Accountancy*, October 1932, pp. 313-314.
Finney, *Introduction to Principles of Accounting*; and Streightoff, *Advanced Accounting. The Journal of Accountancy*, December 1932, pp. 474-475.
Graham and Katz, *Accounting in Law Practice. The Journal of Accountancy*, February 1933, pp. 148-149.
Penndorf, *Luca Pacioli Abhandlung über die Buchhaltung, 1494. The Journal of Accountancy*, December 1933, pp. 475-476.
Staff of the Public Service Commission of Wisconsin, *Depreciation. The Journal of Accountancy*, May 1934, pp. 386-388.
Dewing, *The Financial Policy of Corporations. The California Law Review*, March 1935, pp. 373-374.
Sweeney, *Stabilized Accounting. The Journal of Accountancy*, December 1936, pp. 472-474.
May, *Twenty-five Years of Accounting Responsibility, 1911-1936. The Journal of Accountancy*, January 1937, pp. 77-78.
Peragallo, *Origin and Evolution of Double Entry Bookkeeping. The Journal of Accountancy*, May 1939, pp. 317-318.
MacNeal, *Truth in Accounting*. Research Supplement No. 10 to *The Accountant*, The Accounting Research Association, January 1940, pp. 14-16.
Paton, *Advanced Accounting. The Journal of Accountancy*, February 1942, pp. 183-184.
Taylor, *No Royal Road: Luca Pacioli and His Times. The Accounting Review*, January 1943, pp. 76-77.

TRANSLATION

A History of the Latin Union, by Alfred de Foville. Translated from the French. *Journal of Political Economy*, December 1901, pp. 113-119.

Index

The index covers Chapters 1 through 6. Coverage of the material in the text is comprehensive but, for the most part, only the names of people cited in the endnotes are included in the index. In the alphabetization of entries, the articles, prepositions and conjunctions have generally been ignored.

www.ingramcontent.com/pod-product-compliance
Lightning Source LLC
LaVergne TN
LVHW010655300926
849161LV00005B/1127